IF YOU THINK YOU'VE HEARD IT ALL, YOU PROBABLY HAVEN'T HEARD THIS . . .

The longest recorded boxing fight—between Andy Bowne and Jack Burke—was on April 6, 1893, in New Orleans. It lasted 110 rounds and took 7 hours and 19 minutes!

Aaron Fotheringham successfully landed the first wheelchair back-flip at the Doc Romeo skate park in Las Vegas, Nevada, on October 25, 2008.

The highest denomination currency note is a $100-billion-dollar bill that features 11 zeroes. It was issued in Zimbabwe on July 22, 2008, and because of inflation at that time it was enough to buy three eggs.

Dr. Vijaypat Singhania achieved the altitude record of 68,986 feet in a hot air balloon over Mumbai, India, on November 26, 2005.

Accreditation

Guinness World Records Limited has a very thorough accreditation system for records verification. However, while every effort is made to ensure accuracy, Guinness World Records Limited cannot be held responsible for any errors contained in this work. Feedback from our readers on any point of accuracy is always welcomed.

Abbreviations & Measurements

Guinness World Records Limited uses both metric and imperial measurements. The sole exceptions are for some scientific data where metric measurements only are universally accepted, and for some sports data. Where a specific date is given, the exchange rate is calculated according to the currency values that were in operation at the time. Where only a year date is given, the exchange rate is calculated from December of that year. "One billion" is taken to mean one thousand million. "GDR" (the German Democratic Republic) refers to the East German state, which was unified with West Germany in 1990. The abbreviation is used for sports records broken before 1990. The USSR (Union of Soviet Socialist Republics) split into a number of parts in 1991, the largest of these being Russia. The CIS (Commonwealth of Independent States) replaced it and the abbreviation is used mainly for sporting records broken at the 1992 Olympic Games. Guinness World Records Limited does not claim to own any right, title or interest in the trademarks of others reproduced in this book. Where possible, Guinness World Records recognizes trademarks with a ® or ™ symbol; where these may be absent, this is intended for ease of use by the reader.

General Warning

Attempting to break records or set new records can be dangerous. Appropriate advice should be taken first and all record attempts are undertaken at the participant's risk. In no circumstances will Guinness World Records Limited have any liability for death or injury suffered in any record attempt. Guinness World Records Limited has complete discretion over whether or not to include any particular records in the book. Being a Guinness World Record holder does not guarantee you a place in the book.

GUINNESS WRLD RECORDS 2010

BANTAM BOOKS
NEW YORK • TORONTO • LONDON • SYDNEY • AUCKLAND

2010 Bantam mass market edition

GUINNESS WORLD RECORDS™ 2010
Copyright © 2009 by Guinness World Records Limited.
Published under license.

GUINNESS WORLD RECORDS™ is a trademark of Guinness World Records Limited and is reproduced under license by Bantam Books, an imprint of The Random House Publishing Group, a division of Random House, Inc., New York.

Revised American editions copyright © 2010, 2009, 2008, 2007, 2006, 2005, 2004, 2003, 2002, 2001, 2000, 1999, 1998, 1997, 1996, 1995, 1994, 1993, 1992, 1991, 1990, 1989, 1988, 1987, 1986, 1985, 1984, 1983, 1982, 1981, 1980, 1979, 1978, 1977, 1976, 1975, 1974, 1973, 1972, 1971, 1970, 1969, 1968, 1966, 1965, 1964, 1963, 1962, 1960 by Guinness World Records Ltd.

For more information address: Guinness World Records Ltd.

BANTAM BOOKS and the rooster colophon are registered trademarks of Random House, Inc.

ISBN: 978-0-553-59337-2

Printed in the United States of America

www.bantamdell.com

2 4 6 8 9 7 5 3 1

GUINNESS WORLD RECORDS

RECORDS

EDITOR-IN-CHIEF
Craig Glenday

FIRST . . .

Assassination attempt The earliest recorded assassination attempt was against Amenemhat I, a Pharaoh of the Middle Kingdom of Egypt, around 2000 B.C.

Alphabet The earliest known example of an alphabet—that is, a writing system in which a small number of symbols is used to represent single sounds rather than concepts—dates back to around 1900 B.C. and was found by John Darnell (U.S.A.) in the early 1990s, carved into limestone in Wadi el Hol near Luxor, Egypt.

Currency note Paper money has existed in China since the 9th century, but the first bank to issue a note (or *banco-sedlar*) was the Bank of Palmstruch in Stockholm, Sweden, in July 1661. The oldest surviving note is one of the denomination of five dalers, which is dated December 6, 1662.

Manned flight Frenchman Jean-François Pilâtre de Rozier is widely regarded as the first person ever to have flown. On October 15, 1783, he rose 84 ft. (26 m) into the air in a tethered hot-air balloon built by Joseph and Jacques Montgolfier (France).

Beauty contest The earliest international beauty contest was staged by P. T. Barnum (with the public as the judges) in the U.S.A. in June 1855.

Human cannonball Rosa Richter, a 14-year-old acrobat performing under the stage name "Zazel," became the first human cannonball when she was shot a distance of about 30 ft. (6.1 m) at Westminster Aquarium, London, UK, on April 2, 1877.

BLOCKBUSTER Steven Spielberg's (U.S.A.) movie *Jaws* (U.S.A., 1975)—the story of a small seaside community terrorized by a great white shark—is considered the first summer blockbuster. It became the **first movie to earn over $100 million** at the box office, and won three Oscars—Best Film Editing, Best Music (Original Score) and Best Sound. (It also was nominated for Best Picture.) Fans lined up around the block to see the movie, giving rise to the term "blockbuster."

---

75 FT. (22.8 M): the speed, per minute, of the **first escalator**, installed as a pleasure ride at Coney Island, New York, U.S.A., in 1891.

CLONED ANIMAL A Finn Dorset sheep called Dolly was the first animal to be successfully cloned from an adult cell, as revealed in February 1997 by Dr. Ian Wilmut (UK, pictured left) at the Roslin Institute in Scotland, UK. Born on July 5, 1996, Dolly survived to maturity and gave birth to lambs of her own via natural means. She was euthanized on February 14, 2003, age six and a half, after developing a progressive lung disease.

Nobel prize The first Nobel prizes were awarded on December 10, 1901, for contributions to physics (Wilhelm C. Röntgen, Germany), chemistry (Jacobus H. van't Hoff, the Netherlands), physiology or medicine (Emil A. von Behring, Germany), literature (Sully Prudhomme, France), and peace (Jean H. Dunant, Switzerland, and Frédéric Passy, France).

Million-selling record The first record to sell over 1 million copies was "Vesti la giubba" from Leoncavallo's *I Pagliacci,* sung by Enrico Caruso (Italy, 1873–1921). It was recorded in November 1902. The **first million-selling CD** was Dire Straits' (UK) *Brothers in Arms* in 1985.

Air conditioner U.S. inventor Willis Haviland Carrier designed and built the first air-conditioning system in 1902. It was devised for a printer in New York, U.S.A., who had found that temperature fluctuations were causing his paper to warp.

Feature film The world's first full-length feature film, running for more than an hour, was *The Story of the Kelly Gang,* made in Melbourne, Australia, in 1906. This biopic of the notorious bushranger Ned Kelly (Australia, 1855–80) opened at the Melbourne Town Hall on December 26, 1906. It was produced by local theatrical company J & N Tait on a budget of $2,185 (£450).

SIGNIFICANT FIRSTS

One of the main criteria for a Guinness World Records achievement is that the record must be breakable. The only exception to this rule is when the achievement is considered a "significant first" within that category. For example, the **first ascent of Mount Everest** is significant within the climbing community; the **first person to play the banjo at the top of Everest** is not a significant first within either the music or climbing communities.

First . . .

IN-FLIGHT MOVIE The first movie to be shown on a flight was First National's *The Lost World* (U.S.A., 1925), a dinosaur adventure based on Sir Arthur Conan Doyle's (UK) book of the same name. It was shown during an Imperial Airways flight in a converted Handley-Page bomber, which flew from London, UK, to Paris, France, in April 1925.

The Lost World is also considered the first full-length feature film to use stop-motion animation; the first use of the technique was in the 1908 short *Humpty Dumpty Circus* (U.S.A.).

★**Person to be killed by a powered airplane crash** Lieutenant Thomas Etholen Selfridge (U.S.A.) was an army observer on a plane piloted by Orville Wright (U.S.A.) on September 17, 1908, when, four minutes into the test of the aircraft *Wright Flyer,* the propeller snapped a rudder control wire, which led to the plane nose-diving into a field. Selfridge died from internal injuries and a fractured skull within three hours of the accident.

★**PERSON KILLED IN A CAR ACCIDENT** The first person to be killed by a car was Bridget Driscoll (UK, circled left), when she walked into the path of a vehicle moving at 4 mph (6.4 km/h), in the grounds of Crystal Palace, London, UK, on August 17, 1896.

FERRIS WHEEL The original Ferris wheel was designed by George Washington Gale Ferris Jr. (U.S.A., 1859–96), a bridge and tunnel engineer, and was erected for the World's Columbian Exposition of 1893 in Chicago, Illinois, U.S.A. The "Ferris Wheel," as it became known, reached a maximum height of 264 ft. (80 m), with a diameter of 250 ft. (76 m) and a circumference of 790 ft. (240 m). Each of the 36 fully enclosed gondolas carried up to 40 passengers.

Ascent of Mount Everest The summit of Mount Everest was first reached at 11:30 a.m. on May 29, 1953, by Edmund Percival Hillary (New Zealand) and Sherpa Tenzing Norgay (Nepal).

Reinhold Messner (Italy) and Peter Habeler (Austria) made the **first ascent of Everest without oxygen** on May 8, 1978.

Email In 1971, Ray Tomlinson (U.S.A.), an engineer at the computer company Bolt, Beranek and Newman, sent the very first email. It was an experiment to see if he could get two computers to exchange a message. It was Ray who decided to use the @ symbol to separate the recipient's name from their location. Ray has forgotten what the original message was.

DOG IN ORBIT Laika, a stray Siberian husky-mongrel mix, became the first dog—and the first living Earthling other than microbes—to orbit the Earth, on November 3, 1957, on board Russia's *Sputnik 2.* Laika (which means "barker" in Russian) reached an altitude of 2,000 miles (3,219 km), earning her the nickname of "Muttnik" from the U.S. media. The spacecraft was not designed to return to Earth, and Laika died from overheating and stress just a few hours into the mission—a fact not released by the Russians until October 2002.

CONTENTS

★ **BRAND-NEW RECORDS** are indicated by a solid star, in both the text and record headings

☆ **BROKEN OR UPDATED RECORDS** are indicated by an open star, in both the text and record headings

EXTENDED FEATURES ONLINE

Unlock special extended features on our new-look website whenever you see these symbols:

VIEW THIS CLIP
Watch exclusive video footage of specially selected records.

TOP 100 RECORDS OF THE DECADE
Find out more about the 100 most significant records of the past 10 years. Go online to vote for your top record in each of the 10 categories.

DOWNLOAD IMAGES
Download pictures as a desktop or cell phone wallpaper.

To unlock these exclusive features, visit **www.guinnessworldrecords.com/2010** and enter this key code:

8341159372

Contents   xi

....

124 MILLION: copies sold, to date, of *Guinness World Records*—making it the world's **best-selling copyright book.**

....

SPORTS

★ TOP 10 RECORD HOLDERS OF THE DECADE ★

	RECORD HOLDER	NO. OF RECORDS*	AS SEEN ON . . .
1	Ashrita Furman (U.S.A.)	164	p. 121
2	Alastair Galpin (New Zealand)	38	p. 248
3	Suresh Arulanantham Joachim (Canada)	36	p. 190
4	Paddy Doyle (UK)	25	p. 143
5	Rob Dyrdek (USA)	20	p. xx
6	Jim DeChamp (USA)	14	p. 507
7	Stephen Hyland (UK)	13	p. xxx
8	Anthony Kelly (Australia)	12	p. xxxiv
9	Terry Grant (UK)	10	p. 504
9	Zdenek Bradac (Czech Republic)	10	p. 124

*Figures include only records set between January 1, 2000 and time of press.

It's been a fantastic decade for record breaking and what better way to honor our most prolific achievers than by including 10 of them in our Top 100 Records of the Decade? All 10 record breakers feature at various points in this book, some more than once. Frequent record smasher Ashrita Furman claimed his 100th current Guinness World Records feat on April 14, 2009 when he was one of 111 participants earning the title for the ☆**poem/literary passage recited in the most languages.** Can you beat Ashrita? Turn to p. xxviii to learn how to be a record breaker.

INTRODUCTION

From Skateboard Skills and Titanic Teens to Old Dogs and New Tricks, *Guinness World Records 2010* Reveals Its Annual Snapshot of Our Amazing, Awe-Inspiring, Record-Breaking World. . . .

Hello and welcome to *Guinness World Records 2010*! Here we are once again about to present you with the best of the best from this year's pick of superlative facts and recordworthy feats!

It's been quite some year. Not only did we reveal a new ☆ **tallest man** (from Turkey) but we also found a new ★ **tallest teenage girl** (Thailand), the ☆ **tallest married couple** (UK) and, closer to home in Washington State, the ★ **tallest teenage boy.** A real treat for Editor-in-Chief Craig Glenday was traveling the world measuring these generous, gentle giants. "It's been a real honor to meet these incredible people," he reported. "It's important that we get to meet and measure these unique characters in person. To us, they're

SVETLANA & HE PINGPING GO STATESIDE To celebrate the launch of last year's edition, we got some help from a couple of our most eye-catching record breakers. In the best spirit of GWR, New York played host to He Pingping (China), the world's **smallest mobile man**—standing 28 in. (74.61 cm) from head to toe—and Svetlana Pankratova (Russia), the woman with **longest legs**—a dizzying 51.9 in. (132 cm). It was a formidable affair, making the front pages of the world's newspapers as well as featuring on several daytime TV shows. Many thanks, guys, for all your help!

> **2,802:** the number of new and updated records added to the GWR master database in the past 12 months.

part of the Guinness World Records family." Find our more about why **Size Matters** on p. 112.

As ever, the U.S.A. tops the global list for record-breaking achievements. From the east coast to the west, it seemed no one wanted to be left out. We're really excited to announce a new **longest male fingernails** record from Detroit, Michigan; the ★ **highest rated TV comedy of the decade** (clue: it stars Larry David!); and, of course, we were more than pleased to welcome President Barack Obama into the Guinness World Records family thanks to his historic victory in 2009. You'll find a number of Mr. Obama's achievements listed throughout this year's edition.

So, what else is new in this year's book? As we're approaching a new decade, it seemed the perfect time to look back over the noughties and pick out what we consider the most inspiring, awesome, significant, and world-changing records since the year 2000.

BRENDEN ADAMS Brenden Adams and family welcomed GWR to their home in 2009 for a day of formal measuring. Brenden was just 13 when we visited, and he amazed us with his incredible height—find out more on p. 115.

JAN. 1: Cosmonaut Sergei Avdeyev (Russia), born on the first day of 1956, has completed 11,968 orbits of the Earth during his career—the **most orbits around the world.** Many happy returns!

NITRO CIRCUS One of the highlights of the year was joining the circus . . . not just any circus but the Nitro Circus with Travis Pastrana (U.S.A.) and his gang. Travis is a record-breaking freestyle motorcross rider and he and his pals set over 40 records in a single day! From the ★ longest car drift (4,137 ft.; 1,260 m) to the ★ most BMX bar spins in one minute (62), from the ★ fastest ATV side-wheelie (47 mph; 75.6 km/h) to the ★ longest motorcycle front-flip (47 ft. 8 in.; 14.52 m), Travis and Co.—we salute you!

Online extras To make the most of the last decade, we've loaded extra material onto our website. When you see any of these keys (left) printed in the book, go to www.guinnessworldrecords.com/2010 and use your unique code found on p. x to access special "extended features," such as further details on our Top 100 records and record-holders, downloadable wallpapers, stream-able videos, and exclusive record-holder interviews.

While you're at the site, you'll notice that it's had a bit of a re-fit—there's an expanded community area with a wealth of user-generated videos, competitions, and challenges, constantly updated news stories and Twitter feeds, plus a selection of the most popular record categories. You'll also be able to vote on your favorite Top 100 Records of the Decade, and share your comments with other online visitors. And, as ever, use the site to apply to break a record.

Anyway, back to this year's book. As well as looking back over the triumphs since 2000, we've also tried to keep abreast of current affairs—and look to what's just around the corner and likely to be an up-and-coming issue.

We always want the book to be as fresh, relevant, and up-to-date as humanly possible. To achieve this, we've focused a lot on the subjects that really matter to you—environmental concerns (**Planet in Danger,** p. 270; **Eco-transport,** p. 307), the global economy (**Economy,** p. 274), piracy (**Boats,** p. 315) and **Terrorism and Warfare** (p. 283). We've also logged all the major achieve-

***

JAN. 2: More than 200 million people were left without electricity when a power station failed in Uttar Pradesh, India, on this day in 2001—the **largest power cut** ever.

***

NATIONAL GEOGRAPHIC KIDS Each year, *National Geographic Kids* magazine attempts a record. Last year, led by guest editor Cameron Diaz (see p. 389), they broke the record for the **longest line of shoes**—a string of 10,512 sneakers reaching 8,700 ft. (2,651 m, left). They held on to the record for a few months, until charity Soles4Souls made a line measuring 18,992 ft. (5,788 m).

TEAM AMERICA Meet the team that brings you Guinness World Records in North America: From left to right, Danielle Pontdujour, Jamie Panas, Danny Girton, Laura Plunkett, Carlos Martinez, Stuart Claxton, and Jennifer Gilmour. Based in Manhattan, the GWR team works tirelessly adjudicating records and researching superlatives across the country and beyond. Find out more about our adjudicators on pp. xxviii–xxxii.

JAN. 3: In 2007, Michael Perham (UK, b. March 16, 1992) became the **youngest person to sail the Atlantic solo,** sailing from November 18, 2006 to January 3, 2007, aged 14 years 247 days.

ments in the adventuring world—see the **Travelers' Tales** chapter (pp. 149–172) for more—and the latest scientific innovations, discoveries, and achievements (see **Engineering and Technology** on pp. 305–360).

NBA ALL-STAR JAM SESSION Phoenix, Arizona, played host to the annual stellar event in which the NBA's best of the best come together to answer one question: East or West? Not only that but there was also the little matter of some Guinness World Records that needed to be broken! In total, 18 separate records were set or broken at the event, including the ★ **longest time to spin two basketballs on top of each other**, the ★ **highest slam dunk back flip**, and the videogame record for the ★ **most three pointers in one minute**. Even the stars themselves had a go: Chauncey Billups, Shaquille O'Neal, Devin Harris, and Dwight Howard (pictured) all attempted Guinness World Records. Turn to pp. 455–459 to see who was successful!

X-REF

Are you looking to score the facts on all the top basketball feats? Then shoot on over to pp. 451–459 for some slam dunkin' good records. . . .

JAN. 4: In 1991 on this day, Fu Mingxia (China, b. August 16, 1978) became the **youngest diving world champion,** winning the world title for platform diving at Perth, Australia, aged 12 years 141 days.

MOST SPORT STACKERS It was a sport stacking frenzy in November when once more the World Sport Stacking Association organized 222,560 participants in different locations around the world for Guinness World Records Day on November 26, 2008.

Regular features All your favorite sections are back as usual—including **Sports** (pp. 417–512), **Animal Planet** (pp. 57–85), **The Body** (pp. 87–116), and **Human Achievements** (pp. 117–147). We welcome onboard a new entertainment consultant by the name of Dick Fiddy, the British Film Institute's TV historian, who helped us stay on top of our **TV records** (pp. 372–384). Dick has begun a multi-part series on the history of TV, and has chosen to start with some of his favorite genres: sitcoms and soaps, and game shows and reality TV. He also takes a look at what we're watching today.

As ever, rounding off the book are our **Sports Reference** (pp. 518–547) and **Gazetteer** sections (pp. 173–249). These pages allow us to cover the major sports in depth—for which we'd like to thank all the major inter-

OLDEST DOG Birthday wishes to record-breaking dachshund Chanel, the ☆ **oldest living dog**, who turned an impressive 21 years old on May 6, 2009. To celebrate this milestone, a birthday party was held in her honor at the New York Dog Spa & Hotel. GWR's Jamie Panas (left) attended to present Chanel and her owners with a certificate.

JAN. 5: On January 5, 2008, Los Angeles-born singer/songwriter Josh Groban became the **first artist to have five tracks on the U.S. Top 30 Adult Contemporary chart at once.**

CARNIVAL CRUISES No, GWR's Danny Girtoh Jr. is not a tiny little man—he's standing in front of the world's **largest inflatable beach ball.** The plastic plaything measured 36 ft. (10.99 m) in diameter—giving it a volume of 24,550 cubic feet (695,179 liters) and a surface area of 4084.96 ft.^{2} (379.51 m^2)—and was created by Carnival Cruise Lines (U.S.A.) and bounced down the streets of Dallas, Texas, on October 26, 2008. *See more outsized objects on pp. 340–344.*

X-REF

You want bigger than this beach ball? Then turn to pp. 331–335 for the inside story on the tallest structures throughout history.

national sporting bodies—and offer our overseas researchers the chance to showcase some of the big world records from their particular countries.

Guinness World Records is a truly global arbiter—no one else covers quite as wide a spectrum of topics or geography, as this year's book evidently shows. With so many claims and submissions, it's sometimes hard for us to decide what to include in the book, but we hope you like the results. It's never easy but always most definitely fascinating fun!

Now, before we get stuck into the best-selling copyright book of all time, we'd like to say thanks to a couple of people.

Fantasy factory If there's one man who knows about record-breaking then that would be pro-skateboarder Rob Dyrdek. We were welcomed into the Fantasy Factory where Mr. Dyrdek, his cousin Chris "Drama" Pfaff, and

JAN. 6: The **youngest director of a feature-length film** is Kishan Shrikanth (India, b. January 6, 1996), who directed the movie *C/o Footpath* (India, 2006) when he was 9 years old.

SK8ER BOIS Professional skateboarder and serial record-breaker Rob Dyrdek (on the right in this picture) continued to blaze a trail for record-breaking in the last 12 months—literally in the case of his friend and fellow pro-skater Danny Way (on the left). Driving a Campagna T-Rex, Rob towed Danny along on a skateboard at speeds of 74 mph (119 km/h) in California City, California, on November 4, 2008.

OLDEST WOMAN Our gerontology consultant Robert Young made contact with the world's ☆**oldest living woman** (and the ☆**oldest living person**): 115-year-old Gertrude Baines (b. April 6, 1894) of Shellman, Georgia, who now lives in Los Angeles. Here's Robert surprising Gertrude with a GWR certificate.

ICE TRY Not all record attempts are successful, as NASCAR drivers Dale Earnhardt Jr., Kyle Busch, Carl Edwards, Clint Bowyer, Denny Hamlin, and Jimmie Johnson learned on *Live with Regis & Kelly* when, working in pairs, they failed to beat the record for **most ice-cream scoops thrown and caught in one minute by a team of two (25).**

dogs Meaty and Beefy let us have some superlative Factory fun. Not only did Danny Way pay a visit and set the record for the ★**fastest speed on a towed skateboard** at 74 mph (119 km/h) but Rob himself, with the help of Joe Ciaglia, built the ☆**longest skateboard** in the world—36 ft. 7 in. (10.1 m) long!

Live with Regis & Kelly Mr. Philbin and Ms. Ripa were once again the most gracious of hosts as we celebrated Guinness World Records Week on *Live with Regis & Kelly.* Needless to say, it was a veritable eye-popping feast of record-breaking stunts and feats. There was a bit of everything; a vicar who pulled a 126,200 lb. (57,243 kg) truck over 100 ft. (30.48 m—check out page 119 and page 120 for more on the amazing feats of the Canadian Reverend Kevin Fast), a young lad called Andrew Dahl (U.S.A.) who blew up 308 balloons in one hour with his nose, the ★**most balloons inflated by the nose in one hour,** and a man who could hold his breath for a lung-bursting 17 min. 33 sec. (find out more about the sensational breath control of German Tom Sietas on p. 214).

Not only this, but Regis himself raised the bar even higher when we recognized him for the third year running as the person who has spent the ☆**most time on TV** with a total of 16,100 hours! It took the great man 50

JAN. 7: When he took over as manager of England's national side on this day in 2008, Fabio Capello (Italy) also became the **highest paid soccer manager,** with a reported salary of $11.8 million.

WEEZER Los Angeles rock band Weezer (Rivers Cuomo, Brian Bell, Scott Shriner, and Patrick Wilson, all U.S.A.) went to record-breaking extremes while filming the video for their hit single "Troublemaker" (pictured left). With Guinness World Records adjudicator Stuart Claxton on hand to officiate, the band set new records for the ★ **most people in a custard pie fight** (120), the ★ **most people riding a skateboard** (22) and the ★ **largest game of dodgeball** (100 participants in total split into two teams of 50) among various other attempts on August 21, 2008 in Los Angeles. Well done, Weezer—you've set the bar high, now are there any other musicians out there who think they can set more records?

years to achieve this record, so you'd better start young if you want to try to beat it!

Thanks, indeed, to everyone who has helped make this year's edition so special. Guinness World Records relies not just on the staff in our New York and London offices but on you—the international cast of thousands who make the record-breaking magic happen. Perhaps that's why we're still the number-one records ratification company in the world—because of the unrivaled quality of our record breakers. . . .

The Editors
Guinness World Records

....

JAN. 8: The **largest plasma screen** measures 150 in. (381 cm) diagonally, and was unveiled by Panasonic on this day at the 2008 International Consumer Electronics Show in Las Vegas, U.S.A.

....

THE UNBREAKABLES

MOST GUINNESS WORLD RECORDS ARE BREAKABLE, AS THOUSANDS OF PEOPLE PROVE EVERY YEAR. SOME FEATS STAND THE TEST OF TIME, THOUGH, AND ARE UNLIKELY TO BE BEATEN ANY TIME SOON. WE PRESENT SOME OF HISTORY'S MOST ENDURING RECORDS. . . .

Unbroken for 1,550 years — the longest held record in our archives

Longest pole sit St. Simeon the Stylite (c. A.D. 386–459) spent 39 years on a pillar on the Hill of Wonders, near Aleppo, Syria.

Unbroken for 635 years

Worst dance mania In July 1374, an outbreak of tarantism (dancing mania) in Aachen, Germany, saw thousands quite literally dancing uncontrollably in the streets.

Unbroken for 658 years

Largest pandemic From 1347 to 1351, the pneumonic form of plague, aka the Black Death, killed around 75 million people.

Unbroken for 399 years

Most prolific female murderer From c. 1585 to 1610, Countess Elizabeth Báthory (Hungary) allegedly killed over 600 virgins. She was later locked in her castle, where she died in 1614.

Youngest doctorate On April 13, 1814, Carl Witte of Austria was made a Doctor of Philosophy (Ph.D.) by the University of Giessen, Germany, aged just 12.

Lightest person Lucia Xarate (or Zarate, aka "The Mexican Lilliputian," Mexico, 1863–89), an emaciated ateleiotic dwarf, weighed just 4.7 lb. (2.13 kg) at the age of 17.

Loudest noise Have you heard that the eruption of the island-volcano Krakatoa, in the Sunda Strait, Indonesia, on August 27, 1883, was audible 3,100 miles (5,000 km) away?

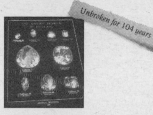

Largest diamond No diamond has ever been found larger than the 3,106-carat Cullinan unearthed on January 26, 1905, at the Premier Diamond Mine in South Africa.

Largest audience to attend a circus Ladies and gentlemen, a round of applause, please, for the largest circus crowd. A total of 52,385 people attended the Ringling Bros. and Barnum & Bailey Circus at the Superdome in New Orleans, Louisiana, U.S.A., on September 14, 1975.

Largest production car When it comes to size, one car leaves its rivals in the dust. First built in 1927, the Bugatti "Royale" type 41 is more than 22 ft. (6.7 m) in length. Its hood is over 7 ft. (2.13 m) long.

4.5 BILLION YEARS AGO: most astronomers now believe that, at around this time, a planet the size of Mars collided with our own world, resulting in the largest ever impact on Earth.

Unbroken for 70 years

Unbroken for 55 years

Highest box office Taking inflation into account, the epic *Gone with the Wind* (U.S.A., 1939) is the top-grossing movie ever, having taken in $5,362,000,000 at the box office.

Bestselling single by a group Recorded on April 12, 1954, "Rock Around the Clock" by Bill Haley and his Comets (U.S.A.) has sold an unaudited 25 million copies. That's what we call a record!

Unbroken for 62 years

Unbroken for 61 years

Largest plane by wingspan The H4 Hercules flying boat, aka the *Spruce Goose,* has a wingspan of 319 ft. 11 in. (97.51 m) and a length of 218 ft. 8 in. (66.65 m). It flew just once, on November 2, 1947.

Highest batting average Australian cricketing legend Sir Donald Bradman holds the highest Test batting average: 99.94 from 52 Tests—or 6,996 runs in 80 innings—from 1928 to 1948. It's unlikely that anyone will catch him. . . .

JAN. 9: Ben Gold (U.S.A.) became the **first video-game world champion** when he won the North American Video Game Olympics in Ottumwa, Iowa, U.S.A., on January 8–9, 1983.

Unbroken for 69 years

TALLEST MAN EVER

He's perhaps the single most famous record holder in the history of GWR. Robert Pershing Wadlow (U.S.A.) was the **tallest man ever recorded**, standing 8 ft. 11.1 in. (272 cm) tall, with a weight of 439 lb. (199 kg) at his peak. Wadlow's hands (unsurprisingly, the **largest hands ever measured**) were 12.75 in. (32.3 cm) from the wrist to the tip of his middle finger and he wore a size-25 ring (pictured). This remarkable man was also the owner of the world's **largest feet**: he wore U.S. size-37AA shoes (or approximately a European size 75), the equivalent to 18.5 in. (47 cm) in length. Indirectly, it was his outsize feet that brought about Wadlow's untimely demise. He died after he developed a blister on his right ankle while he was making a round of public appearances. The blister became infected, Wadlow's health deteriorated dramatically and he died in his sleep on July 15, 1940, aged just 22.

HOW TO BE A RECORD BREAKER

GWR'S ADJUDICATORS SPEND THE WHOLE YEAR TIRELESSLY ROAMING THE GLOBE TO BRING YOU THE HOTTEST RECORDS ON THE PLANET. MEET THE TEAM!

1. Get in touch If you want to set, or break, a world record, the first step is to log on to our website: **www.guinnessworldrecords.com.** Then, click on "Break a Record" and simply follow the instructions. Please tell us as much as possible about your claim.

RMT AT YOUR SERVICE Our dedicated Records Management Team (RMT) assesses, adjudicates, and approves all GWR record attempts. Much of the work takes place at our London, UK, headquarters, but RMT members—10 of whom are seen here—find themselves adjudicating records in all corners of the globe. From left to right: Kaoru, Tzeni, Andrea, Ralph, Marco, Talal, Mariamarta, Gaz, Laura, and Lucia.

JAN. 10: Ann and Claire Recht (both U.S.A.) were measured on January 10, 2007, and each were 6 ft. 7 in. (2.01 m) tall, making them the **tallest twin sisters.**

LONGEST HOT DOG On September 27, 2008, Empacadora Ponderosa (Mexico) created a 375-ft.-long (114.32-m) hot dog in Monterrey, Mexico. GWR's Danny Girton was on hand to measure the oversized snack and to declare it officially as a new world record.

2. Follow the rules Do you want to break an existing world record? If so, we'll send you the guidelines that the current world record holder followed. If you have a brand new record that you're just itching to try—and if we like the sound of it—we'll send a set of new guidelines for you to follow. Once you've got them, you can begin!

☆ **LONGEST SKIS** GWR's Denise Anlander visited Örebro, Sweden, on September 13, 2008, to measure a pair of 1,751-ft. 11-in.-long (534-m) skis. They were worn by 1,043 skiers in an event organized by Danske Bank.

JAN. 11: The **youngest person to trek to the South Pole** without dogs or motor vehicles is Sarah Ann McNair-Landry (Canada, b. May 9, 1986), who was 18 when she reached the pole on this day in 2005.

3. Mail us the evidence After you've completed your record attempt successfully, we'll need you to mail us the evidence. So please remember to video your attempt, take lots of photographs, and have two independent witnesses on hand to certify your achievement. Depending on the nature of your record attempt, we might also need some extra evidence—if we do, though, we'll tell you when we send you our guidelines.

4. Wait This might be the hardest part! You now have to wait while our expert Records Management Team assesses your claim and decides whether or not to award you with a Guinness World Records certificate. Unless, of course, you've already arranged for an adjudicator to be a judge at your record attempt (*see* below). Good luck!

Invite a GWR judge! Arrange for a GWR adjudicator to attend your record attempt and you'll enjoy a very different Guinness World Records experience:

• Instant confirmation that you're an official Guinness World Records holder (if you're successful)—and you'll receive an iconic GWR certificate on the spot.

• International media coverage for your record attempt. You could find yourself becoming one of the headlines of the day!

• A full write-up about your record on our website. See: **www.guinnessworld records.com/register/login.aspx.**

• Expert support: your record attempt will be assigned to a member of our adjudications team, who will guide you through the unique experience of planning and—hopefully—breaking a world record.

• One of our adjudicators will also be available to carry out interviews and press conferences on your big day—a fantastic way to maximize publicity.

Please note that GWR charges a fee for adjudicators to attend record attempts. To find out more about this premium service, visit **www .guinnessworldrecords.com/member/services_adjudications.aspx.**

You can now liaise with us in nine languages—English, French, Italian, German, Spanish, Portuguese, Arabic, Mandarin, and Japanese—via our website. Simply click on the flag of your choice in the top-right corner to find out what's happening in your chosen country.

Finally, don't forget about the *Guinness World Records Gamer's Edition.* If you're aiming for a record-breaking high score, you can have a GWR adjudicator there to make it official!

MARCO FRIGATTI (ITALY) Marco leads RMT, the people who collectively decide what constitutes a record. "It's a massive job," he admits, "with more than 1,000 applications pouring through every week." As well as his native Italian, Marco speaks English, German, French, Dutch, and is learning Mandarin. And what does he most like about his work? "Meeting record holders. They are very passionate about the most disparate things. Record holders are special people I look up to."

ANDREA BÁNFI (HUNGARY) Andrea's role as Adjudications Manager sees her play a key part in setting up record attempts as well as attending them: "I coordinate the company's adjudication service. If a record is witnessed by one of our adjudicators, you can be certain that I am involved in it." For Andrea, adjudications can inspire moments of real magic, too: "Every event has the potential to become the most extraordinary moment in your life." She is fluent in German, English, Romanian, and her native Hungarian.

TALAL OMAR (UK, B. YEMEN) Based in London, Talal specializes in adjudications in the Middle East—appropriately, as he is fluent in both English and Arabic. "The Middle East is one of the fastest-growing areas for record-breaking in the world," he reveals. "The people are passionate about working together to be the best at what they do—such as the team from Al Jana bakers in Qatar, who successfully made the ★ longest pita bread in the world (421.5 ft.; 128.5 m). What does Talal like best about GWR? "You will never have the same day twice!"

CARLOS MARTINEZ (SPAIN) Sports kick-started Carlos's fascination with GWR. His earliest memory of the book was starting a collection of GWR stickers; the sports records always attracted him most. "One of my favorite memories is seeing so many sports greats assembled for the largest gathering of sports titles and awards in Spain," he says. "All my heroes were there." This boundlessly enthusiastic adjudicator speaks Spanish, English, Italian, and Portuguese, and is based in our New York, U.S.A., offices.

LUCIA SINIGAGLIESI (ITALY) "During my high school and college years, I used to take every opportunity I had to travel to different countries," says Lucia. That restless appetite for globetrotting drove this adjudications executive from her home in the Marche, Italy, to London, UK, via much of the rest of the world—and made her a perfect candidate for the GWR team. Lucia speaks three languages—Italian, English, and French—and is based in our London, UK, offices.

DANNY GIRTON (USA) "I love to see history in the making and to personally meet the people who make it happen," says Danny, who handles record attempts from the northernmost stretches of Canada through to the southernmost tip of South America. Danny, who joined GWR some 18 months ago, is based in our New York offices, and speaks English and Spanish.

RECORD-BREAKING TELEVISION

USA British TV star Fearne Cotton (below) flew across the Atlantic to introduce the spectacular countdown show *Guinness World Records Live—Top 100* on NBC. Featuring the 100 greatest records ever seen on TV, the two-hour special culminated in a nerve-wracking, blood-boiling—and live!—attempt at the **longest motorcycle ride through a tunnel of fire**—an incredible 200-ft (60.96-m) stunt by U.S. rider Clint Ewing (top left).

BE ON TV

If you've got a record-worthy skill, body part, plant or pet, then capture it on video and upload it to the GWR community—www.guinnessworldrecords.com/community.

If we like what we see, our talent scouts will get in touch to ensure you get official recognition as a Guinness World Records holder. Get posting!

JAN. 13: The **oldest couple to run a marathon** were Japan's Shigetsugu Anan (83 years 11 days) and his wife Miyoko (78 years 71 days), who ran the Ibusuki Nanohana Marathon on this day in 2008.

23: the **most tennis balls caught in one minute,** achieved by Anthony Kelly (Australia) on the set of *Zheng Da Zong Yi*, Beijing, China, on November 9, 2008.

UNITED KINGDOM Sky1 TV is now officially the home of record-breaking in the UK, thanks to the Outline Production *Guinness World Records Smashed.* This exciting new format, hosted by Steve Jones and Konnie Huq (UK, bottom right), is a high-energy studio show that invites *you,* the public, to prove your record-breaking prowess. Submit your video applications online and you might find yourself on national TV trying to beat Shaeen Sadough's (UK, bottom left) record for the ★most T-shirts worn in 1 minute (83) or Zara Phythian's (UK, above) ★most objects kicked off the head in 1 minute (43).

JAN. 14: Yogesh Sharma (India) shook hands with 31,118 different people in eight hours—the **most handshakes by an individual** in this time period—on January 14, 1996.

GERMANY *Guinness World Records—Die größten Weltrekorde* attracts the best of the international record-breaking community, as well as a host of celebrity guest stars. Pictured are Markus Ferber and Clarissa Beyelschmidt (both Germany) setting the record for the ★ **longest time holding a person vertical overhead** (59.34 seconds), and GWR's Marco and Andrea adjudicating an attempt at the **most eggs crushed with the wrist.**

SPAIN *Guinness World Records: El Show de Los Records* goes from strength to strength with hosts Carmen Alcayde and Luis Muñoz introducing ever more awesome skills and thrills each year. Pictured (clockwise from top right) are *cortadora de jamón* (ham cutter) Nico Jiménez Rodríguez (Spain) creating the ★ longest slice of meat (43 ft. 8 in.; 13.32 m); Daniel Browning Smith (U.S.A.), the world's most flexible man; and Chloe Bruce (UK) performing the ★ most martial arts kicks in one minute using one leg (192).

JAN. 15: Thomas Syta of Van Nuys, California, U.S.A., managed to keep a single Lifesaver candy in his mouth for a record 7 hr. 10 min.—with the hole intact—on this day back in 1983.

ITALY Senior adjudicator Marco Frigatti returns to his native Italy to film *Lo Show dei Record,* a no-expense-spared showcase of talent from a global lineup of record breakers. Claimants from as far afield as China and New Zealand, Finland and Lithuania descend upon Milan for this most glamorous of TV events. Leading the proceedings is host Barbara D'Urso, who introduces records such as ★ most car rolls in 5 minutes (solo)— seven by Austria's Franz Muellner (above left)—and the ☆ most bowls broken by one finger in one minute—102 by the Chinese martial arts expert Fan Weipeng (left).

CHINA Proving that record breaking is a global obsession is *Zheng Da Zong Yi—Guinness World Records Special* on CCTV in China. Pictured is the ever-ready Marco Frigatti awarding a certificate to Chen Yun (China, above) for the ★ most Diabolo juggling catches on the back in 1 minute (67) and scrutinizing Wang Weibao (China, left) as he successfully completes the ★ longest duration standing on four fingers (19.23 seconds).

Canada LARGEST GAME OF LEAPFROG On November 14, 2008, the Toronto Zoo welcomed over 800 participants to leapfrog for five minutes. Despite just falling short of setting a new record for Guinness World Records Day, the event was a great success and helped to raise awareness for amphibian conservation.

USA ★LONGEST DREADLOCKS (FEMALE) When measured in Davenport, Florida, USA, on November 13, 2008, Asha Mandela (U.S.A.) was found to have dreadlocks 8 ft. 6 in. (2.59 m) long.

USA LARGEST DOG WEDDING This record attempt took place in Illinois on November 8, 2008, but freezing temperatures meant that only 87 dog couples attended. The previous record of 178 dog weddings therefore still stands.

JAN. 16: The **largest ice cream cake,** weighing 19,290 lb. (8,750 kg), was made by Beijing Allied Faxi Food Co., Ltd. for Beijing Children's Art Theater Co., Ltd. in Beijing, China, on this day in 2006.

Germany ☆ MOST STEINS CARRIED 40 M BY A WOMAN Anita Schwarz (Germany) carried 19 steins over 40 m (131 ft. 3 in.) in Mesenich on November 9, 2008, to mark Guinness World Records Day.

Ireland ★ LARGEST IMAGE MADE OF LED LIGHTS Tesco Ireland, in conjunction with Disney and Make a Wish Foundation, made an image of Donald Duck using 26,981 LED lights in Dublin on November 13, 2008.

Brazil ☆ LARGEST BREAD A loaf of bread weighing 1.731 tons (1.571 tonnes) was made by Joaquim Goncalves (Brazil) in Curitiba/Parana on November 13, 2008.

. . . .

JAN. 17: The **fastest row across the Atlantic** in any direction, land to land, is 33 days 7 hr. 30 min. A 14-man UK/Irish team rowed from Spain on December 15, 2007, arriving in Barbados on January 17, 2008.

. . . .

103: the **most people dressed as superheroes** gathered at Bournemouth University, Poole, UK, in celebration of GWR Day.

England ★ LARGEST GATHERING OF PEOPLE WEARING UNDERPANTS Raising awareness for the Fair Trade Organization "Pants to Poverty" campaign, 116 people gathered at St. Pancras train station in London wearing just their underwear on Guinness World Records Day, November 13, 2008.

France ★ LONGEST SCOUBIDOU/ BOONDOGGLE A scoubidou (aka boondoggle or gimp) is a lanyard braided and knotted from brightly colored strands of plastic. The longest was made by Manuela Dos Santos (France) and was measured at 1,673 ft. 2 in. (510 m) in Brancourt on November 11, 2008.

England ★ LARGEST CUP OF TEA A cup of tea measuring 4 ft. (1.22 m) in diameter, 4 ft. (1.22 m) in height, and with a volume of 106 gallons (400 liters) was made by Lancashire Tea at an Asda supermarket in Preston, UK, on November 13, 2008.

JAN. 18: The **fastest crossing of the Antarctic continent** (also first **solo and unaided**) was achieved by Børge Ousland (Norway), who completed the 1,675-mile (2,690-km) trek on this day in 1997.

FEATS OF ACHIEVEMENT

• The **farthest golf ball blow** is 19 ft. 1 in. (5.835 m), achieved by Alastair Galpin (New Zealand) in Auckland on November 2, 2008.

• The **most kisses given in a minute** is 94, achieved by Valentin Pasquier (France) in Nantes, France, on November 12, 2008.

• The **longest distance that a person has been pulled by a horse during a full-body burn** is 1,551 ft. 2 in. (472.8 m) by Halapi Roland (Hungary) in Kisoroszi, Hungary, on November 12, 2008.

China ★ HIGHEST WATERFALL DIVE The highest waterfall dive was 39 ft. 11 in. (12.19 m) and was achieved by Di Huanran (China) at the Diaoshuilou Waterfall of Jingbo Lake, Mudanjiang City, on October 5, 2008.

United Arab Emirates ★ MOST CHILDREN READING WITH AN ADULT
The record for the most children reading with an adult is 3,032, which was achieved by The Kindergarten Starters School at Global Village in Dubai, United Arab Emirates, on November 12, 2008.

Turkey CONCRETE BLOCK BREAKING As part of Turkey's celebrations for GWR Day, strongman Ali Bahçetepe (Turkey, above left) set a new record for the ☆ **most concrete blocks broken in a single stack** in Datça, Turkey, on November 14, 2008. At the same event, Norway's Narve Laeret (Norway, above right) broke the record for the ☆ **most concrete blocks broken in 1 minute** with 700 blocks smashed. (Laeret's record has since been broken by Bahçetepe, with 888 on January 9, 2009.)

Check out **guinnessworldrecords.com** to download videos and photos from various GWR Day events.

SPACE

CONTENTS

DEEP SPACE

★ **Oldest brown dwarf** Brown dwarfs are "failed stars," much like gas supergiants that never became large enough to produce the internal pressures necessary for nuclear fusion. One brown dwarf in the sparse halo surrounding our galaxy (the Milky Way) is 2MASS 1626+3925. Measurements of the weak infrared light it emits suggest that this failed star is around 10 billion years old: more than twice as old as our Solar System.

★ **Shortest distance between two black holes** In March 2009, astronomers reported that the quasar (short for "quasi-stellar object") SDSS J153636.22+044127.0, a galaxy emitting vast quantities of electromagnetic energy, appears to contain two black holes (a binary black hole) at its center. The black holes weigh the equivalent of around 50 million and 20 million Suns, respectively, yet are separated by only one-third of a light-year.

☆ **MOST ENDURING MARS ROVER** This image was taken by NASA's *Opportunity* rover, which, along with its twin, *Spirit,* touched down in January 2004. They are both still operational as of March 2009, despite being designed to last just three months.

The photograph shows the rim of the Victoria impact crater. At the top of the crater lies loose, scattered rocks; at the base is hard bedrock. In between is a band of rock geologists believe represents what used to be the surface of the planet, until the impact that created the 2,395-ft.-wide (730-m) crater buried it beneath its ejecta blanket tens of millions of years ago.

★**Densest galaxies** Ultra Compact Dwarf (UCD) galaxies are a class of galaxy discovered in 1999 by a team of astrophysicists led by Dr. Michael Drinkwater (Australia). Dozens of UCD galaxies, which are possibly leftover building blocks that once formed much larger galaxies, are now known to astronomers. These small galaxies contain around a hundred million stars in a space just 200 light-years across, but astronomers suggest that billions of years ago these galaxies had a density of perhaps one million stars per cubic light year—one million times higher than the density of the Milky Way.

★**Galaxy with the highest level of star formation** Astronomers studying the light from the galaxy J1148+5251 have estimated that stars are being formed there at a rate of around 1,000 solar masses per year—roughly a thousand times greater than the rate of star formation in our own galaxy. J1148+5251 is a distant active galaxy known as a quasar. At 12.8 billion light years away, astronomers are watching its star-forming activity as it was 12.8 billion years ago.

★**Fastest approaching galaxy** Despite the overall expansion of the Universe, there are only a small number of galaxies that are approaching our own. M86, a lenticular (lens-shaped) galaxy around 52 million light years away in the Virgo Cluster, is moving toward the Milky Way at 260 miles/s (419 km/s).

☆**Heaviest black hole** In February 2008, astronomers announced their discovery of a black hole in the dwarf galaxy IC 10, which has a mass estimated to be as much as 33 times that of the Sun. With the exception of the supermassive class of black holes at the heart of galaxies, this is more than double the size of any known black hole.

Nearest pulsar Pulsars are a type of neutron star that emit beams of radiation as they rotate. They are formed in supernova explosions where protons and electrons in the atoms of a star's core are fused together into neutrons. Since neutrons comprise much of an atom's mass, neutron stars are small and dense, usually the size of a large city, but containing as much mass as the Sun. Pulsar PSRJ0108-1431, in the constellation of Cetus, is just 280 light-years away from the Earth.

★ LARGEST SPACE MIRROR The primary mirror built for ESA's Herschel Space Observatory measures 11 ft. 6 in. (3.5 m) across. It was constructed from a single piece of silicon carbide ceramic, making it much lighter than glass. The mirror will allow the observatory to study objects in the Solar System as well as in deep space in the infrared spectrum. Successfully launched on May 14, 2009, Herschel is expected to last for three years, with its instruments cooled by liquid helium down to just 2 K (−456.07°F; −271.15°C).

LARGEST LAND-BASED TELESCOPE The twin Keck Telescopes on the summit of Hawaii's dormant Mauna Kea volcano are the world's largest optical and infrared telescopes. Each of these telescopes, designed to observe deep-space objects, is eight stories tall and weighs 300 tons (272 tonnes). Both Kecks have a 32-ft.-wide (10-m) mirror, made up of 36 hexagonal segments that act together to create a single reflective surface.

★ MOST COMMON TYPE OF GALAXY Of the few hundred billion galaxies in the Universe, spiral galaxies—like our own galaxy, the Milky Way—make up roughly 77% of them. They are characterized by spiral arms wound around a brighter core, with about half of all spirals also containing a bar across their centers. Spiral galaxies can contain several hundred million stars, along with dust and gas.

....

JAN. 19: The fastest speed at which a spacecraft has departed from Earth is 36,250 mph (58,338 km/h). It was achieved by NASA's *New Horizons* spacecraft, which launched on this day in 2006.

....

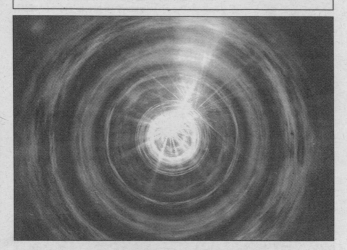

★ **BRIGHTEST ACTIVE GALAXIES** Active galaxies are those that have a highly luminous (bright) center and emit energy over the electromagnetic spectrum. They are also believed to house supermassive black holes at their cores. These black holes are in the process of sucking in matter surrounding them and ejecting jets of ionized gas at close to the speed of light.

When the jet of one of these galaxies is pointing toward the Earth, the galaxy appears more luminous to observations than other galaxies. Such galaxies are known as "blazars." Pictured above is a NASA conceptual image of blazar PKS 2155-304.

☆ **Most distant object in the universe** On April 23, 2009, NASA's *Swift* satellite detected a 10-second-long gamma-ray burst and its subsequent X-ray afterglow eminating from star GRB 090423. Later analysis revealed GRB 090423 to be roughly 13.035 billion light-years away, which means the explosion occurred close to when the Universe is estimated to have formed (see page 7). This also makes GRB 090423 the ★ **oldest object in the Universe** yet detected.

....

JAN. 20: Francis Joyon (France) sailed solo and nonstop around the world in 57 days 13 hr. 34 min. 6 sec. from November 23, 2007, to January 20, 2008—the **fastest circumnavigation sailing solo.**

....

983,571,056 FT./SEC. (299,792,458 M/SEC.): the speed of light in a vacuum, the **fastest speed possible in the Universe.** A light-year is the distance light can travel in a year.

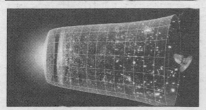

MOST ACCURATE MEASURE OF THE AGE OF THE UNIVERSE The *Wilkinson Microwave Anisotropy Probe* (*WMAP,* pictured above left) was designed to measure the Cosmic Microwave Background of the Universe—the radiation echo of the Big Bang. The first results from *WMAP,* released on February 11, 2003, and pictured below left, reveal minute temperature differences in the early Universe. This has allowed scientists to estimate the age of the Universe at 13.7 billion years old, with a degree of error of just 1%.

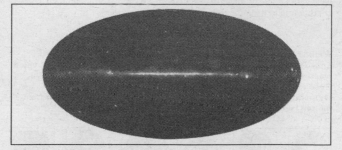

★ **HIGHEST-ENERGY GAMMA-RAYS** Launched on June 11, 2008, NASA's Fermi Gamma-Ray Space Telescope can detect gamma-rays from violent events in the Universe at energies from 8,000 electron volts to greater than 300 billion electron volts, the highest-energy wavelengths yet studied. A map of the whole sky at gamma-ray energies of more than 150 million times greater than visible light (above) was released in March 2009, representing three months of Fermi data.

EXTRASOLAR PLANETS

☆**Lightest extrasolar planet** Gliese 581e, whose discovery was announced in April 2009, is the fourth planet discovered to date orbiting the star Gliese 581. Estimates of its properties reveal that it could have the same mass as just 1.9 Earths; however, this rocky planet orbits too close to its star to have conditions suitable for life.

Generally, extrasolar planets are named after the star they orbit in the order that they are discovered. ("A" is not used as it refers to the star itself.) So, the first planet detected orbiting Gliese 581 is Gliese 581b, and so forth. There are many ways of naming stars, but the system of adding a letter at the end to denote objects in the orbit is standard.

★**Most elongated extrasolar planet orbit** HD 80606b, the first extrasolar planet on which real-time weather changes have been observed (see below), is 190 light years away in the constellation Ursa Major. It has a highly elliptical (oval-shaped) orbit, similar to that of a short period comet. During each orbit, the planet ranges in distance from its star from just 2.8 million miles (4.5 million km) at its closest point to 78 million miles (125 million km) at its most distant point. HD 80606b's solar year—that is, the time it takes the planet to orbit its star—lasts a mere 111 days.

★**Hottest extrasolar planet** HD 149026b is a gas giant orbiting a yellow sub-giant star 257 light years away. Orbiting close to its parent star, it achieves a temperature of around 3,704°F (2,040°C), well above the melting point of iron. The planet is probably metal-rich and very dark and likely to have dark clouds of metal oxides that absorb the star's radiation efficiently, contributing to its immensely high temperature.

★**FIRST REAL-TIME WEATHER CHANGES SEEN ON AN EXOPLANET**
Space telescope observations of the gas giant HD 80606b have revealed weather changes within its atmosphere as it passed close to its star. Over an eight-hour period, the planet's cloud tops went from temperatures of 968°F (520°C) to about 2,228°F (1,220°C)—hotter than molten lava.

JAN. 21: Tommy Clowers of Ramona, California, U.S.A., achieved the **highest jump on a motorcycle** with a leap of 25 ft. (7.62 m) at Van Nuys Airport, California, on this day in 2001.

Oldest extrasolar planet
The oldest planet yet discovered is an extrasolar planet in the globular cluster M4, some 5,600 light-years from Earth. With an estimated age

★ **CLOSEST EXTRASOLAR PLANET TO ITS PARENT STAR** Extrasolar planets, or exoplanets, are any planets that do not orbit our Sun. In 2007, astronomers using the Hubble Space Telescope took part in the Sagittarius Window Eclipsing Extrasolar Planet Search (SWEEPS), a project to monitor 180,000 stars for a week in the direction of the center of the Milky Way. Hubble watched for the dimming of light from the stars caused as planets crossed in front of them. Of the 16 planets discovered in this project, one of them, SWEEPS-10, orbits its star at a distance of only 1.2 million km (745,000 miles). It hurtles around its orbit in only 10 hours. For comparison Mercury takes 88 days to orbit the Sun.

of at least 10 billion years, this distant planet is more than twice as old as our Solar System. Its discovery was announced in July 2003.

★ **Largest star with a planet** In January 2003, astronomers announced their discovery of a planet orbiting the orange giant star HD 47536. This star is expanding at the end of its life and currently measures around 20 million miles (33 million km) across. HD 47536b, one of two planets spotted in the system, is 186 million miles (300 million km) from its star but will eventually be consumed in a few tens of millions of years as the star continues to expand into a red giant.

★ **First map of an extrasolar planet** In 2007, NASA's Spitzer infrared space telescope was pointed at the star HD 189733, and its accompanying planet, HD 189733b, and observed the system for 33 hours. The resulting observations were converted into a temperature map showing a range from 1,292 to 1,724°F (700 to 940°C). The planet was discovered by the transit method, in which the planet passes between the Earth and the planet's star, reducing the light visible from the star by 3%.

★ **FIRST PLANET-HUNTER SPACE MISSION** Designed specifically to find planets around other stars by the French Space Agency CNES, the Convection, Rotation, and Planetary Transits spacecraft (COROT) was launched on December 27, 2006, into a polar orbit 513 miles (827 km) above the Earth. The probe, which uses transits to identify extrasolar planets, reported its first planet discovery, COROT-Exo-1b, in May 2007.

JAN. 22: Happy birthday George Blair (aka Banana George, U.S.A., b. January 22, 1915)! George is the world's **oldest active snowboarder,** snowboarding between 45 and 60 days a year.

> **346:** the number of extrasolar planets discovered by scientists as of April 24, 2009.

moon

Earth

COROT-Exo-7b

★ **SMALLEST EXTRASOLAR PLANET** In February 2009, scientists working with the Convection, Rotation, and Planetary Transits (COROT) satellite announced the discovery of a planet orbiting a star 456 light-years away in the constellation Monoceros. Known as COROT-Exo-7b, this world has a diameter estimated at just 1.7 times that of Earth's.

★ **Coldest extrasolar planet** OGLE-2005-BLG-390Lb, named in part from the Optical Gravitational Lensing Experiment (OGLE) observatory that played a role in its discovery in 2006, orbits a cool red dwarf star 21,000 light-years from Earth. The low energy of its star coupled with the size of its orbit, farther out from its star than Mars is from our Sun, means its surface temperature is just −364°F (−220°C). Its mass is estimated at around five times that of Earth's and it probably has an icy surface, rocky core, and thin atmosphere.

★ **Windiest exoplanets** HD179949b, HD209458b, and 51 Pegasi b are all gas giants orbiting different stars within 150 light years of Earth. Each orbits its star within around 4.5 million miles (8 million km)—far closer than Mercury orbits the Sun. Results released in January 2007 show that the temperature difference between day and night on these planets is tiny. To explain this, some scientists suggest that supersonic winds of up to 9,000 mph (14,500 km/h) are constantly transferring heat from the planets' day sides to their night sides.

JAN. 23: The **deepest manned ocean descent** was achieved by Jacques Piccard (Switzerland) and Donald Walsh (U.S.A.). They descended to 35,797 ft. (10,911 m) in the Mariana Trench on this day in 1960.

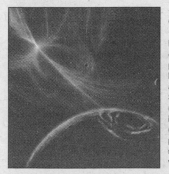

★ **FIRST CONFIRMED DISCOVERY
OF AN EXTRASOLAR PLANET** In
1992, astronomers announced they
had discovered two planets
orbiting pulsar PSR B1257+12. The
pulsar is a supernova remnant 980
light-years from Earth that weighs
around 1.4 times the mass of the
Sun but is only around 18 miles
(30 km) across. It spins once on
its axis in just 6.22 milliseconds
(9,646 rpm). The pulsar was
previously a giant star that went
supernova around 800 million
years ago.

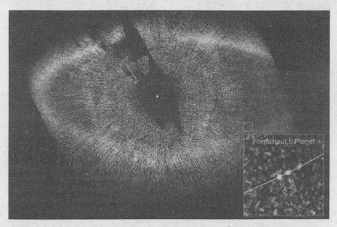

★ **FIRST VISIBLE LIGHT IMAGE OF EXTRASOLAR PLANETS** In November
2008, two discoveries announced at the same time revealed the first
images taken in visible light of planets orbiting other stars. Scientists
using the Hubble Space Telescope captured the dust disk surrounding the
star Formalhaut, 25 light-years from Earth (main picture), and found a
world about the size of Jupiter (inset) orbiting within it. Another team
using the Keck and Gemini telescopes directly imaged three planets
around the star HR 8799, 129 light-years from Earth.

Extrasolar Planets

First detection of an exoplanet atmosphere In November 2001, astronomers used the Hubble Space Telescope to detect light passing through the atmosphere at the edge of the planet HD 209458b as it passed in front of its star. Spectral analysis of this light revealed the presence of sodium in the atmosphere of this scorched gas giant, which orbits its star in just 3.5 days. Subsequent observations of this planet have suggested the presence of water vapor in its atmosphere.

EXPLORING THE SOLAR SYSTEM

★**First thunder heard on another planet** The USSR's *Venera 11* lander touched down on Venus on December 25, 1978. Among its instruments was an acoustic detector capable of registering sound in the Venusian sky and on its surface. During its parachute descent the detector heard the sound of the wind, and it picked up the noises of the lander's other equipment operating just after touchdown. Roughly 32 minutes after landing, another sound of unknown origin with a level of 82 decibels was detected. A Venusian thunder clap is the most likely explanation.

★**First mission to study a dwarf planet** NASA's *Dawn* spacecraft was launched on September 27, 2007. Its goal is to reach the asteroid Vesta in the asteroid belt between Mars and Jupiter, study it from orbit, and then break orbit to rendezvous with Ceres, the largest object in the asteroid belt. Ceres, like Pluto, was reclassified as a dwarf planet in 2006. Despite launching later than NASA had hoped, *Dawn* will reach Ceres in February 2015, five months before the *New Horizons* spacecraft reaches Pluto.

★**Most distant planet studied from orbit** The exploration of the Solar System by unmanned spacecraft began with simple fly-by missions, in which a probe would hurtle past a planet, gathering data. Fly-bys are eventually followed by orbiter missions: as their name suggests, a spacecraft collects planetary data while in orbit. In July 2004, upon the arrival of NASA's *Cassini* orbiter, Saturn (on average 888 million miles; 1.43 billion km from the Sun) became the most distant planet to be studied from orbit.

Fastest departure speed from Earth The fastest speed at which a spacecraft has ever departed from Earth is 36,250 mph (58,338 km/h). It was achieved by NASA's *New Horizons* spacecraft, which launched from Cape Canaveral on January 19, 2006, beginning a nine-year flight to Pluto and its moons Charon, Nix, and Hydra.

JAN. 24: The **largest hora dance** involved 13,828 participants, who danced in the town of Slatina, Romania, on January 24, 2006.

☆**Largest space station** The International Space Station (ISS) has been under construction since its first component, the *Zarya* module, was launched in November 1998. On May 31, 2008, NASA astronauts attached the *Kibo* module, made by the Japan Aerospace Exploration Agency (JAXA), bringing the total mass of the ISS so far to 657,000 lb. (298,000 kg).

Longest comet tail (measured) The longest comet tail ever measured was 350 million miles (570 million km) long and belonged to the comet Hyakutake. This is more than three times the distance from the Earth to the Sun. The tail was discovered by Geraint Jones of Imperial College, London, UK, on September 13, 1999, using data gathered by the ESA/NASA spacecraft *Ulysses*—on a chance encounter with the comet on May 1, 1996. Although other comets undoubtedly have longer tails, this is the longest ever measured.

63: the number of natural satellites that have been discovered orbiting Jupiter, the **planet with the most moons.**

FARTHEST DISTANCE FROM EARTH REACHED BY HUMANS The crew of the ill-fated *Apollo 13* mission (pictured here on Earth with their families) reached a distance of 248,655 miles (400,171 km) above the Earth's surface, at 7:21 p.m. EST on April 14, 1970. An explosion in an oxygen tank on the service module forced the crew to abandon their Moon landing and shift to a free return trajectory enabling them to use the Moon's gravity to slingshot their vessel back to Earth. The maneuver took them to within 158 miles (254 km) of the lunar surface, on the far side of the Moon, and to a distance that is the absolute record for the highest altitude achieved by a human. For more record highs and lows, turn to pp. 151–156.

**MOST REMOTE PLANETARY
LANDING** The European Space
Agency (ESA) probe *Huygens*
landed successfully on Saturn's
largest moon, Titan, on January 14,
2005. It sent back science data and
images of the surface during both
its parachute descent and from the
ground. *Huygens* was carried to
Titan, which is on average 890
million miles (1.433 billion km) from
the Sun, by the NASA spacecraft
Cassini.

☆ **MOST REMOTE MAN-MADE OBJECT**
NASA's *Voyager 1* spacecraft (pictured,
opposite page), launched on September 5,
1977 (left), encountered Jupiter in March
1979, and then Saturn in November 1980.
Those fly-bys flung the probe out of the
plane of the Solar System. As of February 1,
2009, *Voyager 1* was 10.095 billion miles
(16.247 billion km) from the Sun. Still
operational, the craft has enough power
to operate until around 2025.

★ **FIRST DETECTION OF PLANETARY LIFE
BY A SPACE PROBE** When the *Galileo*
spacecraft, bound for Jupiter, made a fly-
by of Earth in December 1990, mission
scientists used *Galileo*'s sensors to study
Earth for signs of life as if it were being
probed for the first time. The spacecraft
detected the infrared signature of
chlorophyll, molecular oxygen, and
methane in the atmosphere, and radio
signals of an unnatural origin—all of
which are key indicators of life.

JAN. 25: Luuk Broos (Netherlands) and his team created the **tallest
Champagne fountain,** consisting of 43,680 glasses, forming 63 stories, in
Wijnegem, Belgium, on this day in 2008.

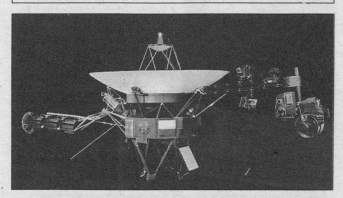

☆ **MOST COMETS DISCOVERED BY A SPACECRAFT** The ESA/NASA spacecraft *SOHO* (Solar and Heliospheric Observatory) was launched in December 1995 to study the Sun from close to the L1 point—a position between the Sun and Earth where the gravities of the two bodies cancel each other out. The probe has produced nearly real-time solar data for space weather prediction, and its discoveries of comets have been incidental. On June 25, 2008, the spacecraft accidentally discovered its 1,500th comet.

SPACE TOURISTS

Businessman Dennis Tito (U.S.A.) became the **first space tourist,** flying to the International Space Station on a trip that lasted from April 28 to May 6, 2001.

Anousheh Ansari (Iran) became the **first female space tourist** on September 18, 2006, with a 10-day visit to the International Space Station.

JAN. 26: The **largest diamond** was found on this date in 1905 at the Premier Diamond Mine near Pretoria, South Africa. Named The Cullinan, it was graded at 3,106 carats.

The ★ **most prolific space tourist** is Charles Simonyi (U.S.A.), who has successfully completed two trips into space. Simonyi departed on his first expedition on April 7, 2007, and his second on March 26, 2009.

★ CLOSEST FLY-BY OF MERCURY
On January 14, 2008, the *MESSENGER* spacecraft performed a gravity-assist fly-by of Mercury, closing to just 124 miles (200 km) above its surface at closest approach. Because Mercury is deep within the Sun's gravity well, achieving orbit is difficult. *MESSENGER* has performed two fly-bys of Mercury so far, with a third due in September 2009. These will adjust the spacecraft's trajectory so it can enter the orbit of Mercury in March 2011.

MARS

☆ **Longest time survived on Mars by a rover** The twin Mars Exploration Rovers, *Spirit* ⑥ and *Opportunity* ⑤ (the **largest planetary rovers**), touched down successfully on the surface of Mars on January 4 and 25, 2004, respectively. Since then, they have each traveled across the Martian surface taking scientific images and measurements. By April 2009, the *Opportunity* rover had traveled 51,853 ft. (15,805 m) over the surface—far farther than it had been originally designed for. As of May 2009, both rovers are still operational.

Largest impact crater One of Mars' most striking features is the stark difference between the low-lying plains of its northern hemisphere and the ancient cratered highlands of its southern hemisphere. Analysis of data from NASA's orbiting probes suggests the whole northern hemisphere could be a vast impact basin 5,300 miles (8,500 km) across—significantly lower than the southern hemisphere. This impact would have happened more than 3.9 billion years ago and would have required an object larger than the dwarf planet Pluto to create.

....

JAN. 27: Clint Ewing (U.S.A.) drove 200 ft. (60.96 m) to complete the **longest motorcycle ride through a tunnel of fire** at Universal City, Los Angeles, U.S.A., on this day in 2008.

....

★Most recent evidence of water on Mars An image taken by *Mars Reconnaissance Orbiter* of a dry gully in the Promethei Highlands suggests liquid water flowed on Mars as recently as 1.25 million years ago. The gully looks like it formed as ice melted, flowed downhill, and deposited sediment before evaporating in the thin Martian atmosphere.

★First successful polar lander NASA's *Phoenix* spacecraft ② landed in the Vastitas Borealis, the great world-wrapping lowland plain of the northern polar region, on May 25, 2008. It entered the atmosphere after a nearly nine-month journey at 13,000 mph (21,000 km/h), using a heat shield, then parachute and retro rockets to slow to just 4.9 mph (8 km/h) for touchdown. Contact was lost with *Phoenix* on November 2, 2008.

Largest canyon in the solar system The Valles Marineris ③ on Mars is the largest canyon in the Solar System. It has an overall length of about 2,800 miles (4,500 km). At its widest, it is 370 miles (600 km) across and is also up to 4.3 miles (7 km) deep. It is named after the *Mariner 9* spacecraft that first discovered it in 1971.

★Most spacecraft orbiting the same planet When NASA's *Mars Reconnaissance Orbiter* entered Martian orbit in March 2006, there were three other functioning spacecraft orbiting the red planet: *Mars Global Surveyor, Mars Odyssey,* and *Mars Express.* In addition, there were two rovers operating on the planet's surface, making the total number of active spacecraft exploring the same planet six.

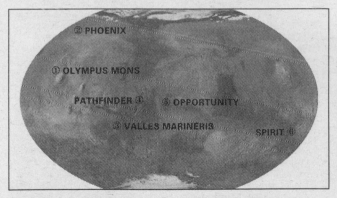

WELCOME TO MARS The fourth planet from the Sun, Mars is a rocky world like Earth but about half the size. Its thin atmosphere of carbon dioxide blankets a dusty surface stained red by iron oxide. In the night sky, Mars' red color is distinctly visible to the naked eye. When space probes began visiting the red planet in the 1960s, they gradually unveiled a world of titanic geology, prehistoric rivers, and conditions that could support primitive life.

★ LARGEST AREA OF SURFACE ICE
Almost all of the ice on Mars' surface is located at the poles. The southern ice cap is the largest of the two and is around 260 miles (420 km) across. It contains enough water to cover the entire planet in a layer 36 ft. (11 m) deep.

Martian ice consists of water ice and a seasonal coating of carbon dioxide "dry" ice, which accumulates during each polar winter. The dry ice can erode the terrain as it sublimates (converts directly from ice to vapor) every spring. The troughs in the image above, captured by the *Mars Reconnaissance Orbiter,* are believed to have been eroded by dust-rich gas flowing beneath the seasonal ice to openings where the gas can escape.

★ FIRST AVALANCHE WITNESSED ON ANOTHER PLANET The HiRiSE camera on NASA's *Mars Reconnaissance Orbiter* took images of a 2,297-ft.-tall (700-m) steep slope near the north pole on February 19, 2007. Upon analysis, it was found that the orbiter had accidentally captured clouds of debris fanning from the base of the slope, where ice and dust had broken loose and fallen just seconds before.

★ First Martian aurora In June 2006, ESA announced that its *Mars Express Orbiter* had detected localized aurorae on Mars. On Earth, the northern and southern lights are caused by charged particles from the Sun interacting with the planet's magnetic field, making parts of the upper atmosphere glow like a neon tube. Mars has no magnetic field; instead, its aurorae are caused by the solar particles interacting with regions of locally magnetized rock—remnants from when Mars had a magnetic field of its own.

....

JAN. 28: At 21 years 155 days, Jamal Lewis (U.S.A., b. August 26, 1979) of the Baltimore Ravens became the **youngest player to ever appear in the Super Bowl** at Super Bowl XXXV on January 28, 2001.

....

▶★ **FIRST MARS ROVER** NASA's Mars *Pathfinder* ④ (see photo p. 17) mission landed in Ares Vallis on July 4, 1997. The lander deployed a small mobile laboratory, or rover, called *Sojourner,* capable of traveling a few hundred yards from the lander. *Sojourner* weighed just over 23 lb. (10.6 kg) and, was able to conduct basic experiments such as measuring the chemical compositions of Martian rocks. *Pathfinder* (pictured above) and the *Sojourner* rover operated until contact was lost on September 27, 1997.

★ **FIRST IMAGE OF A LANDING ON ANOTHER PLANET** While NASA's *Phoenix* polar lander ② (see photo p. 17) was making its descent toward the surface, the orbiting *Mars Reconnaissance Orbiter* used its high-resolution camera to take an oblique snapshot of the event from 192 miles (310 km) above the planet (left). The image shows the lander suspended beneath its parachute, which had opened 46 seconds earlier, with *Phoenix* just 52 seconds away from touchdown.

JAN. 29: The record for the **most consecutive rolls by an airplane** is 408, achieved by Zoltán Veres (Hungary) during the Al Ain Aerobatic Show in Al Ain, UAE, on this day in 2007.

★**FIRST EXTRATERRESTRIAL DUST DEVILS OBSERVED** First seen from orbit by the *Viking* spacecraft in the 1970s, the "dust devils," whirlwinds of dust, on Mars can tower above the landscape. They are produced by the Sun warming the dust and ground, causing the loose dust to rise into clouds with the warm air. A dust devil passed over the *Spirit* rover in 2005, blowing off the dust on its solar panels and improving its power levels.

Most enduring orbiter NASA's *Mars Global Surveyor* was launched in 1996 and entered Martian orbit on September 11, 1997. It was due to spend just two years mapping and monitoring the planet but, because of the success of the mission and the quality of its science, it was granted multiple extensions.

Contact was lost with the spacecraft on November 2, 2006—by which time it had sent more than 250,000 images of the red planet back to Earth after more than nine years in orbit.

HIGHEST MOUNTAIN IN THE SOLAR SYSTEM The peak of the Martian volcano Olympus Mons ① (see photo p. 17) is 15 miles (25 km) above its base—nearly three times the height of Mount Everest. Olympus Mons is designated a shield volcano because of its shape. Despite its great height, it has a very gentle slope—Olympus Mons is over 20 times wider than it is high.

JAN. 30: The **greatest annual net loss by a company** is $98.7 billion, reported by AOL Time Warner on January 30, 2003.

PLANET EARTH

CONTENTS

EUROPE

★ **Oldest land animal** The fossil of a 0.25-in.-long (1-cm) centipede found near Stonehaven, Scotland, UK, by bus driver and amateur paleontologist Mike Newman (UK) is thought to be 428 million years old and the earliest evidence of a creature living on land rather than in the sea. Formally named *Pneumodesmus newmani* in 2004, the anthropod had spiracles—primitive air-breathing structures on the outside of its body—making it the oldest air-breathing creature yet to be discovered.

Newman made his find on the foreshore of Cowie Harbor in 2004 and placed the specimen in the charge of the National Museums of Scotland in Edinburgh, UK.

★ **LARGEST BRACKISH SEA** Brackish water has a salinity (salt level) between that of freshwater and seawater. The Baltic Sea, in northern Europe, with a surface area of about 145,560 miles² (377,000 km²), is the largest area of brackish water in the world. Its salinity ranges from around 0.6% to 1.5%. For comparison, seawater contains around 3.5% salt. The low salinity of the Baltic is due to the mix of seawater with freshwater running off from its surrounding countries.

COMPACT CONTINENT

Europe is the second smallest of the world's seven continents (Oceania is smaller, Asia is the largest), with a land area of approximately 3.9 million miles² (10.1 million km²). This accounts for about 6.8% of Earth's land area.

HIGHEST WATERFALL The Salto Angel ("Angel Falls") in Venezuela, on a branch of the Carrao River in the Canaima National Park, is the highest waterfall (as opposed to vaporized "bridal veil") in the world. It has a total drop of 3,212 ft. (979 m), with the longest single drop being 2,648 ft. (807 m). The Angel Falls were named after the pilot Jimmie Angel (U.S.A., 1899–1956), who recorded them in his log book on November 16, 1933. Known by the natives as Parakupa-vena or Kerepakupai merú, the falls had been reported by Venezuelan explorer Ernesto Sanchez la Cruz as early as 1910.

Largest hot spring The largest boiling river issues from the hot, alkaline Deildartunguhver spring at Reykholtsdalur, north of Reykjavik, Iceland, at a rate of 65 gallons (245 liters) per second. The water, which is piped up to 40 miles (64 km) away to provide heating, is warmed by underground volcanic activity.

Highest cold water geyser The highest cold water geyser is the Geysir Andernach, which typically blows water to heights of 98–196 ft. (30–60 m) in Germany's Mayen-Koblenz district.

Unlike naturally occurring hot water geysers, cold water geysers are formed by cold ground water dissolving large amounts of carbon dioxide (released through cracks from the Earth's upper mantle) and effectively "charging" the water (similar to a soda bottle). This charged underground water then erupts from a drilled well.

The Andernach well is 1,148 ft. (350 m) deep, and the highest eruption of

★ **LOWEST COUNTRY** The Netherlands has a total area of 16,033 miles² (41,526 km²), about 27% of which actually lies below sea level. The country is famous for its extensive systems of dikes, which are either man-made or natural earth walls that hold back the sea and rivers, and protect land for arable and other uses. Humans have been building dikes in the Netherlands for more than 2,000 years.

JAN. 31: Mehmet Ozyurek's (Turkey) nose was 3.46 in. (8.8 cm) long from its bridge to its tip when measured on January 31, 2001, making it the **longest nose** in the world.

the geyser was 201 ft. 9 in. (61.5 m), recorded on September 19, 2002. The average volume of water ejected per eruption is 2,060 gallons (7,800 liters), and the average interval between eruptions is 90–110 minutes. One eruption lasted 7–8 minutes.

Highest raised beach The High Coast in Västernorrland, Sweden, has a shingle beach at 853 ft. (260 m) above sea level. Its high elevation is a result of land rising after the last Ice Age, when the huge weight of the ice sheets was lifted. The region is still rising, at a rate of around 0.39 in. (1 cm) per year, and will continue rising for around another 10,000 years.

Largest coniferous forest The huge coniferous forests of northern Russia, which lie between Lat. 55°N and the Arctic Circle, cover a total area in the region of 1.5 million miles² (4 million km²).

Largest glacial grotto In terms of area, the largest artificial cave cut inside a glacier measures 59,200 ft.² (5,500 m²). It is located inside the Fee Glacier in Switzerland and was constructed by the glaciologist Benedikt Schnyder (Switzerland). The grotto includes a 177-ft.-long (54-m) tunnel that forms an art gallery 26 ft. (8 m) below the surface of the glacier.

★Largest mantle plume Mantle plumes are regions of warmer rock in the Earth's mantle that slowly rise because of their decreased density. The

☆ **DEEPEST CAVE** In September 2007, cavers of the Ukrainian Speleological Association reached a new record depth of 7,188 ft. (2,191 m) inside the Krubera Cave in the Arabika Massif, Georgia. Over 1.5 miles (2.5 km) of new cave passages were explored in this 29-day underground expedition.

The effort of reaching the lowermost chambers of this cave is likened by speleologists to "climbing an inverted Mount Everest."

FEB. 1: Thomas Edison's "Black Maria," a building frame covered in black roofing paper, was completed in West Orange, New Jersey, on this day in 1893—making it the **first movie studio.**

LONGEST PERIOD OF VOLCANIC ERUPTIONS Mt. Etna is a stratovolcano on the Italian island of Sicily. With a summit height of around 10,922 ft. (3,329 m), it is the largest active volcano in Europe. It is also one of the world's most active volcanoes, and has erupted around 200 times since its first recorded eruption in 1500 B.C.

head of the plume can melt upon reaching the surface and they are believed to provide a means for the Earth to lose internal heat. Today, the largest such plume sits beneath Iceland and is responsible for its formation. The Iceland Plume has been studied extensively—particularly using seismic data. It is characterized by an approximately cylindrical structure, about 100–150 miles (160–240 km) across, and extending to a depth of about 248 miles (400 km) or more. Within this region, the rock is some 302–482°F (150–250°C) hotter than the surrounding mantle.

Most tornadoes by area Incredibly, the world's tornado hotspot is the UK, which is hit by a record of one tornado per 2,856 mile^2 (7,397 km^2). The equivalent figure for the U.S.A. is one tornado per 3,345 mile^2 (8,663 km^2).

★Most northerly botanical garden The Tromsø Botanic Garden (69°40′N 18°56′E) in Norway lies within the Arctic Circle but benefits from the warming effects of the Gulf Stream. Operated by the Museum of Tromsø University (the world's **most northerly university**), it houses arctic and alpine plants from across the northern hemisphere.

Deepest shaft Vrtoglavica (meaning "vertigo") is an unbroken vertical shaft that plunges to a depth of 2,110 ft. (643 m) in the Kanin mountain range in Slovenia, making it the world's deepest naturally occurring shaft. It could comfortably accommodate two Eiffel Towers.

X-REF

You've read about Europe's incredible natural extremes. Now find out about the amazing people who live there in the Gazetteer, starting on p. 173.

FEB. 2: The **fastest transatlantic crossing made completely under solar power** is 29 days by the catamaran *sun21* (Switzerland), sailing from Gran Canaria to Martinique and arriving on this in day 2007.

Longest fjord A geological feature evident chiefly along the coastline of Nordic countries, fjords are long, thin inlets that have been carved out by glacial movement and erosion. The longest fjord is Greenland's Nordvest Fjord, which extends 195 miles (313 km) inland from the sea.

Largest island created by volcanic eruptions The entirety of Iceland was formed by volcanic eruptions from the mid-Atlantic Ridge, upon which it sits. With an area of 39,800 miles^2 (64,051 km^2), Iceland is essentially ocean floor exposed above the surface of the ocean.

Lava flow The longest lava flow in historic times reached a distance of 40–43 miles (65–70 km) during the eruption of Laki in southeast Iceland in 1783. The lava was a mixture of pahoehoe (twisted cordlike solidifications) and aa (blocky lava)—both terms taken from Hawaiian.

NORTH AMERICA

Largest grasslands The grasslands of the Great Plains of North America stretch for 1,158,300 miles^2 (3 million km^2) from southern Canada through the U.S.A. to northern Mexico. The Great Plains are the **largest temperate grasslands,** meaning they experience warm, dry summers and are found inland.

By contrast, the **largest tropical grasslands**—that is, grasslands that grow nearer the coast, have higher rainfall, and often include woodland—are the savanna grasslands of northern Australia, which measure just 463,320 miles^2 (1.2 million km^2).

Most cold-tolerant trees The larches (genus *Larix*) are an incredibly hardy group of trees. In particular, the tamarack larch (*L. laricina*), native to northern North America and predominantly Canada, can survive winter temperatures down to at least −85°F (−65°C) and commonly occurs at the Arctic tree line, the most northerly point at which trees grow.

Worst cyclone disaster by damage toll Hurricane Katrina, the category 5 hurricane that devastated the coast of Louisiana, U.S.A., on August 29, 2005, caused damage in the region of $45 billion, according to the insurance company Swiss Re.

☆**Fastest major glacier** The Columbia Glacier, located between Anchorage and Valdez in Alaska, U.S.A., was measured by glaciologists from the University of Colorado to be flowing at an average rate of 80 ft. (24 m) per day in 2005.

Largest waterfall ever About 18,000 years ago, near the end of the last Ice Age, a huge lake was formed in North America, near the present-day city of Missoula, Montana, U.S.A. The lake formed when a huge advancing glacier dammed a river, resulting in a trapped body of water some 500 miles³ (2,000 km³) in volume. When the water broke through the ice dam created by the glacier, the lake, "glacial Lake Missoula," emptied in a catastrophic flood. As the water drained away, some flowed over what is now known as Dry Falls, resulting in a waterfall measuring 3.5 miles (5.6 km) wide by 380 ft. (115 m) high. By comparison, Niagara Falls measures 1 mile (1.6 km) wide by 165 ft. (50 m) high.

★Largest hydrothermal explosion crater Hydrothermal explosions are caused when underground water is subjected to very high temperatures and pressures by interactions with molten rock. When this superheated water moves close to the surface of the Earth, the resulting drop in pressure can cause an explosive expansion of the water into steam. The Mary Bay explosion crater complex in Yellowstone Park, Wyoming, U.S.A., measures 6,330 × 3,100 ft. (1,929 × 944 m) and was formed around 14,000 years ago by a series of hydrothermal explosions.

Largest island Although controlled by Denmark, Greenland forms part of the North American continent and is the world's largest island. It has an area of 2,175,600 km² (840,000 miles²).

★Fastest glacial rebound The weight of ice pressing down on the land in southeast Alaska during the Little Ice Age, roughly between 1300 and 1650, caused it to be squashed downward. When the ice retreated, the land that was covered started to rebound—that is, spring back upward. Global Positioning System measurements reveal that the area is rising at a rate of 1.25 in. (32 mm) every year.

★ MOST CLIMATICALLY SIGNIFICANT ISTHMUS About three million years ago, volcanic activity and sediment deposition closed the gap between North and South America, creating a strip of land called the Isthmus of Panama. This narrow land barrier prevented circulation between the Atlantic and Pacific oceans and forced the formation of the Gulf Stream, which increased the temperature of European winters by around 18°F (10°C).

OLDEST LIVING TREE A bristlecone pine (*Pinus longaeva*) christened "Methuselah" was found by Dr. Edmund Schulman (U.S.A.) in the White Mountains of California, U.S.A., and dated in 1957 as being 4,600 years old, although some scientists claim to have found even older specimens. The location is kept secret to protect the tree from vandalism. The annual growth rings of trees such as bristlecone pines provide an insight into our changing climate.

★ **HIGHEST CONCENTRATION OF PLAYAS** Playas are dry lakebeds with hard, smooth surfaces that generally form in arid and semiarid conditions. They vary in composition from mud flats to salt flats and many contain shallow lakes during the winter. Eastern New Mexico and the southern high plains of Texas, U.S.A., contain almost 22,000 of these features. A playa in the White Sands National Park, New Mexico, U.S.A., is pictured above.

★ **SMALLEST ORCHID** The orchid family is the second-largest family of flowering plants after Compositae (daisies), with about 25,000 species. The world's smallest orchid species is the jungermannia-like platystele (*Platystele jungermannioides*), found in the lower cloud forest of Mexico, Guatemala, Costa Rica, and Panama at an elevation of 656–3,280 ft. (200–1,000 m). Growing around 0.25 in. (6.3 mm) high and 0.78 in. (20 mm) wide, it blooms in the spring with just two or three tiny flowers that are a mere 0.09 in. (2.5 mm) wide.

FEB. 3: The first images from the surface of the Moon were taken by the Soviet robotic lander *Luna* 9, which landed on the lunar surface on this day in 1966.

There is some debate over which countries constitute North America, but Guinness World Records defines it as Canada, the U.S.A., the Caribbean countries, Greenland, and the Central American countries of Belize, Costa Rica, El Salvador, Guatemala, Honduras, Nicaragua, Mexico, and Panama.

★ LONGEST "SAILING STONE" TRAILS The Racetrack Playa in Death Valley on the Nevada-California border is famous for its bizarre "sailing stones." The flat surface of this dry lakebed is home to rocks that seem to have moved across the ground without human intervention, leaving trails in the dried surface. No one has seen these rocks move, but monitoring results published in 1996 revealed that a rock, nicknamed "Diane," had left a 0.5-mile-long (880-m) trail. Strong winds—up to 90 mph (145 km/h)—coupled with occasional wet conditions are the likely causes of this phenomenon.

★ OLDEST ROCK A track of bedrock found on the eastern shore of Canada's Hudson Bay contains the oldest known rocks on Earth, formed 4.28 billion years ago. Some scientists have speculated that the rocks could be remnants of Earth's primordial crust, which formed on the planet's surface as it cooled soon after forming.

FEB. 4: On this day in 1990, the *Voyager* 1 spacecraft took a picture of our home planet from a distance of almost 4 billion miles (6.5 billion km)—making it the **most distant image of Earth.**

Tallest living tree A coast redwood (*Sequoia sempervirens*) was discovered by Chris Atkins and Michael Taylor (both U.S.A.) in the Redwood National Park, California, U.S.A., on August 25, 2006, and named "Hyperion," after the Greek god. The tree currently measures 379 ft. 1 in. (115.5 m) tall.

SOUTH AMERICA

★**Southernmost permanently inhabited place** Except for Antarctic research stations, the farthest south that people permanently live on Earth is the small hamlet of Puerto Toro (55°04′59S) on the island of Navarino at the southern tip of Chile. In the last census taken in the area (2002), its population was recorded as just 36 people.

Highest active volcano Ojos del Salado on the border between Chile and Argentina is the world's highest active volcano at 22,595 ft. (6,887 m). It last saw some minor activity in 1993.

Driest place Between 1964 and 2001, the average annual rainfall at a meteorological station in Quillagua in the Atacama Desert, Chile, was just 0.019 in. (0.5 mm). This discovery was made during the making of the TV series *Going to Extremes* by UK company Keo Films in 2001.

★**Most productive copper mine** The two open pit mines of Escondida and Escondida-Norte in the Atacama Desert, northern Chile, produced 1.634 million tons (1.483 million tonnes) of copper in 2007. In September 2008, the U.S. Geological Survey stated that there may be as much as 826 million tons (750 million tonnes) of undiscovered copper in the Andes Mountains.

Highest lake The highest commercially navigable lake is Lake Titicaca, which lies at an altitude of 12,500 ft. (3,810 m) above sea level on the Andean border between Peru and Bolivia. Its surface area covers approximately 3,200 miles^2 (8,300 km^2) and it has an average depth of around 460–590 ft. (140–180 m). This freshwater lake also sustains an archipelago of more than 40 floating "islands," made entirely from totora reeds, which are home to the indigenous Uros tribe. These islands—the **largest man-made reed islands**—fluctuate in size, as the bottom layers of reeds rot away and their surfaces are constantly replenished.

FEB. 5: Ridden by Captain Alberto Larraguibel Morales (Chile), the horse Huaso ex-Faithful achieved a record 8-ft. 1.25-in.-high (2.47-m) jump on February 5, 1949, the **highest jump by a horse.**

Largest aquatic insect The largest aquatic insect is the giant water bug (*Lethocerus maximus*), a carnivorous species that inhabits Venezuela and Brazil. It has been measured up to 4.5 in. (11.5 cm) long, but, as it is relatively long and narrow, it is not as heavy as some of this continent's burly terrestrial beetles and stick insects.

Widest river While not in flood, the main stretches (i.e., not its tidal reaches, where an estuary/delta can be much wider) of the Amazon River in South America can reach widths of up to 7 miles (11 km) at its widest points.

Greatest species endemism The area of the world considered to have the highest species endemism is the Tropical Andes stretching across Venezuela, Colombia, Ecuador, Peru, Bolivia, and a small section of northern Argentina. So far, scientists have identified 20,000 vascular plants, 677 birds, 68 mammals, 218 reptiles, and 604 amphibians that are endemic to the area, covering 485,700 miles^2 (1,257,957 km^2).

Narrowest country In terms of comparing its length to its width, the narrowest country is Chile. Measuring an average of 2,700 miles (4,345 km) long by 108 miles (175 km) wide, the country forms a ribbon shape that extends down the entire straight western coastline of South America.

LARGEST HERB The puya (*Puya raimondii*, pictured left) is a rare species of giant bromeliad growing at an altitude of around 12,992 ft. (3,960 m) in the Bolivian mountains. Although it is a herbaceous plant, it has a panicle—stalk or trunk—up to 13 ft. (4 m) high, bearing thousands of flowers and millions of seeds. The puya takes about 150 years to bloom, making it the **slowest plant to flower**; once it has blossomed, the plant dies.

FEB. 6: Danny Wainwright (UK) popped the **highest skateboard ollie** at 44.5 in. (113 cm) on this day in 2000 to win the Reese Forbes Ollie Challenge in Long Beach, California, U.S.A.

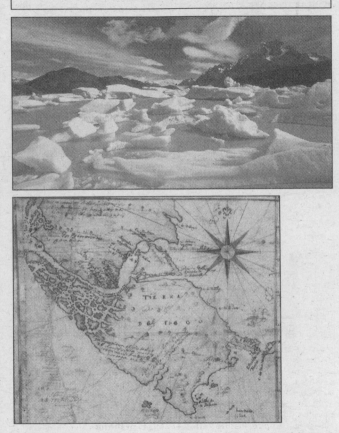

★**SOUTHERNMOST STRAIT** The Strait of Magellan is a natural passage of water separating mainland South America from Tierra del Fuego. Measuring about 329 miles (530 km) long and between 2.4 and 14.9 miles (4 and 24 km) wide, it has historically been the most important shipping route that connects the Atlantic and Pacific oceans. Despite the importance of the man-made Panama Canal, the Strait of Magellan is still used extensively today by ships rounding South America.

LARGEST PRE-COLOMBIAN LINES
The so-called "Nazca lines" are a group of gigantic figures engraved in the ground of the Nazca desert in Peru, representing plants, animals, insects, and a variety of geometric shapes. Most can only be appreciated from the air. The designs occupy a 193-mile^2 (500-km^2) piece of land and average 600 ft. (180 m) in length.

Largest river basin A basin is an area of land where water—usually from rain or melting snow or ice—drains into a significant body of water, typically a river. The largest river basin in the world is the Amazon basin, which covers around 2,720,000 miles^2 (7,045,000 km^2)—almost the size of Australia. It has many tributaries, including the Madeira, which at 2,100 miles (3,380 km) is the world's **longest tributary.**

★ **LARGEST NEW WORLD CIVILIZATION** Owing to their "recent" discovery by Western civilizations, the Americas and Australasia are collectively known as the New World. The most successful and largest empire in these regions before discovery by the West was the Incas, who started as a tribe founded in the city of Cuzco around the year 1200. At their height, around 1460, the Incas ruled over 10 million people throughout an area of western South America similar in size to the Roman Empire. Pictured are the remains of the Inca city of Machu Picchu in Peru.

FEB. 7: Concorde took 2 hr. 52 min. 59 sec. to travel the 3,750 miles (6,035 km) between New York and London on February 7, 1996, the **fastest transatlantic flight by a commercial airplane.**

Longest mountain range The Andes is the world's longest range of mountains. At 4,700 miles (7,600 km) in length, it spans seven countries and includes some of the highest mountains on Earth. Over 50 of the Andes peaks reach over 20,000 ft. (6,000 m) high. The range is around 200 miles (300 km) in width along most of its extent.

Largest swamp Located principally in Brazil, but with small areas within Bolivia and Paraguay, the Pantanal (which is Spanish for "marshland") covers a surface area of 57,915 miles^2 (150,000 km^2)—greater than the total surface area of England. During the rainy season, 80% of the Pantanal is flooded.

☆**Highest rate of deforestation** According to the *2009 State of World's Forests* report by the Food and Agriculture Organization (FAO) of the United Nations, Brazil experiences the greatest rate of deforestation. For the years 2000 to 2005, Brazil underwent a loss of 7,667,680 acres (3,103,000 hectares; 12,000 miles^2, or 31,000 km^2)—an area the size of Belgium—per year.

The report reveals that the planet lost 18.04 million acres (745,000 hectares) of forest between 2000 and 2005, equivalent to 77 miles^2

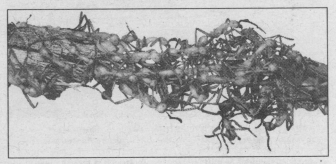

LONGEST COLUMN OF ANTS Army ants of the genus Eciton, from Central and South America, and driver ants of the genus Dorylus, from Africa, have a reputation for traveling in highly organized columns. These can be up to 328 ft. (100 m) long and over 3 ft. 4 in. (1 m) wide, and may contain as many as 600,000 individuals, which frequently take several hours to pass one spot.

....

FEB. 8: On this day in 2005, astronomers from the Harvard-Smithsonian Center for Astrophysics (U.S.A.) announced a star traveling at over 1.5 million mph (2.4 million km/h)—the **fastest recorded star.**
....

(200 km²)—more than 37,000 football fields or the area of Washington, D.C., U.S.A.—every day.

AFRICA

★**Longest inhabited continent** Africa is regarded as the cradle of civilization and is the continent on which human ancestors, as well as the great apes, first evolved millions of years ago. Modern humans, *Homo sapiens,* first appeared there around 200,000 years ago.

Largest desert The Sahara in north Africa is the largest hot desert in the world. At its greatest length, it is 3,200 miles (5,150 km) from east to west; from north to south, it is between 800 and 1,400 miles (1,280 and 2,250 km). The area covered by the desert is about 3.5 million miles² (9.1 million km²). The Sahara also boasts the **highest sand dunes:** in Isaouane-n-Tifernine in east central Algeria, the dunes can reach a height of 1,526 ft. (465 m).

★**SMALLEST PLANT KINGDOM** The South African is the smallest of the six floral kingdoms (Boreal, Neotropical, Paleotropical, South African, Australian, and Antarctic). It also has the ★**highest concentration of plant species,** with over 9,000 species, 6,200 of which are endemic (occur nowhere else), in an area of just 17,750 miles² (46,000 km²). This equates to 1,300 species per 3,861 miles² (10,000 km²). The rainforests of South America contain a concentration of only 400 plant species per the same area.

....

FEB. 9: On this day in 1995, Fred Hale (U.S.A.) became the world's **oldest driver** when he had his license renewed . . . at the grand age of 104 years!

....

★**LARGEST TROPICAL LAKE** With a surface area of 26,500 miles² (68,634 km²), Lake Victoria is the biggest lake in the world that lies within the tropics. Containing some 660 miles³ (2,750 km³) of water, it is ranked as the 7th largest freshwater lake in the world. It is the main source of the Nile River.

Highest recorded temperature The highest shade temperature ever recorded is 136°F (58°C) at Al'Aziziyah in the Sahara Desert, Libya, on September 13, 1922.

★**Highest concentration of heathers** The fynbos (Afrikaans for "fine bush") plant ecosystem, exclusive to South Africa's Cape floristic region, contains more than 600 species of heather (*Erica,* see photograph p. 37). Only 26 species of heather occur in the rest of the world.

★**Highest concentration of endangered plant species** The world's highest concentration of endangered plant species occurs in South Africa's Cape Flats. A total of 15 species per square kilometer in the region are threatened by extinction.

PLATYPUS PLANT

The **leaves with the longest lifespan** belong to the welwitschia (*Welwitschia mirabilis*) of the Namib. This strange plant lives for an estimated 400–1,500 years and produces two leaves per century, which it never sheds, hence its Afrikaans name *tweeblarkanniedood* ("two-leaf-cannot-die").

FEB. 10: The **largest snowball fight** took place on this day in 2006 between 3,745 participants at Michigan Technological University in Houghton, Michigan, U.S.A.

★ **OLDEST DESERT** The Namib Desert, covering some 31,200 miles^2 (80,807 km^2) of Namibia and Angola, has been arid or semiarid for at least 80 million years. A coastal desert, it receives less than 0.4 in. (10 mm) of rain each year. Its hyper-arid state is caused by descending dry air, cooled by the frigid waters of the southern Atlantic's Benguela current. Such conditions lead to thick coastal fogs that provide just enough moisture to support the survival of a number of highly adapted life forms, such as *Welwitschia*, which Darwin named "the vegetable Ornithorhynchus"—the platypus of the plant kingdom.

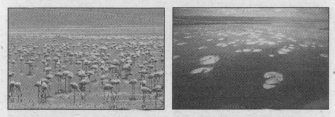

★ **LAKES WITH THE HIGHEST LEVELS OF ALKALINITY** The Magadi-Natron basin in the Rift Valley of Kenya-Tanzania contains saline (salt) bodies of water with temperatures as high as 120°F (50°C) and alkalinity as high as pH 10–12—strong enough to blister or burn the skin. The corrosiveness of these lakes—particularly Natron, Magadi, and Nakuru—is caused by high concentrations of sodium carbonate (soda), sulfur, chlorine, and phosphorus produced by the active volcanoes in this rift system (see p. 40). Lake Natron's characteristic deep red coloration (pictured) is the result of pigments produced by algae thriving in the hypersaline environment. The pigments also account for the pink coloration of the lesser flamingoes (*Phoenicopterus minor*, above left) who feed off the algae.

LONGEST RIFT SYSTEM The East African Rift System is approximately 4,000 miles (6,400 km) long with an average width of 30–40 miles (50–65 km). The escarpments around the edge of the valley have an average height of 2,000–3,000 ft. (600–900 m). Also known as the Great Rift Valley, it begins in Jordan and extends to Mozambique in east Africa. This extensive rift system has been gradually forming for around 30 million years, as the Arabian peninsula has separated from Africa. As a result, the area is dotted with volcanoes, including Oldoinyo Lengai (see Coldest erupting lava, p. 41), hot springs, and highly alkaline lakes.

> **9,387,520 ACRES (3,798,994 HECTARES):** the area of the Kgalagadi Transfrontier Park in Botswana and South Africa, the world's **largest cross-border park.**

Continent most affected by desertification Desertification—the transformation of arable land to desert—has a number of natural causes, such as climate variation and soil erosion. Human activities—including over-intensive farming, deforestation, and even the migration of refugees during wartime—can also give rise to conditions that make desertification possible. The situation is at its worst in Africa, where two-thirds of the continent has been reduced to desert or dry land.

Most thunderous place In the Tororo district of Uganda, an average of 251 days of thunder per annum were recorded for the 10-year period 1967–76, making it the most thunderous place on Earth.

Coldest erupting lava Common basaltic lavas erupt at temperatures of 2,010–2,190°F (1,100–1,200°C), but the natrocarbonatite lava of the volcano Oldoinyo Lengai in Tanzania erupts at just 930–1,110°F (500–600°C). Oldoinyo Lengai is the only active carbonatite volcano on Earth. The bizarre carbonatite lava looks much like melted chocolate upon eruption. It is extremely runny and has the lowest viscosity of any lava. As it cools, it turns white in color.

ASIA

Largest continent Continental masses cover 41.25% of the Earth's surface, or 81,200,000 miles² (210,400,000 km²). The largest of these continental masses is Asia, which covers an area of 17,388,686 miles² (45,036,492 km²).

Largest hydroelectric project The Three Gorges Dam in China is the largest hydroelectric power station in the world, and is set to generate power for China's expanding economy as well as control flooding in the Yangtze River. The huge dam wall, measuring 7,575 ft. (2,309 m) long by 607 ft. (185 m) high was completed in May 2006.

....
FEB. 11: The **first traffic lights** were tested on this day in 1928 in Wolverhampton, UK. Within a month, the first permanently operated lights were turned on in Leeds, West Yorkshire, UK.
....

★ **HIGHEST GLACIER** The head of the Khumbu Glacier, located between the peaks of Mount Everest and the Lhotse-Nuptse Ridge in the Himalayas, is situated at an altitude of around 24,934 ft. (7,600 m) above sea level and runs for 10 miles (17 km) to the west and south, terminating at around 16,076 ft. (4,900 m) above sea level.

Country with the most varied topography China is the world's least flat country, with an altitude range of 29,534 ft. (9,002 m) from the Turpan Depression at 505 ft. (154 m) below sea level to the peak of Mount Everest at 29,028 ft. (8,848 m) above sea level.

★ **Largest vertical extent** Both the highest and lowest points on the Earth's exposed surface are in Asia. Mount Everest, with its peak at 29,028 ft. (8,848 m) above sea level, and the Dead Sea, with its surface at 1,384 ft. (422 m) below sea level, give Asia a vertical extent (that is, the distance between its highest and lowest points) of 30,413 ft. (9,270 m).

COLDEST HOT DESERT In the Gobi desert, winter temperatures can drop below –4°F (–20°C). The Gobi extends over southern Mongolia and certain parts of northern and northwestern China and is the world's fifth largest desert. The Himalayan mountain range prevents rain-laden clouds from reaching the Gobi, which for this reason is referred to as a "rain shadow" desert. Pictured is a bactrian camel, which grows a shaggy winter coat during the colder months.

FEB. 12: On this day in 2002, paleontologists led by Prof. Peter Doyle (UK) announced they had found 160-million-year-old fossilized vomit from an ichthyosaur, a large marine reptile—the **oldest vomit.**

★ MOST CONICAL VOLCANO Mount Mayon (8,077 ft./2,462 m; 13°15'24'N 123°41'6'E) i's the most active volcano in the Philippines. It is almost perfectly conical—with a base 80 miles (130 km) in circumference—and is known to volcanologists as the "Perfect Cone." Situated in Albay on the island of Luzon, the majestic Mayon is a stratovolcano (one composed of layers of erupted material) with a characteristic small crater peak and steep sides. It last erupted between July and October 2006.

★ Largest continental collision zone Around 40–50 million years ago, the Indian subcontinent collided with the Eurasian continent. The collision, which is still ongoing along a zone around 1,491 miles (2,400 km) long, created the Himalayan mountains.

Largest landlocked country Kazakhstan, which has an area of 1,052,100 miles^2 (2,724,900 km^2), is bordered by Russia, China, Kyrgystan, Uzbekistan, Turkmenistan, and the landlocked Caspian Sea. It has no border access to the open ocean.

....

FEB. 13: The **tallest woman ever** was Zeng Jinlian (China, b. June 26, 1964). When she died, on this day in 1982, she measured 8 ft. 1.75 in. (2.48 m).

....

★ **HIGHEST RIVER** Of the world's major rivers, the highest is the Yarlung Zangbo, which begins in Tibet and runs for around 1,242 miles (2,000 km) in China, with an average elevation of around 13,123 ft. (4,000 m), before entering India, where it is known as the Brahmaputra River. It enters the ocean at the Bay of Bengal, where it forms the world's **largest delta.**

Largest lake The largest inland sea or lake in the world is the Caspian Sea (in Azerbaijan, Russia, Kazakhstan, Turkmenistan, and Iran). It is 760 miles (1,225 km) long and it has an area of 143,550 miles^2 (371,800 km^2). Of this total area, some 55,280 miles^2 (143,200 km^2), or 38.5%, is in Iran. Its maximum depth is 3,360 ft. (1,025 m) and the surface is 93.6 ft. (28.5 m) below sea level.

Lake Baikal in the southern part of eastern Siberia, Russia, is the **deepest**

lake. It is 385 miles (620 km) long and between 20 miles and 46 miles (32 km and 74 km) wide. In 1974, the lake's Olkhon Crevice was measured by the Hydrographic Service of the

★ **LARGEST TERRESTRIAL BIOME** Biologists divide the world into major regions of distinctive zones or "biomes," such as desert, tundra, grassland, and mangrove. The largest is the taiga, the great boreal coniferous forest that encircles the world's land south of the northern tundra. It occurs mostly in northern Siberia, where it covers around 2.3 million miles^2 (5.9 million km^2)— around one-third of the world's forested area.

Planet Earth

HIGHEST TREE The highest altitude at which trees have been discovered is 15,000 ft. (4,600 m). A silver fir (*Abies squamata*) was located at this height in southwestern China, and specimens of the closely related *A. spectabilis* have been found at an altitude of 14,000 ft. (4,267 m) in the Himalayas. Himalayan birch trees (*Betula utilis,* left) have also been discovered at these altitudes.

Soviet Pacific Navy and found to be 5,371 ft. (1,637 m) deep, of which 3,875 ft. (1,181 m) is below sea level.

Longest earthquake The Sumatra-Andaman Islands earthquake in the Indian Ocean on December 26, 2004 was the longest-lasting quake ever recorded. Its duration, monitored by seismometers all over the world and announced in the journal *Science* in May 2005, lasted between 500 and 600 seconds. The earthquake had a magnitude of between 9.1 and 9.3 on the Richter scale.

★**Largest frozen peat bog** The western Siberian subarctic region is a vast area of frozen peat bog covering around 386,102 miles^2 (1 million km^2), roughly the area of France and Germany combined. In 2005, scientists discovered that this region is thawing for the first time since its formation 11,000 years ago.

Land farthest from sea The land location most remote from open ocean is at Lat. 46°16.8'N, Long. 86°40.2'E in the Dzungarian Basin, which is in

---

TAKE THE HIGH ROAD

The **highest road** in the world crosses Khardungla pass at an altitude of 18,640 ft. (5,682 m). It is one of three passes on the Leh-Manali road in Kashmir, completed in 1976.

FEB. 14: Valentine's Day! The **longest hug** was achieved by Paul Gerrard and Sandra Brooke (both UK), who hugged for 24 hr. 1 min. at Paddington Station, London, UK, on February 13–14, 2008.

---

the Xinjiang Uygur autonomous region, in the far northwest of China. It is at a great-circle distance of 1,645 miles (2,648 km) from the nearest open sea—Baydaratskaya Guba to the north (Arctic Ocean), Feni Point to the south (Indian Ocean), and Bohai Wan to the east (Yellow Sea).

☆ **Largest natural gas field** The South Pars/North Field gas field covers an underground area of 3,745 miles^2 (9,700 km^2) straddling the jurisdictions of Iran and Qatar. In addition to oil deposits equivalent to 60 billion barrels, its total reserves of natural gas are estimated to be around 1.8 quadrillion ft.^{3} (51 trillion m^3), or enough to fill the fuel tanks of more than 230 million Boeing 747s.

Largest area of dry steppe Steppe land is treeless, savannah grassland with hot, dry summers and cold, snowless winters. The largest area of dry steppe land on Earth is the Kazakh Steppe of central Asia, which measures 310,600 miles^2 (804,500 km^2). Before some areas were cultivated for crop farming in the 1950s, the Kazakh Steppe ran from the Ural River in the west to the Altai foothills in the east.

OCEANIA

★ **Continent with the fewest land borders** Of the major regions of the Earth, Oceania contains the fewest international land borders. According to the United Nations definition of the continent of Oceania, the only land border in the region is that between Papua New Guinea and Indonesia.

★ **RAREST MAMMALS The five species of the order Monotremata are an incredibly rare group of primitive mammals that lay eggs instead of producing live young. The group consists of four species of echidna (a type of spiny anteater) and the only species of platypus (above). The entire Monotreme group is found exclusively in Australia and New Guinea.**

Hottest places On an annual-mean basis, with readings taken over a six year period from 1960 to 1966, the temperature at Dallol, Ethiopia, was 94°F (34°C). In Death Valley, California, U.S.A., maximum temperatures of over 120°F (49°C) were recorded on 43 consecutive days between July 6 and August 17, 1917. But at Marble Bar, Western Australia, 160 consecutive days with maximum temperatures of 100°F (37.8°C) or higher were recorded between October 31, 1923, and April 7, 1924 (maximum 120.5°F; 49.2°C). And at Wyndham, Western Australia, the temperature reached 90°F (32.2°C) or more on 333 days in 1946.

Highest waterspout The highest waterspout of which there is a reliable record was one observed on May 16, 1898, off Eden, New South Wales, Australia. A reading from the shore gave its height as 5,013 ft. (1,528 m). Waterspouts occur when tornadoes appear at sea, sucking a column (vortex) of water into the clouds. Although associated mostly with minor tornadoes, waterspouts pose a significant risk to shipping.

Longest reef The Great Barrier Reef off Queensland, northeastern Australia, is 1,260 miles (2,027 km) in length. It is not actually a single reef but consists of thousands of separate reefs. It is also the **largest marine animal structure,** consisting of countless billions of dead and living stony corals (order Madreporaria or Scleractinia). Over 350 species of coral are currently found there, and its accretion is estimated to have taken 600 million years.

★FLATTEST LANDMASS
Australia is the only major landmass in the world to lack a significant mountain range. The highest point on the Australian mainland is the summit of Mount Kosciuszko (pictured at left) in New South Wales, at an elevation of 7,313 ft. (2,229 m) above sea level. Australia's average elevation is just over 656 ft. (200 m) above sea level.

FEB. 15: On this day in 2003, the **largest anti-war rally** took place in Rome, Italy, where a crowd of 3 million gathered to protest against the U.S.A.'s threat to invade Iraq.

★Most southerly wetlands Home to many rare species, such as the cushion plant Donatia, Waitunu Lagoon and its associated wetlands on the southern tip of South Island, New Zealand, are the southernmost recognized wetlands. Comprising lagoons, ponds, lakes, streams, peatlands, and coastal beaches, the wetlands cover an area of 8,787 acres (3,556 ha).

Largest exposed sandstone monolith Uluru, aka Ayers Rock, is a sandstone monolith that rises to a height of 1,142 ft. (348 m) above the surrounding desert plain in Northern Territory, Australia. It is 1.5 miles (2.5 km) long and 1 mile (1.6 km) wide and is considered sacred by the local Aboriginal people. Only one-third of the rock can be seen—two-thirds of it extends down beneath the surface of the desert. It has a total volume of 0.12 miles^3 (0.54 km^3)—over 215 times that of the Great Pyramid of Giza in Egypt.

HIGHEST DENSITY OF CRABS Around 120 million red crabs (*Gecarcoidea natalis*) live on the 52-mile^2 (135-km^2) Christmas Island, a density of approximately one crab per square yard for the whole island. Each year, millions of the crabs swarm out of their forest burrows to the coast to mate and spawn. Many of the crabs, which are unique to the island, die on the way, but some survive and return to the forest.

> **402,781 ACRES (163,000 HA):** the area of Fraser Island, **the largest sand island,** off the coast of Queensland, Australia.

★**Largest concentration of marsupial species** Marsupials are a group of mammals whose young are not fully developed at birth. Female marsupials, including the kangaroo, wallaby, and koala, carry their newly born young in a pouch. Scientists estimate that there are around 330 species of marsupials, more than two thirds of which are found exclusively in Australia and its surrounding islands.

Longest wilderness horse trail The Australian Bicentennial National Trail is the longest marked horse-trekking trail in the world at 3,312 miles (5,330 km). The trail, which is also used by hikers and mountain bikers, winds through wilderness areas from Cooktown in North Queensland to Healesville in Victoria, following historic coach and stock routes, packhorse trails, and country roads.

★**LARGEST SUBMARINE PLATEAU** The Ontong Java Plateau, a large flat area on the floor of the Pacific Ocean, is a vast volcanic formation north of the Solomon Islands. It covers an area of around 772,204 miles^2 (2 million km^2), roughly the same size as Mexico, and is believed to have formed around 125 million years ago.

FEB. 16: The **most expensive car license plate**—made up of the single digit "1"—was sold to Saeed Abdul Ghaffar Khouri (UAE) for 52.2 million dirhams ($14.2 million) on this day in 2008.

★ **LARGEST HUMAN ART FIGURE** A giant outline of a naked Aborigine man, 2.6 miles (4.2 km) in length and so vast that it can only be seen from the air, appeared at Finniss Springs, near Marree, South Australia, in July 1998. The lines of the figure are 115 ft. (35 m) wide and measure 17 miles (28 km) around. No one has yet owned up to the "Marree Man" and theories about its creation still abound.

★ **Largest submerged microcontinent** New Zealand represents just the highest part of the microcontinent of Zealandia. Although it has an area of some 1,351,357 miles^2 (3,500,000 km^2)—about half the size of Australia—about 93% of Zealandia is under water and forms a shallow coastal shelf around New Zealand. A microcontinent is a fragment of land broken off from a main continental landmass.

OCEANIA

There is much debate as to which countries fall within the continent of Oceania. According to the UN, the continent includes Australia, New Zealand, Papua New Guinea, and the island groups of Melanesia, Micronesia, and Polynesia.

★ **MOST EASTERLY COUNTRY** The Republic of Kiribati is an island nation of around 100,000 people living on a collection of atolls in the Pacific Ocean. In 1995, its government moved the International Dateline so that all of its islands were in the same time zone. As a result, the International Dateline now bulges eastward around Kiribati.

FEB. 17: A group of 72 volunteers built the **largest self-supporting domed igloo** on this day in 2008. The igloo had an internal diameter of 25 ft. 9 in. (7.85 m) and a height of 13 ft. 8 in. (4.17 m).

Most forested country The country with the highest percentage of forested land is the Cook Islands in the South Pacific Ocean, with 95.7% of the country covered as of 2000.

Tallest geyser Waimangu geyser in New Zealand regularly erupted to a height in excess of 1,500 ft. (460 m) every 30–36 hours in 1903. However, in 1904, the geyser fell inactive and has remained so ever since.

Largest cloud Soliton clouds are rare, solitary cloud forms that maintain their shape while moving at a constant velocity. The best-known soliton cloud is Morning Glory, which forms in the Gulf of Carpentaria, Australia. This backward-rolling cloud formation can be 620 miles (1,000 km) long, 3,280 ft. (1 km) high, and can travel at up to 37 mph (60 km/h).

Most remote spot from land An area in the South Pacific, 47°30'S, 120°W, is 1,600 miles (2,575 km) from the nearest points of land, namely Pitcairn Island, Ducie Island, and Peter I Island. Centered on this spot is a massive circle of water with an area of 8,041,200 miles^2 (20,826,800 km^2), which is larger than Russia.

POLAR REGIONS

★**Continent with the fewest countries** The continent of Antarctica has no native population, and no countries are recognized below the latitude of 60°S. Although various countries have claimed parts of Antarctic territory, the Antarctic Treaty, signed by 45 nations in 1959, pledges to keep the continent open for peaceful scientific investigation and precludes military activity.

★**OLDEST CONTINUOUSLY OCCUPIED ANTARCTIC STATION** Mawson Station, operated by the Australian Antarctic Division, is located in Mac Robertson Land, East Antarctica. It was first established as a permanent base on February 13, 1954, and currently houses around 20 people in the winter and 60 during the summer.

....

FEB. 18: The U.S.A.'s Powerball prize stood at $365 million when it was drawn on this day in 2006, the **largest national lottery jackpot** prize.

....

★ **SMALLEST RECORDED ARCTIC ICECAP** The Arctic icecap (above) is mainly composed of sea ice floating on the Arctic Ocean. Because of the changing temperatures across Earth's seasons, this cap shrinks in the summer and grows in the winter. In the summer of 2007, the icecap shrank to a record low extent, covering 1.59 million miles^2 (4.11 million km^2). The average summer area for the Arctic icecap between 1979 and 2000 was 2,6 million miles^2 (6.7 million km^2).

Thickest ice On January 4, 1975, a team of seismologists measured the ice in Wilkes Land in eastern Antarctica and found it to be 15,669 ft. (4,776 m; 2.96 miles; 4.76 km) deep, equivalent to 10 Empire State Buildings!

★ **LARGEST ANTARCTIC BASE** McMurdo Station is the U.S.A.'s permanent research site on the southern tip of Ross Island. It was first established in 1956 and has since grown to be Antarctica's largest permanently inhabited facility. In winter, its population is less than 200 but this grows to around 1,000 during the summer. Its inhabitants are scientists and support personnel. The station contains three airfields, a harbor, and more than 100 buildings, as well as a nine-hole golf course.

★**First aircraft flight over the North Pole** On May 12, 1926, an expedition led by Roald Amundsen (Norway) flew over the North Pole in the airship *Norge,* piloted by its designer, Umberto Nobile (Italy). Among the 16 crew members who undertook the trip was the U.S. explorer Lincoln Ellsworth, who also helped to finance the flight.

★**First expedition to the Antarctic Pole of Inaccessibility on foot** The Antarctic Pole of Inaccessibility is the exact center of the Antarctic land mass. It was first reached on foot (assisted with kite skis) by Henry Cookson, Rupert Longsdon, Rory Sweet (all UK), and Paul Landry (Canada), who dragged their supplies behind them on 264-lb. (120-kg) sleds, on January 19, 2007. The team—N2i—covered 1,056 miles (1,700 km). The Pole of Inaccessibility is more remote and more difficult to reach than the geographic South Pole, and was reached for the first time in 1948 by a Soviet team.

LARGEST . . .

Glacier First discovered by an Australian aircraft crew between 1956 and 1957, the Lambert Glacier has an area of 386,100 miles^2 (1 million km^2). Draining about one fifth of the East Antarctic ice sheet, it is up to 40 miles (64 km) wide and, with its seaward extension (the Amery Ice Shelf), it measures at least 440 miles (700 km) in length, which also makes it the world's **longest glacier.**

Single body of fresh water The Antarctic icecap holds approximately 7.25 million miles^3 (30 million km^3) of fresh water, around 70% of the world's total supply of fresh water.

Area of sea ice During the winter, between 6.5 and 7.7 million miles^2 (17 and 20 million km^2) of the Southern Ocean is covered by sea ice. This area decreases in size to between 1.1 and 1.5 million miles^2 (3 and 4 million km^2) during the summer. The Arctic Ocean, by comparison, is covered by between 5 and 6 million miles^2 (14 and 16 million km^2) of ice in the winter, decreasing to 2.7–3.5 million miles^2 (7–9 million km^2) in the summer.

★ LARGEST RUPTURED EPISHELF LAKE Epishelf lakes are created when an ice shelf blocks the entrance to a saltwater lake or fjord. Fresh water entering the lake is locked in and forms a layer of fresh water above the heavier sea water. The epishelf lake in the 19.8-mile-long (32-km) Disraeli Fjord in Canada had a layer of fresh water 141 ft. (43 m) deep, held in by the Ward Hunt ice shelf. Between 2000 and 2002, fracturing of the shelf caused 105 billion ft.^{3} (3 billion m^3) of fresh water to drain into the ocean.

Subglacial lake Lake Vostok in Antarctica was discovered in 1994 by analyzing radar imagery of the icy continent. Located beneath Russia's Vostok Station, it is buried under 2.5 miles (4 km) of the East Antarctic Ice Sheet and is one of the oldest and most pristine lakes on Earth. It has been completely isolated from the rest of the world for at least 500,000 years and perhaps much longer. Covering an area of some 5,400 miles^2 (14,000 km^2), it is the 18th largest lake in the world and has a depth of at least 330 ft. (100 m).

★ Subglacial mountain range The Gamburtsev Mountains in eastern Antarctica extend for some 745 miles (1,198 km) across the continent. They reach up to 8,858 ft. high and are permanently buried under more than 1,968 ft. (2.69 km) of ice. First discovered by a Soviet team using seismic surveys in 1958, the mountains are believed to be around 500 million years old.

HIGHEST CONTINENT Excluding its ice shelves, Antarctica has an average elevation of 7,198 ft. (2,194 m) above the OSU91A Geoid—a means of measurement similar to, yet more accurate than, measuring from sea level. The highest point on the continent is Vinson Massif, at 16,066 ft. (4,897 m) above sea level.

★ Subglacial river In April 2006, scientists from University College, London and Bristol University (both UK) released the results of satellite studies of lakes under the Antarctic ice. The data showed the lowering of the

....

FEB. 20: Rally driver Juha Kankkunen (Finland) hit a speed of 199.86 mph (321.65 km/h), the **fastest speed for a car on ice,** on the frozen Gulf of Bothnia in Kuivaniemi, Finland, on this day in 2007.

....

ice surface over one subglacial lake by 10 ft. (3 m) and simultaneous bulges over two other lakes 180 miles (290 km) away. The scientists think these observations could be explained by the presence of a subglacial river. A flow of 0.43 miles^3 (1.8 km^3) of water over 16 months could account for the phenomenon.

ANTARCTIC STATIONS

While Antarctica has no permanent population, it has been continuously occupied since 1943 by scientists living at various bases. The seasonal population varies but can reach up to 4,000.

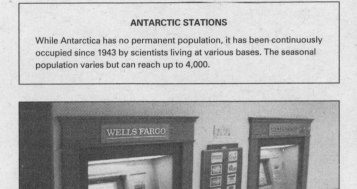

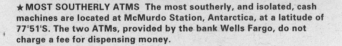

★ **MOST SOUTHERLY ATMS** The most southerly, and isolated, cash machines are located at McMurdo Station, Antarctica, at a latitude of 77°51'S. The two ATMs, provided by the bank Wells Fargo, do not charge a fee for dispensing money.

Iceberg As of April 2005, iceberg B15-A in the Ross Sea off Antarctica measured around 75 miles by 12 miles (120 km by 20 km), with an area of approximately 960 miles^2 (2,500 km^2).

ANIMAL PLANET

CONTENTS

ARTHROPODS

Largest spider A male goliath bird-eating spider (*Theraphosa blondi*) collected by members of the Pablo San Martin Expedition in Rio Cavro, Venezuela, in April 1965 had a leg-span of 11 in. (28 cm) —wide enough to cover a dinner plate.

The **smallest spider** known is *Patu marplesi* of Western Samoa. A male specimen found in moss at Madolelei on the island of Upolu, in January 1965, measured 0.017 in. (0.43 mm) overall—about the size of the period at the end of this sentence. While considered rare, it may just be that *Patu marplesi* is just very difficult to detect and collect.

★**First use of bee-venom therapy** The earliest use of apitherapy (or bee-venom therapy—BVT, the pharmacological use of honeybee products to treat illnesses) was by the ancient Chinese, Greeks, and Romans. Greek physician Galen (A.D. 129–200) is said to have used honey and bee venom to treat baldness. Bees are still used today as a type of "insect acupuncture," and BVT is particularly popular in the alternative treatment of autoimmune diseases such as MS and arthritis.

☆**Largest butterfly farm** Opened in March 1986 and occupying 2 acres (0.8 hectares), the world's largest butterfly farm is on the Malaysian island

☆**LONGEST INSECT** On October 16, 2008, the UK's Natural History Museum announced a new holder for the record of the longest stick insect: *Phobaeticus chani*—aka Chan's megastick—from the rainforests of Borneo. The longest of the three known specimens (pictured with the museum's Orthoptera curator George Beccaloni) measured 22.3 in. (56.6 cm) with its legs stretched; its body alone measured 14 in. (35.5 cm)—also a record for the insect class.

of Penang. It contains over 4,000 living specimens belonging to more than 50 different species.

Smallest butterfly The tiny grass blue (*Zizula hylax*) has a forewing length of 0.25 in. (6 mm). Its upperside is steely blue-gray in color, with a light gray and scattered dark speckling underside.

Newest animal phylum In November 2006, studies of an obscure genus of small, wormlike creatures revealed not one but two species. *Xenoturbella* had first become known to science when dredged up from the Baltic Sea and named in 1949. The two species—*X. bocki* and *X. westbladi*—are so different from all other species of animal that they required the creation of an entirely new phylum—the highest category of animal classification—for themselves; this is a rare occurrence, as only a few new phyla have been discovered in the past 50 years.

Lightest insect The male bloodsucking banded louse (*Enderleinellus zonatus*) and the parasitic wasp *Caraphractus cinctus* each weigh as little as 0.005 mg (5,670,000 to an ounce). Eggs of the latter each weigh 0.0002 mg (141,750,000 to an ounce).

LARGEST MOUTH (LAND ANIMAL) Excuse us! The largest mouth of all land animals belongs to the hippopotamus (*Hippopotamus amphibius*) of Africa, which can open its jaws to almost 180°. In a fully grown male hippo, this equates to an average gape of 4 ft. (1.2 m).

★ **GREATEST COLOR VISION**
Stomatopod crustaceans, which include the mantis shrimps, possess the greatest extent of color vision. Whereas, by comparison, the eyes of most mammals contain two types of color photoreceptor, humans and other primates have three (and most birds and reptiles have four), stomatopod eyes contain no fewer than eight different types of color photoreceptor. These afford the marine coral reef–dwelling crustaceans an unparalleled range of color vision, enabling them to distinguish numerous shades within the electromagnetic spectrum's ultraviolet waveband—which is entirely invisible to humans.

★ **LARGEST FAMILY OF SPIDERS** The largest zoological family of spiders is Salticidae, which contains the jumping spiders. More than 4,400 species are currently known to science, and most live in the tropics. Uncharacteristically for spiders, jumping spiders hardly ever spin webs, catching their prey not by entrapment but by actively leaping at them.

LONGEST INSECT EGG In terms of length, the largest egg laid by an insect belongs to the 6-in.-long (15-cm) Malaysian stick insect *Heteropteryx dilatata*—the Malaysian jungle nymph or giant thorny phasmid—and measures 0.5 in. (1.3 cm). This makes it larger in size than a peanut!

FEB. 21: The **oldest person ever** was Jeanne Louise Calment (France), who lived for 122 years 164 days. She was born on this day in 1875 and died on August 4, 1997.

Heaviest insects The goliath beetles (family Scarabaeidae) of equatorial Africa—*Goliathus regius, G. meleagris, G. goliathus* (*G. giganteus*) and *G. druryi*—are the heaviest insects. In measurements of one series of males (females are smaller), the lengths from the tips of the small frontal horns to the end of the abdomen were up to 4.33 in. (11 cm), with weights of 2.5–3.5 oz. (70–100 g).

Largest marine crustacean A specimen of *taka-ashi-gani* or giant spider crab (*Macrocheira kaempferi*) discovered in Japan in 1836 had a claw-span of 12 ft. 1.5 in. (3.69 m) and weighed 41 lb. (18.6 kg). It is thought to have a life expectancy of up to 100 years.

LARGEST BUTTERFLY Queen Alexandra's birdwing (*Ornithoptera alexandrae*), native to Papua New Guinea, has a wingspan in female specimens in excess of 11 in. (28 cm). The insect is so big (the size of a domestic pigeon) that tribesmen bring it down from the high tree canopies, where it usually flies, by shooting it with a bow and arrow. The first specimen obtained by scientists was brought down using a shotgun! Left is the birdwing's mature larva (caterpillar).

FEB. 22: The **fastest solo unsupported ascent-descent of Mount Kilimanjaro** was completed in a time of 9 hr. 21 min. 47 sec. by Simon Mtuy (Tanzania) on February 22, 2006.

★ **SMALLEST BEE** The world's smallest species of bee is *Perdita minima* (pictured left), a minute species of solitary bee just under 2 mm long and weighing only 0.333 mg. It is native to the southwestern U.S.A., where it constructs a tiny nest in sandy desert soils and feeds upon the nectar and pollen of spurge flowers.

The **largest bee** is the female king bee (*Chalicodoma pluto*), which can attain a total length of 1.5 in. (3.9 cm). This species—found only in the Moluccas Islands of Indonesia—was first discovered in 1859 by naturalist Alfred Russel Wallace (GB), after which no specimen was recorded until February 1981, when two enormous females were seen by entomologist Dr. Adam Messer (U.S.A.).

Largest land crustacean The robber, or coconut, crab (*Birgus latro*), which lives on tropical islands and atolls in the Indo-Pacific, weighs up to 9 lb. (4.1 kg) and has a leg-span of up to 39 in. (1 m), making it the largest land arthropod.

Strongest spider The California trapdoor spider *Bothriocyrtum californicum* has been proven able to resist a force 38 times its own weight when defending its trapdoor: a silken structure covering the entrance to its underground burrow. This equates to a man trying to hold a door closed while it is being pulled on the other side by a small jet plane.

Most dangerous bee The Africanized honey bee (*Apis mellifera scutellata*) will generally only attack when provoked, but it is persistent in pursuit. Its venom is no more potent than that of other bees, but it attacks in swarms and death can result from the sheer number of stings inflicted.

AMPHIBIANS

Smallest frog The world's smallest frog, and the **smallest amphibian,** is *Eleutherodactylus limbatus* of Cuba, which is 0.33–0.47 in. (8.5–12 mm) long from snout to vent when fully grown.

★ **Heaviest frog ever** The heaviest species of frog ever known to have existed was *Beelzebubo ampinga,* which lived in Madagascar during the late Cretaceous Period (65–100 million years ago). Formally described by science in 2008 and currently known from some 75 bones and other fossil

....

FEB. 23: A record 462,572 people took part in the **largest toast at multiple venues** when they gathered in pubs, restaurants, bars, and concert halls across the U.S.A. on this day in 2001.

....

fragments, females of this mega-species may have grown to over 15.7 in. (40 cm) long and weighed 8.8 lb. (4 kg). Its mouth was so expansive that it was probably capable of preying upon small juvenile dinosaurs that co-existed there at the time.

Farthest triple jump by a frog The greatest distance ever covered by a frog in a triple jump is 33 ft. 9 in. (10.3 m)—about half the length of a basketball court! The jump was accomplished by a South African sharp-nosed frog (*Ptychadena oxyrhynchus*) named Santjie at a frog derby held at Lurula Natal Spa, Petersburg, South Africa, on May 21, 1977.

★Most consecutive jumps by a frog An adult spring peeper (*Hyla crucifer*) newly captured on a grassy lawn in the eastern U.S.A. performed 120 consecutive jumps, as documented in 1952 by biologist Stanley A. Rand (U.S.A.). Not surprisingly, the distance covered by each jump gradually decreased, but it remains a prodigious feat of endurance nonetheless.

Farthest gliding amphibian Certain species of flying frog are able to glide up to 50 ft. (15 m) using the extensive webbing on their feet to cause drag and sustain their flight.

FACT

The California newt's typical diet includes snails, slugs, sowbugs, bloodworms, earthworms, and mosquito larvae.

★MOST FERTILE AMPHIBIAN The world's most fecund species of amphibian is the inappropriately named marine toad (*Bufo marinus*), which is not marine. A female can lay up to 35,000 eggs a year.

★MOST POISONOUS NEWT The world's most poisonous species of newt is the California newt (*Taricha torosa*), whose skin, muscles, and blood contain tetrodotoxin, a highly toxic and powerful nerve poison. Although the newt itself is immune to the effects of the poison, one tiny drop of this substance will kill several thousand mice.

Most cold-resistant amphibian The wood frog (*Rana sylvatica*) is the only amphibian able to survive being frozen. These frogs live north of the Arctic Circle and survive for weeks in a frozen state. Glucose in their blood acts as a kind of antifreeze that concentrates on the frogs' vital organs, protecting them from damage while the rest of the body freezes solid.

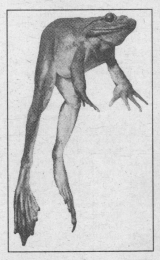

Smallest toad The smallest toad is the subspecies *Bufo taitanus beiranus* of Africa, the largest specimen of which measured 0.94 in. (24 mm) long.

LARGEST FROG A specimen of the African goliath frog (*Conraua goliath*), captured in April 1889 on the Sanaga River, Cameroon, by Andy Koffman of Seattle, Washington, U.S.A., had a snout-to-vent length of 14.5 in. (36.83 cm) and an overall length of 34.5 in. (87.63 cm) with legs extended. On October 30, 1889, it weighed 8 lb. 1 oz. (3.66 kg). The average length for this species is 11.8 in. (30 cm), about the average size of a rabbit.

FEB. 24: The record for the **largest tea party** is 32,681 participants, set by Dainik Bhaskar (India) for the City of Indore, at Nehru Stadium in Indore, India, on this day in 2008.

★ **FIRST LUNGLESS FROG** The first species of lungless frog was confirmed in 2008. Previously known only from two specimens, *Barbourula kalimantanensis,* an aquatic species from Borneo, obtains all of its oxygen by direct absorption through its skin and hence has no need for lungs. This was verified by studies following the recent discovery of two new populations of this species in Kalimantan, Borneo.

★ **LONGEST GESTATION** The longest gestation period for an amphibian, and the ★ **longest gestation for any terrestrial vertebrate,** is 37–38 months by the alpine salamander (*Salamandra atra*), native to the Swiss Alps. This is at least a year longer than that of the Asian elephant, for which the maximum gestation period on record is 25 months, the **longest for any mammal.**

★ **AMPHIBIAN WITH THE MOST RESTRICTED DISTRIBUTION** The Peaks of Otter salamander (*Plethodon hubrichti*) is entirely confined to a 12-mile-long (19-km) expanse of temperate forest in the Blue Mountains of Virginia, U.S.A. This is the most restricted distribution for any species.

FEB. 25: Christopher Eddy (U.S.A.) scored a field goal from a distance of 90 ft. 2.25 in. (27.49 m) on February 25, 1989—the **longest basketball goal ever shot.**

Largest toad The largest known toad is the cane or marine toad (*Bufo marinus*) of tropical South America and Queensland, Australia (introduced). An average specimen weighs 1 lb. (450 g), but the largest ever recorded was a male named Prinsen owned by Håkan Forsberg (Sweden). In March 1991, it weighed 5 lb. 13 oz. (2.65 kg) and measured 1 ft. 3 in. (38 cm) from snout to vent and 1 ft. 9 in. (53.9 cm) when fully extended.

Rarest amphibian The golden toad (*Bufo periglenes*) is notable in its genus for being both sexually dichromatic and visually striking. Male coloration is characteristically bright orange while female pigmentation ranges from greenish-yellow to black. It is found in a small area (less than 4 miles^2; 10 km^2) contained in the Monteverde Cloud Forest Preserve of Costa Rica's Cordillera de Tilaran. Its numbers have mysteriously plummeted, with the last recorded sighting of one specimen between 1988 and 1989.

★**Largest newt** The Spanish ribbed newt (*Pleurodeles waltl*), found in central and southern Iberia and Morocco, ranges in length from 6 in. to 12 in. (15–30 cm). The females are longer and thicker than the males and have smaller tails relative to body length.

The Mexican lungless salamander (*Bolitoglossa mexicana*) is the world's **smallest newt** or salamander. It attains a maximum length of about 1 in. (2.54 cm), including the tail.

Largest caecilian Caecilians are limbless and rarely seen, although they are often mistaken for earthworms. The largest is Thompson's caecilian (*Caecilia thompsoni*) of Colombia, which measures approximately 5 ft. (1.5 m) long and 1.8 in. (3 cm) wide. The ★**smallest caecilian**, *Idiocranium russeli* of west Africa, attains a length of just 3.9–4.1 in. (98–104 mm).

REPTILES

★**Largest snake of all time** The largest snake ever known was *Titanoboa cerrejonensis*, a prehistoric species of boa known from the fossils of 28 specimens found in the coal mines of Cerrejón, in La Guajira, Colombia. They were discovered by an international scientific expedition led by University of Florida vertebrate paleontologist Dr. Jonathan Bloch, and they were formally announced in early 2009. The fossils revealed that the aptly named *Titanoboa,* which lived 58–60 million years ago during the Paleocene Epoch, reached a maximum length of 39 ft. 4 in.–49 ft. 2 in. (12–15 m), measured approximately 3 ft. 3 in. (1 m) across at the thickest portion of its body, and weighed roughly 2,500 lb. (1,135 kg). These measurements dwarf those of both the reticulated python, the world's **longest living snake,** and the anaconda, the world's **heaviest living snake.**

HEAVIEST SNAKE The green anaconda (*Eunectes murinus*) of tropical South America and Trinidad has an average length of 18–20 ft. (5.5–6.1 m). A female shot in Brazil c. 1960 was 27 ft. 9 in. (8.45 m) long with a girth of 44 in. (111 cm) and was estimated to have weighed 500 lb. (227 kg).

BIG SNAKE . . .

Biologists and staff at the biological research station El Frio in Los Llanos, Venezuela, hold a live green anaconda measuring 17 ft. 4 in. (5.3 m), which is about average for an adult of the species.

Fastest lizard The highest burst speed recorded for any reptile on land is 21.7 mph (34.9 km/h), achieved by *Ctenosaura,* a spiny-tailed iguana from Central America.

★ **SMALLEST SNAKE** A species of threadsnake, *Leptotyphlops cariae,* recently discovered on the Caribbean island of Barbados, measures just 4 in. (10 cm) long and is as thin as a strand of spaghetti. This tiny nonvenomous snake is thought to be close to or even at the physiological minimum size possible for any snake.

....

FEB. 26: The record for the **most shrimp eaten in three minutes** is 9.6 oz. (272.1 g), set by William Silver of Asheville, North Carolina, U.S.A., at the Calabash West Restaurant on this day in 2003.

....

★LARGEST TURTLE CONGREGATION The largest congregation of turtles (or, indeed, of any chelonian—turtles, tortoises, and terrapins) ever recorded took place on a 6-mile (10 km) stretch of beach at Gahirmatha, in Orissa, India, in 1991, when 610,000 specimens of olive ridley turtles (*Lepidochelys olivacea*) were counted nesting there. Each February, the turtles emerge from the sea at night to lay their eggs (over 50 million of them) on the beach, returning to the sea by dawn.

Most venomous land snake

The small-scaled snake *Oxyuranus microlepidotus*, which measures 5 ft. 7 in. (1.7 m) and is found mainly in the Diamantina River and Cooper Creek drainage basins in Queensland and western New South Wales, Australia, is the world's most venomous land snake. In a single strike, it can inject 0.00221 oz. (60 mg) of venom, sufficient to kill a small marsupial in seconds, but also more than enough to wipe out several human adults. The average venom yield is 0.00155 oz. (44 mg), but one specimen yielded 0.00385 oz. (110 mg), enough to kill 250,000 mice or 125 men. Fortunately *O. microlepidotus* only lives in the deserts of central eastern Australia and no human death has been reported from its bite.

Most endangered reptile

The Abingdon Island giant tortoise (*Geochelone elephantopus abingdoni*) is represented by a single living specimen, an aged male called "Lonesome George," making it the world's **rarest reptile**.

★NEWEST IGUANA In 2009, it was announced that a new species of iguana, rose-pink (*rosada*) in color and up to 5 ft. 8 in. (1.75 m) long, had been discovered living on a single volcanic mountain called Volcan Wolf on the island of Isabela in the Galapagos chain. Genetic tests confirmed that it is a very distinctive species, dating back over 5 million years. Interestingly, the pink iguana, which has been named *Conolophus rosada,* had first been seen on Isabela in 1986 by park rangers, but had been dismissed as nothing more than a freak variety of the familiar yellow land iguana (*Conolophus subcristatus*).

FEB. 27: The **longest time heading a soccer ball without it dropping** is 8 hr. 32 min. 3 sec. by Tomas Lundman (Sweden) at Gångsatrahallen, Lidingo, Sweden, on this day in 2004.

COLOR CHANGE

It is commonly thought that chameleons change color to blend in with their environment, but this isn't the case. Chameleons can alter the color of their skin, but recent studies indicate that this is a form of communication and not a type of camouflage.

★ **LARGEST & SMALLEST CHAMELEONS** Parson's chameleon (*Chamaeleo parsonii,* above), which is native to small areas of rainforest in eastern and northern Madagascar, is the **largest species of chameleon**, reaching up to 27 in. (68 cm) in length.

The *Brookesia minima* (left), known as the tiny leaf chameleon or the dwarf chameleon, is acknowledged to be the **smallest species of chameleon**, with an average length of 0.7 in. (18 mm) from snout to vent.

Deepest dive by a chelonian In May 1987, Dr. Scott Eckert (U.S.A.) reported that a leatherback turtle (*Dermochelys coriacea*) equipped with a pressure-sensitive recording device reached a depth of 3,937 ft. (1,200 m) off the Virgin Islands.

FEB. 28: The final episode of M*A*S*H aired in the U.S.A. on this day in 1983. An estimated 125 million people tuned in, taking a 77% share of all viewing, the **largest rating share for a TV audience.**

Smallest crocodilian The dwarf caiman (*Paleosuchus palpebrosus*) of northern South America is the world's smallest crocodilian. Females rarely exceed a length of 4 ft. (1.2 m) and males seldom grow to more than 4 ft. 11 in. (1.5 m).

Rarest crocodilian There are fewer than 200 Chinese alligators (*Alligator sinensis*) living in the wild (and some reports put the figure as low as 130), making it one of the most endangered species on Earth. Found in the lower parts of the Yangtze River, China, in wetland habitats, the species can grow to 6.5 ft. (2 m) and weigh 88 lb. (40 kg). Their rapid decline in recent years is the result of habitat destruction and also local farmers who, fearing damage to their land, kill them.

FISH

Largest fish The **largest cartilaginous fish,** and also the **largest living fish** of all, is the whale shark (*Rhincodon typus*). The largest recorded example measured 41 ft. 6 in. (12.65 m) long, 23 ft. (7 m) round the thickest part of the body, and weighed an estimated 33,000–46,200 lb. (16.5–23 tons). It was caught near Karachi, Pakistan, in 1949. Cartilaginous fish (Chondrichthyes) have skeletons made from cartilage and include sharks, rays, and skates. The **heaviest bony fish** in the ocean is the sunfish (*Mola mola*), which has been recorded weighing over 4,400 lb. (2 tons) and measuring 10 ft. (3 m) from fin tip to fin tip. Bony fish (Osteichthyes) are characterized by a mostly calcified skeleton and include sturgeons and most of the common fishes.

★Shortest life span The shortest-lived fishes are various species of toothcarp, including several South American species of the genus *Nothobranchius* that live for only about eight months in the wild. These small

★SMALLEST LAMPREY The Miller Lake lamprey (*Lampetra minima*) is less than 3.9 in. (10 cm) long when mature. Originally known only from Miller Lake in Oregon, U.S.A., this species was believed extinct after 1958. Fortunately, small populations have been found in Oregon's Upper Williamson River and other rivers close by since the early 1990s.

FEB. 29: The **first posthumous Oscar** was awarded to Sidney Howard for his screenplay of *Gone With The Wind* (U.S.A., 1939) on this day in 1940.

fishes thrive in temporary pools of water, such as drainage ditches and even water-filled animal footprints. As soon as these pools dry up, though, the fishes die, but the eggs that they have laid survive in the mud at the bottom of the dried-up pool. And when rain fills them up again, the eggs hatch. The newborn fish rapidly grow to their full size, then spawn before their homes dry out once more.

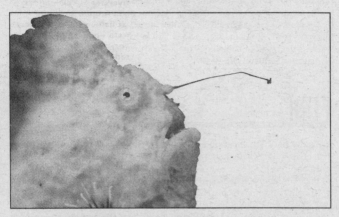

★ **FASTEST-EATING FISH** Frogfishes (family Antennariidae) can open their mouth and engulf prey in under six milliseconds—the fastest recorded time for eating documented for any fish. It was confirmed following frame-by-frame analysis of high-speed cinematography (800–1000 frames per second), as part of research conducted by Theodore Pietsch and David Grobecker (both U.S.A.).

Fish with the most eyes The six-eyed spookfish (*Bathylychnops exilis*), which inhabits depths of 300–3,000 ft. (91–910 m) in the northeastern Pacific, was discovered only in 1958. A slender 17-in.-long (45-cm) pike-like species, it has a pair of large principal eyes and a second, smaller pair (known as secondary globes) positioned within the lower half of its principal eyes, each possessing its own lens and retina. Lastly, located behind the secondary globes is a third pair of eyes, which lack retinas, but divert incoming light into the fish's large principal eyes.

Deepest-living The fish that lives at the greatest recorded depth is the *Abyssobrotula galatheae* species of cusk eel (family Ophidiidae). The 8-in.-

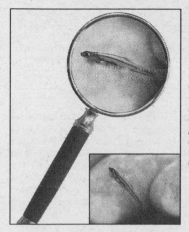

SMALLEST FISH In 2006, the discovery in Indonesia of a fish of the genus *Paedocypris* (left) measuring 0.31 in. (7.9 mm) long was announced. However, according to research published by Prof. Theodore Pietsch of the University of Washington, U.S.A., in August 2005, the smallest fish—and the smallest vertebrate—is a mature male *Photocorynus spiniceps*, collected from the Philippine Sea. The tiny male measured 0.24 in. (6.2 mm) long.

long (20-cm) fish has been collected from the Puerto Rico Trench at a depth of 27,460 ft. (8,370 m).

☆**Strongest bite** The strongest fish bite ever has been estimated at 5,300 N—the equivalent of a downward force of about 1,200 lb. (540 kg). It belonged to the prehistoric *Dunkleosteus terrelli*, an armored fish that lived 360–416 million years ago and grew to lengths of up to 36 ft. (11 m). Scientists Philip S. L. Anderson (U.S.A.) of the University of Chicago and Mark W. Westneat (U.S.A.) of the Field Museum of Natural History created a computer-generated model of *D. terrelli*'s skull based on fossilized jaw bones from the fish, and published their measurements on November 28, 2006.

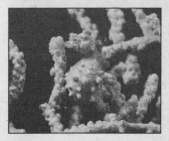

SMALLEST SEAHORSE An adult pygmy seahorse (*Hippocampus denise*) is typically just 0.63 in. (16 mm) long—smaller than an average human fingernail. It is the smallest seahorse on record and a rival to the world's smallest fishes. It was discovered in 2003 in the delicate corals of the Flores Sea, off the coast of Indonesia. It lives among the deeper corals and is a master of camouflage.

MAR. 2: At 1:47 p.m. on this day in 1958, a party of 12 led by Sir Vivian Ernest Fuchs (UK) completed the **first surface crossing of the Antarctic continent.**

Largest sneezing fish The only fish that can sneeze is the hagfish, or slime eel (*Myxine glutinosa*), a primitive species of jawless fish that lacks true fins or scales. The largest known species is *Eptatretus goliath,* with a specimen recorded at 4 ft. 2 in. (127 cm). The hagfish bores inside other fish and eats their internal organs until they are completely hollow. It then slips out of the host by secreting vast amounts of slime to lubricate its body so that it can ease out of its prey's empty carcass. It prevents itself from suffocating in its own slime by sneezing it out of its primitive respiratory slits.

Fish with the greatest sense of smell Sharks have a better sense of smell, with more highly developed scent-detecting organs, than any other fish. Well known for detecting blood from great distances, they can detect just one part of mammalian blood in 100 million parts of water.

★ **LARGEST FISH EVER** The biggest fish ever known to have lived is a specimen of the marine fossil species *Leedsichthys problematicus* that was discovered in claypits near Peterborough, UK, in 2008. Dating back 155 million years, this particular specimen (artist's impression above) was 72 ft. 2 in. (22 m) long, almost twice the length of the whale shark (*Rhincodon typus*), the **largest living fish** (see p. 71). The *Leedsichthys problematicus* was first revealed to science back in the 1800s. It belongs to an extinct group of bony fishes known as the pachycormids, but is believed to have been a plankton feeder, comparable to the basking shark and also the baleen whales.

MAR. 3: The **most goals scored by a National Hockey League team in a single game** is 16, by the Montreal Canadiens in their 16–3 victory over the Quebec Bulldogs on March 3, 1920.

450: the number of marine species, imported from 60 different countries, at Tokyo Central Market, Japan—the **largest fish market.**

★ **FIRST LIVE FISH BIRTH** An extremely well-preserved 9.8-in.-long (25-cm) placoderm (prehistoric armored fish) fossil, uncovered in the Gogo area of Western Australia, clearly shows the presence of an embryo attached to its mother via an umbilical cord. Pictured left is Dr. John Long, Head of Sciences at Museum Victoria, Australia, inspecting a model of the 380-million-year-old placoderm. An artist's impression of the live birth is shown above. The remarkable fossil represents a new species and was named *Materpiscis attenboroughi* after British TV wildlife show host Sir David Attenborough.

★ **Largest placoderm** Placoderms constitute a class of prehistoric armored fish known today only from fossils, and lived from the mid-late Silurian Period to the close of the Devonian Period, 360–416 million years ago. They were characterized by thick articulated plates of armor that covered their head and body. By far the largest species—often looked upon as the world's first vertebrate super-predator—was *Dunkleosteus terrelli*, which measured 26–36 ft. (8–11 m) long and had a near-worldwide distribution.

Most abundant fish The 2.5-in.-long (64-mm) deep-sea bristlemouth (*Cyclothone microdon*) numbers in the billions and has an almost worldwide distribution. It would take about 900 adults to weigh 1 lb. (450 g).

Fish   **75**

Most venomous fish The stonefish (family Synanceiidae), and in particular *Synanceia horrida,* of the tropical waters of the Indo-Pacific have the largest venom glands of any fish. Direct contact with the spines of its fins—which contain a strong neurotoxic poison—can prove fatal.

Largest freshwater fish The Mekong giant catfish (*Pangasius gigas*) of the Mekong River basin, and *P. sanitwongse* of the Chao Phraya River basin, both in southeast Asia, are reputed to attain a length of 9 ft. 10 in. (3 m) and weigh 660 lb. (300 kg). However, *Arapaima giga* of South America is reported to reach 14 ft. 9 in. (4.5 m) long, but weighs only 440 lb. (200 kg).

BIRDS

★**Longest migration by a bird nonstop** A satellite-tagged female bar-tailed godwit (*Limosa lapponica baueri*) known as "E7" was recorded flying directly across the Pacific Ocean from Alaska to New Zealand in a nine-day, nonstop migration flight that covered 7,145 miles (11,500 km) in mid-September 2007. The recording of this migration was made during a study of godwit migration (from their summer breeding grounds in Alaska) by the U.S. Geological Survey, PRBO Conservation Science (U.S.A.), and researchers from New Zealand's Massey University.

★**Largest egg collection** The world's largest scientific collection of bird eggs is that of the Natural History Museum in London, UK, which contains over 1 million different specimens.

★**Most indigenous breeding species (country)** Colombia in South America is home to over 1,700 indigenous breeding species of birds. By comparison, Canada and the U.S.A. combined, yielding a total area vastly in excess of Colombia's, contains fewer than 600 indigenous breeding species.

★**Fewest indigenous breeding species (region)** The most sparsely populated geographical region for birds is the Antarctic (comprising Antarctica and those islands south of the Antarctic Convergence). It supports just three indigenous breeding species of bird. By comparison, the Neotropical region, comprising tropical Mexico, the Caribbean, Central America, and South America, is home to more than 3,400 indigenous breeding species of bird, far more than any other geographical region in the world.

....

MAR. 4: The **longest Oscars acceptance speech** lasted 5 min. 30 sec. and was made by Greer Garson (UK) after winning Best Actress for *Mrs. Miniver* (U.S.A., 1942) on this day in 1943.

....

11 FT. 11 IN. (3.63 M): the wingspan of the male wandering albatross (*Diomedea exulans*), the **largest wingspan of any living bird species.**

★ **FIRST BIRD LEG-RINGED** The earliest known example of a bird being leg-ringed is a grey heron (*Ardea cinerea*) that was ringed during the early 18th century in Turkey (then the Ottoman Empire). The bird was subsequently identified by its ring in 1710 when observed in Germany. In more modern times, the record for the **most birds ringed by a single person** goes to Òskar J. Sigurösson (Iceland), the principle bird-ringer for the Icelandic Institute of Natural History. Since 1953, Sigurösson, lighthouse keeper at Stórhöföi on Heimay in the Westmann Islands, had ringed 65,243 birds as of February 26, 1997.

SMALLEST BIRD Male bee hummingbirds (*Melllsuga helenae*), which inhabit Cuba and the Isle of Youth, measure just 2.24 in (57 mm) in total length, half of which is taken up by the bill and tail, and weigh just 0.056 oz (1.6 g). This is believed to be the lowest weight limit for any warm-blooded animal.

MAR. 5: Ken Edwards (UK) ate 36 cockroaches—the **most cockroaches eaten in one minute**—on the set of *The Big Breakfast* (C4, UK), London, UK, on March 5, 2001.

☆**Rarest bird of prey** According to BirdLife International 2006 and the 2007 IUCN Red List of endangered species, the California condor (*Gymnogyps californianus*) is classified as critically endangered. A conservation program following the species' removal from the wild into captivity in 1987 has seen this condor recently reintroduced into the wild.

Fastest birds

•The **fastest bird in level flight** is the grey-headed albatross (*Thalassarche chrysostoma*); a satellite-tagged specimen sustained a speed of 78.9 mph (127 km/h) for over 8 hours while returning to its nest on Bird Island, South Georgia, in the middle of an Antarctic storm.

•The **fastest bird in a dive** is the peregrine falcon (*Falco peregrinus*), which has been estimated to reach a terminal velocity of approximately 186 mph (300 km/h) when in a diving stoop (the fastest animal on earth).

•The **fastest bird on land** is the (flightless) ostrich (*Struthio camelus*), which can reach speeds of up to 45 mph (72 km/h) when at full stride—up to 23 ft. (7 m) per step.

•The **fastest-running flying bird** is the North American roadrunner (*Geococcyx californianus*), which has been clocked at 26 mph (42 km/h).

•The **fastest swimming bird** is the gentoo penguin (*Pygoscelis papua*), which has a maximum burst speed of 17 mph (27 km/h).

★**FARTHEST HEAD TURN** Several species of owl can rotate their heads by as much as 280° and then swiftly rotate them back again in the opposite direction, creating the appearance of more than 360° rotation. Despite many popular claims, though, no species can rotate its head through a full 360°.

★**LONGEST TIME TO LEARN TO FLY** The longest known interval between hatching from an egg and gaining the ability to fly is exhibited by the wandering albatross (*Diomedea exulans*), whose chicks take 278–280 days on average to make their first flight after hatching. Because it takes so long for the young albatross to take to the air, adults breed only once every two years.

Largest nest A mating pair of bald eagles (*Haliaeetus leucocephalus*) built a nest that measured 9 ft. 6 in. (2.9 m) wide and 20 ft. (6 m) deep near St. Petersburg, Florida, U.S.A. It was examined in 1963 and was estimated to weigh more than 2.2 tons (2 tonnes).

Big birds

•The large-limbed, extinct elephant bird, or vouron patra (*Aepyornis maximus*), that lived in Madagascar had an estimated weight of 1,000 lb. (450 kg)—three times that of the similarly shaped ostrich—and was the **largest modern-day bird.**

•The **largest living bird** is the North African ostrich (*Struthio camelus camelus*). Male examples of this flightless (ratite) subspecies have been recorded up to 9 ft. (2.75 m) tall and weighing 345 lb. (156.5 kg).

•The **heaviest flying bird** was a male kori bustard (*Ardeotis kori*) that weighed 40 lb. (18.2 kg) when documented in 1936.

•The **largest species of penguin** was *Anthropornis nordenskjöldi*, which lived about 24 million years ago. This human-sized penguin stood 5–5 ft. 10 in. (1.5–1.8 m) tall and may have weighed as much as 198–298 lb. (90–135 kg).

★ **STRANGEST DIET** An internal examination conducted on a dead ostrich (*Struthio camelus*) that had been living at London Zoo, UK, revealed that during its life it had swallowed (among other things) an alarm clock, a Belgian franc, a roll of film, three gloves, a handkerchief, and a pencil!

MAR. 6: The **most expensive human skull**—that of Swedish philosopher Emanuel Swedenborg (1688–1772)—was bought by the Royal Swedish Academy of Sciences for $10,664 on this day in 1978.

LARGEST EAGLE Named after the German botanist Georg Steller, the world's largest species of eagle is Steller's sea eagle (*Haliaeetus pelagicus*), which weighs between 11–20 lb. (5 kg and 9 kg) and has a wingspan of between 7 ft. 2 in.–8 ft. 3 in. (2.2 m and 2.45 m). Although it breeds mainly in Russia, where it is a protected species, the eagle has also been spotted in Korea, Alaska in the U.S.A., and in Japan, where it is considered a national symbol. The International Union for the Conservation of Nature classifies the bird as vulnerable with an estimated population of 5,000 specimens.

Highest flying bird A Rüppell's vulture (*Gyps rueppellii*) flying at an altitude of 37,000 ft. (11,300 m) collided with a commercial aircraft over Abidjan, Ivory Coast, on November 29, 1973. The impact damaged one of the aircraft's engines but the plane landed safely. Sufficient feather remains of the bird were recovered to allow the American Museum of Natural History to make a positive identification of this high flier, which is rarely seen above 20,000 ft. (6,000 m).

Most abundant The red-billed quelea (*Quelea quelea*), a seed-eating weaver of sub-Saharan Africa, has an estimated adult breeding population of 1.5 billion. At least 200 million of these birds, sometimes dubbed "feathered locusts," are slaughtered annually without having any impact on this number.

MAMMALS

★**First human-sheep chimera** In March 2007, Prof. Esmail Zanjani from the University of Nevada, U.S.A., announced that his team had created the world's first human-sheep chimera—a sheep that contains sheep cells (85%) and human cells (15%). (Chimera in Greek mythology had a lion's head, a goat's body, and a serpent's tail.) Its creation brings ever closer the prospect of animal organs being transplanted into humans. Zanjani and his team have spent seven years and $7 million perfecting the technique required to produce this chimera, which involves injecting adult human cells into the fetus of a sheep.

★ **Largest mammoth skeleton** Known colloquially as the West Runton elephant, the world's biggest—and most complete—mammoth skeleton was discovered in Cromer, Norfolk, UK, in 1990. *Mammuthus trogontherii* stands 13 ft. 1 in. (4 m) at the shoulder and is approximately 600,000 years old.

☆ **Oldest pig ever** The oldest pig was "Hoofer," who was 18 years 8 months 23 days old when he died, on March 2, 2008. He lived with his owners Shawn Burton Wygrys and Allen Wygrys (both U.S.A.) in Sugar Land, Texas, U.S.A. until his death.

★ **LARGEST INVASIVE SPECIES** Colombian drug baron Pablo Escobar stocked his huge estate with hundreds of exotic animals, including a lake of four African hippopotamuses. After he was killed in 1993, his estate passed into government hands and all the animals disappeared—except for the hippos. They currently number 19, roaming the area at night in search of food.

Mammals

★LONGEST MAMMAL MIGRATION **The humpback whale (*Megaptera novaeangliae*) migrates up to 5,095 miles (8,200 km) each way when journeying back and forth between its warm breeding waters near the equator and the colder, food-rich waters of the Arctic and Antarctic regions.**

☆**Largest prehistoric rodent** The largest rodent ever was a newly identified 2-million-year-old fossil species named *Josephoartigasia monesi*. Although currently known only from a single skull measuring 21 in. (53 cm) long, the complete animal probably weighed a ton (2,000 lb.). Related to today's much smaller pacaraca (*Dinomys branickii*), it lived in coastal Uruguay, in what was then lush forested swampland, and probably fed on soft vegetation as its jaws, though huge, lacked chewing power.

★**Oldest bat ever** The world's oldest bat was an Indian fruit bat (*Pteropus giganteus*) that died at London Zoo, UK, on January 11, 1979, aged 31 years 5 months. In the wild, a little brown mouse-eared bat (*Myotis lucifugus*) found dead in a cave on Mt. Aeolus in Vermont, U.S.A., on April 30, 1960, is known to have been at least 24 years old, because it had been banded back on June 22, 1937, when it was already fully mature.

MAR. 7: Roy Makaay (Netherlands) scored the opening goal for Bayern Munich against Real Madrid in just 10 seconds in Munich, Germany, on March 7, 2007—the **fastest Champions League goal.**

★ **LARGEST SQUIRREL** The Indian, or Malabar, giant squirrel (*Ratufa indica*), found exclusively in the deciduous and evergreen forests of India, can grow to 3 ft. 3 in. (1 m) in total length—about the size of a large domestic cat. Two-thirds of this is represented by its long, bushy tail. Rarely coming down from its home in the upper canopy of the forest, it moves from tree to tree by way of huge leaps of up to 20 ft. (6 m).

LARGEST RODENT The capybara, or carpincho (*Hydrochoerus hydrochaeris*, right) of Argentina, Brazil, and Uruguay, has a head and body length of 3 ft. 3 in.–4 ft. 3 in. (1–1.3 m) and can weigh up to 175 lb. (79 kg). One exceptional cage-fattened specimen attained 249 lb. (113 kg). Several species vie for the title of **smallest rodent.** In particular, the northern pygmy mouse (*Baiomys taylori,* above left) of Mexico, Arizona and Texas, U.S.A., and the Baluchistan pygmy jerboa (*Salpingotus michaelis*) of Pakistan, both have a head-body length of as little as 1.4 in. (3.6 cm) and a tail length of 2.8 in. (7.2 cm).

MAR. 8: The **largest decorated Easter egg,** made by Freeport in Alochete, Portugal, was 48 ft. 6 in. (14.79 m) long and 27 ft. 6 in. (8.40 m) in diameter when measured on March 8, 2008.

★**Rarest elephant** The rarest elephant on record was Motty, a male calf born at Chester Zoo, Cheshire, UK, on July 11, 1978. He is considered the "rarest" because he is the only known example of a hybrid between the African elephant (*Loxodonta africana*) and the Asian elephant (*Elephas maximus*). His father was Jumbolino, a bull African elephant, and his mother was Sheba, a cow Asian elephant, and he lived for 10 days before dying from necrotic enterocolitis and an *E. coli* septicemia.

Motty possessed a fascinating combination of features from both species of elephants and his skin was preserved as a mounted taxiderm specimen, which is housed at the Natural History Museum, London, UK. Until Motty's birth, it was not believed possible that interspecific elephant hybrids could occur, and none has been recorded since.

LARGEST TAPIR The largest of the five known species of tapir, the Malayan tapir usually grows to 6–8 ft. (1.8–2.4 m) long, 3–3 ft. 6 in. (90–107 cm) tall, and typically weigh 550–700 lb. (250–320 kg), although they can weigh up to 1,100 lb. (500 kg).

MAR. 9: The **youngest individual track world record holder** is Wang Yan (China, b. April 9, 1971), who completed the women's 5,000 m walk in 21 min. 33.8 sec., aged 14 years 334 days in China on March 9, 1986.

★ **FIRST RHINO BORN AFTER ARTIFICIAL INSEMINATION** A calf born at Budapest Zoo, Hungary, on January 23, 2007, was the first successful birth of a rhinoceros via artificial insemination. Lulu—the mother of the calf—had already given birth to a dead calf conceived using the same process in 2005. Vets used artificial insemination as there was no chance for natural breeding due to the brother–sister relationship of the zoo's rhinos.

☆ **Oldest pony ever** The oldest pony ever was Sugar Puff (1951–2007), an Exmoor Shetland owned by S. Botting (UK) of Chichester, West Sussex, UK.

★ **Largest orangutan sanctuary** The world's largest sanctuary for orangutans (*Pongo pygmaeus*) is the Sepilok Orangutan Rehabilitation Center in the Malaysian state of Sabah in northern Borneo. Since it opened in 1964, it has rehabilitated over 100 rescued orangutans and returned them to the wild.

The center is also actively involved in public education on conservation, as well as research and assistance in relation to other endangered species. The sanctuary currently employs more than 37 staff, including a wildlife officer, a vet, and wildlife rangers.

★ **Newest tapir** For more than a century, only four species of tapir have been known to science, but a fifth species was identified in 2008. Known as the black dwarf lowland tapir (*Tapirus pygmaeus*), it was found in Brazil's lowland Amazonia by Dutch zoologist Dr. Marc van Roosmalen. It can be distinguished from the common tapir by its smaller size, unique dentition (teeth arrangement), and lack of white marks on its ear tips.

THE BODY

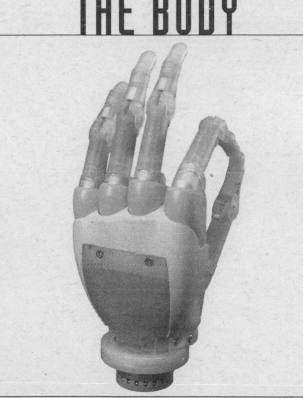

CONTENTS

AMAZING MEN

Largest feet Robert Wadlow (U.S.A., 1918–1940), the **tallest-ever man,** wore U.S. size 37AA shoes, which is equivalent to 18.5 in. (47 cm) long. Wadlow also holds the record for the **largest-ever hands**—his measured 12.75 in. (32.3 cm) from the wrist to the tip of his middle finger. *See p. xxvii for more on Robert Wadlow.*

The ☆**tallest living man,** Sultan Kösen (Turkey, see p. 113), also has the ☆**largest hands** (10.8 in/27.5 cm from wrist to fingertip) and ☆**feet** (14.4 in./36.5 cm, heel to toe) of a living person.

CAN YOU BEAT THIS?

If you think your mustache is longer than Ram Singh Chauhan's, these are the guidelines you'll need to follow if you want to claim the record:

1. Measurements must be made by a suitably qualified individual, such as a medical professional.

2. The total length of the mustache should be measured from tip to tip.

3. Take a photograph of your mustache alongside an accurately calibrated measuring tape.

4. Provide a signed letter confirming the measurement, countersigned by two independent witnesses.

   For full instructions on how to make a claim, go to p. xxviii.

☆**LONGEST MUSTACHE** Ram Singh Chauhan (India), a Rajasthan state tourism official, started growing hair on his upper lip in 1982. When measured in November 2008, his mustache was 11 ft. 6 in. (3.50 m) long.

MAR. 10: The **shortest radio advertisement** lasted 0.954 seconds and was made by BBDO Oslo Reklamebyrå AS. It was first broadcast in Norway on this day in 2006.

1952: the last time that India's Shridhar Chillal (**longest nails on a single hand**) cut the nails of his left hand.

 LONGEST FINGERNAILS We were saddened to hear the news in February 2009 that Lee Redmond (U.S.A.), owner of the world's **longest fingernails on a pair of hands (female)**, had been involved in a car accident that robbed her of her 28-ft. 4-in.-long (8.65-m) nails. A few months before the accident, Lee had joined Guinness World Records in Michigan, U.S.A., to help measure the 29-ft. 8-in. (9.05-m) nails of Melvin Boothe (U.S.A.), the **longest nails on a pair of hands (male)**. The striking photographs taken that day now stand as a beautiful tribute to one of the world's most popular record holders.

★**Most weight lost in a lifetime (male)** The "yoyo" dieting habits of Michael Hebranko (U.S.A.) has resulted in an estimated total weight loss over his lifetime of 5,000 lb. (2,268 kg). His first major documented weight loss—of 709 lb. (321 kg)—was a record at the time (1990). He regained this weight, and more, by 1999, reaching a peak of 1,100 lb. (500 kg). However, his current dieting regime has seen him lose a further 642 lb (291 kg). The accumulated weight that Hebranko has lost over the course of his lifetime equates to that of 35 average males!

Longest hair

•**Nipple:** A hair growing from the nipple of Douglas Williams (U.S.A.) was found to be 5.07 in. (12.9 cm) long when measured in New York City, U.S.A., on May 26, 2007.

•**Leg:** The longest leg hair is 6.5 in. (16.51 cm) in length and belongs to Wesley Pemberton (U.S.A.), as measured on the set of *Lo show dei record* in Madrid, Spain, on February 9, 2008.

•**Arm:** Robert Starrett (U.S.A.) has an arm hair that had grown to a length of 5.31 in (13.5 cm) when measured in Mequon, Wisconsin, U.S.A., on December 7, 2006.

•**Chest:** A chest hair belonging to Richard Condo (U.S.A.) measured 9 in. (22.8 cm) when verified in New Jersey, U.S.A., on April 29, 2007.

•**Eyebrow:** The longest eyebrow hair belongs to Toshie Kawakami (Japan) and was confirmed to be 5.94 in. (15.1 cm) at the Guinness World Records Museum in Tokyo, Japan, on January 22, 2008.

•**Eyelash:** Stuart Muller's (U.S.A.) left upper eyelash was 2.75 in. (6.99 cm) when measured on December 7, 2007.

☆**LONGEST BEARD** After being soaked in water and combed several times, the beard of Sarwan Singh (Canada) measures a record 7 ft. 8 in. (2.33 m) from his chin to the tip of the longest hair. The beard was measured on November 11, 2008. To unveil his whiskers in full, Singh stood on a box and allowed the hairs to flow down freely.

MAR. 11: The youngest person to have a pacemaker implanted is Stephanie Gardiner (UK), who was four hours old when she was given a pacemaker the size of a stamp on March 11, 1995.

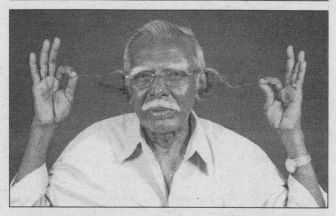

☆ **LONGEST EAR HAIR** Antony Victor (India) has hair sprouting from the center of his outer ears (the middle of the pinna) that measures 7.1 in. (18.1 cm) at its longest point. Victor is a retired school principal from Madurai in the Indian state of Tamil Nadu. He regained his record in 2008, having previously held it in 2002, when his ear hair was measured at 4.5 in. (11.5 cm), signifying a growth of 2.5 in. (6.6 cm) over six years.

MOST TATTOOED MAN Fire-eating, unicycling, chainsaw-juggling Lucky Diamond Rich (Australia) has spent over 1,000 hours having his body modified by tattoo artists. Rich has 100% coverage of black ink, including his eyelids and his gums, and is now being tattooed with white designs on top of the black and colored designs on top of the white!

MAR. 12: Rapper 50 Cent (U.S.A.) had three singles in the U.S. Top 5 on this day in 2005, the **most simultaneous Top 5 hits by a solo artist.** The tracks were "Candy Shop," "How We Do" and "Disco Inferno."

☆ **MOST PIERCED MAN** The world's most pierced man is 78-year-old John Lynch (UK), who was found to have 241 piercings, including 151 in his head and neck, when examined in London, UK, on October 17, 2008. A former Barclays Bank manager, Lynch gave up his "regular" lifestyle in the late 1990s after reading a book on piercings.

★ **Widest tongue** Australian Jay Sloot's tongue measured 3.1 in. (7.9 cm) at its widest point when examined on the set of *Guinness World Records* in Sydney, Australia, on August 23, 2005.

In February 2009, the UK's Stephen Taylor set the record for the ☆ **longest tongue,** measuring 3.85 in. (9.8 cm) from lip to tip.

Longest nose Mehmet Ozyurek's (Turkey) nose measured a record 3.46 in. (8.8 cm) long from the bridge to the top of the philtrum when officially assessed in his home town of Artvin on January 31, 2001.

The **longest nose ever** belonged to circus performer Thomas Wedders (UK, c. 1770s) and was reportedly 7.5 in. (19 cm) long.

SHORTEST LIVING MAN (MOBILE) The shortest known mobile living adult is He Pingping (China, b. 1988), who was measured by a team of doctors in Hohhot, Inner Mongolia, China, and found to be 74.61 cm (2 ft. 5.37 in.) tall on March 22, 2008.

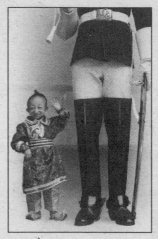

Largest waist Walter Hudson (U.S.A., 1944–91) measured 119 in. (302 cm) around the waist at his peak weight of 1,197 lb. (545 kg).

☆**Most 18-gauge surgical needle body piercings** Robert Jesus Rubio (U.S.A.) had 900 18-gauge, 0.5-in.-long (1.2-cm) surgical needles inserted into his body in Texas, U.S.A., on May 29, 2008. Rubio beat the previous record of 745 needles, held by Benjamin Drucker (U.S.A.), which had stood for five years.

WONDERFUL WOMEN

Shortest living woman Madge Bester (South Africa, b. April 26, 1963) is only 25.5 in. (65 cm) tall. However, she suffers from *osteogenesis imperfecta* (characterized by brittle bones and other deformities of the skeleton) and is confined to a wheelchair. Her mother, Winnie, is not much taller, measuring 27.5 in. (70 cm), and is also confined to a wheelchair.

Shortest woman ever Pauline Musters (Netherlands, b. February 26, 1876) measured 12 in. (30 cm) at birth. At nine years of age, she was just 21.5 in. (55 cm) tall and weighed only 3 lb. 5 oz. (1.5 kg). She died on March 1, 1895, in New York City, U.S.A., at the age of 19, and a postmortem examination showed her to be exactly 24 in. (61 cm) tall—as there was some elongation after death.

MAR. 13: On this day in 2007, the **shortest concert** took place. A performance by The Who (UK) in Tampa, Florida, ended after 13 seconds when lead vocalist Roger Daltrey (UK) realized that he was too ill to sing that night.

Smallest waist Cathie Jung (U.S.A.), who stands 5 ft. 8 in. (1.72 m) tall,
has "trained" her waist to a circumference of 15 in. (38.1 cm) when
corseted. Cathie began tightening her corsets to replicate the narrow hour-
glass shape popular in Victorian England.

Smallest waist ever The smallest waist of a person with normal stature
was 13 in. (33 cm) and was recorded on Ethel Granger (UK, 1905–82). A
measurement of 13 in. (33 cm) was also claimed for the French actress
Emile Marie Bouchand (1881–1939).

Heaviest woman ever Rosalie Bradford (U.S.A., 1943–2006) is
claimed to have registered a peak weight of 1,200 lb. (544 kg) in January
1987. In August of the same year, she developed congestive heart failure
and was rushed to the hospital. She was consequently put on a carefully controlled diet and by February 1994 her weight was down to 283 lb. (128 kg).

LONGEST LEGS Svetlana Pankratova (Russia) has the world's
longest legs, verified as measuring 51.9 in., or nearly 4 ft. 4 in.
(132 cm), in Marbella, Spain, on February 3, 2008. A real estate
agent currently living in Torremolinos, Spain, Svetlana used
to play basketball for Virginia Commonwealth University (U.S.A.) from
1992 to 1995.

MOST PIERCED WOMAN Since her first piercing in January 1997, Elaine Davidson (UK) has had so many additional procedures over and inside her body that she has lost count of them all. When Guinness World Records was last able to examine and count her piercings, in October 2004, she was found to have 2,520 in total.

Lightest person ever Lucia Xarate (or Zarate, Mexico, 1863–89), an emaciated ateleiotic dwarf (a person of short stature with normal human proportions) standing just 26.8 in. (67 cm) tall, weighed 4.7 lb. (2.13 kg) at the age of 17. She managed to increase her weight to 13 lb. (5.9 kg) by her 20th birthday.

Tallest woman ever Zeng Jinlian (China, b. June 26, 1964) of Yujiang village in the Bright Moon Commune, Hunan Province, China, measured 8 ft. 1.75 in. (2.48 m) when she died on February 13, 1982. This figure represented her height with assumed normal spinal curvature because she suffered from severe scoliosis (curvature of the spine) and could not stand up straight.

Tallest twins (female) Ann and Claire Recht (U.S.A., b. February 9, 1988) were measured both horizontally (lying down) and vertically (standing) on three occasions over the course of the day on January 10, 2007, and each was found to have an average overall height of 6 ft. 7 in. (2.01 m).

....

MAR. 14: The **longest-lasting rainbow** was visible for six hours continuously, from 9:00 a.m. to 3:00 p.m., over Wetherby, UK, on March 14, 1994.

....

★**LONGEST DREADLOCKS** The longest dreadlocks belong to Asha Mandela (U.S.A.). When measured in Davenport, Florida, U.S.A., on November 13, 2008, the dreadlocks were 8 ft. 6 in. (2.59 m) long.

Heaviest model U.S. model Teighlor (aka Debra Perkins) reached a peak weight of 719 lb. 0.2 oz. (326.14 kg) in the early 1990s and forged a successful modeling career, appearing in movies, on greeting cards, and in advertisements.

Longest female beard After the death of her mother in 1990, Vivian Wheeler (U.S.A.) stopped trimming her facial hair and grew a full beard. The longest strand of hair was found to be 11 in. (27.9 cm) in 2000. Vivian prefers to tie the beard up, to allow her to continue with her day-to-day routine, and often adorns it with ribbons and bows.

The "bearded lady," Janice Deveree (U.S.A., b. 1842), had the **longest female beard ever**—it measured 14 in. (36 cm) in 1884.

Farthest eyeball pop Kim Goodman (U.S.A.) can pop her eyeballs 0.47 in. (12 mm) beyond her eye sockets—a "talent" she discovered once while yawning! Her eyes were measured most recently in Istanbul, Turkey, on November 2, 2007.

★**OLDEST COMPETITIVE FEMALE BODY BUILDER** At 73 years 4 months of age, Ernestine Shepherd (U.S.A., b. June 16, 1936) is the world's oldest competitive body builder. She did not start training until she was 56, when she wanted to see if she could get her body into shape and delay the aging process.

FACT

Ernestine began her fitness regime by walking every day, which then progressed to running, and she now regularly competes in 5-km and 10-km races.

MAR. 15: David Schummy (Australia) threw a boomerang 1,401 ft. 6 in. (427.2 m) on this day in 2005 in Queensland, Australia—the **farthest distance any object has been thrown by hand.**

Longest toenails Since 1982, Louise Hollis (U.S.A.) has been growing her toenails to great lengths. When measured at their longest, in 1991, the combined length of all 10 toenails was 87 in. (220.9 cm).

Longest hair The world's longest documented hair belongs to Xie Qiuping (China) at 18 ft. 5.54 in. (5.627 m) when measured on May 8, 2004. She has been growing her hair since 1973 from the age of 13.

Largest tummy tuck Surgeons at the Hospital de Cruces in Barakaldo, Spain, removed an "apron" of fat weighing 132 lb. (60 kg) from an obese woman in March 2006. Small cranes were used to help remove the flesh, which hung down to the patient's knees. The excised skin weighed the same as an average 17-year-old girl, and had an energy content of 462,000 calories.

Oldest person to grow a new tooth Mária Magdolna Pozderka (Hungary, b. July 19, 1938) had an upper right canine tooth erupt at the age of 68 in March 2007.

CULTURE SHOCK

★Language with the most sounds !Xóõ (aka Ta'a), which is spoken by about 4,000 Khomani people in southern Africa, contains 74 consonants, 31 vowels, and four tones (pitches).

★First evidence of hominid cannibalism In the foothills of the Sierra de Atapuerca in northern Spain is a series of prehistoric caves in which a human ancestor—*Homosapiens antecessor*—lived up to 800,000 years ago. Among the hominid remains are bones and skulls displaying a

★MOST TATTOOED SENIOR CITIZEN Isobel Varley of Stevenage in Hertfordshire, UK, has an estimated 76% of her body tattooed—everything except her hands, face, neck, and soles of her feet. After 10 years, she has had over 200 designs inked onto her body, including an owl on her leg and tigers on her stomach. The only tattoo she regrets is what she calls an "unrealistic frog" on her stomach. Apparently, the most painful area to have done was her toes!

series of gouges and scars that suggest a tool had been used for skinning, scraping flesh, and extracting marrow from bones. The same pattern of markings is mirrored in animal bones found nearby.

★**Largest voodoo festival** On Voodoo Day, celebrated at the peak of the annual 10-day voodoo festival in Ouida, Benin—the West African home of this ancient religion—about 10,000 worshippers gather for sacrifices, blessings, and prayers. An estimated 60% of Benin's population practices voodoo (more accurately referred to as Vodun), which worships and honors a supreme god as well as ancestors and ancient spirits (loa), each of which is associated—and invoked—with a particular song and dance.

★**Most family members to walk on all fours** Five (out of 19) adult siblings of the Ulas family of Turkey—four sisters and a brother—walk on their feet and the palms of their hands. This quadrupedal gait (known as "bear walk") is unique to the Ulases and is different from the "knuckle walk" witnessed in the great apes. The five siblings also suffer from congenital brain impairment and have trouble balancing on two legs. The condition is known as Uner Tan Syndrome, after the Turkish professor at Çukurova University, Turkey, who first studied the family in 2005.

★**Most isolated tribe** Survival International, a charity dedicated to maintaining tribal societies, points to the inhabitants of the 28-mile^2 (72-km^2) North Sentinel island in the Andaman chain, located in the Bay of Bengal, as the most likely candidates for the most isolated tribe. The Sentinelese—who want no contact with the rest of the world—have inhabited their island for over 60,000 years. Video evidence taken in the aftermath of the 2004 tsunami that destroyed much of the Andaman archipelago confirmed that the tribe continues to cling to life.

★**LONGEST RELIGIOUS CEREMONY** Every 60 years or so, the Dogon peoples of Mali celebrate the Sigui, a mask festival, to mark the handing over of the cult's secrets from one generation to the next. The ceremony takes many years to complete—the last Sigui ran from 1967 to 1973, with the next due in 2032—as the initiates (male only) must learn a secret language and carve a Great Mask, several yards in length. Each initiate wears his own mask and performs in a series of dances from village to village.

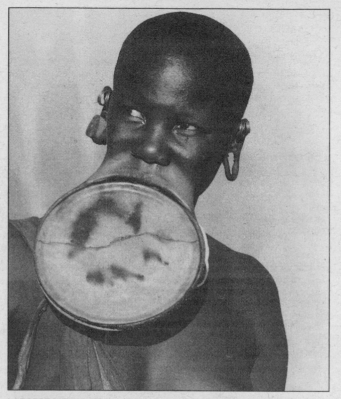

LARGEST LIP PLATES The Surma people of Ethiopia wear lip plates to signify wealth. The process of inserting these plates (made by women from local clay) begins approximately a year before marriage; the final size indicates the number of cattle required by the girl's family from her future husband. Plates typically reach up to 6 in. (15 cm) in diameter, which would require a payment of 50 cattle.

LABRETS

Lip piercings, plugs, and plates are known collectively as labrets (LAY-brits). A small piercing is made in either the upper or lower lip, and a wooden plug inserted. Once the wound heals, increasingly larger plugs are substituted until the lip is stretched wide enough to accommodate a plate.

★ **LARGEST THAIPUSAM FESTIVAL** The Thaipusam Hindu festival, widely celebrated by the Tamils, honors Subrahmanya—aka Murugan—the son of Siva and Parvati. Devotees practice mortification of the flesh by impaling their cheeks with skewers. The largest of the festivals starts at the Sri Mahamariamman Temple in Kuala Lumpur, Malaysia, which attracts up to 1 million devotees.

★ **Most recent tribal "first contact"** There are around 100 known but uncontacted tribes in the world, and the most recent to make contact was a sub-group of the Ayoreo-Totobiegosode peoples of the Chaco, a forest stretching from Paraguay to Bolivia and Argentina. In March 2004, a group of 17 Indians—five men, seven women, and five children—were ousted from the Paraguay forest after cattle ranchers forcibly colonized their territory and occupied their waterholes.

MAR. 16: Wim Hof (Netherlands) swam 188 ft. 6 in. (57.5 m) under ice in a lake near Kolari, Finland, on this day in 2000, the **farthest distance swum under ice without breathing equipment.**

HIGHEST PERCENTAGE OF WOMEN WITH BOUND FEET The practice of foot binding, which began in 10th-century China and persisted until it was banned in 1911, prevented women's feet from growing more than 3.9 in. (10 cm). A study in 1997 of 193 women (93 were over 80 years old, 100 were aged 70–79) in Beijing, by the University of California, San Francisco, U.S.A., found 38% of the women in the over-80 group and 18% in the younger group had feet deformed by foot binding.

Shortest tribe The Mbutsi pygmies from Zaire have an average height of 4 ft. 6 in. (1.37 m) for men and 4 ft. 5 in. (1.35 m) for women, with some groups averaging only 4 ft. 4 in. (1.32 m) for men and 4 ft. 1 in. (1.24 m) for women.

Tallest tribe The tallest major tribe in the world is the Tutsi (also known as the Watussi) of Rwanda and Burundi, Central Africa, whose young adult males average 6 ft. (1.83 m).

Longest neck The maximum known extension of a human neck is 15.75 in. (40 cm), and was created by the successive addition of copper coils, as practiced by the women of the Padaung or Kareni tribe of Burma as a sign of beauty. Their necks eventually become so long and weak that they cannot support their heads without the coils.

Fewest toes The two-toed syndrome exhibited by some members of the Wadomo tribe of the Zambezi Valley, Zimbabwe, and the Kalanga tribe of the eastern Kalahari Desert, Botswana, is hereditary via a single mutated gene.

MAR. 17: The **largest sandwich** weighed 5,440 lb. (2,467.5 kg) and was made by Wild Woody's Chill and Grill, Roseville, Michigan, U.S.A., on this day in 2005.

☆ **MOST ENDANGERED TRIBE** Just six members remain of the Akuntsu tribe of Rondônia state, western Brazil. (Five of the six are pictured left.) They live in a single community, sharing just two malocas (communal houses) made of straw, and cultivate a small garden of corn and manioc. They are also avid hunters of wild pig, tapirs, and agouti. The cause of the tribe's demise was a massacre by cattle ranchers, who bulldozed the forest and caused near genocide among the indigenous population in the 1980s.

MEDICAL MARVELS

★ **First plastic surgery** A World War I gunnery warrant officer named Walter Yeo (UK) was the first person to have plastic surgery. Skin grafts were transferred from his shoulder to his face in order to replace both upper and lower eyelids, which he had lost while manning the guns aboard HMS *Warspite* in 1916 during the Battle of Jutland. The groundbreaking surgery was performed by Sir Harold Gillies (New Zealand), regarded today as the father of plastic surgery.

☆ **Heaviest kidney stone** Wazir Muhammand Jagirani (Pakistan) had this kidney stone (p. 104), weighing 21.87 oz. (620 g), removed from his right kidney at the Nephro-Urology Chandka Medical College Hospital in Sindh, Pakistan, on June 24, 2008.

★ **Longest saliva stone** Saliva stones are mineral deposits that develop in the saliva ducts. They usually measure a few millimeters long, but the longest on record measures 1.45 in. (37 mm). It was removed from a 43-year-old male patient by Dr. Kyprianos Kakouris at the Evangelistria Medical Center in Nicosia, Cyprus, on November 20, 2006.

MAR. 18: The **first spacewalk** was carried out by Lt. Col. (later Maj. Gen.) Alexei Arkhipovich Leonov (USSR), from *Voskhod* 2, on this day in 1965.

MOST EXPENSIVE KIDNEY STONE On January 18, 2006, it was announced that *Star Trek* actor William Shatner (U.S.A.) had sold a kidney stone that he had passed through his body the previous year for $25,000 to online casino GoldenPalace.com. Shatner donated the money to the Habitat for Humanity housing charity.

☆**Highest percentage of body burned, survived** Two people have survived burns to 90% of their bodies. David Chapman (UK) was burned after a gas canister exploded and drenched him with burning fuel on July 2, 1996. Surgeons spent 36 hours following the accident removing his dead skin. Tony Yarijanian (U.S.A.) underwent 25 surgeries, including multiple skin grafts, after suffering similar injuries in an explosion at his wife's beauty spa in California, U.S.A., on February 15, 2004.

★**Heaviest human hairball** A "trichobezoar"—the correct medical term for a hairball—occurs as a result of "trichophagia" or the eating of one's own hair (from the Greek

☆**MOST BLOOD DONATED** A dedicated blood donor, Anthony Davis (UK) has donated a total of 601 units of blood and blood components as of July 3, 2008.

BLOOD BANK

The American Red Cross is the world's **largest provider of blood,** plasma, and tissue products with more than 4.5 million donors supplying 3,000 hospitals.

MAR. 19: Representatives of Swatch Japan cooked the **heaviest Spanish omelette,** which weighed 12.169 tons, in Minato Mirai, Yokohama, Japan, on this day in 1994.

★**FIRST QUINTUPLE KIDNEY TRANSPLANT** The first five-way "domino" organ transplant took place at Johns Hopkins Hospital in Baltimore, U.S.A., in November 2006, led by chief transplant surgeon Robert Montgomery (U.S.A., pictured in front of a chart showing the passage of the five kidneys from patient to patient). It took twelve surgeons, six operating rooms, five donors, and five recipients to achieve the groundbreaking surgery. *See Kidney Swap box (below) for more details.*

KIDNEY SWAP

In this procedure, four patients had a relative willing to offer a kidney. (The fifth was on the waiting list for a dead donor.) But in each case, the donor kidney was incompatible with the patient. With the help of one new donor, enough compatible matches were found to complete a five-way swap simultaneously.

tricha-, hair, and *phagin-*, to eat, also known as Rapunzel syndrome after the Brothers Grimm fairy tale). The largest ever removed from a human was a trichobezoar weighing 10 lb. (4.5 kg), found in the stomach of an 18-year-old woman treated at Rush University Medical Center in Chicago, Illinois, in November 2007. The excised trichobezoar measured $15 \times 7 \times 7$ in. (37.5 $\times 17.5 \times 17.5$ cm).

MAR. 20: Robert G. Davis (U.S.A.) completed the **longest snowmobile journey,** which totaled 12,163 miles (19,574.45 km), on his Yamaha RS Venture snowmobile on this day in 2008.

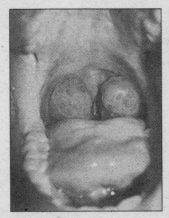

★ LARGEST TONSILS
REMOVED Justin Dodge (U.S.A.)
had tonsils that measured 1.3 in.
(3.2 cm) long, 1 in. (2.6 cm) wide,
and 0.8 in. (2.1 cm) thick when they
were surgically removed at St.
Francis Hospital, Milwaukee,
Wisconsin, U.S.A., on December 18,
2008.

☆ OLDEST UNDISCOVERED
TWIN Sanju Bhagat from Nagpur,
India, lived for 36 years with a
grossly distended stomach that
defied any explanation. In June
1999, his condition became a
medical emergency, as his enlarged
abdomen began to crush his
diaphragm and leave him
breathless. Upon operating, Dr. Ajay
Mehta of Tata Memorial Hospital in
Mumbai, India, encountered the
fetus of Bhagat's unborn twin,
which had continued to grow
parasitically inside his abdomen.
The twin weighed 9 lb.
(4 kg), of which 2 lb. (1 kg) was hair.

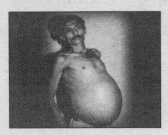

★ Longest confinement in a wheelchair As of November 21, 2008,
William Borrelli (U.S.A., b. March 4, 1925) had been confined to a wheelchair for 76 years 173 days. He was hit by a bus at the age of seven while
running an errand, but has gone on to live a full life, including fathering four
children.

☆ Most tumors removed Dr. Charitesh Gupta (India) removed a total of
nine brain tumors from his 78-year-old patient H.S. Agarwal (India) in a single operation performed at the Himalayan Institute of Medical Sciences in
Dehradun, India, on December 9, 2006.

MAR. 21: The **largest slot machine payout** was $39,713,982.25, won on
the Megabucks slot machine at the Excalibur Hotel-Casino, Las Vegas,
Nevada, U.S.A., on this day in 2003.

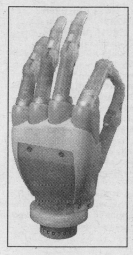

★**FIRST BIONIC HAND** In 2008, the i-limb hand, created by Touch Bionics (UK), became the first commercially available bionic hand. Each finger is powered by its own motor; it has a "credit-card" grip for narrow objects and a power hold for larger objects. It is now used by over 400 patients worldwide.

First successful partial face transplant Isabelle Dinoire (France) underwent a face transplant at Amiens University Hospital, France, on November 27, 2005. Ms. Dinoire was left severely disfigured after being bitten by her dog. Surgeons worked through the night to remove skin, fat, and blood vessels from the donor and then placed them over Ms. Dinoire's skull and muscle before reconnecting the blood vessels.

LIFE STORIES

★**First mother-child supercentenarians** Supercentenarians are people who have attained an age greater than 110. Mary P. Romero Zielke Cota (U.S.A., b. 1870) died in 1982, aged 112 years 17 days; her daughter, Rosabell Zielke Champion Fenstermaker (U.S.A., b. 1893), was equally long-lived and died in 2005, aged 111 years 344 days.

★**Oldest father** The oldest man to father a child was reportedly Les Colley (Australia). Colley was 92 years 10 months old when his ninth child, a son named Oswald, was born. The boy's mother was Colley's third wife, and the couple first met in 1991 through a dating agency when Colley was 90. "I never thought she would get pregnant so easy, but she bloody well did," he told newspaper reporters when the birth was announced.

★**Oldest mother to conceive naturally** On August 20, 1997, Dawn Brooke (UK) became the oldest natural mother when she gave birth to a son by caesarean section at the age of 59 years. She conceived accidentally, having managed to ovulate past her last period.

MAR. 22: Valeriy Poliyakov (Russia) took the **longest manned flight** when he flew to the Mir space station on January 8, 1994, and returned on this day in 1995, a trip lasting 437 days 17 hr. 58 min. 16 sec.

★ MOST CHILDREN SURVIVING FROM A SINGLE BIRTH Nadya Suleman (U.S.A., left) made headlines across the world on January 26, 2009, when she gave birth to six boys and two girls at the Kaiser Permanente Medical Center, Bellflower, California, U.S.A. The babies were conceived with the aid of *in vitro* fertilization (IVF) treatment and were nine weeks premature when they were delivered by cesarean section.

The most children born at a single medically recorded birth is nine, to Geraldine Brodrick (Australia) at the Royal Hospital for Women, Sydney, Australia, on June 13, 1971. None of the children lived for more than six days.

Heaviest birth Anna Bates (Canada, 1846–88), who measured 7 ft. 5.5 in. (2.27 m) tall, gave birth to a boy weighing 23 lb. 12 oz. (10.8 kg) at her home in Seville, Ohio, U.S.A., on January 19, 1879, but the baby died 11 hours later. The **heaviest baby to survive** is a boy born to Carmelina Fedele (Italy) in Aversa, Italy, who weighed 22 lb. 8 oz. (10.2 kg) at birth in September 1955.

★ TOP 10 OLDEST LIVING PEOPLE — AS OF APRIL 16, 2009

	NAME/NATIONALITY	SEX	BORN	AGE
1	Gertrude Baines (U.S.A.)	f	April 6, 1894 ①	115 y 10 d
2	Kama Chinen (Japan)	f	May 10, 1895	113 y 341 d
3	Mary Josephine Ray (U.S.A.)	f	May 17, 1895	113 y 334 d
4	Olivia Patricia Thomas (U.S.A.)	f	June 29, 1895	113 y 291 d
5	Neva Morris (U.S.A.)	f	August 3, 1895	113 y 256 d
6	Chiyo Shiraishi (Japan)	f	August 6, 1895	113 y 253 d
7	Tomoji Tanabe (Japan)	m	September 18, 1895 ②	113 y 210 d
8	Maggie Renfro (U.S.A.)	f	November 14, 1895	113 y 153 d
9	Eugenie Blanchard (France)	f	February 16, 1896	113 y 59 d
10	Lucia Lauria Vigna (Italy)	f	March 4, 1896	113 y 43 d

MAR. 23: *Sen to Chihiro no Kamikakushi*, aka *Spirited Away* (Japan, 2001), is the **first anime to win an Oscar**; it took the prize for Best Animated Feature on this day in 2003.

★ **OLDEST LIVING FATHER** In August 2007, Nanu Ram Jogi (India) celebrated the birth of what he believes is his 21st child, a daughter named Girija, at the grand old age of 90. This achievement makes him the oldest known living dad in the world. He fathered his first child in 1943 and hopes to continue having babies until he reaches 100 years old. His current wife (the fourth) was previously married to one of his sons, who died in 1997.

①

②

Most premature baby to survive The normal human gestation period is around 280 days (roughly 40 weeks); however, James Elgin Gill was born to Brenda and James Gill (all Canada) 128 days premature and weighing just 1 lb. 6 oz. (624 g) on May 20, 1987, in Ottawa, Ontario, Canada. Much of James's body was still developing when he was born, including his skin, hands, ears, and feet. His eyes were still fused shut and he required an operation shortly after his birth to seal off a small artery leading from his heart to his lungs.

★ Oldest mother of triplets In September 2008, an unnamed woman of Asian ethnicity gave birth to triplets at the Cochin Maternity Hospital in Paris, France, at the age of 59 years. The triplets, two boys and a girl, weighed 5 lb. 1 oz. (2.3 kg), 4 lb. 9 oz. (2.1 kg), and 5 lb. 3 oz. (2.4 kg).

First test tube baby Louise Brown (UK) was delivered by caesarean section from Lesley Brown (UK) at Oldham General Hospital, Lancashire, UK, at 11:47 p.m. on July 25, 1978, weighing 5 lb. 12 oz. (2.6 kg). She was externally conceived in a procedure that occurred on November 10, 1977.

Most prolific mother ever The greatest officially recorded number of children born to one mother is 69, to the wife of Feodor Vassilyev (b. 1707–*c*. 1782), a peasant from Shuya, Russia. Amazingly, Vassilyev's wife

---

FACT

On November 13, 2008, Thomas Beatie (below) shocked the world with news of his second pregnancy just months after giving birth to his first child.

★ FIRST MARRIED MAN TO GIVE BIRTH a controversial figure, Thomas Beatie (U.S.A.) was born female but legally became a man in his home state of Oregon, U.S.A. He underwent sex reassignment surgery in 2002, but did not have his female reproductive organs removed. As a man, Beatie was legally able to marry Nancy, his female partner, in 2003. Nancy had previously had a hysterectomy, so when the couple wanted to start a family, it was Thomas who, with the help of an anonymous sperm donor, conceived and carried the child. The couple's daughter, Susan, was born on June 29, 2008.

The ★ **first publicized case of a man giving birth** was that of Matt Rice (U.S.A.). Rice was also born female and became pregnant through artificial insemination, giving birth to a boy named Blake in 1999.

MAR. 24: The **largest inflatable castle** is 39 ft. (12 m) tall and 62 ft.² (19 m²) square at the base, and was first opened to visitors to the Roundhouse in Camden, London, on this day in 1997.

OLDEST WOMAN TO GIVE BIRTH TO HER OWN GRANDCHILDREN At the age of 56, Jacilyn Dalenberg (U.S.A.) acted as surrogate mother for her daughter, Kim Coseno (U.S.A.), carrying and delivering her own grandchildren—three girls named Elizabeth Jacilyn, Carmina Ann, and Gabriella Claire. Born nine weeks early by caesarean section at Hillcrest Hospital in Cleveland, Ohio, U.S.A., on October 11, 2008, the triplets weighed between 2 lb. and 2 lb. 14 oz. (0.9 kg–1.29 kg).

also holds the records for the **most sets of quadruplets born,** with four sets, and the **most sets of twins,** with 16 pairs. While this miraculous mother also gave birth to seven sets of triplets, the record for the **most triplets** is 15 sets, by Maddalena Granata (Italy, 1839–1886).

 Oldest woman to give birth The oldest mother whose age has been verified is Maria del Carmen Bousada Lara (Spain, b. January 5, 1940), who gave birth by caesarean to twin boys, Christian and Pau, aged 66 years 358 days, in Barcelona, Spain, on December 29, 2006.

★**Oldest living single twin** Leona Adams Gleed (U.S.A., b. March 28, 1900) became the oldest living half of a twin on January 27, 2009. Her twin, Leo, died aged 89 in 1990, but the 108-year-old Leona continues to thrive in Norfolk, Nebraska, U.S.A.

★**Oldest ever people to share a birthday** Camille Loiseau (France) and Toyo Endo (Japan) were both born on February 13, 1892 and were the oldest ever people to share a birthday. Toyo was the first to pass away, aged 112 years 325 days on January 3, 2005. Camille was aged 114 years 180 days when she died on August 12, 2006

SIZE MATTERS

8 ft. 11.1 in.: tallest man (ever) Weighing 8.5 lb. (3.85 kg) at birth, Robert Wadlow (U.S.A., see p. xxvii) started growing abnormally at the age of two, following a double hernia operation. His height chart reveals his incredible growth until his death aged 22:

AGE	HEIGHT
5	5 ft. 4 in. (163 cm)
8	6 ft. (183 cm)
10	6 ft. 5 in. (199 cm)
12	6 ft. 10.5 in. (210 cm)
14	7 ft. 5 in. (226 cm)
16	7 ft. 10.24 in. (240 cm)
18	8 ft. 3.5 in. (253 cm)
20	8 ft. 6.75 in. (261 cm)
22.4	8 ft. 11.1 in. (272 cm)*

Still growing while terminally ill

Wadlow died at 1:30 a.m. on July 15, 1940, as a result of a septic blister on his right ankle caused by a brace, which had been poorly attached only a week earlier.

☆ **13 FT. 3.3 IN.: TALLEST MARRIED COUPLE** Wilco (Netherlands) and Keisha van Kleef-Bolton (UK) have a combined average height of 404.7 cm (13 ft. 3.3 in.), making them the world's tallest married couple. They met after Keisha contacted the UK's Tall Persons Club in search of a dance partner. Shortly afterward, the tall twosome were married by the Reverend Brian Shipsides (also pictured) of All Saints Church in Forest Gate, London, UK.

☆ **8 FT. 1 IN.: TALLEST MAN** Sultan Kösen (Turkey) officially reigns supreme as the world's tallest living man—and tallest living human—reaching an average height of 8 ft. 1 in. (246.5 cm) when measured by GWR in Ankara, Turkey, in February 2009. Kösen was born on December 10, 1982, in Kiziltepe Köyü, in the Mardin Province of east Turkey. As a teenager, his height excused him from military service, but drew the attention of scouts from the basketball team Galatasaray; he was signed up to play but proved too ungainly and never made it on to the court.

GROWING PAINS

Sultan has a condition known as "pituitary gigantism," which is the result of excess growth hormone production. Growth hormone is released from the pituitary gland; if the gland is damaged by, for example, a tumor, it can release too much (or too little) hormone. The effects of overproduction include large hands, a thickening of the bones, and painful joints.

---

8 ft. 1.75 in.: tallest woman (ever) Zeng Jinlian (China, 1964–82) measured 8 ft. 1.75 in. tall (248 cm) when she died. This figure represented her height with assumed normal spinal curvature because she suffered from severe scoliosis (curvature of the spine) and could not stand up straight.

Zeng began to grow abnormally from the age of four months and stood 7 ft. 1.5 in. (2.17 m) when she was 13.

3 ft. 10.5 in.–7 ft. 8 in.: most variable stature Adam Rainer (Austria, 1899–1950) measured just 3 ft. 10.5 in. (118 cm) at the age of 21 but suddenly started growing at a rapid rate. By 1931, he had nearly doubled to 7 ft. 1.75 in. (218 cm). He became so weak that he was bedridden for the rest of his life. At the time of his death, he measured 7 ft. 8 in. (234 cm) and was the only person in history to have been both a dwarf and a giant.

7 ft. 6 in.: tallest NBA player With the recent retirement of Gheorghe Muresan (Romania), Yao Ming (China) of the Houston Rockets (U.S.A.)

has become the tallest player in the National Basketball Association (NBA), standing at 7 ft. 6 in. (228.6 cm) tall. He made his pro debut in 1997.

7 ft. 3 in.: tallest male twins

Identical twins Michael and James Lanier (U.S.A., b. November 27, 1969) of Troy, Michigan, both stand 7 ft. 3 in. (223.5 cm). Both men played collegiate basketball—Michael for the University of Denver, Colorado, and James for the University of California in Los Angeles.

7 ft.: tallest WBA heavyweight champion

The tallest person to become the World Boxing Association's Heavyweight Champion is Nicolay Valuev (Russia), who measures 7 ft. (213 cm) tall and weighs 330 lb. (150 kg). Nicknamed the "Beast of the East" by commentators, Valuev is a former basketball player who at the age of 16 had already reached 6 ft. 7 in. (201 cm) tall as a result of a pituitary gland disease.

★ **6 FT 10 IN: TALLEST GIRL** The tallest female under the age of 18 years is Malee Duangdee (Thailand, b. December 22, 1991), whose height of 6 ft. 10 in. (208 cm) is attributable to an inoperable tumor on her pituitary gland. She is pictured here towering above GWR Editor-in-Chief Craig Glenday (5 ft. 7 in.; 170 cm), who measured the teenager at the Chulalongkorn Hospital in Bangkok, Thailand, on January 16, 2009. Drug therapy can slow or even halt Malee's growth, but it is expensive and currently beyond the means of her family.

 ★ 7 FT. 4.6 IN.: TALLEST BOY At just 13 years old, Brenden Adams (U.S.A., b. September 20, 1995) is already 7 ft. 4.6 in. (225.1 cm) tall—taller than Robert Wadlow (**tallest man ever**) was at this age. Although Brenden suffers from a rare chromosomal disorder (he is currently the only known case), his growth rate has slowed to 0.25 in. (0.5 cm) per year.

6 ft. 11 in.: tallest AFL player The tallest man to play in the Australian Football League is Aaron Sandilands (Australia) at 6 ft. 11 in. (211 cm) tall, playing for Freemantle in 2003–05. He shares the record with Tasmanian Peter Street of St. Joseph's.

6 ft. 10 in.: tallest tennis player at Wimbledon Ivo Karlovic (Croatia) measured 6 ft. 10 in. (208 cm) when he played in the 2003 Wimbledon Tennis Championships.

6 ft. 9 in.: tallest NHL player Standing 6 ft. 8.3 in. (204 cm) tall, Zdeno Chara (Slovakia) of the Boston Bruins (U.S.A.) is the tallest player in NHL history.

6 ft. 7 in.: tallest female twins Ann and Claire Recht (U.S.A., b. February 9, 1988) were measured, both horizontally and vertically, three times during January 10, 2007, in Oregon, U.S.A. Each of the twins was found to have an average overall height of 6 ft. 7 in. (201 cm).

☆ 7 FT. 8.9 IN.: TALLEST WOMAN Yao Defens (China) reportedly stands at a height of 7 ft. 8.9 in. (236.2 cm), which would make her the tallest woman on the planet. GWR has yet to confirm her actual height—repeated attempts to measure her have been abandoned due to poor health. Most recently, in April 2009, Ms. Yao was injured in a fall that left her temporarily unable to stand.

6 ft. 5 in.: tallest leading actor Two actors currently hold this title, standing at 6 ft. 5 in. (194 cm)—Christopher Lee (UK), who has played most of the major horror characters in films since 1958; and Vince Vaughn (U.S.A.), whose first leading role was in *Return to Paradise* (U.S.A., 1998). The **tallest actor (ever)** was Matthew McGrory (U.S.A., 1973–2005), who stood at 7 ft. 6 in. (229 cm) when he starred in Tim Burton's *Big Fish* (U.S.A., 2003).

6 ft.: tallest leading actress Margaux Hemingway, Sigourney Weaver, Geena Davis (all U.S.A.), and Brigitte Nielsen (Denmark, see p. 392) all stand at 6 ft. (182 cm) tall.

HUMAN
ACHIEVEMENTS

CONTENTS

STRENGTH

★**Fastest time to pull an articulated bus over 50 m** Pascal Laloux (Belgium) pulled an articulated bus a distance of 164 ft. (50 m) in 3.09 seconds in Namur, Belgium, on April 13, 2008.

☆**Heaviest truck pulled by arm** Using an arm-wrestling move, the Rev. Kevin Fast (Canada) managed to pull a 16,997-lb. (7,710-kg) truck in Cobourg, Ontario, Canada, on February 25, 2008. See p. 120 for another incredible feat of strength by Rev. Fast.

★**Heaviest vehicle pulled by the eyelids** Using ropes attached to hooks that were inserted into his lower eyelids, Dong Changsheng (China) pulled a car weighing 3,307 lb. (1,500 kg) a distance of 33 ft. (10 m) in Changchun, China, on September 26, 2006.

Heaviest vehicle pulled by hair The heaviest vehicle to have been pulled by the hair alone over a distance of 98 ft. (30 m) is a double-decker bus weighing 17,359 lb. (7,874 kg) by Letchemanah Ramasamy (Malaysia) at Bruntingthorpe Proving Ground, Leicestershire, UK, on May 1, 1999.

☆**Heaviest weight lifted by tongue** Thomas Blackthorne (UK) lifted a 27-lb. 8.9-oz. (12.5-kg) weight that had been hooked through his tongue on the set of *El Show Olímpico* in Mexico City, Mexico, on August 1, 2008.

★**LONGEST HOLD OF THE "HUMAN SCALE"** Jessica and Hartmut Held (Germany) maintained the punishing acrobalance position of "human scale" for 38.5 seconds on the set of *Guinness World Records: Die Größten Weltrekorde* in Germany, on December 18, 2008.

....

MAR. 25: Peggy Ashcroft (UK) won an Academy Award for A *Passage to India* (UK/U.S.A., 1984) on this day in 1985, aged 77 years 93 days—the **oldest winner of a Best Supporting Actress Oscar.**

....

16,997 LB. (7,710 KG): the weight of a truck that Kevin Fast pulled using just one arm on February 25, 2008.

  ☆ **HEAVIEST VEHICLE PULLED OVER 100 FT.** Lutheran pastor Reverend Kevin Fast (Canada) started competing in heavy events in 1996 and claimed his first Guinness World Records crown in 1998. Reverend Fast currently holds the record for the heaviest vehicle pulled over a level 100-ft. (30.48-m) course, which he set when he successfully pulled a truck weighing 126,200 lb. (57,243 kg) over that distance on the *Live with Regis & Kelly* television show in New York City, U.S.A., on September 15, 2008.

★ **Heaviest weight lifted by nipples** For five seconds, Sage Werbock (U.S.A.), who performs as "The Great Nippulini," lifted a total weight of 48 lb. 4.2 oz. (21.9 kg) suspended from his pierced nipples at Tritone Bar in Philadelphia, Pennsylvania, U.S.A., on May 20, 2003.

☆ **Heaviest weight supported on the shoulders** Franz Muellner (Austria) supported an average of 1,234 lb. (560 kg) on his shoulders for 30 seconds, while a helicopter landed on a frame which he was partly supporting. The record was achieved in Mexico City, Mexico, on July 31, 2008.

 ☆ **LONGEST TIME SPENT RESTRAINING TWO CESSNA AIRCRAFT** Chad Netherland (U.S.A.) used just his own unaided strength to prevent the takeoff of two Cessna airplanes pulling in opposite directions for 1 min. 0.6 sec.
    The record was set at Richard I. Bong Airport in Superior, Wisconsin, U.S.A., on July 7, 2007.

★ LONGEST TIME TO HOLD A PERSON ABOVE THE HEAD Markus Ferber held Clarissa Beyelschmidt (both Germany) above his head for 59.34 seconds in Cologne, Germany, on September 13, 2008.

☆ Heaviest weight sustained by the body Eduardo Armallo Lasaga (Spain) sustained 71 concrete blocks and four people—3,216.5 lb. (1,459 kg)—on his body in Madrid, Spain, on January 30, 2009.

Heaviest combined weight balanced on the head For one hour, UK strongman and record holder John Evans balanced a total of 11,420 lb. (5,180.09 kg) on his head at Lowestoft Seafront, Suffolk, UK, on July 23, 2000.

★ Most lifts of a 100-kg weight with teeth in one minute Using just his teeth, Georges Christen (Luxembourg) managed to lift a 100-kg (220-lb.) weight 24 times in one minute on the set of *L'Été De Tous Les Records* in Benodet, France, on August 22, 2005.

Greatest weight of bricks lifted Fred Burton (UK) held 20 bricks weighing a total of 226 lb. 7 oz. (102.73 kg) at chest height for two seconds on June 5, 1998, in Cheadle, Staffordshire, UK.

★ Most concrete blocks broken in a single stack with the head The record for the most concrete blocks broken in a single stack using just the head is seven, achieved by Narve Laeret (Norway) in Horten, Vestfold, Norway, on July 3, 2008. Laeret beat his own record of five set the year before.

☆ Giant hula hoop—most rotations in a minute In Jamaica, New York, U.S.A., on April 30, 2008, Ashrita Furman (U.S.A.) rotated a custom-built hula hoop with a diameter of 11 ft. 6 in. (3.5 m) a total of 64 times in one minute.

....

MAR. 26: The **shortest papal reign** was that of Pope Stephen II, who was elected on March 24, 752, following the death of Pope Zacharias . . . and died two days later.

....

★ **HEAVIEST WEIGHT PULLED WITH THE EYE SOCKETS** Chayne Hultgren (Australia) pulled a rickshaw loaded with people, weighing a total of 907 lb. (411.65 kg), using ropes attached to fish hooks that were hooked on to the lacrimal bones underneath his eyes, in Milan, Italy, on April 25, 2009.

☆ **Longest time restraining a car** While appearing on the *El Show Olímpico* television show in Mexico City, Mexico, on July 28, 2008, Franz Muellner (Austria) managed to restrain a Ferrari 360 Modena that was at full throttle for a total of 13.84 seconds.

☆ **Most bench presses of a person** Fernando Saugar (Spain) bench-pressed a person sitting on a specially designed bench with a combined weight of 234 lb. 5 oz. (106.28 kg) 111 times in one minute. Saugar

☆ **TIGHTEST FRYING-PAN ROLLS** Scott Murphy (U.S.A.) took a 12-in. (30-cm) aluminum frying pan and, with his bare hands, rolled it into a tube with a circumference of 6.87 in. (17.46 cm) in 30 seconds. The feat took place at the NXB Team Training Center in Myrtle Beach, South Carolina, U.S.A., on July 30, 2007.

The ★ **tightest circumference of two 12-in. (30-cm) aluminum frying pans** rolled together with bare hands in 30 seconds is 12 in. (30.5 cm), set by Jon Pritikin (U.S.A.) at Rectory Road Park in Sittingbourne, Kent, UK, on July 11, 2007.

MAR. 27: The **longest TV commercial** was for Lipton Ice Tea Green, which lasted for 24 minutes when it was broadcast by the Yorin television channel in the Netherlands on this day in 2005.

580: the number of times Mark Anglesea (UK) lifted the rear of a car clear off the ground in one hour on October 3, 1998.

★ **MOST DOMESTIC APPLIANCES THROWN IN ONE MINUTE** Taking the art of domestic appliance-throwing one stage further, Oliver Gratzer (Austria) tossed 24 different household appliances in one minute on the set of *Guinness World Records—Die größten Weltrekorde* in Cologne, Germany, on September 13, 2008.

achieved the record on the set of *Guinness World Records—El Show de los Records* in Madrid, Spain, on May 25, 2006.

Farthest washing-machine throw by an individual Bill Lyndon (Australia) managed to toss a washing machine weighing 99 lb. (45.3 kg) a distance of 11 ft. 0.24 in. (3.36 m) in Sydney, Australia, on June 26, 2005.

☆**Fastest time to complete the GWR fitness challenge** Robin Simpson (UK) finished a 2-mile swim, a 110-mile cycle ride, a 12-mile run, a 12-mile walk, a 20-mile row, 20 miles of Nordic track (elliptical) training, 300,000 lb. of lifts (no leg lifts), 1,250 push-ups, 3,250 abdominal crunches, 1,250 leg lifts, and 1,250 jumping jacks in 18 hr. 25 min. 40 sec. at the Fitness First gym in Leeds, UK, on November 28, 2008.

☆**Most vehicles to run over the stomach** Tom Owen (U.S.A.) had eight vehicles run over his stomach in Phoenix, Arizona, U.S.A., on October 17, 2008. The total weight of the eight vehicles was 72,000 lb. (32,658 kg).

ODD TALENTS

☆**Loudest burp (male)** Paul Hunn (UK) produced a burp measuring 107.1 dBA on the set of *The New Paul O'Grady Show,* in London, UK, on September 24, 2008.

☆**Fastest time to arrange a deck of playing cards** Zdenek Bradac (Czech Republic) arranged a deck (52 cards) of shuffled playing cards into the order Ace through 10, Jack, Queen, King of Diamonds, Clubs, Hearts, and Spades in 36.16 seconds at Sheffield Castle College, South Yorkshire, UK, on May 15, 2008.

☆**Fastest time to escape from a suitcase** Contortionist Leslie Tipton (U.S.A.) "folded" herself into a standard suitcase, which was then zipped shut. She managed to escape from the case in 7.04 seconds. The feat was

★ **FASTEST 100 M HURDLES WEARING FLIPPERS (FEMALE)** Maren Zänker (Germany) completed the 100 m hurdles wearing flippers in 22.35 seconds on the set of *Guinness World Records—Die Größten Weltrekorde* in Cologne, Germany, on September 13, 2008. The fastest "normal" 100 m hurdles (female) was run in 12.21 sec. by Yordanka Donkova (Bulgaria) in 1988.

MAR. 28: On this day in 1977, the **only posthumous Best Actor Oscar** was awarded to Peter Finch (UK) for his work on *Network* (U.S.A., 1976). He died on January 14, 1977, of a heart attack.

☆ **LONGEST FULL-BODY ICE CONTACT** Wim Hof (Netherlands) spent 1 hr. 42 min. 22 sec. in direct, full-body contact with ice on the set of *Guinness World Records* in Madrid, Spain, on January 23, 2009. Hof has been involved in extreme outdoor activities for over 20 years. He uses the "inner fire" yoga technique to keep his body temperature at a normal 98.6°F (37°C) even in extreme cold.

achieved on May 31, 2008, in Los Angeles, California, U.S.A., during Book Expo America.

☆ **Greatest distance traveled with a pool cue balanced on chin** Ashrita Furman (U.S.A.) traveled one mile (1,668 m) with a pool cue balanced on his chin at the Joe Austin Playground in Jamaica, New York, U.S.A., on July 6, 2008. The 17.6-oz. (500-g) cue was balanced with just the leather tip touching his chin.

Most swords swallowed simultaneously Chayne "Space-cowboy" Hultgren (Australia) swallowed 17 swords in one go at Calder Park Raceway, Melbourne, Australia, on 28 March 2008. The next day he broke the record for the ☆ **heaviest weight dangled from a**

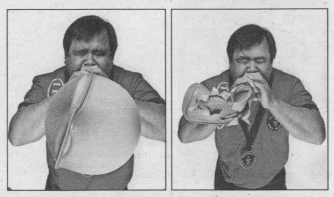

★ **FASTEST TIME TO BURST THREE HOT WATER BOTTLES** Using only his lung power, Brian Jackson (U.S.A.) inflated three hot water bottles until they burst in 1 min. 8 sec., on the set of *Lo Show Dei Record* in Milan, Italy, on April 19, 2009.

☆ **MOST TORCHES EXTINGUISHED WITH THE MOUTH** Hubertus Wawra (Germany), aka "Master of Hellfire," extinguished 68 fire torches with his mouth in one minute on the set of *Guinness World Records: Die Größten Weltrekorde* in Cologne, Germany, on September 13, 2008.

swallowed sword when he swallowed a non-retractable 40.5-cm-long (15.9-in.) sword and then held two gas canisters weighing 22.4 kg (49 lb. 6 oz.) attached to the sword handle for five seconds at the Crusty Demons Night of World Records at the same venue.

☆ **Most candles blown out in one breath** V. Sankaranarayanan (India) blew out 151 candles at the Press Club in Ramnathapuram, India, on January 18, 2008.

★ **Fastest time to ski 100 m backward** Winter sports fanatic Andy Bennett (UK) skied 328 ft. (100 m) backwards downhill, navigating through a course that included four slalom gates, in 9.48 sec. at the SNO!zone in-

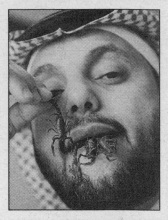

☆ **MOST SCORPIONS HELD IN THE MOUTH** Maged Elmalke (Saudi Arabia) held 22 scorpions in his mouth in Riyadh, Saudi Arabia, on September 1, 2008. Guidelines state that all the scorpions must be in the mouth for at least 10 seconds.

MAR. 29: Henry Fonda (U.S.A.) was the **oldest Best Actor Oscar winner** on this day in 1982 for his performance as Norman Thayer Jr. in *On Golden Pond* (U.S.A., 1981), aged 76 years 317 days.

21: the **most tennis balls held in one hand,** achieved by Rohit Timilsina (Nepal) for 14.32 seconds in Kathmandu, Nepal, on June 14, 2008.

☆ **MOST RATTLESNAKES HELD IN THE MOUTH** Jackie Bibby (U.S.A.) held 11 diamondback rattlesnakes in his mouth by their tails without any assistance for 10 seconds on the set of *Guinness World Records: Die Größten Weltrekorde* in Germany on December 20, 2008. Bibby was born in Texas, U.S.A., in 1950 and has been handling snakes since 1968. He is currently the president of The Heart of Texas Snake Handlers.

door snow slope in Milton Keynes, UK, on April 27, 2009. The challenge was recorded for *Guinness World Records Smashed*.

★ **Most maggots moved with the mouth in one hour** Charlie Bell (UK) shifted 37 lb. 7 oz. (17 kg) of maggots between two containers 3 ft. 3 in. (1 m) apart in one hour on the set of *Guinness World Records Smashed* at Pinewood Studios, London, UK, on April 7, 2009. The hot studio lights prompted the maggots to pupate and turn into flies, making Charlie's challenge even harder!

☆ **Most chainsaw juggling catches** Aaron Gregg (Canada) achieved 88 chainsaw juggling catches on the set of *El Show Olímpico* in Mexico City, Mexico, on July 28, 2008.

MAR. 30: The **greatest amount paid by a single check** was $3,971,821,275. Issued on this date in 1995, the check was a payment by Glaxo plc to Wellcome Trust Nominees Ltd.

☆ **Most M&Ms eaten in one minute by chopsticks** John Muller (U.S.A.) ate 27 M&Ms in one minute using chopsticks in New York City, U.S.A., on November 14, 2008. The record was part of GWR Day 2008 and taped live on the set of *CW11 Morning News*.

☆ **Most juggling catches while suspended** Ashrita Furman (U.S.A.) achieved 601 catches juggling three balls while suspended upside down by gravity boots in Jamaica, New York, U.S.A., on May 6, 2008.

☆ **Most spoons balanced on the face** Joe Allison (UK) balanced 16 spoons on his face simultaneously. This classic cutlery record was achieved in Totnes, Devon, UK, on April 1, 2008.

★ **Most watermelons smashed with a fist** Our UK television show, *Guinness World Records Smashed,* really lived up to its name on April 2, 2009 when Ricky O'Brien (UK) literally smashed his way through 45 watermelons in one minute before a live audience at Pinewood Studios, London, UK.

SUPER STUNTS

★ **Fastest time to throw 10 knives around a human target** The Reverend Dr. David R. Adamovich, aka "The Great Throwdini" (U.S.A.), threw 10 14-in.-long (35-cm) throwing knives around his partner, "Target Girl" Tina Nagy (U.S.A.), in 4.29 seconds on the set of *El Show Olímpico* in Mexico City, Mexico, on July 29, 2008.

★ **Heaviest vehicle pulled using a swallowed sword** Ryan Stock (Canada) swallowed a 17-in.-long (43.18-cm) sword on the TV show *Guinea Pig* filmed in Las Vegas, Nevada, U.S.A., on October 28, 2008. He then tied the sword using ropes to a 2002 Audi A4 that weighed 3,740 lb. (1,696.44 kg) and dragged the car 20 ft. 11 in. (6.38 m) in 20.53 sec.

★ **FASTEST TIME TO RUN THROUGH 10 LOCKED AND BURNING DOORS** In a punishing test of fitness, fearlessness, and foolhardiness, Sandra Kier (Germany) ran through 10 locked, burning doors in just 23 seconds on the set of *Guinness World Records: Die Größten Weltrekorde* in Germany on December 18, 2008.

Human Achievements

201: the number of BASE jumps in 24 hours, by Dan Schilling (U.S.A.) in Twin Falls, Idaho, U.S.A., on July 7–8, 2006.

☆ LONGEST WATERFALL DESCENT BY CANOE The longest descent over a waterfall by canoe is 107 ft. (32.6 m) by Tyler Bradt (U.S.A.) at the Alexandra Falls on the Hay River in Canada's Northwest Territories on September 7, 2007. To succeed in this attempt, Bradt had to remain in his Dagger Nomad kayak at all times.

☆ Highest shallow dive Darren Taylor (U.S.A.) beat his own world record by diving from 35 ft. 6.6 in. (10.83 m) into just 11.8 in. (30 cm) of water in Tokyo, Japan, on December 7, 2008.

☆ Most pine boards broken with the head in 30 seconds The most pine boards broken across the forehead in 30 seconds is 32 by Kevin Shelley (U.S.A.) on the set of *El Show Olímpico* in Mexico City, Mexico, on July 30, 2008.

Highest jump without a parachute on film Movie stuntman A.J. Bakunas (U.S.A., 1950–78) jumped from a height of 232 ft. (70.71 m) without a parachute while doubling for Burt Reynolds in *Hooper* (U.S.A., 1978). He fell onto an air mattress.

Highest freefall on film Working as a stuntman in the film *Highpoint* (Canada, 1979), Dar Robinson (U.S.A.) jumped 1,100 ft. (335 m) from the summit of the CN Tower in Toronto, Canada. His parachute opened just 300 ft. (91 m) from the ground after six seconds of freefalling.

GOING DOWN . . .

Tyler achieved his record-breaking descent (pictured above using multiple exposures) by staying to the far left of the waterfall and landing in a safety zone (or "cushy foam pile" as he called it), where the water pushes away from the waterfall's base. "It was a lot softer landing than I expected," he reported.

MAR. 31: On this day in 1997, Switzerland's Martina Hingis (b. September 30, 1980) became the **youngest woman to be ranked world tennis number one** at the age of 16 years 182 days.

A reverse bungee involves anchoring yourself to the ground, strapping yourself securely to a bungee cord, and stretching the cord upward (usually using a crane) to its limit. Only then do you release the rope, which catapults you high into the air (see below).

★ HIGHEST REVERSE BUNGEE JUMP The greatest height to which a human has been catapulted by reverse bungee is 178 ft. (54.25 m), achieved by Ben Shephard (UK) in London, UK, on October 3, 2008.

Highest skiing base jump on film For a sequence in *The Spy Who Loved Me* (UK, 1977), James Bond—aka stuntman Rick Sylvester (U.S.A.)—skied down a slope and jumped off the edge of a 2,000-ft. (609.6-m) cliff, Asgard Peak on Baffin Island in Canada, before opening his Union Jack canopy.

Lowest death-dive escape Robert Gallup (Australia) was leg-manacled, handcuffed, chained, tied into a secured mail bag, and then locked in a metal cage before being thrown out of a C-123 transport plane at 18,000 ft. (5,486 m) above the Mojave Desert, California, U.S.A. With less than a minute before impact and traveling at 150 mph (240 km/h), Gallup escaped from the sack and cage to reach his parachute secured on the outside of the cage and was able to deploy it with enough altitude to land safely.

APR. 1: The **largest operational mousetrap** was built by Bio Tec-Klute GmbH (Germany) and measured 13 ft. 11.32 in. (4.25 m) long and 6 ft. 10.68 in. (2.10 m) wide when unveiled on April 1, 2007.

★ **LONGEST TIGHTROPE CROSSING BY BICYCLE** Nik Wallenda (U.S.A.), a seventh-generation member of the Flying Wallendas circus acrobat family, cycled 235 ft. (71.63 m) along a tightrope in Newark, New Jersey, U.S.A., on October 15, 2008

FACT

The tightrope was set up between two cranes at a height of 135 ft. (41.15 m)—that's 13 storys high!

★ **Most cars loaded into an aircraft in one hour** The delivery company TNT and the TV show/magazine *TopGear* (both Italy) had just one hour to load a Boeing 747 with Smart cars at Liege Airport in Belgium on October 23, 2008. The team of seven staff actually filled the hold with 30 cars in a time of just 35 min. 45 sec.

★ **SHORTEST GAP BETWEEN AIRPLANE AND MOTORCYCLE DURING A RAMP JUMP** The closest that a motorcycle has ever come to an aircraft during a ramp jump is 7 ft. 11 in. (2.42 m), when Hungary's Veres Zoltán (piloting an Extra 300) and Gulyás Kiss Zoltán (riding a Yamaha YZ250F cross motorcycle) crossed in midair during a stunt in Etyek, Hungary, on September 7, 2008.

MASS PARTICIPATION 1

MOST PEOPLE . . .

☆**In a custard pie fight** The most participants in a single custard pie fight is 120. The feisty pie-flingers did battle during the filming of the music video for the track "Troublemaker" by the band Weezer in Los Angeles, California, U.S.A., on August 21, 2008.

★**Playing dominoes** At the 6th annual World Domino Tournament— hosted by the International Domino Federation and the National Domino Federation (both U.S.A.)—at Walt Disney World in Orlando, Florida, U.S.A., on July 10, 2008, a total of 332 people played dominoes simultaneously.

☆**Dressed as sunflowers** The most people dressed as sunflowers was 116, a record set at The Nursery on the Green in London, UK, on August 13, 2008.

★**Patting their heads and rubbing their stomachs** In total, 159 participants convened at the Windmill Public House in Clapham Common, London, UK, on October 27, 2007, to pat their heads while rubbing their stomachs at the same time.

☆**Sitting on one chair** The most people sitting on one chair is 1,058, in an event organized by the Tampines West Constituency Sports Club at Springfield Secondary School, Singapore, on August 16, 2008. To achieve this record, one person sits on a chair, someone else sits on their lap, another on *their* lap and so on. . . .

★**With team colors painted on the face** A record 29,688 people gathered at the Stade de France in Paris, France, on June 7, 2008, to have their faces painted in the Stade Français Paris Rugby Club colors of blue and pink. The record attempt was organized in collaboration with Fanbrush face paints, the Stade Français Paris, and the Stade de France.

> **1,752:** the number of people at the Wave for Wales event in Margam County Park, UK, dancing the "Locomotion" on June 24, 2007.

APR. 2: Emilio Scotto (Argentina) completed the **longest journey by motorcycle ever** on this day in 1995. He started his trip on January 17, 1985 and covered over 456,700 miles (735,000 km).

★MOST PEOPLE ON HOP BALLS On July 4, 2008, at an event organized by the Shepway School Sport Partnership at the Cheriton Road Sports Ground in Folkestone, Kent, UK, a total of 1,008 people gathered to bounce on their hop balls. Also known as a hoppity-hop, space hopper, and kangaroo ball, the inflatable rubber toy—invented in Italy in the late 1960s—serves no real purpose: they do not allow you to travel higher or faster than you can do on foot!

★Solving crosswords simultaneously On September 28, 2008, 443 people were solving crosswords simultaneously for Gewista Werbeges.m.b.H at the Vienna Recordia event held in Vienna, Austria.

★Dancing the waltz The largest waltz consisted of 242 couples who danced for an event organized by the nonprofit Verein Rueff unter der Patronanz des Verband der Tanzlehrer Österreichs (VTÖ) (Austria) at Austria Center Vienna, Austria, on April 26, 2008.

★Jumping on spring-loaded stilts The Shao Lin Tagou Martial Arts School of Dengfeng City, Henan province, China, organized 103 people to simultaneously jump on spring-loaded stilts on September 17, 2008.

☆MOST PEOPLE DRESSED AS SMURFS On July 18, 2008, at the Muckno Mania Festival in Castleblayney, Co. Monaghan, Ireland, 1,253 people dressed as Smurfs and paraded through the town's streets.

APR. 3: The **first portable telephone handset,** or mobile phone—invented by Martin Cooper (U.S.A.) of Motorola, was used for the first time on this day in 1973.

☆ **LARGEST GATHERING OF WALDOS** If you've been wondering "Where's Waldo?" recently, then you should have had your eyes peeled at the record attempt organized by the ACUITY insurance company at its corporate headquarters in Sheboygan, Wisconsin, U.S.A., on December 10, 2008—a total of 577 people turned up dressed as the elusive children's book character (aka Wally/Walter/Efi/Charlie/Holger, depending on which country you're in)!

☆ **MOST PEOPLE DRESSED AS SUPERMAN** On June 15, 2008, Steven Kirk (U.S.A.) organized an event that was attended by a record 122 people dressed as the "Man of Steel." The Superman celebration was held in Metropolis, Illinois, U.S.A., the self-proclaimed "Hometown of Superman."

APR. 4: The **largest crowd for a basketball game** is 80,000, for the European Cup Winners Cup final in Athens, Greece, between AEK Athens (89) and Slavia Prague (82) on this day in 1968.

★ MOST PEOPLE DANCING WITH HULA HOOPS On April 12, 2008, to celebrate the DVD release of *Alvin and the Chipmunks* (U.S.A., 2007), Twentieth Century Fox organized an event at Chessington World of Adventures, Surrey, UK, during which 342 people danced with hula hoops!

★ Playing mahjong simultaneously A game of mahjong was played by 492 participants at the Hong Kong International Trade & Exhibition Center Rotunda Hall 2 in Hong Kong, China, on July 20, 2008.

★ Playing wood block/Chinese block The record for the most people playing wood (Chinese) block at the same time is 240 participants, at the event Ngong Ping Buddha's Birthday Celebration in Hong Kong, China, on May 11, 2008.

★ Receiving a foot massage A total of 1,000 lucky people received a 40-minute reflexology foot massage at an event organized by the Taiwan Tourism Bureau at Taipei Arena, Taipei, Taiwan, on July 1, 2008.

★ Tossing diabolos A record 223 students and staff at Manor Field Primary School in Burgess Hill, UK, tossed diabolos on July 13, 2008. A diabolo is a spool- or yoyo-like juggling prop that is kept airborne and spinning using a piece of string tied to two sticks; a stick is held in each hand.

☆ In a golf lesson John Roethling (Germany) really got into the swing of teaching when he gave a golf lesson to a record 562 people at Baustert, Rhineland-Palatinate, Germany, on June 8, 2008.

MASS PARTICIPATION 2

LARGEST . . .

★ Speed dating event (multi-venue) At an event organized by Fast Impressions to celebrate the 10th anniversary of the dating organization RSVP, a total of 1,240 single people from across Australia went speed-dating on February 14, 2008, to help raise funds for Drought Relief.

APR. 5: The world's **oldest adopted person** is Jo Anne Benedict Walker (U.S.A.), who was aged 65 years 224 days when she was adopted by Frances Ensor Benedict (U.S.A.) on April 5, 2002.

☆ **LARGEST BALLET CLASS—BARRES On August 24, 2008, 989 dancers from Cape Town City Ballet and 65 ballet schools and studios took part in a single ballet class organized by Andrew Warth (South Africa) at Canal Walk Shopping Center in Cape Town, South Africa.**

☆ **Aqua aerobics display** On April 5, 2008, 273 people took part in the world's largest aqua aerobic display, at LifeCenter Plus health and fitness facility in Hudson, Ohio, U.S.A. The event was organized to raise money for, and awareness of, a diabetes charity.

☆ **Cheerleading cheer** On April 23, 2008, just a few months prior to the Beijing Olympics, a team of 1,200 people dressed in red and took part in a 5-minute-long "I'm Lovin' It When China Wins" cheer at Beijing Olympic Sports Center—a pom-pom's throw from the Bird's Nest Olympic Stadium in Beijing, China.

★ **Air guitar ensemble** An air guitar ensemble involving 318 participants collectively rocked out to "I Believe in a Thing Called Love" by Justin Hawkins (UK) on the set of *Guinness World Records—Smashed* in London, UK, on October 3, 2008.

DANCING BY NUMBERS . . .	
1,217	☆ *Head, Shoulders, Knees and Toes* singalong, Taiwan, July 1, 2008
221	★ Yowla dance, UAE, February 22, 2008
186	★ Long sword dance, UK, September 26, 2003
146	☆ Maypole dance, UK, May 21, 2008

★**Bollywood dance** Organized by Sapnay School of Dance (UK) during *Big Dance 2008,* 278 dancers performed a Bollywood dance routine in Trafalgar Square, London, UK, on July 6, 2008.

☆**Ski lesson** A record 594 skiers were instructed by Hansjürg Gredig (Switzerland) of the Swiss-Snowsport School at Sarn-Heinzenberg (Graubünden), Switzerland, on February 23, 2008.

★**Dance-mat routine** A simultaneous dance-mat routine involving 100 participants established a new Guinness World Record at the NOKIA Theater LA Live in Los Angeles, California, U.S.A., for the FOX television show *So You Think You Can Dance* (U.S.A.) on May 19, 2008.

☆**MOST PEOPLE SPINNING** During the annual Esporta Health & Fitness conference in Gloucester, UK, 412 company employees came together to take part in a 45-minute spinning (static cycling) workout on February 19, 2009.

APR. 6: The **longest recorded boxing fight**—between Andy Bowen and Jack Burke (both U.S.A.)—began on this day in April 1893 in New Orleans, U.S.A. It lasted 110 rounds and took 7 hr. 19 min.!

☆ **LARGEST PARADE OF INLINE SKATERS** On June 15, 2008, a total of 1,188 inline skaters rolled their way into the record books when they came together on the streets of Paris, France. The participants—organized and led by Rollers & Coquillages (France)—skated *en masse* for 12.68 miles (20.4 km) in a circuitous route starting and finishing at the Place de la Bastille.

☆ **LARGEST CPR TRAINING CLASS** A cardiopulmonary resuscitation (CPR) training session involving 3,692 participants was organized by Norwegian Air Ambulance at Valhall indoor stadium in Oslo, Norway, on May 26, 2008.

☆ **LARGEST SANTA GATHERING** In 2007, Christmas came early in Derry City, Northern Ireland, UK, when 13,000 people dressed as Santa gathered in the Guildhall Square on December 9.

APR. 7: The **shortest title of any Oscar-winning movie** is Z (Algeria/France, 1969), directed by Costa-Garvas (Greece), which won two Academy Awards on this day in 1970.

★ LARGEST BHANGRA DANCE On August 31, 2008, a total of 763 dancers from the Nachdi Jawani Association and Punjabi Virsa Arts and Culture Academy (both Canada) participated in a Bhangra dance at the Powerade Center in Brampton, Ontario, Canada.

☆ **Scavenger hunt** A group of 183 participants followed an urban scavenger hunt at the Hanashobu shopping center in Osue-Chou Hikone-Shi, Japan, on June 22, 2008.

☆ **Gathering of zombies** In total, 1,227 people dressed up as zombies in Nottingham, UK, as part of the city's GameCity festival on October 31, 2008.

☆ **Game of dodgeball** Two teams of 50 people (100 total) played against each other during the filming of the pop video "Troublemaker" by Weezer in Los Angeles, California, U.S.A., on August 21, 2008.

★ **Gathering of Ninja Turtles** On April 10, 2008, at Rutgers University in New Jersey, U.S.A., 786 people attended an event wearing full Ninja Turtle costumes.

★ **Gathering of pregnant women** The "Your Baby" show in Johannesburg, South Africa, was the location for a gathering of 1,164 pregnant women on May 17, 2007.

★ **Wine-tasting event (multi-venue)** A wine-tasting event organized by the JD Wetherspoon pub chain saw 17,540 people tasting wine in 409 UK pubs on May 21, 2008.

FACT

On April 13, 2008, Ian Sharman (UK) ran the London Marathon in 3 hr. 12 min. 27 sec.—while dressed as Santa Claus.

APR. 8: On this day in 1998, David Holleran (Australia) completed the **longest triathlon**—a 26-mile (42-km) swim, 1,242-mile (2,000-km) cycle, and 310-mile (500-km) run in 17 days 22 hr. 50 min.

IN AN HOUR

★ **Greatest weight deadlifted (individual)** The greatest weight dead-lifted in one hour is 69,445 lb. (31,500 kg) by Eamonn Keane (Ireland) at Powerhouse Gym in Dublin, Ireland, on September 29, 2007. He also bench-pressed 305,300 lb. (138,480 kg) in an hour at World Gym, Marina del Rey, California, U.S.A., on July 22, 2003—the ★ **greatest weight bench-pressed by an individual in one hour.**

☆ **Greatest distance moonwalked** Krunoslav Budiselic (Croatia) moonwalked for one hour at the Athletic Stadium Mladost in Zagreb, Croatia, on September 10, 2006, and managed to cover 3.265 miles (5.255 km).

☆ **Farthest distance static cycling** Holden Comeau (U.S.A.), from the New York Sports Clubs/Cadence Cycling Team, covered 40.69 miles (65.48 km) in one hour during "Saints & Spinners—The 24-Hour Spin Party and Benefit" in New York City, U.S.A., on January 18, 2008.

☆ **Greatest distance cycling backward** Markus Riese (Germany) cycled 18 miles (29 km) backward in one hour at the VC Darmstadt 1899 e.V. cycling club, Darmstadt, Germany, on May 24, 2003.

MOST . . .

☆ **Balloons inflated by the nose** Andrew Dahl (U.S.A.) inflated 308 balloons using just his nose in one hour on the *Live with Regis & Kelly* TV show in New York City, U.S.A., on September 16, 2008.

☆ **Heads shaved** Anne Armstrong (UK) managed to shave a record 44 heads in one hour at Maginns of Castlewellan in Castlewellan, County Down, UK, on April 25, 2008.

☆ **Chin-ups** Stephen Hyland (UK) achieved 908 successful chin-ups in one hour in Stoneleigh, Surrey, UK, on January 2, 2009.

☆ **MOST KNEE BENDS ON AN EXERCISE BALL** On November 13, 2008, Stephen Buttler (UK) achieved 1,502 knee bends in Shropshire, UK.

24 MILES (38.632 KM): distance traveled by Mauro Guenci (Italy) on inline skates in one hour in Senigallia, Italy, on June 11, 2005.

☆ **MOST PANCAKES MADE BY AN INDIVIDUAL** Bob Blumer (Canada), host and co-creator of the adventure television series *Glutton for Punishment,* made a record-breaking 559 pancakes in one hour at Rope Square in Calgary, Alberta, Canada, on July 10, 2008.

★ **Bungee jumps** Veronica Dean (South Africa) performed 19 bungee jumps in one hour at Bloukrans River Bridge, South Africa, on May 9, 2003. The bungee cord used was approximately 118 ft. (36 m) long.

★ **Basketball layups (team)** UBALL (Utrecht BasketBALL) under-18 boys team recorded 2,640 basketball layups in one hour at Sporthal Galgenwaard, Utrecht, the Netherlands, on May 24, 2008.

☆ **Basketball three-point shots** Vladislav Raiskiy (Russia) made 835 three-pointers in one hour at Tauras-Fitness Ltd, St. Petersburg, Russia, on November 23, 2008.

☆ **Basketball free throws** Appearing on the set of *Unbelievable* at the Fuji TV studios, Tokyo, Japan, Fred Newman (U.S.A.) made 1,663 free throws in one hour on September 17, 2008.

★ **Pizzas made** Donald Mark Rush (U.S.A.) made 142 pizzas in one hour at Domino's Pizza, Gulfport, Mississippi, U.S.A., on August 2, 2008.

FACT

The record for the **largest pancake toss** is 405, achieved by Bram Zwiers in Almere, the Netherlands, on October 24, 2008.

Faces painted Gary Cole (U.S.A.) painted a total of 217 different faces, using a minimum of three colors per face, at Almondvale Shopping Centre in Livingston, West Lothian, UK, on September 1, 2007.

★ **Weight lifted by incline dumbbell flys** An incredible 61,486.9 lb. (27,890 kg) was lifted by Eamonn Keane (Ireland) in one hour at Lough Lannagh Fitness Centre, County Mayo, Ireland, on May 22, 2008. Eamonn also set the record for the ★ **most weight lifted by a barbell upright row in one hour** on June 10, 2008, with 40,752.5 lb. (18,485 kg).

☆ **MOST INVERTS ON A SIT-DOWN HYDROFOIL** Greg Gill (Australia, left) completed 589 inverts in one hour on the Maroochy River in Maroochydore, Queensland, Australia, on June 26, 2008. Gill also performed backside rolls and gainers.

WAVE RIDERS

A sit-down hydrofoil is towed behind a speedboat. When moving across the water, the hydrofoil lifts the rider and board above the surface of the water. Balance is crucial to staying upright, because slight body movements have a great effect on the position of the hydrofoil.

APR. 9: The **oldest voice recording** is that of a woman singing "Au Claire de la Lune" ("By the Light of the Moon"). It was made on April 9, 1860 by Edouard-Leon Scott de Martinville (France).

☆ **MOST STEP-UPS WITH A 40-LB. PACK** The most step-ups completed in one hour with a 40-lb. (18-kg) pack is 1,805 by Arran McLellan (Canada) on a 15-in. (38.1-cm) bench at Club Phoenix Gym in Victoria, B.C., Canada, on February 21, 2009

☆ **Underwater haircuts** The most haircuts given under water in one hour is 27, achieved by David Rae (UK) at the London School of Diving, London, UK, on November 12, 2007.

☆ **Rugby tackles** Students from Scots College (all Australia) in Sydney, New South Wales, Australia, made 4,130 rugby tackles in one hour on March 15, 2007.

☆ **Rubik's cubes solved** David Calvo (Spain) solved 185 Rubik's cubes in one hour while appearing on the Spanish television show *Donde Estas Corazon* on November 14, 2008.

★ **Push-ups (using backs of hands, carrying a 40-lb. pack)** Strongman and multiple record holder Paddy Doyle (UK) performed 663 push-ups on the backs of his hands carrying a 40-lb. (18-kg) pack at Stamina's Boxing Martial Arts Club in Birmingham, UK, on May 13, 2008.

☆ **Weight lifted by standing barbell press** The greatest weight lifted by standing barbell press in one hour is 99,208 lb. (45,000 kg) achieved by Robin Simpson (UK) in Manchester, UK, on October 25, 2008.

☆ **MOST LEGS WAXED IN ONE HOUR** Beautician Susanne Baird (UK) successfully waxed 40 pairs of legs at the Grange Cricket Club in Stockbridge, Edinburgh, UK, on April 14, 2008. She actually managed 42 pairs, but two were rejected as the hair had not been completely removed.

....

APR. 10: Andrzej Makowski (Canada) earned his driver's license on this day in 1974. He passed his test at Namyslow, Poland, aged 14 years 235 days, making him the **youngest licensed driver.**

....

IN A DAY

GREATEST DISTANCE . . .

★ Pushing a car (individual) Record-breaking powerhouse Ashrita Furman (U.S.A.) pushed a car 17.06 miles (27.45 km) in 24 hours at the Old Bridge Township Raceway Park in Englishtown, New Jersey, U.S.A., on March 6, 2008.

Traveled on a skateboard James Peters (U.S.A.) traveled 184 miles (296.12 km) on a skateboard in 24 hours on May 11, 2007. The amazing skating feat was achieved on the Green Lake bike trail in Seattle, Washington, U.S.A.

☆ Covered by wheelchair Mario Trindade (Portugal) covered 113.34 miles (182.4 km) in a wheelchair in 24 hours at the Vila Real Stadium in Vila Real, Portugal, on December 3–4, 2007.

Traveled on a human-powered vehicle In 24 hours, Greg Kolodziejzyk (Canada) covered 647 miles (1,041.24 km) riding *Critical Power,* his specially designed HPV (human-powered vehicle), at Redwood Acres Raceway in Eureka, Alberta, Canada, on July 18, 2006.

☆ FARTHEST DISTANCE TRAVELED ON A HAND-CRANKED CYCLE Keane West (U.S.A.) traveled 322.40 miles (518.85 km) on a hand-cranked cycle in 24 hours during the Bike Sebring 12/24 Hours event in Sebring, Florida, U.S.A., from February 16–17, 2008.

APR. 11: The **largest Rock, Paper, Scissors tournament** featured 793 players in an event organized by Renee Tòmas at Brigham Young University in Provo City, Utah, U.S.A., on April 11, 2008.

★ **GREATEST DISTANCE COVERED IN A PEDAL-POWERED BOAT** Greg Kolodziejzyk (Canada) used pedal power to propel his boat *Critical Power 2* a distance of 152.33 miles (245.16 km) in 24 hours on Whitefish Lake, Montana, U.S.A., from September 8–9, 2008. Greg's next record goal is to pedal his way across the Pacific!

Paddling a bathtub The greatest distance traveled by paddling a hand-propelled bathtub on still water in 24 hours is 90.5 miles (145.6 km) by 13 members of Aldington Prison Officers Social Club, near Ashford, Kent, UK, on May 28–29, 1983.

★ **Three-legged run** The record for the longest distance run three-legged—that is, two people tied together at the ankle—in 24 hours is 62.22 miles (100.13 km), which was achieved by Steven and Suzanne Eltis (both Australia) at Eatons Hill State School in Eatons Hill, Brisbane, Queensland, Australia, on October 24–25, 2008. The husband and wife team attempted the record to raise awareness and funds for Epilepsy Queensland.

★ **MOST TIME SPENT DRIVING A BUMPER CAR** On September 30, 2007, Sebastian Bösch (Austria) spent 24 hours driving a bumper car during the event Vienna Recordia in Vienna, Austria—making it the longest bumper car marathon on record.

APR. 12: The **most expensive car** is a 1931 Bugatti Type 41 "Royale" Sports Coupé by Kellner, which sold for $15 million on this day in 1990.

☆ **MOST TREES PLANTED BY A TEAM**
The record for the most trees planted in 24 hours by a team of 300 people is 348,492, achieved by CONAFOR (Comision Nacional Forestal) and citizens from the state of Durango at Predio San Manuel, Estado Durango, Mexico, on August 29–30, 2008. On hand to present the official GWR certificate was adjudicator Ralph Hannah (pictured, on the left).

MOST . . .

Hair donated to charity The most hair collected for charity in a day is 107 lb. (48.72 kg)—the weight of an average 14-year-old boy—when 881 people donated their ponytails at the Mississippi Institute for Aesthetics, Nail and Cosmetology in Clinton, Mississippi, U.S.A., on May 21, 2007. The event was organized in support of the Pantene Beautiful Lengths campaign, which aims to provide free wigs to women who have lost hair following cancer treatment.

☆ **Holes of miniature golf played (individual)** David Pfefferle (U.S.A.) played 4,729 holes of miniature golf in 24 hours at Westerville Golf Center, Westerville, Ohio, U.S.A., on May 28–29, 2008. During the 24 hours, David—who owns the golf course—walked an estimated 55 miles (88 km) and raised over $6,000 for charity.

★ **MOST COSMETIC MAKEOVERS BY A TEAM** A record 856 cosmetic makeovers were carried out in 24 hours by a team of makeup artists in an event organized by Alpha Marketing Company in Hong Kong, China, on May 3, 2008.

APR. 13: Paula Radcliffe (UK) ran the **fastest marathon by a woman** in London, UK, on April 13, 2003, in a time of 2 hr. 15 min. 25 sec.

☆ **GREATEST DISTANCE TRAVELED RIDING A UNICYCLE** Sam Wakeling (UK) covered 281.85 miles (453.6 km) riding a unicycle during a 24-hour period in Aberystwyth, Wales, UK, from September 29–30, 2007.

☆ **Radio interviews (pair)** On October 31, 2008, Patrick Stump and Pete Wentz (both U.S.A.) from the Chicago-based band Fall Out Boy spoke with 72 different American radio stations. The topic of discussion was the band's new album, *Folie à Deux*, released on December 6, 2008.

★ **Tattoos by a single artist** John McManus (U.S.A.) of the Joker's Tattoo Studio in West Monroe, Louisiana, U.S.A., tattooed 775 two-colored stars in a 24-hour period starting on October 31, 2008. He beat the record of 726 set the previous week by Derek Kastning (U.S.A.) at Rat-A-Tac-Tat Tattoos, in Tyler, Texas, U.S.A.

★ **Visited website within first 24 hours of launch** The most unique (individual) visitors to a website within its first 24 hours is 483,424, registered by MySkip.com on April 30, 2008. The site is a virtual dumpster into which unwanted goods can be dumped or picked up for repurposing.

★ **Weight squat-lifted by an individual** On November 6, 2008, Kevin Machate (U.S.A.) squat-lifted 101,412 lb. (45,999.71 kg) in 24 hours at Gold's Gym in Garland, Texas, U.S.A.

☆ **Consecutive haircuts** The most consecutive haircuts in 24 hours by an individual is 340 and was achieved by Ivan Zoot (U.S.A.) at Men's Grooming Center in Austin, Texas, U.S.A., on August 22–23, 2008. During the course of the day, Ivan also broke Guinness World Records marks for the ☆ **fastest single haircut** (doing so eight times, finally achieving a record time of 55 seconds) and the ★ **most haircuts in one hour** (34).

APR. 14: On this day in 1991, 20 paintings, worth $500 million, were stolen from the Van Gogh Museum in Amsterdam, the Netherlands, in the **greatest art robbery.**

TRAVELERS'
TALES

CONTENTS

UPS & DOWNS

HIGHEST . . .

Altitude (male): 248,655 miles The *Apollo 13* crew of Jack Swigert, Jim Lovell, and Fred Haise (all U.S.A.) traveled beyond the Earth to an altitude of 248,655 miles (400,171 km), farther than any other humans. Turn to p. 13 for the amazing details on this fantastic feat of flight.

Aircraft: 123,523 ft The official FAI (Fédération Aeronautique Internationale) altitude record for an aircraft is 123,523 ft. (37,650 m) by Alexandr Fedotov (USSR) flying a highly modified MIG-25 "Foxbat" (designated E266M) from Podmoskovnoe Aerodrome, Russia, on August 31, 1977.

Parachute escape: 56,102 ft On April 9, 1958, the RAF's J. de Salis and P. Lowe parachuted out of an English Electric Canberra bomber flying at 56,102 ft. (17,100 m) over Monyash, Derby, UK.

 ☆**DEEPEST UNDERWATER CYCLING** Who says you shouldn't cycle when it's wet? The greatest depth for submarine cycling is 214 ft. 10 in. (66.5 m), and it was achieved by Vittorio Innocente (Italy) in Santa Margherita Ligure, Liguria, Italy, on July 21, 2008. He also holds the record for the **farthest distance cycled under water,** having pedaled 1.24 miles (2 km) on a bicycle at the bottom of the Naviglio canal in Milan, Italy, on May 4, 2003, in a time of 36 min. 38.15 sec. Vittorio is pictured here performing an underwater wheelie at the London Aquarium, UK—alongside some of the residents.

205 DAYS: the age at which Vaidehi Thirrupathy (UK, b. May 6, 2008) became the **youngest person to visit all seven continents.** She completed her journey on November 26, 2008, in Antarctica.

HIGHEST HOT AIR BALLOON: 68,986 FT. Dr. Vijaypat Singhania (India) achieved the altitude record of 68,986 ft. (21,027 m) in a Cameron Z-1600 hot air balloon over Mumbai, India, on November 26, 2005.

Glider flight: 50,721 ft. Serial record breaker Steve Fossett (U.S.A.) set the absolute altitude for glider flight record at 50,721 ft. (15,460 m) over El Calafate, Argentina, on August 29, 2006.

Helicopter flight: 40,820 ft. Flying an Aérospatiale SA315B "Lama" helicopter over Istres, France, Jean Bouletan (France) achieved an altitude of 40,820 ft. (12,442 m) on June 21, 1972.

Concert: 40,000 ft. Norwegian performer Magnet (aka Even Johansen) celebrated the launch of his album *The Simple Life!* by performing at an altitude of 40,000 ft. (12,192 m) onboard a flight from Oslo, Norway, to Reykjavik, Iceland, on March 27, 2007.

Cycle ride: 22,992 ft. Siegfried Verheijke, Luc Belet (both Belgium), and Martin Adserballe (Denmark) rode their mountain bikes to an altitude

of 22,992 ft. (7,008 m) on the slopes of the Muztagata peak in the Xinjiang province of China on August 11, 2000.

Dinner party: 22,326 ft. Butler Joshua Heming (UK) served a formal meal to Henry Shelford, Thomas Shelford, Nakul M. Pathak, Robert Aitken, Robert Sully

HIGHEST HEAD-FIRST HIGH DIVE: 115 FT. Professional divers regularly flock to La Quebrada, a cliff top 115 ft. (35 m) high in Acapulco, Mexico, to exhibit their skills. Divers must dive out 27 ft. (8.22 m) from the cliff to ensure they clear the jutting base rocks, and time their dive into the 12-ft. deep (3.65-m) water to coincide with an incoming wave.

(all UK), and Caio Buzzolini (Australia) at 22,326 ft. (6,805 m) on Lhakpa Ri, Tibet, on May 3, 2004.

BASE jump: 21,666 ft. Glenn Singleman and Heather Swan (both Australia) took part in a wingsuit BASE jump from a ledge at an altitude of 21,666 ft. (6,604 m) on Mount Meru, Garwhal Himalaya, India, on May 23, 2006.

Bungee jump: 15,200 ft. Curtis Rivers (UK) performed a bungee jump from a hot air balloon at 15,200 ft. (4,632 m) over Puertollano, Spain, on May 5, 2002. After bouncing five times he freed himself from the cord and parachuted to the ground.

HIGHEST ALTITUDE (FEMALE): 379.757 MILES Kathryn Thornton (U.S.A.) attained an altitude of 379.757 miles (611.16 km) after an orbital engine burn on December 10, 1993, during the space shuttle *Endeavour* mission STS 61. Thornton was the only female crewmember on STS 61, the first shuttle mission to service the Hubble Space Telescope.

DEEPEST SALVAGE (COMMERCIAL): 15,000 FT. On July 20, 1999, the U.S. spacecraft *Liberty Bell 7* was commercially salvaged from the bottom of the Atlantic Ocean, where it had sat since its splashdown on July 21, 1961. The spacecraft rested at a depth of 15,000 ft. (4,500 m) before being raised by the ship *Ocean Project*. The salvage was financed by the Discovery Channel.

Habitation: 21,650 ft. In April 1961, a three-room dwelling believed to date from the late pre-Columbian period *c.* 1480 was discovered at 21,650 ft. (6,600 m) on Cerro Llulllaillaco (22,057 ft.; 6,723 m) on the Argentine–Chilean border.

DEEPEST . . .

Cycle ride: 214 ft. 10 in. Vittorio Innocente (Italy) cycled at a depth of 214 ft. 10 in. (66.5 m) in Santa Margherita Ligure, Liguria, Italy, on July 21, 2008.

Scuba dive (female): 725 ft. Verna van Schaik (South Africa) dived to 725 ft. (221 m) in the Boesmansgat cave in South Africa's Northern Cape province on October 25, 2004. The dive lasted 5 hr. 34 mins., of which only 12 minutes were spent descending.

Scuba dive (male): 1,044 ft. Nuno Gomes (South Africa) dived to a depth of 1,044 ft. (318.25 m) in the Red Sea off Dahab, Egypt, on June 10, 2005. Nuno also achieved the **deepest scuba dive in a freshwater cave** with

DEEPEST RATED DIVING WATCH: 20,000 FT. The 20,000-feet model from CX Swiss Military Watch is a mechanical divers wristwatch made by Montres Charmex SA (Switzerland) that can function, as its name suggests, at depths of 20,000 ft. (6,000 m). The watch was tested for water resistance at the Oceanographic Institute of the University of Southampton, UK, on January 5, 2009, and passed with flying colors.

APR. 15: A team of 12 players at the Castle Mona Pub, Newcastle, UK, knocked down 116,047 table skittles pins to gain the **highest table skittle score in 24 hours** on this day in 1990.

DEEPEST SCUBA DIVE BY A DOG: 13 FT.
Dwane Folsom (U.S.A.) regularly takes his dog, Shadow, scuba diving off the coast of Grand Cayman Island. The deepest the pair usually go is approximately 13 ft. (4 m). When diving, Shadow wears a specially adapted diving suit made up of a helmet, weighted dog jacket, and breathing tube connected to his owner's air tank. Mr. Folsom rescued Shadow, a black mongrel—half retriever, half labrador—as a puppy from a dog pound in Boynton Beach, Florida.

DEEPEST CONCERT: 994 FT.
The deepest concert was performed by Katie Melua (UK) and her band at 994 ft. (303 m) below sea level, in the leg of Statoil's Troll, a gas rig, off the coast of Bergen, Norway, on October 1, 2006. Ms. Melua performed two 30-minute concerts to an audience of 20 rig staff.

a depth of 927 ft. 2 in. (282.6 m) at Boesmansgat cave, South Africa, on August 23, 1996.

Live TV broadcast: 7,920 ft. *Abyss Live* (BBC, UK) was broadcast live from an underwater depth of 1.5 miles (2.4 km) on September 29, 2002. The program, presented by Alastair Fothergill (UK), was broadcast from inside a MIR submersible along the Mid-Atlantic Ridge off the east coast of the U.S.A. The main attraction of the event was live views of hydrothermal vents, fissures in the ocean floor from which mineral-rich water heated by molten rocks flows up in great dark clouds.

Live Internet broadcast: 9,200 ft. On July 24, 2001, live footage of the HMS *Hood* was broadcast over the Internet from a depth of 9,200 ft. (2,800 m) at the bottom of the Denmark Strait, where she sank in 1941. The broadcast, from an ROV (remotely operated vehicle), followed the discovery of the wreck by David Mearns (UK) of Blue Water Recoveries Ltd (UK).

APR. 16: On April 16, 1976, the unmanned spacecraft *Helios* 2 came within 27 million miles (43.5 million km) of the Sun—the **closest approach to the Sun by any spacecraft.**

Salvage: 17,251 ft. The remains of a helicopter that had crashed into the Pacific Ocean in August 1991 with the loss of four lives was salvaged from a depth of 17,251 ft. (5,258 m) by the crew of the U.S.S. *Salvor* and personnel from Eastport International on February 27, 1992. This is the greatest depth at which a salvage operation of any kind has been undertaken and successfully carried out.

Manned descent: 35,797 ft. Dr. Jacques Piccard (Switzerland) and Lt. Donald Walsh (U.S.A.) piloted the Swiss-built U.S. Navy bathyscaphe *Trieste* to a depth of 35,797 ft. (10,911 m) in the Challenger Deep section of the Mariana Trench on January 23, 1960. Challenger Deep is thought to be the **deepest point on Earth** and is situated 250 miles (400 km) southwest of Guam in the Pacific Ocean.

RULING THE WAVES

Youngest person to sail the Atlantic (solo) Michael Perham (UK, b. March 16, 1992) left Gibraltar in his boat *Cheeky Monkey* on November 18, 2006, aged 14 years 247 days, and sailed west across the Atlantic Ocean, arriving in Nelson's Dockyard, Antigua, on January 3, 2007.

★Fastest time to sail the Indian Ocean *Cheyenne,* skippered by Steve Fossett (U.S.A.), sailed across the Indian Ocean at its widest point in a time of 9 days 20 hr. 29 min. from February 25 to March 6, 2004. At 125 ft. (38 m) long and with a beam of 60 ft (18 m), *Cheyenne* is the **largest racing catamaran.**

★Fastest time to sail the Pacific Ocean Olivier de Kersauson (France) sailed from Los Angeles, California, U.S.A., to Honolulu, Hawaii, U.S.A.—

★FASTEST HONG KONG TO LONDON SAILING In September 2008, Lionel Lemonchois (France) and his nine-man crew sailed *Gitana 13* **from Hong Kong, China, to London, UK, in 41 days 21 hr. 26 min. 34 sec. The distance covered was 12,948 nautical miles (14,900.2 miles; 23,979.6 km), giving an average speed of 12.88 knots (14.8 mph; 23.8 km/h).**

APR. 17: The **highest speed attained on a ski-bob** is 125.38 mph (201.79 km/h) by Romuald Bonvin (Switzerland) at Les Arcs, Rhone-Alpes, France, on this day in 2003.

☆ **FASTEST TRANSATLANTIC SAILING** In July 2007, Franck Cammas (France) skippered the trimaran *Groupama 3* across the Atlantic, setting off west to east from Ambrose in New York, U.S.A., to Lizard Point, Land's End, UK, in 4 days 3 hr. 57 min. 54 sec., at an average speed of 29.26 knots (33.6 mph; 54.1 km/h). The crew also broke the record for the **greatest distance sailed in 24 hours: 794 nautical miles (913.7 miles; 1,470 km).**

☆ **GREATEST DISTANCE SAILED IN A MONOHULL YACHT IN 24 HOURS** Torben Grael (Brazil) skippered the monohull yacht *Ericsson 4* for 589 nautical miles (677 miles; 1,090 km) in 24 hours during the first leg (Alicante to Cape Town) of the Volvo Ocean Race in the Southern Atlantic Ocean, on October 29, 2008. This beat the previous record, which had been set during the 2006–07 race, by about 34 nautical miles (39 miles; 63 km).

a total distance of 2,925 nautical miles (3,366 miles; 5,417.1 km)—in 4 days 19 hr. 31 min. 37 sec. in November 2005. His *Geronimo* trimaran achieved an average speed of 19.17 knots (22 mph; 35.5 km/h).

Fastest time to row the Atlantic Ocean The fastest row across the Atlantic in any direction, land to land, is 33 days 7 hr. 30 min. and was achieved by the 14-man crew of *La Mondiale,* led by Leven Brown (UK). The British/Irish team left Puerto Mogan in Gran Canaria, Spain, on December 15, 2007, and arrived at Port St. Charles, Barbados, on January 17, 2008.

APR. 18: The **oldest mother to have quadruplets** is Merryl Thelma Fudel (Australia), who gave birth to three girls and one boy on April 18, 1998, at the age of 55 years 286 days.

1827: the date of the **first powered crossing of the Atlantic by ship.** The *Curaçao* was a 127-ft. (38.7-m) paddle boat that took 22 days to reach the U.S.A. from Rotterdam, the Netherlands.

☆**FASTEST CROSSING OF THE ENGLISH CHANNEL BY AMPHIBIOUS VEHICLE** Professor Hans Georg Näder (Germany) and Captain Henry Hawkins (UK) made a successful crossing of the English Channel between Dover, UK, and Calais, France, in an amphibious vehicle named *Tonic* on July 1, 2008. The record-breaking feat was achieved in a time of 1 hr. 14 min. 20 sec. and broke the previous record of 1 hr. 40 min. 6 sec. set by Sir Richard Branson (UK) in June 2004.

Youngest ocean rower As part of the four-woman crew of *Silver Cloud,* Rachel Flanders (UK, b. September 3, 1990) became the youngest person to row across an ocean. On December 2, 2007, she left La Gomera, Canary Islands, aged 17 years 91 days, and rowed across the Atlantic, reaching Antigua on February 14, 2008.

....
APR. 19: The Boston Marathon, the world's **longest-lasting major marathon,** was first held on this day in 1897, when it was run over a distance of 24.2 miles (39 km).
....

X-REF

If all this talk of water has whet your appetite for more aquatic achievements, dive headfirst into Watersports on p. 499.

★ **GREATEST DISTANCE SAILED SINGLEHANDED IN 24 HOURS** Thomas Colville (France) sailed an unprecedented 628.5 nautical miles (723.2 miles; 1,163.9 km) in his 105-ft. (32-m) trimaran *Sodebo* on December 7, 2008. In doing so, Colville broke his own record, which had been set the year before, of 619 nautical miles (712 miles; 1,146 km).

Youngest ocean rower (solo & unsupported) The youngest person to row the Atlantic solo and unsupported is Oliver Hicks (UK, b. December 3, 1981), who crossed west to east between May 27 and September 28, 2005, on board *Miss Olive, Virgin Atlantic* at the age of 23 years 175 days (at the start). He rowed from Atlantic Highlands, New Jersey, U.S.A., to St. Mary's, Isles of Scilly, UK, in 123 days 22 hr. 8 min., to become the **first person to row from mainland U.S.A. to mainland UK solo and unsupported** and the **youngest person to row any ocean solo and unsupported.**

☆**Fastest speed under sail** The fastest speed sailing (over 1,640 ft.; 500 m) is 49.84 knots (57 mph; 92.3 km/h) and was achieved by Robert Douglas (U.S.A.) at Lüderitz, Namibia, on a kite surfer on September 19, 2008—the first time that a kite surfer has set an outright speed sailing record.

☆ **Fastest speed by a kite sail (female)** Sjoukje Bredenkamp (South Africa) reached a top kite sail speed of 45.20 knots (52 mph; 83.7 km/h) during the Lüderitz Speed Challenge event in Lüderitz, Namibia, in October 2008. This is the third time in succession that Bredenkamp has set the female kite sailing world record, having first claimed the title in 2006.

APR. 20: The **highest human flight using a rocket belt** is 152 ft. (46 m). It was achieved by Eric Scott (U.S.A.) on this day in 2004 in London, UK.

☆ **Longest journey by aquabike (jetski)** Adriaan Marais and Marinus du Plessis (both South Africa) followed the west coast of North America south to the Panama Canal on aquabikes (Yamaha FX Cruisers), setting out from Homer, Alaska, U.S.A., and arriving in Panama City, Panama, after 95 days of navigation. Averaging 10 hours a day, they covered a total of 9,323 nautical miles (10,729 miles; 17,266 km) between June 16 and September 19, 2006.

SCALING THE HEIGHTS

☆ **Oldest person to climb Mount Everest** According to Nepal's Senior Citizen Mt. Everest Expedition (SECEE), Min Bahadur Sherchan (Nepal, b. June 20, 1931) reached the highest point on Earth on May 25, 2008, at the age of 76 years 340 days.

☆ **Most conquests of Mount Everest** Apa Sherpa (Nepal) reached the summit of Mount Everest for the 19th time in 2009, the most times anyone has ever successfully climbed the world's highest mountain.

Fastest time to climb Mount Everest and K2 In 2004, Karl Unterkircher (Italy) became the **first mountaineer to summit the two highest mountains,** Mount Everest and K2, **in the same season without bottled oxygen.** He repeated this feat between May 24 and July 26, 2006, a record time of 63 days.

☆ **DRIVING TO THE HIGHEST ALTITUDE (MOTORCYCLE)** Roland Hess (Chile/Switzerland), German Hess (Chile/Switzerland), Johann Janko (Chile/Austria), and Giovanni Sanguedolce (Argentina/Italy) rode to an altitude of 20,407 ft. (6,220 m) on the slopes of Ojos del Salado, Atacama, Chile, using Honda 4RT 2007 motorcycles, on March 19, 2008.

★ **FASTEST ICE CLIMBER** Pavel Gulyaev (Russia, left) climbed a 49-ft.-high (15-m) vertical ice wall in a record time of 8.748 seconds at the Ice Climbing World Cup held in Bustemi, Romania, on February 8, 2009. Competitors at the Ice Climbing World Cup are each given six attempts to reach a top speed.

☆**Fastest time to climb the Seven Summits—Carstensz list (male)** Henrik Kristiansen (Denmark) climbed the highest peak on each continent (according to the Carstensz list) in 136 days between January 21, 2008 (when he ascended Vinson Massif in Antarctica) and June 5, 2008 (when he conquered Mount McKinley in Alaska, U.S.A., the highest peak in North America).

☆**Fastest time to climb the Seven Summits (both lists) by a married couple** Rob and Joanne Gambi (UK) achieved the fastest (and ☆**first**) Seven Summits ascent by a married couple, climbing the highest peak on each continent in 404 days for the Kosciuszko list (which assumes Mount Kosciuszko as the highest point in Australasia). The couple later climbed the Carstensz Pyramid (aka Puncak Jaya, the continent's highest point if Indonesia is included) in 799 days. Joanne is also the **fastest woman to climb the Seven Summits.**

First person to climb all peaks over 8,000 m Reinhold Messner (Italy) became the first person to climb all 14 peaks over 8,000 m (26,246 ft.) when he summitted Lhotse (27,890 ft.; 8,501 m) on the Nepal/Tibet border on October 16, 1986. His quest started in June 1970.

Fastest ascent of all peaks over 8,000 m Jerzy "Jurek" Kukuczka (Poland) climbed all 14 peaks higher than 8,000 m (26,246 ft.) in 7 years 11 months 16 days between October 4, 1979, when he reached the summit of Lhotse (27,890 ft.; 8,501 m) on the Nepal/Tibet border, and September 18, 1987, when he successfully completed an ascent of Shisha Pangma (26,286 ft.; 8,012 m) in Tibet.

....

APR. 21: Happy birthday to the **longest-reigning living queen.** Her Majesty Queen Elizabeth II (UK, b. April 21, 1926) succeeded to the throne on February 6, 1952, after the death of her father, King George VI.

....

☆ **MOST 8,000-M PEAKS CLIMBED (FEMALE)** Three female climbers share the record for conquering the greatest number of 8,000ers, with 11 each. They are Nives Meroi (Italy, pictured), Gerlinde Kaltenbrunner (Austria), and Edurne Pasaban (Spain).

The term "8,000er" refers to any peak more than 8,000 m (26,246 ft.) high.

★ **FASTEST TIME TO CLIMB EL CAPITAN** Hans Florine (U.S.A., pictured above right) and Yuji Hirayama (Japan, left) climbed the "Nose" of the 3,593-ft.-tall (1,095-m) El Capitan in Yosemite National Park, California, U.S.A., in 2 hr. 48 min. 50 sec. in September 2002. On July 30, 2005, Florine climbed the entire vertical face of El Cap on his own in 11 hr. 41 min., the ★ **fastest solo ascent.**

★ **DEADLIEST MOUNTAIN TO CLIMB** Annapurna I, in the 34-mile-long (55-km) Annapurna Massif, has been climbed by 130 people, 53 of whom died along the way, giving the peak a 41% mortality rate—making it statistically the world's most dangerous mountain. The latest fatality came in 2008 when Iñaki Ochoa de Olza (Spain) had a seizure and pulmonary edema near the summit.

On October 28, 2007, Tomaž Humar (Slovenia, above left) became the ★ **first person to "solo" Annapurna I.** Humar chose to climb a new route along the right side of the south face in a pure "alpine" style (meaning that he carried all of his food and equipment with him), as opposed to "expedition" style (in which the climber benefits from porters and fixed lines).

★ **Most deaths on K2 in one day** ExplorersWeb identifies August 1, 2008, as the deadliest day on K2, with 11 fatalities on the southeast face from an avalanche. A *serac*—a large block or column of ice, often the size of a house—crumbled and fell from an ice field near the summit, killing at least one climber and cutting the lines of a group of climbers descending the dangerous peak, the second highest in the world. Further ice falls claimed

APR. 22: Released on this day in 1993, NCSA Mosaic became the world's first Internet browser.

more lives during the night, while others died trying to recover the dead. The 11 victims hailed from Serbia, Pakistan, Norway, South Korea, Nepal, Ireland, and France.

★**First person to complete the Three Poles Challenge** The first person to reach the North Pole, the South Pole, and the peak of Mount Everest—known as the Three Poles Challenge—was Erling Kagge (Norway), who completed the trio on May 8, 1994. The **first**—and only—**person to complete the challenge without the use of oxygen** on Everest was Antoine De Choudens (France, 1969–2003) between April 25, 1996, and January 10, 1999.

CIRCUMNAVIGATING THE GLOBE

FIRST . . .

Circumnavigation by aircraft without refueling Richard G. "Dick" Rutan and Jeana Yeager (both U.S.A.) circumnavigated the world in a westward direction from Edwards Air Force Base, California, U.S.A., in nine days from December 14–23, 1986, without refueling. The key to their success was their specially constructed aircraft *Voyager*, which was designed and constructed by Dick's brother Burt Rutan, owner of the company Scaled Composites, which achieved the **first private space flight** during 2004.

Circumnavigation by amphibious car Ben Carlin (Australia) made the first, and so far only, circumnavigation of the globe in an amphibious vehicle, driving a modified Ford GPA jeep called *Half-Safe*. He completed the last leg of the Atlantic crossing (the English Channel) on August 24, 1951. He arrived back in Montreal, Canada, on May 8, 1958, having completed a circumnavigation of 39,000 miles (62,765 km) over land and 9,600 miles

---

APR. 23: The **farthest human-powered flight** was by Kanellos Kanellopoulos (Greece), who pedaled his *Daedalus* 88 aircraft 71.52 miles (115.11 km) from Heraklion, Crete, to Santorini, Greece, on this day in 1988.

(15,450 km) by sea and river. He was accompanied on the transatlantic stage by his ex-wife Elinore (U.S.A.) and on the long trans-Pacific stage (Tokyo, Japan to Anchorage, Alaska, U.S.A.) by Boye Lafayette De Mente (U.S.A.).

Solo circumnavigation by balloon Steve Fossett (U.S.A.) circumnavigated the globe in *Bud Light Spirit of Freedom,* a 140-ft.-tall (42.6-m) mixed-gas balloon, from June 19 to July 2, 2002, becoming the first person ever to do so alone. He took off from Northam, Western Australia, and landed at Eromanga, Queensland, Australia, after covering 20,627 miles (33,195 km).

Circumnavigation on foot Proving circumnavigations on foot is notoriously difficult. George Matthew Schilling (U.S.A.) is reputed to have walked round the world between 1897 and 1904. However, the first verified circumnavigation on foot was by David Kunst (U.S.A.), who walked 14,450 miles (23,250 km) through four continents from June 20, 1970, to October 5, 1974.

LAST PERSON TO SAIL AROUND THE WORLD, NONSTOP WESTBOUND, SOLO In April 2008, Tomasz Lewandowski (Poland) became only the sixth sailor ever to successfully circumnavigate the globe single-handedly, sailing east to west, against the prevailing wind.

Lewandowski set out in his Mikado 56, *Luka,* from Ensenada, Baja California, Mexico, on March 6, 2007, and returned on April 1, 2008. His only company for the 28,710-nautical-mile (33,038-mile; 53,170-km) trip was his Jack Russell terrier, Wacek.

FASTEST . . .

Solo circumnavigation by helicopter (female) Jennifer Murray (UK) piloted her Robinson R44 helicopter around the world solo in 99 days from May 31 to September 6, 2000. The journey started and finished at Brooklands airfield in Surrey, UK, and crossed 30 countries. Murray, along with Colin Bodill (UK), also holds the record for the **first** and **fastest circumnavigation via both Poles by helicopter,** which was completed in 170 days 22 hr. 47 min. on May 23, 2007.

Circumnavigation by car The record for the first and fastest man and woman to have circumnavigated the Earth by car, covering six continents under the rules applicable in 1989 and 1991 and embracing more than an equator's length of driving (24,901 road miles; 40,075 km), is held by Saloo Choudhury and his wife Neena Choudhury (both India). The journey took 69

★**LARGEST PASSENGER SHIP TO SAIL AROUND THE WORLD** *Queen Mary II,* at 163,724 tons, is the largest passenger ship to circumnavigate the globe. The last great ocean liner (as opposed to passenger cruiser), towering as high as a 23-story building and covering an area almost as large as four football fields, set off on her first world cruise on January 10, 2007, from Fort Lauderdale, Florida, U.S.A., and completed the trip in 81 days.

APR. 25: The record for the **most heads shaved in an hour** is 44, achieved by Anne Armstrong (UK) in Maginns of Castlewellan in County Down, UK, on April 25, 2008.

FIRST SOLO CIRCUMNAVIGATION BY AIRCRAFT Wiley Post (U.S.A.) made the first solo flight around the world from July 15–22, 1933, in a Lockheed Vega aircraft called *Winnie Mae.* He covered 15,596 miles (25,089 km), starting and ending in Brooklyn, New York, U.S.A. Post is pictured wearing his experimental pressure suit—since the *Winnie Mae* could not be pressurized, Post adapted a diver's helmet and three-layered suit that would allow him to travel at ever greater altitudes.

days 19 hr. 5 min. from September 9 to November 17, 1989. The couple drove a 1989 Hindustan "Contessa Classic," starting and finishing in Delhi, India.

☆ **Solo round-the-world monohull sail (male)** The fastest circumnavigation sailing solo in a monohull is 84 days 3 hr. 9 min. and was achieved by Michel Desjoyeaux (France) for winning the 2008/2009 Vendée Globe single-handed yacht race, starting and finishing at Les Sables d'Olonne, France, from November 9, 2008 to February 1, 2009. This is the second time Desjoyeaux has won this race (becoming the first person to win it twice) and he broke the record in both wins.

★ **YOUNGEST PERSON TO FLY SOLO AROUND THE WORLD** Barrington Irving (Jamaica/ U.S.A.), an aerospace student at Florida Memorial University, U.S.A., circumnavigated the globe in *Inspiration,* an airplane manufactured and assembled by the Columbia Aircraft Manufacturing Company, between March 23 and June 27, 2007. He completed the feat aged 23 years 227 days. His landmark 97-day flight was also the first solo circumnavigation flight by a pilot of Afro-Caribbean ethnicity.

APR. 26: The **largest waltz** consisted of 242 pairs who danced at Austria Center Vienna, Vienna, Austria, on April 26, 2008.

★FIRST FEMALE TO SAIL NONSTOP AROUND THE WORLD IN BOTH DIRECTIONS On February 16, 2009, former gym teacher Dee Caffari (UK) made history when she finished the Vendée Globe around-the-world yacht race in sixth place. This achievement means that Dee is the first woman—and only the fourth person ever—to sail both ways around the world, alone and unaided. The first part of her double world first was achieved between November 2005 and May 2006, when she became the **first solo woman to circumnavigate westward nonstop.**

Circumnavigation by bicycle The fastest circumnavigation by bicycle is 194 days and 17 hours, and was achieved by Mark Beaumont (UK), who cycled a distance of 18,296.74 miles (29,445.81 km) and travelled over 24,916 miles (40,100 km) in total (including transfers). The journey started and finished in Paris (France) from August 5, 2007 to February 15, 2008 and covered Europe, Pakistan, Malaysia, Australia, New Zealand and the U.S.A.

EPIC JOURNEYS

★Longest journey by mouth-controlled motorized wheelchair Chang-Hyun Choi (South Korea) covered 17,398 miles (28,000 km) in a mouth-controlled motorized wheelchair between May 10, 2006, and December 6, 2007. Chang-Hyun Choi, who is affected by cerebral palsy and is paralyzed from the neck down, traveled at a maximum speed of 8 mph (13 km/h) across 35 countries in Europe and the Middle East.

☆Greatest distance traveled by train (24 hours) Corey Pedersen and Michael Kim (both U.S.A.) traveled between Kanazawa and Sendai, Japan, covering 1,802.84 miles (2,901.4 km) without duplicating any part of the journey from October 6–7, 2008.

☆Fastest solo, unsupported, and unassisted journey to the South Pole Todd Carmichael (U.S.A.) completed a solo trek to the South Pole in a record time of 39 days 7 hr. 49 min., arriving on December 21,

APR. 27: The **fastest time to run a mile while balancing an egg on a spoon** is 7 min. 8 sec. by Ashrita Furman (U.S.A.) in Jamaica, New York, U.S.A., on April 27, 2007.

2008. In doing so, Carmichael also became the first American to reach the Pole solo and unaided.

★**Most countries visited in a continuous journey by car** Jim Rogers and Paige Parker (both U.S.A.) visited 111 countries and three territories (Western Sahara, French Polynesia, and Gibraltar) by car between January 1, 1999, and January 5, 2002. They covered more than 152,000 miles (245,000 km) across six continents in their custom-built Mercedes off-road vehicle and trailer.

Longest lawnmower ride Over 260 consecutive days, Gary Hatter (U.S.A.) traveled 14,594.5 miles (23,487.5 km) on his lawnmower. Hatter

---

LONGEST LIFEBOAT JOURNEY

After his ship, the *Endurance,* became trapped in Antarctic sea ice, Sir Ernest Shackleton (UK) escaped with his crew of 28. In three lifeboats, they set course for Elephant Island, around 100 miles (160 km) away. Once there, Shackleton selected five of his best men to take the largest lifeboat toward a whaling station on South Georgia, 800 miles (1,300 km) away. In a journey that is still regarded as one of the greatest in history, Sir Ernest and his men reached the island after 17 days, on May 19, 1916.

☆**LONGEST SNOWMOBILE JOURNEY** Robert G. Davis (U.S.A.) covered 12,163 miles (19,574 km) on his Yamaha RS Venture snowmobile during a 60-day period between January 11, 2008, and March 11, 2008.

APR. 28: The **most participants in a relay race** was 7,841 at the 35th Batavierenrace from Nijmegen to Enschede in the Netherlands on this day in 2007.

★ **LONGEST JOURNEY ON A QUAD BIKE (ATV)** Josh and Anna Hogan (U.S.A.) covered 16,865 miles (27,141 km) on two Top 1 450 Quads (ATV) from August 24, 2007, to March 27, 2008, starting in Mombassa, Kenya, and finishing in Elche, Spain, passing through 17 countries along the way.

QUAD BIKES . . .

The **highest speed on a quad bike** (ATV) is 155.04 mph (249.51 km/h), achieved by Terry Wilmeth (U.S.A.) on the AlbaAction/Fullbore/Powroll Rocket Raptor version 5.0 at Madras Airport, Madras, Oregon, U.S.A., on June 16, 2007.

---

started his drive in Portland, Maine, U.S.A., on May 31, 2000, and passed through all 48 contiguous U.S. states, as well as Canada and Mexico, before arriving in Daytona Beach, Florida, on February 14, 2001.

★ **First winter expedition to the North Pole** Matvey Shparo and Boris Smolin (both Russia) began the first winter expedition to the North Pole on December 22, 2007, the day of the winter solstice, from the Arktichesky Cape on the northern point of the Zevernaya Zemlya Archipelago. They

★ **FASTEST UNSUPPORTED AND UNASSISTED JOURNEY TO THE SOUTH POLE** Ray Zahab (pictured), Kevin Vallely, and Richard Weber (all Canada) reached the South Pole from the Hercules Inlet on January 7, 2009, after just 33 days 23 hr. 30 min.

☆ **LONGEST JOURNEY SWIMMING** Between June 10 and July 30, 2004, Martin Strel (Slovenia) swam the entire length of the Yangtze River, China, covering a record 2,487 miles (4,003 km).

X-REF

You can discover more record-breaking swimming achievements on pp. 536–541.

---

reached the North Pole on March 14, 2008, eight days before the vernal equinox, the official beginning of the polar day. Traveling in complete darkness, the only light source was the light on their headlamps.

First mother and son team to reach a pole At 9:15 p.m. local time (GMT 5 a.m.) on May 2, 2007, Daniel Byles and his mother Jan Meek (both UK) reached the magnetic North Pole (N 78° 35.724', W 104° 11.940') following a 24-day trek on foot and skis from Resolute Bay in Canada—a journey of around 350 miles (560 km).

OLDEST PERSON TO SKI TO BOTH POLES The oldest person to ski to both Poles is Norbert H. Kern (Germany, b. July 26, 1940), who skied to the South Pole on January 18, 2007, and to the North Pole on April 27, 2007, completing the task at the age of 66 years 275 days.

APR. 29: The oldest male tennis player to be ranked number one by the Association of Tennis Professionals is Andre Agassi (U.S.A.), born on this day in 1970. He became the highest seeded men's player on May 11, 2003, aged 33 years 13 days.

☆ **LONGEST JOURNEY ON INLINE SKATES** Khoo Swee Chiow (Singapore) covered 3,782.9 miles (6,088 km) on inline skates, departing from Hanoi, Vietnam, on October 20, 2007, and arriving in Singapore on January 21, 2008.

First person to reach the North Pole (solo) Dr. Jean-Louis Etienne (France) was the first person to reach the North Pole solo and without dogs on May 11, 1986, after 63 days. He had the benefit of resupplies several times during the journey.

★ **Most journeys across the UK, from John O'Groats to Land's End** The UK's most famous journey is from Land's End to John O'Groats (or vice versa), an 874 miles (1,407 km) trip by road (or 1,200 miles; 1,900 km off-road) that has been completed a record 19 times by John Taylor (Australia) on foot, by cycling, or by car from January 14, 1980 to November 29, 2007.

★ **Oldest married couple to visit the North Pole** Heinz G. Fischer (U.S.A., b. March 10, 1929) and his wife Linda G. Burdet (U.S.A., b. November 29, 1931) skied to the North Pole together, aged 79 and 76 respectively, on April 12, 2008. The couple were dropped by helicopter at ice camp Barneo (1 degree south of the pole) and skied 4 miles (6.39 km) to the pole.

★ **Fastest time to visit every sovereign country** Dubai-based businessman Kashi Samaddar (India) visited all 194 United Nations member countries in 12 years 8 months 13 days, between September 15, 1995, and May 27, 2008. The globetrotting Mr. Samaddar—who has actually visited 205 different countries—traveled with an Indian passport, which resulted in extensive delays because of visa issues. He hopes to have visited a total of 250 countries by 2010.

GAZETTEER

CONTENTS

 ★ **FIRST AFRICAN-AMERICAN PRESIDENT OF THE U.S.A.** Barack Hussein Obama II (U.S.A.) was inaugurated as the 44th president of the U.S.A. on January 20, 2009, following a record-breaking campaign. During the September before his election, Obama raised a monthly record of $150 million, taking his fundraising total to over $605 million—also a record. Much of this went to advertising—an unprecedented $250 million was spent on TV ads in just five months. Over 136 million voters turned out on election day—the most since 1960—and more than two million descended on the Capitol in Washington, D.C. for his inauguration (below).

U.S.A.

☆**Largest pub crawl** More than 4,000 participants took part in the SaintPattys.com 11th Annual "Luck of the Irish" St. Patrick's Pub Crawl on March 14, 2009, in Manhattan, New York City, U.S.A. However, only 3,163 of the drinkers followed the official guidelines, which required attendees to have a card stamped at each of the 86 pubs visited along the east side of Manhattan. The route covered more than 5 miles (8 km), and everyone taking part wore green clothing in honor of St. Patrick, the patron saint of Ireland. As per the guidelines, non-alcoholic drinks were allowed.

★**Greatest purchase of property** On November 22, 2006, U.S. private equity firm Blackstone paid $20 billion cash for 580 office buildings across the U.S.A. belonging to Equity Office Property Trust (U.S.A.)—itself part of the largest leveraged buyout in history with a total of $36 billion.

★**Tallest marigold** The tallest marigold measured 10 ft. 1 in. (3.07 m) in December 2007 and was grown by Rebecca Shanks (U.S.A.), who lives in Berlin Heights, Ohio, U.S.A.

First all-talking cartoon Paul Terry's (U.S.A.) *Dinner Time* (U.S.A., 1928) was premiered at the Mark Strand Theater, New York City, U.S.A., on September 1, 1928. The film preceded Disney's *Steamboat Willie* (U.S.A., 1928) by a month.

First cartoon strip The first cartoon strip ever printed is "The Yellow Kid," which first appeared in the *New York Journal* on October 18, 1896.

AT A GLANCE
- **AREA**: 3,794,083 miles² (9,826,630 km²)
- **POPULATION**: 303.8 million
- **HOUSEHOLDS**: 113.9 million
- **KEY FACTS**: The average calorie intake in the U.S.A. is 3,774.1 per day, the highest daily consumption of calories. The country also holds the record for the **highest percentage of gun ownership (country)**—a 1999 survey found that approximately 40% of households contain a gun.

APR. 30: The **largest bonfire** had an overall volume of 60,589 ft.³ (1,715.7 m³). It was built by ŠKD mladi Boštanj and lit on April 30, 2007 in Boštanj, Slovenia, to celebrate Labor Day.

> **$5.3 BILLION:** money raised and spent on the 2008 race for the White House—the **costliest election.**

★ **MOST CHRISTMAS TREES CHOPPED IN TWO MINUTES** Erin Lavoie (U.S.A.) used an axe to cut down 27 Christmas trees in two minutes on the set of *Guinness World Records: Die Größten Weltrekorde* in Germany, on December 19, 2008.

☆ **Largest economy** In terms of Gross Domestic Product (GDP), the U.S.A. has the biggest economy with a figure of $13.8 trillion for 2007, according to the International Monetary Fund.

★ **Fastest time to sail from New York to San Francisco** *Gitana 13,* crewed by a team of nine and skippered by Lionel Lemonchois (France), sailed the Route de l'Or, taking it from New York City to San Francisco via Cape Horn in 43 days 3 min. 18 sec. between January 16 and February 28, 2008.

First privately-funded manned spaceflight On June 21, 2004, *SpaceShipOne,* piloted by Mike Melvill (South Africa) and built by Scaled Composites (U.S.A.), took off from Mojave Airport, California, U.S.A., and reached an altitude of 328,492 ft. (100,124 m), above the 100,000 m threshold set out by the Fédération Aéronautique Internationale (FAI) as the point where space begins. On October 4, 2004, *SpaceShipOne* went on to claim the $10 million Ansari X-Prize for non-government funded manned spaceflight.

★ **FIRST DARK SKY PARK** In April 2007, the International Dark Sky Association named Utah's Natural Bridges National Monument, U.S.A., as the first Dark Sky Park— that is, an area in which the night sky can be viewed clearly, without any "light pollution."

MAY 1: The **tallest maypole** was erected by the town of Eicherloh, Germany, and stood 165 ft. (50.35 m) high on this day in 2005.

★FASTEST LAWNMOWER The fastest speed on an unaltered lawnmower is 61 mph (98 km/h) by Tommy Passemante (U.S.A.) at Miller Motorsports Park in Tooele, Utah, U.S.A., on November 18, 2008. The record attempt was filmed for the MTV show *Nitro Circus*.

Fastest steel roller coaster *Kingda Ka* at Six Flags Great Adventure near Jackson, New Jersey, U.S.A., has a design speed of 128 mph (206 km/h) and opened in the Spring of 2005. It is also the **tallest steel roller coaster,** with riders reaching 456 ft. (139 m) above ground level.

☆**Highest defense budget** The U.S.A. has the highest government budget for defense, with $622 billion approved for the 2007 financial year.

Largest hamburger ever Loran Green and Friends of Hi Line Promotions (all U.S.A.) made a 3-ton (3-tonne) burger at the Sleeping Buffalo Resort at Saco, Montana, U.S.A., on September 5, 1999. The burger was a promotional item and not sold commercially.

Fastest time to run the New York Marathon (male) The fastest time to complete the New York Marathon by a male athlete is 2 hr. 7 min. 43 sec. by Tesfaye Jifar (Ethiopia) on November 5, 2001. The **fastest time to run the New York Marathon by a woman** is 2 hr. 22 min. 31 sec. by Margaret Okayo (Kenya) on November 2, 2003.

MAY 2: The **largest picnic** was set by 8,000 people, who sat down to eat prepared meals brought from home at the Plaza de España, Santa Cruz, Tenerife, Spain, on this day in 1999.

★**Highest-grossing year for Broadway theaters** According to the League of American Theaters and Producers, the highest-grossing year for theaters on Broadway, New York City, was 2006, with an incredible $910 million in ticket sales. Attendance figures matched those of 2005, with over 12 million people going to watch Broadway's musicals and plays.

★**Most performances by an actor in the same role** Theater actor Catherine Russell (U.S.A.) appeared as Margaret Thorne Brent in 8,820 performances of the play *Perfect Crime* in a number of New York City theaters between April 18, 1987 and December 1, 2008.

TALL TALES

The tallest horse ever was Sampson, bred by Thomas Cleaver of Toddington Mills, Bedfordshire, UK. This horse, foaled 1846, measured 21.2½ hands (86.5 in.; 219 cm) in 1850 and is said to have weighed 3,359 lb. (1,524 kg).

TALLEST LIVING HORSE Born in Iowa, U.S.A., in 1998, the tallest living horse is Radar, a Belgian draft horse who was measured at 19 hands 3.5 in. (79.5 in; 202 cm) without shoes on July 27, 2004, at the North American Belgian Championship in London, Ontario, Canada. Radar is owned by Priefert Manufacturing, Inc., in Mount Pleasant, Texas.

★ **LONGEST TAIL ON A HORSE** The longest tail on a horse is 12 ft. 6 in. (381 cm) and was measured on the mare JJS Summer Breeze on August 23, 2007. She is owned by Crystal and Casey Socha (both U.S.A.) of Augusta, Kansas, U.S.A.

First building to have a safety elevator On March 23, 1857, the world's first modern "safety elevator" went into service at a department store in New York City, U.S.A. It was installed by Elisha Otis, who is widely credited with having advanced the development of the modern skyscraper by allowing buildings above five stories to become practical living places for their occupants.

Most stars on the Hollywood Walk of Fame Actor, composer, and songwriter Gene Autry (U.S.A., 1907–98) has five stars on the Hollywood Walk of Fame strip—6,384, 6,520, 6,644, 6,667, and 7,000 Hollywood Boulevard—for Recording, Motion Pictures, Television, Radio, and Theater.

MEXICO

Tallest underwater stalactite Known locally as Tunich Ha, the world's largest underwater stalactite measures 42 ft. (12.8 m) and is found in a cave formation called Sistema Chac Mol in Mexico. Salt water from the Caribbean penetrates the limestone in the region, creating astonishing visual effects as it meets fresh water seeping into the cave.

☆ **Largest soccer tournament (players)** The Copa Telmex was held between February and November 2008 in Mexico and contested by 10,457 teams totaling 172,692 players.

MAY 3: The world's **first spam email** was sent on this day in 1978 by Gary Thuerk (U.S.A.). It was sent to 397 email accounts on the ARPAnet of the U.S. Defense Department.

AT A GLANCE
- **AREA:** 761,603 miles^2 (1,972,545 km^2)
- **POPULATION:** 108.3 million
- **HOUSEHOLDS:** 25.1 million
- **KEY FACTS:** Mexico is home to the world's largest taco, weighing 1,654 lb. (750 kg), and Sistema Sac Actun, the largest explored underwater cave system, which measures 95 miles (153 km) long.

HIGHEST BOX OFFICE GROSS FOR A MEXICAN MOVIE Directed by Guillermo del Toro (Mexico), *El Laberinto del Fauno* (*Pan's Labyrinth*, Mexico/Spain/U.S.A., 2006) made $42.6 million worldwide following its release in 2006.

LARGEST ATTENDANCE AT A BOXING MATCH The greatest paid attendance at any boxing match is 132,274 for four world title fights at the Aztec Stadium, Mexico City, Mexico, on February 20, 1993, headed by the successful WBC super lightweight defense by Julio César Chávez (Mexico) over Greg Haugen (U.S.A.).

★LARGEST BALL COURT The largest ball court in ancient Mesoamerica was the Great Ball Court in Chich'en Itza, Mexico. It was used to play a Mesoamerican ball game, which was a sport with ritual associations played for over 3,000 years by the pre-Columbian peoples. (A modern version of the game, known as Ulama, is still played.) The court measures 545 × 232 ft. (166 × 68 m). The imposing walls are 39 ft. (12 m) high, and in the center, high up on each of the long walls, are rings carved with intertwining serpents.

HAIRIEST FAMILY Victor "Larry" and Gabriel "Danny" Ramos Gomez (both Mexico) are two of a family of 19 that span five generations and all suffer from the rare condition called Congenital Generalized Hypertrichosis, characterized by excessive body hair, particularly on the face and torso. The women are covered with a light to medium coat of hair, while the men of the family have thick hair on approximately 98% of their body except for their hands and feet.

MAY 4: The **most expensive sculpture sold at auction** is Constantin Brancusi's (Romania) *Bird in Space* (1923), which sold at Christie's, New York City, U.S.A., for $27,456,000 on May 4, 2005.

★ Largest display of piñatas A display of 504 piñatas was organized by Union de Locatarios del Mercado Municipal, in Hermosillo, Sonora, Mexico, on April 27, 2008.

Largest drawing "Artistic Electrocardiogram 411" has an overall surface area of 221.97 ft.^{2} (205.5 m^2) and was completed by Filemon Trevino Berlanga of Monterrey, Mexico, on March 13, 2008.

☆ Most games of chess played simultaneously The most simultaneous games of chess ever played in one location is 13,446 on October 21, 2006, during the Third Mexico City Chess Festival in Mexico.

CENTRAL AMERICA & CARIBBEAN

Most people brushing their teeth in a single venue On November 5, 2005, 13,380 people brushed their teeth simultaneously at the Cuscatián Stadium, City of San Salvador, El Salvador, at an event arranged by Colgate Palmolive (Central America) Inc.

Lowest suicide rate According to the World Health Organization's latest figures, for May 2003, Antigua and Barbuda (1995), the Dominican Republic (1994), St. Kitts and Nevis (1995), and St. Vincent and The Grenadines (1986) all recorded the lowest suicide rates with no cases reported in the years shown.

AT A GLANCE
- **AREA: Central America: 202,232 miles^2 (523,780 km^2); Caribbean: 49,325 miles^2 (127,753 km^2)**
- **POPULATION: C. America: 44,934,014; Caribbean: 22,636,621 (2007 est.)**
- **COUNTRIES: C. America:** Belize, Costa Rica, El Salvador, Guatemala, Honduras, Nicaragua, Panama; Caribbean: Anguila, Antigua and Barbuda, Aruba, The Bahamas, Barbados, British Virgin Is., Cayman Is., Cuba, Dominica, Dominican Republic, Grenada, Guadeloupe, Haiti, Jamaica, Martinique, Montserrat, Netherlands Antilles, Puerto Rico, St. Barthélemy, St. Kitts & Nevis, St. Lucia, St. Martin, St. Vincent & The Grenadines, Trinidad & Tobago, Turks & Caicos, U.S. Virgin Isles.

DEEPEST DIVE BY A MAMMAL The deepest authenticated dive by a
mammal was made by a bull sperm whale (*Physeter macrocephalus*) off
the coast of Dominica, in the Caribbean, in 1991. Scientists from the
Woods Hole Oceanographic Institute recorded the dive to be 6,500 ft.
(2,000 m) deep, lasting a total of 1 hour 13 minutes.

Worst cyclone disaster—homeless toll Hurricane Mitch, which
struck Central America (Honduras and Nicaragua) between October 26 and
November 4, 1998, left approximately 2.5 million people dependent on international aid efforts when it destroyed 93,690 dwellings.

Worst oil tanker spill The collision of the *Atlantic Empress* and the
Aegean Captain off the coast of Tobago in the Caribbean Sea on July 19,
1979, resulted in the loss of 42.7 million U.S. gallons (35.55 UK gallons) of
oil.

MAY 5: The **most valuable painting sold at auction** is Pablo Picasso's
Garçon á la Pipe (1905), which was sold to an anonymous buyer for $104
million on this day in 2004 at Sotheby's, New York City, U.S.A.

OLDEST AND YOUNGEST PRESIDENTS Joaquin Balaguer (1906–2002, above left) was president of the Dominican Republic in 1960–62, 1966–78, and 1986–96. When he finally left office at the age of 89, Balaguer was the world's **oldest president** and had held the presidency for more than 23 years in total.

Jean-Claude Duvalier (b. July 3, 1951, above right), became president of Haiti on April 22, 1971, becoming the world's **youngest president**, aged just 19 years 293 days. He served until 1986.

OLDEST PLAYER IN MAJOR LEAGUE BASEBALL (MLB) TO HIT A HOME RUN At 48 years 254 days, Julio Franco (Dominican Republic, b. August 23, 1958) became the oldest player in major league history to hit a home run when he connected off Randy Johnson (U.S.A.) for a two-run home run to help lead the New York Mets (U.S.A.) to a 5–3 win over the Arizona Diamondbacks (U.S.A.) at Chase Field in Phoenix, Arizona, U.S.A., on May 4, 2007.

★ **LARGEST ANCIENT STONE BALLS** Known locally as *Las Bolas Grandes* ("the giant balls"), there are more than 1,000 perfectly spherical granitic globes scattered over the Diquis Delta in Costa Rica. Carved by an unidentified race of pre-Columbian people, the largest of the balls measures 8 ft. 2 in. (2.5 m) in diameter and weighs over 17.6 tons (17.6 tonnes).

SOUTH AMERICA

★**Most balloons deflated in one minute** To celebrate International Women's Day, yoghurt manufacturer Activia Argentina assembled a group of women numbering in their thousands to deflate as many balloons as they could in a minute at Parque Tres de Febrero in Buenos Aires, Argentina, on March 8, 2009. After a 60-second flurry of activity, the band of sisters managed to deflate a grand total of 9,768 balloons, setting a new world record in the process.

AT A GLANCE
- **AREA**: 6,888,062 miles² (17,840,000 km²)
- **POPULATION**: 371 million
- **KEY FACT**: The South American continent (which does not include Central America) covers 3.5% of the Earth's surface.
- **COUNTRIES**: Argentina (fastest turnaround of presidents: five in two weeks in December 2001), Bolivia (highest train station, Cóndor station, at 15,702 ft.; 4,786 m), Brazil, Chile (driest place on Earth is Quillagua, with just 5 mm of rainfall between 1964 and 2001), Colombia, Ecuador, French Guiana, Guyana, Paraguay, Peru, Suriname, Uruguay, and Venezuela.

LARGEST TRUMPET ENSEMBLE On February 19, 2006, at a concert organized by Napoleón Gómez Silva in Oruro, Bolivia, an unprecedented 1,166 participants formed a trumpet ensemble.

MAY 6: The **youngest person to appear in soccer's World Cup** is Souleymane Mamam, who played for Togo against Zambia, aged 13 years 310 days, in a preliminary qualifying game on May 6, 2001.

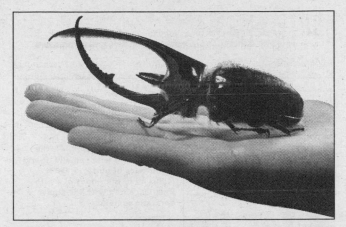

LONGEST BEETLE The longest beetle in terms of body size alone is the titan beetle *Titanus giganteus* of South America, with a body length of 6 in. (15 cm). In terms of total length, the record holder is the hercules beetle *Dynastes hercules* (above), also of South America, which is 7 in. (17.7 cm) long, owing to its pair of horns—one extending from the head, the other from the thorax.

★**Largest charango** The largest charango (South American guitar) ever made measures 20 ft. 1 in. (6.13 m) long and 3 ft. 8 in. (1.13 m) across. It was commissioned by the Town Hall of Belisario Boeto, Villa Serrano, Chuquisaca, Bolivia, and presented on January 15, 2004.

LARGEST SWIMMING POOL The world's largest swimming pool, in terms of area, is the San Alfonso del Mar seawater pool in Algarrobo, Chile. It is 3,324 ft. (1,013 m) long and has an overall area of 19.77 acres (8 ha)—larger than 15 football fields. The prodigious pool was completed in December 2006.

MAY 7: The **fastest guitar player** is Tiago Alberto de Quadros (Brazil), aka Tiago Della Vega, who played "Flight of the Bumblebee" without error at 320 BPM at EM&T, Sao Paulo, Brazil, on this day in 2008.

14: the record number of times Argentina and Uruguay have each won soccer's South American Championship (Copa America) since 1975.

HIGHEST LIVING WILD CAMELID The term "camelid" refers to any member of the family Camelidae, including camels, llamas, and dromedaries. The vicuña (*Vicugna vicugna*) is the highest-living wild camelid, found at altitudes of up to 15,750 ft. (4,800 m) in the Andes of South America, along with the alpaca, a domestic camelid.

☆ **Largest horse parade** On July 29, 2006, at an event organized by Fair of Flowers Cavalgade (Colombia), 8,233 horses and their riders took part in a parade in Medellín, Antioquia, Colombia.

☆ **Highest toll paid for passing through the Panama Canal** The highest toll ever paid for passing through the Panama Canal (the man-made waterway that joins the Atlantic and Pacific oceans, and which opened in 1914) is $226,194.25, by the cruise ship *Coral Princess* on September 25, 2003. *Coral Princess* is 965 ft. (294 m) long and can accommodate a total of 1,974 passengers.

★ **Heaviest potato pie** The heaviest potato pie weighed 5.91 tons (5.36 tonnes) and was created by the District Municipality of Carmen de la Legua Reynoso and displayed in the main square of Miguel Grau Seminario, Carmen de la Legua Reynoso, Callao, Peru, on July 16, 2004.

Most dangerous road The most lethal road in the world is the North Yungas Road, which runs for 43 miles (69 km) from La Paz to Coroico in

MAY 8: Reinhold Messner (Italy) and Peter Habeler (Austria) made the **first successful ascent of Mount Everest without supplemental oxygen** on May 8, 1978.

☆ **LARGEST CEVICHE**
A ceviche (a dish of raw seafood marinated in citrus juices) weighing 14,972 lb. (6,791.3 kg) was served up at the Coliseo Cerrado Miguel Grau del Callao in Callao, Peru, on December 7, 2008. The recipe required 5.5 tons of raw fish (perico or dorado), 1,102 lb. (500 kg) of lemons, 881 lb. (400 kg) of onions, 220 lb. (100 kg) of peppers, and 220 lb. (100 kg) of salt.

Bolivia and is held to be responsible for up to 300 deaths annually—or 6.9 per mile (4.3 per km)! For the majority of the stretch, the single-lane mud road (which caters to two-way traffic) is accompanied by an unbarricaded vertical drop measuring 15,420 ft. (4,700 m) at its highest, which becomes even more deadly during the rainy season.

Highest concert on land The highest concert ever staged on land took place at an altitude of 19,911 ft. (6,069 m) and was performed by Musikkapelle Roggenzell—10 musicians from Germany and Bolivia—on Mount Acotango, Bolivia, on August 6, 2007.

Fastest time to cycle the length of South America Giampietro Marion (Italy) cycled the South American portion of the Pan-American Highway—starting in Chigorodo, Colombia, and finishing in Ushuaia, Argentina—in a time of 59 days between September 17 and November 15,

★ **LARGEST GUINEA PIG FESTIVAL** At the annual Festival of the Cuy (guinea pig) in Huacho, Peru, guinea pig is pitted against guinea pig in a series of contests to find the fattest, fastest, and even best dressed. The stakes are high: only the winners are spared entry to the final contest, the *tastiest* guinea pig of the day, in which they are stuffed, roasted, smoked, and grilled. Guinea pig is a traditional (and almost inexhaustible) source of low-fat protein in the Andes.

2000. Geographically, Chigorodo is the closest town (and road) to the border with Panama, and is therefore a logical starting point for an attempt on the South American portion of the Pan-American Highway.

★ **Largest collection of cachaça bottles** José Moisés de Moura from Pernambuco, Brazil, has collected a total of 6,850 different cachaça bottles since 1986. Cachaça, the most traditional and most consumed spirit in Brazil, is made from sugar cane and is similar to white rum.

CANADA

☆ **Oldest nun** Sister Anne Samson (Canada, b. February 27, 1891) became the oldest nun on May 5, 2003, when, at the age of 112 years 67 days, she beat the record set by Sister Julia (France, b. Augustine Teissier, 1869–1981). Sister Anne died on November 29, 2004, aged 113 years 276 days, at Maison Provinciale Des Filles De Jésus, Moncton, New Brunswick, Canada.

Busiest route for international telephone calls According to TeleGeography, the busiest international telephone route is between the U.S.A. and Canada. In 2002, there were some 10.9 billion minutes of two-way traffic between the two countries.

☆ **Crawling—fastest mile** The fastest time to crawl one mile (1.6 km) is 23 min. 45 sec., set by Suresh Joachim (Canada) in Toronto, Ontario, Canada, on January 23, 2007.

AT A GLANCE
- **AREA**: 3,855,102 miles^2 (9,984,670 km^2)
- **POPULATION**: 33,212,696
- **HOUSEHOLDS**: 12.3 million
- **KEY FACTS**: Canada and the U.S.A. share the **longest boundary**, which (including the Great Lakes boundaries) extends for 3,986 miles (6,416 km). Canada also has the **longest coastline** of anywhere in the world, with 151,489 miles (243,798 km), including islands.

MAY 9: The Chicago White Sox and the Milwaukee Brewers (both U.S.A.) played the **longest baseball game** on this day in 1984. It lasted 8 hr. 6 min. and the Chicago White Sox eventually won 7–6.

LONGEST STREET The longest designated street in the world is Yonge Street, running north and west from Toronto, Canada. The first stretch, completed on February 16, 1796, ran 34 miles (55 km). Its official length, now extended to Rainy River on the Ontario-Minnesota border, is 1,178.3 miles (1,896.3 km).

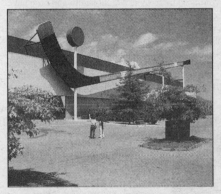

LARGEST HOCKEY STICK The largest hockey stick is 205 ft. (62.48 m) long, weighs 30.9 tons, and was commissioned by Canada's federal government for the Canadian Pavilion at the Expo 1986 in Vancouver, Canada. Since May 21, 1988, the hockey stick has been displayed alongside the Cowichan Community Center in Duncan, Vancouver Island, Canada.

Deepest live radio broadcast On May 24, 2005, Dan Lessard (Canada) of CBC Radio Points North hosted a two-hour show consisting of recorded material, live music, and interviews from a refuge station located 7,680 ft. (2,340 m) beneath Creighton Mine, Sudbury, Ontario, Canada.

MAY 10: The record for the **most people to parachute from a balloon simultaneously** is held by 20 members of the Paraclub Flevo (Netherlands), who jumped from 6,560 ft. (2,000 m) on May 10, 2003.

★ FIRST UFO LANDING PAD The world's first official UFO landing pad was built in the small Canadian prairie town of St. Paul in Alberta, and was formally opened on June 3, 1967. A sign next to the pad includes the following: ". . . future travel in space will be safe for all intergalactic beings; all visitors from earth or otherwise are welcome to this territory and to the Town of St. Paul."

Longest surviving kidney-transplant patient Johanna Leanora Rempel (Canada, b. March 24, 1948) was given a kidney from her identical twin sister, Lana Blatz, on December 28, 1960, in an operation performed at the Peter Bent Brigham Hospital in Boston, Massachusetts, U.S.A. Both Johanna and her sister have continued to enjoy excellent health and both have had healthy children.

Highest blood-sugar level Travis Maynard (Canada, b. May 13, 1960) survived a blood-sugar level of 2,538 milligrams/deciliter (mg/dl), or 141 millimoles/liter (mmol/L), when admitted to the Chalmers Regional Hospital, Fredericton, Canada, in a hyperosmolar non-ketotic coma on February 6, 2003. The normal blood-sugar range is between 80 and 120 mg/dl (4.4–6.6 mmol/L).

☆ FARTHEST DISTANCE ON A SNOWMOBILE ON WATER Riding a snowmobile, Kyle Nelson (Canada) covered 43.04 miles (69.28 km) on Cowan Lake, Canada, on September 3, 2005.

....

MAY 11: Marek Turowski (UK) achieved the record for the **fastest furniture** with a speed of 92 mph (148 km/h), driving a motorized sofa in Leicestershire, UK, on May 11, 2007.
....

MOST EXPENSIVE POP MEMORABILIA John Lennon's (UK) 1965 Phantom V Rolls Royce was acquired for $2,229,000 by Jim Pattison (above left), chairman of the Expo 86 World Fair in Vancouver, Canada, at Sotheby's, New York, U.S.A., on June 29, 1985.

☆**Fastest drive in reverse over 500 miles** Rob Gibney (Canada) covered 501.69 miles (807.39 km) at an average speed of 41.42 mph (66.67 km/h) in a Ford Crown Victoria in Calgary, Canada, on August 22, 2004.

Fastest talker Sean Shannon (Canada) recited Hamlet's soliloquy "To be or not to be" (260 words) in a time of 23.8 seconds (655 words per minute) in Edinburgh, Scotland, on August 30, 1995.

Largest jazz festival The Festival International de Jazz de Montreal in Quebec, Canada, attracted 1,913,868 people for its 25th anniversary year in July 2004.

Highest tide ever A tidal range of 54 ft. 6 in. (16.6 m) was recorded at springs in Leaf Basin, Ungava Bay, Quebec, Canada, in 1953.

Fastest run across Canada (female) Ann Keane (Canada) ran across the country from St. John's, Newfoundland, to Tofino, British Columbia, in 143 days between April 17 and September 8, 2002. She covered a total of 4,866 miles (7,831 km) and ran for all but three of the days.

☆**Longest marathon playing street hockey** The longest street-hockey marathon is 105 hr. 17 min., and was achieved in the fundraiser "Hockey for Life" in Lethbridge, Alberta, Canada, from August 20–24, 2008.

LONGEST CANTILEVER BRIDGE The Quebec Bridge (Pont de Quebec) over the Saint Lawrence River in Canada has the longest cantilever truss span in the world at 1,800 ft. (549 m) between the piers and 3,239 ft. (987 m) overall. It carries a railroad track and two road lanes.

Most bridesmaids to one bride Accompanied by 79 bridesmaids, aged one to 79, bride Christa Rasanayagam married Arulanantham Suresh Joachim (both Canada) at Christ the King Catholic Church, Mississauga, Ontario, Canada, on September 6, 2003.

Most letters to Santa collected in a Christmas season During the Christmas season of 2006, Santa received 1.06 million letters and 44,166 emails. More than 11,000 Canada Post volunteers helped respond to these letters in 11 languages; some were written in braille.

Shortest TV commercial The world's shortest TV commercial is just half a frame (one field) and lasts for ¹⁄₆₀ of a second. Twelve different versions of the commercial were produced, all advertising MuchMusic—a Canadian music and video TV channel—and the first was aired on January 2, 2002.

UK & IRELAND

☆**Largest maypole dance** Maypole dancing, common in England and parts of western Europe, involves dancing around a pole festooned with ribbons and flowers, and is thought to have some basis as a fertility rite. Each

dancer holds a ribbon attached to the top of the pole and braids the pole as they dance around it. The largest maypole dance involved 146 participants at an event organized by Congleton Town Council in Congleton, Cheshire, UK, on May 21, 2008.

☆ **Most styles danced simultaneously to one music track** The most styles danced simultaneously to one music track is 48 during an event organized by One Leicester and Leicester City Council at Humberstone Gate in Leicester, UK, on October 5, 2008.

★ **Longest-working pacemaker (present day)** The longest-working pacemaker still in use (as of July 2008) was given to Lesley Iles (UK) on January 15, 1982. Health-conscious Iles remains active and has even run the London Marathon.

★ **First UFO sighting by a pilot** On January 31, 1916, a British pilot near Rochford, Essex, reported seeing a row of lights, resembling the lighted windows of a train car, rising up into the sky and disappearing. Such "UFO" sightings are common, but those witnessed by pilots are given more credence as they are trained to identify objects in the night sky.

First bus service The first municipal "motor omnibus" service in the world was inaugurated on April 12, 1903, and ran between Eastbourne railroad station and Meads in East Sussex, UK.

Best-selling album in the UK *Greatest Hits* (released November 2, 1981) by UK rock band Queen is the best-selling album of all time in the UK, with sales of 5.75 million copies.

....

MAY 12: The **most expensive house sale** was set by Eric Hotung at 6-10 Black's Link in Hong Kong, China. It sold for HK$778.88 million ($101,909,312) on May 12, 1997.

....

YOUNGEST GAMEKEEPER The youngest gamekeeper is Robert Mandry (UK, b. January 1, 1994), who, at the age of 11 years 312 days, led his first professional shoot on his family's estate, Holdshott Farm, Hampshire, UK, on November 9, 2005. Robert led three further shoots during that season (October 2005–February 2006), all following the retirement of his predecessor, Colin Parsons (UK).

Longest play We were saddened to hear of the death in August 2008 of British writer/performer Ken Campbell (UK), who was known for, among other things, directing the longest recorded theatrical production: *The Warp*.

MOST TRACTORS PLOWING SIMULTANEOUSLY On August 5, 2007, an incredible 4,572 veteran tractors (i.e., older than 30 years) plowed the same field simultaneously in Cooley, County Louth, Ireland. Tractors turned up from more than 30 countries—including South Africa and Australia—and ranged from a 1903 Ivel to dozens of 1977 Massey Fergusons.

MAY 13: The **smallest rowboat to cross an ocean** is *Puffin*, measuring 15 ft. 6 in. (4.65 m) long, which was rowed by Graham Walters (UK) across the Atlantic, east to west, between February 3 and May 13, 2007.

☆ **LARGEST GATHERING OF ROBIN HOODS** Despite high winds and low temperatures, 1,119 people dressed in full Robin Hood costumes gathered at Castle Green, Nottingham, UK, on March 8, 2008. The record attempt celebrated the link that the city has with the legend of Robin Hood—an English folkloric hero whose band of "merry men" famously "stole from the rich to give to the poor."

This ten-part play cycle, written by Neil Oram, was performed for 18 hr. 5 min. at London's Institute of Contemporary Art on January 18–20, 1979.

Fastest selling Booker Prize–winning book Roddy Doyle's (Ireland) 1993 Booker-winning novel *Paddy Clarke Ha Ha Ha* sold 27,000 copies in hardback within 30 minutes of bookstores opening on the day after the prize was awarded.

★ **Largest fishing vessel** The 477-ft. (145.6-m), 14,055 gross-registered-tonnage Irish trawler *Atlantic Dawn* is the world's largest fishing vessel. Built at a cost of $72 million in Norway, she was launched in 2001. She has a crew of 60, is capable of processing 661,386 lb. (300 metric tons) of fish per day, and can carry 7,716 tons (7,000 metric tonnes) of frozen catch.

LARGEST PHOTO MOSAIC The largest photo mosaic measures 9,265 ft.² (860.83 m²) and contains 112,896 individual photographs donated by the public. It was created by The Big Picture project and was unveiled in the Thinktank at the Millennium Point in Birmingham, UK, on August 23, 2008.

14 MIN. 34.69 SEC.: the **fastest three-legged climb up the Canary Wharf Tower**—the UK's tallest building—by Heather Derbyshire and Karen Fingerhut (both UK) on April 6, 2008.

★ **FIRST HABITABLE SAND HOTEL** During summer 2008, vacationers on Weymouth beach in Dorset, UK, could spend the night in a hotel made entirely of sand. A total of 600 hours were needed to build the open-air 50-ft.^{2} (15-m^2) hotel. A family room with full and twin-sized beds and a sea view (but no toilet!) cost £10 ($21) a night. The hotel was the brainchild of sculptor Mark Anderson (UK), who was commissioned by the website LateRooms.com.

Fastest accordion player Liam O'Connor (Ireland) played "Tico Tico" at a speed of 11.67 notes per second on the Rick O'Shea show on 2FM radio in Dublin, Ireland, on November 8, 2006.

★ **LONGEST CAMOGIE MARATHON** A game of camogie—the women's version of the Celtic game hurling—played by Croydon Camogie Club (UK) at Emerald GAA Grounds in Ruislip, UK, on August 23–24, 2008 lasted 24 hr. 7 min.

MAY 14: The **longest steak** was produced by Jean-Yves Renard (France) and a group of butchers from Evron, France. It measured 90 ft. 9 in. (27.68 m) long on May 14, 2002.

☆**Largest hot cross bun** Hot cross buns—spiced fruit buns marked with a cross (thought to represent a crucifix)—are traditionally eaten at Easter. The largest hot cross bun weighed 179 lb. 14 oz. (81.62 kg) and was made by Allied Bakeries Ireland at its factory in Belfast, UK, on March 16, 2005. Staff at the bakery used 82 lb. 10 oz. (37.5 kg) of flour, 37 lb. (16.8 kg) of water, 15 lb. 7 oz. (7 kg) of currants, and 13 lb. 14 oz. (6.3 kg) of sultana raisins to make the bun.

☆**Most siblings to complete a marathon** The 15 siblings of the O'Donoghue family—Willie, Kieran, Teresa, Joseph, Pat, Robert, Mary, Margaret, Noel, Adelaide, James (Jim-Bob), Brenda, Kevin, Louise, and Cronan (all Ireland)—completed the Dublin City Marathon, Dublin, Ireland, on October 29, 2007.

FRANCE

★**Most expensive wallpaper** The most expensive wallpaper is titled "Les Guerres D'Independence" (The Wars of Independence), and in January 2006 was priced at $44,091 (€36,350) for a complete set of 32 panels, each measuring 12 ft. 5 in. (3.8 m) high and 18.5 in. (0.47 m) wide. If the panels could be sold separately, the price per 3 ft.^{2} (1 m^2) would be $766.53 (€631.95). The military scene is created from 19th-century woodblock

AT A GLANCE
- **AREA**: 210,026 miles^2 (543,965 km^2)
- **POPULATION**: 60.7 million
- **HOUSEHOLDS**: 25.5 million
- **KEY FACTS**: According to 2006 figures, France is the most popular country for tourism, with 79.1 million out of a total of 842 million international arrivals. Paris is also the most popular city for tourism, with 31 out of every 150 foreign tourists to the country arriving in the French capital.

★ **MOST KISSES GIVEN IN A MINUTE** Valentin Pasquier (France) kissed 94 people in one minute in Nantes, France, on November 12, 2008. The record for the ★ **most kisses received in one minute** is 108, set by Solene Oudet (France) in Nantes, France, also on November 12, 2008.

prints and takes over one year to finish. The wallpaper is made by Zuber in Rixheim, France, and exports mainly to the U.S.A.

★ **Highest triple backward somersault** Jerry and Jary Souza (France) achieved a triple backward somersault at a height of 34 ft. 4 in. (10.5 m) at the studios of *L'Émission des Records* in Paris, France, on November 30, 2001.

Tallest bridge The 8,070-ft.-long (2,460-m) Millau Viaduct across the Tarn Valley, France, is supported by seven concrete piers, the tallest of which measures 1,095 ft. 4.8 in. (333.88 m). The bridge, which was designed by Foster and Partners (UK) and opened in December 2004, has a maximum height of 1,125 ft. (343 m) from its highest point to the deepest part of the valley below.

Largest festival of films The largest film festival is the Festival International du Film de Cannes held in the south of France every May. The event attracts between 40,000 and 50,000 movie industry workers each year.

LARGEST ATTENDANCE FOR A SPORTS EVENT The largest attendance for a sports event is the estimated crowd of 10 million over a period of three weeks for the annual Tour de France cycling race.

MAY 15: The **largest orchestra** consisted of 6,452 musicians and music students from throughout British Columbia, who gathered in Vancouver, Canada, on May 15, 2000.

LARGEST FASHION SHOW AUDIENCE The Victoria's Secret Fashion Show held in Cannes, France, on May 18, 2000, was watched by more than two million people around the world, who logged on to VictoriasSecret.com. Featuring models Tyra Banks (left), Karen Mulder, and Stephanie Seymour, it raised over $2 million for charity.

LARGEST COLLECTION OF JET FIGHTERS Michel Pont (France) currently owns 110 jet fighters. His hobby started in 1985 and includes Russian MiGs, British Jaguars, and French Mirages. He buys them from foreign governments, but is not allowed to fly them in French airspace.

ITALY

★**Largest cooked ham** The largest cooked ham weighed 56 lb. (25.82 kg) and was made by Magrí SRL in Ancona, Italy, on April 23, 2008.

★**Largest pinzino** A pinzino is a bread made of wheat, flour, water, and lard, fried on both sides. The largest was 39.6 lb. (18 kg) and was made by residents of Vigarano Pieve, Italy, on June 22, 2002.

★**Longest cooked salami** A cooked salami measuring 37 ft. 10 in. (11.55 m) was made by the Pro Loco Association of Viguzzolo, on February 22, 2009.

Youngest opera singer Ginetta Gloria La Bianca (U.S.A., b. May 12, 1934) sang the part of Gilda in *Rigoletto* in Velletri, Italy, on March 24, 1950, aged 15 years 316 days. She also appeared as Rosina in *The Barber of Seville* at the Teatro dell'Opera, Rome, Italy, on May 8, 1950, 45 days later.

Largest accordion The largest playable accordion is 8 ft. 3.5 in. (2.53 m) tall, 6 ft. 2.75 in. (1.9 m) wide, 2 ft. 9.5 in. (85 cm) deep, and weighs approx-

LARGEST CHOCOLATE SCULPTURE Mirco Della Vecchia (Italy) built a chocolate sculpture in the shape of the Dolomite mountains in Limana, Italy, on March 15, 2009. His creation weighed 3.91 tons and measured 8 ft. 2 in. (2.4 m) tall, 9 ft. 10 in. (6.39 m) wide, and 3 ft. 3 in. (1 m) deep.

MAY 16: The **first Academy Awards** were held at the Hollywood Roosevelt, California, U.S.A., on May 16, 1929, for movies made in 1927–28.

LONGEST PORCHETTA Nicola Genobile (Italy) and her team made a porchetta measuring 102 ft. (31.08 m) and weighing 2,926 lb. (1,214 kg). It was presented to the public at the Auchan shopping center in Pescara, Italy, on January 17, 2009.

imately 440 lb. (200 kg). Built by Giancarlo Francenella (Italy), the instrument bears the name "Castelfidardo," after the town of Ancona in which it was constructed.

Fastest canonization St. Peter of Verona, Italy, died on April 6, 1252 and was canonized on March 9, 1253, just 337 days after his death. In modern times, Mother Teresa of Calcutta is the record holder, with her beatification within two years of her death on September 5, 1997.

MOST POINTS BY A TEAM IN A FORMULA ONE SEASON During the 2004 Formula One season, the Ferrari team (Italy) amassed 262 World Championship points. The team's drivers that year were Michael Schumacher (Germany, 148 points) and Rubens Barrichello (Brazil, 114 points). The team won 15 races out of a possible 18: Schumacher with 13 victories and Barrichello chipping in with two.

MAY 17: The **most expensive diamond** is a "D" color Internally Flawless pear-shaped gem weighing 100.10 carats. It was sold at auction for $16,561,171 on this day in 1995.

SPAIN

☆ **Most flamenco taps in one minute (female)** Flamenco dancer Rosario Varela (Spain) performed 1,274 taps in one minute on the set of *Guinness World Records* TV show in Madrid, Spain, on January 23, 2009.

Largest nightclub Privilege nightclub in San Rafael, Ibiza, Spain, can hold up to 10,000 people and covers an area of 69,940 ft.^{2} (6,500 m^2). The club has been the island's main attraction since 1994.

★ **Fastest time to solve five Rubik's cubes one-handed** Using just one hand, David Calvo (Spain) solved five Rubik's Cubes in 2 min. 27.78 sec. on the set of *Guinness World Records* in Madrid, Spain, on January 16, 2009. Calvo is able to solve one cube with one hand in just 28 seconds!

★ **Largest Sevillanas dance** A Sevillanas dance is performed to a type of folk music originating from Seville, in the south of the country. The largest dance was performed by 492 people for an event organized by Embrujo Andaluz (Spain) at Luis Mariano Square, Irun, Spain, on May 11, 2008.

★ **Fastest time to break five bottles with the palm** Alberto Delgado (Spain) broke five glass bottles using the palm of one hand in 40.46 seconds on the set of *Lo Show Dei Record* in Madrid, Spain, on February 23, 2008.

AT A GLANCE
- **AREA**: 194,897 miles^2 (504,782 km^2)
- **POPULATION**: 40.4 million
- **HOUSEHOLDS**: 15.3 million
- **KEY FACTS**: On the last Wednesday in August, the town of Buñol, near Valencia, holds its annual tomato festival, the Tomatina—the largest annual food fight. In 2004, around 38,000 people spent one hour throwing 137.75 tons (124.96 tonnes) of tomatoes at each other.

MAY 18: The volcanic explosion of Mount St. Helens in Washington State, U.S.A., on May 18, 1980, triggered the **fastest recorded avalanche**, with a velocity of 250 mph (402.3 km/h).

LARGEST CHAIR The world's largest chair measures 85 ft. 4 in. (26 m) tall with a seat 32 ft. 10 in. (10 m) wide. The oversized chair was created by the company Grupo Hermanos Huertas to advertise their furniture factory and was completed in April 2005. It was constructed in, and sits outside, the company's factory in Lucena, Spain.

MOST PROLIFIC PAINTER Pablo Diego José Francisco de Paula Juan Nepomuceno de los Remedios Crispín Cipriano de la Santísima Trinidad Ruíz y Picasso (Spain, 1881–1973) was the most prolific of all professional painters, boasting a career that lasted 75 years. Picasso produced an estimated 13,500 paintings and designs, 100,000 prints and engravings, 34,000 book illustrations, and 300 sculptures and ceramics—an output valued at $788 million.

MOST WINS OF THE FOOTBALL (SOCCER) EUROPEAN CUP Real Madrid (Spain) has won the European Champions Cup nine times: 1955–56, 1956–57, 1957–58, 1958–59, 1959–60, 1965–66, 1997–98, 1999–2000, and 2002. It is also the world's ☆ **richest soccer club**, with an income of $577.9 million according to Deloitte's annual Football Money League.

Heaviest mayor José Manuel Barros González, mayor of Porriño, Spain, weighed in at 395 lb. 4 oz. (179.330 kg) in July 1999.

Oldest restaurant Restaurante Botín in Calle de Cuchilleros, Madrid, was opened in 1725 by Jean Botín (France) and his Asturian wife. The restaurant is now run by the third generation of the Gonzalez family, and the original 18th-century interiors and firewood oven remain intact.

PORTUGAL

Largest human logo On July 24, 1999, 34,309 people organized by Realizar Eventos Especias gathered at the National Stadium of Jamor, Lisbon, Portugal, to create the Portuguese logo for Euro 2004, as part of Portugal's bid to UEFA to hold the European soccer championships in 2004.

☆**Largest Easter egg** A giant Easter egg was built and decorated by Freeport in Alcochete, Portugal, in March 2008. The enormous egg was 48 ft. 6 in. (14.79 m) long and 27 ft. 6 in. (8.40 m) in diameter when measured by Guinness World Records.

★**Longest reef-knot chain** On April 14, 2007, 224 participants tied 8,841 reef knots in five minutes, which resulted in a chain measuring a record 25,748 ft. (7,848 m) long. The event was organized by Agrupamento 626—Corpo Nacional de Escutas (Portugal) at the National Stadium in Linda-a-Velha, Portugal.

AT A GLANCE
- **AREA:** 35,672 miles² (92,391 km²)
- **POPULATION:** 10.6 million
- **HOUSEHOLDS:** 3.9 million
- **KEY FACTS:** The longest reign of any European monarch was that of Afonso I. Henriques of Portugal, who ascended the Portuguese throne on April 30, 1112, and died on December 6, 1185, after a reign of 73 years 220 days, first as count and then (after July 25, 1139) as king.

MAY 19: The **largest magazine** measures 35.63 × 40.20 in. (90.5 × 102.1 cm). Created by publisher Bayard Revistas S.A., it was unveiled in the Palacio de Congresos in Madrid, Spain, on this day in 2007.

LARGEST POCKET KNIFE The world's largest pocket knife measures 12 ft. 8 in. (3.9 m) when open and weighs 268 lb. 14 oz. (122 kg). The handle is made of wood, weighs 213 lb. 12 oz. (97 kg), and measures 6 ft. 4 in. (1.95 m); the steel blade also measures 6 ft. 4 in. (1.95 m), but weighs 55 lb. (25 kg). It was designed by Telmo Cadavez of Bragança, Portugal, and handmade by Virgílio, Raúl, and Manuel Pires (all Portugal) on January 9, 2003.

★ **LARGEST SADDLE** Carlos Almeida and Manuel Nogueira (both Portugal) manufactured a saddle 9 ft. 6 in. (2.92 m) long, 3 ft. 11 in. (1.20 m) high at the front, and 5 ft. 1 in (1.55 m) high at the back. It was presented and measured in Torre de Dona Chama, Portugal, on February 3, 2008.

MAY 20: The **most premature baby** was James Elgin Gill (Canada), born to Brenda and James Gill on May 20, 1987, in Ottawa, Ontario, Canada; 128 days premature, he weighed 1 lb. 6 oz. (624 g).

LONGEST LOAF The lengthiest loaf ever baked measured 3,975 ft. (1,211.6 m) and was created by Município de Vagos, Ferneto, Máquinas e Artigos Para a Indústria Alimentar, Lda. and Comissíão de Festas de Vagos in Vagos (Portugal) during the Bread and Bakers' Party on July 10, 2005. Over 100 bakers, mainly from Vagos' municipality, worked for over 60 hours to produce dough for the loaf.

Most watches in a chain A chain of 1,382 Swatch watches buckled together was displayed in Oeiras Parque, Lisbon, Portugal, on December 2, 2003.

Highest underwater mountain face Monte Pico in the Azores, Portugal, has an altitude of 7,711 ft. (2,351 m) above sea level and extends a record 20,000 ft. (6,098 m) from the surface to the sea floor, making it the highest underwater mountain face.

Longest painting A 13,129-ft. 2-in.-long (4,001.8-m) painting was created by the Círculo Artístico e Cultural Artur Bual and the City of Amadora in Amadora, Portugal, on September 15, 2007.

NORDIC COUNTRIES

★**Fastest glider assembly** Kouvola's Glider Association (Finland) assembled a glider and launched it to an altitude of 1,310 ft. (400 m) in 1 min. 40 sec. at Selänpää Airport, Valkeala, Finland, on July 10, 2001.

★**Most northerly fast food restaurant** The most northerly fast food restaurant is The Red Polar Bear, a kebab shop owned by Kazem Ariaiwad (Iran). It is located on the island of Spitsbergen, far within the Arctic Circle, in the Svalbard archipelago 300 miles (482 km) off the northern tip of Norway.

Oldest living tree A 13-ft.-tall (4-m) Norway Spruce discovered in the Dalarna province of Sweden in 2004 has been growing for 9,550 years.

AT A GLANCE

SWEDEN
- **AREA**: 173,732 miles² (449,964 km²)
- **POPULATION**: 9.2 million
- **HOUSEHOLDS**: 4.2 million

FINLAND
- **AREA**: 130,558 miles² (338,145 km²)
- **POPULATION**: 5.3 million
- **HOUSEHOLDS**: 2.4 million

NORWAY
- **AREA**: 125,020 miles² (323,802 km²)
- **POPULATION**: 4.7 million
- **HOUSEHOLDS**: 2.0 million

ICELAND
- **AREA**: 39,768 miles² (103,000 km²)
- **POPULATION**: 319,355
- **HOUSEHOLDS**: 116,000

DENMARK
- **AREA**: 16,638 miles² (43,094 km²)
- **POPULATION**: 5.5 million
- **HOUSEHOLDS**: 2.5 million

GREENLAND
(part of the Kingdom of Denmark)
- **AREA**: 836,330 miles² (2,166,086 km²)
- **POPULATION**: 57,600
- **HOUSEHOLDS**: 21,302

☆**Most peaceful country** According to the 2008 Global Peace Index—which measures internal and external turmoil such as organized conflict and violent crime in an attempt to quantify peace—Iceland ranks as the most peaceful country. Denmark was in second place, with Iraq ranked last.

☆**Highest score on the Human Development Index** The United Nations' Human Development Index takes into account income levels, adult

MAY 21: The **largest walk** was The New Paper Big Walk 2000, which had 77,500 participants and started from the National Stadium, Singapore, on this day in 2000.

literacy rates, number of years schooling, and life expectancy to provide an indicator of quality of life. The most recent study, in 2008, places Iceland and Norway in joint first place, with an index of 0.968 (out of 1). At the end of the list is Sierra Leone, with just 0.329.

☆ **LONGEST SKIS** The world's longest pair of skis measured an incredible 1,751 ft. 11 in. (534 m)—roughly 300 times longer than a regular pair—and were worn by 1,043 skiers simultaneously in an event organized by Danske Bank on Drottninggatan in Örebro, Sweden, on September 13, 2008. Owing to the warm weather conditions, the participants needed artificial snow in order to ski.

☆ **Least corrupt country** As of 2008, the world's least corrupt countries were Denmark, New Zealand, and Sweden, all of which achieved a score of 9.3 on Transparency International's Corruption Perceptions Index. This index compares the misuse of public office for private gain in more than 180 countries, as perceived by business and country analysts. Finland was fifth with a score of 9.0, and Somalia last with 1.0.

MOST PRODUCTIVE ICE FLOE Disko Bay in northern Greenland, 185 miles (300 km) north of the Arctic Circle, produces an average of 20 million tons of ice and icebergs a day. The glacier that produces the ice advances at around 8,298 ft. (2,530 m) per day and produces icebergs from a front 6 miles (10 km) long.

MAY 22: The **youngest successful climber of Mt. Everest** is Ming Kipa Sherpa (Nepal), who reached the summit on May 22, 2003 at the age of 15.

$0: amount spent by Iceland on defense in 2009, the **lowest military spending per capita** of any country in the world.

☆ FASTEST UNSUPPORTED NORTH POLE TREK BY A FEMALE The fastest unsupported trek to the North Pole by a female is 48 days 22 hr. by Cecilie Skog, who left Ward-Hunt Island in the Arctic Ocean with teammates Rolf Bae and Per Henry Borch (all Norway) on March 6, 2006, and reached the North Pole on April 24, 2006.

★ Most Nobel Prize laureates per capita According to the Nobel Foundation, Iceland has 3.36 Nobel laureates for every 1 million heads of population. Sweden runs a close second with 3.33 laureates per million. The foundation, established in 1900, is based on the last will of Alfred Nobel (Sweden, 1833–1896), the inventor of dynamite, and recognizes achievements in physics, chemistry, physiology or medicine, literature, and for peace.

☆ Highest-taxed country In Denmark, the highest rate of personal income tax is, as of 2009, 52%. Overall tax revenue as a percentage of the country's Gross Domestic Product (GDP) is 50.0%.

OLDEST NATIONAL FLAG IN CONTINUOUS USE The oldest continuously used national flag is that of Denmark. The current design of a white Scandinavian cross on a red background was adopted in 1625 and its shape in 1748. In Denmark, it is known as the "Dannebrog" or "Danish cloth."

MAY 23: The **most amount of money paid for a cell phone number** is 10 million QAR ($2.75 million) by an anonymous bidder for the number 666-6666 during a charity auction in Qatar on May 23, 2006.

★ **LARGEST CAT WINGSPAN** So-called "winged cats" are domestic cats suffering from a rare genetic skin disorder called feline cutaneous asthenia (FCA). With this condition, the skin is exceptionally extensible, so that when the cat grooms itself or rubs itself against an object, the skin stretches into long, furry wing-like extensions. Sometimes, these "wings" can contain muscle tissue and can be raised up and down by the cat.

The largest confirmed wingspan was recorded in northern Sweden in June 1949. Examined by the State Museum of Natural History, its wings were 23 in. (58 cm) across. Pictured is a more recent case (2008) of FCA from Sichuan in southern China.

Longest span of electrical overhead powerline The Ameralik Span is the longest electrical overhead powerline in the world. It is situated near Nuuk on Greenland and crosses Ameralik fjord, which is 3.34 miles (5.37 km) wide.

Deepest concert under ground A concert staged 4,170 ft. (1,271 m) below sea level in Pyhäsalmi Mine Oy in Pyhäjärvi, Finland, was performed by Agonizer (Finland) on August 4, 2007.

GERMANY

★ **Largest pet store** The Zoo Zajac, owned and managed by Norbert Zajac (Germany) and situated in Duisburg, Germany, covered an area of 86,867.56 ft.^{2} (8,070.26 m^2) as of September 2005.

Furthest leaning tower The bell tower of the Protestant church in Suurhusen leaned at an angle of inclination of 5.1939 degrees when measured on January 17, 2007.

AT A GLANCE
- •**AREA:** 137,846 miles^2 (357,021 km^2)
- •**POPULATION:** 82.3 million
- •**HOUSEHOLDS:** 39.4 million
- •**KEY FACTS:** Munich's Oktoberfest 99 attracted 7 million visitors—the **largest beer festival.** Germany is a formidable sports nation, winning the **most medals at a winter Olympic Games**—35 at the XIX Winter Games, Salt Lake City, Utah, U.S.A., in 2002.

LARGEST RAT KING A rat king occurs when young rats living close to each other get their tails entangled and encrusted with dirt. The knot tightens when the rats pull and, being trapped, they cannot feed themselves and they die. The rat king with the greatest number of rats was found in a miller's chimney at Buchheim, Germany, in May 1828. It contained 32 individual rats.

★ **Largest Easter egg tree** The record for the largest Easter egg tree was set by Zoo Rostock, Rostock, Germany, who decorated a tree with 76,596 painted hen's eggs on April 8, 2007.

☆ **Largest indoor water park** The Tropical Islands Resort near Berlin, Germany, is situated in a giant former blimp hangar and is 1,181 ft. (360 m) long, 689 ft. (210 m) wide, and covers 710,400 ft.^{2} (66,000 m^2). The facility features a large body of water called the South Sea as well as a smaller lagoon, a rainforest area, and a number of large beaches.

★ **FASTEST VIOLINIST** The fastest recorded violin player is David Garrett (Germany), who played "Flight of the Bumblebee" in 1 min. 5.26 sec. on the set of *Guinness World Records: Die Größten Weltrekorde* in Germany on December 20, 2008.

MAY 24: Kåre Walkert (Sweden), who suffers from apnea, a breathing disorder, recorded the **loudest snore** at 93 dBA, while sleeping at the Örebro Regional Hospital, Sweden, on May 24, 1993.

★ **MOST MILK EXTRACTED FROM A COW IN TWO MINUTES** Gunther Wahl (Germany) squeezed 0.5 gal. (2 liters) of milk from a cow on the set of *Guinness World Records: Die Größten Weltrekorde* in Germany on December 19, 2008.

☆**Largest pretzel** A prodigious pretzel weighing 842 lb. (382 kg), measuring 26 ft. 10 in. (8.20 m) long and 10 ft. 2 in. (3.10 m) wide was made by Olaf Kluy and Manfred Keilwerth of Müller-Brot GmbH (both Germany) in Neufahrn, Germany, on September 21, 2008.

☆**Longest time to hold one's breath** Tom Sietas (Germany) held his breath under water for 17 min. 33 sec. on the set of *Guinness World Records,* in Madrid, Spain, on December 30, 2008. The feat saw Sietas reclaiming the record from the illusionist David Blaine (U.S.A.), who held his breath for 17 min. 4.4 sec. on the set of *The Oprah Winfrey Show* in Chicago, Illinois, U.S.A., on April 30, 2008.

★ **MOST JUICE EXTRACTED FROM GRAPES IN ONE MINUTE** The greatest amount of juice successfully extracted by treading grapes for one minute is 1.43 gal. (5.4 liters). This pressing task was achieved by Martina Servaty (Germany) in Mesenich, Germany, on November 9, 2008, in celebration of Guinness World Records Day.

MAY 25: The **fastest time to score a goal in a Champions League final** is 52 seconds, by Paolo Maldini (Italy) playing for AC Milan against Liverpool on May 25, 2005.

NETHERLANDS

Largest clog dance Introdans Education and Dance and Child International organized a clog dance involving 475 participants at the Spuiplein in the Hague, the Netherlands, on July 8, 2006.

First evidence of *homo erectus* Homo erectus (upright man), the direct ancestor of *Homo sapiens,* was discovered by Eugéne Dubois (Netherlands) at Trinil, Java, in 1891. The Javan *H. erectus* remains were dated 1.8 million years old in 1994.

AT A GLANCE
- **AREA:** 16,033 miles^2 (41,526 km^2)
- **POPULATION:** 16.6 million
- **HOUSEHOLDS:** 7.2 million
- **KEY FACTS:** The largest painting (a seascape) measured 92,419 ft.^{2} (8,586 m^2) and was completed by ID Culture at The Arena, Amsterdam, on August 14, 1996. The largest solar energy roof covered the exposition hall of the Floriade 2002, Haarlemmermeer. It was 281,045 ft.^{2} (26,110 m^2) in size and had a generating capacity of 2.3 MW.

☆ **MOST PEOPLE ON ROWING MACHINES** The largest rowing class consisted of 165 people rowing simultaneously at an event organized by Boekel De Neree Advocaten and civil law notaries at Gustav Mahlerplein in Amsterdam, the Netherlands, on August 14, 2008.

FACT

The **greatest distance covered on a land rowing machine** is 3,280 miles (5,278.5 km), by Rob Bryant of Fort Worth, Texas, U.S.A., who rowed across the U.S.A. in 1990.

MAY 26: On this day in 1969, the crew of the *Apollo* 10 command module reached a speed of 24,790.8 mph (39,897 km/h)—the **fastest speed at which humans have ever traveled.**

★ **TALLEST POPULATION** The Dutch are the world's tallest citizens, with the average male measuring 6 ft. (184 cm) tall. Studies show that by 2012, Dutch men will average 6 ft. 1 in. (186 cm) and Dutch women 5 ft. 7 in. (172 cm). In early 2000, activists persuaded the Dutch government to raise the ceiling levels stipulated in the nation's building codes by 7.8 in. (20 cm).

Greatest art robbery On April 14, 1991, 20 paintings, together estimated to be worth $500 million, were stolen from the Van Gogh Museum in Amsterdam, the Netherlands.

Fastest knitter Miriam Tegels (Netherlands) hand-knitted 118 stitches in one minute at the Swalmen Townhall, the Netherlands, on August 26, 2006.

★ **Longest pergola** A pergola measuring 132 ft. 7 in. (40.42 m) long and covered by leaves and grapes was created by Lidy and Niek Reijnen (both Netherlands). It was measured in Noord Beveland, the Netherlands, on August 22, 2005.

☆ **MOST DOMINOES TOPPLED BY A GROUP** A total of 4,345,027 dominoes were toppled on the set of Domino Day 2008 in Leeuwarden, the Netherlands, on November 14, 2008. At the same event, the ★ **largest domino mosaic** was created, comprising 1,011,732 dominoes and measuring 5,382 ft.^{2} (500 m^2).

Tallest working windmill De Noord Molen at Schiedam, the Netherlands, is a windmill that stands 109 ft. 4 in. (33.33 m) tall. However, there are other—derelict—Dutch windmills that are taller.

EASTERN & CENTRAL EUROPE

★**Largest enamel image** Susanne Zemrosser (Austria) created an enamel mural measuring 166 ft. 1 in. (50.63 m) long and 8 ft. 6 in. (2.61 m) high. It was installed at the Praterstern subway station in Vienna, Austria, on May 10, 2008.

☆**Furthest flight by a paraglider (female)** Petra Krausova (Czech Republic) flew an incredible distance of 188.2 miles (302.9 km) by paraglider from Quixada, Brazil, on November 18, 2005.

★**Largest coffee pot** The food and coffee-processing company Vispak d.d. completed a coffee pot measuring 4 ft. 1 in. (1.24 m) tall with a base diameter of 37.4 in. (95 cm) in Visoko, Bosnia and Herzegovina, in June 2004.

★**Most enduring Olympic torch bearer** Pandelis Konstantinidis (Greece) took part in the 2008 Olympic torch relay procession, 72 years after taking part in the 1936 torch relay.

AT A GLANCE
- **AREA**: 1,372,220 miles² (3,554,034 km²)
- **POPULATION**: 216.8 million
- **COUNTRIES**:
  Central Europe: Austria, Czech Republic, Hungary, Liechtenstein, Poland, Slovakia, Slovenia, and Switzerland.
  Eastern Europe: Belarus, Estonia, Latvia, Lithuania, Moldova, Romania, and Ukraine.
  Southeastern Europe: Albania, Bulgaria, Bosnia and Herzegovina, Croatia, Greece, Kosovo, Macedonia, Montenegro, Serbia, and part of Turkey.

MAY 27: Arie Luyendyk (Netherlands) achieved the **fastest finish in the Indianapolis 500** on this day in 1990, clocking 2 hr. 41 min. 18.404 sec.

LARGEST BEACH TOWEL To celebrate the start of the summer tourist season in Cyprus, Bookcyprus.com & Aeolos Travel organized the creation of a huge beach towel measuring 210 ft. 8 in. (64.2 m) long by 101 ft. 9 in. (31 m) wide. Fittingly, the towel was laid on the beach at Fig Tree Bay in Protaras, Cyprus, for a party held on June 1, 2008.

FACT

After this event, the beach towel was cut into small pieces and given away to all involved as a memento of the occasion.

★**Largest chocolate firework** The food company Nestlé made a chocolate firework measuring 9.8 ft. (3 m) high and 4.9 ft. (1.5 m) in diameter, designed to fire 132 lb. (60 kg) of Swiss Cailler chocolates into the air. The firework was released on December 31, 2002, and showered its chocolatey payload over Hechtplatz in Zürich, Switzerland.

★**LARGEST CORK MOSAIC** Saimir Strati (Albania) built a cork mosaic on the theme "Mediterranea" measuring 42 ft. 6 in. (12.94 m) wide by 23 ft. 4 in. (7.1 m) tall at the Sheraton Tirana Hotel in Tirana, Albania, between August 8 and September 4, 2008. The mosaic, which has an area of 988 ft.^{2} (91.87 m^2), required 229,675 bottle corks.

....

MAY 28: On this day in 2000, the **longest parade of Rolls-Royce cars** took place when 420 vehicles formed a 2-mile (3.2-km) procession on the A55 highway near Chester, UK.

....

50 FT. 11 IN. (15.52 M): the **longest piece of chalk,** made by Vladimir Micenke and staff at his company, Amice Košice, in Košice, Slovakia.

☆**MOST MENTOS & SODA FOUNTAINS Students at the School of Business Administration Turiba in Riga, Latvia, celebrated their school's 15th anniversary by breaking a world record. On June 19, 2008, the students managed to make a total of 1,911 Mentos and soda fountains at the same time.**

☆**Longest straw chain** Petru Pognaru, Marcu Cristi, and 27 students (all Romania) made a straw chain measuring 7 miles (11.29 km) using 58,469 drinking straws. The chain was created at Dacia Square, Buzau, Romania, on July 10, 2008, and covered most of the surface of the square.

☆**Largest parade of fire trucks** Vogt Ltd Fire Service Accessories and Vehicles held a parade of 159 fire trucks in Oberdiessbach, Switzerland, on April 28, 2006.

☆**LARGEST DANCE (COUPLES) A total of 1,635 couples danced the "cha-cha" for five minutes in the market square of Kraków Old Town, Kraków, Poland, for the TV program *You Can Dance* on August 31, 2008.**

MAY 29: At 11:30 a.m. on this day in 1953, Edmund Percival Hillary (New Zealand) and Sherpa Tenzing Norgay (Nepal) became the **first people to reach the summit of Mount Everest.**

★LARGEST RUBBER STAMP A rubber stamp seal measuring 4 ft. 3 in. (1.3 m) tall and 3 ft. 3 in. (1 m) in diameter was unveiled at the Brand of the Year Awards in Kiev, Ukraine, on June 6, 2002. The stamp, which weighs 226 lb. (102.6 kg), was made from rubber and walnut and cherry wood.

☆**Highest rate of unemployment (country)** According to the International Labor Organization definition of unemployment, the country with the highest rate of unemployment is Macedonia, where 36% of the labor force is without a job, despite being available for work.

★Fastest speed with an ice stock Ice stock is a winter sport similar to curling that uses gliding stones with long poles protruding from their middle. Bernhard Patschg (Austria) managed to accelerate his ice stock to an amazing speed of 41.73 mph (67.16 km/h) at Lake Stubenberg, Austria, on January 30, 2005.

★Largest legal document The largest legal document is an insurance policy measuring 29 ft. 4 in. (9 m) tall by 19 ft. 8 in. (6 m) wide, issued by ING Asigurari de Viata of Romania. It was signed in Varna, Bulgaria, on March 15, 2008.

RUSSIA

☆**Largest country** Russia is the largest country in the world. It has an area of 6,592,771 miles^2 (17,075,200 km^2), or 11.5% of the world's total land area. It is 70 times larger than the UK, and had a population of 140,702,096 in July 2008.

Highest personal majority The highest personal majority obtained by any politician was 4,726,112 in the case of Boris Nikolayevich Yeltsin (b. February 1, 1931), the people's deputy candidate for Moscow, in the parliamentary elections held in the Soviet Union on March 26, 1989. Yeltsin received 5,118,745 votes out of the 5,722,937 which were cast in the Moscow constituency; his closest rival obtained 392,633 votes.

MAY 30: Ray Harroun (U.S.A.), driving the Marmon Wasp, was the **first winner of the Indianapolis 500** race (then known as the "International Sweepstakes") on this day in 1911.

AT A GLANCE
- **AREA**: 6,592,771 miles² (17,075,200 km²)
- **POPULATION**: 140.7 million
- **HOUSEHOLDS**: 53.0 million
- **KEY FACTS**: Russia is facing a population crisis, with a growth rate in 2008 of -0.08%. Not only are there more abortions than births, the death rate is considerably higher than in mainland Europe. The average life expectancy for males in Russia is 61.5 years, which is 10 years below the European average.

GREATEST TEMPERATURE RANGE ON EARTH The greatest recorded temperature ranges in the world are around the Siberian "cold pole" in the east of Russia. Temperatures in Verkhoyansk (67°33'N, 133°23'E) have ranged 188°F (105°C), from a coldest point of −90°F (−68°C) to a warmest of 98°F (37°C).

★Largest aerial firefighting force The Avialesookhrana of Russia, established in 1931, is the world's largest aerial firefighting force and was the first of its kind in the world. There are currently 4,000 "smokejumpers" in the force, who cover a forested area of 2 billion acres (809 million ha).

HIGHEST CLOCK Positioned 751 ft. 3 in. (229 m) above street level on top of the Federation Tower "West" in Moscow, Russia, the world's highest clock was activated on April 24, 2008.

MAY 31: The **oldest recorded bride** is Minnie Munro (Australia), who married 83-year-old Dudley Reid at Point Clare, New South Wales, Australia, on this day in 1991, aged 102 years!

MOST TANKS IN ONE ARMY In 2006, the Russian Federation was credited with at least 22,831 Main Battle Tanks (MBT), making it the army with the most tanks in the world. China has about 7,580 MBTs, while the U.S.A. possesses approximately 7,620.

☆ **BUSIEST SUBWAY NETWORK** The Greater Moscow Metro carries up to 9 million passengers a day (compared with 4.5 million in the New York City Subway and 3 million in the UK Tube) between its 177 stations. In all, 9,915 trains run over 12 lines totaling 81 miles (292.2 km) of track.

Longest journey by tractor Vasilii Hazkevich (Russia) covered 13,172 miles (21,199 km) on an unmodified tractor from April 25 to August 6, 2005, starting and finishing in Vladimir, Russia.

☆**Largest board game tournament** A record 1,214 people played chess in the Central Park of Krasnoyarsk in Siberia, Russia, on June 2, 2007. A shot was fired to start the first round of games, and the 32 semifinalists played a knockout lightning tournament. The event was organized with the help of the city's education department.

ISRAEL

Longest-serving prisoner in solitary confinement Mordecai Vanunu (Israel) spent nearly 12 years in a total isolation jail cell—the longest known term of solitary confinement in modern times. Born in 1954, Vanunu was convicted of treason for giving information about Israel's nuclear pro-

AT A GLANCE
- **AREA:** 8,019 miles² (20,770 km²)
- **POPULATION:** 6.8 million
- **HOUSEHOLDS:** 2.1 million
- **KEY FACTS:** Per capita, Israel has the ★ greatest weapons holdings of any country, with 2,646,600 weapons per 1 million people. According to the Center for International Policy, Israel is also the ★ recipient of the most U.S. military exports, with the equivalent of $259.83 spent for every 1,000 people.

gram to *The Sunday Times* (UK) newspaper. He was sentenced to a total of 18 years, and spent from 1986 until March 1998 in total isolation. He remained incarcerated until he was released on April 21, 2004, although he has been arrested several times since then for violating the conditions of his release.

HEAVIEST LEMON The world's heaviest lemon weighed 11 lb. 9.7 oz. (5.265 kg) on January 8, 2003, and was grown by Aharon Shemoel (Israel) on his farm in Kefar Zeitim, Israel. The lemon's circumference was 29 in. (74 cm) and it was 13.7 in. (35 cm) high. The record-breaking citrus fruit grew with another very large lemon.

HIGHEST CONSUMPTION OF PROTEIN (COUNTRY) Israel consumes more protein than any other country, according to the United Nations, with every Israeli eating 4.53 oz. (128.6 g) every day. The world average is 2.65 oz. (75.3 g).

JUNE 1: Herbert Fisher and Zelmyra Fisher (both U.S.A.) achieved the **longest marriage of a living couple** on this day in 2008 with the amazing commitment of 84 years and 50 days!

★ LARGEST *PAPIER-MÂCHÉ* SCULPTURE The largest *papier-mâché* sculpture has a height of 6 ft. 10 in. (2.10 m) and a circumference of 21 ft. 7 in. (6.60 m). This model of the globe was presented at Ma'a Iot Meshulam School in Rehovot, Israel, on May 5, 2008.

★ Largest tabbouleh A bowl of tabbouleh weighing 4,784 lb. (2,170 kg) was made by the citizens of Majdal Shams, Israel, on March 21, 2008.

★ Highest male youth literacy rate In the 15–24 age group, male literacy rates are at a record high of 100% in Israel. According to the World Development Indicators database in 2006, literacy is the ability of a person to "read and write a short, simple statement on their everyday life." Israeli women of the same age score 99.6%. (At No. 1 is Cuba, with a score of 100%.)

★ Most injuries from terrorist attacks In recent years (1968–2006), more Israelis have suffered injuries in terrorist attacks than any other people, with 1,165.73 injuries per 1 million of population, according to the Memorial Institute for the Prevention of Terrorism (MIPT) Terrorism Knowledge Base. Iraq is in second place with 706.49 injuries per million, and the West Bank third with 653.39.

THE MIDDLE EAST

Least taxed country The sovereign countries with the least personal income tax are Bahrain and Qatar, where the rate, regardless of income, is zero.

☆ Lowest rate of death The United Arab Emirates has the fewest deaths per 1,000 population, with a projection of 1.4 per 1,000 for the period 2005–10.

Highest rate of diabetes The United Arab Emirates (UAE) has the highest percentage of type-II diabetes in the population (20% between 20 and 79 years of age). Two other Gulf states feature in the top 10 list of dia-

JUNE 2: The **first radio patent** was granted on this day in 1896 to the Italian-Irish Marchese Guglielmo Marconi GCVO (1874–1937).

betics: Kuwait (12.8%) and Oman (11.4%). At joint second place are Cuba and Puerto Rico, with 13.2%.

☆**Most crowded network of roads** Qatar has 283.6 registered motor vehicles per kilometer (0.62 miles) of road, in theory making its roads the most crowded in the world, according to figures available in 2007.

★**Largest serving platter** A steel serving plate measuring 33 ft. × 6 ft. 7 in. (10.06 m × 2.03 m) was crafted in Liwa, UAE, on July 31, 2008, for the 4th Liwa Festival. The dish was filled with 2.2 tons of dates.

☆**OLDEST PAINTING ON A CONSTRUCTED WALL** On October 2, 2006, the French archaeological mission (leader Eric Coqueugniot, pictured left) at Dja'de al-Mughara—a Neolithic settlement on the Euphrates River near Aleppo, Syria—found walls of a house that bore a series of polychrome geometric paintings. Measuring 6 ft. 6.7 in. × 6 ft. 6.7 in. (2 m × 2 m), the wall is believed to date from *c.* 9,000 B.C.

FACT

The oldest painted wall features a geometric pattern of red (from burnt hematite rock), white (crushed limestone), and black (charcoal) not unlike the Persian art seen in carpets and rugs.

JUNE 3: On this day in 2005, Fu Haifeng (China) hit a shuttlecock at a measured speed of 206 mph (332 km/h), the **fastest recorded speed of a shuttlecock.**

★**FASTEST VEHICLE CROSSING THE GREAT SAND SEA** The record for the fastest crossing of the Great Sand Sea—the Sahara Desert—by a vehicle is 5 hr. 33 min., achieved by Hesham Nessim (Egypt) between the Gilf Kebir Plateau and the Siwa Oasis in Egypt, on March 5, 2009.

★**Largest acrylic panel** The largest single acrylic panel is an aquarium window at The Dubai Mall, Dubai, United Arab Emirates, that measures 107 ft. 10 in. × 27 ft. 2 in. (32.88 m × 8.3 m). It was completed on July 25, 2008.

Largest single humanitarian operation The world's largest and most expensive humanitarian operation was undertaken by the United Nations World Food Program (WFP), feeding the 27.1 million people in Iraq displaced by war. The food-aid operation began on April 1, 2003, and finished in late October 2003 with 4.8 billion lb. (2.4 million tons) of food commodities being delivered under a budget of $1.5 billion.

★**Oldest surviving personal name** The earliest surviving personal name is that of a predynastic king of Upper Egypt *pre*-3050 B.C., who is indicated by the hieroglyphic sign for a scorpion. It has been suggested that the name should be read as Sekhen.

★**Largest mortarboard** A giant mortarboard—a square academic headdress, so named because it resembles a bricklayer's cement palate—was made by HQ Link and the Bahrain Convention & Exhibition Bureau. The cap, which measured 19 ft. 8 in. × 19 ft. 8 in. (6 m × 6 m), was displayed at the Career, Education, and Training Middle East 2006 exhibition in Manama, Bahrain, on April 18, 2006.

☆ **LONGEST PITA BREAD** Pita bread—or Arabic bread, as it's known in the Middle East—is widely used in many Middle Eastern and Mediterranean cuisines. The longest ever made measured 421 ft. 6 in. (128.5 m)—over two and a half times longer than an Olympic swimming pool—and was produced by a team from Jana Bakers, LLC of Doha, Qatar, on December 4, 2008.

Largest item on a menu The largest item on any menu in the world is roasted camel, prepared very occasionally for Bedouin wedding feasts. The elaborate dish includes cooked eggs which are stuffed into fish; the fish are then stuffed into cooked chickens, and the chickens stuffed into a roasted sheep's carcass. Lastly, the sheep is stuffed into the whole camel.

Largest percentage of population to attend a funeral Official estimates gave the size of the crowds lining the 20-mile (32-km) route to Tehran's Behesht-e Zahra cemetery on June 11, 1989, for the funeral of Ayatollah Ruhollah Khomeini as 10,200,000 people. This figure represented one-sixth of Iran's population at that time.

Thickest walls Ur-nammu's city walls at Ur (now Muqayyar, Iraq), destroyed in 2006 B.C., were 88 ft. (27 m) thick and made of mud brick.

Costliest caviar The most expensive of all caviar, and indeed the world's most expensive food, is "Almas," from the Iranian beluga fish. A single kilogram (2 lb. 3 oz.) of this "black gold" is regularly sold for $34,500. Almas is produced from the eggs of a rare albino sturgeon between 60 and 100 years old.

....

JUNE 4: The **largest rideable bicycle,** as measured by the wheel diameter, is "Frankencycle," ridden by Steve Gordon (U.S.A.) on June 4, 1989. The wheel diameter is 10 ft. (3.05 m), and the bike is 11 ft. 1 in. (3.4 m) high.

....

★ **LARGEST BOOK** The world's largest book measures 12 ft. 7 in. × 9 ft. 1 in. (3.85 × 2.77 m), weighs 2,336 lb. 9 oz. (1,060 kg), and consists of 304 pages. It is a re-creation of a bestselling photography book, *Beirut's Memory,* which depicts the changing face of the Lebanese capital between 1991 and 2002. It was made by photographer Ayman Trawi (Lebanon)—the Lebanese Prime Minister Rafic Hariri's personal photographer—and displayed in Beirut on February 27, 2009.

Highest altitude mosque The King Abdullah Mosque on the 77th floor of the Kingdom Centre building in Riyadh, Saudi Arabia, is 600 ft. (183 m) above ground level and was completed on July 5, 2004.

Oldest cultivated plant for drinking Among the oldest cultivated plants that are used primarily for drinking are grapes (*Vitis vinifera*). The earliest evidence proving that grapes were cultivated to make wine dates to 6000 B.C. in Mesopotamia (modern-day Iraq). The earliest physical proof of wine being stored and drunk comes from pottery excavations made in 1968 in Iran and dating to *c.* 5000 B.C. But it was the ancient Egyptians, in 3000 B.C, who first recorded the process of winemaking, known as viticulture.

☆ **HEAVIEST MEDALLION**
A medallion with a 39.37 in. (1 m) diameter and a thickness of 0.9 in. (2.3 cm) weighed in at 409 lb. 12 oz. (185.88 kg) on December 15, 2008. It was made by Damas jewelry (UAE), one of the Middle East's leading jewelry retailers, to mark the 10th anniversary of the Sheikh Hamdan Al Maktoum Medical Science award. The medallion has a value of 1 million UAE dirhams or AED ($272,257) and was made of solid fine silver plated with 22 carat gold. It took 85 jewelers a total of 30 days to craft this unique piece.

AFRICA

★**Highest economic growth (country)** In the period 1996–2006, Equatorial Guinea in Central Africa saw the highest annual percentage increase in real Gross Domestic Product (GDP), with a rise of 33.7%. GDP is the most commonly used indicator of an economy's health and is the combined sum of money made by the wealth-generating sectors of the economy, such as manufacturing, retailing, and service industries.

☆**Lowest rate of car ownership** Of the seven countries with the lowest rate of car ownership in the world, five are African: Burundi, Central African Republic, Ethiopia, Rwanda, and Tanzania; all have a rate of one car per 1,000 population, according to the current figures. By contrast, the wealthy European state, Luxembourg, has 647 cars per 1,000, or one for every 1.5 people.

☆**Highest ratio of patients to doctor (country)** Doctors in Malawi have more patients—49,624 each, according to *The Economist*—than doctors in any other country.

☆**Highest rate of death** Swaziland has a projected death rate of 22.1 deaths per 1,000 population, for the period 2005–10. The landlocked kingdom in southern Africa also has the **lowest life expectancy in the world**—with the average male living to just 39.6 years—and the **highest rate of death from AIDS,** with 1,455 deaths per 100,000 population.

AT A GLANCE
- **AREA: 12,010,859 miles²
(31,107,983 km²)**
- **COUNTRIES: Algeria, Angola, Benin, Botswana, Burkina Faso, Burundi, Cameroon, Cape Verde, Central African Republic, Chad, Comoros, Côte d'Ivoire, D. R. Congo, Djibouti, Equatorial Guinea, Eritrea, Ethiopia, Gabon, Gambia, Ghana, Guinea, Guinea-Bissau, Kenya, Lesotho, Liberia, Libya, Madagascar, Malawi, Mali, Mauritania, Mauritius, Morocco, Mozambique, Namibia, Niger, Nigeria, Republic of the Congo, Réunion, Rwanda, Saint Helena, São Tomé and Príncipe, Senegal, Seychelles, Sierra Leone, Somalia, South Africa, Sudan, Swaziland, Tanzania, Togo, Tunisia, Uganda, Zambia, Zimbabwe.**

FIRST WOMAN TO BE FIRST LADY OF MORE THAN ONE COUNTRY Graca Machel was married to Samora Machel (1933–86), president of Mozambique, from 1975 to 1986. President Machel was killed in a plane crash on October 19, 1986. On July 18, 1998, Graca married Nelson Mandela (seated), president of South Africa, making her the first woman to be "First Lady" of two different countries.

LARGEST SCENTED GARDEN The Kirstenbosch National Botanical Gardens on the slopes of Table Mountain, Cape Town, South Africa, cover 88.9 acres (36 hectares). The Fragrance Garden includes a braille trail and many aromatic plants, offering the opportunity for blind and visually impaired visitors to enjoy the experience.

★ **OLDEST HUMAN ANCESTOR INFANT** "Selam" was a three-year-old female of the species *Australopithecus afarensis,* ancestors of human beings that lived 3.3 million years ago. Her remains were discovered on December 10, 2000, by a team led by Zeresenay Alemseged (Ethiopia) in Dikika, Ethiopia. The remains include a skull, a complete torso, fingers, and a foot.

JUNE 5: On June 5, 1966, N. William Kennedy (Canada) slashed the mooring lines of the 10,639-dwt SS *Orient Trader,* which then became the **largest object stolen by an individual.**

☆ **HIGHEST EDUCATION BUDGET** Lesotho, the landlocked country that is entirely surrounded by the Republic of South Africa, put 13% of its GDP into education, according to the latest annual figures available for 2003–07, which is more than any other nation.

The ★ **lowest budget for education** is Equatorial Guinea with 0.6%, according to the latest available figures.

☆ **Highest birth rate** Based on figures for 2007, the Democratic Republic of the Congo and Guinea-Bissau share the record crude birth rate of 50 births per 1,000 population. By contrast, Germany and Macau have eight births per 1,000 people.

Largest game of pick-up sticks Sticks measuring 29 ft. 10.3 in. (9.10 m) long and 5.7 in. (14.5 cm) in diameter were used in a giant game of pick-up sticks by pupils of St John's Preparatory School in Harare, Zimbabwe, on July 21, 2007.

Longest commercially operated single-drop rappel A single-drop rappel of 670 ft. (204 m) can be experienced down the Maletsunyane waterfall at the Semonkong Lodge in Semonkong, Lesotho. This abseil is commercially operated on a daily basis but, because of the training required, only four people generally make the drop every day.

☆ **HIGHEST FERTILITY RATE (COUNTRY)** Fertility rates are determined by the ratio of children to each adult female. The country with the highest rate is Niger with 6.88 children per female, based on projected averages for 2010–15. Niger has one of the world's fastest-growing populations, with a predicted increase of 41 million from 12 million (2004) to 53 million (2050).

JUNE 6: Minoru Saito (Japan) was 71 when he completed a nonstop solo circumnavigation in his 50-ft. (15-m) yacht *Shuten-doji* II in 2005, becoming the **oldest person to sail around the world.**

★ **YOUNGEST POPULATION** In Uganda, the median age—that is, the age at which there are an equal number of people above and below—is just 14.8 years old. African countries dominate the list of nations with the lowest median ages, according to *The Economist.* Uganda is followed by Niger, with a median age of 15.5 years and Mali with 15.8 years.

SOUTH AFRICA

★ **Longest kebob** A kebob measuring 1.271 miles (2.047 km) was prepared by the ArcelorMittal Newcastle Works on the occasion of the company's annual Community Day in Newcastle, South Africa, on October 11, 2008.

Largest wine cellar The Paarl wine cellar of the Koöperatiewe Wijnbouwers Vereniging in Cape Province, at the center of the wine-growing district of South Africa, covers an area of 54 acres (22 ha)—the equivalent of over 40 football fields—and has a capacity of 32 million gal (121 million liters)—enough to fill approximately 1.5 million bathtubs with wine!

☆ **Largest cardboard box pyramid** The largest cardboard box pyramid consisted of 21,345 Air Wick Freshmatic boxes that were stacked into 20 layers, each measuring 14 ft. 1 in. (4.3 m) tall. It was built by two teams of 10 in an event organized by Air Wick at the East Rand Mall in Bocksburg, South Africa, on September 18, 2008.

★ **Most seafood prepared** A record preparation of 3,835 lb. 1 oz. (1,739.56 kg) of large seafish, sardines, shrimp, mussels, and calamari was cooked by South Coast Tourism and Wozani Africa Events (both South Africa) at Silver Beach in Port Edward, South Africa, on July 19, 2008. The event drew a crowd of 7,200 people.

JUNE 7: The **highest score in a game of** *Space Invaders* is 55,160 points (also the highest possible score on that game), set by Donald Hayes (U.S.A.) on this day in 2003.

CENTRAL & SOUTHERN ASIA

☆ **Largest opium crop** United Nations officials in Afghanistan are hoping that 2008 was a turnaround year for opium production in the country, as output fell by 6% to 8,487 tons (7,700 metric tons). While still the largest opium crop in the world—worth $3.4 billion in illegal heroin trade—it is a sign that government and military pressure (as well as market forces and the weather) is reducing the number of people involved in the growing and selling of poppies (the source of the opium). An estimated 1 million fewer farmers cultivated poppies in 2008, opting instead for the more lucrative wheat and corn, which has risen in price.

★ **MOST FOUNTAIN POOLS** The city with the greatest number of fountain pools in a public place is the Turkmenistan capital city of Ashgabat, where a major intersection near the entrance to the airport contains 27 synchronized, illuminated, and fully programmable fountains covering an area of 36.62 acres (14.82 ha).

AT A GLANCE
- **AREA:** 1,390,080 miles² (3,600,292 km²)
- **POPULATION:** 1.619 billion*
- **COUNTRIES:** Afghanistan, Bangladesh, Bhutan, British Indian Ocean Territories, India, Kazakhstan, Kyrgyzstan, Maldives, Nepal, Pakistan, Sri Lanka, Tajikistan, Turkmenistan, and Uzbekistan.

Population figures are estimated for July 2008; statistics for Iran are included as part of the Middle East—see pp. 224–228.

JUNE 8: The **largest pizza delivery** was made by Papa John's pizza company on this day in 2006, when 13,500 pizzas were delivered to the NASSCO Shipyard in San Diego, California, U.S.A.

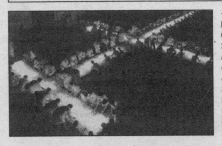

★LARGEST FLAMING IMAGE USING CANDLES A total of 30,500 lit candles were arranged into the shape of a cross at an event organized by the Mar Sleeva Association for Rural Guidance in Irinjalakuda, Kerala, India, on September 8, 2008.

☆**Longest hand-drumming marathon** Kuzhalmannam Ramakrishnan (India) played a mridangam (a double-sided drum played with the hands and fingers) for a total of 301 hours at the Nada Layaa auditorium of the Nehru College of Aeronautics and Applied Sciences, Coimbatore, Tamil Nadu, India, from August 1–13, 2008.

☆**Largest blood donation** A blood-donation drive organized by Dera Sacha Sauda (India) was held at Bapu Ji village in Sriganganagar, India, on October 10, 2004, and attracted 17,921 donors.

★**Longest dosa** A dosa is a rice-flour pancake, and the largest on record was 30 ft. (9.14 m), prepared by chefs at the Sankalp Restaurant in Andheri, Mumbai, India, on February 12, 2006.

☆**LARGEST RANGOLI IMAGE** Nilesh Rajaram Naik (India) made a rangoli painting—a decorative artform using colored powders or sands—measuring 229 × 229 ft. (70 × 70 m) at Murda Ground in Tiswadi, Goa, India, on May 22, 2008. The portrait depicted Shivaji (1627–80), founder of the Maratha Empire.

JUNE 9: The **fastest time to type the alphabet** is exactly 7 seconds, and was achieved by Nick Watson (UK) at the Guinness World Records headquarters in London, UK, on June 9, 2006.

☆ **LARGEST CANOE CREW** It may not be the longest canoe—that record is held by the 149-ft. 1-in.-long (45.44-m) boat built by students of Nokomis Regional High School in Newport, Maine, U.S.A., in 2006—but the 143-ft. 4-in.-long (43.7-m) "Snake Boat" *Aries Punnamada Urukku Chundan* from Alleppey in Kerala, India, had a record crew of 143, which included 118 rowers, two rhythm men, five helmsmen, and 18 singers. It was rowed in Kerala, India, on May 1, 2008.

☆ **Largest tea party** The largest tea party involved 32,681 participants and was organized by Dainik Bhaskar (India) for the City of Indore at Nehru Stadium, Indore, India, on February 24, 2008.

☆ **Largest yoga class** A record 29,973 students from 362 schools performed a sequence of yogic *kriyas* called Suryanamaskar ("Salute to the Sun") simultaneously for 18 minutes, led by Vivekanand Kendra (India) in Gwalior, India, on November 19, 2005.

☆ **Most refugees received (country)** The country that hosts more refugees than any other is Pakistan. According to the United Nations High Commission for Refugees (UNHCR), Pakistan received 1,044,500 refugees in 2006.

Flattest country The country with the lowest point of elevation is the Maldives at just 8 ft. (2.4 m).

☆ **Largest quiz** The largest quiz held at one location was attended by 1,566 participants during a staging of the "TIME Aqua Regia—The Science Quiz" event organized by TIME (Triumphant Institute of Management Education Pvt. Ltd) at Hari Hara Kala Bhavan, Hyderabad, India, on December 3, 2007.

Highest inhabited building The highest inhabited buildings in the world are those in the border fort of Basisi by the Mana Pass (Lat. 31°04'N, Long. 79°24'E) at *c.* 19,700 ft. (6,000 m), which is manned by the Indo-

JUNE 10: On this day in 1989, Alain Ferté (France) set the **fastest lap in the Le Mans 24-hour race:** 3 min. 21.27 sec. (at an average speed of 150.429 mph [242.093 km/h]) in a Jaguar XJR-9LM.

Tibetan Border Police (India). Because of lower air pressures at high altitudes and the corresponding decrease in the amount of oxygen in each breath taken, many people begin to feel the effects of altitude sickness at heights above 8,200 ft. (2,500 m). It takes several days to acclimatize to the altitude at Basisi and most people become ill if airlifted directly to that height.

★ **Largest tunic** Ariel Pakistan (Pakistan) made a kurta—a traditional shirt worn by both men and women in Afghanistan, Bangladesh, India, and Pakistan—measuring 101 ft. (30.78 m) long and 59 ft. 3 in. (18 m) wide in Karachi, Pakistan. It was put on display on January 3, 2008.

★ **Longest horn on a sheep** The longest horn found on a species of sheep measured 75 in. (191 cm) and belonged to a Marco Polo sheep (*Ovis ammon polii*), a species indigenous to the Pamir Mountains bordering Tajikistan, Afghanistan, Pakistan, and China.

Fastest glacier surge In 1953, the Kutiah Glacier in Pakistan advanced more than 7.4 miles (12 km) in three months, averaging 367 ft. (112 m) per day—the fastest glacial surge ever recorded.

Largest landlocked country The largest country with no border access to the open ocean is Kazakhstan, which has an area of 1,052,089 miles^2 (2,724,900 km^2) and is bordered by Russia, China, Kyrgyzstan, Uzbekistan, Turkmenistan, and the landlocked Caspian Sea.

★ **Largest easel** In April 2008, Rajasekharan Parameswaran (India) of Meenachal, Tamilnady, India, unveiled an easel 56 ft. 6 in. (17.22 m) tall and 31 ft. (9.45 m) wide.

☆ **MOST THEATER ADMISSIONS** India—which produces **more feature-length movies than any other country,** with 1,164 films released in 2007—had a total of 3.29 billion theater admissions in 2007, more than double the U.S. figure and 20 times that of the UK. Pictured is Bollywood star Shilpa Shetty (India).

Largest volunteer ambulance organization Abdul Sattar Edhi (Pakistan) began his ambulance service in 1948, ferrying injured people to the hospital. Today, his radio-linked ambulance fleet is 500 vehicles strong and operates all over Pakistan.

SOUTHEAST ASIA

Largest monkey buffet The Kala Temple (also known as Monkey Temple) in Lopburi provence, north of Bangkok, Thailand, provides an annual spread of tropical fruit and vegetables, weighing 6,613 lb. (3,000 kg) for the local population of monkeys, which numbers over 2,000.

★ Most countries in a military tattoo Armed forces from 13 different countries participated in the Brunei Darussalam International Tattoo 2006, which was organized by the Ministry of Defense and the Royal Brunei Armed Forces at the Hassanal Bolkiah National Stadium in Brunei Darussalam from July 29 to August 1, 2006.

★ Highest defense budget (percentage GDP) In 2006, Burma's military government allocated 18.7% of its GDP to defense spending.

Largest legal currency On May 22, 1998, the Central Bank of Manila, the Philippines, issued a special 100,000-peso legal tender currency note measuring 8½ × 12 in. (22 × 33 cm). Only 1,000 notes, which commemorated the centennial of the first declaration of Philippine independence, were issued.

AT A GLANCE
- **AREA**: 1,735,742 miles² (4,495,553 km²)
- **POPULATION**: 585 million
- **COUNTRIES**: Brunei, Burma (home of the Mingun bell, the heaviest bell in use at 101 tons; 92 tonnes), Cambodia, East Timor, Indonesia (site of the largest Buddhist temple at 2,118,880 ft.³; 60,000 m³), Laos, Malaysia (where the world's heaviest mango, weighing an impressive 6 lb. 13 oz./3.1 kg, was grown), the Philippines, Singapore, Thailand, and Vietnam.

JUNE 11: The **largest manufactured pure gold bar** weighs 551 lb. 2 oz. (250 kg) and was made by the Mitsubishi Materials Corporation on this day in 2005.

☆ **RICHEST MONARCH** According to Forbes.com, the richest monarch in the world as of August 2007 was Sultan Haji Hassanal Bolkiah of Brunei, with an estimated wealth of $22 billion. In addition to being ruler of the oil-rich state, the 29th sultan of Brunei inherited much of his wealth.

★ **Largest donation can** A 19-ft. 7-in.-high (6-m) and 13-ft.-wide (4-m) donation can was displayed by the Nanyang Technological University Students' Union and y.e.s. 93.3 fm at the Civic Plaza, Ngee Ann City, Singapore, on July 10, 1998. The can was on show for three days to help raise money for a variety of local charities.

MOST PEOPLE IN A MINI A classic challenge, the most people crammed into a Mini Cooper is 21, and it was achieved by students of INTI College Subang Jaya at their campus in Selangor, Malaysia, on June 17, 2006. The rules for this record state that at the end of the attempt all participants must be within the car and all doors and windows must be fully closed.

★ **HEAVIEST JICAMA** The jicama, or yam bean, is an edible root vegetable used in southeast Asian food. The heaviest jicama weighed 46 lb. 4.8 oz. (21 kg). It was grown by Leo Sutisna (Indonesia) in Bandung, West Java, Indonesia, and was weighed on January 25, 2008.

JUNE 12: The **longest rabbit jump** is 9 ft. 9.6 in. (3 m) and was achieved by a rabbit called Yabo in Horsens, Denmark, on this day in 1999. Yabo was handled by Maria Brunn Jensen (Denmark).

☆ **LARGEST STICKER On September 5, 2008, Focal Point Advertising and Golden Touch Imaging displayed a sticker made to advertise Levi Strauss jeans on the ESL Tower Building in Makati City, the Philippines. The sticker measured 200 ft. × 233 ft. (61 × 71.26 m) and had a total area of 46,995 ft.² (4,366.46 m²).**

DID YOU KNOW?

Makati City, above, is the major financial, commercial, and economic hub of the Philippines.

☆ **Fastest text message** Jeremy Sng Gim (Singapore) typed a prescribed 160-character text on his cell phone in 41.40 seconds during the SingTel SMS Shootout 2008, held at Clarke Quay, Singapore, on February 24, 2008.

★ **Most diabetes readings** The record for the most diabetes readings taken in 24 hours is 503, a feat that was achieved by Grace Galindez-Gupana, president of HalleluYAH Prophetic Global Foundation Philippines, with the sponsorship of ABS Gen Herbs International Corporation at the HalleluYAH Prayer Mountain for All Nations, in San Mateo, Rizal, the Philippines, on March 15, 2008.

☆**LARGEST OBSERVATION WHEEL** Located in Marina Bay, Singapore, the Singapore Flyer observation wheel comprises a 492-ft. (150-m) diameter wheel, built over a three-story terminal building. The wheel has a total height of 541 ft. (165 m).

★**Highest owner occupancy (country)** According to the data available to the United Nations Human Settlement Program, UN-Habitat, as of 1998, Cambodia had an amazing 95.3% of its population living in homes that they owned.

Largest earwig sanctuary The largest, and only, earwig sanctuary is inside the Great Cave at Niah in Sarawak, northern Borneo. The species protected is the hairy earwig (*Arixenia esau*); the insects live in a single block of wood, which was fenced off in the early 1960s, thereby creating the sanctuary.

★**Fastest game of hopscotch** Multiple record holder Ashrita Furman (U.S.A.) completed the fastest single game of hopscotch in just 1 min. 23 sec. at the fitness center of the Awana Kijal Resort and Spa in Kijal, Malaysia, on January 19, 2006.

☆**Longest barbecue** The longest barbecue measured 12,480 ft. 2 in. (3,803.96 m) and was created by Municipality of Santo Tomas (Philippines)

★**FASTEST GROWING CITY** Naypyitaw, the new capital of Burma, was built in the scrublands of central Burma, 300 miles (460 km) north of the old capital, Rangoon. Most of the construction workers involved in building it have to travel great distances to reach the city. Naypyitaw is projected to have grown an amazing 57.8% in the period 2005–10, making it the fastest growing of all conurbations in the world, with a population exceeding 750,000.

JUNE 13: The **most children born at a single birth** to be medically recorded is nine, born to Geraldine Brodrick (Australia) at the Royal Hospital for Women, Sydney, Australia, on this day in 1971.

in Santo Tomas, Pangasinan, the Philippines, on February 11, 2008. The record-breaking meal required more than 3,500 cooks.

★ Largest exporter of rice According to information from the Food and Agriculture Organization of the United Nations, Thailand exported 8,922,107 tons (8,094,000 metric tons) of rice in 2007, giving it a 27% share of the global rice market.

NORTHEAST ASIA

☆ **Heaviest vehicle pulled using earrings** Gao Lin (China) attached a Volkswagen car weighing 3,443 lb. (1,562 kg) to his earrings by means of a rope and pulled it for 33 ft. (10 m). This lobe-stretching feat of strength was achieved on the set of *Zheng Da Zong Yi—Guinness World Records Special* in Beijing, China, on December 19, 2006.

☆ **Largest airport cargo terminal** With a total floor area of 3,019,277 ft.² (280,500 m²), Hong Kong Air Cargo Terminals Limited (HACTL) SuperTerminal 1 is the world's largest cargo terminal under one roof. The terminal has a design capacity of 2.8 million tons (2.6 million tonnes) per year. Hong Kong also boasts the **largest airport passenger terminal building** in the form of the Hong Kong International Airport passenger terminal building, a massive 0.8-mile-long (1.3-km) structure, covering 5,920,150 ft.² (550,000 m²).

AT A GLANCE
- **AREA**: 4,554,087 miles² (11,795,031 km²)
- **POPULATION**: 1.63 billion*
- **COUNTRIES**: China (the most populous country with 1.3 billion inhabitants), which includes two Special Administrative Regions (SARs): Macau (home of the Venetian Macau, the largest casino, with a 550,000-ft.²; 51,100-m² gambling area) and Hong Kong (the busiest container port, handling 22 million containers in 2004), Japan, Mongolia, North Korea, South Korea, and Taiwan (which saw the largest parade of bicycles, consisting of 2,284 bikes, on February 21, 2009).

*only includes figures for China, Hong Kong, Japan, South Korea, and Taiwan.

X-REF

You've seen the youngest, but what about the oldest? Read all about some fascinating life stories on pp. 107–111. . . .

★ **LARGEST TAMBOURINE ENSEMBLE** The largest gathering of people playing the tambourine involved 9,902 participants in an event organized by Taipei County government in Taipei, Taiwan, on January 1, 2008.

★ **YOUNGEST PROFESSIONAL GUITARIST** As of August 4, 2008, Yuto Miyazawa (Japan) was aged 8 years 165 days and had played numerous paid engagements on national television throughout the world. Yuto started playing guitar when he was three and has played with many musicians, including the American jazz guitar legend Les Paul.

★ **MOST MAGAZINE COVERS DESIGNED** Keizo Tsukamoto (Japan) has illustrated the cover of *Shukan Manga Times* for 38 years and 5 months as of July 2008 without missing a single issue. During that time, Tsukamoto produced a grand total of 1,937 magazine covers.

JUNE 14: The **first nonstop flight across the Atlantic,** in a Vickers Vimy biplane, took 16 hr. 12 min. on this day in 1919 by John William Alcock and Arthur Whitten Brown (both UK).

> **3,063:** hot springs visited by Takashi Kasori (Japan) between November 1, 2006, and October 31, 2007, the **most hot springs visited in one year.**

★FASTEST 100 M ON ALL FOURS The fastest time to run 100 m on all fours is 18.58 seconds and was set by Kenichi Ito (Japan) at Setagaya Kuritsu Sogo Undojyo, Tokyo, Japan, on November 13, 2008. Ito came up with the idea of sprinting on all fours when he saw monkeys running very quickly in a zoo, and he trained every day for five years in preparation for the challenge.

★First confirmed survivor of two nuclear attacks Tsutomu Yamaguchi (Japan) was in Hiroshima on a business trip on August 6, 1945, when a U.S. B-29 aeroplane dropped the 12–15-kiloton "Little Boy" atomic bomb on the city, killing 140,000 people. Suffering burns to his upper body, Tsutomu managed to return to his hometown of Nagasaki on August 8. The next day the U.S. Army dropped "Fat Man," a 20–22-kiloton bomb on the city, the **★first use of a plutonium weapon.** Around 73,000 people died in the attack, but Tsutomu again managed to survive with minor injuries. In both cities he was within 1.8 miles (3 km) of ground zero.

☆Most bouts won in a year by a sumo wrestler In 2005, Yokozuna Asashoryu Akinori (Mongolia, birth name: Dolgorsuren Dagvadorj) won 84 of the 90 regulation bouts that top sumo wrestlers, or *rikishi,* fight annually.

☆LONGEST MODELING CONTRACT The actress and model Shima Iwashita (b. January 3, 1941) of Japan has been a house model for the Japanese cosmetic company Menard since 1972. She first signed with them on April 1, 1972, and her contract has continued to be renewed every year since.

JUNE 15: The **largest violin ensemble,** consisting of 4,000 child violinists playing "Recollections of England—Selection," performed at Crystal Palace, London, UK, on this day in 1925.

☆ **OLDEST POPULATION** According to the latest population figures available, the median age—that is, the age at which there are an equal number of people above and below—in Japan was at the record high of 42.9 in 2007. In terms of Asian countries, Japan is exceptional in its high median age and is the only non-European country in the top 10. Italy has the second highest at 42.3 years.

★ **Most couples hugging** A total of 1,451 couples hugged simultaneously at a World Children's Day charity event organized by McDonald's Restaurants, Taiwan, at Taipei Arena, Taipei, Taiwan, on November 18, 2007.

★ **Most books written by an individual in a year** The most books written in one year by an individual is six by Shinichi Kobayashi (Japan), who wrote and published the novels between October 1, 2007 and September 15, 2008.

☆ **Largest producer of energy (country)** China is the largest producer of energy with 1,641.0 Mtoe (million tonnes of oil equivalent) as of 2005.

★ **Largest Mahjong tournament** The largest Mahjong tournament was the First Super Cup Mahjong Tournament held by Gi Tiene International Co. Ltd (Taiwan) between December 8, 2007 and February 3, 2008. The competition featured 14,886 individual players from all over Taiwan.

☆ **Longest firework waterfall** The world's longest fireworks waterfall was the "Niagara Falls," which measured 11,539 ft. 5 in. (3,517.23 m) when ignited on August 23, 2008, at the Ariake Seas Fireworks Festival, Fukuoka, Japan.

★ **Largest shipbuilder** The world's largest shipbuilder is the Hyundai Heavy Industries Co. Ltd of Ulsan, South Korea, which in 1999 accounted for 13% of world ship production. In 2000, it produced 59 vessels with a

JUNE 16: The **first woman in space** was Valentina Tereshkova (USSR) on this day in 1963. Born March 6, 1937, she was 26 years 102 days old at the time, also making her the **youngest woman in space**.

gross deadweight of 4.6 million tons (4.2 million tonnes) and a total value of $3.8 billion. Hyundai's shipyard has nine dry docks, the largest of which is 2,100 ft. (640 m) long and can hold several huge ships at once.

AUSTRALIA

☆**Fastest time to climb the equivalent height of Everest on a machine (male)** Richard Pemberton (Australia) climbed the equivalent of the height of Mount Everest (29,028 ft.; 8,848 m) on a "Versaclimber" machine in 2 hr. 53 min. 47 sec. at Executive Fitness Management Gym, Adelaide, Australia, on November 25, 2006.

★**Fastest time to shear one merino lamb** Dwayne Black (Australia) successfully sheared a single merino lamb in 53.88 seconds on the set of *Zheng Da Zong Yi—Guinness World Records Special* in Beijing, China, on September 20, 2007.

☆**LARGEST HUMAN WHEELBARROW RACE** With 1,044 participants splitting up into 522 pairs, the largest human wheelbarrow race took place at the sports campus of Carey Baptist Grammar School, in Melbourne, Victoria, Australia, on September 9, 2008.

AT A GLANCE
•**AREA**: 2,967,909 miles^2 (7,686,850 km^2)
•**POPULATION**: 21 million
•**HOUSEHOLDS**: 7.7 million
•**KEY FACTS**: Australia is the largest producer of raw wool, with an output of 360,455.8 tons (327,000 tonnes) in 2006. China is the second largest producer of raw wool and New Zealand is third, with 185,188 tons (168,000 tonnes).

JUNE 17: The **first successful human kidney transplant** was performed by R. H. Lawler (U.S.A.) at Little Company of Mary Hospital, Chicago, Illinois, U.S.A., on June 17, 1950.

★ **LARGEST SHEEP STATUE** A giant statue of a merino ram measuring 49 ft. tall, 59 ft. long, and 13 ft. wide (15 × 18 × 4 m) towers above the freeway in Goulburn, New South Wales, Australia. Named "Big Merino" but better known as "Rambo," the 106-ton beast is constructed from steel and reinforced concrete and houses a gift shop and a wool exhibition. It opened to the public on September 20, 1985.

Longest road train On February 18, 2006, a road train with a total length of 4,836 ft. 11 in. (1,474.3 m) was put together for an event sponsored by Hogs Breath Café in Clifton, Queensland, Australia. A single Mack Titan prime mover (road tractor), driven by 70-year-old veteran trucker John Atkinson (Australia), towed the 113 trailers weighing 2,865,980 lb. (1,299,986 kg) for a distance of approximately 490 ft. (150 m).

★ **Fastest circumnavigation of Australia by aquabike** Paul Fua, Randall Jones, and Lynden Parmenter (all Australia) circumnavigated Australia on an aquabike (jet ski) in 106 days. They set out from Sydney Harbor on August 20, 2000, and covered around 10,250 miles (16,500 km) in a clockwise direction before arriving back in Sydney on December 3, 2000.

★ **Most whistle blowers** On September 5, 2008, a total of 37,552 people blew whistles simultaneously at an event organized by the Asthma Foundation of Queensland at Suncorp Stadium in Brisbane.

☆ **Fastest 100 m wheelbarrow race** Otis Gowa (Australia) pushed Stacey Maisel, who weighed 110 lb. (50 kg), in a wheelbarrow across 328 ft.

★ **MOST EXPENSIVE CRICKET BAT** A cricket bat used by Sir Donald Bradman (Australia) in his debut test match was sold for A$145,000 ($120,350) at Leski Auctions, Melbourne, Australia, on September 24, 2008. Arguably the world's greatest cricketer, Bradman made his debut in the 1928/29 Ashes series. He scored just 18 runs in the first innings and 1 run in the second innings.

(100 m) in a record time of 14 seconds. The wheelbarrow race was filmed on location for *Guinness World Records* at Davis Park, Mareeba, Queensland, on May 15, 2005.

NEW ZEALAND

★ **Tap dancing—most taps in a minute** Tony Adams (New Zealand) achieved 602 taps in one minute (averaging a fraction over 10 taps per second), live on Television New Zealand's *Good Morning Show* at Studio 11 in Wellington, New Zealand, on August 4, 2008.

☆ **Fastest coal shoveling by a team of two** The record for filling a 0.5-ton (508-kg) hopper with coal using a banjo shovel by a team of two is 14.8 seconds, by Brian Coghlan and Piet Groot (both New Zealand) at the opening of the Brunner Bridge, South Island, New Zealand, on March 27, 2004.

☆ **Highest bungee jump from a building** A. J. Hackett (New Zealand) leaped 652 ft. 10 in. (199 m) off a platform situated at 764 ft. 5 in. (233 m) on the Macau Tower, Macau, China, on December 17, 2006.

Largest demolition derby A demolition derby with 123 participants took place at Todd & Pollock Speedway, Mount Maunganui, New Zealand, on March 16, 2002. It took 47 minutes of mass automotive mayhem before the winner—the last car still moving—emerged.

☆ **Fastest text message blindfolded** Elliot Nicholls (New Zealand) completed a 160-character text message, without error, while blindfolded in 45.09 seconds. The record was achieved at the Telecom shop on Filluel Street, in Dunedin, New Zealand, on November 17, 2007.

AT A GLANCE
- **AREA: 103,737 miles²**
(268,680 km²)
- **POPULATION:** 4.1 million
- **HOUSEHOLDS:** 1.5 million
- **KEY FACTS:** According to the latest available figures, which were released in 2006, New Zealand has more CD players per member of the population than any other country, with 88.5 per 100 people. The United Kingdom is only just behind New Zealand with 88.4 per 100.

X-REF

Can't get enough rugby records? Then tackle the Rugby section on pp. 490–494.

★ **COIN FLICKING—FARTHEST DISTANCE** New Zealand's serial record breaker Alastair Galpin flicked a NZ$0.10 coin a distance of 34 ft. 10 in. (10.64 m) at the Old Homestead Community House in Auckland, New Zealand, on November 2, 2008.

☆ **MOST TRI NATIONS WINS** The Tri Nations, the annual rugby union tournament contested between Australia, New Zealand, and South Africa, has been won a record nine times by New Zealand, which was victorious in 1996–97, 1999, 2002–03, and each year from 2005 to 2008.

JUNE 18: On this day in 2005, Phil Naylor (UK) played the first hole of the Devlin course at St. Andrews Bay Golf Resort and Spa, St. Andrews, UK, in 1 min. 52 sec., the **fastest single hole of golf.**

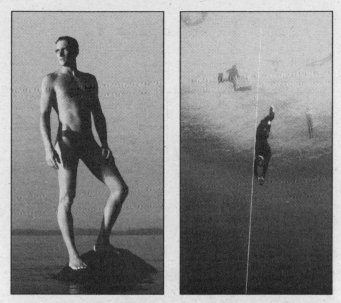

☆ **FREEDIVING—CONSTANT WEIGHT NO FINS (MEN)** New Zealander William Trubridge dived to a depth of 282 ft. (86 m) in the constant weight no fins category at the Vertical Blue 2008 Invitational Freediving competition, held at Dean's Blue Hole, Long Island, The Bahamas, on April 10, 2008. Constant weight no fins involves a totally unassisted descent and ascent (right).

☆**Heaviest colossal squid** On February 22, 2007, it was announced that fishermen in the Ross Sea of Antarctica had caught an adult male colossal squid (*Mesonychoteuthis hamiltoni*) weighing approximately 990 lb. (450 kg) and measuring 33 ft. (10 m). The squid was taken to New Zealand to be studied. Rarely-caught aquatic beasts, colossal squid are usually shorter than giant squid, but are much heavier.

....
JUNE 19: The **youngest scorer in a FIFA World Cup finals tournament** is Pelé, who was aged 17 years 239 days when he scored for Brazil against Wales at Gothenburg, Sweden, on June 19, 1958.
....

MODERN WORLD

CONTENTS

MAN'S BEST FRIEND

★ **Most dogs jumping over the same rope** On May 23, 2007, Uchida Geinousha's "Super Wan Wan Circus" achieved the incredible canine feat of getting 12 dogs to jump together over the same rope at an event held for Sanyo Bussan Co. Ltd, in Tokyo, Japan.

☆ **Fastest time to pop 100 balloons by a dog** Anastasia, a Jack Russell terrier owned by Doree Sitterly (U.S.A.), popped 100 balloons in 44.49 seconds on the set of *Live with Regis and Kelly* in Los Angeles, U.S.A., on February 24, 2008. The balloons that Anastasia popped were standard party balloons inflated to a diameter of at least 8 in. (20 cm).

☆ **Largest dog walk** A leash-straining 10,272 dogs took part in the Butchers Great North Dog Walk, organized by Anthony Carlisle (UK). The walk was held in South Shields, UK, on June 17, 2007.

☆ **Largest dog wedding ceremony** A "wedding" ceremony featuring 178 dog pairs took place at the "Bow Wow Vows" event organized by the Aspen Grove Lifestyle Center in Littleton, Colorado, U.S.A., on May 19, 2007. The poochy partners sealed their marriage with a bark to the notes of the wedding march.

☆ **Oldest dog (living)** A dachshund called Chanel, who is owned by Karl and Denise Shaughnessy (both U.S.A.) of Port Jefferson Station, New York, U.S.A., has a confirmed age of 20 years as of May 6, 2008.

Oldest dog (ever) The greatest reliable age recorded for a dog is 29 years 5 months for an Australian cattle-dog named Bluey, owned by Les Hall of Rochester, Victoria, Australia. Bluey was obtained as a puppy in 1910 and worked among cattle and sheep for nearly 20 years before being put to sleep on November 14, 1939.

 Tallest dog living Gibson, a harlequin Great Dane, measured 42.2 in. (107 cm) tall on August 31, 2004. He was born on April 26, 2002, is owned by Sandy Hall of Grass Valley, California, U.S.A., and currently works as a therapy dog, providing affection to people with special needs.

☆ **Fastest pole weaving** Alma, owned by Emilio Pedrazuela Cólliga (Spain), weaved through 24 poles in 5.88 seconds on the set of *Guinness World Records,* recorded in Madrid, Spain, on January 16, 2009. Alma was attempting the record as part of a three-dog challenge, with each dog having two attempts. Her first attempt was 6.10 seconds. The best attempts by the other two dogs, Yuna and King, were 6.79 seconds and 6.66 seconds, respectively.

★**LARGEST COLLECTION OF** *POOH & FRIENDS* **MEMORABILIA** When Deb Hoffmann's (U.S.A.) collection of *Pooh & Friends* memorabilia was counted on February 23, 2009, it was found to contain 4,405 different items. Deb began her collection in 1967.

THE WET NOSE OF THE LAW

The ★ **first dog trained to identify illegal mobile phones** was Murphy, a springer spaniel who was trained by the Eastern Area Drug Dog team, UK, to identify a certain scent emitted by mobile phones. Murphy began work with his handler, Mel Barker (UK), in autumn 2006 in an initiative to detect such contraband items among prisoners at Norwich Prison (HMP Norwich), Norfolk, UK. Murphy can even differentiate between prison officers' and prisoners' mobile phones, as well as locate phones that have been hidden in wall cavities or wrapped in plastic bags.

JUNE 20: Bertha Wood (UK) became the **oldest person to have a debut book published** when *Fresh Air and Fun: The Story of a Blackpool Holiday Camp* came out on her 100th birthday on June 20, 2005.

 MOST ROPE JUMPS BY A DOG IN ONE MINUTE Sweet Pea, an Australian Shepherd/Border Collie cross, performed 75 rope jumps in one minute on the set of *Live with Regis and Kelly* in New York City, U.S.A., on August 8, 2007. Sweet Pea's owner Alex Rothaker (U.S.A.) helped out by swinging the rope.

Largest litter of puppies Tia, a Neopolitan mastiff owned by Damian Ward (UK) and Anne Kellegher (Ireland) of Manea, Cambridgeshire, UK, gave birth to 24 puppies on November 29, 2004.

WELL BALANCED Sweet Pea (left) also holds the record for the most steps climbed by a dog balancing a glass of water on the snout. She successfully walked up 17 steps on the set of *Live with Regis and Kelly,* in New York City, U.S.A., on August 8, 2007.

JUNE 21: The **highest recorded altitude in a helicopter** is 40,820 ft. (12,442 m) by Jean Bouletan (France) flying an Aérospatiale SA315B "Lama" over Istres, France, on June 21, 1972.

LONGEST EARS ON A DOG Tigger, a bloodhound owned by Bryan and Christina Flessner of St. Joseph, Illinois, U.S.A., has the longest ears of any dog. When measured on September 29, 2004, Tigger's right ear was found to be 13.75 in. (34.9 cm) in length, while his left ear was slightly shorter at 13.5 in. (34.2 cm).

HEAVIEST BREEDS OF DOG The heaviest breeds of domestic dog *Canis familiaris* are the mastiff (pictured left) and the St. Bernard, with males of both species regularly weighing 165–200 lb. (75–90 kg). In its breed guidelines, the Kennel Club (UK) states that the ideal mastiff should have "a large, powerful, well-knit frame," displaying "a combination of grandeur and courage."

FACT

Pictured above are mastiffs Simba and Jorden, who appeared on a German Guinness World Records TV show in 2008 representing the world's **heaviest dog breed**.

JUNE 22: Hip-hop producer Irv Gotti (U.S.A.) produced the No. 1 single on the U.S. Hot 100 pop chart for a record 19 successive weeks between February 23 and June 22, 2002.

BIG FOOD

LARGEST . . .

★**Biryani** A spicy biryani dish weighing 30,996 lb. (14,059 kg) was prepared by Kohinoor Foods Ltd (India) in Delhi, India, on March 1, 2008.

★**Bougatsa bread** Bougatsa is a pastry stuffed with custard, cheese, or minced meat. The largest ever made weighed 401 lb. 11 oz. (182.2 kg) and was served in Serres, Greece, on June 1, 2008.

★**Gazpacho** The Municipality of Campohermoso in Almeria, Spain, made a 1,196-gal. (4,520-liter) gazpacho—a chilled tomato soup—on August 2, 2008.

★**Jambalaya** The Jambalaya Festival Association (U.S.A.) prepared a 3,041-lb. (1,379.3-kg) jambalaya (a rice dish with meat and vegetables) in Gonzales, Louisiana, U.S.A., on May 24, 2008.

☆**Meatball** A 72-lb. 9-oz. (32.93-kg) mass of meat was prepared and cooked at Meatball Mike's in Cranston, Rhode Island, U.S.A., on June 6, 2008.

☆**Pizza** The world's largest *commercially available* pizza has an area of 14 ft.^{2} (1.3 m^2) and has been on sale at Mama Lena's Pizza House in McKees Rocks, Pennsylvania, U.S.A., since March 20, 2006.

The **largest pizza ever cooked** weighed 26,883 lb. (12.19 metric tons) and was prepared in Norwood, South Africa, in 1990.

☆**LARGEST CHEESECAKE** A cheesecake weighing 4,703 lb. (2,133.5 kg) was made by Philadelphia Kraft Foods Mexico at the Universidad del Claustro de Sor Juana in Mexico DF, Mexico, on January 25, 2009. The cheesecake had a diameter of 8 ft. 2 in. (2.5 m), a height of 22 in. (56 cm), and included 1,763 lb. 11 oz. (800 kg) of cheese, 220 lb. 7 lb. (100 kg) of strawberries, and 1,763 lb. (800 kg) of yogurt!

JUNE 23: The **first brain cell transplant** was performed by a team of doctors from the University of Pittsburgh Medical Center, Pennsylvania, U.S.A., on this day in 1998.

LARGEST SCOTCH EGG "Scotch egg" is the name given to a hard-boiled egg that is encased in spicy sausage meat, covered in breadcrumbs, then deep-fried. The largest on record weighed 13 lb. 10 oz. (6.2 kg) and was made by Clarence Court (UK) and Lee Streeton (UK, pictured with his creation) at Rocco Forte Brown's Hotel in London, UK, on July 30, 2008. The entire cooking process took more than eight hours, with 90 minutes alone spent boiling the ostrich egg. The scotch egg is not a Scottish invention—it was conceived at the London food store Fortnum & Mason in 1738.

INGREDIENTS . . .

- 3 lb. 11 oz. (1.7 kg) ostrich egg
- 8 lb. 13 oz. (4 kg) sausage meat
- 2 lb. 1 oz. (940 g) haggis
- 1 lb. 12 oz. (800 g) breadcrumbs

TALLEST . . .

☆ **Stack of poppadoms** Nahim Aslam and Fayaz Aslam (UK) stacked poppadoms to a height of 4 ft. 10 in. (1.48 m) at the Indian Ocean restaurant, Ashton-Under-Lyne, Lancashire, UK, on October 9, 2007.

☆ **Cookie tower** The Mt. Wilson Vista Council Girl Scouts erected a 5-ft. 4-in. (1.62-m) cookie tower at Paseo Colorado, Pasadena, California, U.S.A., on February 29, 2008.

☆ **LARGEST RESTAURANT** The Bawabet Dimashq (Damascus Gate) restaurant in Damascus, Syria, has 6,014 seats and employs up to 1,800 staff during peak seasons. "In this part of the world, all people care about is their stomachs," says general manager Muhannad Samman, "so the food has to be the best."

☆ **Stack of pancakes** Krunoslav Budiselic (Croatia) created a free-standing stack of 627 pancakes—each 9–10 in. (23–25 cm) wide—at the Grand Hotel Toplice in Terme Catez, Slovenia, on August 26, 2008. The stack took 22 hours to complete and reached a total height of 2 ft. 5 in. (74 cm).

☆ **Champagne-glass pyramid** Luuk Broos (Netherlands) and his team created a Champagne fountain comprising 43,680 glasses, layered in an incredible 63 stories, at the Wijnegem Shopping Center in Belgium on January 25, 2008.

☆ **Chocolate sculpture** A chocolate Christmas tree measuring 21 ft. 4 in. (6.5 m) tall was created by pastry chef Justo Almendrote (Spain) and unveiled in Madrid, Spain, on December 10, 2008. Approximately 661 lb. (300 kg) of white chocolate was used.

LONGEST . . .

☆ **Hot dog** A hot dog measuring 375 ft. (114.32 m) was made by Empacadora Ponderosa (Mexico) in Monterrey, Mexico, on September 27, 2008.

★ **Line of sandwiches** A line of sandwiches measuring 5,609 ft. 11 in. (1,545.3 m) was made by the Serravalle Scrivia shopping center on March 8, 2009, in Alessandria, Italy.

★ **LARGEST SCONE** A scone weighing 110 lb. (49.89 kg) and measuring 3 ft. 2 in. (1 m) in diameter was made by Mary, Nick, and Amy Lovering of Sandford's Bakery in Torrington, Devon, UK, on January 21, 2009. The ingredients included 58 lb. (26.3 kg) of flour, 35 lb. (15.87 kg) of clotted cream, and 12 lb. (5.44 kg) of strawberry jam.

★**String of licorice** The Junee Licorice and Chocolate Factory (Australia) made a licorice string measuring 800 ft. 6 in. (244 m) in Junee, New South Wales, Australia, on March 8, 2008.

☆**Line of pizzas** Chicago Town Pizzas (UK) produced a line of pizzas measuring 1,161 ft. (353.9 m) in Preston, UK, on December 10, 2008.

HEAVIEST . . .

Pumpkin Joseph Jutras (U.S.A.) presented a pumpkin weighing 1,689 lb. (766.12 kg) at the Topsfield Fair in Topsfield, Massachusetts, U.S.A., on September 29, 2007.

☆ **LARGEST BOTTLE OF WINE The world's largest bottle of wine measures 7 ft. 10 in. (2.40 m) tall and contains 127 gal. (480 liters). The production of the wine bottle was organized by Emil Eberle (Switzerland) and Weinlaubenhof Kracher (Austria). The bottle was filled with 2005 Grand Cuvée TBA NV no. 7 wine in Rehetobel, Switzerland, on October 9, 2007. The bottle has a diameter of 2 ft. 2 in. (68 cm) and weighs 1,388 lb. (630 kg).**

JUNE 24: Wazir Muhammand, son of Abbass Ali Jagirani (Pakistan), had the world's **heaviest kidney stone** at 21.87 oz. (620 g). It was removed from his right kidney in Sindh, Pakistan, on this day in 2008.

☆**LARGEST BURGER COMMERCIALLY AVAILABLE** A burger weighing a jaw-dropping 164.8 lb. (74.75 kg) is available for $399 on the menu at Mallie's Sports Grill & Bar in Southgate, Michigan, U.S.A., as of August 29, 2008. If you're feeling hungry, please notify the restaurant 24 hours in advance!

FOOD FEATS

Largest feasts

★**Cooked meat:** A giant banquet of chicken, lamb, pork, and beef weighing 57,639 lb. (26,145 kg) was prepared by La Pastoral Social y Amigos for a charity event at La Asociacion Rural de Paraguay in Mariano Roque Alonso, Paraguay, on October 26, 2008.

★**Ceviche:** See p. 189

★**Cooked fish:** The Polish Union of America and visitors to the Polish Heritage Festival (both U.S.A.) ate 2,552 fish dishes, all provided by Krolick's Bar-B-Q, in Hamburg, New York, U.S.A., on May 30, 2008.

★**Mixed seafood:** South Coast Tourism and Wozani Africa Events (both South Africa) prepared 3,834 lb. (1,739 kg) of large sea fish, sardines, prawns, mussels, and calamari and served it to 7,200 visitors at an outdoor event held at Silver Beach, Port Edward, South Africa, on July 19, 2008.

20: the **most eggs held by hand,** achieved by Zdenek Bradac (Czech Republic) at Sheffield Castle College, Sheffield, South Yorkshire, UK, on December 20, 2007.

☆Farthest Curly Wurly stretch Helen Weddle (UK) stretched a Curly Wurly—a chocolate-covered caramel candy bar—a distance of 5 ft. 1 in. (156.8 cm) at Magna Science Centre, Rotherham, UK, on July 26, 2007. Cadbury's candy usually measures 7.4–7.8 in. (19–20 cm) long, despite its advertising slogan of "miles of chewy toffee . . ."!

★Most noodle portions prepared (3 minutes) Noodle chef Fei Wang (China) of Inn Noodle (London) prepared eight noodle portions in three minutes at Borough Market, London, UK, on October 10, 2008. The record was attempted as part of the *Gordon Ramsay's Cookalong Live* TV show.

During the same series of shows—in which chef Ramsay attempted (and failed) various head-to-head culinary challenges—Paul Kelly (UK) of Kelly Turkey Farms set the record for the **★fastest time to pluck three turkeys,** doing so in 11 min. 30.16 sec. at Little Claydon Farm, Essex, UK, on November 13, 2008.

Salmon monger Darren Matson (UK) of H. Forman & Son appeared on the show and established the **★fastest time to bone and slice a salmon** (1 min. 24.18 sec.), also at Borough Market on October 10, 2008.

★Fastest time to fillet a 40-lb. fish It took fish vendor Duncan Lucas (UK) just 4 min. 25.31 sec. to fillet and portion a 40-lb. (18-kg) fish—at M & J Seafood, London, UK, on October 1, 2008.

☆TALLEST CAKE Students and staff at the Hakasima-Nilasari Culinary School baked a 108-ft. 3-in.-tall (33-m) cake to celebrate the Amazing Christmas event in Senayan City, Jakarta, Indonesia, from November 28 to December 8, 2008. The cake weighed 19.99 tons (18.14 metric tonnes) and included:
- 3,571 lb. (1,620 kg) sugar
- 3,571 lb. (1,620 kg) margarine
- 357 lb. (162 kg) milk powder
- 535 lb. (243 kg) chocolate powder
- 7,143 lb. (3,240 kg) eggs
- 211 pints (100 liters) liquid sugar.

JUNE 25: The **highest Scrabble score** recorded is 1,049, accomplished by Phil Appleby (UK). The winning match was played on June 25, 1989 at Wormley, Hertfordshire, UK.

☆ **LONGEST CURRY DELIVERY**
Newspaper journalists Jon Wise and James Crisp (both UK, left and right, respectively) ordered a vegetable biryani and pilau rice from The Raj Mahal Restaurant in Christchurch, New Zealand, to the *Daily Sport* offices in Manchester, UK, where the pair work. Measuring the distance between the two points in a straight line, the curry traveled more than 11,701 miles (18,830 km) by the time it arrived at its destination on February 29, 2008.

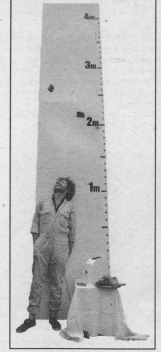

★ **Largest fruit mosaic** The People's Government of Pingyuan County and the local committee of the Communist Party of China created a mosaic consisting of 372,525 fruits in Pingyuan County, Guangdong Province, China, on December 1, 2008. The mosaic was created for the county's Fourth Navel Orange Tourism Festival, had an area of 23,895 ft.^{2} (2,220 m^2), and showed the county's flower and pictograms commemorating the achievement of its fruit growers.

☆ **Most Big Macs consumed** Donald Gorske (U.S.A.) consumed his 23,000th McDonald's Big Mac on August 17, 2008. He is now in his 37th consecutive year of eating Big Macs on a daily basis.

★ **HIGHEST-POPPING TOASTER** Freddie Yauner (UK) designed and built a toaster that can toast a slice of bread and eject it to a height of 8 ft. 6 in. (2.60 m), as verified at the Guinness World Records offices in London, UK, on June 13, 2008. Just the thing for a high-class breakfast!

JUNE 26: Jennifer Capriati (U.S.A., b. March 29, 1976) was just 14 years 89 days old when she competed in her first match on June 26, 1990, and became the **youngest person to win a match at Wimbledon.**

Fastest Eaters

★ **Chocolate orange:** A chocolate orange is a ball of chocolate mixed with orange oil that is divided into 20 segments. Robert Jones (UK) unwrapped and ate an entire chocolate orange in 4 min. 34.25 sec. at the Balham Bowls Club in London, UK, on November 29, 2008.

☆ **Lemon (1):** Ashrita Furman (U.S.A.) peeled and ate a lemon in 10.97 seconds at the Panorama Café in Jamaica, New York City, U.S.A., on August 24, 2007.

☆ **Lemon (3):** Gekidan Hitori (Japan) peeled and ate three lemons in 1 min. 33 sec. on the set of *Waratte Iitomo! Zokango* at Studio Alta, Tokyo, Japan, on April 28, 2008.

★ **MOST COCKTAILS MADE IN AN HOUR** Christopher Raph (U.S.A.) made 662 cocktails in one hour in Minneapolis, Minnesota, U.S.A., on April 16, 2009. All the drinks were different and included at least three ingredients.

☆ **MOST PEOPLE TOSSING PANCAKES** A record 405 people took part in a pancake toss hosted by Bram Zwiers on the television show *Mooi! Weer de Leeuw* in Almere, the Netherlands, on October 24, 2008.

JUNE 27: The world's **first electronic cash dispenser** was installed at a branch of Barclays Bank in Enfield, Middlesex, UK, on this day in 1967.

☆ MOST EGGS CRUSHED WITH THE HEAD IN ONE MINUTE Serial record breaker Ashrita Furman (U.S.A.) crushed 80 eggs with his head in one minute at the Panorama Café, Jamaica, New York City, U.S.A. on December 10, 2008. But this achievement is no flash in the frying pan—Furman also has the distinction of holding the **most Guinness World Records**, with a grand total of 164 records set, broken, or re-established.

★ **Pickled eggs (3):** Jonathan Armstrong (UK) ate three medium-sized pickled hen's eggs in 2 min. 27.02 sec. on August 19, 2008, at the Jeremy Bentham pub in London, UK.

★ **Hamburgers (3 min.):** The most hamburgers eaten in three minutes is five, by Sean Durnal (U.S.A.) in Fort Scott, Kansas, U.S.A., on July 11, 2008.

Cream crackers: This food challenge is a classic Guinness World Records achievement that for years stood at about the 3-minute mark. Ambrose Mendy (UK), however, smashed this time by eating three crackers in 34.78 seconds at the studios of LBC radio, London, UK, on May 9, 2005.

☆ **Longest line of satay** Staff at the Kopitiam Group (Singapore) put together a chicken satay measuring 459 ft. 4 in. (140.02 m) at Lau Pa Sat, Singapore, on July 21, 2007. Over 330 lb. (150 kg) of chicken and 700 bamboo sticks were used to make the satay.

★ **Longest chocolate bar** Bakers Pasticceria Beddini created a ludicrously lengthy chocolate bar measuring 22 ft. 10 in. (6.98 m) long and 3 ft. 4 in. (1.01 m) wide for the Piazza Umbra shopping center in Trevi, Italy, on April 5, 2009.

★ **Tallest sugar sculpture** The tallest sugar sculpture ever (created in 11 hours) measured 16 ft. 4.3 in. (4.97 m) and was made by Regis Courivaud (France) in Minneapolis, Minnesota, U.S.A., on April 21, 2006, during the filming of Guinness World Records Week for the Food Network channel.

★ **Parmesan wheels cracked** When it comes to cracking cheese, none can beat Whole Foods Market (U.S.A.). Staff at 176 Whole Foods Market stores cracked open 176 parmigiano reggiano wheels simultaneously at stores across North America and the UK on April 12, 2008.

JUN. 28: The **largest band** ever assembled was formed of 20,100 members at the Ullevaal Stadium in Oslo, Norway, from Norges Musikkorps Forbund bands on this day in 1964.

MOST EXPENSIVE . . .

★**Computer** The Japanese-owned Earth Simulator, which was completed in May 2002, cost an incredible $400,000,000. Although no longer the most powerful computer in the world, at the time of its construction, the *New York Times* reported it to be "so powerful that it matches the raw processing power of the 20 fastest American computers combined." The Earth Simulator is available to international projects that need to simulate atmospheric, climate, or oceanographic conditions.

☆**Internet address domain name** The internet domain name sex.com was sold by Gary Kremen (U.S.A.) for a reported $12 million in 2005, according to *Forbes*. The rights to this lucrative URL were fought over in court for many years.

★**Lunch date sold at auction** A Hong Kong–based investor paid $2.1 million on June 28, 2008 for a lunch date with billionaire investor Warren Buffett. Zhao Danyang (Hong Kong) enjoyed a meal for himself and seven friends accompanied by Mr. Buffett at Smith & Wollensky's steakhouse in New York City, U.S.A. All proceeds from the auction went to charity.

MOST EXPENSIVE VINTAGE CAR SOLD AT AUCTION A UK collector paid £3,521,500 ($7,242,916) for the world's oldest surviving Rolls-Royce at Bonhams auctioneers, London, UK, on December 3, 2007. The two-seater, 10-hp car was manufactured in Manchester, UK, in 1904, which puts it in the "veteran" (pre-1905) category.

Batman memorabilia sold at auction A Batmobile used in *Batman Forever* (U.S.A., 1995) sold at the Kruse International collector car auction in Las Vegas, U.S.A., in September 2006 for $335,000 to John O'Quinn (U.S.A.). O'Quinn spent $690,000 on a 1975 Ford Escort GL once owned by Pope John Paul II at the 1995 Kruse auction.

★Book A book titled *Michelangelo: La Dotta Mano* costs $155,000 (€100,000) per single edition. Each handmade copy takes six months to create and weighs 62 lb. (28.1 kg), as the front cover is made from white marble.

★Turntable The price of the Continuum Caliburn turntable, manufactured by Continuum Audio Laboratories (Australia), reaches $112,000, depending on the finish. The tone arm alone costs an additional $12,000. The magnesium platter is magnetically levitated and suspended in a vacuum to ensure that the playing disc is unaffected by external vibrations.

Insect A giant 3-in. (80-mm) stag beetle (*Dorcus hopei*) was reported to have been sold for ¥10,035,000 ($90,000) at a store in Tokyo, Japan, on August 19, 1999.

★Vacuum cleaner Vacuum cleaner manufacturer Electrolux celebrated its award-winning ErgoRapido model by teaming up with Gronowalski Crystal Fashion and designer Lukasz Jemiol (Poland) to make a unique Swarovski crystal encrusted cleaner. The bejewelled ErgoRapido comes with 3,730 Swarovski sparklers mounted on its body and is valued at $19,340.

BICYCLE A 24-carat gold-plated bicycle decorated with Swarovski crystals and featuring a hand-sewn leather saddle is sold by design firm Aurumania (Denmark) for €80,000 ($103,803), making it the most expensive bicycle commercially available. A limited edition of 10 bikes will be made.

FACT

A cheaper version without the crystals, and with the rims, handlebars, wheels, and chain made of hand-polished aluminum, is available for €20,000 ($25,930).

Most Expensive . . .

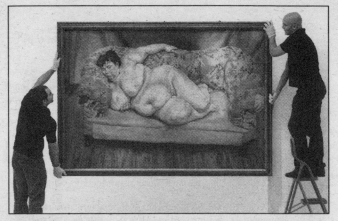

PAINTING BY A LIVING ARTIST SOLD AT AUCTION Lucian Freud's (UK, b. 1922) painting *Benefits Supervisor Sleeping*, painted in 1995, sold for $33.64 million at an auction held at Christie's in Manhattan, U.S.A., on May 13, 2008, making it the most expensive painting sold attributed to a living artist. The buyer was Russian billionaire Roman Abramovich.

Wine The most expensive wine commercially available is the Chateau d'Yquem Sauternes (1787), a sweet, golden yellow dessert wine from Bordeaux, France, priced at an average of $60,000, depending on the retailer.

★Computer mouse Swiss manufacturer Pat Says Now produces the world's most expensive computer mouse. Cast from 18-carat white gold and set with 59 individual diamonds, the mouse retails for $24,180.

☆ POP STAR'S COSTUME SOLD AT AUCTION Elvis Presley's (U.S.A.) white peacock jumpsuit was bought for $300,000 in a sale by online auctioneer GottaHaveIt.com on August 7, 2008. The costume, which he wore on stage extensively during a five-month tour in 1974, was one of Elvis' favorites.

JUNE 29: The **jigsaw puzzle with the most pieces** featured 212,323 pieces and had an overall measurement of 35 ft. 5 in. × 38 ft. 4 in. (10.8 × 11.68 m) when assembled in Singapore on June 29, 2002.

★ **BABY'S PACIFIER** A $17,000 solid white-gold pacifier, studded with 278 diamonds, is available for sale from American company www.personalizedpacifiers.com. Although not recommended for actual use, the pacifier does feature a silicone nipple and moving handle.

★ **BOTTLE OF WATER SOLD AT AUCTION** A 1-liter bottle of Evian natural mineral water sold for $23,000 to Shazzie Hoss (UAE) at an auction held in Dubai, UAE, on November 12, 2008. The handcrafted bottle, produced by French designer Christian Lacroix, was sold to raise funds for the Dubai Autism Center.

PIZZA A pizza topped with onion puree, white truffle paste, fontina cheese, baby mozzarella, pancetta, cep mushrooms, and wild mizuna lettuce, and garnished with fresh shavings of a rare Italian white truffle, is regularly sold for $178 (£100) in Gordon Ramsay's Maze restaurant, London, UK.

JUNE 30: Jean François Gravelet, aka Charles Blòndin (France), made the first crossing of the Niagara Falls on a 3-in. (76-mm) rope 1,100 ft. (335 m) long and 160 ft. (47.75 m) above the falls on June 30, 1859.

★**Computer keyboard** The Happy Hacking Keyboard Professional HP Japan, produced by an affiliate of Fujitsu, retails at $4,240. Its extreme price is due in part to the fact that its keys are hand-coated in Urushi lacquer and then dusted with gold.

PLANET IN DANGER

☆**Largest consumer of electricity** It is estimated that the United States consumed 3.892 billion KW/hr in 2007, which amounts to nearly a quarter of the whole world's consumption of electricity in that year, which came to 17.480 billion KW/hr. China was the second-largest consumer with a rate of 3.271 trillion KW/hr.

☆**Largest producer of carbon dioxide per capita** Citizens of Qatar were responsible for the emission of 56.40 tons of carbon dioxide per person in 2004. Overall, in the same year, the U.S.A. produced more CO_2 than any other country, with emissions reaching 6.48 billion tons. CO_2 is a potent greenhouse gas produced during the combustion of solid, liquid, and gaseous fuels.

★**COUNTRY WITH THE MOST THREATENED MAMMALS** Indonesia has an estimated 667 mammal species—more than any other country—of which 146 are considered by the United Nations to be "threatened." The International Union for Conservation of Nature and Natural Resources lists 1,104 mammal species that face "a higher risk of global extinction"; Indonesia's threatened mammals, therefore, represent about 13% of the world total.

··

JULY 1: The **youngest female golfer to score a hole-in-one** is Soona Lee-Tolley (U.S.A.), aged 5 years 103 days at the par 3 7th at Manhattan Woods Golf Club, West Nyack, New York, U.S.A., on July 1, 2007.

··

★ COUNTRY WITH THE LARGEST AREA OF PROTECTED LAND
According to the United Nations Environment Program World Conservation Monitoring Center (UNEP-WCMC), a total of 34.2% of the land in Venezuela is protected. A protected area is defined as "an area of land and/or sea especially dedicated to the protection and maintenance of biological diversity, and of natural and associated cultural resources, and managed through legal or other effective means."

☆ **Highest levels of carbon dioxide** According to the World Meteorological Organization, the atmospheric abundance of carbon dioxide, a powerful greenhouse gas, was 383.1 ppm (parts per million) in 2007. This is the highest in recorded history and represents a 37% increase since the mid-18th century.

★ **Largest producer of sulfur dioxide** China is responsible for the greatest production of sulfur dioxide—the primary contributor to acid rain—pumping out over 37.6 million tons yearly.

Sulfur dioxide forms when fuel containing sulfur, such as coal and oil, is burned, when gasoline is extracted from oil, or when metals are extracted from ore.

LAST CHANCE TO SEE . . .

Among the species under threat in Indonesia are: the binturong (*Arctictis binturong,* opposite page left), also known as the Asian bearcat; the Bornean orangutan (*Pongo pygmaeus,* opposite page center); and the Javan rhino (*Rhinoceros sondaicus,* opposite page right), with fewer than 60 in existence.

JULY 2: On this day in 2002, Steve Fossett (U.S.A.) completed the **fastest solo circumnavigation of the globe in a balloon,** taking *Bud Light Spirit of Freedom* around the world in 13 days 8 hr. 33 min.

★ COUNTRY WITH THE LOWEST WATER POVERTY INDEX (WPI) The Water Poverty Index (WPI) measures the impact of water scarcity and water provision on human populations. The WPI is a number between 0 and 100, where a low score indicates water poverty and a high score indicates good water provision. Niger is recognized by the Food and Agriculture Organization of the United Nations as having the lowest Water Poverty Index, with a mark of 35.2, and is followed closely by Ethiopia with 35.4. WPI is based on five factors: resources, access, capacity, use, and environment. Finland has the highest Water Poverty Index with 78.0, while Canada sits in second place with a WPI of 77.7.

☆**Highest rate of glass recycling** In 2007, the people of Switzerland recycled 352,000 tons of glass, which is 95% of the 370,000 tons of glass products they consumed—the highest rate of glass recycling in the world. By comparison, Germany recycled 87% of its glass and the UK managed 57%.

Largest reforestation
The Chinese State Forestry Administration announced the beginning of a 10-year reforestation project to plant up an area the size of Sweden in May 2002. The replanted area, representing 5% of China's land mass, will measure about 169,884 miles^2 (440,000 km^2) and should offset some of the environmental problems caused by logging in China.

★ Greatest ocean pollutant According to the UN Environment Program, plastic bags account for over 50% of all marine litter, with 46,000 pieces of plastic for every 1 mile^2 (2.5 km^2) of ocean. The Blue Ocean Society for Marine Conservation estimates that more than 1 million birds and 100,000 marine mammals die each year because of this plastic.

JULY 3: The **first transmission of color television** occurred on this day in 1928 when John Logie Baird (UK) completed a demonstration at his studios in Long Acre, London, UK.

MOST UBIQUITOUS CONSUMER ITEM

Estimates for the global manufacture of plastic bags number in the trillions, making them the most abundant consumer product in the world. In the USA alone, consumers throw away 100 billion plastic bags every year; as plastic bags are manufactured from petroleum, this is equivalent to dumping nearly 12 million barrels of oil annually.

★ **LARGEST BOTTLE ISLAND** The world's largest island made entirely from plastic bottles has been created just off Mexico by British expatriate Richard Sowa. The island is composed of over 100,000 empty, discarded plastic bottles held together in fishing nets and currently measures 47 ft. 10 in. × 41 ft. 11 in. (14.6 m × 12.8 m). The waterborne construction is growing ever larger in spiraling loops each day as Sowa canoes back and forth between his artificial island and the Mexican mainland, bringing more bottles to add to it. It even has a sand beach, a cabana, and a compost toilet.

JULY 4: The **fastest time to boardsail across the English Channel** is 1 hr. 4 min. 33 sec., set by Baron Arnaud de Rosnay (France) on this day in

☆ **FASTEST GROWING COMPONENT OF MUNICIPAL WASTE** According to the World Resources Institute, electronic waste is the fastest growing component of municipal waste worldwide with 22–55 million tons generated annually. In the U.S. alone, 14–20 million PCs are thrown out each year.

Warmest year A NASA report from January 2008 reveals that 2005 was the planet's warmest year on record. The report also revealed that Earth's 14 warmest years have all occurred since 1990.

THE ECONOMY

☆**FTSE 100** *The Financial Times Stock Exchange (FTSE) 100 index is a stock index of the UK's 100 most valuable companies, as listed on the London Stock Exchange, and is the most commonly used indicator of the health of the UK market.*

•The ☆**biggest rise of the FTSE 100** was posted on November 24, 2008, when it rose 372.00 to 4,152.96, a surge of 9.84%. It came on the back of news that the U.S. Treasury had pumped over $13 billion into the troubled banking giant Citigroup.

•The FTSE 100 closed at the end of 2008 at a level of 4,423.34, down from its opening level of 6,456.90—the ☆**greatest annual percentage fall of the FTSE 100.** This is a fall of more than 30%, making it the ☆**index's**

....

JULY 5: On this day in 2001, six diners at Petrus, London, UK, spent £44,007 ($61,941) on one meal, making it the **most expensive meal per head.** The majority of the bill went on five bottles of wine.

....

worst year in its 24-year history. This is the UK's second largest slide of all
time, overshadowed only by the 55.3% fall of the FTSE All-Share Index in
1974.
•The **largest daily points loss on the FTSE 100** occurred on September 11,
2001, following the terrorist attacks in the U.S.A., when the index dropped
287.70 points.

☆**Dow Jones Industrial Average** *The Dow Jones Industrial Average
(DJIA) is an index compiled to monitor the health of the U.S. stock market;
it is based on the stock prices of 30 of the country's biggest companies.*
•On October 10, 2008, the DJIA swung during the day from a low of
7,882.51 to a high of 8,901.28, the ☆**largest swing ever recorded on the
DJIA.** The day closed at 8,451.19, down 128.00. The top 10 largest swings
ever on the DJIA occurred during the financial crises of 2008.
•The Dow closed on October 13, 2008, at 9,387.61, following a gain of
936.42—the ☆**largest daily points gain on the DJIA.**
•On October 9, 2007, the Dow closed at a record high of 14,164.53—the
☆**highest closing of the DJIA** on record. Two days later, it peaked intraday
at 14,198.10 but had fallen below the October 9 figure by the close of day.

☆**Country with the most billionaires** According to *Forbes,* 42% of
the world's billionaires live in the U.S.A. Of the 1,125 world billionaires
identified, 469 are from the U.S.A.

OUR NATIONAL DEBT:
$10,149,940,844,092.
YOUR *Family share* $86,019.
THE NATIONAL DEBT CLOCK

☆**LARGEST NATIONAL DEBT** The U.S. national debt surpassed the
**$10-trillion mark for the first time on September 30, 2008—rendering
the famous Durst National Debt Clock in Times Square, New York City,
U.S.A., redundant. The sign, which clocks up the debt with every
passing second, ran out of digits and required a hasty makeover.**

CASH CAREFUL . . .

Warren Buffett is an investor and CEO of the conglomerate Berkshire Hathaway. Despite his great wealth, Buffett is notoriously frugal. He still lives in the same modest house in Omaha, Nebraska, U.S.A., that he bought in 1958, and when he married his second wife, Astrid, in 2006, he purchased the wedding ring from a discount jewelery store.

☆ **RICHEST PERSON** On March 5, 2008, Warren Buffett (U.S.A., pictured) ousted Microsoft's Bill Gates (U.S.A.) from the top of the *Forbes* rich list for the first time in 13 years. Buffet's wealth was estimated at $62 billion while Gates' was a mere $58 billion. But the global credit crunch hit Buffett's fortune hard, reducing his wealth to $37 billion, while Gates fared slightly better and by April 2009 was once again the world's richest man with a $40-billion fortune.

★ **Greatest budget deficit** According to a White House estimate released in July 2008, the federal budget deficit will reach $482 billion by the end of 2009. A deficit occurs when a country spends more money than it makes. Between 1998 and 2001, the U.S.A. was in surplus—the opposite, making more than it spent—but the sagging economy has sent debts through the roof.

★ **COUNTRY WITH THE GREATEST ECONOMIC FREEDOM** According to the 2009 Economic Freedom Index, the citizens of Hong Kong, China, enjoy the most economic freedom. This is defined by the index as "the fundamental right of every human to control his or her own labor and property . . . to work, produce, consume, and invest in any way they please, with that freedom both protected and unconstrained by the state." Hong Kong has held its position at the top of the chart for 15 consecutive years.

JULY 6: The **oldest main draw Wimbledon tennis champion** is Martina Navratilova (U.S.A.), who was 46 years 261 days when she won the mixed doubles with Leander Paes (India) on this day in 2003.

☆**LARGEST POINTS FALL ON THE DOW JONES INDUSTRIAL AVERAGE (DJIA)** On September 20, 2008—"Dark Monday"— the DJIA suffered a loss of 777.68 points, the largest one-day drop in its 114-year history. A dive of over 700 points was recorded shortly before 2 p.m. when the U.S. Congress began to vote on the federal government's $700-billion "bailout bill" designed to protect the financial markets and taxpayers.

☆ **MOST ZEROS ON A BANKNOTE** The highest denomination currency note is a $100-billion-dollar bill that featured 11 zeroes. It was issued in Zimbabwe on July 22, 2008, and because of inflation at that time it was enough to buy three eggs.

★**Poorest citizens** According to the World Resources Institute's Earth-trends report for the period 1989–2004, a total of 70.8% of the people of Nigeria existed on less than $1 a day (the equivalent today of $1.55), making it the nation with the poorest citizens.

The poorest nation, when based on the per person share of all monies made by a country's economic activity—that is, the ☆**country with the lowest Gross Domestic Product (GDP) per head of population**—is Burundi in Africa, with a figure of just $120 per head (as of 2006). By contrast, Luxembourg has the ☆**highest GDP per citizen,** with a figure of $87,490 per head.

★ **Lowest price for fuel** Given the large oil reserves in Venezuela, drivers in that country pay 3.5 cents per liter. The same amount of unleaded fuel cost U.S. drivers 51 cents in February 2009.

RUNNERS-UP

The other top 10 countries listed by the OECD are:

2.	Japan	127	7.	U.S.A.	109
3.	Norway	123	8.	UK	107
4.	Denmark	117	9.	Ireland	105
5.	Iceland	112	10.	Finland	101
6.	Sweden	110			

CRIME

★ **Largest ship hijacked** On November 15, 2008, pirates captured one of the world's largest oil tankers, the MV *Sirius Star* (UAE), off the coast of Somalia, East Africa. The 1,100-ft.-long (330-m) VLCC (very large crude carrier)—which has a gross tonnage of 162,252 tons (147,192 metric tons)—was bound for the U.S.A. with a crew of 25 and a load of crude oil valued at $110 million. The ship was taken to the Somali port of Haradheere and a ransom was demanded from the owners. The ship was eventually released on January 9, 2009, after an undisclosed sum was paid.

★ **First use of Nintendo for criminal investigation** Japanese police have used the Nintendo Wii Channel to generate a "wanted" poster of a hit-and-run suspect. Police authorities usually employ artists or photofit soft-

★ FIRST ARREST FOR MURDER OF A VIRTUAL VICTIM In October 2008, a 43-year-old piano teacher was arrested in Miyazáki, Japan, after killing her online husband. The woman had been unexpectedly "divorced" in the context of the role-playing game *Maple Story*, in which avatars (such as the one pictured left) can marry. She was jailed on suspicion of illegally accessing a computer and manipulating data using her gaming partner's ID and password to log on to the game and "murder" her partner. If convicted, she could be jailed or fined up to $5,000.

ware for such purposes. However, by selecting a range of face shapes, hairstyles, ears, and other features using the Nintendo "Mii" customizable avatar facility, police were able to create the mugshot of the male suspect. The wanted poster was displayed at the scene of the car accident next to a photograph of the type of car involved.

★ First legal summons served online In December 2008, Australian lawyers Mark MacCormack and Jason Oliver created Internet and legal history when they used the Facebook social networking site to serve legal documents on a couple who had defaulted on their mortgage. A Supreme Court judge in the Australia Capital Territory ruled that court notices served on the site were binding. Having tracked down one of the missing people by putting their email address into Facebook, the lawyers found information that was identical to that on the mortgage application, and also details of the second defendant.

★ BIGGEST MILITARY COMPUTER HACK In 2002, Gary McKinnon (UK) was accused of hacking into 97 U.S. military computers, as well as rendering 300 computers at a U.S. Navy weapons station unusable after the 9/11 terrorist attacks in New York. In 2005, the U.S. began extradition proceedings, alleging that McKinnon caused damage in the order of $800,000. McKinnon has admitted that his hacking constituted an offense in the UK and, as of March 2009, is contesting the extradition request in the UK courts.

JULY 7: Col. Ernest Loftus (Zimbabwe) had the **longest-kept daily diary.** He began on May 4, 1896, at the age of 12 and continued it until his death 91 years later, on this day in 1987, aged 103 years 178 days.

EXECUTIONS 2008

	COUNTRY	NUMBER	METHOD
1	China	1,718*	Lethal injection, shooting
2	Iran	346*	Hanging
3	Saudi Arabia	102*	Beheading
4	U.S.A.	37	Injection, electrocution
5	Pakistan	36*	Hanging
6	Iraq	34*	Hanging
7	Vietnam	19*	Shooting
8	Afghanistan	17	Shooting
9	North Korea	15*	Shooting
10	Japan	15	Hanging

*Confirmed figure, actual figure may be higher
Source: Amnesty International
In total, 2,390 people were executed in 2008 and at least 8,864 people were sentenced to death.

★ **Country with the most murders** According to the Tenth United Nations Survey of Crime Trends and Operations of Criminal Justice Systems Report, the country with the highest number of intentional homicides in 2006, the latest year for which information is available, is India with 32,481. The U.S.A. was in second place with 17,034. Not all nations respond to the survey.

★ **HIGHEST INCIDENCE OF PIRACY (YEAR)** According to the International Maritime Bureau, piracy and armed robbery attacks against ships grew significantly in 2008 with a total of 293 incidents—an increase of 11.4% on the previous year and an all-time high for modern piracy.

HIGHEST HIJACK RANSOM

The *MV Faina* (*pictured above*), a Ukrainian vessel loaded with Russian tanks, was hijacked off the coast of Somalia by Somali pirates on September 25, 2008. The ship was eventually released after a ransom of $3.2 million was paid on February 5, 2009.

JULY 8: Svetlana Pankratova (Russia) has the world's **longest legs,** which were verified as measuring 51.9 in. (132 cm) long in Torremolinos, Spain, on July 8, 2003.

★**FIRST INTERNATIONAL CRIMINAL COURT** The International Criminal Court (ICC) came into being on July 1, 2002, and is the world's only permanent international criminal court. The ICC deals with the most serious crimes of international concern such as genocide and war crimes. The official seat of the court is in The Hague, the Netherlands (above left).

The ★first trial at the ICC began on January 26, 2009, when Congolese warlord Thomas Lubanga (above right) appeared on war crimes charges for his role in the civil war in the Democratic Republic of Congo.

DID YOU KNOW?

Although the official seat of the ICC is in The Hague, International Criminal Court proceedings may take place anywhere.

★**Richest drug dealer** Joaquin Guzman Loera (Mexico), head of the Sinaloa Cartel and Mexico's most wanted man, has amassed a fortune of $1 billion from drug trafficking. The U.S. government is offering a $5 million reward for the capture of the 5-ft.-tall (152-cm) Loera, who escaped from a Mexican prison in 2001 in a laundry van. He is the second alleged drug dealer to make *Forbes'* annual billionaire list—Colombia's Pablo Escobar was the world's seventh richest man in 1989.

JULY 9: The **largest limbo dance** involved 1,150 participants at the Music Under the Stars World Festival 2006 at the Chamizal National Memorial in El Paso, Texas, U.S.A., on July 9, 2006.

★ **LARGEST PONZI FRAUD** A "Ponzi" scheme is a form of fraudulent investment in which returns are paid for by subsequent investors and not by the profit on real investments. They are named after Charles Ponzi (Italy/U.S.A., above right) who, in 1920, became notorious for establishing such a scheme.

The ★ **largest Ponzi fraud** was perpetrated by Bernard Lawrence Madoff (U.S.A., above left), a former chairman of the NASDAQ stock market and hedge fund manager. According to a complaint filed in December 2008 by the U.S. Attorney's Office and the FBI, Madoff told at least three employees that he had operated a giant "Ponzi" scheme that had lost investors $50 billion (£35 billion).

★ **Largest hashish haul** On June 9, 2008, 261 tons of hashish were seized in Khandahar, Afghanistan, by the UK's Special Boat Service and local commandos. Weighing the equivalent of 30 double-decker buses, the haul had a street value of $338 million.

★ **Largest ecstasy haul** The largest ecstasy haul ever recovered consisted of 15 million pills imported into Australia as 3,000 cans of tomatoes. Announced on August 8, 2008, the 4.8-ton shipment was believed to have come from Italy and had an estimated street value of A$440 million ($400.3 million).

★ **Most advanced biometric security method** A new biometric system from the Hitachi Company (Japan) is able to identify people from the unique pattern of veins inside their fingers, and it has been introduced into security systems in Europe and Japan. It is the fastest, and most secure, biometric method of identifying people.

★ **Largest reward for counter-terrorism** Osama bin Laden (Saudi Arabia), the terrorist leader of Al-Qaeda, has been on the FBI top ten wanted list since 1999, with a price of $25 million on his head. In July 2008,

JULY 10: When Willie Jones (U.S.A.) was admitted to a hospital in Atlanta, Georgia, U.S.A., on this day in 1980, his temperature was found to be 115.7°F (46.5°C), the **highest body temperature ever recorded.**

With fears growing that the threat from Al-Qaeda was stronger than at the time of the 9/11 terror attacks, the U.S. Senate voted to double the reward for the death or capture of bin Laden to $50 million.

☆**Greatest bank robbery** A gang of 6–10 robbers, previously "operating" as a landscape company at a nearby building, dug a tunnel measuring 256 ft. (78 m) long at 13 ft. (4 m) below street level, which ended directly below the Banco Central in Fortaleza, Brazil. On the weekend of August 6–7, 2005, the robbers broke through 3 ft. 7 in. (1.1 m) of steel-reinforced concrete to enter the bank vault and steal an estimated 164,755,150 Brazilian reais ($71.3 million).

TERRORISM & WARFARE

★**First European Union task force mission** In response to the growing problem of piracy off the coast of Somalia, the European Union, the political super-bloc of Europe consisting of 27 member states, took the decision to deploy a naval force to the area as of December 15, 2008, to take over the NATO mission there. It is the first naval task force in the bloc's history and it will assist in the delivery of food aid to Somalia, as well as increasing maritime security in the hazardous Somali waters.

★**First female combat pilot** Sabiha Gökçen (Turkey, b. March 21, 1913) enrolled in the Military Aviation Academy in Eskisehir, Turkey, in 1936 and undertook training at the First Aircraft Regiment there. She went on to fly fighter and bomber planes to become the first Turkish female aviator and the world's first female combat pilot.

★**Largest contributor to UN forces** In 2008, Pakistan was the largest contributor of police, military observers, and troops to UN peacekeeping missions, with a total of 11,135 personnel. It was closely followed by Bangladesh with 9,567 and India with 8,693.

JULY 11: The **most hamburgers eaten in three minutes** is five, and it was achieved by Sean Durnal (U.S.A.) in Fort Scott, Kansas, U.S.A., on July 11, 2008.

★ **OLDEST RESISTANCE HERO** On February 3, 2009, Andrée Peel (France) celebrated her 104th birthday, making her the oldest known surviving female member of the French Resistance. Known as Agent Rose, she helped to save 102 Allied pilots in a three-year period working for the Resistance during World War II.

☆**Highest defense budget** The U.S.A. has the world's largest defense budget, reported as $622 billion by the International Institute for Strategic Studies in 2007. The budget request for 2009 will see it maintain that position, as the White House is seeking a record $711 billion. The U.S. accounts for 48% of the world's military spending—its defense budget is greater than the next 44 highest-spending countries combined.

★**Most prolific executioner** Personally selected in 1926 by Stalin, leader of the former USSR, Vasili M. Blokhin (USSR) acted as chief executioner to the NKVD (People's Commissariat of Internal Affairs), where he led a company of executioners. Under him, they carried out most of the exe-

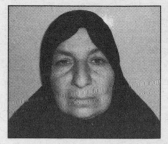

★ **MOST FEMALE SUICIDE BOMBERS RECRUITED** On January 21, 2009, in Baghdad, Iraq, Samira Ahmed Jassim (Iraq) was arrested on suspicion of recruiting more than 80 women to become suicide bombers. In a taped confession, Jassim—nicknamed "Mother of the Believers"— confirmed that at least 28 of the recruits had carried out attacks.

cutions ordered by Stalin. Not only is he recorded as having executed all significant prisoners of the regime, as well as many others by his own hand, he also personally executed 7,000 Polish officers at the Ostachkov prison camp in 1940 over precisely 28 nights—250 executions a night—thereby ranking him as the world's most prolific official executioner. He died in 1955.

★ **Largest EU mission** On December 9, 2008, the European Union (EU) commenced its largest mission ever, EULEX, when it deployed the first of nearly 1,900 officials to take over police, customs, and justice responsibilities from the United Nations staff in Kosovo. The EU officials will be supported by 1,100 local staff, and the aim is not to govern but to oversee the running of the courts, police, and customs services as well as helping the authorities to combat organized crime.

★ **Worst effect of weather in war** The worst weather, in military terms, was the extremely bad winter of 1941–42 during World War II, when Germany invaded Russia. The troops were badly equipped for the cold, with temperatures dropping to at least –40°F (–40°C)—bad by even Russian standards. Casualty figures for the German campaign and the Siege of Stalingrad vary; but for both sides by the beginning of 1943 the total casualty figure was probably over 250,000, with troops dying from the effects of cold weather, disease, starvation, exhaustion, and fighting.

MOST WANTED TERRORIST Osama bin Laden (Saudi Arabia), figurehead of the terrorist organization Al-Qaeda, is sought by many nations for terrorist activities. He is also alleged to have been an inspiration for those responsible for the terrorist attacks on the U.S.A. on September 11, 2001. According to the official count from the authorities, 2,749 people died as a result of the attacks, the **most individuals killed in a terrorist act.** A total of 157 people died aboard the two aircraft that crashed into the twin towers and a further 233 died in two other aircraft hijacked the same day.

★ **FIRST FEMALE FOUR-STAR GENERAL** On Friday, November 14, 2008, after 33 years in the U.S. Army and at the age of 55, Ann E. Dunwoody (U.S.A.) was promoted to full general rank—four stars—the first in the history of the U.S. armed forces.

★**Largest naval raid** On March 28, 1942, during World War II, the British Royal Navy initiated *Operation Chariot* to destroy the Normandie dock in St. Nazaire, France, the largest dry dock in the world at that time. HMS *Campbeltown,* an obsolete 1,090-ton (1,107-metric tonne) destroyer, was stripped out to reduce her draft for transit through the shallow waters to the dock, and the bows were packed with 4.9 tons (4.5 metric tonnes) of

★ **MOST U.N. MISSIONS (CONTINENT)** Africa is currently home to seven authorized United Nations peacekeeping operations: Central African Republic and Chad; Darfur; Sudan; Côte d'Ivoire; Liberia; DR Congo; and Western Sahara. In Europe and the Middle East there are three each, while there are two in Asia and the Pacific and one in the Americas. Pictured are Nigerian peacekeepers with the U.N. on a mission to Darfur.

JULY 12: The **highest speed to crash a motorcycle and survive** is an estimated 200 mph (322 km/h) by Ron Cook (U.S.A.) at El Mirage Dry Lake, California, U.S.A., on July 12, 1998.

★ **WORST YEAR OF AFGHAN INSURGENCY** With a total of 294 coalition military deaths, 2008 was the worst year of the Afghan insurgency since NATO operations started there. Civilian deaths are more difficult to ascertain; it has nonetheless been estimated that, based on media reports, the number of civilian deaths ranges from 4,800 to 7,000 since October 2001.

AFGHANISTAN

Afghanistan produced around 87% of the world's opium crop in 2005. More than 90% of the heroin in Britain alone comes from this one country.

---

high explosive attached to delayed fuses. At 1:34 a.m., the ship rammed the dock gates, and in the hours that followed, the ship was examined by German soldiers; at 11:35 a.m., the explosives blew up, killing the soldiers, destroying the dock, and putting it out of action until 1948.

★ **Most advanced long-range airborne surveillance system** With the introduction of the fifth and final new Sentinel R1 (spy jet) into Royal Air Force service on February 10, 2009, the UK armed forces have gained a long-range battlefield intelligence, target imaging, and surveillance capability that is the most advanced of its kind in the world. Located at RAF Waddington, Lincolnshire, UK, No. 5 (Army Cooperation) Squadron now has five modified Bombardier Global Express aircraft equipped with the Raytheon Airborne Stand-off Radar (ASTOR). This will provide high-quality radar images of a surveyed area, while the Moving Target Indicator (MTI) will detect moving vehicles operating in the area.

···

JULY 13: The **longest walk by a funambulist** (tightrope walker) is 11,368 ft. (3,465 m) by Henri Rochetain (France). The wire was placed across a gorge at Clermont Ferrand, France, on July 13, 1969.

···

GOLD

Most ductile element Gold is not only a precious metal, it's also exceptionally malleable and can even be spun into a thread suitable for embroidery. One gram of gold can be drawn to 1.4 miles (2.4 km), or 1 oz. to 43 miles (69.2 km).

Largest gold nugget The Holtermann Nugget, which weighed 7,257 oz. (7,560 troy oz.), was found on October 19, 1872, in the Beyers Holtermann Star of Hope mine in New South Wales, Australia. It contained some 2,534 oz. (2,640 troy oz.) of gold.

Largest bar of gold The largest manufactured pure gold bar weighs 551 lb. 2 oz. (250 kg) and was created by the Mitsubishi Materials Corporation on June 11, 2005, at the Naoshima Smelter & Refinery in Kagawa Prefecture, Japan.

Deepest mine With a depth of 12,391 ft. (3,777 m) as of 2005, the Savuka Mine in South Africa is the largest and deepest gold mine. Miners extract rock that contains about 1.2 in. (20 cm) of gold in each cubic yard.

☆ **Largest producer of gold** China mined 303 tons (9.7 million oz.) of gold in 2007, representing one-tenth of the world supply. This was the first time since 1905 that South Africa was not responsible for the greatest output.

The ☆ **largest gold production company** is Barrick (Canada), with 27 mines on five continents and over 20,000 personnel. It also has the ☆ **largest gold reserves for a company,** with 124.6 million oz.

☆ **Largest gold reserves** The United States Treasury currently holds 8,133.5 tons of gold, worth $241 billion at July 2008 prices—the largest reserve of any single country.

★ **MOST EXPENSIVE SNEAKERS** Ken Courtney (U.S.A.), founder of fashion label Ju$t Another Rich Kid, created these high-top Nike Dunks dipped in 18-carat gold as part of a fashion show in New York in 2007. Five pairs were made, costing $4,053 each.

JULY 14: Richard Presley (U.S.A.) spent 69 days 19 min. in a module under water—the **longest time spent living under water**—at a lagoon in Key Largo, Florida, U.S.A., from May 6 to July 14, 1992.

MOST EXPENSIVE BATHROOM In October 2008, we heard the sad news of the death of self-made jewelry tycoon Lam Saiwing at the age of just 53. Lam was famous for spending HK$27 million ($3.5 million) on a lavish bathroom for his Hong Kong shop. The toilet bowls, sinks, mirror frames, wall tiles, floors, and doors are all made out of solid 24-carat gold. Not everyone can use the facilities at Lam's, however—only customers spending over a certain amount in his store!

★**Largest known gold repository** The Federal Reserve Bank of New York, at 33 Liberty Street, Manhattan, holds an estimated 5,000 tons of gold bullion, worth $160 billion as of March 2008. The vault—which lies 86 ft. (26 m) below sea level—is only the largest *known* repository; Swiss banks famous for not revealing details of their gold stocks may hold more.

Largest transaction for a numismatic item The largest known transaction for a single numismatic item (i.e., one relating to coins, currency, or medals) took place on November 7, 2001, when an 80-lb. (30-kg) pioneer gold bar retrieved from the SS *Central America,* wrecked in 1857, was bought anonymously for $8 million.

Deepest salvage with divers HM cruiser *Edinburgh* sank on May 2, 1942, off northern Norway in 803 ft. (245 m) of water. For a period of 31 days (from September 7 to October 7, 1981), 12 divers worked on the wreck in pairs, recovering 460 gold ingots in all.

JULY 15: The **largest firework** was the Universe I Part II, exploded in Hokkaido, Japan, on July 15, 1988. The 1,543-lb. (700-kg) shell was 54.75 in. (139 cm) in diameter.

145,000 TONS: the weight of all the gold ever mined as of 2001. This would form a solid gold cube with a length of 66 ft. (20 m) and, at October 2008 prices, be worth $3.39 trillion!

MOST EXPENSIVE COIN SOLD AT AUCTION The most expensive coin in the world is the 1933 Double Eagle, a $20 gold piece that was auctioned at Sotheby's, New York City, U.S.A., on July 30, 2002, and which secured substantially more than $20—$7,590,020, in fact, including buyer's premium.

LARGEST GOLD RING The Najmat Taiba (which means "Star of Taiba") was created by Taiba (United Arab Emirates) for the Gold and Jewelry Co. Ltd of Saudi Arabia. No ordinary piece of finger jewelry, this ring is 27.5 in. (70 cm) wide— the same diameter as a hula hoop!—and weighs 140 lb. 12 oz. (63.8 kg), about the same as a fully grown man! It consists of 11.39 lb. (5.17 kg) of precious jewels set on a 129-lb. 5-oz. (58.68-kg), 21-carat gold ring. It took 55 workers 45 days to construct.

LARGEST COIN You'd need a pretty big pocket for the world's largest coin. It weighs 220 lb. (100 kg), measures 19.6 in. (50 cm) in diameter and 1.1 in. (3 cm) in thickness, and is made from bullion with a purity of 99.999%. The legal-tender coin was introduced on May 3, 2007, by the Royal Canadian Mint and has a face value of CAN$1 million ($900,375).

Heaviest gold hoard On January 25, 1917, the White Star Liner HMS *Laurentic* sank after striking a mine in 132 ft. (40 m) of water off Malin Head, Donegal, Ireland. A hoard of gold ingots weighing 96,320 lb. (48 tons), and worth $23.8 million in 1917, has been recovered from the wreck over the years.

Most valuable shipwreck Mel Fisher (U.S.A.), one of the most famous treasure hunters of the 20th century, found the *Nuestra Señora de Atocha* off Florida, U.S.A., on July 20, 1985. When it sank in a hurricane in 1622, it had been carrying a cargo worth hundreds of millions of dollars: among it 40 tons (44 tonnes) of gold and silver, some 70 lb. (31.75 kg) of emeralds, 20 bronze cannons, 525 bales of tobacco, and countless items left unregistered to avoid taxation. So vast was the cargo that it had taken two months to load; and it was no surprise that it all sank in a matter of minutes.

★ **FIRST GOLD-PLATED PORSCHE** In 2005, German company Visualis commissioned an artist to gild a Porsche Boxster in 22-carat beaten gold. There are now plans to release a limited-edition model and plate nine further Porsches, though a price for this ultimate symbol of wealth and luxury has not yet been determined.

JULY 16: The **greatest recorded crowd at any soccer match** was 199,854 for the Brazil vs. Uruguay World Cup match in Rio de Janeiro, Brazil, on July 16, 1950.

Most valuable religious artifact The 15th-century gold Buddha in Wat Trimitr Temple in Bangkok, Thailand, measures 10 ft. (3 m) tall and weighs an estimated 12,125 lb. (6 tons). At the December 2008 price of $821.48 per fine ounce, its intrinsic worth was over $159 million. The gold was only discovered under a layer of plaster in 1954.

★**Most expensive mug** A 23-carat gold mug made by Yoo Long Kim Kee Gold Store (Thailand) was bought for 1,000,023 Thai Baht ($33,842) by Nestlé Thai Ltd on January 9, 2008.

Most lead turned into gold In 1980, the reknowned scientist Glenn Seaborg (U.S.A.) transmuted several thousand atoms of lead into gold at the Lawrence Berkeley Laboratory in California, U.S.A. His experimental technique, which uses nuclear physics to remove protons and neutrons from the lead atoms, is far too expensive to enable routine manufacturing of gold from lead. Even so, Seaborg's work is the closest thing yet to the Philosopher's Stone—a mythical object that would reputedly turn base metal into gold.

TOYS & GAMES

☆**Largest marble tournament** The largest marble tournament hosted 677 participants playing the game Ringer for an event organized by the Toy & Miniature Museum of Kansas City in Missouri, U.S.A., on August 23, 2008.

☆ **FASTEST TIME TO SOLVE A RUBIK'S CUBE BY A ROBOT** Invented by Peter Redmond (Ireland), "Rubot2" solved a Rubik's cube in 1 min. 4 sec. at the BT Young Scientist & Technology Exhibition, Dublin, Ireland, on January 8, 2009.

FACT

The fastest time to solve a Rubik's cube is just 9.55 sec., set by Ron van Bruchem (Netherlands) on November 24, 2007.

JULY 17: Professional stuntman Ted A. Batchelor (U.S.A.) endured the **longest full-body burn (without oxygen)** for 2 min. 38 sec. on an island at Ledges Quarry Park, Nelson, Ohio, U.S.A., on July 17, 2004.

☆**Largest teddy bear mosaic** A teddy bear mosaic measuring 614 ft.^{2} (57.04 m^2) was made by the Chelsea Teddy Bear Company in Chelsea, Michigan, U.S.A., on July 26, 2008. Members of the public contributed bears to help create a large peace symbol mosaic in the company parking lot.

☆**Most traveled toy mascot** A bear called Rex Lancaster, owned by Rex Travel Organization Inc. (U.S.A.), traveled 281,516 miles (453,056 km) from November 9, 2005, to May 5, 2006, passing through seven continents and 30 countries on his journey.

★**Fastest slot car** A Scalextric Honda F1 replica reached a speed of 983.88 scale mph (1,583.4 scale km/h) when it was controlled by Dallas Campbell (UK) of *The Gadget Show* at the Chatsworth Rally Show, Chatsworth, UK, on June 6, 2008.

☆**Most expensive toy car** A red-and-green model delivery van, with the name W. E. Boyce on the side, sold for a record £19,975 (or $39,852) in March 2008. First sold in the 1930s for about £0.10 (then $0.30), the van was sold by Vectis Auctions of Teeside, UK.

☆**LARGEST GATHERING OF SOFT TOYS** The Girl Scouts of Southeast Florida (U.S.A.) organized a record-breaking gathering of 5,884 soft toys at Roger Dean Stadium in Jupiter, Florida, U.S.A., on September 6, 2008.

HAND-IN-PAW

The **longest human/soft toy chain** included 2,623 people, each with a soft toy, and was achieved at an event organized by the J.J. van der Merwe Primary School in Ermelo, South Africa, on August 29, 2008.

☆ **TALLEST LEGO STRUCTURE** The tallest structure built from Lego was 96 ft. 8 in. (29.48 m) high and was constructed by Per K. Knudsen, Finn Flou Laursen, and Karsten Niebuhr (all Denmark) from Lego CE, in collaboration with Die Kinderfreunde at the Rathausplatz in Vienna, Austria, October 2–5, 2008. The tower used more than 450,000 blocks, almost all of them having eight studs. The blocks were put together by the Viennese children, and the architects placed them in the tower.

★ **LARGEST DISPLAY OF LEGO *STAR WARS* CLONE TROOPERS** The world's largest construction and display of Lego *Star Wars* Clone Troopers was composed of 35,210 individual models and was built by Lego in Slough, UK, on June 27, 2008.

Largest image built with Lego

A picture made from 1.2 million Lego bricks was found to have an area of 80.84 m² (870.15 ft.²) when measured on October 24, 2007. Completed by The Toy Museum during August 2007 in Bellaire, Ohio, U.S.A., the picture was 13.61 × 5.95 m (44 ft. 8 in. × 19 ft. 6 in.) in size and took over 2,000 hours to complete. The image was essentially that of a truck with different designs created in the "cargo" being carried by the vehicle.

JULY 18: Michael O'Shaughnessy (U.S.A.) completed the **fastest crossing of the English Channel by paddleboard** in a time of 5 hr. 9 min. on this day in 2006.

☆ **LARGEST PLAYABLE TWISTER BOARD** A playable Twister board measuring 128 ft. (39 m) long and 119 ft. (36.2 m) wide was put together at the University of Tulsa in Oklahoma, U.S.A., on October 23, 2008. In total, 600 standard Twister boards were used, covering an area of 15,232 ft.² (1,415.1 m²).

☆ **Largest teddy bear (stitched)** Dana Warren (U.S.A.) constructed a stitched teddy bear measuring a record 55 ft. 4 in. (16.86 m) in length. The bear was completed on June 6, 2008, and displayed at the Exploration Place, Wichita, Kansas, U.S.A.

☆ **Longest toy train track** A wooden toy train track measuring 5,413 ft. 10 in. (1,650.14 m)—that's 1.02 miles (1.65 km) long—was built by Friends of Thomas "Team Japan" in collaboration with Fuji Television Network Inc., Fuji Television Kids Entertainment Inc., and Sony Creative Products Inc. at Mediage/Aqua City Odaiba, Japan, on August 23, 2006.

☆ **Scrabble, most simultaneous opponents** On November 7, 2007, Ganesh Asirvatham (Malaysia) played Scrabble against 25 opponents simultaneously, winning 21 of the 25 games. The attempt took place in Mumbai, India, and was organized by Mattel Toys (India) Pvt. Ltd.

☆ **MOST HOOPS HULA-HOOPING** Jin Linlin (China) successfully hula-hooped 105 hoops on the set of *Zheng Da Zong Yi—Guinness World Records Special* in Beijing, China, on October 28, 2007. The guidelines require three full revolutions of standard-size hula-hoops between the shoulders and hips.

JULY 19: The **largest rocking horse** measured 15 ft. 7 in. × 15 ft. 7 in. × 8 ft. 9 in. (4.8 m × 4.8 m × 2.7 m). The horse was made by citizens of Hanno, Saitama, Japan, and completed on July 19, 2004.

☆ Most expensive toy soldier sold at auction The most valuable toy soldier in the world is the first handcrafted 1963 G.I. Joe prototype, which was sold on August 7, 2003, by its creator Don Levine to businessman Stephen A. Geppi (U.S.A.) for $200,000 during an auction conducted by Heritage Comics Auctions of Dallas, Texas, U.S.A.

Earliest cartoon merchandise Pat Sullivan's (U.S.A.) Felix the Cat, who appeared in 1919 as the animal that "kept on walking," was not only the first cartoon character to attain the celebrity of a human star but also the first to be used as an image on packaging, in 1924. Felix was also merchandised as a hugely successful cuddly toy two years later.

CLOTHES

LARGEST . . .

Hawaiian shirt In March 1999, Hilo Hattie (U.S.A.), a retailer of Hawaiian fashions in Hawaii, U.S.A., created an aloha shirt with a chest measurement of 14 ft. (4.26 m), a waist of 11 ft. 5 in. (3.5 m), and a neck of 5 ft. (1.53 m).

Trousers Trousers measuring 35 ft. 6 in. (10.83 m) long with a 20-ft. 10-in. (6.4-m) waist were made by Value Planning Co., Ltd, on December 27, 2006.

☆ LARGEST PAIR OF JEANS Workers from textile company Corporacion Wama Pieers (Peru) created a pair of jeans measuring 131 ft. (40 m) long, 98 ft. (30 m) wide, and weighing more than 2.2 tons (2 tonnes). The jeans, which were cut from 9,842 ft. (3,000 m) of cloth, were unveiled in Lima, Peru, on October 30, 2008.

FACT

The most expensive pair of jeans (commercially available) are Escada's Couture Swarovski Crystal Jeans, which could be bought from Neiman Marcus stores in 2006 for a mere $10,000!

☆ **LARGEST HIKING BOOT** A hiking boot measuring 23 ft. 5 in. (7.1 m) long, 8 ft. 2 in. (2.5 m) wide, and 13 ft. 9 in. (4.2 m) tall was made by Schuh Marke (Germany) and presented in Hauenstein, Germany, on September 30, 2006. The boot weighs 3,306 lb. (1,500 kg), the leather used weighs 661 lb. (300 kg), and the shoelace is 114 ft. 9 in. (35 m) in length. Pictured measuring the boot are Guinness World Records adjudicators Kristian (top) and Andrea.

BEST FOOT FORWARD

The ★ **largest cowboy boot** measures 8 ft. 2 in. (2.50 m) in height and 7 ft. 9 in. (2.38 m) in length and was made by Belachew Tola Buta (Ethiopia). The boot was measured in Addis Ababa, Ethiopia, on January 24, 2008.

★ **Apron** A kitchen apron measuring 57 ft. 8 in. (17.6 m) long and 50 ft. 6 in. (15.4 m) wide—and weighing 110 lb. (50 kg)—was manufactured by Ignacio Rodriguez (Spain) in San Sebastian, Spain, on January 15, 2007.

Pair of socks A pair of long nylon socks, measuring 45 in. (114 cm) from top to toe and 10 in. (25 cm) wide, were made by Michael Roy Layne (U.S.A.) in October 1986 and displayed outside City Hall in Boston, MA, U.S.A., to celebrate the Red Sox entering the World Series.

Bra In September 1990, Triumph International Japan Ltd developed a brassiere with an underbust measurement of 78 ft. 8 in. (24 m) and a bust measurement of 91 ft. 10 in. (28 m).

☆ **Underpants** Giant underpants measuring 58 ft. 3 in. (17.75 m) across the waist and 38 ft. 9 in. (11.82 m) from waistband to crotch were manufactured by Angajala Venkata Giri (India). They were presented and measured in Jeypore, India, on December 15, 2007.

....

JULY 20: The **largest mirrored disco ball** measured 24 ft. 1.3 in. (7.35 m) in diameter. It was made by Raf Frateur of Frateur Events and displayed at "Studio 54" in Antwerp, Belgium, on this day in 2007.

....

★MOST UNDERWEAR AT THE SAME TIME Carl Saville (UK, left) wore 137 pairs of underpants at the same time on the set of *Guinness World Records—Smashed,* in London, UK, on October 3, 2008.

Jef Van Dijck (Belgium, above) holds the record for the ☆ **most T-shirts worn at the same time**—a total of 227—at an attempt organized by Unizo in Brecht, Belgium, on April 24, 2008.

T-shirt A T-shirt measuring 187 ft. 7 in. (57.19 m) long and 134 ft. 1 in. (40.88 m) wide was made by OMO Safe Detergent in Ho Chi Minh City, Vietnam, and displayed on March 9, 2006.

★Retailers of men's suits Aoyama Trading Company (Japan) is the largest menswear retailers of suits in the world. From January to December 2007, the company sold 2,725,359 men's suits.

MOST . . .

☆ **Expensive costume from a môvie** A black cocktail dress designed by Hubert de Givenchy (France) and worn by Audrey Hepburn (Belgium) in the iconic film *Breakfast at Tiffany's* (U.S.A., 1961) was sold to an anonymous bidder by the author Dominique Lapierre (France) at Christie's, London, UK, for £467,200 (or $924,401) on December 5, 2006.

JULY 21: A temperature of −128.6°F (−89.2°C) was registered at Vostok, Antarctica, on July 21, 1983, the **lowest recorded temperature on Earth.**

LARGEST MEN'S SUIT Between February 14 and March 7, 2001, tailors from Raymond Ltd constructed the world's largest men's suit at their factory in Mumbai, India. From shoulder to trouser hem, the suit measured 64 ft. (19.5 m) long.

Expensive jacket sold at auction

The most valuable jacket sold at auction belonged to rock legend Jimi Hendrix (U.S.A.) and was sold to the Hard Rock Cafe chain on September 19, 2000, for $49,185. The sale was organized by Sotheby's at the London, UK, branch of the Hard Rock Cafe.

Expensive jeans

An original pair of 115-year-old Levi Strauss & Co. (U.S.A.) 501 jeans were sold by Randy Knight (U.S.A.) to an anonymous collector from Japan for $60,000 through internet auction site eBay on June 15, 2005.

★**Socks sorted in one minute** Kristina Ilieva (Bulgaria) sorted socks into 16 correct pairs at the Guinness World Records Pavilion in Global Village, Dubai, United Arab Emirates, on November 24, 2008.

☆**Gloves worn on one hand** Multiple record-holder Alastair Galpin (New Zealand) was able to get 24 gloves onto one hand at the Old Homestead Community House in Auckland, New Zealand, on November 2, 2008.

Socks worn on one foot Alastair Galpin (New Zealand) managed to fit 74 socks on one foot for Guinness World Records Day in Auckland, New Zealand, on November 7, 2006.

Expensive dress sold at auction The flesh-colored beaded Jean Louis (France) gown worn by actress Marilyn Monroe (U.S.A.) when she sang "Happy Birthday" to President John F. Kennedy on May 19, 1962, was sold at auction on October 27, 1999, for $1,267,000 at Christie's, New York, U.S.A. It was sold to New York dealers Robert Schagrin and Peter Siegel of Gotta Have It! Collectibles. The sale, of more than 100 of Monroe's belongings, raised $13,405,785.

....

JULY 22: The **oldest panda ever** in captivity was Dudu, who was born in 1962 and lived for most of her life in Wuhan Zoo, Chengdu, China, until her death on July 22, 1999, aged 37 years.

....

★ **MOST GARTERS REMOVED WITH THE TEETH** Ivo Grosche (Germany) removed 26 garter belts from the legs of willing volunteers using just his teeth in a period of two minutes on the set of *Guinness World Records: Die Größten Weltrekörde* in Germany, on December 18, 2008.

Expensive shoes from a movie sold at auction The ruby slippers worn by Judy Garland (U.S.A.) in the film *The Wizard of Oz* (U.S.A., 1939) sold at Christie's, New York, U.S.A., on May 24, 2000, for $666,000. Made by Innes Shoe Co., Los Angeles, the shoes are constructed from red silk faille overlaid with hand-sequined georgette and lined with white kid leather.

COLLECTIONS

☆**Badges** As of June 19, 2008, Seppo Mäkinen (Finland) had collected 30,105 different badges from over 50 countries.

★**Donald Duck Memorabilia** The largest collection of Donald Duck memorabilia belongs to Mary Brooks (U.S.A.), with 1,285 different items as of May 28, 2008. Her collection is over 30 years old.

★**Demitasse cups** Paul Pisasale (Australia) had a collection of 650 different demitasse cups, as of March 11, 2008. Pisasale has been collecting the cups, which are used to serve espresso, since 1993.

★**Elephants** Janet Mallernee-Briley (U.S.A.)—aka The Elephant Lady—has a collection of elephant-related items that numbered 5,779 as of April 8, 2008. The previous holder—Sandy Rosen-Hazen (U.S.A.)—died in May 2007, leaving behind a collection of 4,233 objects, but not before the two women could meet in an online elephant-collecting community.

★**POKÉMON** As of April 1, 2008, Belle Starenchak (U.S.A.) of Dunnellon, Florida, U.S.A., had amassed 5,456 different items of Pokémon memorabilia over 10 years of collecting. Starenchak's favorite Pokémon is Pikachu, and her collection boasts one of the official Volkswagen beetle Pikachu Cars, which she named "PikaBug."

★**Miniature chairs** Barbara Hartsfield (U.S.A.) has collected miniature chairs for over 10 years and owned 3,000 examples as of March 13, 2008.

★**Mobile phones** Carsten Tews (Germany) had 1,260 different mobile phones, as of April 12, 2008, collected over the past decade. The oldest item in his collection is a TeKaDe BSA 31 car phone.

★**DALMATIANS** Kazzy Ferrier (UK) has been collecting dotted dalmatian-related objects since 1992, when Ditto, a real dalmation puppy, entered her life. She currently owns over 5,000 items, including teapots, snow globes, curtains, keyrings, toilet paper, and 1,117 different ornaments. She even drives a spotted Smart car!

JULY 23: The **heaviest combined weight balanced on the head in one hour** is 11,420 lb. 2 oz. (5,180.09 kg) by John Evans (UK) in Lowestoft, Suffolk, UK, on July 23, 2000.

> **20,202:** the number of unique items in Mark Hendrickx's (Netherlands) ☆ **largest collection of beer bottles.** It includes bottles from 2,302 breweries across 120 countries.

☆ **"DO NOT DISTURB" SIGNS** Jean-François Vernetti (Switzerland) has collected 8,888 different "Do Not Disturb" signs from hotels in 189 countries across the world since 1985. Jean-François began his collection after spotting a spelling error on a "Do Not Disturb" sign he was using at a hotel in Sheffield, UK.

★ **Mouse pads** As of April 19, 2008, Daniel Evans (UK) had 3,673 different mouse pads, amassed since 2001. His first pad was a gift from his mother, who had won it in a competition.

☆ **Penguins** Birgit Berends (Germany) had a 5,098-strong penguin collection, as of March 12, 2008. Birgit started her collection in 1990 because of the animated series *Pingu*. Her favorite penguin is a real living specimen named Alfred, whom she has adopted in the Cuxhaven Kurpark in Germany.

★ **Panda items** Janice Kennedy (New Zealand) has been collecting panda items since 1960 and had a total of 252 as of August 7, 2008.

CAN YOU BEAT THIS?

Is *your* collection a world record? Contact us if:

1. You've amassed the items personally over time (not just inherited or bought the group).

2. Every object is different.

3. You have a logbook in which the items are numbered and described.

Find out more about how to be a record breaker on p. xxviii or visit www.guinnessworldrecords.com

---

JULY 24: The **longest inverted flight** lasted 4 hr. 38 min. 10 sec., and was performed by Joann Osterud (Canada) flying from Vancouver to Vanderhoof, Canada, on July 24, 1991.

☆ **CLOCKS** One man with time on his hands—or at least walls—is Jack Schoff (U.S.A.), owner of a record 1,094 working timepieces of varying types as of June 17, 2008. "Collecting clocks keeps me sane," says Jack.

★ **Silver coins** The largest collection of silver coins consists of 1,600 non-duplicate coins from around the world. The collection—which was assessed in person by a Guinness World Records adjudicator on July 1, 2008—belongs to a Mexican man who does not want his name published for fear of being kidnapped or having his collection stolen.

☆ **Snow globes** Wendy Suen's (China) love of snow globes—and in particular mini globes no larger than a golf ball—has resulted in a unique collection that numbered 1,888 as of April 7, 2008.

★ **Stamps featuring eyeglasses** Jane Lippert Hushea (U.S.A.) of Pompano Beach, Florida, U.S.A., has a total of 1,476 stamps featuring people wearing eyeglasses, an unusual collection that she started in 1952.

☆ **Motion sickness bags** Niek Vermeulen's (Netherlands) collection of airline sickness bags has now grown to an incredible 5,468. He has accumulated these sacks since the 1970s from 1,065 different airlines—as well as from the Space Shuttle and *Air Force One*.

JULY 25: Louise Brown (UK), the **first test-tube baby,** was delivered by Caesarean section from Lesley Brown (UK) in Oldham General Hospital, Lancashire, UK, on this day in 1978.

TROLLS Sophie Marie Cross's (UK) army of 490 different trolls is the largest in the world. She started collecting the cute little critters in 2003. A troll can be identified by its colorful, long, wild hair, its squashed nose, and its forward-pointing ears.

★**Thimbles** Donna Decator (U.S.A.) has been collecting thimbles since 1986 and owned a grand total of 4,930 unique items as of October 15, 2008.

★**Toothbrushes** Grigori Fleicher (Russia) owns 1,320 different toothbrushes; he has also amassed over 3,000 other dental healthcare products.

ENGINEERING & TECHNOLOGY

CONTENTS

ECO TRANSPORT

★**Lowest fuel consumption across 48 U.S. states** Between September 3 and 25, 2008, Helen and John Taylor (both Australia) achieved an average fuel consumption of 62 miles per gallon (3.9 liters/100 km) while driving a 2009 VW Jetta TDI powered with Shell diesel over 9,419 miles (15,158 km) through all 48 contiguous U.S. states.

The Taylors also set the record for the ★**lowest fuel consumption driving around Australia** when they covered a distance of 9,059 miles (14,580 km) on just 119.91 gallons (453.94 liters) of Shell diesel, in a Peugeot 308 HDi, between February 3 and 26, 2008—a fuel consumption of just 0.83 gallons over each 62 miles (or 3.13 liters/100 km).

☆**Largest pedal-powered vehicle** The largest pedal-powered vehicle is capable of carrying 104 riders and was built by Alloy Fabweld in conjunction with the Great Dunmow Round Table at Duxford Airfield, Cambridgeshire, UK, on September 22, 2007.

☆ **MOST FUEL-EFFICIENT CAR** The PAC-Car II from the Swiss Federal Institute of Technology Zurich used 0.0049 gallons (0.01857 liters) of gas over 62 miles (100 km), equivalent to 15,212 mpg (24,481 km/g) on June 26, 2005.

JULY 26: The **largest permanent Monopoly board** measures 31 × 31 ft. (9.44 × 9.44 m). Located in San Jose, California, U.S.A., it was officially opened to the public on this day in 2002.

☆ **TALLEST STRUCTURE** On January 17, 2009, the Burj Dubai ("Dubai Tower"; architects: Skidmore, Owings & Merrill LLP) in Dubai, United Arab Emirates, topped out at a record-breaking 2,684 ft. (818 m), making it the ☆ **tallest man-made structure** on Earth, surpassing the 1,815-ft. 5-in.-tall (628.8-m) KVLY-TV mast in North Dakota, U.S.A. It is also the ☆ **tallest man-made structure ever** (surpassing the 2,120-ft. 8-in.-tall [646.38-m] Warszawa radio mast in Poland, which fell down during renovation in 1991) and the ☆ **tallest free-standing structure** (beating the 1,815-ft. 5-in.-tall [553.34-m] CN Tower in Canada). The construction also established a new record for the ☆ **highest vertical concrete pumping** (1,972 ft.; 601 m), beating the 1,745 ft. (532 m) height achieved during the building of the Riva del Garda hydroelectric plant in Italy.

At the time of going to press (May 2009), the Burj Dubai had yet to be named as the world's **tallest building** as it had not been officially opened—a key criteria for the Guinness World Record, as agreed with the Council on Tall Buildings and Urban Habitat. At press time, Taipei 101 in Taiwan remains the record holder at 1,666 ft. (508 m).

★ **Longest journey on an electric mobility vehicle (scooter)** John Duckworth (UK) traveled 1,654.6 miles (2,662.8 km) around mainland UK on a Horizon Mayan electric mobility scooter between June 20 and July 27, 2004, finishing in Hincaster, Cumbria, UK.

☆ **Best-selling hybrid car** Global sales of the Toyota Prius exceeded the 1 million mark in 2008, with a total of 1,028,000 sold by the end of April. As of February 2009, U.S. sales alone reached 1 million. "Hybrid" vehicles use two or more power sources, typically an internal combustion engine and electric motor(s).

★ **First flight by a commercial airliner using natural gas fuel** On February 1, 2008, an Airbus A-380 MSN004—the world's **largest passenger airliner**—successfully completed the first flight ever by a commercial aircraft using a liquid fuel processed from natural gas (a GTL, or "gas to liquid" fuel). The flight from Filton in Bristol, UK, to Toulouse, France, took three hours. The aircraft uses Rolls-Royce Trent 900 engines, and Shell International Petroleum provided the GTL jet fuel. During the flight, one engine was fed with a blend of GTL and jet fuel while the remaining three were fed with standard jet fuel.

The flight marks the start of a program to evaluate sustainable alternative fuels for the future. Airbus predicts that about 25% of fuel used in aviation will come from alternative sources by 2025.

★ **First jet aircraft powered by biodiesel** On October 2, 2007, the first flight of a jet fighter powered only with 100% biodiesel fuel took place in Reno, Nevada, U.S.A. The aircraft was an unmodified Czech Delfin L-29 (Albatross). It reached an altitude of 17,000 ft. (5,181 m) without any significant loss of performance compared with a flight using conventional fuel.

A series of tests had been undertaken with a blend of jet fuel and biodiesel and the amount of biodiesel was gradually increased until test data with 100% biodiesel—from vegetable oil used to make french fries—was found to be acceptable.

245.523 MPH (395.821 KM/H): the highest speed achieved by an electric vehicle, set by Patrick Rummerfield (U.S.A.) on October 22, 1999.

★ **FASTEST ELECTRIC MOTORCYCLE** The *KillaCycle* electric motorcycle can accelerate from 0 to 60 mph in less than a second and is powered by a lithium ion phosphate battery pack. It has a top speed of 168 mph (270 km/h) and covers a quarter of a mile in 7.95 seconds (500 m in 9.85 seconds).

★ **MOST FUEL-EFFICIENT 40-TON TRUCK** The Mercedes Benz Actros used 8.28 gallons per 100 miles (19.44 liters per 100 km) under test drive conditions at the high-speed track of Nardò in Brindisi, Italy, in May 2008. This average was established by driving the truck for one week—24 hours a day—over 7,908 miles (12,728 km) of track.

★ **FIRST HYDROGEN FUEL CELL CAR** The FCX Clarity was developed by Honda and introduced in 2008. Its hydrogen fuel cell (the unit pictured at right) produces no carbon monoxide (CO), carbon dioxide (CO_2), hydrocarbons (HC), or oxides of nitrogen (NOx)—its only emissions are heat and water vapor (H_2O). The company plans to lease 200 of the cars between 2008 and 2010.

LONGEST JOURNEY BY SOLAR ELECTRIC VEHICLE
The *Midnight Sun* solar car team from the University of Waterloo in Ontario, Canada, traveled 9,364 miles (15,070 km) through Canada and the U.S.A., departing from Waterloo on August 7 and finishing back in Ottawa on September 15, 2004.

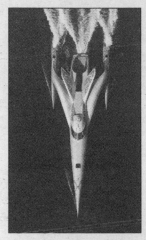

★ **FASTEST BIODIESEL-FUELED BOAT**
Running entirely on biodiesel, and incorporating hemp for the first time in any boat construction, *Earthrace* is one of the most environmentally friendly vessels in the world. Skippered by Pete Bethune (New Zealand), the wave-piercing trimaran completed an around-the-world trip on June 27, 2008, after just 60 days 23 hr. 49 min., shaving 13 days off the record for powerboats.

CARS & BIKES

☆**Fastest police car in service** With a top speed of 230 mph (370 km/h) and a power output of 500 hp (372 kW), the fastest police car is the Lamborghini Gallardo LP560-4, which is in service with the Italian state police. A pool of just 30 policemen and women are permitted to drive the car after taking special training.

....

JULY 28: The **largest button mosaic** measured 720 ft.² (66.89 m²), contained 296,981 buttons, and was made at Maritime Square, Tsing Yi District, Hong Kong, between July 23 and 28, 2006.

5.234 TONS (4.749 TONNES): the weight of the **heaviest motorcycle,** the *Harzer Bike Schmiede,* built by Tilo and Wilfried Niebel of Zilly, Germany.

★ **FASTEST SPEED ON A TOP FUEL DRAGBIKE** Top Fuel Dragbiker Larry "Spiderman" McBride (U.S.A., pictured) achieved a speed of 245.36 mph (394.87 km/h) over a quarter of a mile, a record for Top Fuel Dragbike racing, on March 6, 2006, at South Georgia Motorsports Park, Valdosta, Georgia, U.S.A.

★**Farthest reverse ramp jump by car** A stuntman reversed an Austin Allegro car up a ramp, clearing a distance of 61 ft. 2 in. (18.62 m) over a "cushion" of cars in Woodbridge, Suffolk, UK, on May 27, 2008. The Allegro that was used in the stunt, which was filmed for the motor vehicle—based television program *Top Gear* (BBC, UK), was modified only with a roll-cage and cleared 10 cars before smashing into the 11th. The anonymous stuntman was unhurt.

Longest car Jay Ohrberg of Burbank, California, U.S.A., designed a 26-wheel limousine measuring 100 ft. (30.5 m) long. A truly luxurious vehicle, the car includes a swimming pool with diving board and a king-sized water bed.

☆**Cheapest production car** The cheapest production car is the Tata Nano, a four-door, five-seat family car with a 33 hp, 623 cc rear engine (with a maximum speed of 43 mph, or 70 km/h), which went on sale on March 23, 2009, for 100,000 rupees ($1,979). Tata Motors (India) launched the car at the 9th Auto Expo in New Delhi, India, on January 10, 2008, with the aim of providing car ownership to millions of people across the developing world.

....

JULY 29: Born on this day in 1977, Balamurali Ambati (U.S.A.) became the world's **youngest doctor** on May 19, 1995, at the age of 17 years 294 days when he graduated from medical school.

....

LONGEST MOTORCYCLE
Colin Furze (UK) built a motorcycle that was found to be 46 ft. 3 in. (14.03 m) long when measured at Saltby Aerodrome in Leicestershire, UK, on October 14, 2008. Furze's bike, made from two 50 cc Honda Sky mopeds and an aluminum trellis, was long in the making—he found he was constantly walking from one end of his creation to the other to find his tools!

★**Largest automated truck** Engineers from Caterpillar Inc. (U.S.A.) and computer scientists from Carnegie Mellon University (U.S.A.) are working together to automate 700-ton (635-metric ton) Caterpillar trucks designed to haul loads up to 240 tons (217.7 metric tons) as part of the U.S. Defense Advanced Research Projects Agency (DARPA) Urban Challenge. The goal is to use automation technology including Global Positioning Satellite (GPS) receivers to improve efficiency and reduce the risk of injury to people in the hazardous environments in which high-capacity trucks operate.

Largest monster truck *Bigfoot 5* is 15 ft. 6 in. (4.7 m) tall with 10-ft.-high (3-m) tires and weighs 38,000 lb. (17,236 kg). Built in the summer of 1986, the monster truck is one of a fleet of 17 Bigfoot vehicles created by Bob Chandler of St. Louis, Missouri, U.S.A.

SMALLEST PRODUCTION CAR Smaller than an average fairground "dodgem" car, the Peel P50 is 53 in. (134 cm) long, 39 in. (99 cm) wide, and 53 in. (134 cm) high. The vehicle, which weighs a mere 130 lb. (59 kg) and has a top speed of 38 mph (61 km/h), was constructed by Peel Engineering Co. in Peel, Isle of Man, between 1962 and 1965.

JULY 30: Between June 10 and July 30, 2004, Martin Strel (Slovenia) swam the entire length of the Yangtze River, China, covering 2,487 miles (4,003 km)—**the longest journey ever swum.**

Fastest production car An Ultimate Aero TT Super Car, manufactured by Shelby Supercars (U.S.A.), achieved two-way timed speeds in excess of 256.14 mph (412 km/h) on Highway 221 in Washington, U.S.A., on September 13, 2007.

Fastest land speed On October 15, 1997, Andy Green (UK) achieved a speed of 763.035 mph (1,227,985 km/h) over a distance of one mile in his car *Thrust SSC* in the Black Rock Desert of Nevada, U.S.A.

Fastest steam car On August 19, 1985, Robert E. Barber (U.S.A.) broke the 79-year-old record for a steam car when *Steamin' Demon,* built by Barber-Nichols Engineering Co., reached a speed of 145.58 mph (234.33 km/h) at Bonneville Salt Flats, Utah, U.S.A.

★ **FIRST "ROADABLE" AIRCRAFT** The *Terrafugia Transition,* an airplane described by its manufacturers, Terrafugia (U.S.A.), as "roadable" because it can become a car, successfully completed its first flight at Plattsburgh International Airport in Plattsburgh, New York, U.S.A., on March 5, 2009. The two-seat aircraft has a range of 450 miles (724 km) and can reach speeds of 115 mph (185 km/h). The plane converts into a car in just 15 seconds, with the wings folding automatically at the touch of a button.

★ **SMALLEST ALL-TERRAIN ARMORED VEHICLE** Built by Howe and Howe Technologies and measuring less than 3 ft. 3 in. (1 m) wide, the *PAV1 Badger* is the world's smallest all-terrain armored vehicle. Powerful enough to break down doors but small enough to fit in an elevator, the vehicle was designed to increase officer safety in SWAT team duties and was commissioned by Civil Protection Services (CPS) of California, U.S.A.

JULY 31: The **highest recorded jump by an insect,** reported on this day in 2003, is 28 in. (70 cm) by the froghopper (*Philaenus spumarius*). When jumping, it accelerates at 13,000 ft. (4,000 m) per second.

Largest car parades

★**Ferrari:** Cornes & Company Ltd assembled 490 Ferrari cars at the Fuji Speedway Circuit, Shizuoka, Japan, on May 11, 2008.

★**Mitsubishi:** Mitsubishi Lancer Register (UK) arranged 273 Mitsubishi cars in Chippenham, Wiltshire, UK, on July 12, 2008.

★**Mustang:** Michel Bourassa (Canada) organized 620 Mustangs to be driven between St.-Eulalie and Victoriaville, Québec, Canada, on June 7, 2008.

★**Mini:** The Dutch Mini People gathered 884 Mini cars of varying types in Lelystad, the Netherlands, on May 11, 2008.

BOATS

★**Fastest production diesel boat** The fastest diesel boat currently in production is the XSR48, a 48-ft. (14.63-m) stiff Kevlar/carbon-fibre monocoque-hull, luxury superboat, which can achieve speeds in excess of 100 mph (161 km/h) with its 1,900 hp race-tuned engine option. Developed by XSMG World Ltd (UK) and launched in Lymington, Hampshire, UK, in December 2006, production will be limited to 100 models, and prices start around $1.5 million.

★**First catamaran made from plastic** In spring of 2009, David de Rothschild (UK), founder of Adventure Ecology, will set sail in a 60-ft. (18-m) catamaran made entirely from plastic bottles, self-reinforcing plastic (polyethylene terephthalate), and recycled waste products. His 12,083-mile (19,446-km; 10,506-nautical mile) voyage across the Pacific from San Francisco, U.S.A., to Sydney, Australia, takes him through an area popularly termed the "great Pacific garbage patch," a mass of floating debris five times the size of the UK that sits just below the surface between California and Hawaii. The aim of the voyage is to highlight the threat of pollution.

★**LARGEST CARBON FIBER SHIP** The first of five new Swedish *Visby* class corvettes came into service in January 2009, having completed sea trials in 2008. The vessel is the largest ship to be made of carbon fiber—an extremely hard, lightweight material that enables it to be faster and lighter than a conventional ship, which makes it one of the stealthiest afloat. The *Visby* is 239 ft. 6 in. (73 m) long, weighs 661 tons—about half the weight of a conventional corvette—and has a crew of 43.

FACT

The *Visby* class is designed principally for anti-submarine operations and has a top speed of 35 knots (40 mph; 64 km/h). The vessel costs $150 million.

★ **LARGEST CHARTERED YACHT** The largest private yacht that is available for charter is the 407-ft. (124-m) *Savarona,* built for Mrs. Emily Roebling Cadwallader (U.S.A.) in 1931. It was sold to the Turkish government in 1938, but privatized in 1992. It features a swimming pool, jacuzzis, two separate saunas and steam rooms, and a Turkish bath built from 286 tons of carved marble.

☆ **LARGEST PASSENGER LINER** Weighing 160,000 gross tons and measuring 1,112 ft. (338.9 m) in length and 237 ft. (72 m) in height, the 15-deck *Independence of the Seas* is the world's largest passenger liner. The boat, registered in Nassau, The Bahamas, can carry 5,700 passengers and crew, and its ammenities include a theater, water park, wave simulator, rock-climbing wall, an ice-skating rink, and a boxing ring.

The MS *Oasis of the Seas,* due to take its maiden voyage on December 1, 2009, will be even bigger. It resembles a floating city, complete with tropical gardens, a 328-ft. long (100-m) landscaped park, and seven "neighborhoods" that can support over 6,500 people. Some of the facilities can be seen in the artist's impression at right.

★ **Largest marine engine** The Wärtsilä RT-flex96C is a turbocharged, two-stroke reciprocating diesel engine designed to power large container ships. Built in the Aioi Works of Japan's Diesel United Ltd, it has a length of 88 ft. 7 in. (27 m), is 44 ft. 4 in. (13.5 m) high, and weighs over 2,535 tons. In 2008, the power output of the 14-cylinder version of this engine attained 114,800 hp (84.42 megawatts).

....

AUG. 1: The first men to row the Atlantic were George Harbo and Frank Samuelson (both Norway), who departed on June 6, 1896 and arrived on this day after rowing 3,270 miles (5,262 km).

....

A. ZIPLINE (*not on artwork*) Thrillseekers can try out the 82-ft.-long (25-m) zipline suspended nine decks above the boardwalk.

B. 2,700 STATEROOMS The ship can accommodate 5,400 passengers in its staterooms.

C. DIVING PLATFORMS Two 33-ft.-high (10-m) platforms connected by a bridge that also supports a trapeze for evening circus acts.

D. AQUATHEATER POOL By day: Largest and deepest freshwater pool at sea—21 × 51 ft. (6.6 × 15.7 m) with a depth of 17 ft. (5.4 m).

E. WATER & LIGHT SHOW By night: Programmable nozzles provide a colorful, synchronized water show with 65-ft.-high (20-m) fountains.

F. CLIMBING WALL *Oasis of the Seas* has two rock-climbing walls; they flank each side of the AquaTheater, facing aft toward the wake.

G. SHOPS & RESTAURANTS Cafes, restaurants, a jazz bar, snack bar, wine bar, steakhouse, and a three-deck cocktail bar.

H. AMPHITHEATER The size of a football field, the outdoor amphitheater has its own microclimate.

I. GIANT LED SCREENS Two giant Barco LED screens flank the AquaTheater pool, displaying images filmed by cameras located under the water.

★ FIRST LITTORAL COMBAT SHIP In order to operate more effectively in coastal (littoral, or near shore) waters, the U.S. Navy has created a new class of littoral combat ship. The first version, known as *Sea Fighter*, is a high-speed aluminum catamaran that will test a variety of technologies designed for greater operational effectiveness in littoral waters. It weighs 1,047 tons, is 262 ft. (79.9 m) long with a beam of 72 ft. (22 m), and has a top speed of around 50 knots (57.5 mph; 92.5 km/h). It has been in service since May 2005.

Largest container ship At 1,300 ft. (397 m) long and with a beam of 184 ft. (56 m), the MV *Emma Maersk* is the largest container vessel in the world. The 20-story ship has a top speed in excess of 25 knots (28.7 mph; 46.2 km/h).

Largest ship The world's largest ship of any kind is the oil tanker *Jahre Viking* at 622,544 tons deadweight and 260,815 grt. The tanker is 1,504 ft. (458.45 m) long, has a beam of 226 ft. (68.8 m), and a draft of 80 ft. 9 in. (24.61 m). The ship went out of service in 2004, and is currently a permanently moored storage tanker. It also has a new name: the *Knock Nevis*.

AIRCRAFT

★ Most expensive aircraft loss On February 23, 2008, a USAF B-2 Spirit bomber crashed due to moisture in three of its 24 air-pressure sensors giving false readings to its flight computer. The incident marked the first crash of a B-2 bomber. Introduced into service in 1997 at a unit cost of around $737 million, the aircraft were so expensive that only 21 were made.

★ **LARGEST AIRLIFT OF PENGUINS**
On the weekend of July 1–2, 2000, between 15,000 and 20,000 penguins were airlifted by helicopter after an oil spill off the coast of western South Africa. The operation to save the birds, part of the largest colony of African penguins, was mobilized by the International Fund for Animal Welfare (IFAW).

★ **MOST SUCCESSFUL AIRCRAFT DITCHING** The "success" of an aircraft ditching into water can be judged by the number of passengers who survive. The most successful ditch, therefore, was U.S. Airways Airbus A320 flight 1549, flown by Captain Chesley B. "Sully" Sullenberger (above), which landed in the Hudson River, New York, U.S.A., on January 15, 2009. All of the 155 passengers and crew survived the incident, caused by birds flying into the aircraft's engines.

FACT

Sullenberger, an ex-U.S. Air Force fighter pilot and avid glider pilot, received the key to New York City in recognition of his fantastic flying.

★ **FIRST MANNED HYDROGEN-POWERED AIRCRAFT** A two-seat Dimona motor glider, powered by a modified exchange membrane fuel cell/lithium battery hybrid system designed by Boeing Research and Technology Europe Proton, flew in tests from an airfield at Ocana, Spain, during February and March 2008.

....

AUG 2: Excluding singalongs by stadium crowds, the **greatest choir** was one of 60,000, which sang at a choral contest in Breslau, Germany (now Wroclaw, Poland), on August 2, 1937.

....

★ **LONGEST PRODUCTION RUN FOR A MILITARY AIRCRAFT** The Lockheed C-130 first flew on August 23, 1954, and was introduced into service with the USAF in December 1956. It has been in continuous production ever since, with more than 40 different models produced, serving the air forces of over 50 nations.

According to experts, if the U.S. military were to replace the B-2 the cost would be around $1.4 billion.

★ **First supersonic flight with synthetic fuel blend** On March 19, 2008, a Boeing B-1B Lancer from the 9th Bomb Squadron at Dyess Air Force Base in Texas, U.S.A., became the first aircraft to fly at supersonic speed using synthetic fuel. The fuel is a 50/50 blend of synthetic gas derived from natural gases and standard petroleum gas. It is being tested as part of a United States Air Force program to help the environment and reduce reliance on imported fuels. The flight was made in the airspace over the White Sands Missile Range in New Mexico, U.S.A.

★ **Highest altitude by an autogyro** Andrew Keech (U.S.A.) flew a Little Wing LW-5 autogyro to an altitude of 26,407 ft. (8,049 m) in Frederick, Maryland, U.S.A., on April 20, 2004. Invented by Juan de la Cierva, autogyros are aircraft that achieve lift using rotating wings.

★ **FIRST FLIGHT FROM HAWAII TO NORTH AMERICA** On January 11, 1935, Amelia Earhart (U.S.A.) flew a Lockheed Vega 5b solo from Wheeler Field, Honolulu, Hawaii, to Oakland Airport in Oakland, California, U.S.A. The flight lasted 18 hours, covered a distance of 2,400 miles (3,862 km), and netted the pilot a $10,000 prize for her achievement. Earhart disappeared two years later, on July 2, 1937, somewhere in the South Pacific while attempting to fly around the world.

AUG. 3: The **oldest cat ever** was Creme Puff, who was born on August 3, 1967 and lived until August 6, 2005—38 years 3 days in total. Creme Puff lived with her owner, Jake Perry, in Austin, Texas, U.S.A.

☆ **Most expensive private jet** The Airbus A380 purchased by HRH Prince Waleed Bin Talal of Saudi Arabia in November 2007 for his personal use (the first private sale of an A380) had a list price of $319 million. The world's **largest private jet,** it has a wingspan of 261 ft. 8 in. (79.8 m) and a maximum takeoff weight of 617 tons. Rumor has it that the prince has asked for the double-decker plane to be equipped with a marble dining area, a sauna, and a gym—as well as having the exterior covered in gold leaf.

☆ **Largest airline** As of June 2007, the airline with the largest fleet of active aircraft was American Airlines, with 978 planes, including 47 Boeing 777s. Orders have also been placed for 42 Boeing 787-9 Dreamliners for 2012.

★ **FIRST JET WING FLIGHT ACROSS THE ENGLISH CHANNEL** On September 26, 2008, Yves "Jet Man" Rossy, a Swiss pilot and inventor, took just 9 min. 7 sec. to cross the English Channel wearing a jet wing. Rossy attained a speed of 186 mph (299 km/h) during the flight.

AUG. 4: The **longest standing jump on a motorcycle** is 13.77 ft. (4 m 20 cm), a mark held jointly by Jeroni Fajardo and Toni Bou (both Spain) who both achieved the record on this day in 2004.

★ **MOST ADVANCED MILITARY AIRLIFTER** The C-17 Globemaster III is the most advanced military airlifter in service today, with a strategic, unrefueled range of 2,400 nautical miles carrying a payload of 169,000 lb. (78,657 kg), and a speed of 450 knots (Mach 0.76). It can airdrop 102 paratroops with their equipment and operate on airfields with runways as short as 3,500 ft. (1,066 m). There are currently around 190 C-17s, which are 174 ft. (53 m long) and have a wingspan of 169 ft. 9 in. (51.75 m), operational worldwide.

★ **Longest flight by an unmanned aerial vehicle (UAV)** On March 21, 2001, a Northrop Grumman Ryan Aeronautical RQ-4A Global Hawk flew for a total of 30 hr. 24 min. 1 sec. at Edwards Air Force Base, California, U.S.A. It was 44 ft. 3 in. (13.5 m) long, had a wingspan of 114 ft. 9 in. (35 m), and a gross takeoff weight of 23,600 lb. (10,704 kg). The Global Hawk later became the **first UAV to fly across the Pacific Ocean.**

★ **Largest model aircraft by length** *Dyna Might* is a 1:4.9 scale model of the B-29 Superfortress, built by Vercruyesse Bart, Honore Ignace, and Lamaire Pieter (all Belgium). The plane—which has a wingspan of 28 ft. 10 in. (8.8 m), is 19 ft. 10 in. (6.05 m) long, and weighs 441 lb (200 kg)—made its maiden flight on May 22, 1998.

★ **Smallest coaxial helicopter** The GEN H-4 made by Gen Corporation (Japan) has a rotor length of only 13 ft. (4 m). The aircraft weighs just 154 lb. 5 oz. (70 kg) and consists of a single seat, a basic landing gear, and a single power unit. Unlike more traditional helicopters, it has two coaxial (mounted on a common axis) contra-rotating rotors, which eliminate the need for a tail rotor for balancing.

AUG. 5: The **most participants in a didgeridoo ensemble** was 238 musicians, all participating at Didge Fest UK, held in Escot Park, Devon, UK, on this day in 2006.

TRAINS

FASTEST . . .

★**Scheduled speed between two train stations** Between the French stations of Lorraine and Champagne-Ardennes, trains reach an average speed of 173 mph (279.4 km/h), covering the 104-mile (167.6-km) route in 36 minutes, according to the last official *Railway Gazette International* World Speed Survey study in 2005. While this figure is almost half the speed of the **fastest train speed ever**—357.2 mph (574.8 km/h) achieved by a French SNCF modified version of the TGV called V150 (with larger wheels than usual and two engines driving three double-decker cars) on April 3, 2007—it represents a realistic, affordable, environmentally sound, and safe top speed.

★**Tunnel boring** During construction of a 4.2-mile (6.9-km) underground route between Atocha and Chamartin stations in Madrid, Spain, in August 2008, a tunneling speed record of 304 ft. 5 in. (92.8 m) per day was reached using a double-shield tunnel-boring machine.

★**FASTEST ELECTRIC LOCOMOTIVE** The multisystem electric 1216 050 (type ES 64 U4), built by Siemens and owned by Austrian Federal Railways (ÖBB) is the fastest electric locomotive on record.

On September 2, 2006, the locomotive reached a speed of 221.8 mph (357.0 km/h) while being driven by Alex Dworaczek of Munich (Germany), on the high-speed line between Ingolstadt and Nuremberg, Germany.

FACT

The Siemens-built locomotive (above) needed just 18.6 miles (30 km) of free track to first set the record at 213.7 mph (344 km/h) and then raise it to 221.8 mph (357 km/h).

AUG. 6: The **first website** was launched on this day in 1991. The site— http://nxoc01.cern.ch/hypertext/WWW/TheProject.html/—was created by Tim Berners-Lee (UK) to explain the World Wide Web.

Maglev train The MLX01, a manned superconducting, magnetically levitated (maglev) train, operated by the Central Japan Railway Company and Railway Technical Research Institute, reached a record high speed of 361 mph (581 km/h) on the Yamanashi Maglev Test Line, Yamanashi Prefecture, Japan, on December 2, 2003.

Train in regular public service The maglev train linking China's Shanghai International Airport and the city's financial district reaches a top speed of 267.8 mph (431 km/h) on each 18-mile (30-km) run. The train, built by Germany's Transrapid International, had its official maiden run on December 31, 2002.

34,270,820 LB. (15,545 METRIC TONS): the weight of the **heaviest train ever hauled by a single engine,** on the Erie Railroad in the U.S.A. from 1914 until 1929.

★**FASTEST MAXIMUM OPERATING SPEED FOR A TRAIN** On the 70.84-mile-long (114-km) Beijing-Tianjin Intercity Rail line in China, trains run at a maximum operating speed of 217.48 mph (350 km/h). Tests have shown an unmodified capability of 244.82 mph (394 km/h), but the speed has been limited for safety reasons.

LONGEST . . .

Exhibition train The Opel *Millennium Express* is the world's longest exhibition train and measures 931 ft. (284 m) in length. It was "rolled out" at the Opel plant at Russelsheim, Germany, on July 28, 1999. The *Millennium Express,* which is made up of 14 wagons, was created to celebrate the 100th anniversary of Opel car production.

AUG. 7: The **longest sandwich** measured 2,081 ft. (634.50 m) and was created by Pietro Catucci and Antonio Latte of EuroSpin in Mottola, Taranto, Italy, on August 7, 2004.

★ **HEAVIEST HAUL RAILROAD** On May 14, 2008, the Fortescue Metals Group (Australia) completed 142 miles (230 km) of single-track rail line from their Cloudbreak iron ore mine in Pilbara to Port Hedland. The track is capable of running trains of up to 1.55 miles (2.5 km) long, hauling a gross load of up to 38,400 metric tons of ore. The fleet of 15 locomotives and 976 ore cars make up four trains, with each of the ore cars designed to operate at a nominal 44-ton axle load.

Freight train A freight train measuring 4.5 miles (7.35 km) long and consisting of 682 ore cars pushed by eight powerful diesel-electric locomotives was assembled by BHP Iron Ore. The train traveled 171 miles (275 km) from the company's Newman and Yandi mines to Port Hedland, Western Australia, on June 21, 2001.

Hospital train journey The Indian Army, as a part of its contribution to the Golden Jubilee celebrations of India's independence, organized a hospital train that provided specialized medical treatment to retired personnel of the Indian Army Forces in 11 Indian states. The train departed from New Delhi on August 15, 1997, and returned five months later, on January 13, 1998.

AUG. 8: The **longest skateboard ramp jump** was performed by Danny Way (U.S.A.) with a 79-ft. (24-m) 360 air on his Mega Ramp at X Games X in Los Angeles, California, U.S.A., on August 8, 2004.

★ **MOST EXPENSIVE HIGH-SPEED RAIL LINK** The 67-mile-long (108-km) Channel Tunnel Rail Link connecting the UK end of the Channel Tunnel with London cost £5.8 billion (or $11.6 billion) and is the world's most expensive high-speed rail link. The finding came after construction costs were investigated for Britain's Commission for Integrated Transport.

Suspended monorail The Chiba Urban Monorail near Tokyo, Japan, is the longest suspended monorail train system in the world, at 9.45 miles (15.2 km). The first 2-mile (3.2-km) stretch opened on March 20, 1979, and the line has been expanded three times since.

Passenger train A passenger train created by the National Belgian Railway Company measured 5,685 ft. (1,732.9 m) and consisted of 70 coaches pulled by one electric locomotive. It traveled 38.9 miles (62.5 km) from Ghent to Ostend, Belgium, on April 27, 1991.

Nonstop international train journey Leaving London, UK, at 9:40 a.m. on May 16, 2006, a Eurostar train traveled the 883 miles (1,421 km) to Cannes, France, in 7 hr. 25 min. without stopping. The journey was part of an event promoting *The Da Vinci Code* (U.S.A., 2006) movie, and the film's stars Tom Hanks and Audrey Tatou were on board.

· ·

AUG. 9: The **longest-running advertising campaign** features Smokey the Bear, a mascot of the United States Forest Service, who was first portrayed on a fire-prevention poster displayed on August 9, 1944.

· ·

Distance covered by a runaway train A record run of 100 miles (161 km) was made on the Chicago, Burlington & Quincy Railroad east of Denver, Colorado, U.S.A., on March 26, 1884, when a wind of great force set eight coal cars on the move in Akron, Colorado. The cars ran on to the main line, where the wind drove them along at around 40 mph (64 km/h). A freight engine eventually brought the cars under control in just under three hours.

WEAPONS

★**First deployed battlefield ray gun** The Zeus ray gun, named after the Greek god of the sky and thunder, is used to neutralize explosives such as roadside bombs and unexploded ordnance at a safe distance (984 ft.; 300 m). The weapon, which was field-tested in Afghanistan in 2003, has since been sent to Iraq, and approximately 12 more are likely to be deployed by the end of 2009.

★**Oldest sample of weapons-grade plutonium** The oldest known sample of weapons-grade plutonium was produced in 1944 at the Hanford nuclear site in Washington, U.S.A., from the spent nuclear fuel that came from the prototype X-10 reactor at Oak Ridge in Tennessee, U.S.A. The sample—a jar of white liquid slurry that had been locked in a safe and deposited in a trench at the Hanford nuclear site—was rediscovered in 2004 by workers attempting to clean up the contaminated facility where the first nuclear weapons were built.

★**FIRST WEARABLE SNIPER DETECTOR**
The EARS sniper detection system is a device designed for soldiers fighting in urban war zones or other places where enemy snipers are likely to be present. Weighing under 6 oz. (170 g), the device is based on a single miniature integrated acoustic sensor and uses just 1 watt of power to give the soldier audio-visual alerts to identify the direction and distance of small-arms fire from a variety of weapons.

AUG. 10: The **longest surfboard ridable by one person** is 30 ft. 2 in. (9.2 m) long and was built by Murasaki Sports at Hama Atsuma, Tomakomai, Japan, on this day in 2008.

★ **FIRST MACHINE GUN** In 1862, Richard Gatling (U.S.A.) produced the first workable, hand-cranked, multiple-barrel machine gun. Deployed during the American Civil War of 1861–65, loose cartridges were gravity fed into the open breach from a top-mounted funnel device. It was this feature rather than the multi-rotating barrels that permitted unskilled operators to achieve high rates of fire.

★ **Most advanced night vision system** The BugEye developed by BAE Systems for missile-tracking applications is based on the eyes of the male wasp parasite *Xenos peckii*. The parasite's visual system—not found in any other living creature—uses 50 lenses to provide a 120° field of vision. The BugEye is not quite so advanced yet, using nine lenses to create 60° of peripheral vision, but that is still far more than the 20° field of vision currently available on most standard lighter cameras for missile-tracking systems.

★ **Most advanced sniper rifle** First operationally deployed by the British Army's 16 Air Assault Brigade in Afghanistan in May 2008, the L115A3 sniper rifle made by Accuracy International weighs just 15 lb. (6.8 kg). It fires large 8.59-mm caliber rounds that are less likely to be deflected over extremely long ranges. Under optimal conditions, it can achieve a first-round hit at 1,968 ft. (600 m) and harassing fire at a range of more than 3,608 ft. (1,100 m).

★ **FIRST TRUE AUTOMATIC WEAPON** In 1883, Hiram Maxim (later Sir Hiram Maxim) developed and built the first self-powered, single-barreled machine gun. It used the recoil force of the fired round to extract the fired case and place another in the chamber, cocking the action in the process. By holding the trigger down, the gun fired continuously.

AUG. 11: The **lowest resting heart rate** on record is 27 bpm by Martin Brady (UK), recorded on this day in 2005.

★**Most expensive tank** The K2 Black Panther Main Battle Tank, developed and produced in South Korea, costs around 8.3 billion Korean won ($8.5 million) per unit. The tank, which requires a three-man crew, has a 1,500 hp engine and can travel at 43.5 mph (70 km/h) on paved roads and 31 mph (50 km/h) off-road. The Republic of Korea Army currently has 390 K2 Black Panthers on order.

★**Most lethal iPod application** On December 22, 2008, Runaway Technology Inc. released BulletFlight, an application for the iPhone and iPod Touch that helps marksmen make more accurate shots. The application turns the iPod into a ballistics computer and allows users to input various factors, such as weather conditions and distance, while the accelerometer measures angles to the target, providing detailed data on how to set up the ideal shot at distances of up to 6,561.67 ft. (2,000 m). The program also has built-in profiles for three major sniper rifles, including the M110 semi-automatic, and allows the user to add further profiles to suit their needs.

A.

B.

★**SAFEST PRESIDENTIAL LIMOUSINE** Nicknamed "Cadillac One" or "the Beast," the presidential limousine built for Barack Obama (U.S.A.) is an extended Cadillac DTS built by General Motors. The exact technical specifications are confidential for security reasons, but defense technology includes: Kevlar reinforced run-flat tires that are shred- and puncture-proof; 8-in.-thick (20-cm) armor-plated doors with bulletproof windows; and a 5-in.-thick (12.7-cm) bomb-proof reinforced steel plate chassis. The cabin area is believed to be sealed against chemical attacks and contains a coded communications suite. The mobile fortress is unlikely to manage more than 8 miles (12.8 km) to the gallon.
A. WINDOWS The car's tinted windows are tough enough to withstand armor-piercing bullets. The passenger windows are all sealed to protect against the risk of chemical or biological attack.
B. DOOR Each door is thought to have 8-in.-thick (20-cm) armor plating, and a 5-in.-thick (12.7-cm) steel alloy plate under the car to provide bomb protection.
C. BODYWORK The mixed metal and ceramic bodywork is designed to break up projectiles.

★ **MOST DURABLE MILITARY ROBOT** The Dragon Runner is a robot that can be thrown into caves and buildings to perform mine clearance, explosives disposal, and reconnaissance tasks. Weighing 19.8 lb. (9 kg), it has all its electronics encased in a tough plastic shell and can operate either side up. It can be further equipped with a manipulator arm with rotating grippers.

★ **MOST UAVS SHOT DOWN BY A LASER WEAPON SYSTEM** In December 2008, a Humvee-mounted laser weapon system, dubbed the Laser Avenger by its manufacturer, Boeing Combat Systems, shot down three small Unmanned Aerial Vehicles (UAVs) at the White Sands Missile Range, New Mexico, U.S.A.

....

AUG. 12: The **youngest chess player to qualify as an International Grand Master** is Sergey Karjakin (Ukraine, b. January 12, 1990), aged 12 years 212 days on this day in 2002.

....

SUPERSTRUCTURES

LOFTY AMBITIONS

The history of the world's **tallest structures** tells the story of man's towering ambitions. The earliest superstructures were grandiose final resting places for Ancient Egyptian pharaohs. As Christianity flowered across Europe in the Middle Ages, gargantuan churches and cathedrals rose up as epic paeans to God. The skyscrapers of the modern era are a tribute both to leaps in technology and to good old-fashioned human ingenuity. So, if you've got a head for heights, sit back and let us take you on a tour of history's larger-than-life structures. *Note: dates in parenthesis indicate the building's period as tallest in the world.*

A. COLOGNE CATHEDRAL (1880–84) Although construction of Cologne Cathedral began in 1248, this striking example of Gothic architecture was not completed until 1880. From that year until 1884, the cathedral was the world's tallest building—until it was superseded by the Washington Monument. Only Ulm Cathedral has taller spires than those of Cologne, which top out at 515 ft. (157 m)—more than 10 times the height of a London double-decker bus. It has now been designated a World Heritage Site.

B. RED PYRAMID OF SNEFERU (c. 2600–2560 B.C.E.) So called because of the pinkish limestone from which it is constructed, this 341-ft. (104-m) pyramid is one of three at the Dahshur Necropolis in Egypt. Built by the fourth-dynasty pharaoh Sneferu, who ruled c. 2613–2589 B.C.E., it remained the world's tallest man-made structure until overtaken by the Great Pyramid of Giza.

C. ST. MARY'S CHURCH (1625–47) Located in Stralsund, Germany, and another famous example of Gothic architecture, St. Mary's Church stretched to a height of 495 ft. (151 m). This pre-1400 construction finally lost its title as the world's tallest building when its tower (which had already been rebuilt after a storm toppled it) was destroyed by a lightning strike in 1647. (The baton then passed to Strasbourg Cathedral.) It currently rises to a relatively modest 341 ft. (104 m).

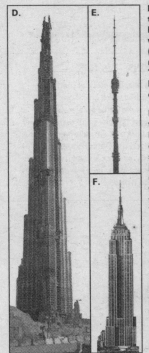

D. BURJ DUBAI (2009–) The world's ☆ **tallest structure** is currently the Burj Dubai in Dubai, United Arab Emirates, which reached a vertiginous 2,257 ft. (688 m) on September 1, 2008. That's more than twice the height of the Eiffel Tower! It is due to reach its maximum height of 2,684 ft. (818 m) upon completion in September 2009.

E. OSTANKINO TOWER (1967–75) Still the tallest man-made structure in Europe—and the first structure to exceed 1,640 ft. (500 m)—this free-standing TV and radio tower in Moscow, Russia, is 1,772 ft. (540 m) tall. Construction began in 1963 and lasted four years. It finally lost its title as the tallest structure on land to Toronto's CN Tower.

F. EMPIRE STATE BUILDING (1931–67) This iconic New York landmark was the first building to exceed 100 stories and is today officially one of the Seven Wonders of the Modern World, as put forward by the American Society of Civil Engineers in 1994. Completed in 1931 and topping out at 1,250 ft. (381 m), it was succeeded as the world's tallest structure by the Ostankino Tower in 1967.

CITY LIMITS

The Washington Monument is the tallest building in Washington, D.C., U.S.A.—and will remain so. How can we be so sure? It's the law. The 1910 Heights of Buildings Act restricted the height of any new building in the city to the width of the adjacent street, plus an additional 20 ft. (6.1 m).

AUG. 13: On this day in 2003, Scott Hammell (Canada) executed the **highest suspension straitjacket escape** dangling from a hot-air balloon 7,200 ft. (2,194.5 m) over Knoxville, Tennessee, U.S.A.

G. EIFFEL TOWER (1889–1930) This much-loved Parisian landmark—named after its designer, Gustave Eiffel (France)—was originally intended to serve as a grand gateway to the city's Universal Exhibition and was planned to stand for just 20 years. (It took two years to erect, finally opening in 1889.) Despite provoking a storm of outrage, the tower—which at 1,063 ft. (324 m) is three times the height of London's St. Paul's Cathedral—swiftly became a tourist favorite. The Chrysler Building took its crown in 1930.

H. LINCOLN CATHEDRAL (1311–1549) Built between 1185 and 1311, and with a 525-ft.-tall (160-m) central spire, Lincoln Cathedral is commonly regarded as having been the world's tallest structure until 1549. In that year, the spire burned down and its record was assumed by St. Olaf's Church in Tallinn, Estonia.

I. PYRAMID OF DJOSER (c. **2700–**c. **2600 B.C.E.)** Located in Egypt's Saqqara Necropolis and built for the eponymous pharaoh in the 27th century B.C.E., this pyramid reached 203 ft. (62 m) in height—or about the same as that of the sculpted heads of the four U.S. presidents immortalized on Mount Rushmore. In around 2600 B.C.E., it was superseded by the Red Pyramid of Sneferu.

J. ST. NIKOLAI (1874–76) Located in Hamburg, Germany, this gargantuan Gothic Revival building was the world's tallest for just two years before it was overtaken by Rouen Cathedral. Several buildings dedicated to St. Nikolai, the earliest dating back to the 11th century, had been erected on the spot, but this church—whose spire topped out at 483 ft. 3 in. (147.3 m)—was built between 1846 and 1874.

AUG. 14: Svetlana Masterkova (Russia) ran the **fastest mile by a woman**—in a time of 4 min. 12.56 sec.—in Zurich, Switzerland, on August 14, 1996.

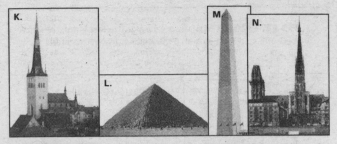

K. ST. OLAF'S CHURCH (1549–1625) Dating from the 12th century and located in Tallinn, Estonia, St. Olaf's Church was the tallest building in the world from 1549 to 1625, when St. Mary's Church in Stralsund claimed its throne. It was originally 522 ft. (159 m) tall; after repeated lightning strikes and reconstructions, today it reaches only 404 ft. (123 m).

L. GREAT PYRAMID OF GIZA (c. 2560 B.C.E.–1311) Egypt's largest pyramid once rose to 479 ft. (146 m), though erosion has now reduced its height. Also known as the Pyramid of Cheops (or Khufu), it is one of three pyramids at the Giza Necropolis near Cairo, Egypt. Completed c. 2560 B.C.E., it was the world's tallest structure for more than 3,800 years, until the erection of Lincoln Cathedral.

M. WASHINGTON MONUMENT (1884–89) Opened in 1888, but officially the world's tallest structure for four years previously, this striking obelisk rises to 555 ft. 5.1 in. (169.29 m). In 1889, the Eiffel Tower took its record. *(For more about this famous monument, see p.333.)*

N. STRASBOURG CATHEDRAL (1647–1874) At 465 ft. (142 m) tall, the spire of Strasbourg Cathedral is 9 ft. 10 in. (3 m) taller than the Sydney Harbor Bridge. The building was the tallest structure in the world from 1647 (when Stralsund's St. Mary's Church lost its spire) to 1874 (when it was overtaken by St. Nikolai's Church in Hamburg).

  This much-revered Gothic cathedral was begun in 1015 and completed in 1439.

AUG. 15: When it opened on August 15, 1956, the Algiers Drive-in of Detroit, Michigan, U.S.A., had a screen measuring 216 ft. (65.8 m) wide and covering 4,800 ft.² (445.9 m²)—the **largest drive-in movie screen.**

O. ROUEN CATHEDRAL (1876–80) Officially the Cathédrale Notre-Dame de Rouen, this splendid Gothic cathedral was built between 1202 and 1880 and was the tallest building in the world for the last four years of this period, after which it was overtaken by Cologne Cathedral. Its spire topped out at 495 ft. (161 m).

P. CN TOWER (1975–2009) At a dizzying 1,815 ft. 5 in. (553.33 m), Toronto's CN Tower overtook Moscow's Ostankino Tower as the tallest structure in 1975, during its construction. It was completed the following year and held its title for an impressive 32 years until the Burj Dubai took its place. Like the Empire State Building, the CN Tower has been voted one of the Seven Wonders of the Modern World.

Q. CHRYSLER BUILDING (1930–31) An Art Deco masterpiece, this famous Manhattan skyscraper was erected between 1928 and 1930 and reached 1,046 ft. (318.9 m) in height—over three times the height of the Red Pyramid of Sneferu. It was the world's tallest building for less than a year, before losing its title to another New York icon—the Empire State Building.

ATOM SMASHERS

★ **Largest silicon detector** The Compact Muon Solenoid 2 (CMS2) Silicon Stop Tracking Detector is designed to track the three-dimensional positions of particles produced in collisions inside the LHC's Compact Muon Solenoid experiment ③. This array has a total surface area of 2,206 ft.² (205 m²)—roughly the size of a tennis court.

★ **Largest superconducting magnet** The Barrel Toroid consists of eight magnet coils in an array 82 ft. long and 16 ft. wide (25 × 5 m). It weighs 110 tons (100 metric tonnes). Part of the Atlas Detector ①, it was first tested in 2006 at an operating temperature of −452.2°F (−269°C) and is designed to use a 4-Tesla magnetic field to bend the paths of particles produced in the collisions in the LHC.

100 MILLION: the number of sensors in the ATLAS detector, part of the Large Hadron Collider. ATLAS is the **largest particle detector** at 150.9 ft. long and 82 ft. wide.

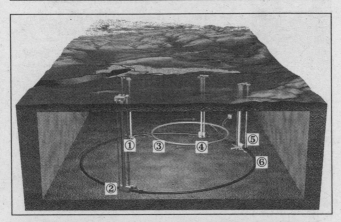

★ **HIGHEST-ENERGY PARTICLES IN A PARTICLE ACCELERATOR** The proton beams in the LHC can be accelerated by magnets up to within about one-millionth of a percent of the speed of light (983,571,056 ft./s.; 299,792,458 m/s), circumnavigating the accelerator 11,245 times per second. This means each proton will have around 7 TeV of energy (7 tera electron volts), equivalent to the energy used by seven flying mosquitoes. Combined, all the protons in the active beams have the energy equivalent to 900 cars traveling at 62 mph (100 km/h).

① **LHCb** Large Hadron Collider beauty—to study the b-quark ("beauty quark")

② **CMS** Compact Muon Solenoid—a general particle detector with a solenoid magnet

③ **SUPER PROTON SYNCHROTRON** 4.3-mile-long (7-km) particle pre-injector

④ **ATLAS** A Toroidal LHC ApparatuS—a general particle detector with a giant, doughnut-shaped magnet

⑤ **ALICE** A Large Ion Collider Experiment—to recreate conditions just after the Big Bang

⑥ **ACCELERATOR** Protons race around a 16.7 mile (27-km) track 11.245 times every second

AUG. 16: Usain Bolt (Jamaica) ran the **fastest men's 100 m ever** in 9.69 seconds in The Bird's Nest, Beijing, China, during the Olympic Games on this day in 2008.

★ **LARGEST MACHINE EVER BUILT** The Large Hadron Collider (LHC) is not just the world's largest particle accelerator—it's the largest and most complex machine ever built (and the largest fridge!). Located on the Franco-Swiss border near Geneva, Switzerland, it consists of a 16.7-mile (27-km-long) circular tunnel under the ground.

The LHC was built with the aim of smashing together two opposing beams of protons at extremely high energies in order to witness the results of their collisions. The most famous goal of this experiment is to find the theorized Higgs boson—the so-called "God particle"—which so far has eluded discovery. The first beam of protons was steered around the LHC on September 10, 2008, but operations were halted on September 19 when a fault was discovered.

On these pages are a selection of the world records established by this extraordinary science project.

LARGE HADRON COLLIDER The LHC and its four detectors are located between 164 and 490 ft. (50 and 150 m) underground.

★ **HEAVIEST PARTICLE DETECTOR** The Compact Muon Solenoid (CMS) ② is one of the general-purpose detectors in the LHC. Built around a huge solenoid magnet, the whole detector is 68 ft. 10 in. long, 49 ft. 2 in. wide, and 49 ft. 2 in. high (21 m × 15 m × 15 m), and weighs 13,778 tons (12,500 metric tonnes). Its job is to observe aspects of high-energy physics including the possibility of extra dimensions.

★ **MOST COMMON PARTICLE ACCELERATOR** The television set in its earliest form is based on a cathode ray tube, in which electrons are emitted from a hot metal cathode, accelerated by electric fields and directed by magnets onto the inside of the screen, making the individual pixels glow to form a moving image. Estimates of the number of these "domestic particle accelerators" range from 1 to 2 billion globally.

LONGEST LINEAR ACCELERATOR The Stanford Linear Accelerator Center (SLAC) in California, U.S.A., is a particle accelerator some 2 miles (3.2 km) long. Since beginning operations in 1966, its key achievements include the discovery of the charm quark and tau lepton subatomic particles. The accelerator is located underground and is among the world's longest and straightest objects.

★ **Largest refrigerator** The 9,300 magnets inside the Large Hadron Collider are designed to be refrigerated for operational use. Around 11,111 tons (10,080 metric tonnes) of liquid nitrogen are needed to cool them down to just −315.76°F (−193.2°C) before they are filled with nearly 66 tons of liquid helium, which cools them further to just −456.34°F (−271.3°C).

MOST SENSITIVE GAMMA RAY DETECTOR Gammasphere at the Argonne National Laboratory, Illinois, U.S.A., is the most sensitive gamma ray "microscope" in the world. It is a cylinder measuring 10 ft. (3 m) and high-pierced with 110 gamma ray detectors. These focus on a central target area that is blasted with ions. Gammasphere is so sensitive that it can detect gamma rays produced in these collisions that are 300,000 times weaker than the strongest produced in the collisions.

★ **LARGEST COMPUTING GRID** In order to tackle the vast amounts of data from the LHC, scientists around the world have collaborated to create the Worldwide LHC Computing Grid. It consists of 100,000 computers across 140 computer centers in 33 countries and was unveiled in October 2008. The LHC detectors are expected to generate 300 gigabytes of data (equivalent to 35 full-length DVDs) per second.

....

AUG. 17: The **largest mosaic of wrapped bubblegums** measured 209 ft.² (19.4 m²) and was created in Johannesburg, South Africa, on this day in 2004.

....

★ **LARGEST CYCLOTRON** Cyclotrons are a type of particle accelerator in which charged particles, such as protons, are accelerated using a high-frequency alternating voltage. The particles move in a spiral so that they meet the same accelerating voltage numerous times. The largest is the 59-ft. (18-m) diameter machine at TRIUMF, the Canadian lab for particle and nuclear physics. The protons inside this cyclotron travel 27.9 miles (45 km) as they spiral outward, gradually reaching their maximum energy of 520 mega electron volts. The TRIUMF cyclotron has been in operation since 1974.

★ **Longest vacuum system** The beams of particles that travel around the accelerator ring at the Large Hadron Collider must operate in a vacuum in order to avoid collisions with gas molecules. In total, the LHC contains a vacuum some 33.5 miles (54 km) long and is rated as a UHV, or Ultra High Vacuum—which means that it has 10 times *less* gas pressure than the almost-vacuum conditions experienced at the surface of the Moon.

★ **Highest-energy operational accelerator** The LHC is due to become operational toward the end of 2009, so as of June 2009, the Tevatron at the Fermi National Accelerator Laboratory in Batavia, Illinois, U.S.A., remains the world's most powerful particle accelerator. The Tevatron is a "synchrotron," the most powerful type of accelerator using synchronized magnetic and electric fields that can accelerate protons and antiprotons in a ring 3.9 miles (6.3 km) long up to energies of 1 tera electron volt.

....
AUG. 18: The **largest ukulele ensemble** involved 401 participants at "Ukulele 07" on Långholmen Island in Stockholm, Sweden, on August 18, 2007.
....

★ **Last major undiscovered particle** The current theory of particles, such as the proton, neutron and electron, and how they interact, is known as the Standard Model. All major high-energy physics experiments since the mid-20th century have yielded discoveries or results that agree with this theory. It is, however, incomplete. One phenomenon that remains unexplained is exactly why these particles have mass. The Higgs boson is a theoretical particle which, if it exists, would explain why matter in the Universe has mass at all. Its existence is predicted by the Standard Model, and it remains the last such predicted particle to be undiscovered by science. One of the major goals of the Large Hadron Collider project is to discover the Higgs boson.

THINK BIG!

LARGEST . . .

☆ **Toilet paper roll** Kimberly-Clark Perú unveiled a roll of toilet paper with a diameter of 5 ft. 6 in. (1.7 m) in Lima, Peru, on June 7, 2008. With a surface area of 602,000 ft.^{2} (56,000 m^2), it has enough paper to last the average human 100 years.

☆ **Bed** A bed measuring 77 ft. (23.47 m) long and 46 ft. 6 in. (14.17 m) wide was created by Mark Gerrick (U.S.A.) and Royal Sleep Products in Fort Worth, Texas, U.S.A., on September 11, 2008.

☆ **Pillow** Every big bed needs a big pillow. The largest ever measured 2,422 ft.^{2} (225 m^2) and was created by AAROVA vzw (Belgium) in Oudenaarde, Belgium, on October 3, 2008.

★ **LARGEST WHOOPEE CUSHION** In order to demonstrate the scientific principles behind wind instruments, Steve Mesure (UK) crafted a giant whoopee cushion measuring 10 ft. (3.05 m) in diameter. It was made on behalf of the Street Vibe Festival of Sound held at The Scoop near Tower Bridge in London, UK, on June 14, 2008.

AUG. 19: The **oldest functioning car** is La Marquise, a steam-powered vehicle manufactured in France in 1884. It was sold for $3,520,000 on this day back in 2007.

 LARGEST SKATEBOARD A skateboard measuring 31 ft. 0.5 in. (9.4 m) long, 8 ft. (2.4 m) wide, and 47 in. (1.19 m) high was designed and produced by a team of students attending Jerry Havill's Team Problem Solving course at Bay de Noc Community College in Escanaba, Michigan, U.S.A., on August 17, 2007.

☆ **TALLEST SNOWMAN** Olympia—a snowman, or more accurately a snowwoman, built by residents of Bethel in Maine, U.S.A., and its surrounding towns—measured 122 ft. (37.21 m) tall. She was built over a period of one month, and was completed on February 26, 2008.
BODY 6,500 tons (5,890 tonnes) of snow packed into concentric rings; cranes used to lift snow to a height of 114 ft. (35 m)—just 30 ft. (9 m) shorter than the Statue of Liberty!
ARMS Made from two 30-ft.-tall (9-m) spruce trees
EYELASHES Made from 16 skis
EYES Made from giant Christmas wreaths
NOSE 8 ft. (2.5 m) long
MOUTH Made from five car tires painted red
SCARF 100 ft. (30 m) long

....

AUG. 20: The **largest soft drink** contained 1,000 gallons (3,791.4 liters) of lemonade and was created by Arthur Greeno and Chick-fil-A (both U.S.A.) on this day in 2008.

....

Think Big!

☆ **LARGEST RUBBER BAND BALL** An estimated 700,000 rubber bands have gone into Joel Waul's (U.S.A.) giant band ball. "Megaton," as Joel calls it, was measured in Lauderhill, Florida, U.S.A., on November 13, 2008, and found to weigh 9,032 lb. (4,097 kg)—about the same as a young bull elephant! It is 6 ft. 7 in. (2 m) high and 25 ft. 4 in. (7.72 m) in diameter.

☆ **LARGEST BALL OF PLASTIC WRAP** At the beginning of 2006, Jake Lonsway's (U.S.A.) plastic wrap ball was the size of a softball; as of June 14, 2007, it had grown to 11 ft. 6 in. (3.51 m) wide and weighed 281 lb. 8 oz. (127.7 kg)—five times heavier than Jake!

☆ **Cup of coffee** On October 11, 2007, Mauricio Cadavid (Colombia) created a 1,096-gal. (4,143-liter) cup of coffee—enough to fill over 50 bathtubs or 17,511 cups! It contained an estimated 1.5 million mg of caffeine.

★ **Beach ball** An inflatable beach ball measuring 36 ft. wide (10.99 m)—about three stories—was made by Carnival Cruise Lines (U.S.A.) and bounced through the streets of Dallas, Texas, U.S.A. on October 26, 2008.

★ **Knitting needles** Knitting needles measuring 11 ft. 5.8 in. (3.5 m) long, with a diameter of 3.15 in. (8 cm), were used by Ingrid Wagner (UK) to knit a tension square of ten stitches by ten rows at the Metro Radio Arena, Newcastle upon Tyne, UK, on March 10, 2008.

AUG. 21: The **oldest athlete to win an Olympic gold** was Patrick Joseph "Babe" McDonald (U.S.A.), who was 42 years 26 days when he won the 56-lb.-weight (25.4-kg) throw in Antwerp, Belgium, today in 1920.

☆**Canned food structure** On July 4, 2008, students from the School of Architecture at Montana State University—in partnership with nonprofit organization Conscious Alliance (both U.S.A.)—used 45,725 cans of food to build a structure in the shape of a human hand. The sculpture measured 32 ft. (9.75 m) long, 16 ft. (4.88 m) wide, and 10 ft. (3.05 m) tall.

★**Flute of sparkling wine** The world's largest wine flute was filled with 4.37 gallons (16.5 liters) of sparkling wine by Fede & Tinto at the Vini nel Mondo 2008 wine-lovers event in Spoleto, Umbria, Italy, on May 30, 2008.

Pair of scissors A pair of scissors measuring 5 ft. 10 in. (1.78 m) from tip to handle were manufactured by Michael Fish (Canada) and his team from Keir Surgical Ltd. The scissors were displayed at the Operating Room Nurses Association of Canada's (ORNAC) 20th National Conference in Victoria, Canada, on April 24, 2007.

LARGEST CHAINSAW A working chainsaw measuring 22 ft. 11 in. (6.98 m) long, 6 ft. (1.83 m) high and powered by a V-8 engine was made by Moran Iron Works, Inc., of Onaway, Michigan, U.S.A., in 1996. Named "Big Gus," it was put on display by James A. DeCaine (U.S.A.) at Da Yoopers Tourist Trap at Ishpeming, Michigan, U.S.A. DeCaine calls items such as this—and his **largest rifle** (see below)—"Yoopervations": novelty items built not out of necessity but "out of whimsy."

★**LARGEST WORKING RIFLE** On display at Da Yoopers Tourist Trap at Ishpeming, Michigan, U.S.A., is a working rifle 33 ft. 4 in. (10.18 m) long belonging to James A. DeCaine (U.S.A.). It can shoot projectiles by using propane and oxygen, and is capable of firing a rock wrapped in duct tape a distance of 2.5 miles (4 km).

★**Glass of beer** A glass of beer containing 101.5 gallons (384.21 liters)—that's about 813 pints—of Budweiser was produced by Harry Caray's Restaurant Group and WLS AM 890 (both U.S.A.) in Chicago, Illinois, U.S.A., on February 21, 2008.

★**Lantern** A stone lantern built for the Nenbutsushu Sanpouzan Muryojuji Temple in Kato City, Hyogo, Japan, measured 39 ft. 4 in. (12 m) tall and 24 ft. 3 in. (7.4 m) wide on March 10, 2008.

ALTERNATIVE ENERGIES

SOLAR POWER

★**Largest investment in renewable energies** Germany's investment in renewable energies increased to over $14 million in 2007, mostly for solar photovoltaics and wind power.

★**Fastest-growing energy technology** Grid-connected solar photovoltaic technology—the harnessing of solar power—witnessed a 50% annual increase in installed capacity in 2006–07, reaching an estimated 7.8 gigawatts (GW). Hydro power remains the ★**largest contributor to renewable energy,** reaching a capacity of 770 GW in 2007.

★**Most widely deployed solar technology** At the beginning of 2007, the installed capacity for solar water heating was approximately 154 GW. Israel has the **highest per capita use of solar-power heaters,** with one heater for every 10 people.

★**MOST POWERFUL PUMPED STORAGE STATION** The Bath County Pumped Storage Station in Virginia, U.S.A., consists of a pumping station and two reservoirs, separated in height by 1,247 ft. (380 m). When demand on the electricity grid is low, excess power pumps water from the lower into the higher reservoir. When demand is high, water is released back into the lower, via turbines, which can generate 2,100 megawatts of power at maximum flow, at a rate of 32,242 ft.^{3} (915 m^3) per second.

....

AUG. 22: At 92 years 156 days, Smoky Dawson (Australia, b. March 19, 1913) is the **oldest person to release a new album of original material** when Homestead of My Dreams came out on this day in 2005.

....

★LARGEST WIND FARM In terms of absolute numbers, Altamont Pass in California, U.S.A., has the largest concentration of wind turbines in the world. With around 7,300 turbines spread over an area of 54 miles^2 (140 km^2, or twice the size of Manhattan in New York, U.S.A.), it has a maximum generating capacity of 576 megawatts—that is, an annual generation of about 1.1 terawatt-hours (TWh) of electricity. Construction of the first turbines began in 1981 as a reaction to the 1970s energy crisis, making them among the oldest in the U.S.A.

Largest solar power facility In terms of capacity, the Harper Lake Site (LSP 8 & 9) in the Mojave Desert, California, U.S.A., which is operated by UC Operating Services, is the largest solar electric power facility in the world. Its two solar electric-generating stations have a nominal capacity of 160 megawatts (80 megawatts each). The station site covers 1,280 acres (2 miles^2; 5.2 km^2) and houses 400,000 solar collectors (mirrors that concentrate solar energy) over an area equal to 750 football fields.

A WHAT? NO, A WATT

A watt is a unit of measurement used to describe the rate at which electrical power flows—a 100-watt lightbulb, for example, uses up 100 joules of energy every second. A 100 megawatt (mega = 1,000,000) power station therefore produces 100,000,000 joules of energy per second—a lot of lightbulbs! Here is a rough guide to the outputs of various forms of technology:

- Wind turbines: 1–5 MW
- Geothermal: 1–100 MW
- Solar: 10–500 MW
- Hydro: 1–18,000 MW

Alternative Energies

★ **HIGHEST POWER OUTPUT FROM A TIDAL STREAM TURBINE In December 2008, Marine Current Turbines (UK) announced the successful operation of its SeaGen turbine. Operating like an underwater wind farm, its two huge turbines are driven by the tidal flow in Strangford Lough, UK. SeaGen can generate up to 1.2 megawatts of power.**

★ **Highest solar efficiency** In July 2007, a team led by the University of Delaware, U.S.A., announced it had managed to produce a photovoltaic cell system with an energy efficiency of 42.8%. Currently, mass-produced cells have an efficiency of 15–20%, while high-end cells operate at roughly 25%.

The U.S. Defense Advanced Research Projects Agency (DARPA) considers the potential of solar cells so great—primarily for lightening the load of soldiers on the battlefield—that it initiated the Very High Efficiency Solar Cell (VHESC) program to develop cells that are at least 50% efficient. The market value of cells is around $100 million.

Largest solar-slate roof A former barn in Berne, Switzerland, has been redesigned with a roof measuring 22,066 ft.² (2,050 m²) and containing 16,650 photovoltaic-cell-embedded slates known as "sunslates." The project was engineered by Atlantis Energy Ltd and is expected to generate 167,000 kWh (kilowatt-hours) of electrical energy.

Most powerful solar chimney Enviromission's (Australia) solar-chimney power station in Manzanares, Spain, produced 50 kilowatts between 1982 and 1989. It consisted of a large area of greenhouses in which air, heated by the sun, expanded upward through a central tower, powering turbines as it escaped into the atmosphere.

GEO, HYDRO, TIDAL, & WIND

Greatest geothermal generating capacity The U.S.A. has the world's largest geothermal generating capacity. It can produce 2,700 megawatts of electricity directly from the Earth. ("Geothermal" comes from the Greek for "earth-heat.")

The Geysers Power Plant in California, U.S.A., is the world's **largest complex of geothermal plants.** The 22 power plants on site draw on the power from 350 steam wells and are capable of generating 1,700 megawatts of electricity.

★ **MOST POWERFUL SOLAR POWER TOWER** The PS10 power plant near Seville, Spain, uses a total of 624 moveable mirrors (heliostats), each with an area of 1,292 ft.² (120 m²), to focus the sun's light onto the top of a 377-ft.-high (115-m) tower, where the combined heat drives a turbine to produce electricity. With a maximum generating capacity of 11 megawatts, the PS10—which became operational in March 2007—has the potential capacity to power up to 60,000 homes.

AUG. 23: The **largest Mexican wave** involved a total of 157,574 participants and was achieved by the TUMS wave at Bristol Motor Speedway in Bristol, Tennessee, U.S.A., on August 23, 2008.

★ HIGHEST-CAPACITY CHICKEN MANURE POWER STATION In September 2008, a biomass power plant in Moerdijk, the Netherlands, was opened to convert chicken manure into electricity. With a generating capacity of 36.5 megawatts, the plant is carbon neutral since the burning of the manure releases less greenhouse gases than if it were spread on fields. The plant consumes around 440,925 tons (440,000 metric tons) of chicken manure each year—around a third of the annual production in the Netherlands.

Most powerful hydroelectric station The Itaipu hydroelectric power station, on the border between Paraguay and Brazil, can generate 12,600 megawatts of electricity—or enough to power the state of California, U.S.A.

Most powerful tidal power station The La Rance tidal barrage, which is situated at the mouth of the La Rance River estuary in Bretagne, France, has been operating since 1966. It generates 240 megawatts of electricity from its 24 turbines, which are driven by the rising and falling tides. The electricity generated would meet the power needs of a city of 300,000 people.

Largest wind generator With a hub height of 443 ft. (135 m) and a rotor diameter of 416 ft. (127 m), the Enercon E-126 is the world's largest wind turbine. Its capacity is rated at 6 megawatts (or 20 million kilowatt-hours each year)—enough to fuel 5,000 European households of four! The wind generator was manufactured by Enercon GmbH (Germany) and installed on the Rysumer Nacken in Emden, Germany. It began operation in November 2007.

★ Highest-capacity wind farm The Horse Hollow Wind Energy Center consists of 421 wind turbines spread over nearly 73 miles^2 (190 km^2) in Texas, U.S.A. At its peak, it can produce 735.5 megawatts of electricity. The wind farm is owned by Florida Power & Light (FPL) Energy, which owns 47 such sites providing power for nearly 1 million U.S. homes.

AUG. 24: The **fastest swim of the English Channel** is 6 hr. 57 min. 50 sec. by Petar Stoychev (Bulgaria), who crossed from Shakespeare Beach, UK, to Cap Gris Nez, France, on August 24, 2007.

CUTTING-EDGE SCIENCE

★**Highest achieved RPM (revolutions per minute)** Researchers from the Department of Power Electronics at the Swiss Federal Institute of Technology, Zürich, announced in November 2008 that they had created a drive system that can spin at a rate of one million revolutions per minute. The drive system—which has applications in drill and compressor technology—has a titanium shell that prevents it from flying apart.

★**Fastest transistor** In 2007, U.S. security company Northrop Grumman announced that it had created a transistor with an operating frequency of over 1,000 gigahertz. Transistors are the basic elements of electronic components, amplifying, detecting, or switching electrical signals. "These advancements will enable a new generation of military and commercial applications that operate at higher frequencies with improved performance," said Dwight Streit, vice president at the company's Space Technology sector.

☆ **STRONGEST ROBOTIC ARM** The M-2000iA/1,200—an industrial robot created by Fanuc Robotics (U.S.A.) and unveiled in October 2008—can lift a payload of 2,645 lb. (1,199 kg). "Armed" with artificial intelligence sensors and video cameras, the M-2000iA can lift a ton of metal 20 ft. (6 m) into the air.

BEND OVER BACKWARD

The M-2000iA has six axes of motion—equivalent, says Fanuc, to a human waist, shoulder, elbow, wrist and fingers; it is even more flexible than a human shoulder, being able to contort into any position.

AUG. 25: The **youngest sports commentator** is Zach Spedden (U.S.A., b. July 8, 1992), who called an entire nine-inning baseball game aged 10 years 48 days on this day in 2002.

6 BILLION: approximate number of "letters" in the genetic makeup of Dr. Craig Venter (U.S.A.)—the first person to publish the human genome in its entirety, in September 2007.

★ **SMALLEST ELECTRIC MOTOR** In 2005, U.S. researchers at the Lawrence Berkeley National Laboratory and University of California at Berkeley, U.S.A., unveiled a motor that operates by moving atoms between two molten droplets of metal. Completely contained within a carbon nanotube, the motor measures less than 200 nanometers across—hundreds of times smaller than the width of a human hair.

★ **Highest intensity positron beam** Positrons are the antimatter equivalent of electrons, and the two annihilate each other upon collision. The PULSTAR nuclear reactor, operated by North Carolina State University, uses the intense radiation in the vicinity of its reactor core to produce a low-energy beam of positrons with an intensity of 600 million positrons per second. Positrons are used to detect damage in nuclear reactors, as well as probe the scale of nanotechnological materials.

★ **MOST COMPLEX LASER SYSTEM** The goal of the National Ignition Facility (NIF) at the Lawrence Livermore National Laboratory in California, U.S.A., is "creating a miniature star on Earth." To do this, 192 laser beams housed in a 10-story chamber will focus 2 million joules of energy onto a tiny target (inset) containing hydrogen fuel. This will fuse (ignite) the atoms' nuclei and re-create the conditions that exist in the cores of stars. The practical aim of the project is self-sustaining nuclear fusion in the laboratory.

AUG. 26: The **youngest club DJ** is Jack Hill (UK, b. May 20, 2000), who played at CK's Bar and Club in Weston-Super-Mare, UK, on August 26, 2007, aged 7 years and 98 days.

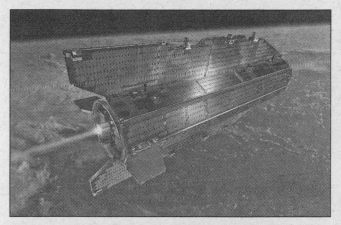

★ MOST ACCURATE GRAVITY MAPPING SATELLITE The European Space Agency's Gravity field and steady-state Ocean Circulation Explorer (GOCE, artist's impression above) satellite was launched on March 17, 2009. Its mission is to orbit the Earth while performing very high resolution measurements of Earth's gravity field. GOCE will, over 24 months, provide a map of Earth's "geoid" (that is, its idealized shape—smooth but irregular—based on the varying strength of gravity across the globe) with an accuracy of just 0.5 in. (2 cm) of altitude and 62 miles (100 km) across. The GOCE map will provide an advanced baseline from which sea-level changes and ice-sheet evolution can be monitored with very high accuracy.

NANOTECHNOLOGY

★ **Heaviest man-made water strider** In 2008, a team led by Wei Pan at Tsinghua University in Beijing, China, announced the development of a technique for coating the wire legs of an artificial water strider with extremely water repellent polymer nanofibers. This makes the strider's legs so hydrophobic that they do not break the surface tension of water even when holding a weight of 1 gram—around 100 times heavier than a real water strider.

★ **Smallest nano calligraphy** In 1991, scientists at the Hitachi Central Research Laboratory (Japan) reproduced the message "Peace 91 HCRL" on the surface of a molybdenum disulfide crystal using a scanning tunneling microscope to blast out atoms of sulfur from the crystal one at a time. The letters are less than 1.5 nanometers in height.

AUG. 27: The **loudest noise ever recorded** occurred when the island-volcano Krakatoa exploded in an eruption on this day in 1883. The sound was heard 3,100 miles (5,000 km) away.

★ **SMALLEST NANOCAR** In 2005, scientists at Rice University in Texas, U.S.A., led by James Tour, revealed a "car" made from a single molecule of mostly carbon atoms. It contains a chassis, axles, and four wheels made from "buckyballs" (a sphere of 60 carbon atoms). The entire assemblage—which "rolls on four wheels in a direction perpendicular to its axles," according to Tour—measures just 3–4 nanometers across, slightly wider than a strand of DNA. The car is moved using a scanning tunnel microscopy (STM) probe.

★ **Strongest carbon nanotube** In 2008, a team led by Alan Windle (UK) at the University of Cambridge, UK, announced it had developed a method of making carbon nanotubes around 0.4 in. (1 cm) long with a tensile strength of 9 gigapascals. This corresponds to about four times stronger than Kevlar, the strong synthetic fiber used in body armor. Further refinements of this material could theoretically make it the best candidate for the construction of a space elevator for reaching space without the use of rockets.

★ **Largest graphene sheet** Scientists at UCLA, California, U.S.A., reported the successful fabrication of sheets of graphene with surface areas up to 0.0000012 in.^{2} (800 microns). The sheets are just one atom of carbon in thickness and, at the atomic scale, resemble a chain-link fence.

Graphene, a nanofabric, is the **thinnest man-made material.** Graphene is similar to carbon nanotubes and buckyball carbon-60 molecules, but can exist as a single sheet of theoretically an infinite size.

INTERNET

☆ **Largest fine for spamming** Three U.S. companies were together ordered to pay $1.08 billion to Robert Kramer (U.S.A.) for spamming the customers of his Iowa-based Internet Service Provider with junk email between August and December 2003, breaking local anti-spam law. Since the federal CAN-SPAM Act became U.S. law in January 2004, the largest damages for spamming are $873 million, which were awarded to Facebook against Adam Guerbuez (Canada) in 2008.

★ **Largest social network** In April 2008, social networking websites Facebook and MySpace both had 115 million unique viewers using their services. By May 2009, Facebook surged ahead of its rival to claim over 200 million users, with 100 million logging on once a day.

☆ **LARGEST VIDEO-SHARING SERVICE** Founded in February 2005 and bought by Google in November 2006 for $1.65 billion (£863 million), YouTube allows Internet users to upload and watch video clips. As of 2009, around 13 hours of video are uploaded every minute. In July 2008, U.S. users watched more than 558 million hours of video on the site.

★**Most cyber-dissidents imprisoned (country)** According to Reporters Without Borders, the country that has incarcerated the most people for violating its web-surfing laws is China, with 69 people in prison as of March 13, 2009.

★**Most Internet "friends"** Tom Anderson (U.S.A.), president and cofounder of MySpace, is automatically added as your first "friend" when you open a MySpace account. Because of this, Anderson had a total of 262,838,285 "friends" on his contacts list as of May 31, 2009.

★**Most visited personal blog in 24 hours** Japanese TV presenter Yusuke Kamiji's personal weblog attracted 230,755 unique visitors on April 12, 2008.

★ **HIGHEST-ALTITUDE COMPUTER VIRUS** In August 2008, NASA revealed that laptops orbiting the Earth at an altitude of around 217 miles (350 km) on board the International Space Station had been infected with a virus. The laptops were for email and minor experiments only and were not integral to the space station. According to SpaceRef.com, the virus was the W32.Gammima.AG worm, which installs malware that steals online game data.

★ **LONGEST-RUNNING HACKER CONVENTION** Originally started in 1993 as a party for members of "Platinum Net," a now-defunct Canada-based hacking network, DEFCON is the oldest continuously running hacker convention. Held at the Riviera Hotel & Casino in Las Vegas, Nevada, U.S.A., the event regularly attracts crowds of 5,000–7,000. Tickets cost $120 and can be purchased only at the door, in cash, to avoid attempts by police to track attendees through their credit card details.

FACT

DEFCON usually features talks, events, and a Wi-Fi network where attendees can show off their hacking skills to their peers.

AUG. 28: The **oldest person to visit the North Pole** is Dorothy Davenhill Hirsch (U.S.A., b. May 11, 1915), who visited the Pole on the Russian nuclear icebreaker *Yamal* on this day in 2004.

☆ **MOST SEARCHED-FOR NEWS ITEM** Alaska governor Sarah Palin (U.S.A., left) was named the most searched-for person on the internet in 2008, according to the Google Zeitgeist list, which identifies the fastest-growing global search terms. Palin, the Republican Party's vice-president nominee in the 2008 presidential elections, may have lost at the polls but she beat even President Barack Obama (U.S.A.) to the top of the list—as well as ousting last year's No. 1, Britney Spears (U.S.A.), from the top spot!

★ **LARGEST "RICKROLL"** "Rickrolling" is an Internet phenomenon where links purporting to lead somewhere else instead lead to a music video of '80s music star Rick Astley (UK) singing "Never Gonna Give You Up." The ★ **biggest online "Rickroll"** occurred on April 1, 2008, when all the featured links on YouTube's front page linked to the music video. The same month, Survey U.S.A. estimated that at least 18 million Americans had been "Rickrolled."

☆ **Highest broadband coverage per capita** According to figures published by the Organization for Economic Cooperation and Development (OECD) in July 2007, Denmark has the highest broadband coverage per capita, with 34.3 per 100 people having internet connections with download speeds equal to or faster than 256 kbit/s.

Youngest billionaire Facebook CEO Mark Zuckerberg (U.S.A., b. May 14, 1984) had an estimated net worth of $1.5 billion when listed on Forbes.com on March 5, 2008, aged just 23 years 296 days.

....

AUG. 29: Sir Ranulph Fiennes and Charles Burton (both UK) completed the **first surface circumnavigation via both the geographical poles** on this day in 1982.

....

★ **FIRST U.S. PRESIDENT WITH REGULAR EMAIL ACCESS** Among the first few announcements made when Barack Obama took office in January 2009 was the news that the president, an avid emailer, would use email to stay in touch with senior staff and personal friends during his term of office.

However, the title for the ★ **first U.S. president to use email in office** goes to Bill Clinton (U.S.A.), who sent one email as a test and another, with the help of his staff, to astronaut John Glenn while he was in orbit on the Space Shuttle.

☆ **LONGEST BROADBAND WI-FI CONNECTION** In April 2007, Ermanno Pietrosemoli (Venezuela) shot an 802.11 wireless signal 237 miles (382 km) between two mountains in the Venezuelan Andes. Pietrosemoli—president of the Latin American networking association Escuela Latino-america de Redes—sent a signal with a data throughput of 3 Mb/s.

★ **Largest online and interactive map** Launched under its current title in 2005, Google Earth is an Internet-linked application that produces a virtual 3D globe depicting the entire Earth from satellite data. Since 2005, Google Earth has been expanded to include areas under the sea and in space. It has also added new applications to its suite of map services, including Google Street View, which provides 360° horizontal and 290° vertical panoramic photographic views of streets of major cities in Australia, France, Italy, Japan, Netherlands, New Zealand, Spain, the UK, and U.S.A.

★ **Most software downloads in 24 hours** Mozilla's Firefox 3.0 is a free web browser that was developed by a team of volunteer programmers. It was downloaded 8,002,530 times on June 17–18, 2008, the launch day of the new Firefox web browser.

....

AUG. 30: Carl F. Haupt (U.S.A., b. April 21, 1926) became the **oldest climber to summit Mount Kilimanjaro** in Tanzania, on August 30, 2004, aged 78 years 131 days.

....

GADGETS

★**First USB prosthetic** In May 2008, Finnish computer programmer Jerry Jalava lost part of a finger in a motorcycle accident. To "replace" the lost digit, Jalava made a prosthetic finger, inside which he installed a 2-GB USB memory stick, allowing him to carry his data around with him constantly. The idea came to him when doctors, having learned of his profession, joked that he should make a "finger drive" for his hand.

☆**Smallest color scanner** Planon System Solutions (Canada) has produced a pen-sized (8.9-in.-long × 0.5-in.-thick; 226 mm × 12 mm) color scanner that can digitize a sheet of paper in four seconds. The DocuPen RC800 has 8 MB of flash memory supplemented by a 1-GB micro CD card.

★**First GPS projectile tracking device** StarChase is a tracking system developed by a U.S. company of the same name. It is a small cannon that fires a golf ball–sized sticky projectile at a vehicle being pursued by law-enforcement personnel. The projectile contains a small GPS tracker, receiver, and power supply and allows the police to track fugitives without having to enter into a car chase.

☆**Fastest computer** Built by IBM (U.S.) for the U.S. National Nuclear Security Administration, the Roadrunner computer, unveiled on June 10, 2008, is capable of operating at one petaflop (1,000 trillion floating point operations per second).

★**Largest Bluetooth device** In February 2007, London's Tower Bridge was modified to be a giant Bluetooth-enabled device. Bluetooth detectors on the bridge scanned people crossing below 15 times per second and displayed the location of people with Bluetooth devices as brightly colored pixels on a lighting array in the bridge's upper walkway, allowing spectators to watch the movement of people along the bridge.

★**MOST SECURE SMARTPHONE** The Sectera Edge is the first and only smartphone/PDA to be certified by the U.S. National Security Agency as able to connect to classified U.S. government networks. With a touch of one button, users can switch between unclassified and classified (secret and top secret) phone calls using the NSA Type 1 encryption algorithms. It was developed and built by General Dynamics (U.S.A.) to meet U.S. military standards for ruggedness, including water, shock, and temperature resistance.

1 BILLION: the number of iPod/iTouch software downloads from Apple's App Store, as of April 2009—just nine months after opening. It would reportedly cost you $71,442 (£49,386) to buy all 25,000 Apps.

SMALLEST FUEL CELL In January 2009, chemical engineers at the University of Illinois, U.S.A., revealed a prototype fuel cell measuring just $0.11 \times 0.11 \times 0.33$ in. ($3 \times 3 \times 1$ mm). The metal hydride fuel cell contains just four components: a metal hydride chamber, a water reservoir, a thin membrane separating them, and an electrode assembly. It can generate 0.7 volts and 0.2 milliamps for 30 hours before refueling.

★ **Haptic jacket with the most actuators** Philips Electronics (Netherlands) has produced a "haptic" feedback system attached to a wearable jacket. The jacket is lined with 64 actuators—vibration motors—that provide the wearer with the sensation of being touched, adding heightened interaction with movies or video games. Two AA batteries are sufficient to replicate the feel of a punch, a shiver running up the spine, or the beating of a heart.

☆ **Best-selling smartphone** According to the analysts iSuppli, Apple's iPhone outsold all other models of smartphone in the U.S.A. in July 2007, its first full month on sale. In the last four months of 2007, Apple sold 2,315,000 units, helping to push its net quarterly profits to $1.58 billion and making the iPhone the fastest-selling feature phone ever. As of March 2009, global sales have reached 17 million units.

★ **QUADRUPED ROBOT, FARTHEST DISTANCE** BigDog, developed by Boston Dynamics (U.S.A.) in 2005, is a four-legged robot designed to be a "pack mule" for soldiers traveling on rough terrain. It measures 3.2×2.2 ft. (1×0.7 m) and weighs 165 lb. (75 kg). In February 2009, the developers announced that it had walked 12.8 miles (20.5 km) autonomously, using GPS tracking.

AUG. 31: The **longest distance swum without flippers in open water** is 139.8 miles (225 km) by Veljko Rogosic (Croatia) in the Adriatic Sea from Grado to Riccinoe (both Italy) from August 29–31, 2006.

★LONGEST RANGE BLUESNARF
Bluesnarfing is the act of stealing data such as telephone numbers and addresses from insecure Bluetooth devices. In 2004, mobile security expert John Hering (U.S.A.) used an antenna attached to a gunlike stock to bluesnarf a cell phone from a distance of 1.1 miles (1.7 km). As part of the experiment, he used "exploits" (cell phone hacks) to attack the phone, steal its contact list, and send sms messages from it. The attack was performed on one of the phones owned by the wireless research and development company that Hering worked for, in order to demonstrate vulnerabilities in Bluetooth devices at the time.

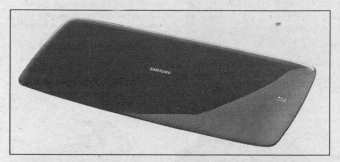

★THINNEST BLU-RAY PLAYER In January 2009, at the Consumer Electronics Show in Las Vegas, Nevada, U.S.A., Samsung (South Korea) revealed its wall-mountable, Wi-Fi-enabled, BDP 4600 Blu-ray player, which has a thickness of just 1.5 in. (39 mm).

☆FARTHEST DISTANCE FLOWN WITH ROCKET BELT On November 24, 2008, Eric Scott (U.S.A.) flew 1,500 ft. (457 m) over a 1,053-ft.-deep (320-m) part of the Royal Gorge, Colorado, U.S.A., using a rocket belt. He completed the flight, without a parachute, in 21 seconds, leaving just 12 seconds of reserve fuel.

SEPT. 1: The Burj Dubai tower in Dubai, United Arab Emirates, reached a height of 2,257 ft. (688 m) on this day in 2008, making it the **world's tallest building**.

★**Most expensive ice-cream maker** The G Series ice-cream makers made by NitroCream LLC (U.S.A.) are customized and signed by artists. Prices start at $75,000 for these machines, which are designed for restaurants or home kitchens. They use liquid nitrogen to create ice cream almost instantly, by mixing the nitrogen, which turns into gas at −321°F (−196°C), directly with the ice cream mixture. The G Series was launched in March 2009, but for those with a smaller wallet, a cheaper version, the N2-G4, costs just $34,900.

SMALLEST CAMERA PLANE In July 2008, researchers at the University of Delft, the Netherlands, unveiled the DelFly Micro. The dragonfly-shaped prototype aerial drone weighs just 0.1 oz. (3 g) and has a wingspan of 4 in. (10 cm). It carries a camera that transmits live video to a controller on the ground. The camera and transmitter weigh 0.015 oz. (0.4 g), and the onboard lithium ion battery can keep the plane flying for up to three minutes.

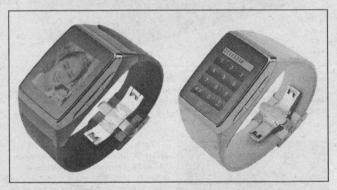

★**FIRST VIDEO WATCH PHONE** With a thickness of 0.55 in. (1.39 cm) and a 1.43-in. (3.6-cm) color screen, the LG GD910 Watch Phone is the first model in the world that allows video calls. First announced at the Consumer Electronics Show in Las Vegas, Nevada, U.S.A., the phone includes features such as a touchscreen, voice recognition, and Bluetooth. It is due to be available to the public sometime in 2009.

SEPT. 2: The **longest carrot** measured 19 ft. 1.96 in. (5.841 m) and was grown by Joe Atherton (UK). The carrot was measured in Somerset, UK, on September 2, 2007.

ART & MEDIA

CONTENTS

ART & SCULPTURE

MOSAICS . . .

☆**Stone** On July 29, 2001, a team of 2,001 students, teachers, and parents completed a stone mosaic depicting three figures hand-in-hand (parent, student, teacher) dancing on six beans representing the cultivation of youth. The mosaic, which was organized by HK Talent Foundation Ltd and HK United Youth Association Ltd, has a surface area of 50,805.65 ft.^{2} (4,720 m^2) and is located in the Luozuling Park, Shiyan Town, Shenzhen, China.

☆**Candy** About 5,000 schoolchildren and customers created a mosaic of the Haribo logo measuring 49 ft. (15 m) in length and 10 ft. (3 m) in height using 350,000 Haribo candies for the Centro Commerciale Curno shopping center and Aldino srl (both Italy) in Curno, Bergamo, Italy, on November 2, 2008.

☆**Car** Rally organizer Tequenitune (Japan) arranged a car mosaic of the Subaru company logo covering an area of 40,849 ft.^{2} (3,795 m^2) and made from 339 Subaru cars at Ryugasaki Airfield, Ibaraki, Japan, on March 7, 2009.

★**Cookie** Visual artist Laurent Gagnon (Canada) designed a cookie mosaic measuring 177.9 ft.^{2} (16.53 m^2) to celebrate the 400th anniversary of the founding of Québec City, using cookies provided by the Canadian baking company Leclerc in St.-Augustin-de-Desmaures, Québec, Canada, on June 26, 2008.

★**Confetti** Nikki Douthwaite (UK) created an 8 × 5-ft. (2.4 × 1.5-m) portrait of Formula 1 driver Lewis Hamilton (UK) from 250,000 discarded hole-punched dots in October 2008.

★**MOST EXPENSIVE ILLUSTRATION SOLD AT AUCTION** An anonymous British collector bought a Beatrix Potter (UK) watercolor titled "The Rabbits' Christmas Party" for £289,250 ($575,400) at Sotheby's in London, UK, in July 2008. The illustration, created in the 1890s, had been part of the collection of the artist's brother, Bertram Potter.

SEPT. 3: On this day in 1906, Joe Gans (U.S.A.) beat Oscar Nelson (Denmark) after an epic 2-hr. 6-min., 42-round boxing match, the **longest world boxing title fight,** in Goldfield, Nevada, U.S.A.

★ **LARGEST ANAMORPHIC PAVEMENT ART** Covering an area of more than 2,906 ft.² (270 m²), *Waterfall* is the largest piece of 3D pavement art ever created. Artist Edgar Mueller (Germany) turned River Street in Moose Jaw, Saskatchewan, Canada, into a virtual raging torrent of a river during the city's Prairie Arts Festival in summer 2008. Mueller's work celebrates the phenomenon and technique of "perspectival anamorphosis"; this involves creating a distorted image that can only be seen properly from one view point.

SEPT. 4: The **most consecutive boomerang catches** from juggling two boomerangs, keeping at least one aloft at all times, is 555, by Yannick Charles (France) at Strasbourg, France, on this day in 1995.

120,000 FT.³ (3,398 m³): the volume of the **largest snow sculpture,** built by a team of 600 sculptors in Heilongjiang Province, China, in December 2007.

★ **LARGEST PAPIER-MÂCHÉ PANDA DISPLAY** The World Wildlife Fund (WWF) set up a display of 1,600 papier-mâché pandas in Paris on October 18, 2008, to draw attention to the continuing plight of giant pandas, the emblem of the organization, and to encourage the protection of their environment. The number of papier-mâché pandas represented the number of the animals remaining in the wild.

LARGEST . . .

☆ **Handprint painting** Erdem Örnek and students of Tevfik Kusoglu Primary Education School (all Turkey) in Kayseri, Turkey, created a handprint painting measuring 31,695.5 ft.² (2,944.62 m²) on June 20, 2008.

Mural by one artist Pontus Andersson (Sweden) created a mural measuring 7,494.9 ft.² (696.3 m²) depicting the north and south waterfronts of Gothenburg in Gothenburg, Sweden, on September 4, 2007.

★ **MOST MONEY MADE AT AUCTION BY A SINGLE ARTIST** Damien Hirst (UK) made £111 million ($200.8 million) during a two-day auction of his works on September 15–16, 2008. Only three of the 167 items on sale at Sotheby's in London, UK, went unsold at the end of the auction.

SEPT. 5: Employees of Pidy, a company based in Ypres, Belgium, completed a cream-puff pastry, or mille-feuille, 3,403 ft. (1,037.25 m) in length on this day in 1992, the **longest mille-feuille.**

☆ **LARGEST ORIGAMI MOSAIC** More than 2,000 children trained by 150 origami experts assembled a mosaic measuring 3,453 ft.^{2} (320.87 m^2) at an event to celebrate the Beijing Olympics. It was organized by the Hong Kong Youth Visual Art Association, Chinese Arts Festival, Lo Fung Art Gallery Ltd, and the Union of Visual Artists Limited, at Hiu Kwong Street Sports Center, in Kwun Tong, Hong Kong, China, on July 26, 2008.

☆ **Painting by numbers** A group of 2,409 volunteers created a paint-by-numbers picture measuring 14,300 ft.^{2} (1,328.52 m^2) during the "Lilly Global Day of Service" on May 15, 2008, in Indianapolis, Indiana, U.S.A.

☆ **Permanent coin mural** Jin Jeonggun (South Korea) created a permanent coin mural depicting the South Korean flag consisting of 110,000 10-won coins measuring 258.33 ft.^{2} (24 m^2) in Seoul, South Korea, on April 16, 2008.

★ **Art competition** The Federal Ministry of Transport, Building, and Urban Affairs of Germany organized an art competition to promote traffic safety among young children that attracted a total of 122,942 entries from children from all over Germany. The pictures were eventually displayed at the Olympiastadion in Berlin, Germany, on June 3, 2008, in an event organized by 2sense event GmbH and Zeitgeist Media (both Germany).

☆ **Cardboard box sculpture** Volunteers from Cheney and surrounding areas, and Allpak Containers, Inc., in Cheney, Washington, U.S.A., built a replica of a medieval castle measuring 111 ft. 9 in. × 6 ft. 8 in. × 72 ft. 4 in. (34.06 m × 2.03 m × 22.04 m) out of cardboard boxes on August 18, 2007. A total of 147 boxes were used in the sculpture.

★ **LARGEST COFFEE CUP MOSAIC** Documentary film makers assembled a mosaic depicting a huge, steaming cup of coffee made up of 77,244 coffee cups outside the Brandenburg Gate, Berlin, Germany, to illustrate the amount of coffee consumed by an average German in a lifetime, in September 2008.

☆**LARGEST ICE HOTEL** The Ice Hotel in Jukkasjärvi, Sweden, has a total floor area of between 43,000 and 64,000 ft.² (4,000 m²–6,000 m²), and in the winter of 2008–09 featured 80 rooms, many decorated with ice sculptures, as well as an ice bar and an ice church. Lying 120 miles (200 km) north of the Arctic circle, the hotel has been re-created (and enlarged) for the winter season every December since 1990.

☆**Picture made of Lite-Brite** Representatives from advertising agency Vitrorobertson LLC and ASICS America Corporation (both U.S.A.) created a Lite-Brite picture of an ASICS Gel-Lyte III shoe using 347,004 Lite-Brite pegs in New York City, U.S.A., on October 7, 2008.

☆**Wooden sculpture** Michel Schmid (Switzerland) built a 75-ft. 2-in. (22.92-m) wooden Sioux tribal head in Porrentruy, Switzerland, on August 19, 2008.

TALLEST . . .

☆**Chocolate sculpture** Pastry chef Justo Almendrote (Spain) created a chocolate sculpture measuring 21 ft. 4 in. (6.5 m) in the shape of a Christmas tree. It was unveiled to the public in Madrid, Spain, on December 10, 2008.

Stained-glass window The tallest stained-glass window in the world is the 135-ft.-high (41.14-m), 29-ft. 6-in.-wide (9-m) backlit glass mural installed in 1979 in the atrium of the Ramada Hotel, Dubai, United Arab Emirates.

☆ **LARGEST CHALK PAVEMENT ART** The largest chalk pavement art measured 8,361.31 m² (90,000 ft.²) and was created by 5,678 children from schools in Alameda, California, U.S.A., for the Kids' Chalk Art Project between 27 May and 7 June 2008.

LONGEST . . .

☆ **Graffiti scroll** The longest graffiti scroll measured 2,299 ft. 7 in. (700.92 m) and was crafted by children's charity "To hamogelo tou pediou" in an event organized by Anemos Events in Kerkyra, Greece, on December 15, 2008.

☆ **Painting by an individual** The longest painting by an individual measured 6,587 ft. 10 in. (2,008 m) and was created by Tommes Nentwig (Germany) in Vechta, Germany, on July 10, 2008.

Gum wrapper chain Since March 11, 1965, Gary Duschl of Virginia, U.S.A., has been making a gum wrapper chain which currently measures 44,378 ft. (13,526 m). The chain is made up of 2,071,148 links from 1,036,574 wrappers.

☆ **Cartoon strip** Pupils of De Eindhovense School in Eindhoven, the Netherlands, created a cartoon strip measuring 1,016 ft. 8 in. (309.90 m) long and 2 ft. 3 in. (70 cm) high titled "Look at us—De Eindhovense School" on January 25, 2008.

PHOTOGRAPHY

★ **Largest daguerreotype** David Burder (UK) built *Big Bertha,* a 6.5-ft.² (2-m²) camera capable of taking daguerreotype images measuring up to 4 × 2 ft. (0.6 × 2.12 m). Daguerreotype—named after its inventor, Louis Jacques Mandé Daguerre (France, 1789–1851)—was the first truly successful form of photography, with the subjects captured on light-sensitive, silver-coated copper plates.

....

SEPT. 6: The worldwide TV audience for the funeral of Diana, Princess of Wales (UK, 1961–97) on this day in 1997 was estimated at 2.5 billion—the **largest TV audience for a live broadcast.**

....

☆ **LARGEST PHOTOGRAPHIC EXHIBITION** A photographic exhibition entitled "The Running Line" featured a record 138,355 photographs, all taken by the people of Tyneside, UK, during the 2006 Great North Run half marathon. The images were mounted side by side on a roll and draped around Saltwell Park in Gateshead, UK, on October 19, 2007.

☆ **OLDEST SURVIVING PHOTOGRAPH** The grainy image left shows the view from the window of the home of inventor Joseph Niépce (France, 1765–1833). To look at, it is far from special until you realize that it was taken in 1827 using a *camera obscura* and is in fact the oldest known surviving photograph. (Beneath it is the pewter plate onto which the image was originally exposed.) Rediscovered by the historian Helmut Gernsheim in 1952, it is now in the Gernsheim Collection at the University of Texas, Austin, U.S.A.

CAMERA OBSCURA

View from the Window at Le Gras (middle photo above) took eight hours to expose using a precursor of the camera called a *camera obscura* ("veiled chamber"). A simple box with a pinhole lens, light enters and exposes a plate coated with light-sensitive bitumen.

SEPT. 7: The **highest speed reached on a conventional motorcycle** is 252.662 mph (406.62 km/h), by John Noonan (U.S.A.) at Bonneville Salt Flats, Utah, U.S.A., on this day in 2005.

★ FIRST DIGITAL CAMERA Steve Sasson (U.S.A.) of Kodak built the first digital camera prototype in 1975. It weighed 8 lb. (3.6 kg) and was the size of a toaster. The camera took black-and-white images with a resolution of 0.01 megapixels and its on-board storage medium was magnetic tape. Images were viewed by removing the tape and placing it in a cassette-reader playback device, which then displayed images on a TV monitor.

A. LENS The lens was salvaged from a used-parts bin on the Kodak Super-8 movie-camera production line. The camera's resolution of just .01 megapixels—which is 10,000 pixels of image data—resulted in a 100-line black-and-white image.

B. DIGITAL TAPE A "portable digital instrumentation recorder"—i.e. a regular cassette tape—was used to store images. It took 23 seconds to record an image to tape and another 23 seconds to read the tape and display the image on a television screen.

C. CCD CHIPS Charge-coupled devices (CCD)—electronic sensors used to gather the optical information—had just been introduced in 1973 and were the inspiration behind the digital camera.

D. CIRCUITRY Steve Sasson, the camera's inventor, amassed "several dozen digital and analogue circuits all wired together on approximately half a dozen circuit boards."

E. A/D CONVERTER An analogue-to-digital converter was cannibalized from a Motorola digital voltmeter.

☆ **Largest panoramic digital photograph** Michael Høeltermand of SUN-ADvertising (Denmark) snapped a panoramic digital photograph of 15.33 gigapixels—that is, containing 15.33 billion "picture elements." The image, which covers an area of 42,608 ft.² (3,958.5 m²)—half the size of a regular football field—was created for "Event 2006" on May 20, 2006, which was held at the Messecenter Herning, Denmark.

SEPT. 8: The **fastest harmonica player** is Nicky Shane (U.S.A.) who played "Oh When the Saints Go Marching In" at a speed of 285 bpm in SRS Studios, Santa Barbara, California, U.S.A., on this day in 2005.

★ MOST EXPENSIVE CELEBRITY PHOTOS *People* magazine and *Hello!* magazine each paid $6.08 million (£3.5 million)—$12.16 million (£7 million) in total—to Brad Pitt and Angelina Jolie (both U.S.A.) for images of their twins Vivienne and Knox Jolie-Pitt when they were three weeks old in July 2008. It is thought the money was donated to a foundation created by Pitt and Jolie that helps children in need around the world.

LARGEST NUDE PHOTO SHOOT

A total of 18,000 people volunteered to collectively pose naked in Zocalo Square, Mexico City, Mexico, for photographer Spencer Tunick (U.S.A.) on May 6, 2007.

First JPEGs The well-known digital image format JPEG—which stands for Joint Photographic Experts Group—was developed in order to standardize the techniques for digital image compression and is used on the Internet and by digital cameras. The first images that used the JPEG compression method are a set of four test images used by the JPEG group called "Boats," "Barbara," "Toys," and "Zelda," created on June 18, 1987 in Copenhagen, Denmark.

★ Largest pinhole camera A pinhole camera created from a 45 × 160 × 80 ft. (13.71 × 48.76 × 24.38 m) aircraft hangar in El Toro, California, U.S.A., produced a photograph on canvas measuring 31 ft. 7 in. × 111 ft. (9.62 × 33.83 m) in June 2006. A pinhole camera works on the same principle as a *camera obscura* (see p. 369).

★ Longest photographic career GHF Atkins (UK) had his first photograph published in 1927 and had photos published in every subsequent decade until he retired in 2004. He specialized in photographs of buses.

☆ Largest photo album A photo album measuring 13 ft. 1 in. × 16 ft. 4 in. (4 m × 5 m) was created by Johnson's Baby China and unveiled in Beijing, China, on June 10, 2008.

☆ Most expensive photograph sold at auction German photographer Andreas Gursky's image *99 Cent II, Diptych* (2001) is a chromogenic color print of the interior of a discount store, showing racks of packaged food. One of six copies of the photograph, which measures 81.1 × 134.2 in. (206 × 341 cm), was sold at auction by Sotheby's, London, UK, on February 7, 2007 for £1,700,000 ($3,351,720), including premium.

LARGEST COLLECTION OF CAMERAS (STILLS PHOTOGRAPHY) Dilish Parekh of Mumbai, India, has a collection of 4,425 antique cameras that he has amassed since 1977. Parekh, who works as a photojournalist, has within his collection cameras made by Rolliflex, Canon, Nikon, and a Royal Mail postage stamp camera that dates back to 1907.

Most successful instant camera In 1947, Edwin Land (U.S.A.), created the Polaroid instant camera, which used the principle of diffusion transfer to reproduce the image recorded by the camera lens directly onto a photosensitive surface; this was then dispensed from the camera "instantly" as a photograph. In 1998, the Polaroid Corporation generated revenue of $1.86 billion (£1.12 billion), with sales peaking at $3 billion (£2.04 billion) in 1991. The company stopped making the film used in their cameras in 2008, after digital photography took over the market and made the Polaroid concept largely redundant.

Most expensive book by a single photographer *Helmut Newton's Sumo,* a retrospective of German-born Australian photographer Helmut Newton's work, retails at $8,563 (£6,000) on the website of the book's publisher Taschen.

☆**Most expensive camera sold at auction** An 1839 daguerreotype camera, made by Susse Freres, was sold at auction in Vienna, Austria, on May 26, 2007 for €588,613 ($792,000; £399,385).

The wooden box structure, which was in its original state, had been lying forgotten in a loft in Munich, Germany, since 1940 until the owner of the premises accidentally came across it.

WHAT'S ON TV

☆**Most watched TV event of the year (2008)** The Nielsen Company estimated that—worldwide—up to 4.7 billion viewers tuned into the Beijing Olympics at some point. This equates to approximately 70% of the global population.

•The **most watched TV show of the year in the UK** was *Wallace and Gromit: A Matter of Loaf and Death* (BBC), which aired on Christmas Day and attracted an audience of 16.15 million.

•The **most watched TV show of the year in the U.S.A.** was Super Bowl XLII (Fox), in which the New York Giants achieved a thrilling win over the New England Patriots. This was the **largest TV audience for a Super Bowl** ever; the huge average viewing figures of 97.5 million places this Super

★ **MOST WINS OF THE ESPN ULTIMATE COUCH POTATO** The ESPN Ultimate Couch Potato is awarded for watching a continuous sports TV broadcast from a recliner for as long as possible without falling asleep. Three Americans have each won twice: Jason Pisarik (lasting 32 hr. and 39 hr. 55 min.), Jeff Miller (40 hr. 30 min. and 39 hr. 2 min.), and Stan Friedman (pictured, 29 hr. and 19 hr. 48 min.).

Bowl second only to the *M*A*S*H* series finale in the list of all-time viewing figures (see TV Comedies & Soaps on pp. 376–380).

★ **Most watched national network TV broadcast** China Central Television's New Year's Eve Gala (aka *Spring Festival*) regularly attracts viewing figures of over 300 million. The 2009 broadcast of song, dance, and news review was seen by 95.6% of all families watching television in China.

Internationally broadcast events (such as Live Aid) or global sporting events (such as the Olympics and the soccer World Cup) attract higher viewing figures.

☆ **Highest TV advertising rate (single day)** On February 1, 2009, NBC Sports (U.S.A.) secured a record $206 million in TV advertising from its slots during the Super Bowl XLIII game between the Pittsburgh Steelers and Arizona Cardinals (both U.S.A.). Many of the 69 available 30-second time slots sold for $2–3 million. All 69 slots were sold to 32 advertisers; this, plus pre- and post-game advertising, resulted in a record day's sale of $261 million.

☆ **HIGHEST-PAID TV STARS** *Two and a Half Men* (CBS, U.S.A., 2003–present) star Charlie Sheen (U.S.A.) is currently the highest-paid actor on TV, earning $20 million for his role as eternal bachelor Charlie Harper in the hit comedy show.

The highest-paid actress on TV is Katherine Heigl (U.S.A.), who portrays Dr. Izzie Stevens from *Grey's Anatomy* (ABC, U.S.A., 2005–present). According to *Forbes,* she earned $13 million in 2007–08.

SEPT. 9: The record for the **longest distance walked over hot plates** is 62 ft. 7 in. (19.10 m), achieved by Rolf Iven (Germany) in Cologne, Germany, on this day in 2006.

★ **HIGHEST-RATED TV SCI-FI** The re-imagined sci-fi series *Battlestar Galactica* (2004–2009) was currently the highest-rated science-fiction and fantasy show on TV, according to an aggregation of reviewers' ratings. The past three seasons (out of four) appear in the Metacritic.com sci-fi top 10, with Season 3 peaking in ratings with a score of 9.4/10.

★ **Greatest product placement (TV series)** Product placement involves promoting a branded product or service subtly (or sometimes not so subtly) within the context of a TV show. There were a record 6,248 incidences of product placement throughout 2008 on the TV series *Biggest Loser* (NBC, U.S.A., 2004–present), according to a study by Nielsen. In this game show, obese contestants compete for cash prizes by losing as much weight as possible.

★ **Largest DVD box set** The 2007 DVD release of *Prisoner—Cell Block H: The Complete Collection* (Australia, 1979–1986) comprises 179 discs containing 692 episodes. The gritty women's-prison drama series has an overall running time of 22 days 14 hr. 4 min.

LONGEST RUNNING SCI-FI TV SERIES *Doctor Who* (BBC, UK) has chalked up 753 episodes to date (April 2009), encompassing 204 storylines, numerous specials, five spin-off series, and 10 official Doctors. The relaunched show is set to return for a fifth season in 2010 with 26-year-old Matt Smith (pictured) as the eleventh—and youngest—Doctor.

SEPT. 10: The **longest measured home run in a major league game** is 634 ft. (193 m) by Mickey Mantle (U.S.A.) for the New York Yankees at Briggs Stadium, Detroit, Michigan, U.S.A., on this day in 1960.

☆ **HIGHEST-RATED TV SERIES** The fourth season of the Baltimore-set crime drama *The Wire* (HBO, U.S.A., 2002–09) achieved a record high rating of 98/100 on the aggregator website Metacritic.com, making it the highest-rated series on TV. Season five also appears in the top 10 list of highest-rated shows. Created by David Simon (U.S.A.), the multi-award-winning series explores the nature of street and drug crime from various points of view, and was heralded as a unique—and most successful—take on the "cop show" genre.

★ **Longest TV ad** To celebrate the launch of its new route from Dubai, UAE, to São Paulo, Brazil, the Emirates airline created a TV commercial lasting 14 hr. 40 min.—the same length of time as the journey itself. It features Fernando Ferreira (Brazil, aka Nonstop Fernando), who talks (without cuts) for the entire time about the delights of his home country and the benefits of flying Emirates.

★ **Most successful feature film spin-off** The most successful feature film spin-off from a TV show is *Transformers* (U.S.A., 2007), based on the syndicated 1984–87 TV series of the same name. The movie grossed over $700 million worldwide and was a live-action version of the 1980s cartoon series, which itself was based on the Hasbro toy line.

•The ★ **most successful feature film spin-off from a live-action TV show** is *Mission Impossible II* (U.S.A., 2000), based on the *Mission Impossible* series (U.S.A., CBS 1966–73; ABC 1988–90). The second and most lucrative installment in the feature-film series grossed over $545 million worldwide.

SEPT. 11: The **youngest astronaut** is Major (later Lt.-Gen.) Gherman Stepanovich Titov (Russia, born on this day in 1935), who was aged 25 years 329 days when launched in *Vostok* 2 on August 6, 1961.

★ **MOST PORTRAYED SUPERHERO ON TV** The character of Superman has featured in four live-action TV series and been played by five different U.S. actors: George Reeves (*The Adventures of Superman,* syndicated 1951–57, pictured above left); John Haymes Newton and Gerard Christopher (*Superboy,* syndicated 1988–91); Dean Cain (*Lois & Clark: The New Adventures of Superman,* ABC 1993–97); and Tom Welling (*Smallville,* Warner Bros., later CW, 2001–present, pictured above right). A sixth actor, Johnny Rockwell (U.S.A.), played the character in *The Adventures of Superboy* (1961), an untransmitted pilot for an unrealized series.

The characters of Superman and Batman have also appeared in numerous movie serials and animated TV series over the years.

TV COMEDIES & SOAPS

COMEDIES

★ **First TV sitcom** The first television sitcom was *Pinwright's Progress* (BBC, UK, 1946–47) starring character actor James Hayter (UK) as J. Pinwright, owner of the smallest chain store in the world. The show ran for 10 half-hour episodes, which were broadcast every other week, live from studios at Alexandra Palace, London, UK.

★ **Longest-running sitcom (longevity)** The longest-running sitcom is *Last of the Summer Wine* (BBC, UK), which debuted in 1973 and is still on air. Having completed its 30th season, it boasts 292 episodes, all written by the show's creator, Roy Clarke.

★ **BIGGEST-SELLING TV SHOW ON DVD**
(2008) The hour-long season six premier
special *Family Guy: Blue Harvest* (FOX, U.S.A.)
achieved DVD sales of 1,141,575—of which a
record 442,000 were Blu-ray—in 2008. The DVD
of the show's seventh season occupied the
number two spot, making *Family Guy* the TV
comedy show of the year in terms of home
entertainment sales. "Blue Harvest" was the
working title used to maintain the secrecy of
the making of *Star Wars VI: Return of the Jedi*
(USA, 1983).

★**Most popular comedy of the decade** According to TV.com, *Scrubs*
(NBC/ABC, U.S.A., 2001–present) was the most popular comedy on TV in
the 2000s. Its average visitor review score of 9.2 out of 10 was also the highest for this period, a record shared with *Friends* (NBC).

In terms of reviewer ratings collated on Metacritic.com, the ★**highest-
rated comedy of the decade** was season five of *Curb Your Enthusiasm*
(HBO, U.S.A., 2000–present) starring *Seinfeld* co-creator Larry David
(U.S.A.) as a fictional version of himself.

★**Most Emmy awards for Best Comedy Series** *Frasier* (NBC,
U.S.A., 1993–2004) won a record 37 Emmys during its run, including five
consecutive wins for Best Comedy Series. Its star, Kelsey Grammer
(U.S.A.), appeared in three different shows as Dr. Frasier Crane, and for
each series received Emmy acknowledgement: twice for *Cheers* (NBC,
U.S.A.), once for his guest appearance on *Wings* (NBC, U.S.A.), and nine
times (winning four) for *Frasier*—the **most TV shows to receive Emmy
nominations for the same character.**

★**LONGEST UNINTERRUPTED
TRANSMISSION OF A TV SERIES** From
June 7–11, 2008, the German pay TV
channel Sat.1 Comedy broadcast—without
any interruptions—all 236 episodes of the
U.S. TV series *Friends*. The comedy
marathon was broadcast primarily to give
viewers the chance to watch something
other than Euro 2008, the UEFA European
Football Championship, in which Germany
finished as runners-up.

SEPT. 12: The **longest contract in National Hockey League history** is
the 15-year deal given to goaltender Rick DiPietro (U.S.A.) by the New York
Islanders (U.S.A.) on this day in 2006.

 ★LONGEST-RUNNING SITCOM (MOST EPISODES) During its 20th season (2008–09), *The Simpsons* (U.S.A.) became the longest-running TV sitcom by number of episodes broadcast. The classic cartoon sitcom, which first broadcast on Fox (U.S.A.) on December 17, 1989, has now seen 443 episodes (and counting) aired, overtaking the 435 episodes of former record holder *The Adventures of Ozzie and Harriet* (ABC, U.S.A.), which ran from 1952 to 1966.

Largest TV audience for a comedy show The 2.5-hour-long finale of *M*A*S*H* (CBS, U.S.A.)—*Goodbye, Farewell and Amen*—had an estimated audience of 125 million (from 50.15 million households) on February 28, 1983. The black comedy/medical drama recounted the experiences of field doctors in the Korean War, and the final episode was seen by 77% of the viewing public—or 60.2% of all U.S. households.

 ★MOST SUCCESSFUL TELENOVELA In terms of its global reach, the most successful telenovela is *Yo Soy Betty, La Fea* ("I am Ugly Betty"), created by Fernando Gaitán (Colombia), which aired on Colombia's RCN Television network from 1999 to 2001. It has gone on to be the first truly global telenovela, being shown in its original form throughout Latin America and Spain, and dubbed for at least 15 other countries. Adaptations or remakes have also been produced in 19 other languages, with the U.S. remake alone showing on at least 50 TV networks around the world.

SEPT. 13: The **fastest production car** is an Ultimate Aero TT Super Car that achieved a speed of 256.14 mph (412 km/h) on Highway 221 in Washington, U.S.A., on September 13, 2007.

MOST BAFTA NOMINATIONS The British Academy of Film and Television Arts (BAFTA) TV awards are the UK equivalent of the Emmys, and the most frequent nominee is comedienne Victoria Wood (UK), whose record 12th nomination came in 2007 for her role in *Housewife, 49* (ITV, UK).

SOAP OPERAS

★**First soap opera** Soap operas began life on U.S. radio in the 1930s; the name refers to the soap manufacturers that often sponsored these continuing dramas. The mother of the soap opera was Irna Phillips (U.S.A., 1901–73), who created the first radio soap, *Painted Dreams,* which debuted on October 20, 1930. Phillips would later go on to create three giants in the field: *The Guiding Light* (U.S.A., NBC Radio, 1937–1956; CBS TV, 1952–2009), *As the World Turns* (U.S.A., CBS TV, 1956–present), and *Another World* (U.S.A., NBC TV, 1964–1999).

★**First TV soap opera** In 1944, Lever Brothers sponsored TV versions of two radio soaps—*Big Sister* and *Aunt Jenny's Real Life Stories*—on Dumont's New York station. Two years later, *Faraway Hill* (October 2 to December 18, 1946) became the first networked soap opera.

★**Longest-running soap opera** *The Guiding Light* (later just *Guiding Light*) began on NBC radio on January 25, 1937, and first aired on television on June 30, 1952. The classic soap, which is based around the central themes of family, love, romance, community, and the trials and tribulations of human life, ran until September 18, 2009, on U.S. TV (CBS).

The longest-running soap on UK television is *Coronation Street* (ITV), which debuted on December 9, 1960, and is still on air today.

MOST SUCCESSFUL TV SOAP *Dallas* (CBS, U.S.A.) began in 1978 as a mini-series and went on to become the most successful soap opera of all time. By 1980, it was watched by an estimated 83 million people in the U.S.A.—giving it a record 76% share of the TV audience—and had been seen in more than 90 countries. The final episode was broadcast in the U.S.A. on May 3, 1991.

Longest-serving soap star Helen Wagner (U.S.A.) has played Nancy McClosky in *As the World Turns* (U.S.A., CBS) since it premiered on April 2, 1956. Britain's longest-serving soap star is William Roache (UK), who has played Ken Barlow in *Coronation Street* (ITV) since its first episode on December 9, 1960.

★**Most prolific soap opera producer** Telenovelas (the Latin American version of soap opera) are the most widely watched shows in Latin America and are exported in huge numbers to many different territories. It's estimated that telenovelas from Mexico and Brazil are more globally popular than U.S., British, and Australian soap operas combined. The market leader in this field is Mexico's Televisa, closely followed by Brazil's Globo.

★**Most popular soap** *The Young and the Restless* (CBS, U.S.A., 1973–present) rated as the most watched soap of the 2007–08 TV season in the U.S.A.—and the **most watched soap of the decade** (and the 1990s). The daytime drama—shown in 22 countries—has rated no. 1 every week for over 1,000 consecutive weeks in U.S. daytime ratings.

GAME SHOWS & REALITY TV

★**First game show** Canada-based journalist and former teacher Roy Ward Dickson (UK, 1910–78) effectively invented the game show when he adapted quizzes he had written for his pupils to the radio. *Professor Dick and His Question Box* aired on CKCL Radio on May 15, 1935, and Dickson went on to produce many pioneering game show formats, including the first panel game, *Claim to Fame*.

★ MOST SUCCESSFUL REALITY TV FORMAT The UK's *Strictly Come Dancing,* which pairs celebrities with professional dancers and asks the public to vote on which of the couples is the best dancing duo, has spawned more international spin-offs than any other program.

The BBC format has been sold to 38 countries as *Dancing With the Stars,* including the U.S.A. where the eighth season's premiere had 22.8 million viewers on March 9, 2009, which was a record for the show.

★ First TV game show *Spelling Bee* was first transmitted on BBC television at 10:00 p.m. on May 31, 1938. Beamed live from Alexandra Palace, London, UK, the 15-minute show involved host Freddie Grisewood (UK) asking adult contestants to spell various words and was based on a successful radio format adapted by the BBC from the U.S. schools' Spelling Bee competitions. The show ran monthly for just five episodes.

★ First game show contestant to win $100,000 U.S. television networks were required to cap game show winnings after a series of scandals in the 1950s, but NBC limited its contestants' earnings by capping the number of games that could be played by a champion. On the 1980s version of NBC's *Sale of the Century* (U.S.A.), contestant Barbara Phillips (U.S.A.) retired with winnings of over $150,000.

The ☆ **largest cash prize won on a TV game show** is $2,520,700 by Ken Jennings of Salt Lake City, Utah, U.S.A., on the CBS show *Jeopardy!,* winning 74 games between June 2 and November 30, 2004.

★ MOST PROLIFIC TV GAME SHOW HOST (U.S.A.) Bill Cullen (U.S.A., 1920–90) hosted 23 different game shows during a television career that spanned five decades. Cullen's shows included *Winner Take All* (his first, in 1952), *The Price is Right, Blockbusters,* and *The Joker's Wild.* The Bill Cullen Career Achievement Award is now awarded by The Game Show Congress, a nonprofit organization that promotes the game show industry.

SEPT. 15: 171 members of the Chilli Club International (Australia) performed at the opening of the Sydney Olympics, Australia, on September 15, 2000—the **most people simultaneously fire-eating.**

★ **LARGEST OFCOM FINE** In May 2008, ITV pic (UK) was fined a record £5,675,000 ($11,218,000) for irregularities and misconduct over its premium phone line services by Ofcom, the independent regulator for the communication industries in the UK. "Serious editorial issues" were raised over *Ant & Dec's Saturday Night Takeaway* (pictured), *Gameshow Marathon,* and *Soapstar Superstar.* Uncounted votes to the value of £7.8 million ($15.4 million) were logged. ITV pledged to return the missing sum to charity.

★ **Most prolific producers** Together, Mark Goodson and Bill Todman (both U.S.A.) created more than 25 game show formats, producing over 21,830 hours of TV. Goodson alone produced over 39,000 shows.

★ **Costliest game show production error** The Plinko minigame on *The Price is Right* requires the contestant to drop a token down a board studded with pegs; as the chip falls, it is deflected by the pegs and ends up in one of a number of slots worth various amounts of prize money. During the filming of an episode on July 22, 2008, the producers forgot that the Plinko board had been rigged to always result in a $10,000 win and the contestant managed three wins before the fault was detected. The contestant was allowed to keep the $30,000.

★ **MOST SYSTEMATIC GAME SHOW STUDY** Economists eager to understand decision-making processes have analyzed clips from the game show *Deal or No Deal* (Endemol, 2002, UK version pictured). The resulting paper, *Deal or No Deal? Decision Making under Risk in a Large-Payoff Game Show* (Post, Van den Assem, Baltussen, and Thaler; March 2008), explores the choices made by 151 contestants on the show. The conclusion? Players who suffer setbacks early in the game take more risks later on, rather than making decisions based on guaranteed returns—an established economic concept known as "prospect theory."

SEPT. 16: The **largest school reunion** involved 3,299 former pupils of Stadium High School, Tacoma, Washington, U.S.A., attending its centennial event on this day in 2006.

★ **MOST SYNDICATED GAME SHOW** *Who Wants to be a Millionaire?,* created by Celador (UK) and first broadcast in the UK in 1998, can now be seen in over 100 countries around the world. Pictured is U.S. host Regis Philbin (U.S.A.), who won the 2001 Daytime Emmy Award for Outstanding Game Show Host. Most recently, the Indian version of the show featured in the Oscar-winning hit movie *Slumdog Millionaire* (UK, 2008).

FIRST REALITY TV SHOW The first TV show to regularly feature members of the public as its stars was the U.S.A.'s *Candid Camera,* which premiered (as *Candid Microphone*) in 1948. The premise was to perform practical jokes on members of the public and film their reactions.

★ **LARGEST GAME SHOW SET** Hosted by Richard O'Brien (UK, left), British game show *The Crystal Maze* (Chatsworth Television/Channel 4) boasted the world's largest game show set, which was, at the time, the largest TV set in Europe. Technically not a maze but a set of four interconnected "time zones," the Crystal Maze was the size of two football fields and cost about $480,000 to build.

SEPT. 17: The **shortest radio show** is *The Maurie Show,* presented by Maurie Sherman (Canada), which lasts one minute and was first broadcast on Virgin Radio Toronto, Canada, on September 17, 2008.

☆ **FASTEST-SELLING DOWNLOAD SINGLE (UK)** UK reality TV talent show *The X Factor* has been producing record breakers ever since it first hit the small screen in 2004. Series winners Shayne Ward, Leona Lewis, and Alexandra Burke (all UK) have each held the record for **fastest-selling download single in the UK**, with Burke's (pictured) track "Hallelujah" being the current holder with 289,621 downloads sold in the week ending December 27, 2008.

Highest death toll from a game show On February 4, 2006, at least 74 people died during a stampede for tickets for the Filipino game show *Wowowee* (ABS-CBN). The chance to win 1 million pesos ($19,300) led to 30,000 people vying to be at the front of a line leading into the Ultra Stadium in Manila, the Philippines. When the gates finally gave way, hundreds were crushed by the desperate mob.

★**First fly-on-the-wall reality TV series** The 12-part *An American Family* (PBS, filmed 1971; aired 1973) is considered to be the first TV show to feature a prolonged fly-on-the-wall look at real people. Over 10 million viewers would tune in each week to watch as the "stars"—the Louds, a typical nuclear family from Santa Barbara, California, U.S.A.—went about their everyday lives. Viewing figures peaked when mother Ann asked father Bill for a divorce.

HOLLYWOOD HEROES

★**Most overpaid actor** *Forbes* magazine has named Tom Cruise (U.S.A.) the world's most overpaid actor, based on the relationship between the profitability of his movies and the size of his fees. Cruise—named as the most powerful actor in Hollywood in 2008—had a recent run of movies that underperformed at the box office, including *Lions for Lambs* (U.S.A.,

SEPT. 18: In 2006, Anousheh Ansari (Iran) spent $20 million to become the **first female space tourist,** blasting off on this day for an eight-day stay on the International Space Station.

TOM CRUISE With 20 movies in his filmography classed as "blockbusters," Tom Cruise has appeared in the ★ **most $100-million grossing movies.** His first blockbuster was *Top Gun* (U.S.A., 1986), which earned $345 million; his most recent *Valkyrie* (U.S.A./Germany, 2008), a real-life story about the attempted assassination of Adolf Hitler—grossed just over $165 million. Despite this, Cruise was named as the ★ **most overpaid actor** of the year (see p. 384).

2007), which earned just $1.88 for every $1 he was paid. For his last three movies (plus their first three months of DVD sales), Cruise grossed an average of $4 for every $1 he was paid. See *Screen Goddesses* on p. 388 for a full explanation of the formula *Forbes* used to come to this ruling.

HIT MAN

Following his role in *The Dark Knight* (U.S.A., 2008), his death at just 28, and his posthumous Oscar award, Heath Ledger (Australia) topped the list of ★ **"fastest rising" male searched for on Google in 2008.**

JAMES DEAN & HEATH LEDGER In 2009, Heath Ledger (Australia, 1979–2008, above left) became only the second person ever to win an acting Oscar after his death (for the role of The Joker in the 2008 blockbuster *The Dark Knight,* U.S.A.). **The first actor to win an acting Oscar posthumously** was Peter Finch (UK) for his role as Howard Beale in *Network* (U.S.A., 1975). The ★ **most posthumous Oscar nominations for an actor** is two, for James Dean (U.S.A., 1931–55, above) as Cal Trask in *East of Eden* (U.S.A., 1955) and as Jett Rink in *Giant* (U.S.A., 1956).

DANIEL RADCLIFFE Daniel Radcliffe's (UK) starring roles in the five *Harry Potter* movies—plus parts in *The Tailor of Panama* (U.S.A./Ireland, 2001) and *December Boys* (Australia, 2007)—means that he remains unbeaten as the ☆ **highest-average-grossing box-office star in a leading role**, raking in an average of $558 million (£383 million) per film. He is also, therefore, the ★ **highest-grossing actor of the decade.**

☆**Highest paid actor** Keanu Reeves (U.S.A.) received a salary of $15 million for each of the two *Matrix* sequels, *Reloaded* and *Revolutions* (both U.S.A./Australia, 2003), plus 15% of the box-office gross. *The Matrix* (U.S.A./Australia, 1999) earned the actor $10 million plus 10% of the gross, putting his earnings for the trilogy at an estimated $260 million—an average of $87 million per movie.

☆ **Most academy awards (Oscars) for best actor** With his win for portraying gay activist Harvey Milk in *Milk* (U.S.A., 2008), Sean Penn (U.S.A.) became the ninth actor to share the accolade of winning two Oscar trophies for Best Actor; his other was for *Mystic River* (U.S.A., 2003). Marlon Brando (U.S.A.), Gary Cooper (U.S.A.), Daniel Day-Lewis (UK), Tom Hanks (U.S.A.), Dustin Hoffman (U.S.A.), Fredric March (U.S.A.), Jack Nicholson (U.S.A.), and Spencer Tracy (U.S.A.) round out the list.

★**Shortest screen time for a best actor Oscar win** Anthony Hopkins (UK) won a Best Actor Oscar for his performance in *The Silence of the Lambs* (U.S.A., 1991), despite appearing on screen for little more than 16 minutes.

MAGIC TOUCH . . .

According to the UK *Daily Mail* newspaper, Daniel Radcliffe will earn $50 million for reprising his role as Harry Potter in the last two movies of the series—not bad, considering that his first Potter paycheck was for just $362,000!

SEPT. 19: The **pumpkin-chuckin' world record** was set on this day in 1998 when an Aludium Q-36 Pumpkin Modulator was used to fire a pumpkin 4,491 ft. (1,368 m) in Morton, Illinois, U.S.A.

BEST ACTOR: MOST OSCAR NOMINATIONS FOR A CHARACTER One character has inspired more Best Actor Oscar nominations than any other: Henry VIII of England (1491–1547). Pictured right to left are Charles Laughton (UK) in *The Private Life of Henry VIII* (UK, 1933), for which he won the Oscar; Robert Shaw in *A Man for All Seasons* (UK, 1966); and Richard Burton (UK) in *Anne of the Thousand Days* (UK, 1969).

★ **Most Razzie nominations** Sylvester Stallone (U.S.A.) has the dubious honor of being nominated for the annual Golden Raspberry "Worst in Film" Awards a record 30 times (winning 10); nine of the nominations (1984–92) were consecutive, also a record. The Razzies were first awarded in 1981 by U.S. copywriter John Wilson as a lighthearted complement to the American Academy Awards (Oscars).

JOHNNY DEPP *Pirates* star Johnny Depp (U.S.A.) regains his position this year as the ☆ **most powerful actor** in Hollywood. Candidates for this role are assessed on their salary, web hits, news agency and magazine coverage, Celebdaq rating, IMDb star rating, and so on, for a 12-month period.

SEPT. 20: The **first world circumnavigation** was completed on this day in 1522—not by Ferdinand Magellan, as commonly thought (he was murdered in the Philippines), but by his navigator, Juan Sebastián Elcano.

MARLON BRANDO The ★ **first actor to break the $1 million dollar threshold** was Marlon Brando (U.S.A.), who was paid $1.25 million—equivalent today to $8.8 million—for his starring role as Fletcher Christian in *Mutiny on the Bounty* (U.S.A., 1962).

With his small part as Jor-El in *Superman* (1978), he also broke the $3 million mark; he also negotiated a share of the profits, thereby earning $14 million ($46 million today) for just 10 minutes of screen time.

★ **Most Razzie nominations in a single year** In 2004, Ben Stiller (U.S.A.) received a record five Golden Raspberry Worst Actor nominations in one year, for *Along Came Polly, Anchorman, Dodgeball, Envy,* and *Starsky & Hutch* (all U.S.A.).

•In 2007, Eddie Murphy (U.S.A.) won five Razzie nominations for just one film: *Norbert* (U.S.A.). He played three characters, all of whom won a Worst Actor trophy; two of the characters were nominated for Worst Couple, and Murphy was nominated for Worst Screenplay.

☆ **Highest-grossing actor** Over the past year, the movies of Samuel L. Jackson (U.S.A.) have grossed a further $150.3 million at the box office, taking his total career box-office gross to $7.57 billion.

SCREEN GODDESSES

☆ **Most powerful actress** Angelina Jolie (U.S.A.) has retained her position as the top actress in Hollywood's power league thanks to her Oscar-nominated performance in *Changeling* (U.S.A., 2008) and the public's seemingly endless appetite for stories about her relationship with Brad Pitt (U.S.A.) and their ever-expanding family—including the couple's most recent additions, twins Knox Léon and Vivienne Marcheline.

☆ **Most consecutive $100 million-gross movies** Jada Pinkett (U.S.A.) has appeared in seven movies with a domestic gross of over $100 million, four of which were consecutive, a record for an actress: *The Matrix Reloaded* (U.S.A., 2003), *The Matrix Revolutions* (U.S.A., 2003), *Collateral* (U.S.A., 2004) and *Madagascar* (U.S.A., 2005). Her other +$100 mil-

SEPT. 21: The **fastest time to play a concert in each of the 50 states of the U.S.A.** is 50 days by Adam Brodsky (U.S.A.) between August 3 and September 21, 2003.

lion movies were *Scream 2* (U.S.A., 1997), *The Nutty Professor* (U.S.A., 1996) and *Madagascar: Escape 2 Africa* (U.S.A., 2008).

Highest salary per movie In February 2006, it was revealed that Reese Witherspoon (U.S.A.) had struck a pay deal worth $29 million to star in and produce horror movie *Our Family Trouble* (U.S.A., 2009). The deal is based on her wage as an actress, plus a percentage of box-office earnings. This beats the $25 million earned by Julia Roberts (U.S.A.) for *Mona Lisa Smile* (U.S.A., 2003).

★**Most screen credits for a living actress** Marianne Stone (UK) has been credited for appearances in a record-breaking 159 movies from 1943 to 1985. Usually appearing in supporting roles or as a bit-part actress, she is best known for her regular appearances in the *Carry On . . .* movies.

OSCARS

★**Shortest role to win an acting Oscar** Beatrice Straight (U.S.A., 1914–2001) won the Best Actress in a Supporting Role award at the 1977

Academy Awards for her portrayal of Louise Schumacher in *Network* (U.S.A., 1976)—despite appearing on screen for a mere 5 min. 40 sec.!

CAMERON DIAZ The ☆**highest annual earnings for an actress in 2007–08** was $50 million by Cameron Diaz (U.S.A., above left—she's the one on the right, obviously, next to Princess Fiona from *Shrek*). Since her debut in *The Mask* (U.S.A., 1994), Diaz has appeared in a string of hit movies, including *My Best Friend's Wedding* (U.S.A., 1997), *Charlie's Angels* (U.S.A., 2000) and its sequel, and most recently *What Happens in Vegas* (U.S.A., 2008, above right), as well as providing the voice of Fiona in the *Shrek* movies. *(See p. 391 for a list of the 10 wealthiest actresses in Hollywood.)*

....

SEPT. 22: The **most people to perform a synchronized swimming routine** was 105 at the Big Sync in London, UK, on this day in 2007.

....

 A DECADE OF SUCCESS As of June 2008, Emma Watson (UK, above left) had starred in six movies and grossed an average $753,700,000 per movie—the ★ **highest average box-office gross for an actress.** The reason for Watson's incredible success? The five phenomenally successful *Harry Potter* movies that she has starred in since 2001.

Keira Knightley (UK, above right) has starred in 15 movies since 2000, including the three films in the amazing hit series *Pirates of the Caribbean.* According to the Internet Movie Database, the total box-office gross for Knightley's movies in the last decade is $3.42 billion, which is the ★ **highest box-office gross for an actress in multiple roles** (three or more).

 **NICOLE KIDMAN** According to data supplied by Forbes, the ★ **most overpaid actress** is Nicole Kidman (Australia), with a box-office gross of $1 for every $1 paid in salary. To calculate this "payback," the following formula is applied to the star's last three movies to gross over $5 million:

$$\frac{\left(\frac{\text{worldwide box-office}}{2}\right)^* + \text{first 3 months} - \text{budget} \atop \text{of DVD sales}}{\text{salary}} = \text{payback}$$

The box-office figure is halved to approximate the studios' return on each ticket sold

With *The Golden Compass* (U.S.A., 2007), *Invasion* (U.S.A., 2007) and *Bewitched* (U.S.A., 2005) all underperforming, Kidman appears to have had a run of bad luck!

....

SEPT. 23: The **youngest winner of golf's Open championship** is Tom Morris Jr. (UK, b. April 20, 1851). He was 17 years 156 days old when he won the Open at Prestwick Golf Club, Prestwick, UK, on this date in 1868.

....

MILEY CYRUS The ☆ **highest-earning child actor** is currently Miley Cyrus (U.S.A., b. November 23, 1992), who earned an estimated $25 million in 2008 according to *Forbes.* Born Destiny Hope Cyrus (her father is the U.S. country singer Billy Ray Cyrus), the singer-songwriter shot to fame in 2006 as the star of the Disney Channel's *Hannah Montana* series. She subsequently released two solo studio LPs—*Meet Miley Cyrus* (2007) and *Breakout* (2008)—both of which entered the *Billboard* 200 at No. 1. In 2008, *Time* magazine declared her to be one of the 100 Most Influential People in the World.

★ **Most Oscar nominations for the same character in one movie** Only two movie characters have ever had two Oscar nominations for the same film: Rose DeWitt Bukater in *Titanic* (U.S.A., 1997) led to nominations for both Kate Winslet (UK) and Gloria Stuart (U.S.A.); and Iris Murdoch, played by nominees Dame Judi Dench (UK) and Winslet again, in *Iris* (UK/U.S.A., 2001).

WEALTHIEST ACTRESSES (2007–08)

1. Cameron Diaz (U.S.A.) $50 m

2. Keira Knightley (UK) $32 m

3. Jennifer Aniston (U.S.A.) $27 m

4. (tied) Reese Witherspoon and Gwyneth Paltrow (both U.S.A.) $25 m

6. Jodie Foster (U.S.A.) $23 m

7. Sarah Jessica Parker (U.S.A.) $18 m

8. Meryl Streep (U.S.A.) $16 m

9. Amy Adams (U.S.A.) $14.5 m

10. Angelina Jolie (U.S.A.) $14 m

Source: *Forbes*

BRIGITTE NIELSEN When it comes to actresses, almost everyone looks up to Brigitte Nielsen (Denmark, b. July 15, 1963)—literally. Along with Sigourney Weaver (U.S.A., b. October 8, 1949), Margaux Hemingway (U.S.A., 1955–96), and Geena Davis (U.S.A., b. January 21, 1957), the statuesque blonde tops out at 6 ft. (1.82 m). All four share the record for **tallest actress in a leading role.**

Most nominations Meryl Streep (U.S.A., b. June 22, 1949) was nominated for a total of 15 Oscars from 1979 to 2008. She has been nominated 12 times for Best Actress, winning in 1983 for *Sophie's Choice* (U.S.A., 1982), and three for Best Actress in a Supporting Role, winning in 1980 for *Kramer vs. Kramer* (U.S.A., 1979). Her 15th nomination followed her starring role in *Doubt* (U.S.A., 2008).

Most Best Actress wins Katharine Hepburn (U.S.A., 1907–2003) won four Best Actress Oscars, for *Morning Glory* (U.S.A., 1933) in 1934, *Guess Who's Coming to Dinner* (U.S.A., 1967) in 1968, *The Lion in Winter* (UK, 1968) in 1969, and *On Golden Pond* (U.S.A., 1981) in 1982.

Oldest Best Actress Jessica Tandy (UK, 1909–94) won the Best Actress Oscar for *Driving Miss Daisy* (U.S.A., 1989) on March 29, 1990, at the age of 80 years 295 days. The **youngest winner of a Best Actress Academy Award** was Marlee Matlin (U.S.A., b. August 24, 1965), who won on March 30, 1987, for her role as Sarah Norman in *Children of a Lesser God* (U.S.A., 1986), aged 21 years 218 days.

AT THE MOVIES

☆**Most Oscars won by a film** Three films have won 11 Oscars. The first to achieve the record was *Ben-Hur* (U.S.A., 1959), which won from 12 nominations on April 4, 1960, followed by *Titanic* (U.S.A., 1997) from 14 nominations on March 23, 1998, and *The Lord of the Rings: The Return of the King* (NZ/U.S.A., 2003), which completed a clean sweep to win all 11 of its nominations on February 29, 2004.

....

SEPT. 24: The **fastest tennis serve by a man** is 155 mph (249.4 km/h) by Andy Roddick (U.S.A.) during the Davis Cup semifinal match on September 24, 2006.

....

★ **HIGHEST-GROSSING MOVIE BY A FEMALE DIRECTOR** With a global box-office gross of over $351 million, *Twilight* (U.S.A., 2008), directed by Catherine Hardwicke (U.S.A.), is the highest-grossing movie directed by a woman. Based on the best-selling novel by Stephenie Meyer, *Twilight* explores the relationship between a teenage schoolgirl and her vampire boyfriend. A sequel, *The Twilight Saga: New Moon* (2009), is currently in theaters.

☆ **Highest-grossing studio** In 2008, over 248 million tickets were sold for the 31 movies released by Warner Bros., earning them a gross of $1.78 billion (£1.22 billion) and a record 18.13% market share.

★ **Most popular film genre** Comedies accounted for 30.26% of the movies released in 2008, the highest market share of any genre. Analyzing the box-office results from this year's releases, it is possible to formulate the elements for the ideal Hollywood movie: a contemporary, live-action, adult (but PG-13-rated) comedy based on an original screenplay.

★ **FIRST FULL-LENGTH FEATURE FILMED IN DIGITAL HIGH RES** The French movie *Vidocq* (2001)—about the life of Eugène François Vidocq, founder of the *Sûreté Nationale*, France's National Police—was the first theatrical release of a movie shot on digital 1080p24 cameras. This revolutionary film was released a whole year before *Star Wars II—Attack of the Clones* (U.S.A., 2002) made it to the screen.

SEPT. 25: The **most valuable chocolate bar**—a piece from Robert Scott's (UK) 1901–04 D*iscovery* expedition to the Antarctic—sold at auction in London, UK, on this day in 2001 for £470 (then $687).

★ **FIRST FULLY DIGITAL FEATURE FILM** *The Rescuers Down Under* (U.S.A., 1990), the first animated sequel made by Disney (U.S.A.), was also the first movie to be made using the Computer Animation Production System (CAPS)—Disney's digital ink-and-paint system developed with Pixar (U.S.A.). CAPS allowed for, among other things, the digital colorization of scanned elements, multi-plane backgrounds, and complex camera movements never before available to animators.

★ **MOST DOWNLOADED MOVIE TRAILER (24 HOURS)** The trailer for J. J. Abram's (U.S.A.) reboot of the *Star Trek* (U.S.A., 2009) series was downloaded from Apple.com a record 1.8 million times in 24 hours, starting on March 6, 2009. It became the site's most popular high-definition (HD) download ever, with more than five million downloads in its first five days. The movie, which opened on May 8, 2009, returns to the roots of the TV series and follows the characters as they first meet.

 ☆ **HIGHEST BOX-OFFICE GROSS (OPENING DAY)** With a worldwide box-office gross of $997 million, *Batman: The Dark Knight* (U.S.A., 2008) is the second most successful movie of all time, behind *Titanic* (U.S.A., 1997). *The Dark Knight* opened on July 18, 2008, and raked in $66.4 million, setting new box-office records for ☆ **opening-** and ☆ **single-day** **earnings.** *See table on p. 395 for more* Dark Knight *achievements.*

★ **FIRST ANIMATION NOMINATED FOR BEST FOREIGN FILM** *Vals Im Bashir* (*Waltz with Bashir*, Israel/Germany/France/U.S.A., 2008) was the first animation to be Oscar-nominated for Best Foreign Language Film. The movie, directed by Ari Folman (Israel), tells the story of an ex-soldier piecing together his shattered memories of an Israeli Army mission in the First Lebanon War (1982).

☆ **Highest earnings for a film producer** TV and movie producer Jerry Bruckheimer (U.S.A.)—the man responsible for bringing *Pirates of the Caribbean: At World's End* (U.S.A., 2008) and *National Treasure: Book of Secrets* (U.S.A., 2008) to the big screen, as well as *CSI, Cold Case,* and *Without a Trace* to the small screen—has overtaken Stephen Spielberg as

THE DARK KNIGHT RECORDS

•Highest-grossing opening day	$66.4 million
•Highest-grossing single day	$66.4 million
•Highest-grossing weekend	$158 million
•Highest gross from a midnight screening	$18.5 million
•Highest-grossing PG-13	$997 million
•Widest film release in a single country	4,366 screens (U.S.A.)
•Highest-grossing first release on IMAX	$55 million
•Fastest time to gross $100 million	2 days
•Fastest time to gross $200 million	5 days
•Fastest time to gross $500 million	45 days

SEPT. 26: The **longest speech made in the United Nations** lasted 4 hr. 29 min. It was made on this day in 1960 by President Fidel Castro Ruz (Cuba).

Hollywood's highest-earning mogul. The *Forbes* Celebrity 100 estimated his earnings for 2007–08 at a cool $145 million.

Spielberg, however, remains the **most powerful person in motion pictures** according to *Forbes*, having recently produced *Transformers* (U.S.A., 2007) and directed *Indiana Jones and the Kingdom of the Crystal Skull* (U.S.A., 2008).

★**Most Golden Raspberries won by a movie** Three cinematic clangers share the record for winning nine trophies at the Golden Raspberry Awards, which celebrate the worst in Hollywood movie making. The most recent was *I Know Who Killed Me* (U.S.A., 2007), starring Lindsay Lohan (U.S.A.), who earned two Razzies for both the roles she played; the other two were John Travolta's (U.S.A.) *Battlefield Earth* (U.S.A., 2000), and *Showgirls* (U.S.A., 1995).

SPECIAL EFFECTS

First special-effects shot in a movie The silent, minute-long *Execution of Mary, Queen of Scots* (U.S.A., 1895), shot at the Edison Laboratories in West Orange, New Jersey, U.S.A., was the first piece of film footage to use stop-action, giving the impression of a beheading. The scene was so compelling that some viewers at the time believed an actress had given her life to film it!

★**First CG character with realistic hair/fur** Kitty, the saber-toothed tiger created by Industrial Light & Magic for the live-action movie version of *The Flintstones* (U.S.A., 1994), was the first computer-generated character covered with realistic fur.

☆**Most Oscar nominations for visual effects** Dennis Muren (U.S.A.) has been nominated for an Oscar on 13 occasions, the first being in 1982 for *Dragonslayer* (U.S.A., 1981) and the most recent being in 2006 for *War of the Worlds* (U.S.A., 2005). During his career, he has received an Academy Special Achievement Award for *Star Wars: Episode V—The Empire Strikes Back* (U.S.A., 1980) in 1981 and a Technical Achievement Award "for the development of a Motion Picture Figure Mover for animation photography" in 1982. He also holds the record for the **most Oscars won by a visual-effects artist** (8) and is the only FX artist with a star on the Hollywood Walk of Fame.

....

SEPT. 27: The **longest hot dog** measured 375 ft. 0.7 in. (114.32 m) and it was made by Empacadora Ponderosa (Mexico) in Monterrey, Mexico, on September 27, 2008.

....

★**FIRST FILM WITH DIGITAL WATER** The first movie to use computer software to simulate the properties of water was Dreamworks' *Antz* (U.S.A., 1998). Prior to this, computer-generated fluid effects were drawn, frame by frame, using graphics programs. Realistic water effects require powerful, physics-based computer simulations—at the time *Antz* was released, the only detailed studies of fluid dynamics were being carried out by scientists at the Los Alamos National Laboratory in New Mexico, U.S.A., researching the flow of particles after a nuclear strike.

★**First use of Claymation** The Oscar-winning movie *Closed Mondays* (U.S.A., 1975)—the directorial debut of Will Vinton (U.S.A.)—saw the first use of the Claymation process, in which modeling clay is animated using stop-motion. Vinton patented the process and went on to create two decades of colorful work, including the famous California Raisins and many MTV commercials.

★**FIRST TV SERIES TO FEATURE 3D CG MODELS** The first computer-generated 3D spacecraft on TV were those conceived by Ron Thornton (U.S.A.) and his effects company Foundation Imaging for *Babylon 5* (1993–1998). The pilot show—*The Gathering*—won an Emmy for its special effects (and another for its makeup).

SEPT. 28: On this day in 2008, Haile Gebrselassie (Ethiopia) ran the **fastest marathon** with a time of 2 hr. 3 min. 59 sec. He performed this record-breaking feat at the Berlin Marathon, Germany.

★ **FIRST USE OF "CARI" ANIMATION** Effects house Industrial Light & Magic (ILM) created the CARI (short for "caricature") animation program to render skin and muscle tissue onto animated characters. Its rollout was for the movie *Dragonheart* (U.S.A., 1996), in which it was used to give life to Draco, a dragon voiced by Sean Connery (UK).

★ **MOST EFFECTS SHOTS IN A MOVIE** Peter Jackson's *King Kong* (NZ/U.S.A./Germany, 2005) featured 2,510 visual effects shots, with a further 279 included in the extended DVD version. A total of 3,809 FX shots were created, although not all were used. The movie won an Oscar for Best Visual Effects in 2006.

FACT

Young Sherlock Holmes (U.S.A./UK, 1985) was the **first full-length movie to feature a completely computer-generated character.** To achieve the effect of a stained-glass knight emerging from a window, animator John Lassiter (U.S.A.), who would go on to create *Toy Story* (U.S.A., 1995), relied solely on computer graphics.

SEPT. 29: The **largest bouquet** was made from 156,940 roses. It was created by and displayed in NordWestZentrum shopping mall in Frankfurt am Main, Germany, on September 29, 2005.

370: hours of footage shot for Peter Jackson's *King Kong* (2005)— over 378 miles (609 km) of film—123 times more than the final cut.

FACT

Industrial Light & Magic also used their CARI software to create the all-CG Martians in Tim Burton's *Mars Attacks!* (U.S.A., 1996).

☆**MOST SPOT POINTS IN FACIAL MOTION CAPTURE** The facial expressions of Dr. Manhattan in *Watchmen* (U.S.A., 2009) were captured by Sony Pictures Imageworks (U.S.A.) using 165 spot points marked onto the face of actor Billy Crudup (U.S.A., left). According to the Motion Capture Society, the suit worn by Crudup during the filming of the movie—a suit covered in 2,500 LEDs to give the character his blue glow—was also the "most original mocap [motion capture] suit" yet designed.

TELEVISION FX

★**Largest makeup budget** *Buffy the Vampire Slayer* (1997–2003) had the largest makeup budget for a TV show, with a weekly average of $3,000 allocated for contact lenses, foam-rubber appliances, and false teeth; the cost of whole-body transformations, however, could exceed $30,000.

A total of $1 million was budgeted for makeup in *Planet of the Apes* (U.S.A., 1968)—the **largest makeup budget for a movie**—equal to $4.95 million today. This amount represents nearly 17% of the film's total production cost of $5.8 million—equivalent to $28.71 million today.

★**Most digital effects in a TV series** Brian Henson's (U.S.A.) *Farscape* (1999–2003) employed about 25 computer artists to create between 40 and 50 effects shots per episode. The effects teams had just seven days to work on each episode, at a rate of 22 episodes per year. The third season alone featured 1,109 digital effects.

Dinotopia (2002)—the tale of a hidden continent where humans and dinosaurs live together—needed 1,800 visual effects shots: the ★ **most digital effects in a TV mini-series.** The show cost $80 million to produce and featured the largest sets ever constructed in Europe at the time.

★ **MOST COMPLEX CG HUMAN** The character of Aki Ross in *Final Fantasy: The Spirits Within* (U.S.A., 2001) is composed of over 100,000 subdivided polygons; she has 60,000 hairs, each individually modeled and animated, taking up a quarter of the computer processing power, and 16 motion-capture cameras were used to create and animate her body.

★ **First Emmy for special effects** The 13-part documentary series *Cosmos* (1980), produced and presented by astrophysicist Carl Sagan (U.S.A.), utilized the skills of effects technicians who had previously worked on *Star Wars* (1977) to create a "spaceship of the imagination"—an impressive set that replicated the inside of a space station with portholes looking out onto the Universe. The project took two years to plan, earning the show the first ever Emmy award for special effects.

THE NAME'S BOND . . .

Most appearances as James Bond Sean Connery (UK, b. August 25, 1930) and Roger Moore (UK, b. October 14, 1927) have each appeared as 007 seven times. Connery starred in the first Bond movie, *Dr. No* (UK, 1962); Moore debuted in 1973's *Live and Let Die.*

★ **First "astro spiral" in a movie** *The Man with the Golden Gun* (1974) featured a revolutionary "astro spiral" jump, in which an AMC Hornet X hatchback drives up a corkscrewed ramp and spins 360° about its length, connecting with a landing ramp on the other side of a river. Loren "Bumps" Willert (U.S.A.) performed the spiral stunt.

SEPT. 30: The **first daily TV service** began on this day in 1929, when programs by John Logie Baird (UK) were transmitted by the BBC from the Long Acre Studio in London, UK.

★TOP 10 STUNTS [AS VOTED FOR BY READERS OF *RADIO TIMES*]

FILM	STUNT
1. *Casino Royale* (UK/U.S.A., 2006)	Crane-to-crane jump
2. *The Spy Who Loved Me* (UK, 1977)	Ski jump/parachute jump
3. *The Man with the Golden Gun* (UK, 1974)	Aston spiral ramp jump
4. *Live and Let Die* (UK, 1973)	Speedboat leap
5. *The World Is Not Enough* (UK/U.S.A., 1999)	River Thames speedboat chase
6. *Goldfinger* (UK, 1964)	Aston Martin ejector seat trick
7. *GoldenEye* (UK/U.S.A., 1995)	Dive off the Verzasca Dam
8. *On Her Majesty's Secret Service* (UK, 1969)	Ski chase
9. *Live and Let Die* (UK, 1973)	Jumping over crocodiles
10. *Tomorrow Never Dies* (UK/U.S.A., 1997)	Motorcycle jump over a helicopter

Longest speedboat jump in a movie In a truly iconic Bond stunt, Jerry Comeaux (U.S.A.) jumped a 1972 Glastron GT-150 speedboat over a road for a distance of 120 ft. (36.5 m) in *Live and Let Die* (1973).

Largest film studio stage The 007 stage at Pinewood Studios in Iver Heath, UK, measures 336 × 139 × 41 ft. (102 × 42 × 12 m). Designed in

OCT. 1: Disney World, the world's **largest amusement resort,** is set in 12,140 ha (30,000 acres) of Orange and Osceola Counties, Florida, U.S.A. It was opened this day in 1971.

1976 for *The Spy Who Loved Me* (1977) it accommodates 1.2 million gallons (4.5 million liters) of water, a full-scale section of a 600,000-ton supertanker and three scaled-down submarines.

☆ **Most expensive James Bond movie memorabilia** An anonymous Swiss collector paid $1.9 million (£1.1 million) for the 1965 Aston Martin DB5 featured in *Goldfinger* and *Thunderball*. The gadget-packed car was sold at auction in Phoenix, Arizona, U.S.A., on January 20, 2006.

★ **First Bond theme nominated for a best original song Oscar** With "Live and Let Die," Paul McCartney (UK) and Wings—aided by producer George Martin (UK)—created the first Bond theme song to receive an Oscar nomination for Best Original Song (1973). It charted at No. 2 in the U.S.A. and No. 7 in the UK, but lost the Oscar to "The Way We Were," from the movie of the same name. To date, no Bond music has won an Oscar.

SEAN CONNERY Played Bond in six of the first seven official movies, and in the one-off non-EON film *Never Say Never Again* (UK, 1983).

GEORGE LAZENBY (Australia, b. September 5, 1939) Lazenby has the distinction of being the only actor to play 007 just once in the official series—in *On Her Majesty's Secret Service* (1969).

ROGER MOORE Moore rose to stardom on British TV in the 1960s with his eponymous portrayal of *The Saint*. He assumed the role of Bond in 1973, playing the part for 12 years—longer than any other actor.

OCT. 2: The **highest speed in an aircraft propelled only by human power** is 27.5 mph (44.26 km/h) by Holger Rochelt (Germany) in M*usculair* II at Oberschleissheim, Germany, on this date in 1985.

BEST BOND . . .

Based on box-office figures adjusted for inflation, the ★ **most popular James Bond** is Sean Connery, grossing an average of $618.04 million per movie at current prices. This compares with the average of $559.87 million for Daniel Craig, who occupies second place.

TIMOTHY DALTON (UK, b. March 21, 1946) **Played Bond twice, in** *The Living Daylights* **(UK/U.S.A., 1987) and** *Licence to Kill* **(UK/U.S.A., 1989). He had been mooted for the role as early as 1969's** *On Her Majesty's Secret Service.*

PIERCE BROSNAN (Ireland/U.S.A., b. May 16, 1953) **Played Bond four times, revitalizing the series, and bowing out with 2002's** *Die Another Day* **(UK/U.S.A.).**

DANIEL CRAIG (UK, b. March 2, 1968) **The "Blond Bond" overcame the doubters with a killer performance in** *Casino Royale* **(2006).**

Highest-grossing Bond movie As of March 2006, *Casino Royale* (2006)—the 21st installment of the James Bond franchise by EON Productions—had grossed a worldwide total of $594,239,066 (£304,693,332). It was the first Bond movie to feature Daniel Craig (UK) in the lead role.

....

OCT. 3: The **largest printed map** measured 19 ft. 8 in. × 36 ft. 1 in. (6 × 11 m) and was unveiled this day by the State Geodetic Administration of the Republic of Croatia in Dubrovnik, Croatia, in 2007.

....

MOST CANNON ROLLS Stuntman Adam Kirley (UK, left) carried out seven cannon rolls—in which a vehicle flips onto its roof and rolls over repeatedly—in an Aston Martin DBS (above), for 2006 Bond outing *Casino Royale.* The head-spinning stunt took place at Millbrook Proving Ground in Milton Keynes, UK, in July 2006.

★ **Most prolific Bond composer** In total, eight composers have created soundtracks for the Bond movies, the most prolific being John Barry (UK), with 11 movies to his name (plus his arrangement of Monty Norman's classic opening theme for *Dr. No*).

★ **Most prolific James Bond author** Perhaps surprisingly, Ian Fleming was not the most prolific writer of James Bond novels. Between 1981 and 1996, John Gardner (UK) wrote 14 Bond novels and two screenplay adaptations, surpassing Fleming's output of 12 novels and two short-story collections.

MUSIC

☆ **Bestselling download single in the U.S.A.** "Low," by rappers Flo Rida and T-Pain (both U.S.A.), which topped the chart in December 2007, had sold over 4.4 million downloads in the U.S.A. by December 2008.

Having topped the U.S. Hot Digital Songs chart for 13 consecutive weeks between December 15, 2007, and March 8, 2008, the track also holds the record for the ★ **most weeks at No.1 on the U.S. digital chart.**

★ **LONGEST TOP 10 UK CHART RUN BY A GROUP** After an unprecedented run of 22 successive Top 10 singles in the UK, Oasis (UK) had to settle with a peak position of No. 12 for their December 2008 release, "I'm Outta Time." Oasis was the UK's most successful band in the 1990s, and its debut album *Definitely Maybe* (1994) was the fastest-selling UK debut LP of all time when released. Pictured is singer Liam Gallagher.

X-REF

If you're a gamer, you won't want to miss the feast of facts and figures on our Video Gaming spread—flip to p. 412 now!

Flo Rida's "Right Round" sold 636,000 downloads in its first week of release, making it the ☆ **bestselling download single in the U.S. in one week.** The record-breaking single entered the U.S. digital chart at No. 1 on February 28, 2009.

★ **Most downloaded free track in a week** For one week only, starting April 28, 2008, British rock band Coldplay offered the track "Violet Hill" as a free download. That week it was downloaded 2 million times.

★ **Most successful digital singles sales year in the U.S.A.** In 2008, 1.04 billion digital tracks were sold in the U.S.A. The biggest individual seller that year was "Bleeding Love" by Leona Lewis (UK), which sold 3.3 million copies.

☆ **Most consecutive no. 1 singles** KinKi Kids (Japan) had 28 consecutive singles debut at No. 1 on the Japanese chart between July 28, 1997, and January 28, 2009. The duo scored their 28th successive No. 1 with "Yakusoku" ("Promise").

★ **Most hits on Billboard's Hot 100 by the same manager** The Billboard Hot 100 chart of June 7, 2008, featured a total of 17 songs recorded by musicians who were managed by Simon Fuller (UK), 14 of which debuted that week. All 17 hits were by artists launched on the TV series *American Idol*, created by Fuller.

★ **BEST START ON THE US DIGITAL CHART BY A FEMALE ARTIST** Katy Perry (U.S.A.) is the only female artist to have sold over 3 million downloads of her first two releases. They were "I Kissed A Girl" and "Hot N Cold," both released in 2008.

OCT. 4: The record for the **longest backward motorcycle ride** is 93.21 miles (150 km), achieved by Hou Xiaobin (China) in Binzhou City, China, on October 4, 2006.

★ **MOST SIMULTANEOUS NEW ENTRIES ON THE HOT 100 BY A SOLO ACT** *American Idol* winner David Cook (U.S.A.) secured an unprecedented 11 simultaneous new entries on the Billboard Hot 100 chart of June 7, 2008. Cook's highest entry, "The Time Of My Life," entered the Hot 100 at No. 3. *See p. 408 for more on David's chart successes.*

★ **Best-selling single in the UK (female)** The 2008 *X Factor* winner Alexandra Burke (UK) is the only female soloist to have sold in excess of 1 million copies of a single in the UK. She achieved this landmark in January 2009 with her first release, a cover of Leonard Cohen's (Canada) "Hallelujah."

★ **Most hit singles on the UK chart by a British act** Cliff Richard (UK) had his first UK hit in October 1958 with "Move It." He scored his 134th chart entry 50 years later with "Thank You For A Lifetime" in September 2008. It was also a record 123rd Top 40 entry by the British singer, who has sold over 21 million singles in the UK.

★ **Most US Top 10 entries** When "4 Minutes" increased Madonna's (U.S.A.) number of U.S. Hot 100 Top 10 entries to 37 on April 12, 2008, she took a record that Elvis Presley had held for almost 36 years.

On August 9, 2008, Madonna notched up her 39th No. 1 hit on the U.S. Club Chart with her sixth successive chart topper, "Give It 2 Me." In doing so, the star also established a new record for the ★ **most No. 1s on the U.S. Dance/Club Play chart.**

When Madonna's 2008 single "Miles Away" peaked at No. 39, it ended her run of 64 UK Top 20 entries in a row (59 of which had reached the Top 10)—the ★ **longest run of Top 20 hits by a solo artist.**

☆ **Most No. 1 albums by a country music artist** George Strait (U.S.A.) scored his 22nd No. 1 country album in the U.S.A. on April 19, 2008 with *Troubadour,* which also gave him his fourth No. 1 album on the pop chart. On April 18, 2009, Strait notched up his 44th No. 1 single with "River of Love," a record for the ☆ **most No. 1 entries on the U.S. Hot Country Songs chart.**

★ **MOST NO.1S FROM A MUSIC TV TALENT SHOW** When David Cook's (U.S.A.) "The Time Of My Life" debuted at No. 1 on Billboard's Hot Digital Songs and Hot Digital Tracks charts, it brought the total of No. 1 hits by artists discovered on U.S. TV talent show *American Idol* to 179. Kelly Clarkson (U.S.A.) had the first *American Idol* No. 1 in October 2002 with "A Moment Like This."

140: the **most guitars smashed on tour,** by Matt Bellamy (UK) of Muse, during concerts in 2004.

★ MOST SINGLES TO ENTER STRAIGHT INTO THE U.S. TOP 20 IN A YEAR BY A GROUP In 2008, the Jonas Brothers (U.S.A., Kevin, Nick, and Joe, pictured left to right) had five separate tracks enter the U.S. Hot 100 in the Top 20: "Play My Music" (No. 20), "Pushin' Me Away" (No. 16), "Burnin' Up" (No. 5, their biggest U.S. hit as of April 2009), "Tonight" (No. 8), and "A Little Bit Longer" (No. 11). The band shot to fame on the Disney Channel TV network.

★Best start on the U.S. country chart by a female artist *American Idol* winner Carrie Underwood (U.S.A.) had her seventh solo U.S. country No. 1 hit with "Just A Dream" on November 8, 2008, just 3 years 5 months after her first solo Hot Country Songs chart entry.

★Most simultaneous R&B hits in the U.S. On August 9, 2008, rapper Lil Wayne (U.S.A.) had 13 tracks in the U.S. R&B Top 100. This included five hits in the Top 40.

☆YOUNGEST FEMALE TO HAVE FIVE NO. 1 STUDIO ALBUMS IN THE U.S.A. In December 2008, *Circus* topped the U.S. album chart, making Britney Spears (U.S.A.) the youngest female artist in history to have five of her albums reach No. 1. Before she turned 20 years old on December 2, 2001, Spears had sold an unprecedented 37 million records around the world, making her the all-time bestselling teenage artist.

OCT. 5: The **youngest Oscar nominee for Best Actor** was Jackie Cooper (U.S.A., b. September 15, 1922), nominated for playing Skippy Skinner in *Skippy* (U.S.A., 1931) on October 5, 1931, aged 9 years 20 days.

★ **OLDEST TOP 10 ALBUM DEBUT IN THE UK** U.S. blues singer Seasick Steve (born Steve Wold) made his UK Top 10 album debut on October 11, 2008, at the age of 68, with *I Started Out With Nothin And I Still Got Most Of It Left.*

☆ **Most downloads from one company** In June 2008, Apple iTunes—which in February 2008 replaced Wal-Mart as the biggest-selling U.S. music retailer—announced that it had sold its 6 billionth downloaded track. The company has a catalog of over 8 million tracks.

☆ **Highest annual earnings for a band** The Police (UK) earned an estimated $115 million in 2007–08, according to the *Forbes* Celebrity 100 list.

★ **Best-selling act with no concert appearances** Irish singer/songwriter Enya, who has sold 70 million albums since 1988, had (up to the end of 2008) never performed a solo concert.

★ **Highest climb to No. 1 on the Billboard Hot 100** Kelly Clarkson's (U.S.A.) single "My Life Would Suck Without You" rose from No. 97 to No. 1 after it sold 280,000 downloads in its first week of release on February 7, 2009.

★ **Most new entries on the Billboard Hot Digital Songs chart** David Cook (U.S.A.) registered 14 new entries on the Hot Digital Songs chart of June 7, 2008, including the No. 1 "The Time Of My Life," which sold 260,000 downloads.

☆ **BEST-SELLING UK ALBUM SERIES BY VARIOUS ARTISTS** Sales of the *Now!* series of albums passed the 85-million mark in August 2008. At that point, 70 albums had been released in the series, which began in October 1983. *Now! 70* sold a record 383,002 copies in its first week of release. The artist with the most tracks featured in the series is Robbie Williams (UK), with 28.

OCT. 6: The **longest bridal wedding veil** was worn by Ingrid Schlott at her wedding to Michael Stöpke (both Germany) on October 6, 2007, in Loxstedt-Dedesdorf, Germany. It was 10,393 ft. 8 in. (3,168 m) long.

★ **FASTEST-SELLING SOUNDTRACK ALBUM IN THE UK** The soundtrack LP to *High School Musical 3* sold 97,972 copies in its first week of release (week ending November 1, 2008). The three *High School Musical* movies to date have been hugely popular: the first in the series is the most successful film ever produced by Disney Channel Original Movie (DCOM).

★ **Most simultaneous top 10 albums on U.S. Pop Catalog chart** On November 8, 2008, Australian rock band AC/DC became the first act to hold five of the top 6 places on the U.S. Pop Catalog album chart. The group found its name after a band member's sister read the label on a vacuum cleaner.

☆ **BIGGEST-SELLING DIGITAL DOWNLOAD SINGLE IN THE UK** "Sex On Fire" by Kings of Leon (U.S.A.) had sold 560,000 digital copies in the UK as of March 2009. Their 2008 album *Only By The Night* is the best-selling digital album in the UK, with download sales in excess of 152,000.

OCT. 7: The **oldest college graduate,** Allan Stewart (Australia, b. March 7, 1915), received a law degree, aged 91 years 214 days, from the University of New England, NSW, Australia, on October 7, 2006.

13.5 MILLION: copies of The Beatles' LP I sold in its first month, making it the **fastest-selling album.**

★ **BEST-SELLING DOWNLOAD ALBUM IN THE UK** *Viva La Vida Or Death And All His Friends* by Coldplay (UK) is the top-selling digital album in the UK with sales of 115,000 to the end of 2008. The album sold 30,378 copies in the first week it went on sale (week ending June 21, 2008).

★ **BEST-SELLING DOWNLOAD FEMALE ARTIST IN THE UK** Barbados-born Rihanna (Robyn Rihanna Fenty) sold over 2.5 million downloads in the UK from September 2005 to December 2008. She has scored U.S./UK No. 1 singles with "Umbrella" and "Take a Bow," and U.S. No. 1s with "SOS" and "Disturbia."

X-REF

If your pinups are movie legends rather than pop stars, take a trip down our own Walk of Fame, starting with Hollywood Heroes on p. 384.

OCT. 8: The **level-flight duration record for a hand-launched paper aircraft** is 27.6 seconds, by Ken Blackburn (U.S.A.) at the Georgia Dome, Atlanta, Georgia, U.S.A., on October 8, 1998.

Art & Media

★ FASTEST-SELLING UK TOUR All 600,000 tickets for British band Take That's 2009 UK tour sold out within five hours when they went on sale on October 31, 2008. Originally five people, including Robbie Williams (UK), the current incarnation (pictured left, left to right) comprises Howard Donald, Mark Owen, Gary Barlow, and Jason Orange (all UK).

★ Most entries in the U.S. Top 20 in a year by a solo artist In 2008, Taylor Swift (U.S.A.) had six tracks enter the Top 20 in their first week on the Hot 100: "Change," "Love Story," "Fearless," "You're Not Sorry," "You Belong With Me," and "White Horse." In total that year, Taylor had 13 Top 100 entries.

★ Fastest-selling download single in the UK In its first week of release (week ending December 27, 2008), *X Factor* winner Alexandra Burke's (UK) cover of "Hallelujah" sold a record 289,621 downloads. Before the end of the year, it had sold 409,002 downloads.

Burke's "Hallelujah" sold 576,046 copies (physical sales and downloads combined) in its first week, the ☆ **best-selling single in the UK chart in one week by a female artist.**

★ Best-selling singles week in the UK For the first time, more than 4 million singles were sold (actually 4.028 million) in the UK in one week—that ending December 27, 2008. This was the highest total since accurate records were kept. The figure (of which 93.5% were downloads) included a record-breaking 338,203 complete album downloads.

In the same year, an unprecedented 115.1 million singles were sold in the UK, making 2008 the **★ most successful singles sales year in the UK.** This figure beat the previous record, set in 1979, by 26 million. Downloads accounted for 95.8% of the 2008 total.

☆ **Oldest person to reach No. 1 on the U.S. album chart with a new release** At the age of 67 years, Bob Dylan (U.S.A.) had a No. 1 hit in the UK and U.S.A. with *Together Through Life,* his 33rd studio album, released April 28, 2009. Despite his phenomenal global success, Dylan has yet to secure a No. 1 single in the UK.

★ Oldest album to top the UK chart On August 9, 2008, Abba's (Sweden) album *Gold: Greatest Hits* topped the UK chart 16 years after it was first released. It had previously reached No. 1 in both 1992 and 1999.

VIDEO GAMING

★**Best-selling video game series (stealth)** The best-selling stealth video game series is *Metal Gear*, which sold over 22 million units in the 20 years between its launch in 1987 and March 2009.

★**Best-selling adventure game series on Nintendo DS** The best-selling point-and-click adventure game series for Nintendo DS is the *Ace Attorney* game, based on the role of a defense attorney in a fictional courtroom setting, which has sold over 2.8 million copies as of May 2008.

★**Largest collection of playable gaming systems** Richard Lecce (U.S.A.) owns 483 unique video gaming systems, including a variety of home consoles, portable games, and LCD mini-systems, as of August 2008.

★**MOST POPULAR MMORPG GAME** In terms of online subscriber numbers, *World of Warcraft* is the most popular Massively Multiplayer Online Role-Playing Game (MMORPG), with 11.6 million subscribers as of January 2009. According to developers Blizzard Entertainment, *WoW* hosts over 2 million subscribers in Europe, more than 2.5 million in the U.S.A., and around 5.5 million in Asia.

★**FASTEST COMPLETION OF *H2OVERDRIVE* (FROZEN TUNDRA COURSE)** The fastest completion of the Frozen Tundra course on *H2Overdrive* (Arcade, 2009) is 1 min. 34.35 sec., achieved by Kevin Williams (UK) at the Arcades Trade Exhibition International (ATEI), Earls Court, London, UK, on January 27, 2009.

OCT. 9: The **largest free-floating soap bubble,** made using a wand, had a volume of 105.4 ft.³ (2.98 m³). It was produced by XTREME Bubbles LLC in Farmington, Minnesota, U.S.A., on this day in 2005.

★ **LARGEST IN-GAME SOUNDTRACK** *Grand Theft Auto IV* boasts 214 licensed tracks played over 18 in-game radio stations. This beats the previous record of 156 licensed songs featured in *GTA: San Andreas*.

The release of *GTA IV*, on April 29, 2008, is also the **most successful entertainment product launch**, generating $310 million worth of first-day sales worldwide.

★ **Highest score for an original *Donkey Kong* arcade game** The highest recorded score ever is 1,050,200 points, set by Billy Mitchell (U.S.A.) on July 16, 2007, in a game lasting 2 hr. 39 min. He beat previous record holder Steve Wiebe (U.S.A.) by just 1,100 points; but, unlike Wiebe, he did not play the game through to completion.

The titanic struggle between these gaming giants served as the basis for the film *The King of Kong* (U.S.A., 2007), the ★ **highest grossing video game documentary.** Mitchell offered $10,000 to anyone who could beat his score at the 2007 Classic Gaming Expo.

★ **Longest winning streak on *Street Fighter IV*** Zack Bennett (UK) remained unbeaten for 108 matches of *Street Fighter IV* at HMV, Oxford Street in London, UK, on February 20, 2009.

☆ **MOST OFFICIAL REAL-LIFE STAND-INS FOR A VIDEO GAME** The most real-life video game stand-ins are for the *Tomb Raider* series. Lara Croft has been officially portrayed by 10 different models since 1996, including actress Rhona Mitra and TV presenter Nell McAndrew (both UK). The current real-life Lara is UK gymnast/model Allison Carroll (pictured left).

OCT. 10: On this day in 1993, a total of 44,158 people descended on Warwick Farm Racecourse, Sydney, Australia, for a huge barbecue, the **largest attendance for a one-day barbecue.**

★**FASTEST COMPLETION OF *RESIDENT EVIL 4*** Derek Taylor (UK) completed *Resident Evil 4* (Wii) in 2 hr. 12 sec. at the Nottingham GameCity event in Nottingham, UK, on October 31, 2008.

★**First protein named after a video game character** In July 2008, biologists from the Osaka Bioscience Institute in Suita, Osaka Prefecture, Japan, identified a protein that is necessary to efficiently transmit visual information to the brain. Having determined that the protein is used in kinetic vision (being able to detect fast-moving objects), they named it pikachurin after Pikachu, who is also known for high speed.

☆**Highest score for a single track on Guitar Hero III (XBOX 360)** Former *Guitar Hero III* record holder Danny Johnson (U.S.A.) reclaimed his title in style on February 4, 2009, scoring 965,364 points playing *Through the Fire and the Flames,* the game's hardest track, on the set of *Pix 11 Morning News,* in New York City, New York, U.S.A.

Johnson then went on to break his own record, scoring 973,954 points at the Best Buy electronics store, also in New York, later the same day.

★**BEST-SELLING VIDEO GAME *Wii Sports,*** which comes bundled with the Wii console, has achieved worldwide sales of over 43 million copies since its launch in 2006. This eclipses the previous record held for over 20 years by another Nintendo favorite, *Super Mario Bros.,* with 40 million copies sold worldwide.

OCT. 11: The **fastest time to make an omelette** is 49 seconds. It was achieved by Howard Helmer (U.S.A.) on the set of *This Morning* (ITV) at the London Studios, London, UK, on this day in 2006.

YOUNGEST PRO GAMER The youngest professional video gamer is Lil Poison. Born on May 6, 1998, Victor De Leon III—aka Lil Poison—started gaming at the age of two and took part in his first competition at the age of four. Major league gaming recruiters signed him as a Pro Gamer when he was just six, making him the world's youngest signed professional gamer.

★**Most expensive home flight simulator cockpit** Matthew Sheil (Australia) has spent eight years constructing a flight simulator cockpit based round the 747-400. The project has cost $300,000 and features 12 computers controlling motion, audio, and the flight simulator game itself. Motion is provided by a hydraulic system fitted to the cockpit.

★**Fastest completion of *Sonic the Hedgehog 3*** James Richards (UK) of Maidstone, Kent, UK, completed *Sonic the Hedgehog 3* in 49 min. 1 sec. on the Sega Genesis/Mega Drive using Sonic as his character on August 9, 2008.

GUINNESS WORLD RECORDS: THE VIDEOGAME

(Wii leaderboards as of March 9, 2009)

CHALLENGE	ACHIEVEMENT	HOLDER	COUNTRY	DATE
One minute melon smash	*198 melons smashed*	Romaap	Netherlands	12/13/2008
Plane eating	*19.10 sec.*	DBER87	U.S.A.	02/27/2009
Plunger throwing	*157 plungers*	CACA	UK	02/03/2009
Phone book tearing	*29.44 sec.*	rsimpson	UK	01/14/2009
Longest fingernails	*28 m 37 cm*	siddic	UK	01/01/2009
Human cannonball	*790.02 m*	TITOU	France	12/30/2008
Plane pulling	*11.62 m*	Wiinner	UK	11/23/2008
Turkey plucking	*11.05 sec.*	CASE123	UK	01/03/2009
Cockroach eating	*14.71 sec.*	MELLORS	UK	01/02/2009
Most tattooed person	*5,001 cm²*	SANDRE	France	11/29/2008

SPORTS

CONTENTS

ACTION SPORTS

★ **Fastest 20-cone slalom on inline skates** Guo Fang (China) negotiated a 20-cone slalom course on inline skates in 5.04 seconds on the set of *Zheng Da Zong Yi—Guinness World Records Special* in Beijing, China, on November 14, 2008.

☆ **Longest journey kite-surfing (male)** The longest continuous kite-surfing journey by a male was 149.05 nautical miles (171.52 statute miles; 276.04 km) by Philipp Knecht (Switzerland), who traveled from Cumbuco through Jericoacoara to Camocim (Brazil) in 12 hr. 9 min. on November 6, 2006.

☆ **LIGHTNING BOLT** After setting a world record time of 9.72 seconds for the 100 m in May 2008, Jamaican sprinter Usain Bolt went to the Beijing Olympic Games in August of that year as the huge favorite to take the gold medal in the blue riband track event. "Lightning" Bolt didn't disappoint: in the Olympic 100 m final on August 16, he lowered his record to 9.69 seconds, even though he eased up before the finish line (pictured). But Bolt's record breaking had only just begun—on August 20, the world's fastest man won the 200 m gold with a record time of 19.30 seconds, and two days later he was part of the Jamaica 4 × 100 m relay team (Bolt, Asafa Powell, Michael Frater, Nesta Carter) that won gold in a new world record time of 37.10 seconds.

★ **OLDEST BUNGEE JUMPER** The oldest person to bungee jump is Helmut Wirz (Germany, b. December 2, 1924), who was 83 years 8 months and 7 days on the date of his latest jump in Duisburg, Germany, on August 9, 2008. He took up the extreme sport when he retired from work and could no longer afford his hobby of flying a Cesna light aircraft.

★ **Most continuous loops with a paraglider** Multiple paragliding world champion Raul Rodriguez (Spain) achieved a record 108 continuous loops with a paraglider in Passy Plaine Joux, France, on June 15, 2006.

★ **Lowest indoor parachute jump** The lowest-ever indoor parachute jump was performed by Andy Smith and Paul Smith (both U.S.A.) from a height of just 192 ft. (58.5 m) in the Houston Astrodome, Texas, U.S.A., on January 17, 1982.

★ **Longest rail grind on a snowboard** Luis Chamarro "Toto" (Spain) ground his snowboard for 193 ft. 11 in. (59.10 m) at Madrid SnowZone in Madrid, Spain, on September 27, 2008.

★ **Greatest distance in 24 hours on a snowmobile (woman)** Roxann Weidner (U.S.A.) covered 1,019.12 miles (1,640.11 km) on a snowmobile in 24 hours on a circular course in Tug Hill, New York, U.S.A., on January 24–25, 2001. She made 118 laps of the course, which was just short of 9 miles (14 km) long, at an average speed of 42.25 mph (68 km/h).

★ **Fastest speed on a snowmobile** Chris Hanson (U.S.A.) reached 172.2 mph (277.13 km/h) on Lake Nipissing in North Bay, Ontario, Canada, on March 13, 2004.

OCT. 12: The **greatest number of theatrical performances** is 47,250 for *The Golden Horseshoe Revue* staged in Anaheim, California, U.S.A., from July 16, 1955 to October 12, 1986.

BACKFLIPS . . .

Aaron Fotheringham is 16 years old and suffers from spina bifida. He has been in a wheelchair since he was 13, and began practicing stunts and tricks soon after. His unofficial record is six consecutive backflips.

★**FIRST WHEELCHAIR BACKFLIP** Aaron Fotheringham (U.S.A.) successfully landed the first wheelchair backflip at the Doc Romeo skate park in Las Vegas, Nevada, U.S.A., on October 25, 2008.

★**LONGEST SOMERSAULT ON SPRING-LOADED STILTS** John Simkins (UK) of Team 101 bounced to a height of 14 ft. 11 in. (4.57 m) on the set of *Guinness World Records* in Madrid, Spain, on December 23, 2008, using spring-loaded stilts.

Spring-loaded stilts consist of a footplate with ski-type bindings, a rubber footpad, and a fiberglass leaf spring to produce lift. They date back as far as 1957, when acrobats Bill Gafney and Tom Weaver demonstrated a type of pogo stick/stilt in the pages of *Time* magazine. Today, the sport is known as "powerbocking," after Alexander Böck (Germany), who originally obtained the patent.

☆ **LARGEST CANOPY FORMATION** The largest canopy formation consisted of 100 parachutes and was formed by an international team over Lake Wales, Florida, U.S.A., on November 21, 2007. The formation was in the shape of a diamond, with each parachutist in contact with the canopy of the person below.

☆ **HIGHEST JUMP ON A POGO STICK** David Barabé (Canada)— a mechanical engineering student— achieved 8 ft. (243.84 cm) on a customized pogo stick at the Université de Sherbrooke in Québec, Canada, on April 24, 2008. The pogo stick used for the attempt was a Vurtego modified with an air-injection system.

☆ **Fastest speed by a male paraglider (25-km course)** The highest speed achieved over a 25-km (15.53-mile) triangular course for an official Fédération Aéronautique Internationale (FAI) world record is 25.56 mph (41.15 km/h) by Charles Cazaux (France) at Aiguebelette, France, on July 23, 2006.

☆ **Fastest speed by a female paraglider (25-km course)** The highest average speed achieved over a 25-km (15.53-mile) triangular course for an official FAI world record by a woman is 15.2 mph (24.5 km/h) by Fiona Macaskill (UK) at Plaine Joux, France, on April 17, 2007.

Highest altitude balloon skywalk Mike Howard (UK) walked on a beam between two balloons at an altitude of 21,397 ft. (6,522 m) near Yeovil, Somerset, UK, on September 1, 2004, as part of a recording for the *Guinness World Records: 50 Years, 50 Records* television show.

OCT. 14: The **first supersonic flight** was achieved on this day in 1947 by Captain Charles "Chuck" Elwood Yeager (U.S.A.), with a speed of Mach 1.015 (670 mph; 1,078 km/h).

★**Fastest speed for a towed skateboard** Professional skateboarder Danny Way (U.S.A.)—the first person to jump the Great Wall of China on a skateboard—was towed to a speed of 74 mph (119 km/h) in California City, California, U.S.A., on November 4, 2008.

☆**Fastest speed on a gravity-powered street luge** Tom Mason (U.S.A.) reached a speed of 81.28 mph (130.8 km/h) on a street luge at Mount Whitney, California, U.S.A., on May 29, 1998.

★**Fastest 50-cone slalom on a skateboard** The fastest time to slalom 50 cones with a skateboard is 12.83 seconds, achieved by Martin Drayton (Trinidad and Tobago) in Hyde Park, London, UK, on October 2, 2007.

★**Smallest parachute** The smallest parachute canopy used for a jump is the JVX-37 measuring 37 ft.^{2} (3.43 m^2), which was landed by Luigi Cani (Brazil) on February 1, 2008, in Perris Valley, California, U.S.A.

FOOTBALL

★**Longest touchdown in a Super Bowl** The longest touchdown in Super Bowl history is 100 yards, scored by James Harrison (U.S.A.) of the Pittsburgh Steelers (U.S.A.) in Super Bowl XLIII at the Raymond James Stadium, Tampa, Florida, U.S.A., on February 1, 2009. The linebacker intercepted a throw from Kurt Warner (U.S.A.) of the Arizona Cardinals (U.S.A.) and ran the full length of the field to score at the end of the first half. Pittsburgh went on to win the game 27–23.

★**Fastest time to reach 2,000 rushing yards in an NFL career** Adrian Peterson (U.S.A.) of the Minnesota Vikings (U.S.A.) topped 2,000 career rushing yards during the 2008 season. Peterson reached the milestone in 21 games, becoming the fastest player in NFL history to reach 2,000 career rushing yards.

Peterson also holds the record for the ☆**most yards gained rushing in an NFL game:** he rushed 296 yards against the San Diego Chargers (U.S.A.) at the Metrodome in Minneapolis, Minnesota, U.S.A., on November 4, 2007.

 First undefeated season by an NFL team The New England Patriots (U.S.A.) scored a 16–0 record in 2007, the first team to go undefeated in a regular season since the league went to a 16-game schedule in 1978.

OCT. 15: The official **land-speed record** (measured over one mile) is 763.035 mph (1,227.985 km/h), set by Andy Green (UK) in the car Thrust SSC, on October 15, 1997, in the Black Rock Desert, Nevada, U.S.A.

☆**LONGEST NFL INTERCEPTION RETURN** The longest interception return for a touchdown was one of 107 yards by Ed Reed (U.S.A., right), playing for the Baltimore Ravens against the Philadelphia Eagles (both U.S.A.) on November 23, 2008. Reed broke his own record of 106 yards set against the Cleveland Browns (U.S.A.) on November 7, 2004.

MOST CONSECUTIVE NFL GAMES PLAYED Punter Jeff Feagles (U.S.A.) has played 336 NFL games, for the New England Patriots (1988–89), Philadelphia Eagles (1990–93), Arizona Cardinals (1994–97), Seattle Seahawks (1998–2002), and New York Giants (2002–08) (all U.S.A.). Feagles is also the **oldest player in Super Bowl history**—he was 41 years 333 days old when he appeared for the New York Giants in Super Bowl XLII on February 3, 2008.

Youngest NFL coach The youngest coach ever hired in the NFL's modern era is Lane Kiffin (U.S.A., b. May 9, 1975), who was 31 years 259 days old when he signed on to coach the Oakland Raiders (U.S.A.) on January 23, 2007. He was controversially dismissed in September 2008, having lost 15 out of 20 regular season games.

★**Most consecutive playoffs by a head coach** Superstar coach Tony Dungy (U.S.A.) has led his teams, Tampa Bay Buccaneers (1999–2001) and Indianapolis Colts (2002–08) (both U.S.A.), into the playoffs for 10 consecutive seasons.

OCT. 16: The **tallest free-standing house of cards** measured 25 ft. 9 in. (7.86 m) and was built by Bryan Berg (U.S.A.) on this day in 2007 in Dallas, Texas, U.S.A.

★MOST CONSECUTIVE NFL GAMES RECORDING A SACK Two players have gained the distinction of sacking the quarterback in 10 consecutive games. DeMarcus Ware (U.S.A., pictured above) of the Dallas Cowboys (U.S.A.) got his 10 from December 16, 2007, to October 19, 2008; Simon Fletcher (U.S.A.) of the Denver Broncos (U.S.A.) took down his quarterbacks between November 15, 1992, and September 20, 1993.

★Most consecutive NFL playoff games throwing a touchdown pass Brett Favre (U.S.A.) threw at least one touchdown pass in 18 postseason games while playing for the Green Bay Packers (U.S.A.) from 1992 to 2007.

★Most touchdown catches in an NFL postseason Playing for the Arizona Cardinals (U.S.A.), wide receiver Larry Fitzgerald (U.S.A.)

★MOST RECEPTIONS, NFL POSTSEASON The most receptions in one postseason is 30 by Larry Fitzgerald (U.S.A.) playing for the Arizona Cardinals (U.S.A.) during the 2008 postseason (four games).

☆ **MOST SUPER BOWL WINS** The **Pittsburgh Steelers (U.S.A.) have recorded more Super Bowl victories than any other team, with a total of six titles**, winning in the 1974, 1975, 1978, 1979, 2005, and 2008 seasons.

At 36 years 323 days, the Steelers' Mike Tomlin (U.S.A., b. March 15, 1972) is the ☆ **youngest head coach to lead his team to a Super Bowl win**, when the Steelers defeated the Arizona Cardinals (U.S.A.) 27–23 in Tampa, Florida, U.S.A., on February 1, 2009.

scored seven touchdown catches during the four games of the 2008 post-season.

☆ **Most seasons passing 4,000 yards in an NFL career** Peyton Manning (U.S.A.) of the Indianapolis Colts (U.S.A.) reached 4,000 passing yards in a season nine times in his career. During the 2008 season, Manning also extended his record streak of consecutive seasons with at least 25 touchdown passes to 11 years.

★ **Most watched NFL championship game** The New York Giants' 17–14 upset of the New England Patriots (both U.S.A.) in Super Bowl XLII on February 3, 2008, was the most watched NFL championship game ever. It was seen by an average of 97.5 million viewers, according to Nielsen Media Research. The game beat the previous Super Bowl record of 94.08 million, set when the Dallas Cowboys defeated the Pittsburgh Steelers (both U.S.A.) in 1996.

Most wins in an NFL career as a starting quarterback Brett Favre (U.S.A.) had 169 victories as a starting quarterback between 1992 and 2008.

OCT. 17: A total of 43,716,440 participants—in 6,540 global events—took part in the **largest stand up in 24 hours**, as part of the UN's "Stand Up Against Poverty 2007": the largest record ever staged.

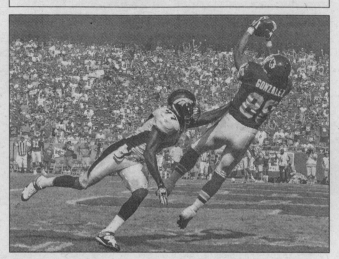

★ **MOST TOUCHDOWNS BY A TIGHT END IN AN NFL CAREER** Tight end Tony Gonzalez (U.S.A., above right) of the Kansas City Chiefs (U.S.A.) has scored 76 touchdowns in his career through to the end of the 2008 season. He also holds career records for the ☆ **most catches** (916) and ☆ **most receiving yards by a tight end** (10,940).

★ **Fewest turnovers in an NFL season (team)** The fewest turnovers in a 16-game season by a team is 13 by the New York Giants and Miami Dolphins (both U.S.A.) in 2008.

★ **Oldest player** Paul L. Morton (U.S.A., b. January 12, 1941) was 67 years old when he played a regular season game for the semi-professional Stateline Miners (U.S.A.) in 2008.

TRACK & FIELD

★ **Most 20 km World Race Walking Cup wins (female)** The 20 km event at the women's World Race Walking Cup has been contested five times and been won by a different athlete on each occasion: Liu Hongyu

☆**FASTEST 50 KM RACE WALK (MALE)** Denis Nizhegorodov (Russia) completed the 50 km race walk at the World Cup in Cheboksary, Russia, in a new record time of 3 hr. 34 min. 14 sec., on May 11, 2008. Italy's Alex Schwazer finished the World Cup race in second place, trailing by 2 min. 50 sec., but went on to win the gold medal in the event at the Beijing Olympic Games.

(China) in 1999, Erica Alfridi (Italy) in 2002, Yelena Nikolayeva (Russia) in 2004, Ryta Turava (Belarus) in 2006, and Olga Kaniskina (Russia) in 2008.

★ **Most medals won at a single World Race Walking Cup (country)** At the 2008 World Race Walking Cup held in the streets of Cheboksary in Chuvashia, Russia, the home nation collected a record 15 out of a possible 20 medals: six individual golds, three silvers, and a bronze, plus five team golds.

★**Most team golds won at the World Championships** The track & field World Championships were inaugurated in 1983, when they were held in Helsinki, Finland. The championships were originally held every four years, but this changed in 1991, when the event became biennial. To date, the most golds won by a team is 114 by the U.S.A. between 1983 and 2007. Far behind in second place is Russia with 33 golds.

The U.S.A. also boasts the ★**most medals won at the World Championships** with 234 (compare this with Russia's 121).

★**Most athletes to compete in the World Championships** A record 1,978 athletes took part in the track & field World Championships held in Osaka, Japan, from August 24 to September 2, 2007—the 11th staging of the competition.

For a comprehensive list of all IAAF track & field world records, please turn to the Sports Reference section on pp. 518–529.

OCT. 18: The **largest cobweb** was discovered by Ken Thompson (UK) on October 18, 1998. It covered the entire 11.23-acre (4.54-hectare) playing field at Kineton High School, Kineton, Warwick, UK.

☆ **FASTEST 110 M HURDLES (MALE)** On June 12, 2008, Dayron Robles (Cuba) shaved 0.01 seconds off the world best for the 110 m hurdles in Ostrava, Czech Republic, setting a new record time of 12.87 seconds. Later that year, Robles added the Olympic title to his world record, winning the final of the event at the 29th Olympic Games held at the National Stadium, Beijing, China, in 12.93 seconds on August 21, 2008.

Most track & field world records set on one day Jesse Owens (U.S.A., 1913–80) set five world records in 45 minutes in Ann Arbor, Michigan, U.S.A., on May 25, 1935. At 3:15 p.m., he equaled the world record for the 100-yard dash with a 9.4-second sprint; he achieved a 26-ft. 8.25-in. (8.13-m) long jump at 3:25 p.m.; a 20.3-second 220 yards (and 200 m, although this is considered a separate race) at 3:45 p.m., and a 22.6-second 220-yard low hurdles (and 200 m) at 4:00 p.m.

☆ **Most people running 100 m in a 24-hour relay** A record 3,807 participants took part in a 24-hour 100-m relay for Latvia's 90th Anniversary Celebrations at the Daugava Stadium in Riga, Latvia, on October 19, 2008. The youngest participant on the day was a one-year-old toddler!

OCT. 19: On October 19, 2002, the **world's longest line of firecrackers** was detonated in Sueca, Valencia, Spain, measuring 6.83 miles (11 km) long.

☆ **MOST TEAM WINS OF THE EUROPEAN CUP** Three teams have won the European Cup a record six times: East Germany in 1970 and 1975–83 (when it was held biennially); Germany in 1994–96, 1999, and 2004–05; and Great Britain in 1989, 1997–98, 2000, 2002, and 2008 (pictured).

Russia holds the record for the **most European Cup wins by a women's team** with 14 victories, in 1993, 1995, 1997–2008. From 2009, the Cup will be replaced by the European Team Championships.

☆ **Fastest 100 miles on a treadmill (team)** On November 13, 2008, a team of 12 set a record in Bickershaw, Wigan, UK, when they ran 100 miles (160 km) on a treadmill in 9 hr. 5 min. 17 sec. The team consisted of Adam Balmer, Anthony Battersby, Adam Bibby, Michael Dawes, Joseph Donald, Lee Double, Mark Foster, Ray Hill, Simon Holland, Farrell Kilbane, Mark Livingston, and Steven Turnbull (all UK).

☆ **Greatest distance run in 48 hours on a treadmill** Tony Mangan (Ireland) covered 251.79 miles (405.22 km) on a treadmill at St Mel's College in Longford, Ireland, from August 22–24, 2008.

☆ **Fastest 1,000 × 400 m** The fastest time for 1,000 runners to run 400 m in a relay is 21 hr. 57 min. 46 sec., and was achieved by Turn und Sportgemeinde (Germany) in Lollar, Germany, on July 14–15, 2008.

OCT. 20: The **lowest note by a human voice** was achieved on this day in 2000 by Tim Storms (U.S.A.), who produced a recognizable B-2 note that was measured electronically at 8Hz.

30.86 SECONDS: the time that 100-year-old Philip Rabinowitz (South Africa) took to run the 100 m in July 2004.

☆ **FASTEST 3,000 M STEEPLECHASE (FEMALE)** In an event that was new to the Olympic Games, Russia's Gulnara Galkina (née Samitova) won the 3,000 m steeplechase final in a record time of 8 min. 58.81 sec. at the National Stadium, Beijing, China, on August 17, 2008.

☆ **HIGHEST POLE VAULT (FEMALE)** Having set new world records of 5.03 m in Rome, Italy, on July 11, 2008, and 5.04 m in Monaco on July 29, 2008, Yelena Isinbayeva (Russia) capped an amazing couple of months of pole-vaulting excellence by securing the gold medal at the Beijing Olympics with another world best of 5.05 m, at the National Stadium, Beijing, China, on August 18, 2008.

☆**FASTEST 5,000 M (FEMALE)** On June 6, 2008, at the Exxon Mobil Bislett Games in Oslo, Norway, Tirunesh Dibaba (Ethiopia) smashed the world record for the 5,000 m when she recorded a time of 14 min. 11.15 sec. Dibaba's time beat the previous best time, set by Meseret Defar (Ethiopia), by more than 5 seconds.

★**Longest hammer throw (Highland Games)** The longest throw of the light hammer (16 lb.; 7.25 kg) is 156 ft. 8.5 in. (47.76 m) by Bruce Aitken (UK) at the Aboyne Games, Aberdeenshire, UK, in August 2000. Other challenges at the Highland Games include caber tossing (throwing a large wooden pole), stone putting (similar to the shot put but using actual stones), tug o' war, and bagpiping.

Combined events *The World Combined Events Challenge is an annual worldwide competition series for Decathlon (Men) and Heptathlon (Women). The three best scores of the year are accumulated to find out who has the highest points total.*

•The ★ **most points scored in the World Combined Events Challenge by a male** is 26,476, by Tomáš Dvořák (Czech Republic) in 1999.

•The ★ **most points scored by a female** is 20,541, by Carolina Kluft (Sweden) in 2004.

•The ★ **most wins by a female** is four by Carolina Kluft (Sweden), who claimed the title each year from 2003 to 2006.

•The ★ **most wins by a male** is four, by Roman Šebrle (Czech Republic) in 2002, 2004–05, and 2007.

MARATHONS

★**Fastest marathon (female)** Paula Radcliffe (UK) ran the fastest marathon ever recorded by a woman when she completed the 2003 London Marathon in 2 hr. 15 min. 25 sec. in London, UK, on April 13, 2003.

••

OCT. 21: The **world's largest shoe** measured 17 ft. 4 in. long, 7 ft. 8 in. wide, and 6 ft. 7 in. high (5.29 m × 2.37 m × 2.03 m) and was unveiled in Marikina City, Philippines, on this day in 2002.

••

FASTEST HALF MARATHON WITH A STROLLER (FEMALE) Nancy Schubring (U.S.A.) ran a half marathon in 1 hr. 30 min. 51 sec. while pushing a stroller at the Mike May Races Half Marathon in Vassar, Michigan, U.S.A., on September 15, 2001. For comparison, Lornah Kiplagat (Netherlands) ran the **fastest half marathon (female)** in 1 hr. 6 min. 25 sec. in Udine, Italy, on October 14, 2007.

☆**Fastest aggregate time to complete a marathon on each continent (male)** The fastest aggregate time to complete a marathon on each of the seven continents is 23 hr. 43 min. 55 sec., which was achieved by David Smith (UK) who ran marathons around the world between November 12, 1995, and March 5, 2008. With a fastest time of 2 hr. 52 min. 43 sec. and a slowest of 3 hr. 45 min. 19 sec., Smith averaged just over 3 hr. 23 min. for each race.

FASTEST MARATHON (MALE) On September 28, 2008, at the age of 35, Haile Gebrselassie won the Berlin Marathon in Berlin, Germany, with a world record time of 2 hr. 3 min. 59 sec., breaking his own world best time by 27 seconds. It was the first occasion that anyone had run under 2 hr. 4 min. for the race over 26 miles 385 yards (42.195 km).

★ MOST POINTS SCORED TO WIN THE WORLD MARATHON MAJORS Inaugurated in 2006, the World Marathon Majors championship encompasses the five annual marathon races in Boston (U.S.A.), London (UK), Berlin (Germany), Chicago, and New York City (both U.S.A.), with athletes scoring points for top five finishes over two calendar years. The World Championship and Olympic marathons are also included in the years they are run. Gete Wami (Ethiopia) won the 2006–07 women's competition with 80 points. Robert Cheruiyot (Kenya, above) won the men's competition in 2006–07, also scoring 80 points.

☆ **Youngest person to complete a marathon on all seven continents (male)** Timothy Harris (UK, b. February 26, 1983) was 23 years 339 days old when he completed the Marrakech Marathon, Marrakech, Morocco, on January 28, 2007, in a time of 3 hr. 34 min. It was the final race in a sequence of seven marathons that Harris ran on each of the seven continents, which began at the K42 Patagonia Mountain Marathon in Neuquen, Argentina, on October 29, 2006 (a race that Harris completed in 4 hr. 45 min.).

★ **Most marathons run on consecutive days (female)** Michelle Atkins (UK) ran 10 marathons on consecutive days in Brathay, UK, from May 9–18, 2008.

★ **Most marathons run on consecutive days (male)** Enzo Caporaso (Italy) ran 51 marathons on consecutive days in Turin, Italy, from February 23 to April 13, 2008.

....

OCT. 22: The **fastest speed at which a car has been driven in reverse** is 102.58 mph (165.08 km/h) by Darren Manning (UK) in a Caterham 7 Fireblade in Gloucester, UK, on this day in 2001.

....

★ FASTEST TIMES FOR THE FIVE MAJOR MARATHONS ★

M: Male **F:** Female

MARATHON	ATHLETE	TIME	DATE
Berlin (Germany)	**M:** Haile Gebrselassie (Ethiopia)	2:03:59	Sep. 28, 2008
	F: Mizuki Noguchi (Japan)	2:19:12	Sep. 25, 2005
Boston (U.S.A.)	**M:** Robert Cheruiyot (Kenya)	2:07:14	Apr. 17, 2006
	F: Margaret Okayo (Kenya)	2:20:43	Apr. 15, 2002
Chicago (USA)	**M:** Khalid Khannouchi (Morocco)	2:05:42	Oct. 24, 1999
	F: Paula Radcliffe (UK)	2:17:18	Oct. 13, 2002
London (UK)	**M:** Martin Lei (Kenya)	2:05:15	Apr. 13, 2008
	F: Paula Radcliffe (UK)	2:15:25	Apr. 13, 2003
New York City (U.S.A.)	**M:** Tesfaye Jifar (Ethiopia)	2:07:43	Nov. 4, 2001
	F: Margaret Okayo (Kenya)	2:22:31	Nov. 2, 2003

FLORA LONDON MARATHON 2009

The 2009 Flora London Marathon took place on April 26 on the streets of London, UK. On a day of stifling heat, there were more Guinness World Records attempts than ever in the marathon's history: over 60 runners took part in 29 official record attempts, and 11 new Guinness World Records were achieved. All of the new record holders are featured on pp. 436–38—well done to them and everyone who took part.

FULL SUIT & MOVIE CHARACTER Thomas Day (UK, far left) completed the race in 4 hr. 19 min. 37 sec.—the ★fastest marathon dressed in a full suit. Ian Benskin (UK, left) dressed as a Thunderbird to run the ☆fastest marathon in a movie character costume (male) in 3 hr. 11 min. 50 sec.

3 HR. 50 MIN. 31 SEC.: the ★ **fastest marathon in military desert uniform** by Jennifer Jenks (UK) at the Flora London Marathon 2009.

MOST PEOPLE LINKED TOGETHER Neal Gardner (UK) and 29 of his friends set the record for the ☆ **most people linked together to run a marathon.** The 30 runners set a time of 6 hr. 18 min. 41 sec.

A. FRUIT Sally Orange (UK), wearing an orange costume, ran the ★ **fastest marathon dressed as a fruit** in 4 hr. 32 min. 28 sec.

B. LEPRECHAUN Jack Lyons (UK) ran the ★ **fastest marathon dressed as a leprechaun** in 4 hr. 22 min. 8 sec.

C. VEGETABLE Robert Prothero (UK) wore a carrot costume to run the ★ **fastest marathon dressed as a vegetable** in 3 hr. 34 min. 55 sec.

D. ANIMAL COSTUME Alastair Martin (UK) ran the ★ **fastest marathon in an animal costume (male)**, in 3 hr. 42 min. 27 sec. while dressed as an ostrich.

E. BACKPACK Gordon Chaplin (UK) achieved the ★ **fastest marathon carrying a 40-lb. pack** when he recorded a time of 5 hr. 35 min. 19 sec.

....

OCT. 23: The **world's largest doner kebab** weighed 910 lb. 7 oz. (413 kg) and was made by the Maroosh Lebanese Café at the Applause Festival, Albury, New South Wales, Australia, on this day in 2004.

....

★**Fastest marathon backward on inline skates** Werner Fischer (Germany) completed a marathon traveling backward on inline skates in 1 hr. 45 min. 56 sec. at the 2006 Berlin Marathon, Berlin, Germany, on September 23, 2006.

AUTOSPORTS

FORMULA ONE

•The record for the **most wins in a Formula One season by a rookie** is four, set by Jacques Villeneuve (Canada) in 1996 and equaled by Lewis Hamilton (UK) in 2007.

•Italian constructor Ferrari has amassed a total of 209 Grands Prix, the ☆**most Grand Prix wins by a manufacturer,** between 1961 and 2008.

•A Formula One legend, Michael Schumacher (Germany) recorded 148 points in the 2004 season, the **most points by a driver in a single season.** Schumacher dominated Formula One in the 1990s and 2000s and also holds the records for the **most Grand Prix wins by a driver,** with 84 checkered flags between 1991 and 2005, and the **most points scored in a Formula**

GLOSSARY

FIA: Fédération Internationale de l'Automobile

NASCAR: National Association for Stock Car Auto Racing

NHRA: National Hot Rod Association

TT: Touring Trophy

★FIRST NASCAR WIN FOR A JAPANESE AUTOMAKER Kyle Busch (U.S.A.) gave Toyota its first NASCAR Sprint Cup victory, winning the Kobalt Tools 500 at Atlanta Motor Speedway on March 9, 2008. The win came in Toyota's 40th race and is the first NASCAR victory by a foreign manufacturer since Al Keller (U.S.A.) drove a Jaguar (UK) to a road-course win in 1954.

One career, with an intimidating total of 1,248 points scored between 1991 and 2005.

• The **oldest Formula One World Champion** was Juan Manuel Fangio (Argentina, b. June 24, 1911), who won his last World Championship on August 4, 1957, aged 46 years 41 days.

• Rubens Barrichello (Brazil) holds the record for ☆ **most Formula One Grand Prix starts** with 257 starts from 1993 to 2008. Barrichello has raced for Jordan (1993–96), Stewart Grand Prix (1997–99), Ferrari (2000–05), and Honda (2006–08). He has amassed 519 career points including nine wins and 61 podium finishes. The driver is said to have grown up idolizing the multiple Formula One World Champion and fellow Brazilian Ayrton Senna (1960–1994).

☆ MOST CONSECUTIVE WORLD RALLY CHAMPIONSHIP TITLES The most consecutive FIA World Rally Championship titles wins is five, by Sébastien Loeb (France) between 2004 and 2008. Loeb won all of his titles driving for the Citroën team.

OCT. 24: The **youngest player in a baseball World Series** was Fred Lindstrom, who was 18 years 339 days old when he played for the New York Giants (NL) on this day in 1924.

NASCAR TRUCK SERIES

•Ted Musgrave (U.S.A.) won his first NASCAR title in 2005, taking that year's NASCAR Craftsman Truck Series championship. It was the ★**first vehicle carrying the number "1" to win a NASCAR championship** in any of NASCAR's three national touring series.

•Jack Sprague (U.S.A.) earned $7,276,475 (£4,952,165) in the 2008 Truck Series season, giving him the distinction of the ☆**highest earnings in a NASCAR career.** Sprague also claimed the ★**greatest prize money from one series race,** taking home a purse of $93,375 at Daytona on February 16, 2007.

•Mike Skinner (U.S.A.) recorded 47 poles in the 2008 season, an achievement that gave him the **most career poles won in the NASCAR Truck Series.** A trucking king, Skinner currently drives the #5 Exide Toyota Tundra for Randy Moss Motorsports in the NASCAR Camping World Truck Series.

NHRA DRAG RACING

•John Force (U.S.A.) is the first drag racer to win 1,000 career rounds, the ★**most Funny Car rounds won in a career.** Force attained this landmark achievement at the Gateway International Raceway in Madison, Illinois, U.S.A., on May 4, 2008. Force also holds the records for the ★**most career finals for a drag racer,** with 202 appearances, and the ★**most career wins for a drag racer,** with 126 race victories.

•Mike Ashley (U.S.A.) hit a terminal velocity of 356.06 mph (573.02 km/h) from a standing start over 440 yd. (402 m) in a Dodge Charger in Las Vegas, Nevada, U.S.A., on April 13, 2007, the **fastest speed in an NHRA Funny Car drag race.**

•Melanie Troxel (U.S.A.) reached a terminal velocity of 330.31 mph (531.58 km/h) after a 440-yd. (402-m) run at the Texas Motorplex in Dallas, U.S.A., in October 2005—the ★**fastest speed in Top Fuel NHRA drag racing (female).**

★**FIRST FEMALE INDYCAR WINNER**
When Danica Patrick (U.S.A.) won the Indy Japan 300 in Motegi, Japan, on April 20, 2008, she became the first woman to take the checkered flag in the history of IndyCar racing.

Patrick was also the **first woman to lead the Indianapolis 500 race** when she headed the field for 19 laps in the May 2005 event.

OCT. 25: Verna van Schaik (South Africa) dived to a depth of 725 ft. (221 m) in a cave in South Africa's Northern Cape province on October 25, 2004—the **deepest scuba dive by a woman.**

> **$100,695,731:** total earned by Jeff Gordon (U.S.A.) by 2008, the **highest NASCAR career earnings.**

☆ **MOST CONSECUTIVE NASCAR TITLES** Jimmy Johnson (left) and Cale Yarborough (both U.S.A.) are the only drivers to win three consecutive NASCAR Cup championships. Jimmy took his third straight title in 2008; Cale accomplished the feat in 1978.

☆ **YOUNGEST F1 WORLD CHAMPION** Lewis Hamilton (UK, b. January 7, 1985) won his first F1 World Championship on November 2, 2008, at Interlagos, Brazil, aged 23 years and 298 days. Hamilton, driving for McLaren Mercedes, won the title by just one point from Brazilian Felipe Massa.

OCT. 26: The **fastest ascent of Mount Kilimanjaro** is by Gerard Bavato (France), who ran the 21.1 miles (34 km) from the base to the summit in a time of 5 hr. 26 min. 40 sec. on October 26, 2007.

TT RACES

- Joey Dunlop (Ireland, 1952–2000) accumulated the **most Isle of Man TT race wins in a career,** with 26 victories between 1977 and 2000.
- Maria Costello (UK) lapped the 37.75-mile (60.75-km) Isle of Man TT course in a time of 19 min. 43.8 sec., at an average speed of 114.73 mph (184.64 km/h), on June 8, 2004, the ★ **fastest lap time for a female driver.**
- The **highest lap speed for the Isle of Man TT races** is 129.45 mph (208.33 km/h) by John McGuinness (UK, riding for England). McGuinness achieved this feat in a Honda CBR1000 Fireblade on June 9, 2006.

BALL SPORTS

Australian football league

- The ★ **most AFL games coached** is 713, by Jock McHale (Australia) for Collingwood between 1912 and 1949.
- Charlie Ricketts (Australia) was 24 years 91 days old when he coached South Melbourne in 1909, making him the AFL's ★ **youngest coach.**
- The ★ **oldest AFL coach** was Allan Jeans (Australia), who coached Hawthorn in a 1989 match, aged 56 years 9 days.

- Fred Fanning (Australia) holds the record for the ★ **most goals kicked in a match,** scoring 18 goals for Melbourne against St. Kilda in a single AFL match in 1947.

★ MOST EUROPEAN KORFBALL CHAMPIONSHIPS (TEAM)
Korfball is played in over 50 countries worldwide. It is similar to basketball but played with mixed teams, either indoors or outdoors. ("Korf" refers to the basket into which teams attempt to shoot a ball.) The Netherlands has won the European Korfball Championships a record three times, in 1998, 2002, and 2006.

OCT. 27: An audience at the BBC's Big Bash event held between October 24 and 27, 1997, at the NEC, Birmingham, UK, clapped to a level of 100 dB—the **loudest applause ever measured.**

★ MOST WINS OF THE ANZ CHAMPIONSHIP The ANZ Championship is the newly created elite netball competition in Australia and New Zealand, replacing Australia's Commonwealth Bank Cup and New Zealand's National Bank Trophy. It was contested for the first time in 2008 between 10 teams from each country. At the inaugural event, the New South Wales Swifts (Australia) beat the Waikato-Bay of Plenty Magic (New Zealand, in black) 65–56.

Beach handball The men's world championships has been staged three times, and the ☆ **most wins** is just one, by three countries: Egypt (2004), Brazil (2006), and Croatia (2008).

Beach volleyball

•The ☆ **most tournament titles won by a woman** is 105, by Misty May-Treanor (U.S.A.) between 2000 and 2008.

•The beach volleyball World Championships have been held biennially since 1997. The ★ **most wins by a women's team** is three, by Brazil (1997, 1999, and 2001), and the U.S.A. (2003, 2005, and 2007).

•The ☆ **most men's beach volleyball World Tour titles won by the same pair** is five, consecutively, by Emanuel Rego and Ricardo Santos (both Brazil) in 2003–07.

•Beach volleyball has been part of the Olympic Games since 1996, and the ☆ **most Olympic wins by a men's team** is three, by the U.S.A.: Karch Kiraly

☆ HIGHEST CAREER EARNINGS FROM THE BEACH VOLLEYBALL AVP TOUR (WOMEN) Misty May-Treanor (U.S.A.) has won a record $1,824,158 in official Association of Volleyball Professionals (AVP) Tour earnings through to the end of the 2008 season.

OCT. 28: The record for **hula-hooping the most hoops at once** is 105 and was set by Jin Linlin (China) on the set of *Zheng Da Zong Yi—Guinness World Records Special* in Beijing, China, on this day in 2007.

☆ MOST BEACH HANDBALL CHAMPIONSHIPS (FEMALE) The women's beach handball world championships has been staged on three occasions. Three countries share the record for the most wins, with one each: Russia in 2004, Brazil in 2006 (pictured), and Croatia in 2008.

and Kent Steffes in 1996; Dain Balanton and Eric Fonoimoana in 2000; and Phil Dalhausser and Todd Rogers in 2008.

Canadian football league

• The ★ most kicks blocked in a CFL career is 12, by Gerald Vaughn (Canada) playing for the Calgary Stampeders, Winnipeg Blue Bombers, and Hamilton Tiger-Cats, between 1993 and 2004.

• The Grey Cup is the name of the trophy given to the CFL champions and also the name of the championship itself. The player who has won the ★ most consecutive Grey Cup Final Most Valuable Players awards is Doug Flutie (U.S.A.) who picked up two awards playing for the Toronto Argonauts in 1996–97.

• The ★ most career fumbles returned for touchdowns is five, by Michael Allen (U.S.A.) for the Winnipeg Blue Bombers in 1988–93.

☆ MOST ALL-IRELAND HURLING FINALS The greatest number of All-Ireland hurling championships won by a team is 31, by Kilkenny between 1904 and 2008.

FACT

Kilkenny's Philip Larkin (above left) tackles Cork's Ben O'Connor during the All-Ireland Hurling Final at Croke Park Stadium September 12, 1999.

Handball
•The **highest score in an international handball match** occurred when the USSR beat Afghanistan 86–2 in the "Friendly Army Tournament" at Miskolc, Hungary, in August 1981.
•The ☆ **most wins of the women's European Championships** is four, by Norway—in 1998, 2004, 2006, and 2008.

Hockey (field)
•The Champions Trophy was first held in 1978, and since 1980 it has been played annually by the top six men's teams in the world. The ☆ **most wins of the men's hockey Champions Trophy** is nine and was achieved by Australia in 1983–85, 1989–90, 1993, 1999, 2005, and 2008.

Germany also has a tally of nine victories, but three of these wins occurred before reunification: 1986–88 (as West Germany) and 1991–92, 1995, 1997, 2001, and 2007 (as Germany).
•The Asia Cup was introduced by the Asia Hockey Foundation (ASHF) in 1982 (with the first women's tournament following in 1985). The ★ **most Asia Cup wins by a men's team** is three, by Pakistan in 1982, 1985, and 1989. The ★ **most wins by a women's team** is also three, by South Korea in 1985, 1993, and 1999.
•Anne Graves (UK, b. March 5, 1935) is the ☆ **oldest regular hockey player.** She played the majority of the 2008/09 season for the Stevenage Ladies 5s in the Five Counties Division 7 Hockey League in Stevenage, UK, aged 74.

Korfball The ☆ **most team wins in the korfball world championships** (instituted 1978) is seven, by the Netherlands, in 1978, 1984, 1987, 1995, 1999, 2003, and 2007.

★ **MOST PASSING YARDS IN GREY CUP FINALS** Canadian football quarterback Anthony Calvillo (U.S.A.)—the League's Most Outstanding Player of 2008—achieved a record 1,458 passing yards in Grey Cup finals games between 2000 and 2006.

OCT. 29: On this day in 2007, Beverley Lateo (Italy) paid £8,000 (or $16,420) for the **most expensive haircut** on the rate card at the Stuart Phillips Salon in Covent Garden, London, UK.

Netball

•The ☆ **most international appearances** is 164, recorded by Irene van Dyk (New Zealand) playing for South Africa and New Zealand between 1994 and 2008.

Volleyball

•The ☆ **most wins of the volleyball Grand Prix**—a women-only tournament played annually since 1993—is seven by Brazil in 1994, 1996, 1998, 2004–06, and 2008.

•The ☆ **most wins of the men's Olympic volleyball title** is three, by the USSR in 1964, 1968, and 1980, and the U.S.A. in 1984, 1988, and 2008.

•The ☆ **most medals won in the volleyball World League** is 13, by Italy and Brazil. Italy has the **most gold medals in the World League,** with eight.

BASEBALL

★**Highest baseball team payroll** The New York Yankees (U.S.A.) had a payroll of $218.3 million for the 2007 season, a Major League Baseball (MLB) record for a single season. The Yankees have had the highest payroll for nine straight years. The team's total rose $10.8 million, up from the previous high of $207.5 million in 2006.

★**Most games played at shortstop—career** Omar Vizquel (Venezuela) played in 2,654 games with the Seattle Mariners, Cleveland Indians, and San Francisco Giants (all U.S.A.) from 1989 to 2008.

★ **MOST CONSECUTIVE SEASONS HITTING 35 HOME RUNS** Alex Rodriguez (U.S.A.) has played 11 consecutive seasons where he has scored at least 35 home runs while batting for the Seattle Mariners, Texas Rangers, and New York Yankees (all U.S.A.) from 1998 to 2008.

OCT. 30: Matthew "Matt the Knife" Cassiere (U.S.A.) achieved the **fastest handcuff escape** with a time of five seconds at Rhode Island, U.S.A., on this day in 2004.

★ **MOST CONSECUTIVE BASEBALL CROWD SELLOUTS** The Boston Red Sox (U.S.A.) reached 468 consecutive sellouts, for every home game at Fenway Park since May 15, 2003. The Cleveland Indians (U.S.A.) held the previous record—455 consecutive sellouts—at Jacobs Field from June 12, 1995, to April 4, 2001.

FACT

Fenway Park in Boston, U.S.A., has been the Red Sox's home since 1912. It has a capacity of 37,400 (night) and 36,984 (day) as of 2008.

★ **Most consecutive games without an error—first base** Kevin Youkilis (U.S.A.) played 238 consecutive games as a first baseman for the Boston Red Sox (U.S.A.) in 2007 and 2008. Youkilis also handled a record 2,002 consecutive catches at first base without an error.

★ **Most enduring bat boy** Stan Bronson Jr. (U.S.A.) began his service for the Memphis Tigers (U.S.A.) baseball team on February 15, 1958, at the age of 29 years 211 days and continues to do so.

★ **Most consecutive scoreless innings by a relief pitcher** Brad Ziegler (U.S.A.) had 39 scoreless innings playing for the Oakland Athletics

OCT. 31: The **largest jack o'lantern** was carved by Scott Cully (U.S.A.) from the world's **largest pumpkin,** weighing 1,469 lb. (666.32 kg), on October 31, 2005 in Northern Cambria, Pennsylvania, U.S.A.

★MOST SAVES IN A MAJOR LEAGUE BASEBALL SEASON The Major League Baseball (MLB) record for most saves in a season is 62, by Francisco Rodriguez (Venezuela) playing for the Los Angeles Angels (U.S.A.) in 2008.

(U.S.A.) in 2008. Ziegler also broke the mark for the **longest shutout streak for any pitcher at the start of his career.**

★Most career postseason runs batted in Bernie Williams (Puerto Rico) had 80 career postseason runs batted in while playing for the New York Yankees (U.S.A.) from 1991 to 2006.

☆Most saves in an MLB career Trevor Hoffman (U.S.A.) recorded 554 career saves playing for the Florida Marlins and San Diego Padres (both U.S.A.) from 1993 to 2008.

☆Most strikeouts in an MLB career by a left-handed pitcher Randy Johnson (U.S.A.) recorded 4,789 strikeouts playing for the Montreal Expos (Canada), Seattle Mariners, Houston Astros, Arizona Diamondbacks, and New York Yankees (all U.S.A.) from 1988 to 2008.

★Most double plays in an MLB career by a pitcher Greg Maddux (U.S.A.) participated in 98 double plays in his career with the Chicago Cubs, Atlanta Braves, Los Angeles Dodgers, and San Diego Padres (all U.S.A.) from 1986 to 2008.

★FASTEST BASEBALL PITCH (FEMALE) The fastest pitch by a woman is 65 mph (104.6 km/h) achieved by Lauren Boden (U.S.A.) at Lakeside High School, Atlanta, Georgia, U.S.A., on April 19, 2008.

NOV. 1: Eugene Andreev (USSR) experienced the **longest free-fall parachute jump,** falling 80,380 ft. (24,500 m) after jumping from a balloon at 25,458 m (83,523 ft.) near Saratov, Russia, in 1962.

☆ **MOST STRIKEOUTS IN A GAME BY A BATTER** Many players have equaled the record of five strikeouts in a game, but the most recent is Craig Monroe (U.S.A.) of the Detroit Tigers (U.S.A.). Craig is pictured looking at the home plate umpire after a called second strike in the ninth inning of a 6–5 loss to the Milwaukee Brewers (U.S.A.) in a game on June 14, 2007.

★ **Most double plays in an MLB career by a shortstop** Omar Vizquel (Venezuela) participated in 1,698 double plays in his career with the Seattle Mariners, Cleveland Indians, and San Francisco Giants (all U.S.A.) from 1989 to 2008.

☆ **Most ejections in an MLB career** Bobby Cox (U.S.A.), manager of the Toronto Blue Jays (Canada) and Atlanta Braves (U.S.A.) from 1978 to 2008, has been ejected from 143 games.

Most runs scored in an MLB season by a switch hitter Switch hitter Mark Teixeira (U.S.A.) scored 144 runs for the Texas Rangers (U.S.A.) in 2005.

★ **Most home runs leading off games** Rickey Henderson (U.S.A.) achieved a record-breaking 81 home runs leading off games while playing for the Oakland Athletics, New York Yankees, San Diego Padres, Anaheim Angels, New York Mets, Seattle Mariners, Boston Red Sox, Los Angeles Dodgers (all U.S.A.), and the Toronto Blue Jays (Canada) from 1979 to 2003.

☆ **Most home runs scored all for one manager in an MLB career** Chipper Jones (U.S.A.) recorded all 408 of his career home runs playing for manager Bobby Cox (U.S.A.) of the Atlanta Braves (U.S.A.) from 1993 to 2008. Jones' 408 home runs are the most ever hit by a National League switch hitter.

☆ **MOST GOLD GLOVE AWARDS IN AN MLB CAREER** The Rawlings Gold Glove Award (usually known just as the Gold Glove) is given annually to the MLB player judged to have the most "superior individual fielding performance." Greg Maddux (U.S.A.) has been awarded 18 while playing for the Chicago Cubs, Atlanta Braves, Los Angeles Dodgers, and San Diego Padres (all U.S.A.) from 1986 to 2008.

★ **Most home runs hit in one postseason** Carlos Beltran (Puerto Rico) hit eight home runs in one postseason playing for the Houston Astros (U.S.A.) in 2004. This record is shared with Barry Bonds (U.S.A.), who played for the San Francisco Giants (U.S.A.) in the 2002 postseason.

☆ **Most consecutive seasons with 200 or more hits** Ichiro Suzuki (Japan) had at least 200 hits in eight consecutive seasons playing for the Seattle Mariners (U.S.A.) from 2001 to 2008, equaling Wee Willie Keeler's (U.S.A.) record in 1894–1901.

☆ **Most strikeouts in an MLB season by a batter** Mark Reynolds (U.S.A.) suffered 204 strikeouts playing for the Arizona Diamondbacks (U.S.A.) in the 2008 season.

☆ **Most home runs in an MLB career by a designated hitter** Frank Thomas (U.S.A.) scored 269 home runs in his career as a designated hitter playing for the Chicago White Sox, Oakland Athletics (both U.S.A.), and the Toronto Blue Jays (Canada) from 1990 to 2008.

★ **Most wild pitches thrown in an inning** This record is held by various pitchers, with four wild throws—most recently by R. A. Dickey (U.S.A.) playing for the Seattle Mariners (U.S.A.) on August 17, 2008.

☆ **Most home runs hit in a postseason baseball career** The record for the most career home runs hit during the postseason is 25 by Manny Ramirez (Dominican Republic) playing for the Cleveland Indians, Boston Red Sox, and Los Angeles Dodgers (all U.S.A.) since 1995.

☆ **Most times hit by a pitch in a baseball game** Several players have been hit three times by a pitch. The most recent were Nomar Garciaparra (U.S.A.), playing for the Los Angeles Dodgers (U.S.A.) on July 3, 2006; Reed Johnson (U.S.A.), playing for the Toronto Blue Jays (Canada) on April 29, 2006; Manny Ramirez (Dominican Republic), playing for the Boston Red Sox (U.S.A.) on July 5, 2008; and Chase Utley (U.S.A.), playing for the Philadelphia Phillies (U.S.A.) on April 8, 2008.

BASKETBALL

NBA

★ **Best single-season improvement (team)** The biggest single-season turnaround is 42 wins by the Boston Celtics (U.S.A.) during the 2007–08 season. The Celtics won 24 games in 2006–07, but improved to 66 wins in 2007–08.

★ **Best 30-game start (team)** The Boston Celtics also achieved a 27–3 record with their 97–93 win over the Houston Rockets (U.S.A.) on January 2, 2008, which ties them with five other teams for the best start in NBA history after 30 games. The 1966–67 Philadelphia 76ers, 1969–70 New York Knicks, 1971–72 Los Angeles Lakers, 1990–91 Portland Trail Blazers, and 1995–96 Chicago Bulls (all U.S.A.) each began the season 27–3.

☆ **Most three-point field goals in an NBA game (team)** The Orlando Magic scored 23 three-point shots in an NBA game against the Sacramento Kings (both U.S.A.) on January 13, 2009.

☆ **Highest percentage of three-point field goals** Since 2003, Jason Kapono (U.S.A.) has shot a 45.6 percentage for three-points with the Cleveland Cavaliers, Charlotte Hornets, Miami Heat (all U.S.A.), and Toronto Raptors (Canada).

★ **FIRST TWINS SELECTED IN THE FIRST ROUND OF THE SAME NBA DRAFT** Twins Brook (right) and Robin Lopez (left) from North Hollywood, California, U.S.A., are the first twins selected in the opening round of the same NBA draft. Brook was the 10th overall selection by the New Jersey Nets and Robin was the 15th overall pick by the Phoenix Suns (both U.S.A.) in 2008.

★ **YOUNGEST PLAYER TO APPEAR IN 1,000 GAMES (NBA CAREER)** At the age of 32 years 165 days, Kevin Garnett (U.S.A., b. May 19, 1976) became the youngest individual to appear in 1,000 NBA career games. He achieved this landmark while playing for the Boston Celtics in a 96–80 victory over the Chicago Bulls (U.S.A.) on October 31, 2008, breaking Shawn Kemp's (U.S.A.) record of 33 years 24 days set in December 2002.

★ **Fewest field goals scored in a game (team)** The Miami Heat (U.S.A.) scored 17 baskets in an 88–62 loss against the Boston Celtics on March 30, 2008.

☆ **Most playoff games won by a coach** Phil Jackson (U.S.A.) recorded 193 playoff game wins while coaching the Chicago Bulls (1989–97) and the Los Angeles Lakers (1999–2008).

Fewest points scored in a half (team) The New Orleans Hornets scored 16 points in the second half of their 89–67 loss to the Los Angeles Clippers (both U.S.A.) on March 1, 2006.

★ **Most playoff game appearances (individual)** Robert Horry (U.S.A.) has made 244 playoff appearances playing for the Houston Rockets, Los Angeles Lakers, and San Antonio Spurs (all U.S.A.) from 1992 to 2008.

★ **Most steals in a final** The Boston Celtics achieved 18 steals in Game 7 of the NBA Finals against the Los Angeles Lakers on June 17, 2008.

★ **MOST POINTS SCORED IN ONE QUARTER BY AN INDIVIDUAL, NBA** Carmelo Anthony (U.S.A.) scored 33 points in the third quarter playing for the Denver Nuggets against the Minnesota Timberwolves (both U.S.A.) on December 10, 2008. Anthony tied the mark set by George Gervin (U.S.A.) playing for the San Antonio Spurs against the New Orleans Jazz (both U.S.A.) on April 9, 1978.

NOV. 2: The world's **largest truffle** was a white truffle weighing 2 lb. 8 oz. (1.31 kg), found by Giancarlo Zigante (Croatia) on November 2, 1999. It was estimated to be worth $5,080.

34: the **most points scored in a WNBA debut game**—by Candace Parker (U.S.A.), playing for the Los Angeles Sparks (U.S.A.) on May 18, 2008.

★ LONGEST-TENURED NBA COACH Jerry Sloan (U.S.A.) has spent 22 seasons coaching the Utah Jazz (U.S.A.), a post he took up in 1988. Jerry also holds the record for the **most technical fouls in an NBA career**. As of March 15, 2007, he was whistled for 413 fouls in his career as a player—with the Baltimore Bullets and Chicago Bulls—and as a coach—with the Bulls and Utah Jazz (all U.S.A.).

Most three-point field goals in an NBA career Reggie Miller (U.S.A.) scored 2,560 three-point field goals for the Indiana Pacers (U.S.A.) between 1987 and 2005, a career record for an NBA player.

WNBA

☆**Most games played** Vickie Johnson (U.S.A.) has played in 378 games during her Women's National Basketball Association (WNBA) career with

the New York Liberty (U.S.A.) between 1997 and 2005, and the San Antonio Silver Stars (U.S.A.) between 2006 and 2008. Johnson also holds the record for the ☆**most minutes played in a WNBA career** with a total of 11,698 minutes played over the same period.

☆**MOST BLOCKS IN A WNBA CAREER** Margo Dydek (Poland) achieved 877 blocks in 323 games playing for the Utah Starzz (1998–2002), San Antonio Silver Stars (2003–04), Connecticut Sun (2005–07), and Los Angeles Sparks (2008). She also holds the record for the **most blocks per game**, with a 2.72 average.

NOV. 3: The first known attack using an unmanned aerial vehicle occurred in Yemen on November 3, 2002, when a CIA-operated AGM-114 Hellfire missile was fired at six alleged Al-Qaeda operatives.

★ **YOUNGEST INDIVIDUAL TO SCORE 12,000 POINTS** At 24 years 35 days, Lebron James (U.S.A.), (b. December 30, 1984) is the youngest player in NBA history to score 12,000 career points. James reached the mark while playing for the Cleveland Cavaliers (U.S.A.) on February 3, 2009.

★ **Highest point-scoring average** Named Rookie of the Year in her 2006 debut season, Seimone Augustus (U.S.A.) has scored 2,104 points in 99 games for the Minnesota Lynx (U.S.A.) since starting her professional career, giving her a record point-scoring average of 21.3.

☆ **Most assists** Ticha Penicheiro (Portugal) provided 2,023 assists in 339 games playing for the Sacramento Monarchs (U.S.A.) between 1998 and 2008.

☆ **Most points scored** Lisa Leslie (U.S.A.) scored a record-breaking 5,909 points playing for the Los Angeles Sparks (U.S.A.) from 1997 to

NOV. 4: The record for the **most yo-yos spun simultaneously** was set by Eric Lindeen (Sweden), who managed to spin nine yo-yos up on hooks in Stockholm, Sweden, on November 4, 2006.

2008. A four-time women's basketball Olympic gold medalist, Leslie also holds three other records: the ☆ **most field goals,** with 2,188; the ☆ **most free throws made,** with 1,412; and the ☆ **most rebounds,** with 3,156—all achieved over the course of her career with the Los Angeles Sparks.

☆ **Most minutes played per game in a WNBA career** Veteran WNBA player Katie Smith (U.S.A.) averaged 34.8 minutes per game over the course of her career with the Minnesota Lynx (U.S.A.) from 1995 to 2005 and the Detroit Shock (U.S.A.) from 2005 to 2008. She also racked up the ☆ **most three-point field goals in an WNBA career,** with 674 three-pointers over the same period.

NBA ALL-STAR JAM SESSION

LONGEST TIME . . .

★ **Spinning a basketball on the head** Harlem Globetrotter Scooter Christensen (U.S.A.) spun a basketball on his head for 6.07 seconds at NBA All-Star Jam Session in Phoenix, Arizona, U.S.A., on February 12, 2009. Christensen also broke the record for the ☆ **longest time spinning a basketball on the nose,** doing so for 5 seconds.

☆ **Spinning a basketball on one finger** Joseph Odhiambo (U.S.A.) spun a basketball on one finger, using one hand and giving the ball just one

---

NBA ALL-STAR JAM SESSION PHOENIX 2009
PRESENTED BY ADIDAS

NBA All-Star Jam Session provides fans the once-in-a-lifetime experience of participating in NBA All-Star excitement, where the chance to meet and collect free autographs from NBA Players and Legends is just the beginning. With over 500,000 ft². (46,451 m²) of NBA All-Star action, Jam Session is non-stop basketball nirvana! Fans of all ages can shoot, slam, and dribble all day on several different courts; compete against their friends in skills challenges; watch mascots, dance teams, and celebrities compete in basketball competitions; or get basketball tips from NBA Players and Legends.

NOV. 5: On November 5, 2001, Tesfaye Jifar (Ethiopia) achieved the **fastest time to finish the New York Marathon by a male athlete,** completing the course in just 2 hr. 7 min. 43 sec.

★ **FASTEST BASELINE TO BASELINE DRIBBLE** Basketball pro Devin Harris (U.S.A.) of the New Jersey Nets (U.S.A.) showed the crowd his athletic power by dribbling the length of the court, baseline to baseline, in just 3.93 seconds during NBA All-Star Jam Session on February 16, 2009.

BALL ACROBATICS Athletic basketball performers Team Acrodunk (U.S.A.) set two records at the NBA All-Star Jam Session 2009. The ★ **most backboard passes to a dunk in 30 seconds using a trampoline (team)** saw four of the group complete 35 passes on the trampoline before finishing off with a slam dunk. The ★ **farthest six-person tandem using a trampoline** saw the team passing the ball on a trampoline 20 ft. (6 m) from the basket before hitting a slam dunk.

spin, for 1 min. 54.88 sec. on February 14, 2009, at NBA All-Star Jam Session in Phoenix, Arizona, U.S.A., breaking his previous record of 37.46 seconds, set at the 2008 event.

A renowned basketball freestyler, Odhiambo has a number of world records to his name, including the **longest time to spin a basketball on one finger, maintaining spin**—an impressive 4 hr. 15 min. on February 19, 2006, in Houston, Texas, U.S.A., during NBA All-Star Jam Session.

MOST . . .

★ **Blindfolded free throws in two minutes** Australian basketball legend Ed Palubinskas is so well known for shooting, he even set up the Palubinskas Basketball Academy to teach players to improve their shooting skills. At NBA All-Star Jam Session in Phoenix, Arizona, U.S.A., on February 16, 2009, he really put himself to the test, netting a record eight free throws in two minutes—not all that impressive until you realize that he was blindfolded at the time!

NOV. 6: The world's **largest Hindu temple**—the BAPS Swaminarayan Akshardham in New Delhi, India—has a total area of 86,342 ft². (8,021.43 m²) and was inaugurated on this day in 2005.

TWO BALLS A-SPINNING Basketball skills specialist Tommy Baker (UK) spun out the record for the ★**longest duration spinning two basketballs on one hand** to 32.88 seconds at NBA All-Star Jam Session in Phoenix, Arizona, U.S.A., on February 14, 2009.

★**Basketball headers while spinning two basketballs** Ball skills entertainer Tommy Baker (UK, left) managed 40 basketball headers while spinning another basketball on each of his hands at NBA All-Star Jam Session in Phoenix, Arizona, U.S.A., on February 16, 2009.

Baker also set the record for the ★**most consecutive chest and head rolls using three basketballs** at the same event, keeping three basketballs rolling in a circular motion—around his arms, up his shoulders, and over his head—a total of 10 times.

★**Basketball neck catches in one minute** Luis "Trikz" Da Silva Jr. (U.S.A.) really got it in the neck at NBA All-Star Jam Session—he caught an impressive total of 24 basketballs with his neck in one minute on February 14, 2009.

Consecutive free throws from a wheelchair National Wheelchair Basketball Association (NWBA) player Jeff Griffin (U.S.A.) scored three consecutive free throws from a wheelchair at NBA All-Star Jam Session in Phoenix, Arizona, U.S.A., on February 12, 2009.

★**Three-pointers scored in one minute on *NBA 2k9*** Video gamer Chad Heathcote (U.S.A.) scored 26 three-point shots in one minute on

★**HIGHEST SLAM DUNK WITH A BACK FLIP** Jerry Burrell (U.S.A.), a member of the acrobatic basketball skills group Team Acrodunk, thrilled the crowds at NBA All-Star Jam Session when he sank a slam dunk while back flipping from a platform 15 ft. 4 in. (4.67 m) high in Phoenix, Arizona, U.S.A., on February 16, 2009.

NOV. 7: The **most expensive dessert** is the Frrrozen Haute Chocolate ice cream sundae, added to the menu at Serendipity 3 in New York City, U.S.A., on November 7, 2007—at a cost of $25,000!

☆ **MOST BLINDFOLDED FREE THROWS IN ONE MINUTE** Chauncey Billups (U.S.A.) equaled Jack Ryan's (U.S.A.) record of five free throws scored blindfolded in one minute at NBA All-Star Jam Session in Phoenix, Arizona, U.S.A., on February 14, 2009.

NBA 2K9 at NBA All-Star Jam Session in Phoenix, Arizona, U.S.A., on February 12, 2009. Heathcote used the player Steve Nash to beat off strong competition and triumph in the record-breaking video game challenge.

★**Consecutive free throws on *NBA 2k9*** Blaine Griffin (U.S.A.) showed off his video-gaming skills by racking up 15 consecutive free throws on *NBA 2K9* at NBA All-Star Jam Session in Phoenix, Arizona, U.S.A., on February 15, 2009.

★**Free throws scored in one minute on *NBA 2k9*** Just a minute was all it took for Phil Ramirez (U.S.A.) to score 13 free throws on *NBA 2K9* at NBA All-Star Jam Session on February 13, 2009.

★ **MOST CONSECUTIVE THREE-POINTERS ON** *NBA 2K9* The 2K9 Sports Gaming Area was a popular venue with video game fans throughout NBA All-Star Jam Session. It was here, on February 14, 2009, that Marcus Platt (U.S.A., far left) established a new world record by scoring a total of eight three-pointers on the run in the video game *NBA 2K9.*

COMBAT SPORTS

KARATE

☆ **Most team Kata World Championships (female)** Kata is the detailed choreographed patterns of karate moves, practiced either solo or in pairs. In competitive kata, Japan has won the Karate Kata World Championships on eight occasions between 1988 and 2008.

★ **Most consecutive Kata World Championships (female)** Atsuko Wakai (Japan) has won four consecutive World Karate Federation (WKF) World Championships, in 1998, 2000, 2002, and 2004.

★ **MOST WINS OF THE WKF WORLD KARATE CHAMPIONSHIPS KATA CLASS (MALE)** The most titles won by a man is three, a record shared by Tsuguo Sakumoto (Japan) in 1984, 1986, and 1988; Michael Milan (France) in 1994, 1996, and 2000; and Luca Valdesi (Italy, left) in 2004, 2006, and 2008.

☆ **MOST GOLD MEDALS WON AT THE OLYMPICS FOR WRESTLING (MALE)** Five men have each won three Olympic wrestling titles: Carl Westergren (Sweden) in 1920, 1924, and 1932; Ivar Johansson (Sweden) in 1932 (twice) and 1936; Aleksandr Vasilyevich Medved (USSR) in 1964, 1968, and 1972; Aleksandr Karelin (Russia) in 1988, 1992, and 1996; and Buvaysa Saytiev (Russia) in 1996, 2004, and 2008.

FACT

Pictured is Russia's Buvaysa Saytiev battling Uzbekistan's Soslan Tiglev during the 2008 Beijing Olympic Games.

☆ **Fastest 100-Man Kumite karate** The 100-Man Kumite is the ultimate test in full-contact karate. It involves 100 opponents in full-contact knockdown fighting, with each bout lasting two minutes. On June 9, 2002, Paddy Doyle (UK) took just 3 hr. 6 min. to defeat his 100 opponents. He won 59 fights by Ippon (full points) and 29 by decision, drew 12, and did not lose a single fight.

JUDO

★ **Most World Championship medals won (male)** Judo, which means "gentle way," uses only throws in combat, with no punching, kicking, or striking. The most medals won by an individual male at a World Championships is seven, by two judoka: Naoya Ogawa (Japan), with four gold and three bronze between 1987 and 1995; and Robert Van de Walle (Belgium) with two silver and five bronze between 1979 and 1989.

....

NOV. 8: The **smallest newspaper,** measuring 1.25 × 0.86 in. (32 × 22 mm), was an edition of the children's newspaper *First News* (UK) published on November 8, 2007.

....

☆ **MOST CONSECUTIVE WORLD SUPER-MIDDLEWEIGHT TITLE DEFENSES** Joe Calzaghe (UK, right) successfully defended his super-middleweight world title on 21 occasions. He completed his 21st defense by beating Mikkel Kessler (Denmark, left) on points in Cardiff, UK, on November 3, 2007.

★ **MOST WORLD JUDO CHAMPIONSHIP TEAM COMPETITION WINS (FEMALE)** The Japan women's team has won the World Judo Championships on two occasions, in 2002 and 2008 (pictured).

★**Most World Championship medals won (female)** For an individual female judoka, the record for the most Judo World Championships medals won is 11, by Ingrid Berghmans (Belgium), with six gold, four silver, and one bronze between 1980 and 1989.

Ryoko Tani (Japan) has won the **most World Championship titles (female)**, with seven wins in the -48 kg category between 1993 and 2007.

TAEKWONDO

★**Most World Cup heavyweight wins (male)** Taekwondo is the national sport of Korea and one of the most widely practiced martial arts in the world. The most Taekwondo World Cup heavyweight class wins by a man is three, by Pascal Gentil (France) from 2000 to 2002.

★**Most World Cup heavyweight wins (female)** Myoung Sook Jung (Korea) recorded three World Cup heavyweight class wins, in 1997, 2000, and 2001.

★**Most World Cup lightweight wins (male)** Hadi Saeibonehkohal (Iran) has more World Cup lightweight class wins than any other competitor, triumphing on four occasions, first in 1998 and then from 2000 to 2002.

★**Most World Cup lightweight wins (female)** Eun Kyung Jun (South Korea) has won the World Cup lightweight class on two occasions, in 2002 and 2006.

☆**Most countries competing at a Taekwondo World Championships** The 18th (11th Women's) World Taekwondo Championships held between May 18 and 22, 2007, in Beijing, China, welcomed a record 116 participating nations.

UFC

☆**Most heavyweight championships** Ultimate Fighting Championship (UFC) is a U.S.-based mixed martial arts competition. Randy Cou-

☆**MOST WINS OF THE WORLD WRESTLING ENTERTAINMENT CHAMPIONSHIP (MALE)** One male wrestler has won the World Wrestling Entertainment (WWE) Championship on eight occasions: Triple H (U.S.A., b. Paul Levesque, pictured left) took the title between 1999 and 2008.

ture (U.S.A.) won seven UFC heavyweight championship bouts between 1997 and 2008.

☆**Heaviest fighter** Teila Tuli (U.S.A.) weighed 414 lb. (188 kg) for his one and only UFC career fight. He lost to Gerard Gordeau (Netherlands) at UFC 1 on November 12, 1993, despite far outweighing his opponent.

☆**Lightest fighter** Thiago Alves (Brazil), Jeff Curran, Jens Pulver, and Leonard Garcia (all U.S.A.) each weigh in at 140 lb. (63.5 kg), making them the lightest UFC fighters.

☆**Most UFC middleweight championships** Anderson Silva (Brazil) has won five UFC middleweight championship bouts, which is the most by an individual fighter. Silva set the record between 2006 and 2008. The middleweight championship was reinstituted in 2001 when the old middleweight championship became the light-heavyweight championship.

★**Largest audience for a UFC television show** UFC 66, held at the MGM Arena in Las Vegas, U.S.A., on December 30, 2006, attracted a pay-per-view television audience of 1 million viewers. The event was headlined by a bout between Chuck Liddell and Tito Ortiz (both U.S.A.), in which Liddell defeated Ortiz to retain the UFC light-heavyweight championship.

LONGEST BOXING MATCH

Andy Bowen boxed Jack Burke (both U.S.A.) in New Orleans, Louisiana, U.S.A., on April 6–7, 1893. The match lasted 110 rounds—or 7 hr. 19 min.—before being declared a no contest.

CRICKET

TWENTY20 MATCHES

★**Highest individual score in an innings** Brendon McCullum (New Zealand) scored 158 not out (from 73 deliveries) for the Kolkata Knight Riders against Bangalore Royal Challengers in a Twenty20 match in Bangalore, India, on April 18, 2008.

★**Highest individual score in an international innings** Chris Gayle (Jamaica) scored 117 (from 57 deliveries) for the West Indies against South Africa in a Twenty20 match in Johannesburg, South Africa, on September 11, 2007. Gayle hit 10 sixes in his innings—the ★ **most sixes in an international Twenty20 innings.**

☆**Most catches by a fielder in an international career** Ross Taylor (New Zealand) has taken 13 catches for New Zealand in Twenty20 internationals spanning 17 matches between 2006 and 2008.

★**Most sixes in an innings** Graham Napier (UK) hit 16 sixes in his innings of 152 not out (from 58 deliveries) for the Essex Eagles in a Twenty20 match against Sussex Sharks in Chelmsford, UK, on June 24, 2008.

☆ **MOST WICKETS IN A TWENTY20 INTERNATIONAL CAREER** Daniel Vettori (New Zealand, pictured left) has taken 21 wickets in Twenty20 internationals, playing for New Zealand between 2007 and 2009.

NOV. 10: The record for the **largest salad** is 22,619 lb. 6 oz. (10,260 kg) and was achieved by the Sde Warburg Agricultural Association in Sde Warburg, Israel, on November 10, 2007.

★**Most wickets in a Twenty20 career** Tyron Henderson (South Africa) has taken 74 wickets in Twenty20 spanning 62 matches from April 13, 2004, to October 30, 2008.

ONE-DAY INTERNATIONAL (ODI) MATCHES

☆**Highest margin of victory (runs)** New Zealand scored 402–3 to beat Ireland (112 all out) by 290 runs in an ODI match at Aberdeen, UK, on July 1, 2008.

☆**Most catches by a fielder in an ODI career** Mahela Jayawardene (Sri Lanka) held 159 catches in 299 ODI matches between 1998 and 2009, an average of 0.535 catches per match.

☆**Most ODI matches played** Sanath Jayasuriya (Sri Lanka) played a record 432 ODI matches for his country between 1989 and 2009.

FACT

Gibbs (below) hit six sixes in an over against the Netherlands in the 2007 World Cup in St. Kitts—the first person to achieve the feat in an international match.

★**MOST FOURS IN A TWENTY20 INTERNATIONAL INNINGS** Herschelle Gibbs (South Africa) hit 14 fours in his innings of 90 (from 55 deliveries) for South Africa against the West Indies in Johannesburg, South Africa, on September 11, 2007. No other player has scored more fours in an international Twenty20 innings.

NOV. 11: The **largest animal sculpture** (a cow), measuring 46 ft. 6 in. (14.18 m) tall, 38 ft. 7 in. (11.77 m) wide, and 69 ft. 8 in. (21.24 m) long, was created by Milka (Germany) in Berlin, Germany, on this day in 2007.

★ **YOUNGEST PLAYER TO SCORE 1,000 RUNS IN ONE-DAY INTERNATIONALS (FEMALE)** When Sarah Taylor (UK, b. May 20, 1989) scored her 1,000th run in women's One-Day International cricket at the age of 19 years 104 days, she became the youngest woman to reach that milestone in the one-day form of the game. Taylor achieved the feat playing for England against India at the County Ground, Taunton, Somerset, UK, on September 1, 2008.

☆ **Most wicket-keeping dismissals in an ODI career** Wicketkeeper Adam Gilchrist (Australia) secured a total of 472 dismissals (417 catches, 55 stumpings) in 287 ODI matches from 1996 to 2008.

Gilchrist also holds the record for the **most wicket-keeping dismissals in a cricket World Cup career** with 52 in 31 matches in World Cup tournaments from 1992 to 2007.

☆ **Most wickets taken in a one-day international career** Muttiah "Murali" Muralitharan (Sri Lanka) has taken 505 wickets (at an average of 22.74 per wicket) in 329 ODI matches for Sri Lanka, Asia, and the ICC World XI. His tally was amassed in matches between August 12, 1993 and February 8, 2009.

TEST MATCHES

★ **Most double centuries in a Test series** Sir Donald Bradman (Australia) scored three double centuries in the 1930 Ashes series against England—the most by an individual batsman in a Test match series.

★ **Most appearances as a Test match referee** Ranjan Madugalle (Sri Lanka) has officiated at a total of 110 Test matches as referee between 1993 and 2009.

☆ **Most times to score in the 90s** The most Test match scores in the 90s by an individual batsman is 10, by "Iceman" Steve Waugh (Australia)

....

NOV. 12: Paul McCartney (UK) became the **first singer to broadcast live to space** when he sent a "wake-up call" to the International Space Station during a concert on this day in 2005.

....

MOST CENTURIES IN A CAREER In a One-day International (ODI) career that has encompassed 425 matches between December 1989 and March 2009, modern-day cricket marvel Sachin Tendulkar (India) has scored 43 centuries, the ☆ **most centuries scored in an individual ODI career.**

Tendulkar, known as "Little Master" by his fans, also holds the record for the ☆ **most centuries scored by an individual batsman in Test matches**—42 in 159 Tests between November 1989 and April 2009.

RUN MACHINE . . .

In his incredible career, Sachin Tendulkar has scored the **most runs in One-Day Internationals,** with 16,684; the **most runs in Test cricket,** with 12,773; and the **most runs in the Cricket World Cup,** with 1,796 in World Cup tournaments from 1992 to 2007.

---

between 1985 and 2004, and Rahul Dravid (India) between 1996 and 2009. A score in the 90s is unenviable as it means getting out before reaching the milestone of a century.

☆**Most wickets taken** Muttiah Muralitharan (Sri Lanka) is the leading Test match wicket-taker, with 770 wickets (at an average of 22.18 runs per wicket) in 127 matches from August 28, 1992, to March 5, 2009.

....

NOV. 13: The **largest teepee** stands 51 ft. 2 in. (15.61 m) high and is 53 ft. 7 in. (16.34 m) in diameter. It was constructed by the firefighters of Horgenberg, Switzerland, on this day in 2004.

....

TEST NATIONS

There are currently 10 Test cricket playing nations: Australia, Bangladesh, England, India, New Zealand, Pakistan, Sri Lanka, South Africa, West Indies, and Zimbabwe (Zimbabwe has not played a Test match since 2005).

☆ **MOST WICKET-KEEPING CATCHES IN A TEST CAREER** Wicket-keeper Mark Boucher (South Africa) took 453 catches in 126 matches playing Test cricket for South Africa between October 1997 and March 2009.

Add 22 stumpings to that figure and you get a career total of 475 Test dismissals, the ☆ most wicket-keeping dismissals in a Test cricket career.

★**Most centuries in a Test series** Clyde Walcott (Barbados) hit five centuries for the West Indies in the 1955 series against Australia from March 26 to June 17, 1955.

★**Most consecutive innings before scoring first duck** A. B. de Villiers (South Africa) batted for 78 innings before scoring his first duck (zero runs) between December 17, 2004, and November 27, 2008.

☆**Most triple centuries in a Test career** Only three batsmen in the history of Test match cricket have scored two innings of more than 300 runs: Sir Don Bradman (Australia) hit 334 against England in 1930, and 304 against England in 1934, both scores coming at Leeds, UK; Brian Lara (Trinidad and Tobago), playing for the West Indies, hit 375 against England at St. Johns, Antigua, in 1994, and 400 against England at the same ground in 2004; and Virender Sehwag (India) scored 309 against Pakistan in Multan, Pakistan, in 2004, and 319 against South Africa in Chennai, India, in 2009.

☆**Most Man of the Match awards** Jaques Kallis (South Africa) has won 20 Test match Man of the Match awards between 1985 and 2009.

CYCLING

OLYMPIC CYCLING

•The ☆ **most Olympic cycling medals won (male)** is five, shared by Daniel Morelon (France) and Chris Hoy (UK). Hoy also set the ★ **fastest Olympic 1-km standing start race win** with a time of 1 min. 0.711 sec.

•Leontien Zijlaard-Van Moorsel (Netherlands) has won four individual gold medals at two Olympic Games—the **most Olympic cycling gold medals (female)**. She struck gold in the road race, time trial, and pursuit categories at the 2000 Sydney Olympics and in the time trial at the 2004 Athens Olympics. Her tally of six medals also gives her the record for the **most Olympic cycling medals** overall.

MOUNTAIN BIKING

•Nicolas Vouilloz (France) achieved the **most downhill World Championship wins (male)** with a total of 10 titles—three in the junior championships (1992–94) and seven in the senior class (1995–99 and 2001–02). Vouilloz also holds the **most downhill World Cup titles (male)** with five, winning in 1995–96 and 1998–2000.

•The **most mountain biking cross-country World Championships wins (female)** is four, achieved by Gunn-Rita Dahle Flesjå (Norway) in 2002 and 2004–06. A truly extraordinary record-breaking cyclist, she's also won the

MOST FOUR-CROSS MOUNTAIN BIKING WORLD CUPS (MALE) Four-cross mountain bike events feature four riders racing simultaneously down a prepared track, with the first rider down winning the race. Brian Lopes (U.S.A.) won three four-cross World Cups, in 2002, 2005, and 2007, and holds the record for the ☆ **most four-cross mountain biking World Championship titles by a man**, with three wins also in 2002, 2005, and 2007.

☆ **MOST UCI BMX WORLD TITLES (MALE)** Kyle Bennett (U.S.A., left) racked up a record three Union Cycliste Internationale (UCI) BMX World Championship titles, in 2002–03 and 2007. Bennett also jointly holds the record for the ☆ **most consecutive BMX World Championship titles** with Gary Ellis (U.S.A.), who won the title in both 1987 and 1988. The most UCI BMX World Championships (female) is three, held by Gabriela Diaz (Argentina), who won in 2001, 2002, and 2004.

most mountain biking cross-country World Cups (female), with four consecutive victories from 2003 to 2006.

Flesjå's nearly total dominance of women's cross-country mountain biking is challenged only by Pia Sundstedt (Finland), who gained the **most wins of the UCI Mountain Bike Marathon World Cup (female)** with a grand total of three victories between 2006 and 2008.

•In the men's marathon categories, Thomas Frischknecht (Switzerland) scored victories in 2003 and 2005 to claim the **most wins of the UCI Mountain Bike Marathon World Championship (male)**. Meanwhile, Leonardo Paez (Colombia) has the distinction of the **most wins of the UCI Mountain Bike Marathon World Cup (male)**, with titles in 2006 and 2008.

•In the field of women's four-cross mountain biking, Jill Kintner (U.S.A.) and Anneke Beerten (Netherlands) rule the roost, each winning two World

Cups; Kintner in 2005–06 and Beerten in 2007–08. This distinction makes them joint holders of the record for the ☆ **most four-cross mountain biking World Cup titles (female)**.

★ **GREATEST DISTANCE CYCLED (24 HR)** Extreme cyclist Marko Baloh (Slovenia) cycled a total of 553.14 miles (890.2 km), solo and unpaced, over 24 hours in Lenart, Slovenia, on September 6–7, 2008.

NOV. 14: Frank Brown, Marcelo Prieto, and Rafael Monteiro Saladini (all Brazil) paraglided 286.8 miles (461.6 km), the **farthest flight in a paraglider,** on this day in 2007.

★ **MOST MOUNTAIN BIKE MARATHON WORLD CHAMPIONSHIPS (FEMALE)** Norwegian cyclist Gunn-Rita Dahle Flesjå has achieved four wins of the Union Cycliste Internationale mountain bike marathon World Championship. Flesjå took the top title in 2004–06 and, after illness impeded her performance in 2007, came back fighting to claim victory in 2008.

ROAD CYCLING

•Rubén Plaza Molina (Spain), riding for team Comunidad Valenciana Puerta Castalla, averaged a record 34.932 mph (56.218 km/h) over the 24.1-mile (38.9-km) time trial from Guadalajara to Alcalá de Henares in the 2005 Vuelta a España (Tour of Spain), the **fastest time trial of a major Tour.**

•The **most stage wins of the Tour of Spain** is 39, by Delio Rodriguez (Spain), between 1941 and 1947. The **most wins of the Tour of Spain** is three, with honor for this achievement shared between Tony Rominger (Switzerland), who won in 1992–94, and Roberto Heras Hernandez (Spain),

★ **FIRST CYCLIST TO BE KNIGHTED** Chris Hoy (UK) became the first cyclist to be knighted, when honored by Her Majesty Queen Elizabeth II in the 2009 New Year Honors List. Hoy's knighthood came shortly after he won three gold medals at the 2008 Olympic Games and was in recognition of his service to sports.

....

NOV. 15: On this day in 2005, an anonymous U.S. collector paid $690,000 for an original poster for the film *Metropolis* (Germany, 1927), the **most money paid for a poster.**

....

> **48,615:** total participants in Udine Pedala 2000 in Udine, Italy, the **largest cycling event** in the world.

FACT

Years before finding Olympic success, Chris Hoy raced BMX bikes, becoming the Scottish champion in his early teens.

☆ **FASTEST 4-KM TEAM PURSUIT** The GB team of Ed Clancy, Bradley Wiggins, Paul Manning, and Geraint Thomas scored a world record, and Olympic gold, with a time of 3 min. 53.31 sec. in Beijing, China, on August 18, 2008.

who won in 2000 and 2003–04. Heras Hernandez also won the race in 2005, but he tested positive for a banned substance and his victory was handed to Denis Menchov (Russia).

•Mathias Clemens (Luxembourg) won five Tours of Luxembourg (1935–37, 1939, and 1947)—the ★ **most wins of the Tour of Luxembourg.**

•Lance Armstrong (USA) has the **most wins in the Tour de France,** with seven titles between 1999 and 2005.

•Three cyclists can claim the record for the **most wins of the Tour of Italy,** with five titles apiece for: Alfredo Binda (Italy, 1925, 1927–9, 1933); Fausto Coppi (Italy, 1940, 1947, 1949, 1952–3); and Eddy Merckx (Belgium, 1968, 1970, 1972–4). In the points competition, it is a

NOV. 16: The **greatest recorded meteor shower** occurred on this night in November 1966, when the Leonid meteors were visible between western North America and eastern Russia (then USSR).

different story, with two riders having scored a record four points wins: Francesco Moser (Italy) in 1976–78 and 1982 and Giuseppe Saronni (Italy) in 1979–81 and 1983 are both able to claim the ★ **most Tour of Italy points competition victories.**

CYCLO-CROSS

•Hanka Kupfernagel (Germany) has won the **most cyclo-cross World Championships (female)**, with four title victories in 2000–01, 2005, and 2008.

•In the men's event, Eric De Vlaeminck (Belgium) still holds the record for the **most cyclo-cross World Championships (male)**, with seven wins, in 1966 and 1968–73.

TRIALS

•Karin Moor (Switzerland) has won seven cycling World Championships trials titles, with consecutive wins from 2001 to 2007, earning her the record for **most trials cycling World Championship titles (female).**

•The rider with the **most wins of the trials cycling World Championships (male, elite)** is Benito Ros Charral (Spain), who racked up five titles in 2003–05 and 2007–08.

SOCCER

CLUB SOCCER

☆**Most UEFA Champions League goals** Raúl González Blanco (Spain) scored 64 goals in UEFA Champions League matches playing for Real Madrid (Spain) between 1995 and 2009. Raúl also holds the record for the ☆ **most UEFA Champions League appearances,** having played in 125 matches since his debut on September 13, 1995.

Most UEFA Champions League titles won by an individual player Clarence Seedorf (Suriname) claimed his fourth UEFA Champions League winning title as a player when his team, AC Milan (Italy), beat Liverpool in Athens, Greece, on May 23, 2007. Seedorf also won with AC Milan in 2003 and triumphed with two other clubs: Ajax (Netherlands) in 1995 and Real Madrid (Spain) in 1998.

★**Youngest player in the Champions League** Celestine Babayaro (Nigeria) was 16 years 87 days old when he played for Anderlecht (Belgium) against Steaua Bucharest (Romania) in a UEFA Champions League match on November 23, 1994. The **oldest player in the UEFA Champions League** is Marco Ballota (Italy), who was 43 years 252 days when he played for Lazio (Italy) against Real Madrid (Spain) on December 11, 2007.

★ **MOST APPEARANCES IN THE UEFA EUROPEAN CHAMPIONSHIPS**
Both defender Lilian Thuram (France) and goalkeeper Edwin van der Sar
(Netherlands, pictured above) have played in 16 UEFA European
Championship matches. Both players' international careers spanned the
tournaments played from 1996 to 2008.

Highest transfer fee Zinedine Zidane (France) moved from Juventus (Italy) to Real Madrid (Spain) for a reported 13,033,000,000 Spanish pesetas ($66.36 million) on July 9, 2001.

★**Most wins of the top division in English soccer by a female team** The FA Women's Premier League is the top division of league soccer competition in England for women and has been won a record 11 times by Arsenal Ladies between 1993 and 2009.

....

NOV. 17: The **fastest time to pluck a turkey** is 1 min. 30 sec. by Vincent Pilkington of Cootehill, Co. Cavan, Ireland, who achieved the feat on RTE television in Dublin, Ireland, on this day in 1980.

....

☆ **MOST GOALS SCORED IN AN MLS CAREER** Jamie Moreno (Bolivia) scored 112 goals in 295 Major League Soccer (MLS) games playing for D.C. United and MetroStars (both U.S.A.) between 1996 and 2007.

Youngest person to play in the top division of English soccer The youngest player to appear in the English Premier League, which is the top division of English professional soccer, is Matthew Briggs (UK, b. March 9, 1991), who came on as a substitute playing for Fulham in the team's 3–1 defeat against Middlesbrough on May 13, 2007, aged 16 years 65 days.

★ **Most English Premier League red cards** The most red cards received by an individual player in the English Premier League is eight, by three players: Richard Dunne (Ireland) playing for Everton and Manchester City between 1996 and 2008; Duncan Ferguson (UK) playing for Everton and Newcastle between 1994 and 2006; and Patrick Vieira (France), who played for Arsenal between 1996 and 2005.

INTERNATIONALS

★ **Most goals scored in a single FIFA Confederations Cup tournament** The most goals scored by an individual player in a single Confederations Cup tournament is seven by Romario (Brazil) in 1997.

☆ **MOST CONSECUTIVE ENGLISH PREMIER LEAGUE APPEARANCES** U.S. goalkeeping veteran Brad Friedel (U.S.A.) has recorded 188 consecutive appearances in the English Premier League, playing for Blackburn Rovers and Aston Villa, between August 14, 2004, and January 31, 2009.

NOV. 18: The **most couples hugging simultaneously** is 1,451 at a World Children's Day charity event held at Taipei Arena, Taipei, Taiwan, on this day in 2007.

★ **MOST UEFA EUROPEAN CHAMPIONSHIP MATCHES PLAYED** The most matches played by a team in all UEFA European Championships is 38 by Germany (West Germany 1960–88) between 1960 and 2008.

The German national team has also won the ★ **most matches by a team in all UEFA European Championships** with a total of 19 victories, which included titles, in 1972, 1980, and 1996.

★ **Most UEFA European Championship goals scored by an individual** Michel Platini (France) has scored a record nine goals in UEFA European Championship finals tournaments. Platini scored all nine goals playing in midfield for France in the 1984 European Championships, which were held in his home country from June 12–27, 1984.

Longest-running soccer competition for national teams The oldest surviving international soccer competition in which national teams compete is the South American Championship (known as the Copa America since 1975), organized by the South American Football Confederation, Conmebol. The competition was first held in Argentina in 1916, with Venezuela hosting Copa America 2007, its 42nd tournament. Argentina and Uruguay have each won the tournament on 14 occasions.

★ **Oldest international soccer field** The Racecourse Ground in Wrexham, Wales, UK, is the oldest international soccer field that is still in use. The first international match was played at the Racecourse on March 5, 1877, when Scotland beat Wales 2–0.

Wales is the third-oldest international soccer team after England and Scotland.

☆ **MOST GOALS SCORED IN EUROPEAN CLUB COMPETITIONS** Between 1995 and February 19, 2009, Filippo Inzaghi (Italy) scored a record 66 goals playing in European club competitions for Parma, Juventus, and AC Milan (all Italy).

NOV. 19: A total of 1.6 million tickets, valued at $142,825,258.47, were sold on November 19, 2005, for Robbie Williams's 2006 World Tour—**the most tour tickets sold in a day.**

31–0: the **highest score in an international match,** by Australia against American Samoa at Coffs Harbor, NSW, Australia on April 11, 2001.

★ **YOUNGEST PLAYER IN ENGLISH LEAGUE SOCCER** Reuben Noble-Lazarus (UK, b. August 16, 1993, pictured at far left) came on as a substitute for Barnsley, aged 15 years 45 days, at Portman Road, Ipswich, UK, on September 30, 2008, making him the youngest player to appear in an English league match.

☆ **MOST INTERNATIONAL CAPS WON (FEMALE)** Kristine Lilly (U.S.A., b. July 22, 1971) has played in 342 international matches for the U.S. women's soccer team, a record for any international soccer player, male or female. Lilly's debut for her national team took place on August 3, 1987, just 12 days after her 16th birthday, in a match against China.

SOCCER: WORLD CUP

★ **First hat-trick scored in the FIFA World Cup** Bert Patenaude (U.S.A.) was the first player to score a hat-trick (three goals) in a World Cup Finals match, playing for the U.S.A. against Paraguay in Montevideo, Uruguay, on July 17, 1930. Until 2006, Argentinian Guillermo Stabile was credited with the record, having scored three times in his country's 6–3 victory over Mexico on July 19, 1930. But research by FIFA indicated that a goal that was initially credited to the U.S.A.'s Tom Florie in the match against Paraguay should instead be attributed to Patenaude, thus confirming his hat-trick.

★Highest goal average in a FIFA World Cup Finals At the 1954 World Cup Finals in Switzerland, 16 teams competed in a total of 26 matches, during which an incredible 140 goals were scored at an average of 5.38 goals per match. Hungary alone scored 25 goals in four matches to progress to the final, where it lost 3–2 to West Germany.

The **★lowest goal average** was 2.21 per game at the 1990 finals in Italy. The overall average for the 18 World Cup Finals is 2.91 goals per match.

★Largest attendance at a FIFA World Cup Finals The 52 matches played during the 1994 World Cup Finals tournament in the U.S.A., held from June 17 to July 17, 1994, attracted a total of 3,587,538 spectators at a record high average of 68,991 spectators per game.

The 1994 World Cup Finals also had the **★largest television audience of any World Cup Finals tournament,** when a record 32,115,652 viewers in 188 broadcast countries watched a total of 16,392 hours 37 minutes of transmission.

MOST WINS OF THE FIFA WORLD CUP The Fédération Internationale de Football Association (FIFA) instituted the first World Cup on July 13, 1930 in Montevideo, Uruguay. Brazil has won the tournament, which is held every four years, on five occasions: in 1958, 1962, 1970, 1994, and 2002. After winning its third title, Brazil was awarded the original World Cup trophy, the Jules Rimet Trophy (far left), to keep. In 1974, a new trophy, the FIFA World Cup Trophy (left), was introduced.

☆ MOST FIFA WORLD CUP CLEAN SHEETS Two goalkeepers have each achieved 10 clean sheets (a match in which they have conceded no goals) in their World Cup Finals career. Peter Shilton (UK) achieved the feat playing for England from 1982 to 1990 and Fabien Barthez (France) (left) equaled the record playing for France in finals from 1998 to 2006.

NOV. 20: The **largest serving of currywurst** weighed 330 lb. 13 oz. (150.07 kg) and was made at an event organized by Volkswagen AG (Germany) in Wolfsburg, Germany, on November 20, 2008.

MOST CONSECUTIVE WINS IN WORLD CUP FINALS (TEAM) Between 2002 and 2006, Brazil won a record 11 World Cup Finals matches in a row. The sequence began on June 3, 2002, with a 2–1 victory over Turkey in Ulsan, South Korea, and ended on June 27, 2006, when the Brazilian team beat Ghana 3–0 in Dortmund, Germany. The winning streak included the 2002 World Cup Final in Tokyo, Japan, on June 30, 2002, in which Brazil defeated Germany 2–0 to secure its fifth World Cup (pictured).

★**Oldest referee at the FIFA World Cup Finals** George Reader (UK) was 53 years 236 days old when he officiated the final match of the 1950 World Cup Finals at the Maracana stadium in Rio de Janeiro, Brazil, on July 16, 1950. The match was won by Uruguay, which beat the hosts, Brazil, 2–1.

★**FIRST FIFA WORLD CUP GOAL** Lucien Laurent (France, circled left), scored the first World Cup goal ever, playing for France against Mexico in Montevideo, Uruguay, on July 13, 1930. The goal, a 19th-minute volley, was the opener in France's 4–1 victory over Mexico. France lost its two remaining group games and were eliminated from the tournament after the group stages.

NOV. 21: The **oldest known divorcee** was 101-year-old Harry Bidwell of East Sussex, UK. He divorced his 65-year-old wife on this day in 1980.

MOST CARDS ISSUED IN A FIFA WORLD CUP FINALS MATCH An incredible 20 cards (16 yellow and four red) were issued during the Portugal vs. Netherlands match played in Nuremburg, Germany on June 25, 2006, during the 2006 FIFA World Cup Finals. The four red cards issued were the **most red cards in a single World Cup Finals tournament match,** with each team having two players sent off the field.

FIRST PERSON TO WIN THE FIFA WORLD CUP AS BOTH CAPTAIN AND COACH Franz Beckenbauer (Germany) captained West Germany to a 2–1 victory in the FIFA World Cup Final match against the Netherlands in Munich, Germany, on July 7, 1974. On July 8, 1990, Beckenbauer coached the German team to a 1–0 win in the FIFA World Cup Final match against Argentina in Rome, Italy.

NOV. 22: The highest average speed achieved in a glider by a woman is 141.54 mph (227.8 km/h) by Ghislaine Facon (France) at Chos Malal, Argentina, on this day in 2005.

MOST MINUTES PLAYED IN WORLD CUP FINALS Italian defender Paolo Maldini has played for a total of 2,217 minutes in World Cup Finals, playing for Italy in the 1990, 1994, 1998, and 2002 tournaments.

★**Most FIFA World Cup Finals matches refereed** Joel Quiniou (France) refereed eight World Cup Finals matches in a career that spanned the 1986, 1990, and 1994 tournaments.

Quiniou took charge of his first match on June 13, 1986, when Uruguay drew 0–0 with Scotland, and sent off Uruguay's José Batista after just one minute, which was the **fastest red card in a FIFA World Cup Finals** match.

GOLF

★**Most PGA Champions Tour major tournament victories** Jack Nicklaus (U.S.A.) secured an unprecedented eight victories in PGA Champions Tour major tournaments between the years 1990 and 1996.

★**Highest career earnings on the European Senior Tour** The European Senior Tour career earnings record stands at $2,336,395 (€1,799,375) and was achieved by Carl Mason (UK) between 2003 and 2008.

☆**Highest season's earnings for the U.S. LPGA** The season's record for earnings on the U.S. Ladies Professional Golf Association (LPGA) Tour is $4,364,994 by Lorena Ochoa (Mexico) in 2007.

☆**Greatest prize money for a golf tournament** The PGA Tour Players Championship, contested between May 8 and 11, 2008, at Sawgrass, Florida, U.S.A., had a total prize pool of $9,500,000, with $1,710,000 going to the winner.

☆ **HIGHEST EUROPEAN TOUR CAREER EARNINGS (MALE)** The European Tour career earnings record stands at €23,595,864 ($30,638,010) and is held by Colin Montgomerie (UK) for the years 1986–2009.

THE OPEN/U.S. OPEN

★ **Most appearances at the Open Championship** The greatest number of appearances at the annual Open Championship (known as the Open, or—outside the UK—as the British Open), is 46 by Gary Player (South Africa), between 1956 and 2001. The Open is the sole major golf tournament to be staged outside the U.S.A.

★ **Most times to host the Open Championship by a course** The Royal and Ancient Golf Club of St. Andrews (UK) has hosted the Open Championship on 27 occasions between 1873 and 2005.

★ **MOST PGA CHAMPIONS TOUR WINS** Between 1995 and 2008, Hale Irwin (U.S.A.) secured 45 victories in Professional Golfers' Association (PGA) Champions Tour events. The Champions Tour is held in the UK and U.S. and is open to golfers aged 50 and over.

Irwin is also the ★ **oldest U.S. Open golf champion.** He was aged 45 years 15 days when he won the tournament at Medinah Country Club, Illinois, U.S.A., in 1990.

☆**FASTEST GOLF ROUND (TEAM)** The fastest round of golf took 7 min. 56 sec. and was achieved by the News/Talk 760 WJR team of golfers (U.S.A.) at the Monument Course, Boyne Mountain, Michigan, U.S.A., on July 20, 2008. In total, 22 players and 19 volunteers took part in the event.

GREAT LENGTHS

The par-77 International GC in Bolton, Massachusetts, U.S.A., is the world's **longest golf course** at 8,325 yd./7,612 m (24,973 ft.)—that's over 4.7 miles or 7.6 km long! The course was remodeled in 1969 by prolific golf course architect Robert Trent Jones (U.S.A.).

★**Oldest champion** The oldest winner of the Open is Tom Morris Sr. (UK, b. June 16, 1821), who was aged 46 years 99 days when he won the 1867 Championship at Prestwick Golf Club, Prestwick, UK, on September 26, 1867.

★**Youngest champion** The youngest Open Championship winner is Tom Morris Jr. (UK, b. April 20, 1851), who was 17 years 156 days old when he won the 1868 Open Championship at Prestwick, UK, on September 23, 1868. Tom also holds the record for the ★**most consecutive wins of the Open Championship,** with four from 1868 to 1872. (There was no competition in 1871.)

....

NOV. 23: The **greatest number of plates spun simultaneously** is 108, achieved by Dave Spathaky (UK) for the *Tarm Pai Du* television program in Thailand on November 23, 1992.

....

The ladies' Curtis Cup competition, held between the U.S.A. and a combined team of Great Britain and Ireland, was first staged in 1932 and won by the U.S.A. The U.S.A. has subsequently won the tournament on 27 occasions, up to 2008.

★ **Oldest competitor** The oldest competitor at the Open Championship was Gene Sarazen (U.S.A., b. February 27, 1902). He entered the 1976 Championship, aged 74 years 132 days, at Royal Birkdale Golf Course, Southport, UK, on July 10, 1976.

Most U.S. Open titles Four U.S. players have won the U.S. Open four times: Willie Anderson (1901, 1903–05), Bobby Jones Jr. (1923, 1926, 1929, 1930), Ben Hogan (1948, 1950, 1951, 1953), and Jack Nicklaus (1962, 1967, 1972, 1980).

Two women jointly share the record for the **most U.S. Women's Open titles** with four victories: Betsy Earle-Rawls (U.S.A.) in 1951, 1953, 1957, and 1960, and Mickey Wright (U.S.A.) in 1958, 1959, 1961, and 1964.

With four wins (1958, 1960–61, 1963), Wright also holds the record for the **most LPGA Championships won (individual)**.

☆ **HIGHEST CAREER EARNINGS ON THE U.S. PGA TOUR** The all-time career earnings record on the U.S. PGA circuit is held by Tiger Woods (U.S.A.) with $82,354,376, between 1996 and 2009.

Among other records, Woods also achieved the ★ **lowest score under par after four rounds at the Open Championship**: a score of −19 (19 under par) at St. Andrews, UK, on July 23, 2000.

NOV. 24: The **fastest time to solve a Rubik's Cube** is 9.55 seconds by Ron van Bruchem (Netherlands) in the Dutch Championship 2007 Rubik's Cube competition held on this day in 2007.

☆**HIGHEST U.S. LPGA TOUR CAREER EARNINGS** Annika Sorenstam (Sweden) won a record **$22,573,192 on the U.S. LPGA Tour in a career stretching from 1993 to 2009.**

★**Most wins of the Senior British Open** Two golfers share this record. Gary Player (South Africa) won the Senior British Open three times, in 1988, 1990, and 1997. Tom Watson (U.S.A.) achieved the same feat in 2003, 2005, and 2007.

RYDER CUP

☆**Most match wins (team)** Instituted in 1927, the Ryder Cup is staged every two years between the U.S.A. and Europe (British Isles or Great Britain prior to 1979). The U.S.A. has won 25 to 10 (with two draws) up to 2008.

★**Most consecutive Cup wins (team)** The U.S.A. has won the Ryder Cup seven times consecutively on two separate occasions, first from 1935 to 1955, and most recently from 1971 to 1983.

Most match wins (individual) The most Ryder Cup match wins by an individual is 23 (out of 46) by Nick Faldo (UK). The Brit also holds the world record for the **most Ryder Cup tournaments played,** with 11. (The U.S. record is eight, shared by Billy Casper, Ray Floyd, and Lanny Wadkins.)

★**Most consecutive match wins (individual)** Two players share the record for the longest unbeaten streak at the Ryder Cup, each going undefeated for 12 matches. Lee Westwood (UK) was unbeaten from 2002 to 2008 and Arnold Palmer (U.S.A.) from 1965 to 1971.

★**Most matches halved by an individual** Two golfers have halved eight matches in their Ryder Cup careers: Tony Jacklin (UK) from 1967 to 1979, and Gene Littler (U.S.A.) from 1961 to 1975. A match is halved when all competitors record the same score and thus share the match points.

★**Youngest captain** Arnold Palmer (U.S.A.) captained the United States team at the age of 34 years 1 month 1 day at East Lake Country Club, Atlanta, Georgia, U.S.A., in the 1963 competition.

ICE HOCKEY

☆**Highest score in an ice hockey game** The highest score in an international ice hockey game occurred when Slovakia beat Bulgaria 82–0 in a pre-Olympic women's qualification game that took place in Liepaja, Latvia, on September 6, 2008.

☆**Largest ice hockey tournament—players** The Hockey Calgary 37th Annual Minor Hockey Week Tournament was played by 664 teams totaling 10,922 players in Calgary, Alberta, Canada, from January 5 to January 13, 2007.

MOST . . .

★**Stanley Cup playoff games played** Chris Chelios (U.S.A.) has played 248 games in the Stanley Cup playoffs, for the Montreal Canadiens (Canada), Chicago Blackhawks, and Detroit Red Wings (both U.S.A.) in the National Hockey League since 1984. Chelios also holds the record for the ☆**most seasons playing in the postseason,** with 23.

★**YOUNGEST PLAYER TO APPEAR IN 200 NHL GAMES** At 20 years 111 days, Jordan Staal (Canada, b. September 10, 1988) became the youngest player to appear in 200 National Hockey League (NHL) games while playing for the Pittsburgh Penguins (U.S.A.) since the 2006–07 season. Staal also holds the rookie record for most shorthanded goals scored in a season, with seven in 2006–07.

★MOST OVERTIME GOALS SCORED IN A SEASON Daniel Sedin (Sweden, left), playing for the Vancouver Canucks (Canada) during the 2006–07 season, and Patrik Elias (Czech Republic), playing for the New Jersey Devils (U.S.A.) in the 2003–04 season, each scored a record four National Hockey League (NHL) goals in overtime.

Chelios's amazing career longevity has seen him rack up 1,629 games in the NHL up to February 8, 2009, the ☆most NHL games played by an American-born player.

★Goals scored by a player in a first NHL game Fabian Brunnstrom (Sweden) scored three goals in his first NHL game playing for the Dallas Stars against the Nashville Predators (both U.S.A.) on October 15, 2008. Only two other players have scored a hat-trick in their debut game: Alex Smart of the Montreal Canadiens (both Canada) on January 14, 1943; and Real Cloutier of the Quebec Nordiques (both Canada) on October 10, 1979.

☆Men's ice hockey world championships Canada has won 24 men's ice hockey world titles: 1920, 1924, 1928, 1930–32, 1934–35, 1937–39, 1948, 1950–52, 1955, 1958–59, 1961, 1994, 1997, 2003–04, and 2007.

☆LONGEST ICE HOCKEY MARATHON Brent Saik (Canada) and friends played ice hockey for 241 hr. 21 min. from February 8–18, 2008, at Saiker's Acres, Strathcona, Alberta, Canada.

NOV. 26: The **largest serving of risotto** weighed 8.27 tons (7.51 tonnes) and was made by the Ricegrowers' Association of Australia and displayed on this day in 2004.

> **6 FT. 9 IN. (2.06 M):** the height of Zdeno Chara (Czech Republic) of the Boston Bruins (U.S.A.)—the **tallest NHL player ever.**

Enduring ice hockey player John Burnosky (U.S.A.) played ice hockey on a regular basis for 76 years. He began playing at Kelvin Technical High School, Winnipeg, Manitoba, Canada, in 1929 and continued playing until 2005.

Goals scored in a season Alex Ovechkin (Russia) scored 65 goals playing in the NHL for the Washington Capitols (U.S.A.) during the 2007–08 season, the ☆ **most goals scored by a left wing in a season.**

Brett Hull (Canada) scored 86 goals playing right wing for the St. Louis Blues (U.S.A.) during the 1990–91 season, the ☆ **most goals scored by a right wing in a season.**

Multiple record holder Wayne Gretzky (Canada) scored 92 goals playing as center for the Edmonton Oilers (Canada) during the 1981–82 season, the ☆ **most goals scored by a center in a season.**

Art Ross Trophy wins The Art Ross Trophy is awarded each year to the player who has scored the most points in NHL regular season play. The most Art Ross Trophies won by an individual player is 10 by the legendary Wayne Gretzky (Canada) between 1981 and 1994.

★Overtime goals scored in a career The NHL record for the most overtime goals scored in a regular season career stands at 15 and is shared by three players: Patrik Elias (Czech Republic) playing for the New Jersey Devils (U.S.A.) since the 1997–98 season; Mats Sundin (Sweden) playing

★FASTEST SHOT IN NHL HISTORY Zdeno Chara (Czech Republic) of the Boston Bruins (U.S.A.) hit a slap shot measured at 105.4 mph (169.7 km/h) during the SuperSkills competition at the NHL All-Star Weekend in Montreal, Canada, on January 25, 2009. Chara broke Al Iafrate's 16-year-old record of 105.2 mph (169.3 km/h).

NOV. 27: The **highest start to a marathon** is for the Everest Marathon, first run on November 27, 1987. It begins at Gorak Shep, at 17,100 ft. (5,212 m) and ends at Namche Bazar, at 11,300 ft. (3,444 m).

★ **BEST 30-GAME START BY A TEAM** The best start through 30 games in National Hockey League history is 52 points by the San Jose Sharks (U.S.A.) at the beginning of the 2008–09 season. The Sharks won 25 games to equal the record set by the Boston Bruins (U.S.A.) in 1929–30 for **most victories in the first 30 games of the season.**

for the Quebec Nordiques and Toronto Maple Leafs (both Canada) since the 1990–91 season; and Jaromir Jagr (Czech Republic) playing for the Pittsburgh Penguins, Washington Capitols, and New York Rangers (all U.S.A.) from the 1990–91 season to the 2007–08 season.

★**Saves in a shutout** Goaltender Craig Anderson (U.S.A.) made 53 saves while guarding the net for the Florida Panthers (U.S.A.) in a 1–0 victory over the New York Islanders (U.S.A.) on March 2, 2008. Anderson also has the **most saves in consecutive shutouts,** 93, when he made another 40 saves in a 1–0 win over the Boston Bruins (U.S.A.) on March 4, 2008.

★**Shootout victories in a season by an NHL team** The Edmonton Oilers (Canada) recorded 15 shootout victories playing in the NHL during the 2007–08 season.

★**Team shutouts in a season** The single-season record for being shut out is 16 by the Columbus Blue Jackets (U.S.A.) during the 2006–07 season.

★ **MOST CONSECUTIVE SEASONS WINNING 40 GAMES BY AN NHL GOALTENDER** Martin Brodeur (Canada), the goaltender for the New Jersey Devils (U.S.A.), had three consecutive seasons winning at least 40 games: in 2005–06, 2006–07, and 2007–08. Brodeur also has the ★ **most 40-win seasons for a goaltender** with seven: 1997–98, 1999–2000, 2000–01, 2002–03, 2005–06, 2006–07, and 2007–08.

NOV. 28: On this day in 2000, Madonna (U.S.A.) performed a concert that was broadcast live on the Internet by Microsoft Network and was watched by 11 million people online, making it the **largest Internet pop concert.**

Goals scored by a player in an international game Chris Bourque (U.S.A.) scored five goals to help the U.S.A. beat Norway 11–2 during the International Ice Hockey Federation World Junior Championship, in Vancouver, Canada, on December 26, 2005. Bourque equaled the U.S.A. Hockey record first set by Wally Chapman (U.S.A.) in January 1984.

RUGBY

RUGBY UNION

★**Fastest try in the English Premiership** Lee Blackett (UK) scored a try in 8.28 seconds playing for Leeds Carnegie against Newcastle Falcons at Headingley, Leeds, UK, on March 21, 2008. Leeds went on to win the game 16–15.

★**Most penalties in an international career** The reliable boot of Welshman Neil Jenkins kicked 248 penalties in 91 matches for his country between 1991 and 2002.

☆**Most Hong Kong Sevens wins** First held in 1976, the Hong Kong Sevens seven-a-side tournament has been won 12 times by Fiji, in 1977–78, 1980, 1984, 1990–92, 1997–99, 2005, and 2009.

★HIGHEST ATTENDANCE FOR A GUINNESS PREMIERSHIP RUGBY UNION MATCH The largest paying attendance for a single Guinness Premiership regular season match was 50,000 for a Harlequins match against Leicester (pictured) on December 27, 2008.

★ MOST SUPER LEAGUE TRIES "Try Machine" Keith Senior (UK) scored 169 tries playing rugby league for Sheffield Eagles and Leeds Rhinos (both UK) in Europe's Super League from 1996 to 2009.

★ Most conversions in one hour (team) Haddington Rugby Football Club Under 17s scored 374 conversions in one hour at Neilson Park, Haddington, Scotland, UK, on November 15, 2008. The team's achievement broke the previous record of 124 held by Bicester Rugby Union Club Under 12s.

★ Most tries in a British Lions & Irish Lions career Tony O'Reilly (Ireland) scored six tries playing for the British & Irish Lions in Test matches in 1955 and 1959.

☆ Most tries in an IRB sevens career Santiago Gomez Cora (Argentina) scored 213 tries in International Rugby Board (IRB) Sevens competitions between 1999 and 2009. However, the record for the ☆ **most points in an IRB Sevens career** goes to Ben Gollings (UK), who scored 1,889 points while playing for England from 2001 to 2009.

☆ Most Super Rugby titles The Canterbury Crusaders (New Zealand) won seven Super Rugby titles between 1998 and 2008. The Super Rugby competition is the largest team rugby competition in the southern hemisphere. It was renamed the Super 14 competition from the Super 12 for the 2006 season with the admission of two new teams.

★ OLDEST RUGBY LEAGUE PLAYER Dennis Gleeson (Australia, b. August 17, 1936) was 70 years 9 days old when he played for the State Rail Apprentice RLFC in the New South Wales Tertiary Student Rugby League Competition at the Peter Hislop Oval, Auburn, Australia, on August 26, 2006.

NOV. 29: Rajat Kumar Mishra (India, b. November 28, 1992) played a tabla, a traditional Indian hand drum, live on All India Radio at the age of seven, making him the **youngest tabla player.**

★ **MOST TRIES IN A TRI-NATIONS MATCH** Jongikhaya "Jongi" Nokwe of South Africa scored four tries against Australia at Ellis Park, Johannesburg, South Africa, on August 30, 2008. The Springboks romped home to an emphatic 53–8 victory against the Wallabies.

☆ **Most Six Nations wins** The top northern hemisphere competition was renamed from the Five Nations to the Six Nations in 2000 when Italy was invited to join the series. England has won the championship 25 times over the event's history. The ☆ **most Grand Slams**, where one team wins against all the other teams, is 12, also held by England.

★ **Largest attendance at a club match** A crowd of 81,600 watched the Guinness Premiership final between Leicester Tigers and London Wasps (both UK) at Twickenham Stadium, London, UK, on May 31, 2008. The Wasps won 26–16.

★ **Most conversions in an international career** Andrew Mehrtens (New Zealand) kicked 169 conversions in 70 matches for the All Blacks in a career than ran between 1995 and 2004.

★ **MOST TRIES IN AN INTERNATIONAL RUGBY UNION CAREER** Speedy winger Daisuke Ohata (Japan), who started his career playing Rugby Sevens, scored an amazing 69 tries for his country in 68 internationals between 1996 and 2006, an average of more than one try per game. Since 2006, Ohata has been dogged by injuries, first to his left Achilles tendon and then to his right. The first of these cost him the chance to compete in the 2007 Rugby World Cup.

NOV. 30: The **most concerts performed in 24 hours** was 50 by N. Karthik (India) at venues in and around Bangalore, India, on November 29–30, 2005.

★ **MOST POINTS IN AN ENGLISH PREMIERSHIP CAREER** Charlie Hodgson (UK) broke rival fly-half Jonny Wilkinson's record for the most points in an English Premiership Rugby Union career with a 65th-minute penalty scored for Sale Sharks against Newcastle Falcons (coincidentally, Wilkinson's team) at Edgeley Park, Newcastle, UK, on March 8, 2009. By the end of the match, Hodgson had amassed an impressive career total of 1,492 points. Despite this feat, Sale still lost the game 32–25.

RUGBY LEAGUE

Most consecutive hat-tricks The most consecutive matches in which an individual player scored three tries is 12 by Richard Lopag of Deighton New Saracens, Huddersfield, West Yorkshire, UK, in the 2000/01 season.

★ **Most tries in a National Rugby League season** Terry Lamb (Australia) scored 38 tries playing for Eastern Suburbs, Sydney, Australia, in the 1938 season.

★ **Most international appearances** New Zealander Ruben Wiki made 55 international appearances for his country between 1994 and 2006.

★ **Most appearances in a National Rugby League career** Dave Brown (Australia) made 349 appearances for Western Suburbs and Canterbury-Bankstown between 1980 and 1996.

☆ **Most State of Origin series wins** Australia's State of Origin series is an annual best-of-three fought between Queensland and New South Wales. Queensland has seen the most wins, with 17 between 1980 and 2008.

DEC. 1: The **fastest piggyback race** over 1 mile (1.61 km) is 13 min. 1 sec., set by Ashrita Furman (U.S.A.) carrying Bipin Larkin at the Egilshöll Sports Complex, Reykjavik, Iceland, on this day in 2006.

MOST HEINEKEN CUP TITLE WINS Inaugurated in 1995, the Heineken Cup, or H-cup, is Rugby Union's premier European team competition. It has been won three times by Toulouse (France), in 1996, 2003, and 2005.

Most points in a National League career Andrew Johns (Australia) scored 2,176 points in league matches between 1993 and 2007, playing for the Newcastle Knights, but the record for the **most points in a National League season** belongs to Hazem El Masri (Lebanon), who scored 342 points in the 2004 season playing for the Canterbury Bulldogs.

TENNIS & RACKET SPORTS

BADMINTON

Longest match In the men's singles final at the World Championships in Glasgow, UK, on June 1, 1997, Peter Rasmussen (Denmark) beat Sun Jun (China) 16/17, 18/13, 15/10 in a match lasting 2 hr. 4 min.

★**Most nations in the Sudirman Cup** A total of 59 nations competed in the 1997 staging of the Sudirman Cup, named after the famous Indonesian player Dick Sudirman.

☆ **MOST BADMINTON SINGLES WINS (MALE)** Two players have won the Badminton World Championships men's singles title twice: Yang Yang (China) in 1987 and 1989, and, more recently, Lin Dan (China, left) in 2006 and 2007.

MOST WINS . . .

- **Overall championships:** five, by Park Joo-bong (South Korea): men's doubles (1985, 1991), mixed doubles (1985, 1989, 1991).
- **Badminton World Championships singles (female):** two, by China's Li Lingwei (1983, 1989), Han Aiping (1985, 1987), Ye Zhaoying (1995, 1997), and Xie Xingfang (2003, 2006).
- **Sudirman Cup,** from 1989, held every two years (**World Mixed Team Badminton Championship**): six, by China, 1995–2001.
- ☆**Uber Cup,** from 1956 (**World Team Badminton Championships— female**): 11, by China, between 1984 and 2008.

REAL TENNIS

☆**Most World Championships (men)** Jacques Edmond Barre (France) held the title for a record 33 years from 1829 to 1862; however, the **first recorded real tennis world champion** was a Frenchman known only as Clerg c. 1740. Since 1996, the competition has been held biennially on even-numbered years. The record for the ☆ **most defenses of the real tennis world championships** belongs to Robert Fahey (Australia), who fought off strong opposition to retain the title on nine occasions between 1994 and 2008.

Most World Championships (women) Penny Lumley (UK, born as Fellows) has won the Women's World Championships (from 1985) six times between 1989 and 2003.

TABLE TENNIS

Olympic games The **most women's medals won** is four, by Deng Yaping (China) with four golds (1992–96), which is also the **most women's gold medals won;** and by Yoo Nam-kyu (South Korea) with one gold and three bronze (1988–96).

The ☆**most men's gold medals** is two by Liu Guoliang (China) for singles and doubles (1996); and Ma Lin (China) for singles and team (2008).

The ☆ **most men's team gold medals won** is eight by China, from 1988 to 2008. The ☆ **most women's team gold medals won** is nine, also by the Chinese team and also from 1988 to 2008.

World Table Tennis Championships (team) In addition to its strong performances in the Olympics, China also dominates the World Table Tennis Championships. Between 1961 and 2008, China won the Swaythling Cup (from 1926) 17 times, the ☆**most men's team titles.**

China also won the Corbillon Cup (from 1926) 18 times between 1965 and 2008, the ☆**most women's team titles.**

....

DEC. 2: The **largest game of bingo** involved a total of 70,080 participants and took place at an event organized by Almacenes Exito S.A. in Bogotá, Colombia, on December 2, 2006.

....

☆ **OLDEST TABLE TENNIS PLAYER** Dorothy de Low (Australia, b. October 5, 1910) was aged 97 years 232 days when she represented Australia at the XIV World Veterans Table Tennis Championships in Rio de Janeiro, Brazil, on May 25, 2008. She won the gold medal at the 1992 championships in Dublin, Ireland, in the Over-80s Women's Singles category.

★ **MOST MONEY WON IN A TENNIS CAREER (FEMALE)** Lindsay Davenport (U.S.A.) has really cashed in on her tennis success, winning an impressive $22,144,735 in tournament play over the course of her professional tennis career between 1993 and 2008.

TEAM LEADER

The ☆ **largest annual team competition in sport** is the Davis Cup, organized by the International Tennis Federation (ITF), which is based in London, UK. An elimination competition, the 2007 event saw 137 countries enter, with Spain emerging victorious.

DEC. 3: The **largest group of carol singers** comprised 7,514 people who performed at the Bob Jones University, South Carolina, U.S.A., on December 3, 2004.

16 YEARS 182 DAYS: the age at which Martina Hingis (Switzerland) became the **youngest person to be ranked tennis number one.**

X-REF

Do sports statistics make you ecstatic? Then turn to p. 518 for our **Sports Reference** section—a numerical nirvana of sports facts and figures!

TENNIS

★**Highest annual earnings (from all sources)** Roger Federer (Switzerland) earned an estimated $35 million between June 2007 and June 2008.

He also holds the record for the ☆ **most money won in a tennis career (male):** $44,644,857 between 1998 and 2008.

The ★**highest annual earnings for a female** is an estimated $26 million, which was earned by Maria Sharapova (Russia) between June 2007 and June 2008.

☆**LONGEST RALLY** Ettore Rossetti and Angelo Rossetti (both U.S.A., seen here with GWR's Stuart Claxton) played a tennis rally of 25,944 strokes at North Haven Tennis & Racquet in North Haven, Connecticut, U.S.A., on August 9, 2008.

DEC. 4: The **greatest distance traveled by wheelchair in 24 hours** is 113.34 miles (182.4 km), by Mario Trindade (Portugal) at the Vila Real Stadium in Vila Real, Portugal, on December 3–4, 2007.

★ MOST CONSECUTIVE FRENCH OPEN SINGLES TITLES (MALE) The French Open is the tennis world's premier clay court tournament. Two players have each won the French Open four times consecutively: Björn Borg (Sweden) in 1978–81 and Rafael Nadal (Spain, left) in 2005–08. Nadal's record on clay is formidable—he has also scored the **most consecutive clay-court men's singles wins**, with 60 victories.

★ Most consecutive U.S. Open singles titles (male) Richard Dudley "Dick" Sears (U.S.A.) won seven consecutive U.S. Open singles tennis titles from 1881 to 1887 while still a student. His 18-match unbeaten streak remained a record until 1921.

Most French Open titles Between 1962 and 1973, Margaret Court (Australia) won a record 13 French Open tennis titles: five singles titles, four doubles titles, and four mixed doubles titles.

The **greatest number of French Open tennis titles won by a man** is nine, by Henri Cochet (France): four singles titles, three doubles titles, and two mixed doubles titles, between 1926 and 1930.

★ Most consecutive U.S. Open singles titles (female) Three women have won four consecutive U.S. Open singles titles each: Molla Mallory (Norway) in 1915–18, Helen Jacobs (U.S.A.) in 1932–35, and Chris Evert (U.S.A.) in 1975–78.

GREATEST EVER?

Roger Federer's record for the **most consecutive finals victories** (24 back-to-back wins between October 2003 and September 2005) is considered one of the greatest achievements of the Open era. It is also one of our Top 100 Records of the decade.

Most Wimbledon singles titles Martina Navratilova (U.S.A.) won a record nine Wimbledon singles tennis titles, in 1978–79, 1982–87, and 1990.

Two players hold the record for the **most men's Wimbledon singles titles,** with a total of seven each: W. C. Renshaw (UK), with wins in 1881–86 and 1889, and more recently Pete Sampras (U.S.A.), with victories in 1993–95 and 1997–2000.

★ **Longest final (male singles)** Rafael Nadal (Spain) beat Roger Federer (Switzerland) 6–4, 6–4, 6–7(5), 6–7(8), 9–7 in a match lasting 4 hr. 48 min. at the Wimbledon Championships in London, UK, on July 6, 2008.

WATERSPORTS

DIVING

Most world championships Greg Louganis (U.S.A.) has won a record five world titles; highboard in 1978, and both highboard and springboard in 1982 and 1986. Louganis shares the record for the ★ **most consecutive FINA championship titles** with Philip Boggs (U.S.A.), who scored springboard wins in 1973, 1975, and 1978.

Highest dive from a diving board (male) The world record high dive from a diving board is 176 ft. 10 in. (53.9 m) by Olivier Favre (Switzerland) at Villers-le-Lac, France, on August 30, 1987. The record **highest dive from a diving board (female)** is 120 ft. 9 in. (36.80 m) by Lucy Wardle (U.S.A.) at Ocean Park, Hong Kong, China, on April 6, 1985.

···
DEC. 5: A total of 23,930 people attended the premiere of *Brewster McCloud* (U.S.A., 1970) at the Houston Astrodome, Texas, U.S.A., on December 5, 1970, the **largest premiere for any movie.**
···

★ **MOST GOLD MEDALS WON AT A SINGLE OLYMPIC GAMES (MALE)** The most gold medals won at a single Olympic Games is eight by Michael Phelps (U.S.A.), who won gold in the following swimming disciplines at the 2008 Beijing Olympics, between August 9 and 17, 2008: 400 m individual medley, 4 × 100 m freestyle relay, 200 m freestyle, 200 m butterfly, 4 × 200 m freestyle relay, 200 m individual medley, 100 m butterfly, and the 4 × 100 m medley relay.

☆ **MOST GOLDS WON (MALE)** The most Olympic gold medals won is 14, achieved by swimmer Michael Phelps (U.S.A.). He won six gold medals at the 2004 Olympics and eight gold medals at the 2008 Olympics.

FACT

Phelps earns an estimated $5 million (£3.4 million) per year through endorsements, including a deal to be the face of Mazda in China.

Most FINA Grand Prix men's Springboard titles The most Fédération Internationale de Natation Diving Grand Prix Springboard titles won by an individual male diver is seven by Dmitri Sautin (Russia) in 1995–2001. Sautin also holds the record for the ★ **most FINA Grand Prix men's Platform titles,** with four in 1995–96, 1998, and 2000.

★ **Most FINA Grand Prix women's 10 m Platform titles** Na Li (China) has won the Grand Prix 10 m Platform title three times (1999–2000, 2002).

DEC. 6: The **most coconuts smashed in 1 minute with one hand** is 81, set by Muhamed Kahrimanovic (Germany) in Hamburg, Germany, on this day in 2007.

6: the **most synchronized swimming Olympic golds won,** by Russia between 1984 and 2008.

FASTEST SWIM, LONG COURSE, 800 M FREESTYLE (FEMALE) Rebecca Adlington (UK) set a time of 8 min. 14.10 sec. to complete the 800 m on August 16, 2008, at the Beijing Olympics, China. She was a full 6 seconds ahead of the silver medalist and 2 seconds ahead of the former world record held by Janet Evans (U.S.A.)—a record set in 1989, the year Rebecca was born.

☆**Most Olympic diving medals won (male)** Dmitri Sautin (Russia) won a total of eight Olympic medals, two gold, two silver, and four bronze, between 1992 and 2008. His most recent was a silver in the men's synchronized springboard event.

Youngest gold medalist The youngest individual Olympic winner was Marjorie Gestring (U.S.A., b. November 18, 1922), who took the springboard diving title at the age of 13 years 268 days at the Olympic Games in Berlin, Germany, on August 12, 1936.

FASTEST SWIM, LONG COURSE RELAY 4 × 100 M FREESTYLE (FEMALE) The Netherlands team (Inge Dekker, Ranomi Kromowidjojo, Femke Heemskerk, and Marleen Veldhuis) completed the 4 × 100 m freestyle in a record-breaking time of 3 min. 33.62 sec. in Eindhoven, the Netherlands, on March 18, 2008.

★ **MOST OLYMPIC WATER POLO TITLES WON (WOMEN)** Since women's water polo was introduced at the 2000 Olympic Games, the winners have been Australia in 2000, Italy in 2004 (Manuela Zanchi is pictured above right), and the Netherlands (Danielle de Bruijn, above left) in 2008.

WATER POLO

☆ **Most Olympic wins** Hungary's men's team has won the Olympic tournament most often, with nine wins between 1932 and 2008. With an additional three silver medals and three bronze, the Hungarians also top the table for the most Olympic water polo medals, with 15.

ROWING

☆ **Fastest 2,000 m, rowing eight (female)** The women's record time for 2,000 m on non-tidal water is 5 min. 55.50 sec. by a U.S.A. eight in Eton, UK, on August 27, 2006.

☆ **Most Olympic golds (female)** The most Olympic golds for rowing won by a woman is five, a record shared by Elisabeta Lipa (Romania), who won in 1984, 1992, 1996, 2000, and 2004, and Georgeta Damian (Romania) in 2000 (two golds), 2004 (two golds), and 2008.

....

DEC. 7: The band Grabowsky (Germany) was applauded for 1 hr. 30 min. after a performance at Altes-Brauhaus-Musicclub in Frankenthal, Germany, on December 7, 2002—the **longest applause.**

....

★ **FASTEST CANOE/ KAYAK K1 500 M FLATWATER (MALE)** Adam van Koeverden (Canada) completed the men's kayak K1 500 m flatwater event in 1 min. 35.55 sec. in Beijing, China, on August 19, 2008.

WINDSURFING

★ **Most Formula World Championships (male)** Formula windsurfing is a class of race windsurfing that has developed over the past 15 years in order to surf in light and moderate winds. The most World Championships won by a man is two, by four sailors: Wojtek Brzozowski (Poland) in 2000 and 2008; Kevin Pritchard (U.S.A.) in 2001–02; Steve Allen (Australia) in 2003 and 2006; and Antoine Albeau (France) in 2005 and 2007.

The ★ **most Formula Windsurfing World Championships won by a woman** is four, by Dorota Staszewska (Poland) in 2000–02 and 2004.

WHEEL SKILLS

★ **First skateboard trick** The ollie is a skateboarding trick in which the skateboarder pops the board into the air, making him appear to be jumping with the skateboard stuck to his or her feet. It was first performed by Alan "Ollie" Gelfand (U.S.A.) in 1976, and was known as a "no-hands aerial."

★ **Most ollies in one minute** Rob Dyrdek (U.S.A.) popped 42 skateboard ollies in a minute on MTV's *The Rob & Big Show* in Los Angeles, California, U.S.A., on September 17, 2007. On the same show, on the same day, Rob managed the ★ **most consecutive ollies,** with 215 nonstop, the ★ **most frontside ollies in one minute** (32) and the ★ **most backside, back-foot ollie-impossibles** (15).

☆ **FASTEST SKATEBOARD SPEED (STANDING)** Douglas da Silva (Brazil) reached a speed of 70.21 mph (113 km/h) on a skateboard in a standing position at Teutonia, Rio Grande do Sul, Brazil, on October 20, 2007. The run was a qualifier for the International Downhill Malarrara Pro Teutonia and was measured using a radar speed gun.

★ **TIGHTEST PARALLEL PARKING IN REVERSE** Terry Grant (UK) parked a Renault Twingo GT in reverse in a space that was only 5 in. (15 cm) longer than the car, at ExCel London, UK, on February 3, 2008.

★ **Most consecutive kick flips on a skateboard** Zach Kral (U.S.A.) pulled off 1,546 consecutive kick flips at 4 Seasons Skate Park, Milwaukee, Wisconsin, U.S.A., on November 30, 2008.

Longest one-wheel manual (wheelie) Stefan Akesson (Sweden) wheelied for 224 ft. 10 in. (68.54 m) at the Gallerian Shopping Center, Stockholm, Sweden, on November 2, 2007.

★ **Longest continuous unicycle ride** On October 18, 2004, Joze Voros (Slovenia) unicycled for 89.14 miles (143.46 km) without his feet touching the ground.

Fastest 100 m on a unicycle Peter Rosendahl (Sweden) set a sprint record for 100 m of 12.11 seconds (18.47 mph; 29.72 km/h) from a standing start in Las Vegas, Nevada, U.S.A., on March 25, 1994.

....

DEC. 8: The **highest score in any NFL game** is 73 by the Chicago Bears against the Washington Redskins (0) in the NFL Championship game in Washington D.C., U.S.A., on December 8, 1940.

....

100 FT. 5 IN. (30.62 M): the **longest skateboard slide,** set by Rob Dyrdek (U.S.A.) on September 17, 2007.

★FASTEST MOTORCYCLE HANDLEBAR WHEELIE Enda Wright (Ireland) reached a speed of 108 mph (173.81 km/h) while performing a handlebar or "highchair" wheelie in Elvington, York, UK, on July 11, 2006. To perform a handlebar wheelie, the rider sits on the gas tank with his or her legs hanging over the handlebars.

★LONGEST RAMP-TO-RAMP BACKFLIP ON A MOTORCYCLE Cameron Sinclair (Australia) achieved a ramp-to-ramp motorcycle backflip of 129 ft. 7 in. (39.49 m) at the Crusty Demons Night of World Records at Calder Park Raceway in Melbourne, Victoria, Australia, on March 29, 2008.

☆**Longest motorcycle ramp jump** Robbie Maddison (Australia) achieved a 351-ft. (106.98-m) ramp jump in Melbourne, Australia, on March 29, 2008.

DEC. 9: The **largest Santa Claus gathering** was achieved by 13,000 participants in the Guildhall Square in Derry City, Northern Ireland, UK, on December 9, 2007.

☆ **LONGEST RAMP-TO-RAMP JUMP ON A QUADBIKE** Jon Guetter
(U.S.A.) jumped a distance of 176 ft. 11 in. (53.92 m) ramp to ramp on a
quadbike at the Crusty Demons Night of World Records at Calder Park
Raceway in Melbourne, Victoria, Australia, on March 29, 2008. Guetter
smashed the previous record of 148 ft. 11 in. (45.38 m).

☆ **Tightest gap driven through on two wheels** Filmed for *Zheng Da
Zong Yi—Guinness World Records Special,* the Zhengzhi Driving School
drove through a gap 2 ft. 1 in. (66 cm) wide on two wheels in Linyi City,
Shandong Province, China, on November 2, 2008.

★ **Longest mini-bike jump with a backflip** Ben Fiez (Australia)
jumped 66 ft. 4 in. (20.21 m) while performing a backflip on a Honda CRF
at Calder Park Raceway in Melbourne, Australia, on March 29, 2008.

DEC. 10: The **oldest message in a bottle** spent 92 years 229 days at sea.
It was released by the Marine Laboratory, Aberdeen, UK, on April 25, 1914
and recovered by Mark Anderson (UK) on this day in 2006.

★**MOST CONSECUTIVE BACKFLIPS ON INLINE SKATES (HALFPIPE)**
Kevin Lopez (Belgium) achieved a record 31 consecutive backflips on
inline skates in a halfpipe at ZDF Inliner Days 2007, Mainz, Germany, on
September 23, 2007.

Longest bicycle wheelie journey Kurt Osburn (U.S.A.) traveled
2,839.6 miles (4,569 km) from the Guinness World of Records Museum in
Hollywood, California, U.S.A., to the Guinness World of Records Museum
in Orlando, Florida, U.S.A., between April 13 and June 25, 1999. He wheelied all the way!

★**Fastest ATV side-wheelie** Travis Pastrana (U.S.A.) proved that it was
possible to perform a side-wheelie on an all-terrain vehicle (ATV) at a speed
of 47 mph (75.6 km/h) at the Miller Motorsports Park in Tooele, Utah,
U.S.A., on November 18, 2008.
    At the same event, Pastrana and Jolene Van Vugt (U.S.A.) performed the
★**longest tandem ATV side-wheelie,** covering 3.29 miles (5.29 km).

★**Longest UTV wheelie** Andy Bell (U.S.A.) performed a 960-ft
(1,544.97-m) wheelie on a utility terrain vehicle (UTV) at the Miller Motorsports Park in Tooele, Utah, U.S.A., on November 18, 2008.

★**Longest bicycle no-foot wheelie (back wheel)** The longest no-
foot wheelie on a mountain bike is 173 ft. 8 in. (52.93 m) by Jim DeChamp
(U.S.A.) at Miller Motorsports Park in Tooele, Utah, U.S.A., on November 18, 2008, for the MTV show *Nitro Circus*.

X GAMES

Oldest X Games athlete Angelika Casteneda (U.S.A.) was 53 years old when she competed in the X Venture Race in 1996. Angelika was part of a three-person team (which also included John Howard and Keith Murray, both U.S.A.) that won the six-day, 350-mile (563-km) event, making her the **oldest athlete to win an X Games gold medal.**

Youngest X Games athlete Nyjah Huston (b. November 30, 1994, U.S.A.) was just 11 years 246 days old when he made his debut at X Games 12 in Los Angeles, California, U.S.A., on August 3–6, 2006. He competed in Men's Skateboard Street. In the finals, Huston placed eighth out of the 19 skaters taking part in the event.

Youngest X Games gold medalist Ryan Sheckler (U.S.A., b. December 30, 1989) was 13 years 230 days old when he won the Skateboard Park gold medal at ESPN X Games 9 in Los Angeles, California, U.S.A., on August 17, 2003.

Longest BMX 360 ramp jump Mike Escamilla (U.S.A., aka "Rooftop") completed a 50-ft. 6-in. (15.39-m) BMX 360-degree ramp jump on the Mega Ramp at X Games 11 in Los Angeles, California, U.S.A., on August 3, 2005.

MOST WINTER X GAMES MEDALS WON (FEMALE) Barrett Christy (U.S.A.) won 10 Winter X Games medals in a variety of snowboard disciplines between 1997 and 2001. For Slopestyle, she won gold in 1997, silver in 1998 and 1999, and bronze in 2000 and 2002; in Big Air, she won gold in 1997 and 1999, and silver in 1998 and 2001; finally, she earned a silver for SuperPipe in 2000.

DEC. 11: The **oldest permanent circus building** is Cirque d'Hiver (originally Cirque Napoléon), which opened in Paris, France, on this day in 1852.

☆ **MOST WINTER X GAMES MEDALS WON (MALE)** Shaun White (U.S.A.) has won 14 Winter X Games medals in snowboard disciplines between 2002 and 2009: for Slopestyle, he won silver (2002), five golds (2003, 2006, and 2009), and two more bronze (2007–2008); and, for SuperPipe, he won two silvers (2002, 2007) and four golds (2003, 2006, and 2008–2009).

Longest handstand on a snowskate board Trenton R. Schindler (U.S.A.) performed a snowskate-board handstand lasting a record 4.38 seconds during the GWR Break Fest at Winter X Games 11 in Aspen, Colorado, U.S.A., on January 28, 2007.

First "900" on a skateboard Skateboard legend Tony Hawk (U.S.A.) became the first person to achieve a "900" (two and a half airborne rotations) in competition at the ESPN X Games 5 in San Francisco, California, U.S.A., on June 27, 1999. The so-called "900" is regarded as one of the most difficult tricks in vert skateboarding.

Most X Games medals (skateboard) Skateboarders Andy Macdonald and Tony Hawk (both U.S.A.) have each won 16 X Games medals during their careers.

★ **MOST KICK FLIPS IN 30 SECONDS** Zachary Kovacs (U.S.A., far left) and Michael Sohheh (U.S.A., left) each completed 13 kick flips in 30 seconds at the X Games 14 Guinness World Records Break Fest in Los Angeles, California, U.S.A., on August 2, 2008.

DEC. 12: The **greatest dressed weight for a turkey** is 86 lb. (39.09 kg) for a stag reared by Philip Cook of Leacroft Turkeys Ltd, Peterborough, UK, which was weighed on December 12, 1989.

Guinness World Records is proud to partner with the X Games—the world's largest action sports event. At X Games 14 in August 2008, for example, we sponsored the GWR Break Fest and challenged all comers to break records for the most ollies in 30 seconds and the most kick flips in 30 seconds (pictured).

First non-U.S. snowboarder to earn SuperPipe gold at an X Games Antii Autti (Finland) became the first snowboarder from outside

the U.S.A. to earn a gold medal in SuperPipe. He landed back-to-back 1080s (three full 360° rotations) in Aspen, Colorado, U.S.A., in 2005, at Winter X Games 9, to take the top spot over Danny Kass and Shaun White (both U.S.A.).

Moto X highest step up jump The greatest height achieved in the X Games Moto X Step Up event is 35 ft. (10.67 m), by Tommy Clowers (U.S.A.) in August 2000. Essentially a "high jump" on a motorcycle, riders must try to clear a bar placed at the top of a steep takeoff ramp. The height obtained is the equivalent of jumping onto the roof of a two-story building.

MOST OLLIES IN 30 SECONDS Willy Apodaca (U.S.A.) completed 33 ollies in 30 seconds at the X Games 14 Guinness World Records Break Fest in Los Angeles, California, U.S.A., on August 2, 2008.

X-REF

Like incredible achievements with a watery theme? Turn to pp. 499–503 and check out the exciting Watersports records.

MOST WAKEBOARDING MEDALS WON America's Darin Shapiro (left), Dallas Friday, and Tara Hamilton (below left) have each earned six Summer X Games medals in the sport of wakeboarding, a pursuit that employs a combination of water-skiing, snowboarding, and surfing techniques.

KING OF SNOWSKATE On consecutive days in January 2007, snowskate-boarder Phil Smage (U.S.A.) set three new ollie records during the GWR Break Fest at Winter X Games 11 in Aspen, Colorado, U.S.A. On January 25, Smage achieved the **most consecutive ollies on a snowskate board**, making 14 in a row. The next day, he achieved the **highest ollie on a snowskate board** with a height of 27.75 in. (70.5 cm). On January 27, Smage made the **longest ollie on a snowskate board** with an effort measured at 11 ft. 4 in. (3.45 m).

DEC. 13: The **oldest movie director,** Manoel de Oliveira (Portugal), made his most recent film, *Cristóvão Colombo—O Enigma* (Portugal, 2007) at the age of 99 years 2 days.

Longest Moto X dirt-to-dirt back flip Jeremy Stenberg and Nate Adams (both U.S.A.) did a dirt-to-dirt back flip measuring 100 ft. (30.48 m) in the Moto X Freestyle finals at X Games 11 in Los Angeles, California, U.S.A., on August 6, 2005.

Longest skateboard ramp jump The longest skateboard ramp jump was performed by professional skateboarder Danny Way (U.S.A.) with a 79-ft. (24-m) 360° air on his Mega Ramp at X Games 10 in Los Angeles, California, U.S.A., on August 8, 2004.

CRAZY CONTESTS

Fastest racing snail The World Snail Racing Championship has been held every July since 1970 in Congham, Norfolk, UK, where races are conducted over a 13-in. (33-cm) course located outside the local church. The all-time record holder is a snail named Archie, trained by Carl Bramham (UK), who sprinted to the winning post in 2 min. 20 sec. in 1995.

★Fastest time to run 150 m in high-heeled shoes Jill Stamison (U.S.A.) ran 150 m (492 ft.) in high-heeled shoes in 21.95 seconds during the "High-Heel-a-Thon" on *Live with Regis and Kelly* on July 9, 2008, in New York City, U.S.A.

★FASTEST COMPLETION OF THE WORLD BOG SNORKELING TRIATHLON The fastest female to complete the bog snorkeling triathlon course is Natalie Bent (UK, pictured), who got through the grueling challenge in 3 hr. 9 min. 59 sec. at the 2008 World Bog Snorkeling Triathlon, Llanwrtyd Wells, UK, on July 6, 2008. Natalie's brother Daniel Bent (UK) holds the male record for the event, having completed the triathlon in 2 hr. 23 min. 46 sec. on the same day.

☆ **MOST PEOPLE RUNNING IN HIGH-HEELED SHOES** In an event organized by Gillette Venus Embrace and *Shop Til You Drop* magazine, 265 people took part in a 492-ft. (150-m) race wearing high-heeled shoes in Sydney, Australia, on September 2, 2008. Heels had to be at least 2.75 in. (7 cm) high and no more than 0.6 in. (1.5 cm) wide at the tip.

☆**Fastest Wife-Carrying Championships win** The World Wife-Carrying Championships is held annually in Sonkajärvi, Finland (first held 1992). The contest is a race in which each contestant carries his/her wife over an 831-ft. (253.5-m) obstacle course as quickly as possible. The record time is 56.9 seconds by Margo Uusarj and Sandra Kullas (both Estonia) on July 1, 2006. This is the fastest time for the event since a minimum wife-weight of 108 lb. (49 kg) was introduced in 2002.

☆ **Largest tournament of Rock, Paper, Scissors** A Rock, Paper, Scissors tournament with 793 participants was organized by Renee Tomas at Brigham Young University, Provo, Utah, U.S.A., on April 11, 2008.

Most worms charmed At the first World Worm Charming Championship held in Cheshire, UK, on July 5, 1980, Tom Shufflebotham (UK) charmed 511 worms out of a 32-ft². (3-m²) plot in the allotted time of 30 minutes.

....

DEC. 14: The South Pole was first reached at 11:00 a.m. on this day in 1911 by a Norwegian party of five men led by Captain Roald Amundsen (Norway), after a 53-day march with dog sleds.

....

☆ **MOST OYSTERS EATEN IN THREE MINUTES** Colin Shirlow (UK) ate 233 oysters in three minutes at the World Oyster Eating Championship held in Hillsborough, County Down, UK, on September 3, 2005.

Fastest speed for a Morse code transmission On May 6, 2003, Andrei Bindasov (Belarus) transmitted 216 Morse code marks of mixed text in one minute. The attempt was part of the International Amateur Radio Union's 5th World Championship in High Speed Telegraphy.

☆ **Largest rubber boot race** A record 1,022 "wellie"-boot-wearing participants completed a 1.24-mile (2-km) course in Callendar Park, Falkirk, UK, for an event organized by Kidney Kids Scotland on May 17, 2007.

★ **MOST WINS OF THE WORLD SAUNA CHAMPIONSHIPS** The World Sauna Championships, held in Heinola, Finland, challenges contestants to see who can stay in a sauna for the longest time. Two men have won this competition four times each: Leo Pusa (Finland, pictured) won in 2000–02 and 2004, and Timo Kaukonen (Finland) won in 2003 and 2005–07.

DEC. 15: The **farthest accurate archery shot** was 656 ft. (200 m), and was made on this day in 2005 by Peter Terry (Australia) at the Kalamunda Governor Stirling Archery Club, Perth, Australia.

☆**Farthest grape spit** Anders Rasmussen (Norway) spat a grape a record distance of 28 ft. 7.25 in. (8.72 m) in Myra, Arendal, Norway, on September 4, 2004.

★**Farthest match throw** Michael Ottosson (Sweden) threw a matchstick measuring 1.85 in. (4.7 cm) long and weighing 0.16 oz. (4.8 g) a distance of 61 ft. 6 in. (18.75 m) at Smögens tennis hall in Stockholm, Sweden, on January 31, 2001.

Farthest cowpat throw Records in the sport of throwing dried cowpats or "chips" depend on whether or not the projectile may be "molded into a spherical shape." The greatest distance achieved under the "nonsphericalization and 100 % organic" rule (established in 1970) is 266 ft. (81.1 m) by Steve Urner (U.S.A.) at the Mountain Festival in Tehachapi, California, U.S.A., on August 14, 1981.

MOST AIR GUITAR WORLD CHAMPIONSHIP WINS The Oulu Music Video Festival's Air Guitar World Championships have been held annually in Finland since 1996. Zac "The Magnet" Monro (UK), who rocked his way to the title in 2001 and 2002, is the only person to have won the event more than once since its inauguration.

★ OLDEST ROACH RACES
According to local legend, the Story
Bridge Hotel Cockroach Races were
started when two bar regulars
argued over which suburb had the
biggest and fastest roaches. Races
have now been held at the Story
Bridge Hotel, Brisbane, Australia,
on January 26 (Australia Day) every
year for 28 years. Races are held on
a circular track and roaches are
released in the middle . . . the first
to the edge is the winner.

Farthest tobacco spit David O'Dell (U.S.A.) spat a tobacco wad 53 ft.
3 in. (16.23 m) at the World Tobacco Spitting Championships held in California, U.S.A., on March 22, 1997.

First Sheep Counting Championships The first National Sheep
Counting Championships were held in New South Wales, Australia, on September 14–15, 2002. Sheep are herded past competitors, who try to guess
the precise figure. Peter Desailly (Australia) took the inaugural title by cor-
rectly counting 277 sheep.

....
DEC. 16: Many happy returns today to Dexter Dunworth (Australia), the
oldest licensed boxer. He was 52 years 139 days old at the time of his
most recent bout in May 2008.
....

Fastest time to boil a billy can Frank Ryder (Australia) boiled a billy can (a lightweight cooking pot used on a campfire) containing 0.53 gallons (2 liters) of water in 7 min. 29.3 sec. at a competition held in Queensland, Australia, on June 3, 1989.

Most Elephant Polo World Championships The Tiger Top Tuskers have won the World Elephant Polo Association Championships on eight occasions: 1983–85, 1987, 1992, 1998, 2000, and 2003. The invitational tournament is held every December in Megauly, on the edge of the Royal Chitwan National Park in Nepal.

SPORTS REFERENCE

★ TRACK & FIELD—OUTDOOR TRACK EVENTS ★

MEN	TIME/DISTANCE	NAME & NATIONALITY
☆ 100 m	9.69	Usain Bolt (Jamaica)
☆ 200 m	19.30	Usain Bolt (Jamaica)
400 m	43.18	Michael Johnson (U.S.A.)
800 m	1:41.11	Wilson Kipketer (Denmark)
1,000 m	2:11.96	Noah Ngeny (Kenya)
1,500 m	3:26.00	Hicham El Guerrouj (Morocco)
1 mile	3:43.13	Hicham El Guerrouj (Morocco)
2,000 m	4:44.79	Hicham El Guerrouj (Morocco)
3,000 m	7:20.67	Daniel Komen (Kenya)
5,000 m	12:37.35	Kenenisa Bekele (Ethiopia)
10,000 m	26:17.53	Kenenisa Bekele (Ethiopia)
20,000 m	56:26.00	Haile Gebrselassie (Ethiopia)
1 hour	21,285 m	Haile Gebrselassie (Ethiopia)
25,000 m	1:13:55.80	Toshihiko Seko (Japan)
30,000 m	1:29:18.80	Toshihiko Seko (Japan)
3,000 m steeplechase	7:53.63	Saif Saaeed Shaheen (Qatar)
☆ 110 m hurdles	12.87	Dayron Robles (Cuba)
400 m hurdles	46.78	Kevin Young (U.S.A.)
☆ 4 x 100 m relay	37.10	Jamaica (Asafa Powell, Nesta Carter, Usain Bolt, Michael Frater)
4 x 200 m relay	1:18.68	Santa Monica Track Club, U.S.A. (Michael Marsh, Leroy Burrell, Floyd Heard, Carl Lewis)
4 x 400 m relay	2:54.29	U.S.A. (Andrew Valmon, Quincy Watts, Harry Reynolds, Michael Johnson)
4 x 800 m relay	7:02.43	Kenya (Joseph Mutua, William Yiampoy, Ismael Kombich, Wilfred Bungei)
4 x 1,500 m relay	14:38.80	West Germany (Thomas Wessinghage, Harald Hudak, Michael Lederer, Karl Fleschen)

WOMEN	TIME/DISTANCE	NAME & NATIONALITY
100 m	10.49	Florence Griffith-Joyner (U.S.A.)
200 m	21.34	Florence Griffith-Joyner (U.S.A.)
400 m	47.60	Marita Koch (GDR)
800 m	1:53.28	Jarmila Kratochvílová (Czechoslovakia)
1,000 m	2:28.98	Svetlana Masterkova (Russia)
1,500 m	3:50.46	Qu Yunxia (China)
1 mile	4:12.56	Svetlana Masterkova (Russia)
2,000 m	5:25.36	Sonia O'Sullivan (Ireland)
3,000 m	8:06.11	Wang Junxia (China)
☆ 5,000 m	14:11.15	Tirunesh Dibaba (Ethiopia)

LOCATION	DATE
Beijing, China	Aug. 16, 2008
Beijing, China	Aug. 20, 2008
Seville, Spain	Aug. 26, 1999
Cologne, Germany	Aug. 24, 1997
Rieti, Italy	Sep. 5, 1999
Rome, Italy	Jul. 14, 1998
Rome, Italy	Jul. 7, 1999
Berlin, Germany	Sep. 7, 1999
Rieti, Italy	Sep. 1, 1996
Hengelo, the Netherlands	May 31, 2004
Brussels, Belgium	Aug. 26, 2005
Ostrava, Czech Republic	Jun. 26, 2007
Ostrava, Czech Republic	Jun. 27, 2007
Christchurch, New Zealand	Mar. 22, 1981
Christchurch, New Zealand	Mar. 22 1981
Brussels, Belgium	Sep. 3, 2004
Ostrava, Czech Republic	Jun. 12, 2008
Barcelona, Spain	Aug. 6, 1992
Beijing, China	Aug. 22, 2008
Walnut, U.S.A.	Apr. 17, 1994
Stuttgart, Germany	Aug. 22, 1993
Brussels, Belgium	Aug. 25, 2006
Cologne, Germany	Aug. 17, 1977

☆ MEN'S 4 × 100 M RELAY Asafa Powell, Nesta Carter, Usain Bolt, and Michael Frater (all Jamaica) celebrate after winning the gold medal in the 4 × 100 m relay final on August 22, 2008, at the Beijing Olympics.

LOCATION	DATE
Indianapolis, U.S.A.	Jul. 16, 1988
Seoul, South Korea	Sep. 29, 1988
Canberra, Australia	Oct. 6, 1985
Munich, Germany	Jul. 26, 1983
Brussels, Belgium	Aug. 23, 1996
Beijing, China	Sep. 11, 1993
Zürich, Switzerland	Aug. 14, 1996
Edinburgh, UK	Jul. 8, 1994
Beijing, China	Sep. 13, 1993
Oslo, Norway	Jun. 6, 2008

★ TRACK & FIELD—OUTDOOR TRACK EVENTS ★

WOMEN	TIME/DISTANCE	NAME & NATIONALITY
10,000 m	29:31.78	Wang Junxia (China)
20,000 m	1:05:26.60	Tegla Loroupe (Kenya)
☆1 hour	18,517 m	Dire Tune (Ethiopia)
25,000 m	1:27:05.90	Tegla Loroupe (Kenya)
30,000 m	1:45:50.00	Tegla Loroupe (Kenya)
☆3,000 m steeplechase	8:58.81	Gulnara Samitova-Galkina (Russia)
100 m hurdles	12.21	Yordanka Donkova (Bulgaria)
400 m hurdles	52.34	Yuliya Pechonkina (Russia)
4 x 100 m relay	41.37	GDR (Silke Gladisch, Sabine Rieger, Ingrid Auerswald, Marlies Göhr)
4 x 200 m relay	1:27.46	United States "Blue" (LaTasha Jenkins, LaTasha Colander-Richardson, Nanceen Perry, Marion Jones)
4 x 400 m relay	3:15.17	USSR (Tatyana Ledovskaya, Olga Nazarova, Maria Pinigina, Olga Bryzgina)
4 x 800 m relay	7:50.17	USSR (Nadezhda Olizarenko, Lyubov Gurina, Lyudmila Borisova, Irina Podyalovskaya)

★ TRACK & FIELD—INDOOR TRACK EVENTS ★

MEN	TIME	NAME & NATIONALITY
50 m	5.56	Donovan Bailey (Canada)
60 m	6.39	Maurice Green (U.S.A.)
	6.39	Maurice Green (U.S.A.)
200 m	19.92	Frankie Fredericks (Namibia)
400 m	44.57	Kerron Clement (U.S.A.)
800 m	1:42.67	Wilson Kipketer (Denmark)
1,000 m	2:14.96	Wilson Kipketer (Denmark)
1,500 m	3:31.18	Hicham El Guerrouj (Morocco)
1 mile	3:48.45	Hicham El Guerrouj (Morocco)
3,000 m	7:24.90	Daniel Komen (Kenya)
5,000 m	12:49.60	Kenenisa Bekele (Ethiopia)
50 m hurdles	6.25	Mark McKoy (Canada)
60 m hurdles	7.30	Colin Jackson (GB)
4 x 200 m relay	1:22.11	Great Britain & N. Ireland (Linford Christie, Darren Braithwaite, Ade Mafe, John Regis)
4 x 400 m relay	3:02.83	U.S.A. (Andre Morris, Dameon Johnson, Deon Minor, Milton Campbell)
4 x 800 m relay	7:13.94	Global Athletics & Marketing, U.S.A. (Joey Woody, Karl Paranya, Rich Kenah, David Krummenacker)
5,000 m walk	18:07.08	Mikhail Shchennikov (Russia)

DEC. 17: The **first controlled and sustained power-driven flight** occurred at 10:35 a.m. on December 17, 1903, when Orville Wright flew the 12-hp (9-kW) Flyer I for a distance of 120 ft. (36.5 m).

LOCATION	DATE
Beijing, China	Sep. 8, 1993
Borgholzhausen, Germany	Sep. 3, 2000
Ostrava, Czech Republic	Jun. 12, 2008
Mengerskirchen, Germany	Sep. 21, 2002
Warstein, Germany	Jun. 6, 2003
Daijing, China	Aug. 17, 2008
Stara Zagora, Bulgaria	Aug. 20, 1988
Tula, Russia	Aug. 8, 2003
Canberra, Australia	Oct. 6, 1985
Philadelphia, U.S.A.	Apr. 29, 2000
Seoul, South Korea	Oct. 1, 1988
Moscow, Russia	Aug. 5, 1984

☆ **WOMEN'S
1 HOUR** Dire Tune
(Ethiopia) in the
1-hour event at the
IAAF World Athletics
Grand Prix on June
12, 2008 in Ostrava,
Czech Republic,
where she ran a
record 18,517 m.

LOCATION	DATE
Reno, U.S.A.	Feb. 9, 1996
Madrid, Spain	Feb. 3, 1998
Atlanta, U.S.A.	Mar. 3, 2001
Liévin, France	Feb. 18, 1996
Fayetteville, U.S.A.	Mar. 12, 2005
Paris, France	Mar. 9, 1997
Birmingham, UK	Feb. 20, 2000
Stuttgart, Germany	Feb. 2, 1997
Ghent, Belgium	Feb. 12, 1997
Budapest, Hungary	Feb. 6, 1998
Birmingham, UK	Feb. 20, 2004
Kobe, Japan	Mar. 5, 1986
Sindelfingen, Germany	Mar. 6, 1994
Glasgow, UK	Mar. 3, 1991
Maebashi, Japan	Mar. 7, 1999
Boston, U.S.A.	Feb. 6, 2000
Moscow, Russia	Feb. 14, 1995

DEC. 18: The **largest secret Santa game** involved 1,270 participants in an event organized by Boots UK Limited in Nottingham, UK, on December 18, 2008.

★ TRACK & FIELD——INDOOR TRACK EVENTS ★

WOMEN	TIME	NAME & NATIONALITY
50 m	5.96	Irina Privalova (Russia)
60 m	6.92	Irina Privalova (Russia)
	6.92	Irina Privalova (Russia)
200 m	21.87	Merlene Ottey (Jamaica)
400 m	49.59	Jarmila Kratochvílová (Czechoslovakia)
800 m	1:55.82	Jolanda Ceplak (Slovenia)
1,000 m	2:30.94	Maria de Lurdes Mutola (Mozambique)
☆1,500 m	3:58.28	Yelena Soboleva (Russia)
1 mile	4:17.14	Doina Melinte (Romania)
3,000 m	8:23.72	Meseret Defar (Ethiopia)
☆5,000 m	14:24.37	Meseret Defar (Ethiopia)
50 m hurdles	6.58	Cornelia Oschkenat (GDR)
60 m hurdles	7.68	Susanna Kallur (Sweden)
4 x 200 m relay	1:32.41	Russia (Yekaterina Kondratyeva, Irina Khabarova, Yuliya Pechonkina, Yulia Gushchina)
4 x 400 m relay	3:23.37	Russia (Yulia Gushchina, Olga Kotlyarova, Olga Zaytseva, Olesya Krasnomovets)
4 x 800 m relay	8:18.54	Moskovskaya Region (Anna Balakshina, Natalya Pantelyeva, Anna Emashova, Olesya Chumakova)
3,000 m walk	11:40.33	Claudia Stef (Romania)

★ TRACK & FIELD——ULTRA-LONG DISTANCE [TRACK] ★

MEN	TIME/DISTANCE	NAME & NATIONALITY
50 km	2:48:06	Jeff Norman (GB)
100 km	6:10:20	Donald Ritchie (GB)
100 miles	11:28:03	Oleg Kharitonov (Russia)
☆1,000 km	5 days 16:17:00	Yiannis Kouros (Greece)
1,000 miles	11 days 13:54:58	Peter Silkinas (Lithuania)
☆6 hours	97.2 km (60.4 miles)	Donald Ritchie (GB)
☆12 hours	162.4 km (100.91 miles)	Yiannis Kouros (Greece)
24 hours	303.506 km (188.59 miles)	Yiannis Kouros (Greece)
48 hours	473.495 km (294.21 miles)	Yiannis Kouros (Greece)
☆6 days	1,038.851 km (645.51 miles)	Yiannis Kouros (Greece)

WOMEN	TIME/DISTANCE	NAME & NATIONALITY
50 km	3:18:52	Carolyn Hunter-Rowe (GB)
☆100 km	7:00:27	Norimi Sakurai (Japan)
100 miles	14:25:45	Edit Berces (Hungary)
☆1,000 km	7 days 01:28:29	Eleanor Robinson (GB)
1,000 miles	13 days 1:54:02	Eleanor Robinson (GB)
☆6 hours	83.2 km (57.7 miles)	Norimi Sakurai (Japan)
12 hours	147.6 km (91.71 miles)	Ann Trason (U.S.A.)
24 hours	250.106 km (155.40 miles)	Edit Berces (Hungary)
☆48 hours	382.777 km (237.85 miles)	Inagaki Sumie (Japan)
6 days	883.631 km (549.06 miles)	Sandra Barwick (New Zealand)

LOCATION	DATE
Madrid, Spain	Feb. 9, 1995
Madrid, Spain	Feb. 11, 1993
Madrid, Spain	Feb. 9, 1995
Liévin, France	Feb. 13, 1993
Milan, Italy	Mar. 7, 1982
Vienna, Austria	Mar. 3, 2002
Stockholm, Sweden	Feb. 25, 1999
Moscow, Russia	Feb. 18, 2006
East Rutherford, U.S.A.	Feb. 9, 1990
Stuttgart, Germany	Feb. 3, 2007
Stockholm, Sweden	Feb. 18, 2009
Berlin, Germany	Feb. 20, 1988
Karlsruhe, Germany	Feb. 10, 2008
Glasgow, UK	Jan. 29, 2005
Glasgow, UK	Jan. 28, 2006
Volgograd, Russia	Feb. 11, 2007
Bucharest, Romania	Jan. 30, 1999

> **29:** years that ultrarunner Jeff Norman (UK) has held the 50 km track world record of 2 hr. 48 min. 6 sec.

LOCATION	DATE
Timperley, UK	Jun. 7, 1980
London, UK	Oct. 28, 1978
London, UK	Oct. 20, 2002
Colac, Australia	Nov. 26–Dec. 1, 1984
Nanango, Australia	Mar. 11–23, 1998
London, UK	Oct. 28, 1978
Montauban, France	Mar. 15–16, 1985
Adelaide, Australia	Oct. 4–5, 1997
Surgères, France	May 3–5, 1996
Colac, Australia	Nov. 20–25, 2005

LOCATION	DATE
Barry, South Wales, UK	Mar. 3, 1996
Winschoten, the Netherlands	Sep. 8, 2007
Verona, Italy	Sep. 21–22, 2002
Nanango, Australia	Mar. 11–18, 1998
Nanango, Australia	Mar. 11–23, 1998
Verona, Italy	Sep. 27, 2003
Hayward, U.S.A.	Aug. 3–4, 1991
Verona, Italy	Sep. 21–22, 2002
Surgères, France	May 16–18, 2008
Campbelltown, Australia	Nov. 18–24, 1990

OFFICIAL WEBSITES

TRACK & FIELD:
www.iaaf.org

ULTRARUNNING:
www.iau.org.tw

★ TRACK & FIELD—ROAD RACE ★

MEN	TIME	NAME & NATIONALITY
10 km	27:02	Haile Gebrselassie (Ethiopia)
15 km	41:29	Felix Limo (Kenya)
	•41:29	Deriba Merga (Ethiopia)
20 km	55:48	Haile Gebrselassie (Ethiopia)
Half marathon	58:33	Samuel Wanjiru (Kenya)
25 km	1:12:45	Paul Malakwen Kosgei (Kenya)
30 km	1:28:00	Takayuki Matsumiya (Japan)
☆ Marathon	2:03:59	Haile Gebrselassie (Ethiopia)
100 km	6:13:33	Takahiro Sunada (Japan)
Road relay	1:57:06	Kenya (Josephat Ndambiri, Martin Mathathi, Daniel Mwangi, Mekubo Mogusu, Onesmus Nyerere, John Kariuki)

WOMEN	TIME	NAME & NATIONALITY
10 km	30:21	Paula Radcliffe (GB)
15 km	46:55	Kayoko Fukushi (Japan)
20 km	1:02:57	Lornah Kiplagat (the Netherlands)
Half marathon	1:06:25	Lornah Kiplagat (the Netherlands)
25 km	1:22:13	Mizuki Noguchi (Japan)
30 km	1:38:49	Mizuki Noguchi (Japan)
Marathon	2:15:25	Paula Radcliffe (GB)
100 km	6:33:11	Tomoe Abe (Japan)
Road relay	2:11:41	China (Jiang Bo, Dong Yanmei, Zhao Fengdi, Ma Zaijie, Lan Lixin, Li Na)

•still awaiting ratification at the time of going to press

★ TRACK & FIELD—RACE WALKING ★

MEN	TIME	NAME & NATIONALITY
20,000 m	1:17:25.6	Bernardo Segura (Mexico)
20 km (road)	1:17:16	Vladimir Kanaykin (Russia)
30,000 m	2:01:44.1	Maurizio Damilano (Italy)
50,000 m	3:40:57.9	Thierry Toutain (France)
☆ 50 km (road)	3:34:14	Denis Nizhegorodov (Russia)

WOMEN	TIME	NAME & NATIONALITY
10,000 m	41.56.23	Nadezhda Ryashkina (USSR)
20,000 m	1:26:52.3	Olimpiada Ivanova (Russia)
20 km (road)	1:25:41	Olimpiada Ivanova (Russia)

....
DEC. 19: The **heaviest vehicle pulled using earrings** is 3,443 lb. (1,562 kg), achieved by Gao Lin (China) who attached a car to his earrings by means of a rope and pulled it for 33 ft. (10 m) on this day in 2006.
....

LOCATION	DATE
Hoha, Qatar	Dec. 11, 2002
Nijmegen, the Netherlands	Nov. 11, 2001
Ras Al Khaimah, UAE	Feb. 20, 2009
Phoenix, U.S.A.	Jan. 15, 2006
The Hague, the Netherlands	Mar. 17, 2007
Berlin, Germany	May 9, 2004
Kumamoto, Japan	Feb. 27, 2005
Berlin, Germany	Sep. 28, 2008
Tokoro, Japan	Jun. 21, 1998
Chiba, Japan	Nov. 23, 2005

LOCATION	DATE
San Juan, Puerto Rico	Feb. 23, 2003
Marugame, Japan	Feb. 5, 2006
Udine, Italy	Oct. 14, 2007
Udine, Italy	Oct. 14, 2007
Berlin, Germany	Sep. 25, 2005
Berlin, Germany	Sep. 25, 2005
London, UK	Apr. 13, 2003
Tokoro, Japan	Jun. 25, 2000
Beijing, China	Feb. 28, 1998

☆ **15 KM ROAD RACE**
Deriba Merga (Ethiopia)
runs the marathon at the
2008 Olympic Games in
Beijing, China. On
February 20, 2009, Merga
equaled Kenyan Felix
Limo's 15 km road race
record in a time of
41 min. 29 sec. in Ras
Al Khaimah, UAE.

LOCATION	DATE
Bergen, Norway	May 7, 1994
Saransk, Russia	Sep. 29, 2007
Cuneo, Italy	Oct. 3, 1992
Héricourt, France	Sep. 29, 1996
Cheboksary, Russia	May 11, 2008

LOCATION	DATE
Seattle, U.S.A.	Jul. 24, 1990
Brisbane, Australia	Sep. 6, 2001
Helsinki, Finland	Aug. 7, 2005

....

DEC. 20: The world's **largest Christmas cracker** measured 207 ft. (63.1 m)
long and 13 ft. (4 m) in diameter and was made at Ley Hill School, Chesham,
Buckinghamshire, UK, on December 20, 2001.

....

★ TRACK & FIELD—INDOOR FIELD EVENTS ★

MEN	RECORD	NAME & NATIONALITY
High jump	2.43 m (7 ft. 11.66 in.)	Javier Sotomayor (Cuba)
Pole vault	6.15 m (20 ft. 2.12 in.)	Sergei Bubka (Ukraine)
Long jump	8.79 m (28 ft. 10.06 in.)	Carl Lewis (U.S.A.)
Triple jump	17.83 m (58 ft. 5.96 in.)	Aliecer Urrutia (Cuba)
	17.83 m (58 ft. 5.96 in.)	Christian Olsson (Sweden)
Shot	22.66 m (74 ft. 4.12 in.)	Randy Barnes (U.S.A.)
Heptathlon*	6,476 points	Dan O'Brien (U.S.A.)

*60 m 6.67 seconds; long jump 7.84 m; shot 16.02 m; high jump 2.13 m; 60 m hurdles 7.85 seconds; pole vault 5.20 m; 1,000 m 2 min. 57.96 sec.

WOMEN	RECORD	NAME & NATIONALITY
High jump	2.08 m (6 ft. 9.8 in.)	Kajsa Bergqvist (Sweden)
☆ Pole vault	•5.00 m (16 ft. 4 in.)	Yelena Isinbayeva (Russia)
Long jump	7.37 m (24 ft. 2.15 in.)	Heike Drechsler (GDR)
Triple jump	15.36 m (50 ft. 4.72 in.)	Tatyana Lebedeva (Russia)
Shot	22.50 m (73 ft. 9.82 in.)	Helena Fibingerová (Czechoslovakia)
Pentathlon†	4,991 points	Irina Belova (Russia)

†60 m hurdles 8.22 seconds; high jump 1.93 m; shot 13.25 m; long jump 6.67 m; 800 m 2 min. 10.26 sec.

•still awaiting ratification at time of going to press

★ TRACK & FIELD—OUTDOOR FIELD EVENTS ★

MEN	RECORD	NAME & NATIONALITY
High jump	2.45 m (8 ft. 0.45 in.)	Javier Sotomayor (Cuba)
Pole vault	6.14 m (20 ft. 1.73 in.)	Sergei Bubka (Ukraine)
Long jump	8.95 m (29 ft. 4.36 in.)	Mike Powell (U.S.A.)
Triple jump	18.29 m (60 ft. 0.78 in.)	Jonathan Edwards (GB)
Shot	23.12 m (75 ft. 10.23 in.)	Randy Barnes (U.S.A.)
Discus	74.08 m (243 ft. 0.53 in.)	Jürgen Schult (USSR)
Hammer	86.74 m (284 ft. 7 in.)	Yuriy Sedykh (USSR)
Javelin	98.48 m (323 ft. 1.16 in.)	Jan Železný (Czech Republic)
Decathlon*	9,026 points	Roman Šebrle (Czech Republic)

*100 m 10.64 seconds; long jump 8.11 m; shot 15.33 m; high jump 2.12 m; 400 m 47.79 seconds; 110 m hurdles 13.92 seconds; discus 47.92 m; pole vault 4.80 m; javelin 70.16 m; 1,500 m 4 min. 21.98 sec.

DEC. 21: The **first crossword clue** appeared in the U.S. newspaper *New York World* on December 21, 1913. The clue was "What bargain hunters enjoy." The answer? "Sales."

LOCATION	DATE
Budapest, Hungary	Mar. 4, 1989
Donetsk, Ukraine	Feb. 21, 1993
New York City, U.S.A.	Jan. 27, 1984
Sindelfingen, Germany	Mar. 1, 1997
Budapest, Hungary	Mar. 7, 2004
Los Angeles, U.S.A.	Jan. 20, 1989
Toronto, Canada	Mar. 14, 1993

26: Guinness World Records broken by Haile Gebrselassie (Ethiopia), making him one of the greatest distance runners in history.

LOCATION	DATE
Arnstadt, Germany	Feb. 4, 2006
Donetsk, Ukraine	Feb. 15, 2009
Vienna, Austria	Feb. 13, 1988
Budapest, Hungary	Mar. 6, 2004
Jablonec, Czechoslovakia	Feb. 19, 1977
Berlin, Germany	Feb. 15, 1992

LOCATION	DATE
Salamanca, Spain	Jul. 27, 1993
Sestriere, Italy	Jul. 31, 1994
Tokyo, Japan	Aug. 30, 1991
Gothenburg, Sweden	Aug. 7, 1995
Los Angeles, U.S.A.	May 20, 1990
Neubrandenburg, Germany	Jun. 6, 1986
Stuttgart, Germany	Aug. 30, 1986
Jena, Germany	May 25, 1996
Götzis, Austria	May 27, 2001

OFFICIAL WEBSITES

TRACK & RACE WALKING:
www.iaaf.org

CYCLING:
www.uci.ch

....

DEC. 22: The record for the **most lights lit simultaneously on a Christmas tree** is 150,000 by RTL Television GmbH, Germany, on December 22, 2006, at Cologne Cathedral, Cologne, Germany.

....

★ TRACK & FIELD—OUTDOOR FIELD EVENTS ★

WOMEN	RECORD	NAME & NATIONALITY
High jump	2.09 m (6 ft. 10.28 in.)	Stefka Kostadinova (Bulgaria)
☆ Pole vault	5.05 m (16 ft. 6 in.)	Yelena Isinbayeva (Russia)
Long jump	7.52 m (24 ft. 8.06 in.)	Galina Chistyakova (USSR)
Triple jump	15.50 m (50 ft. 10.23 in.)	Inessa Kravets (Ukraine)
Shot	22.63 m (74 ft. 2.94 in.)	Natalya Lisovskaya (USSR)
Discus	76.80 m (252 ft.)	Gabriele Reinsch (GDR)
Hammer	77.80 m (255 ft. 3 in.)	Tatyana Lysenko (Russia)
☆ Javelin	72.28 m (253 ft. 6 in.)	Barbora Spotáková (Czech Republic)
Heptathlon†	7,291 points	Jacqueline Joyner-Kersee (U.S.A.)
Decathlon**	8,358 points	Austra Skujyte (Lithuania)

†100 m hurdles 12.69 seconds; high jump 1.86 m; shot 15.80 m; 200 m 22.56 seconds; long jump 7.27 m; javelin 45.66 m; 800 m 2 min. 8.51 sec.

**100 m 12.49 seconds; long jump 6.12 m; shot 16.42 m; high jump 1.78 m; 400 m; 57.19 seconds; 100 m hurdles 14.22 seconds; discus 46.19 m; pole vault 3.10 m; javelin 48.78 m; 1,500 m 5 min. 15.86 sec.

★ CYCLING—ABSOLUTE TRACK ★

MEN	TIME/DISTANCE	NAME & NATIONALITY
200 m (flying start)	9.772	Theo Bos (Netherlands)
500 m (flying start)	24.758	Chris Hoy (GB)
1 km (standing start)	58.875	Arnaud Tournant (France)
4 km (standing start)	4:11.114	Christopher Boardman (GB)
☆ Team 4 km (standing start)	3:53.314	Great Britain (Ed Clancy, Paul Manning, Geraint Thomas, Bradley Wiggins)
1 hour	*49.7 km	Ondrej Sosenka (Czech Republic)

WOMEN	TIME/DISTANCE	NAME & NATIONALITY
200 m (flying start)	10.831	Olga Slioussareva (Russia)
500 m (flying start)	29.655	Erika Salumäe (Estonia)
500 m (standing start)	33.588	Anna Meares (Australia)
3 km (standing start)	3:24.537	Sarah Ulmer (New Zealand)
1 hour	*46.065 km	Leontien Zijlaard-Van Moorsel (Netherlands)

*Some athletes achieved better distances within an hour with bicycles that are no longer allowed by the Union Cycliste Internationale (UCI). The 1-hour records given here are in accordance with the new UCI rules.

DEC. 23: The **youngest band to have a recording banned** from radio play is Who's Ya Daddy? (Australia; average age 12 years 26 days). "I Like Fat Chicks" was banned from ZZZ FM on December 23, 2004.

LOCATION	DATE
Rome, Italy	Aug. 30, 1987
Beijing, China	Aug. 18, 2008
St. Petersburg, Russia	Jun. 11, 1988
Gothenburg, Sweden	Aug. 10, 1995
Moscow, Russia	Jun. 7, 1987
Neubrandenburg, Germany	Jul. 9, 1988
Tallinn, Estonia	Aug. 15, 2006
Stuttgart, Germany	Sep. 13, 2008
Seoul, South Korea	Sep. 24, 1988
Columbia, U.S.A.	Apr. 15, 2005

LOCATION	DATE
Moscow Russia	Dec. 16, 2006
La Paz, Bolivia	May 13, 2007
La Paz, Bolivia	Oct. 10, 2001
Manchester, UK	Aug. 29, 1996
Beijing, China	Aug. 18, 2008
Moscow, Russia	Jul. 19, 2005

LOCATION	DATE
Moscow, Russia	Apr. 25, 1993
Moscow, Russia	Aug. 6, 1987
Palma de Mallorca, Spain	Mar. 31, 2007
Athens, Greece	Aug. 22, 2004
Mexico City, Mexico	Oct. 1, 2003

☆ **4 KM TEAM CYCLING** Gold medalists Paul Manning, Ed Clancy, Geraint Thomas, and Bradley Wiggins (all GB) celebrate after the men's team pursuit finals at the Laoshan Velodrome on Day 10 of the 2008 Olympic Games on August 18, 2008, in Beijing, China. They achieved a time of 3 min. 53.314 sec.

DEC. 24: The world's **first passenger-carrying car** was a steam-powered road vehicle carrying eight passengers, built by Richard Trevithick (GB). It first ran at Camborne, Cornwall, UK, on December 24, 1801.

★ FREEDIVING ★

MEN'S DEPTH DISCIPLINES	DEPTH/TIME	NAME & NATIONALITY
☆ Constant weight with fins	120 m (393 ft. 8 in.)	Herbert Nitsch (Austria)
☆ Constant weight without fins	88 m (288 ft. 8 in.)	William Trubridge (New Zealand)
Variable weight	140 m (259 ft. 4 in.)	Carlos Coste (Venezuela)
No limit	214 m (702 ft.)	Herbert Nitsch (Austria)
☆ Free immersion	109 m (357 ft. 7 in.)	Herbert Nitsch (Austria)

MEN'S DYNAMIC APNEA

☆ With fins	250 m (800 ft. 2 in.)	Alexey Molchanov (Russia)
☆ Without fins	213 m (698 ft. 9 in.)	Tom Sietas (Germany)
☆	213 m (698 ft. 9 in.)	Dave Mullins (New Zealand)

MEN'S STATIC APNEA

☆ Duration	10 min. 12 sec.	Tom Sietas (Germany)

WOMEN'S DEPTH DISCIPLINES

☆ Constant weight with fins	96 m (314 ft. 11 in.)	Sara Campbell (UK)
☆ Constant weight without fins	60 m (196 ft. 10 in.)	Natalia Molchanova (Russia)
Variable weight	122 m (400 ft. 3 in.)	Tanya Streeter (U.S.A.)
No limit	160 m (524 ft. 11 in.)	Tanya Streeter (U.S.A.)
☆ Free immersion	85 m (278 ft. 10 in.)	Natalia Molchanova (Russia)

•Please note that these records were still awaiting ratification at the time of going to press.

WOMEN'S DYNAMIC APNEA

☆ With fins	214 m (702 ft. 1 in.)	Natalia Molchanova (Russia)
☆ Without fins	151 m (495 ft. 4 in.)	Kathryn McPhee (New Zealand)

WOMEN'S STATIC APNEA

Duration	8 min. 0 sec.	Natalia Molchanova (Russia)

LOCATION	DATE
The Bahamas	Apr. 11, 2009
The Bahamas	Apr. 10, 2009
Sharm el Sheikh, Egypt	May 9, 2006
Spetses, Greece	Jun. 14, 2007
The Bahamas	Apr. 6, 2009
Lignano, Italy	Oct. 5, 2008
Hamburg, Germany	Jul. 2, 2008
Wellington, New Zealand	Aug. 12, 2008
Athens, Greece	Jun. 7, 2008
The Bahamas	Apr. 2, 2009
Dahab, Egypt	Jun. 12, 2008
Turks and Caicos Islands	Jul. 19, 2003
Turks and Caicos Islands	Aug. 17, 2002
Crete, Greece	Jul. 27, 2008
Lignano, Italy	Oct. 5, 2008
Wellington, New Zealand	Aug. 9, 2008
Maribor, Slovenia	Jul. 6, 2007

☆ **MEN'S DEPTH Herbert Nitsch (Austria) dives at Dean's Blue Hole, The Bahamas. He holds the world record in three depth disciplines: constant weight with fins, no limit, as well as free immersion.**

OFFICIAL WEBSITES

FREEDIVING:
www.aida-international.org

ROWING:
www.worldrowing.com

SPEED SKATING:
www.isu.org

★ ROWING ★

MEN	TIME	NAME & NATIONALITY
Single sculls	6:35.40	Mahe Drysdale (New Zealand)
Double sculls	6:03.25	Jean-Baptiste, Adrien Hardy (France)
☆ Quadruple sculls	5:36.20	Christopher Morgan, James McRae, Brendan Long, Daniel Noonan (Australia)
Coxless pairs	6:14.27	Matthew Pinsent, James Cracknell (GB)
Coxless fours	5:41.35	Sebastian Thormann, Paul Dienstbach, Philipp Stüer, Bernd Heidicker (Germany)
Coxed pairs*	6:42.16	Igor Boraska, Tihomir Frankovic, Milan Razov (Croatia)
Coxed fours*	5:58.96	Matthias Ungemach, Armin Eichholz, Armin Weyrauch, Bahne Rabe, Jörg Dederding (Germany)
Coxed eights	5:19.85	Deakin, Beery, Hoopman, Volpenhein, Cipollone, Read, Allen, Ahrens, Hansen (U.S.A.)

LIGHTWEIGHT

Single sculls*	6:47.82	Zac Purchase (GB)
Double sculls	6:10.02	Mads Rasmussen and Rasmus Quist (Denmark)
Quadruple sculls*	5:45.18	Francesco Esposito, Massimo Lana, Michaelangelo Crispi, Massimo Guglielmi (Italy)
Coxless pairs*	6:26.61	Tony O'Connor, Neville Maxwell (Ireland)
Coxless fours	5:45.60	Thomas Poulsen, Thomas Ebert, Eskild Ebbesen, Victo Feddersen (Denmark)
Coxed eights*	5:30.24	Altena, Dahlke, Kobor, Stomporowski, Melges, März, Buchheit, Von Warburg, Kaska (Germany)

WOMEN

Single sculls	7:07.71	Rumyana Neykova (Bulgaria)
Double sculls	6:38.78	Georgina and Caroline Evers-Swindell (New Zealand)
Quadruple sculls	6:10.80	Kathrin Boron, Katrin Rutschow-Stomporowski, Jana Sorgers, Kerstin Köppen (Germany)
Coxless pairs	6:53.80	Georgeta Andrunache, Viorica Susanu (Romania)
Coxless fours*	6:25.35	Robyn Selby Smith, Jo Lutz, Amber Bradley, Kate Hornsey (Australia)
Coxed eights	5:55.50	Mickelson, Whipple, Lind, Goodale, Sickler, Cooke, Shoop, Francia, Davies (U.S.A.)

LIGHTWEIGHT

Single sculls*	7:28.15	Constanta Pipota (Romania)
Double sculls	6:49.77	Dongxiang Xu, Shimin Yan (China)
Quadruple sculls*	6:23.95	Hua Yu, Haixia Chen, Xuefei Fan, Jing Liu (China)
Coxless pairs*	7:18.32	Eliza Blair, Justine Joyce (Australia)

*Denotes non-Olympic boat classes

LOCATION	DATE
Eton, UK	Aug. 26, 2006
Poznan, Poland	Jun. 17, 2006
Beijing, China	Aug. 10, 2008
Seville, Spain	Sep. 21, 2002
Seville, Spain	Sep. 21, 2002
Indianapolis, U.S.A.	Sep. 18, 1994
Vienna, Austria	Aug. 24, 1991
Athens, Greece	Aug. 15, 2004

> **8:** minutes that Natalia Molchanova (Russia) can hold her breath without using supplemental oxygen.

LOCATION	DATE
Eton, UK	Aug. 26, 2006
Amsterdam, the Netherlands	Jun. 23, 2007
Montreal, Canada	Aug. 1992
Paris, France	1994
Lucerne, Switzerland	Jul. 9, 1999
Montreal, Canada	Aug. 1992

LOCATION	DATE
Seville, Spain	Sep. 21, 2002
Seville, Spain	Sep. 21, 2002
Duisburg, Germany	May 19, 1996
Seville, Spain	Sep. 21, 2002
Eton, UK	Aug. 26, 2006
Eton, UK	Aug. 27, 2006

LOCATION	DATE
Paris, France	Jun. 19, 1994
Poznan, Poland	Jun. 17, 2006
Eton, UK	Aug. 27, 2006
Aiguebelette-le-Lac, France	Sep. 7, 1997

★ SPEED SKATING—LONG TRACK ★

MEN	TIME/POINTS	NAME & NATIONALITY
500 m	34.03	Jeremy Wotherspoon (Canada)
2 x 500 m	68.31	Jeremy Wotherspoon (Canada)
☆ 1,000 m	1:06.42	Shani Davis (U.S.A.)
☆ 1,500 m	1:41.80	Shani Davis (U.S.A.)
3,000 m	3:37.28	Eskil Ervik (Norway)
5,000 m	6:03.32	Sven Kramer (Netherlands)
10,000 m	12:41.69	Sven Kramer (Netherlands)
500/1,000/500/1,000 m	137.230 points	Jeremy Wotherspoon (Canada)
500/3,000/1,500/5,000 m	146.365 points	Erben Wennemars (Netherlands)
500/5,000/1,500/10,000 m	145.742 points	Shani Davis (U.S.A.)
Team pursuit (8 laps)	3:37.80	Netherlands (Sven Kramer, Carl Verheijen, Erben Wennemars)

WOMEN	TIME/POINTS	NAME & NATIONALITY
500 m	37.02	Jenny Wolf (Germany)
2 x 500 m	74.42	Jenny Wolf (Germany)
1,000 m	1:13.11	Cindy Klassen (Canada)
1,500 m	1:51.79	Cindy Klassen (Canada)
3,000 m	3:53.34	Cindy Klassen (Canada)
5,000 m	6:45.61	Martina Sáblíková (Czech Republic)
500/1,000/500/1,000 m	149.305 points	Monique Garbrecht-Enfeldt (Germany)
	149.305 points	Cindy Klassen (Canada)
500/1,500/1,000/3,000 m	155.576 points	Cindy Klassen (Canada)
500/3,000/1,500/5,000 m	154.580 points	Cindy Klassen (Canada)
Team pursuit (8 laps)	2:56.04	Germany (Daniela Anschütz, Anni Friesinger, Claudia Pechstein)

★ SPEED SKATING—SHORT TRACK ★

MEN	TIME	NAME & NATIONALITY
500 m	41.051	Sung Si-Bak (South Korea)
☆ 1,000 m	•1:23.454	Charles Hamelin (Canada)
1,500 m	2:10.639	Ahn Hyun-Soo (South Korea)
3,000 m	4:32.646	Ahn Hyun-Soo (South Korea)
☆ 5,000 m relay	•6:38.486	South Korea (Kwak Yoon-Gy, Lee Ho-Suk, Lee Jung-Su, Sung Si-Bak)

WOMEN	TIME	NAME & NATIONALITY
☆ 500 m	•42.609	Wang Meng (China)
1,000 m	1:29.495	Wang Meng (China)
1,500 m	2:16.729	Zhou Yang (China)
3,000 m	4:46.983	Jung Eun-Ju (South Korea)
☆ 3,000 m relay	•4:07.179	China (Liu Qiuhong, Wang Meng, Zhang Hui, Zhou Yang)

•still awaiting ratification at time of going to press

LOCATION	DATE
Salt Lake City, U.S.A.	Nov. 9, 2007
Calgary, Canada	Mar. 15, 2008
Salt Lake City, U.S.A.	Mar. 7, 2009
Salt Lake City, U.S.A.	Mar. 6, 2009
Calgary, Canada	Nov. 5, 2005
Calgary, Canada	Nov. 17, 2007
Salt Lake City, U.S.A.	Mar. 10, 2007
Calgary, Canada	Jan. 18–19, 2003
Calgary, Canada	Aug. 12–13, 2005
Calgary, Canada	Mar. 18–19, 2006
Salt Lake City, U.S.A.	Mar. 11, 2007

LOCATION	DATE
Calgary, Canada	Nov. 16, 2007
Salt Lake City, U.S.A.	Mar. 10, 2007
Calgary, Canada	Mar. 25, 2006
Salt Lake City, U.S.A.	Nov. 20, 2005
Calgary, Canada	Mar. 18, 2006
Salt Lake City, U.S.A.	Mar. 11, 2007
Salt Lake City, U.S.A.	Jan. 11–12, 2003
Calgary, Canada	Mar. 24–25, 2006
Calgary, Canada	Mar. 15–17, 2001
Calgary, Canada	Mar. 18–19, 2006
Calgary, Canada	Nov. 13, 2005

MEN'S 500 M SHORT TRACK Sung Si-Bak (South Korea) competes at the Samsung ISU Short Track World Cup 2008 in Nagano, Japan. On February 10, 2008, he achieved a time of 41.051 seconds in the 500 m event. He was also part of the team that holds the 5,000 m relay record.

LOCATION	DATE
Salt Lake City, U.S.A.	Feb. 10, 2008
Montreal, Canada	Jan. 18, 2009
Marquette, U.S.A.	Oct. 24, 2003
Beijing, China	Dec. 7, 2003
Salt Lake City, U.S.A.	Oct. 19, 2008

LOCATION	DATE
Beijing, China	Nov. 29, 2008
Harbin, China	Mar. 15, 2008
Salt Lake City, U.S.A.	Feb. 9, 2008
Harbin, China	Mar. 15, 2008
Salt Lake City, U.S.A.	Oct. 18, 2008

☆ **WOMEN'S 1,500 M SHORT TRACK** China's Zhou Yang leads, followed by Katherine Reutter (U.S.A.) and Jung Eun-Ju (South Korea), in the women's 1,500 m finals at the 2008 ISU Short Track World Cup on February 9, 2008. Zhou Yang won in a time of 2 min. 16.729 sec.

★ SWIMMING—LONG COURSE [50 M POOL] ★

MEN	TIME	NAME & NATIONALITY
☆ 50 m freestyle	•20.94	Frederick Bousquet (France)
☆ 100 m freestyle	•46.94	Alain Bernard (France)
☆ 200 m freestyle	1:42.96	Michael Phelps (U.S.A.)
400 m freestyle	3:40.08	Ian Thorpe (Australia)
800 m freestyle	7:38.65	Grant Hackett (Australia)
1,500 m freestyle	14:34.56	Grant Hackett (Australia)
☆ 4 x 100 m freestyle relay	3:08.24	U.S.A. (Michael Phelps, Garrett Weber-Gale, Cullen Jones, Jason Lezak)
☆ 4 x 200 m freestyle relay	6:58.56	U.S.A. (Michael Phelps, Ryan Lochte, Ricky Berens, Peter Vanderkaay)
50 m butterfly	•22.43	Rafael Muñoz (Spain)
100 m butterfly	50.40	Ian Crocker (U.S.A.)
☆ 200 m butterfly	1:52.03	Michael Phelps (U.S.A.)
☆ 50 m backstroke	24.33	Randall Bal (U.S.A.)
☆ 100 m backstroke	52.54	Aaron Peirsol (U.S.A.)
☆ 200 m backstroke	•1:52.86	Ryosuke Irie (Japan)
50 m breaststroke	•27.06	Cameron van der Burgh (South Africa)
☆ 100 m breaststroke	58.91	Kosuke Kitajima (Japan)
☆ 200 m breaststroke	2:07.51	Kosuke Kitajima (Japan)
☆ 200 m medley	1:54.23	Michael Phelps (U.S.A.)
☆ 400 m medley	4:03.84	Michael Phelps (U.S.A.)
☆ 4 x 100 m medley relay	3:29.34	U.S.A. (Aaron Peirsol, Brendan Hansen, Michael Phelps, Jason Lezak)

WOMEN	TIME	NAME & NATIONALITY
☆ 50 m freestyle	•23.96	Marleen Veldhuis (Netherlands)
☆ 100 m freestyle	52.88	Lisbeth Trickett (Australia)
☆ 200 m freestyle	•1:54.47	Federica Pellegrini (Italy)
☆ 400 m freestyle	•4:00.66	Joanne Jackson (UK)
☆ 800 m freestyle	8:14.10	Rebecca Adlington (UK)
1,500 m freestyle	15:42.54	Kate Ziegler (U.S.A.)
☆ 4 x 100 m freestyle relay	3:33.62	Netherlands (Inge Dekker, Ranomi Kromowidjojo, Femke Heemskerk, Marleen Veldhuis)
☆ 4 x 200 m freestyle relay	7:44.31	Australia (Stephanie Rice, Bronte Barratt, Kylie Palmer, Linda Mackenzie)
50 m butterfly	•25.33	Marleen Veldhuis (Netherlands)
100 m butterfly	56.61	Inge de Bruijn (Netherlands)
☆ 200 m butterfly	2:04.18	Liu Zige (China)
☆ 50 m backstroke	27.67	Sophie Edington (Australia)
☆ 100 m backstroke	58.77	Kirsty Coventry (Zimbabwe)
☆ 200 m backstroke	2:05.24	Kirsty Coventry (Zimbabwe)

•still awaiting ratification at time of going to press

....

DEC. 25: From 1922 to December 25, 1973, Tommy Chambers (UK, 1903–84) rode a verified total of 799,405 miles (1,286,517 km), the **greatest distance cycled in a lifetime.**

....

LOCATION	DATE
Montpellier, France	Apr. 26, 2009
Montpellier, France	Apr. 23, 2009
Beijing, China	Aug. 12, 2008
Manchester, UK	Jul. 30, 2002
Montreal, Canada	Jul. 27, 2005
Fukuoka, Japan	Jul. 29, 2001
Beijing, China	Aug. 11, 2008
Beijing, China	Aug. 13, 2008
Malaga, Spain	Apr. 5, 2009
Montreal, Canada	Jul. 30, 2005
Beijing, China	Aug. 13, 2008
Eindhoven, the Netherlands	Dec. 5, 2008
Beijing, China	Aug. 12, 2008
Canberra, Australia	May 10, 2009
Durban, South Africa	Apr. 18, 2009
Beijing, China	Aug. 11, 2008
Tokyo, Japan	Jun. 8, 2008
Beijing, China	Aug. 15, 2008
Beijing, China	Aug. 10, 2008
Beijing, China	Aug. 17, 2008

LOCATION	DATE
Amsterdam, the Netherlands	Apr. 19, 2009
Sydney, Australia	Mar. 27, 2008
Riccione, Italy	Mar. 8, 2009
Sheffield, UK	Mar. 16, 2009
Beijing, China	Aug. 16, 2008
Mission Viejo, U.S.A.	Jun. 17, 2007
Eindhoven, the Netherlands	Mar. 18, 2008
Beijing, China	Aug. 13, 2008
Amsterdam, Netherlands	Apr. 19, 2009
Sydney, Australia	Sep. 17, 2000
Beijing, China	Aug. 14, 2008
Sydney, Australia	Mar. 23, 2008
Beijing, China	Aug. 11, 2008
Beijing, China	Aug. 16, 2008

☆ **MEN'S 100 M FREESTYLE** French swimmer Alain Bernard (above) celebrates setting a new world record after winning the semi-final of the men's 100 m freestyle (long course) with a time of 46.94 seconds, during the French Swimming Championships on April 23, 2009 in Montpellier, France.

Three days later, at the same event, Frederick Bousquet (France) set a new world best for the 50 m freestyle with a time of 20.94 seconds.

☆ **WOMEN'S 200 M BUTTERFLY** Liu Zige (China) swims in the 200 m butterfly final on Day 6 of the 2008 Olympic Games on August 14, 2008, in Beijing, China. She won the race and set a new record of 2 min. 4.18 sec.

★ SWIMMING—LONG COURSE [50 M POOL] ★

WOMEN	TIME	NAME & NATIONALITY
50 m breaststroke	30.31	Jade Edmistone (Australia)
100 m breaststroke	1:05.09	Leisel Jones (Australia)
☆ 200 m breaststroke	2:20.22	Rebecca Soni (U.S.A.)
☆ 200 m medley	2:08.45	Stephanie Rice (Australia)
☆ 400 m medley	4:29.45	Stephanie Rice (Australia)
☆ 4 x 100 m medley relay	3:52.69	Australia (Emily Seebohm, Leisel Jones, Jessicah Schipper, Lisbeth Trickett)

★ SWIMMING—SHORT COURSE [25 M POOL] ★

MEN	TIME	NAME & NATIONALITY
☆ 50 m freestyle	20.48	Amaury Leveaux (France)
☆ 100 m freestyle	44.94	Amaury Leveaux (France)
☆ 200 m freestyle	1:40.83	Paul Biederman (Germany)
400 m freestyle	3:34.58	Grant Hackett (Australia)
☆ 800 m freestyle	7:23.42	Grant Hackett (Australia)
1,500 m freestyle	14:10.10	Grant Hackett (Australia)
☆ 4 x 100 m freestyle relay	3:04.98	France (Grégory Mallet, Fabien Gilot, William Meynard, Frédérick Bousquet)
4 x 200 m freestyle relay	6:52.66	Australia (Kirk Palmer, Grant Hackett, Grant Brits, Kenrick Monk)
☆ 50 m butterfly	22.18	Amaury Leveaux (France)
100 m butterfly	49.07	Ian Crocker (U.S.A.)
☆ 200 m butterfly	•1:50.53	Nikolay Skvortsov (Russia)
☆ 50 m backstroke	22.87	Randall Bal (U.S.A.)
☆ 100 m backstroke	49.20	Aschwin Wildeboer (Spain)
☆ 200 m backstroke	1:47.84	Markus Rogan (Australia)
☆ 50 m breaststroke	25.94	Cameron van der Burgh (South Africa)
☆ 100 m breaststroke	56.88	Cameron van der Burgh (South Africa)
200 m breaststroke	2:02.92	Ed Moses (U.S.A.)
☆ 100 m medley	51.15	Ryan Lochte (U.S.A.)
☆ 200 m medley	1:51.56	Ryan Lochte (U.S.A.)
400 m medley	3:59.33	Laszlo Cseh (Hungary)
☆ 4 x 100 m medley relay	3:24.29	Russia (Stanislav Donets, Sergey Geybel, Evgeny Korotyshkin, Alexander Sukhorukov)

WOMEN	TIME	NAME & NATIONALITY
☆ 50 m freestyle	23.25	Marleen Veldhuis (Netherlands)
100 m freestyle	51.70	Lisbeth Lenton (later Trickett, Australia)
☆ 200 m freestyle	1:51.85	Federica Pellegrini (Italy)
400 m freestyle	3:56.09	Laure Manaudou (France)
☆ 800 m freestyle	8:04.53	Alessia Filippi (Italy)

•still awaiting ratification at time of going to press

···

DEC. 26: On December 26, 2005, at the age of three years, Cranston Chipperfield (UK) became the **youngest person to take the stage as a circus ringmaster** at the Circus Royale, Lanarkshire, UK.

···

LOCATION	DATE
Melbourne, Australia	Jan. 30, 2006
Melbourne, Australia	Mar. 20, 2006
Beijing, China	Aug. 15, 2008
Beijing, China	Aug. 13, 2008
Beijing, China	Aug. 10, 2008
Beijing, China	Aug. 17, 2008

25: swimming world records broken at the Olympic Games held in Beijing, China, during August 2008.

LOCATION	DATE
Rijeka, Croatia	Dec. 11, 2008
Rijeka, Croatia	Dec. 13, 2008
Berlin, Germany	Nov. 16, 2008
Sydney, Australia	Jul. 18, 2002
Melbourne, Australia	Jul. 20, 2008
Perth, Australia	Aug. 7, 2001
Istres, France	Dec. 20, 2008
Melbourne, Australia	Jul. 31, 2007
Rijeka, Croatia	Dec. 14, 2008
New York City, U.S.A.	Mar. 26, 2004
St. Petersburg, Russia	Feb. 11, 2009
Berlin, Germany	Nov. 16, 2008
Madrid, Spain	Dec. 21, 2008
Manchester, UK	Apr. 13, 2008
Stockholm, Sweden	Nov. 11, 2008
Moscow, Russia	Nov. 9, 2008
Berlin, Germany	Jan. 17, 2004
Manchester, UK	Apr. 13, 2008
Manchester, UK	Apr. 11, 2008
Debrecen, Hungary	Dec. 14, 2007
Manchester, UK	Apr. 13, 2008

☆ **MEN'S 50 M & 100 M BREASTSTROKE** Cameron van der Burgh (South Africa) dives in for the 50 m breaststroke on November 11, 2008, at the Short Course World Cup held in Stockholm, Sweden. He swam the event in a record 25.94 seconds.

Two days earlier, on November 9, 2008, van der Burgh also broke the 100 m breaststroke (short course) record by swimming it in 56.88 seconds in Moscow, Russia.

LOCATION	DATE
Manchester, UK	Apr. 13, 2008
Melbourne, Australia	Aug. 9, 2005
Rijeka, Croatia	Dec. 14, 2008
Helsinki, Finland	Dec. 9, 2006
Rijeka, Croatia	Dec. 12, 2008

DEC. 27: Vesta Gueschkova (Bulgaria) was launched 75 ft. (22.9 m) from a crossbow in Tampa, Florida, U.S.A., on December 27, 1995—the **longest distance a human has been fired as an arrow.**

★ SWIMMING—SHORT COURSE [25 M POOL] ★

WOMEN	TIME	NAME & NATIONALITY
1,500 m freestyle	15:32.90	Kate Ziegler (U.S.A.)
☆ 4 x 100 m freestyle relay	3:28.22	Netherlands (Hinkelien Schreuder, Inge Dekker, Ranomi Kromowidjojo, Marleen Veldhuis)
☆ 4 x 200 m freestyle relay	7:38.90	Netherlands (Inge Dekker, Femke Heemskerk, Marleen Veldhuis, Ranomi Kromowidjojo)
☆ 50 m butterfly	24.99	Marieke Guehrer (Australia)
☆ 100 m butterfly	55.74	Lisbeth Trickett (Australia)
☆ 200 m butterfly	2:03.12	Nakanishi Yuko (Japan)
☆ 50 m backstroke	26.23	Sanja Jovanovic (Croatia)
☆ 100 m backstroke	56.15	Sakai Shiho (Japan)
☆ 200 m backstroke	2:00.91	Kirsty Coventry (Zimbabwe)
☆ 50 m breaststroke	29.58	Jessica Hardy (U.S.A.)
☆ 100 m breaststroke	1:03.72	Leisel Jones (Australia)
☆ 200 m breaststroke	•2:17.50	Annamay Pierse (Canada)
100 m medley	58.80	Natalie Coughlin (U.S.A.)
☆ 200 m medley	2:06.13	Kirsty Coventry (Zimbabwe)
☆ 400 m medley	4:25.06	Mireia Belmonte (Spain)
☆ 4 x 100 m medley relay	3:51.36	U.S.A. (Margaret Hoelzer, Jessica Hardy, Rachel Komisarz, Kara Denby)

•still awaiting ratification at time of going to press

★ WEIGHTLIFTING ★

MEN	CATEGORY	WEIGHT LIFTED	NAME & NATIONALITY
56 kg	Snatch	138 kg	Halil Mutlu (Turkey)
	Clean & jerk	168 kg	Halil Mutlu (Turkey)
	Total	306 kg	Halil Mutlu (Turkey)
62 kg	Snatch	153 kg	Shi Zhiyong (China)
	Clean & jerk	182 kg	Le Maosheng (China)
	☆ Total	326 kg	Zhang Jie (China)
69 kg	Snatch	165 kg	Georgi Markov (Bulgaria)
	Clean & jerk	197 kg	Zhang Guozheng (China)
	Total	357 kg	Galabin Boevski (Bulgaria)
77 kg	Snatch	173 kg	Sergey Filimonov (Kazakhstan)
	Clean & jerk	210 kg	Oleg Perepetchenov (Russia)
	Total	377 kg	Plamen Jelyazkov (Bulgaria)
85 kg	Snatch	187 kg	Andrei Rybakou (Belarus)
	Clean & jerk	218 kg	Zhang Yong (China)
	☆ Total	394 kg	Andrei Rybakou (Belarus)
94 kg	Snatch	188 kg	Akakios Kakhiasvilis (Greece)
	Clean & jerk	232 kg	Szymon Kolecki (Poland)
	☆ Total	412 kg	Akakios Kakhiasvilis (Greece)
105 kg	☆ Snatch	200 kg	Andrei Aramnau (Belarus)
	☆ Clean & jerk	237 kg	Alan Tsagaev (Bulgaria)
	☆ Total	436 kg	Andrei Aramnau (Belarus)

LOCATION	DATE
Essen, Germany	Oct. 19, 2007
Amsterdam, the Netherlands	Dec. 19, 2008
Manchester, UK	Apr. 9, 2008
Berlin, Germany	Nov. 16, 2008
Canberra, Australia	Apr. 26, 2008
Tokyo, Japan	Feb. 23, 2008
Rijeka, Croatia	Dec. 13, 2008
Tokyo, Japan	Feb. 22, 2009
Manchester, UK	Apr. 11, 2008
Manchester, UK	Apr. 10, 2008
Canberra, Australia	Apr. 26, 2008
Toronto, Canada	Mar. 14, 2009
New York City, U.S.A.	Nov. 23, 2002
Manchester, UK	Apr. 12, 2008
Rijeka, Croatia	Dec. 14, 2008
Manchester, UK	Apr. 11, 2008

☆ **WOMEN'S 50 M BUTTERFLY** A jubilant Marieke Guehrer (Australia) after swimming the women's 50 m butterfly at the FINA Short Course Swimming World Cup on November 16, 2008, in Berlin, Germany, in a time of 24.99 seconds.

LOCATION	DATE
Antalya, Turkey	Nov. 4, 2001
Trencín, Slovakia	Apr. 24, 2001
Sydney, Australia	Sep. 16, 2000
Izmir, Turkey	Jun. 28, 2002
Busan, South Korea	Oct. 2, 2002
Kanazawa, Japan	Apr. 28, 2008
Sydney, Australia	Sep. 20, 2000
Qinhuangdao, China	Sep. 11, 2003
Athens, Greece	Nov. 24, 1999
Almaty, Kazakhstan	April 9, 2004
Trencín, Slovakia	April 27, 2001
Doha, Qatar	Mar. 27, 2002
Chiang Mai, Thailand	Sep. 22, 2007
Ramat Gan, Israel	Apr. 25, 1998
Beijing, China	Aug. 15, 2008
Athens, Greece	Nov. 27, 1999
Sofia, Bulgaria	Apr. 29, 2000
Athens, Greece	Nov. 27, 1999
Beijing, China	Aug. 18, 2008
Kiev, Ukraine	Apr. 25, 2004
Beijing, China	Aug. 18, 2008

☆ **MEN'S 105 KG SNATCH** Andrei Aramnau (Belarus) competes in the men's 105 kg group at the 2008 Olympic Games in Beijing, China. He holds the snatch record of 200 kg as well as the total of 436 kg, both achieved at the Beijing Olympics on August 18, 2008.

★ WEIGHTLIFTING ★

MEN	CATEGORY	WEIGHT LIFTED	NAME & NATIONALITY
105+ kg	Snatch	213 kg	Hossein Rezazadeh (Iran)
	Clean & jerk	263 kg	Hossein Rezazadeh (Iran)
	Total	476 kg	Hossein Rezazadeh (Iran)

WOMEN	CATEGORY	WEIGHT LIFTED	NAME & NATIONALITY
48 kg	Snatch	98 kg	Yang Lian (China)
	Clean & jerk	120 kg	Chen Xiexia (China)
	Total	217 kg	Yang Lian (China)
53 kg	Snatch	102 kg	Ri Song-Hui (North Korea)
	Clean & jerk	129 kg	Li Ping (China)
	Total	226 kg	Qiu Hongxia (China)
58 kg	Snatch	111 kg	Chen Yanqing (China)
	Clean & jerk	141 kg	Qiu Hongmei (China)
	Total	251 kg	Chen Yanqing (China)
63 kg	Snatch	116 kg	Pawina Thongsuk (Thailand)
	Clean & jerk	142 kg	Pawina Thongsuk (Thailand)
	Total	257 kg	Liu Haixia (China)
69 kg	☆ Snatch	128 kg	Liu Chunhong (China)
	☆ Clean & jerk	158 kg	Liu Chunhong (China)
	☆ Total	286 kg	Liu Chunhong (China)
75 kg	Snatch	131 kg	Natalia Zabolotnaia (Russia)
	Clean & jerk	159 kg	Liu Chunhong (China)
	Total	286 kg	Svetlana Podobedova (Russia)
75+ kg	☆ Snatch	140 kg	Jang Mi-Ran (South Korea)
	☆ Clean & jerk	186 kg	Jang Mi-Ran (South Korea)
	☆ Total	326 kg	Jang Mi-Ran (South Korea)

OFFICIAL WEBSITE
WEIGHTLIFTING:
www.iwf.net

DEC. 28: The **first operating movie theater** was the Cinématographe Lumière at the Salon Indien in Paris, France, opened by Clément Maurice (France) on December 28, 1895.

LOCATION	DATE
Qinhuangdao, China	Sep. 14, 2003
Athens, Greece	Aug. 25, 2004
Sydney, Australia	Sep. 26, 2000

LOCATION	DATE
Santo Domingo, Dominican Republic	Oct. 1, 2006
Taian City, China	Apr. 21, 2007
Santo Domingo, Dominican Republic	Oct. 1, 2006
Busan, South Korea	Oct. 1, 2002
Taian City, China	Apr. 22, 2007
Santo Domingo, Dominican Republic	Oct. 2, 2006
Doha, Qatar	Dec. 3, 2006
Taian City, China	Apr. 23, 2007
Doha, Qatar	Dec. 3, 2006
Doha, Qatar	Nov. 12, 2005
Doha, Qatar	Dec. 4, 2006
Chiang Mai, Thailand	Sep. 23, 2007
Beijing, China	Aug. 13, 2008
Beijing, China	Aug. 13, 2008
Beijing, China	Aug. 13, 2008
Chiang Mai, Thailand	Sep. 25, 2007
Doha, Qatar	Nov. 13, 2005
Hangzhou, China	Jun. 2, 2006
Beijing, China	Aug. 16, 2008
Beijing, China	Aug. 16, 2008
Beijing, China	Aug. 16, 2008

☆ **WOMEN'S 69 KG Weightlifter Liu Chunhong (China)** shows off the gold medal she was awarded for a lift of 128 kg during the women's 69 kg snatch on Day 5 of the 2008 Olympic Games on August 13, 2008, in Beijing, China. She holds all the world records in this weight category: she also lifted 158 kg in the clean & jerk at the same event, and so achieved a total of 286 kg.

DEC. 29: The **oldest mother** is Maria del Carmen Bousada Lara (Spain). She was 66 years 358 days old when she gave birth to twin boys, Christian and Pau, in Barcelona, Spain, on December 29, 2006.

★ WATERSKIING ★

MEN	RECORD	NAME & NATIONALITY
Slalom	1.5 buoy/9.75-m line/ 58 km/h	Chris Parrish (U.S.A.)
Barefoot slalom	20.6 crossings of wake in 30 sec.	Keith St. Onge (U.S.A.)
Tricks	12,400 points	Nicolas Le Forestier (France)
Barefoot tricks	10,880 points	Keith St. Onge (U.S.A.)
Jump	74.2 m (243 ft. 5 in.)	Freddy Krueger (U.S.A.)
Barefoot jump	27.4 m (89 ft. 11 in.)	David Small (GB)
Ski fly	91.1 m (298 ft. 10 in.)	Jaret Llewellyn (Canada)
Overall	2,818.01 points*	Jaret Llewellyn (Canada)

*5@11.25 m, 10,730 tricks, 71.7 m jump

WOMEN	RECORD	NAME & NATIONALITY
Slalom	1 buoy/10.25-m line/ 55 km/h	Kristi Overton Johnson (U.S.A.)
☆		Karina Nowlan (Australia)
Barefoot slalom	17.0 crossings of wake in 30 sec.	Nadine de Villiers (South Africa)
Tricks	8,740 points	Mandy Nightingale (U.S.A.)
Barefoot tricks	4,400 points	Nadine de Villiers (South Africa)
Jump	56.6 m (186 ft.)	Elena Milakova (Russia)
Barefoot jump	20.6 m (67 ft. 7 in.)	Nadine de Villiers (South Africa)
Ski fly	69.4 m (227 ft. 8.2 in.)	Elena Milakova (Russia)
Overall	2,850.11 points**	Clementine Lucine (France)

**4@11.25 m, 8,680 tricks, 52.1 m jump; calculated with the 2006 scoring method

★ LONGEST SPORTS MARATHONS ★

SPORT	TIME	NAME & NATIONALITY
Aerobics	24 hours	Duberney Trujillo (Colombia)
Archery	27 hours	Micheal Henri Dames (South Africa)
☆ Baseball	33 hr. 15 min. 45 sec.	Boys of Slumber (U.S.A.)
☆ Basketball	81 hr. 1 min.	La Cuesta Youth Association LV Movement (Spain)
Basketball (wheelchair)	26 hr. 3 min.	University of Omaha students and staff (U.S.A.)
Bowling (tenpin)	120 hours	Andy Milne (Canada)
Bowls (indoor)	36 hours	Arnos Bowling Club (UK)
☆ Bowls (outdoor)	168 hours	Lloyd Hotel Bowling Club (UK)
☆ Cricket	66 hr. 16 min.	Raymond Terrace District Cricket Club (Australia)
Curling	40 hr. 23 min.	B. Huston, C. McCarthy, G. Poole, K. McCarthy, K. Martin, M. Witherspoon, R. Martin, T. Gouldie, T. Teskey, W. From (Canada)

DEC. 30: In the week ending December 30, 2007, almost 43 million tracks were legally downloaded in the U.S.A.—a figure 42.5% higher than the record set in the same week the previous year.

LOCATION	DATE
Trophy Lakes, U.S.A.	Aug. 28, 2005
Bronkhorstspruit, South Africa	Jan. 6, 2006
Lac de Joux, Switzerland	Sep. 4, 2005
Adna, U.S.A.	Sep. 17, 2006
Seffner, U.S.A.	Nov. 5, 2006
Mulwala, Australia	Feb. 8, 2004
Orlando, U.S.A.	May 14, 2000
Seffner, U.S.A.	Sep. 29, 2002

☆ **WOMEN'S SLALOM** Karina Nowlan (Australia) competes in the women's jump finals at the 2007 Waterskiing World Championships. She is joint world record holder in the women's slalom event after equaling Kristi Overton Johnson's (U.S.A.) feat on September 22, 2008, in Sacramento, U.S.A.

LOCATION	DATE
West Palm Beach, U.S.A.	Sep. 14, 1996
Sacramento, U.S.A.	Sep. 22, 2008
Witbank, South Africa	Jan. 5, 2001
Santa Rosa, U.S.A.	Jun. 10, 2006
Witbank, South Africa	Jan. 5, 2001
Rio Linda, U.S.A.	Jul. 21, 2002
Pretoria, South Africa	Mar. 4, 2000
Pine Mountain, U.S.A.	May 26, 2002
Lacanau, France	Jul. 9, 2006

OFFICIAL WEBSITE

WATERSKIING:
www.iwsf.com

LOCATION	DATE
Dosquebradas, Colombia	Feb. 26–27, 2005
Grahamstown, South Africa	Aug. 8–9, 2005
Long Island, U.S.A.	May 24–26, 2008
Tenerife, Spain	Jul. 1–4, 2008
Omaha, Nebraska, U.S.A.	Sep. 24–25, 2004
Mississauga, Ontario, Canada	Oct. 24–29, 2005
Southgate, UK	Apr. 20–21, 2002
Manchester, UK	Oct. 25–Nov. 1, 2008
Raymond Terrace, Australia	Jan. 24–27, 2009
Brandon, Manitoba, Canada	Mar. 9–10, 2007

DEC. 31: The former Soviet Tupolev Tu-144 first flew on December 31, 1968, thereby becoming the **first supersonic airliner to fly.**

★ LONGEST SPORTS MARATHONS ★

SPORT	TIME	NAME & NATIONALITY
☆Darts (doubles)	27 hr. 22 min.	Jeff Garland, Tony Gafa, Ian van Veen, John Goggin (Australia)
☆Darts (singles)	26 hr. 42 min.	Stephen Wilson and Robert Henderson (UK)
Fistball (indoor)	24 hours	TG 1855 Neustadt bei Coburg e.V. (Germany)
Floorball	24 hr. 15 min.	TRM Floorball and Hornets Regio Moosseedorf Worblental (Switzerland)
☆Football	33 hr. 36 min.	Adesa & Stantec teams (Canada)
Football (five a side)	24 hr. 30 min.	Rossendale Mavericks and the Fearns Community Sports College (UK)
Handball	70 hours	HV Mighty/Stevo team (Netherlands)
☆Hockey (ice)	241 hr. 21 min.	Brent Saik and friends (Canada)
☆Hockey (indoor)	50 hours	Bert & Macs and Mid-Town Certigard teams (Canada)
Hockey (inline/roller)	24 hours	8K Roller Hockey League (U.S.A.)
☆Hockey (street)	105 hr. 17 min.	Molson Canadian and Canadian Tire teams (Canada)
☆Korfball	30 hr. 2 min.	Kingfisher Korfball Club (UK)
☆Netball	58 hours	Sleaford Netball Club (UK)
Parasailing	24 hr. 10 min.	Berne Persson (Sweden)
Pétanque (boules)	40 hr. 9 min.	Bevenser Boule-Freunde (Germany)
☆Pool (singles)	53 hr. 25 min.	Brian Lilly and Daniel Maloney (U.S.A.)
Skiing	202 hr. 1 min.	Nicky Willey (Australia)
Snowboarding	180 hr. 34 min.	Bernhard Mair (Austria)
☆Spinning (static cycling)	185 hr. 42 min.	Tom Seabourne (U.S.A.)
☆Table football	51 hr. 52 min.	Alexander Gruber, Roman Schelling, Enrico Lechtaler, Christian Nägele (Austria)
Table tennis (doubles)	101 hr. 1 min. 11 sec.	Lance, Phil and Mark Warren and Bill Weir (U.S.A.)
Table tennis (singles)	132 hr. 31 min.	Danny Price and Randy Nunes (U.S.A.)
☆Tai chi	25 hr. 5 min.	Ken Dickenson and Kevin Bartolo (Australia)
Tennis (doubles)	50 hr. 0 min. 8 sec.	Vince Johnson, Bill Geideman, Brad Ansley, and Allen Finley (U.S.A.)
☆Tennis (singles)	31 hr. 35 min. 30 sec.	George L Bolter and Athos Rostan III (U.S.A.)
☆Volleyball (beach)	24 hr. 10 min.	K. Garbulski, M. Fuks, A. Jankowski, and T. Konior (Poland)
☆Volleyball (indoor)	55 hr. 3 min.	SVU Volleybal (Netherlands)
Wakeboarding	6 hr. 17 min.	Ian Taylor (UK)

PLEASE NOTE: GWR sports marathon guidelines are constantly updated—please contact us for information before attempting a record.

LOCATION	DATE
Wyee Point, Australia	Aug. 30–31, 2008
Palnackie, Scotland, UK	Jun. 20–21, 2008
Frankehalle, Neustadt, Germany	Apr. 16–17, 2005
Zollikofen, Switzerland	Apr. 27–28, 2007
Edmonton, Alberta, Canada	Aug. 9–10, 2008
Waterfoot Rossendale, UK	Nov. 23–24, 2007
Tubbergen, the Netherlands	Aug. 30–Sep. 2, 2001
Strathcona, Alberta, Canada	Feb. 8–18, 2008
Lethbridge, Alberta, Canada	Mar. 25–27, 2008
Eastpointe, Michigan, U.S.A.	Sep. 13–14, 2002
Lethbridge, Alberta, Canada	Aug. 20–24, 2008
Larkfield, Kent, UK	Jun. 14–15, 2008
Sleaford, Lincolnshire, UK	Jul. 25–27, 2008
Lake Graningesjön, Sweden	Jul. 19–20, 2002
Bad Bevensen, Germany	Jul. 22–23, 2006
Spring Lake, North Carolina, U.S.A.	Oct. 10–12, 2008
Thredbo, NSW, Australia	Sep. 2–10, 2005
Bad Kleinkirchheim, Austria	Jan. 9–16, 2004
Mt Pleasant, Texas, U.S.A.	Dec. 5–12, 2008
Bregenz, Austria	Jun. 27–29, 2008
Sacramento, California, U.S.A.	Apr. 9–13, 1979
Cherry Hill, New Jersey, U.S.A.	Aug. 20–26, 1978
Sutherland, NSW, Australia	Mar. 17–18, 2006
Hickory, North Carolina, U.S.A.	Nov. 7–9, 2008
Hickory, North Carolina, U.S.A.	Nov. 8–9, 2008
Ustka, Poland	Jun. 27–28, 2008
Amsterdam, the Netherlands	Dec. 20–22, 2008
Milton Keynes, UK	Sep. 1, 2004

56: consecutive hours that Michael Kinzel (Germany) tobogganed in Kirchhundem, Germany, on May 4–6, 2002.

INDEX

A

accordions 198, 202
acid rain 271
action sports 419–424
actors & actresses 179;
   movie 180, 384–386, 388–391;
   TV 373
adoption 135
advertising 89, 122, 194, 326, 373, 375
aerobics 544
Afghanistan 287
Africa 37–41, 229–232, 286
air conditioners vii
aircraft xxvi, 131, 318–322
   altitude 151;
   camera plane 360;
   car loading 131;
   circumnavigation 164, 167;
   Concorde 592;
   crashes viii, 318, 319;
   eco 309;
   human-powered 402;
   military 201, 284, 287, 320, 322;
   model 322;
   paper 410;
   restrained 120;
   roadable 314;
   rolls xxxvii;
   supersonic 545
air guitar 136, 515
airlines 179, 321
airports 241
albatrosses 78
alligators 71
alphabets vi
alternative energies 344–348
altitude 151–156
amazing men 89–94
Amazon River 33, 35
ambulances 237
American Airlines 321
America's Army 414
amphibians 63–67
amphibious vehicles 158, 164
Andes 36
Angel Falls, Venezuela 24
ANIMAL PLANET 59–85
animals 23, 59–85, 465
   cloned vii;
   endangered 69, 270
animation viii, 108, 176, 395, 398
Annapurna 163
Antarctica xl, 51, 53, 73, 76
ants 36
Apollo missions 13, 151, 215, 593

applause 502
aprons 297
aqua aerobics 136
aquabikes (jetskis) 160, 246
Arabian Desert 227
arcade games 413
archery 514, 544
Arctic 52
Argentina 186
arm, robotic 349
arm hair 91
armies 222, 237
armored vehicles 314
art 205, 363–368
   competitions 366;
   pavement 364, 368;
   thefts 147, 216;
   see also painting;
   sculpture
ART & MEDIA 363–415
art & sculpture 363–368
Art Ross Trophy (ice hockey) 488
arthropods 59–63
artificial insemination 85
Asia 41–46
Asia Cup (Hockey) 445
assassinations vi, 594
astronauts, xv, 244, 375
at the movies 392–396
Atacama Desert, Chile 32
atom smashers 335–340
Atlantic crossings 158;
   flights 35, 242;
   rowing xxxix, 157, 316;
   sailing xvii, 27, 156, 157
Atlas Detector 336
   attendances 200
   barbecue 413;
   basketball 134;
   boxing 181;
   circus xxv;
   funeral 227;
   rugby 490, 492;
   soccer 291, 478
ATV (All-terrain vehicle) 506, 507
audiences:
   fashion show 201;
   TV 70, 368, 372, 427, 478
auroras 18
Australia 47, 48, 49, 245–247
authors 244, 254, 404, 590
autogyros 320
autosports 438–442
   IndyCars 220, 440;
   Le Mans 235
avalanches 18, 204

I

ice 18, 52, 53, 125, 210
  climbing 161;
  hotel 367;
  swimming under 101
icebergs 53, 55
ice caps 52
ice cream xxxviii, 360, 457
ice hockey 74, 377, **486–490**
ice stocks 220
Iceland 25, 26, 28, 209, 210
igloos 50
iguanas 69
images xxxix, 234, 294
Imperial Airways viii
in a day 144–147
in an hour 140–143
Incas 35
India 43
Indian Ocean 156
Indianapolis 500 217, 221, 440
Indonesia 237, 270
IndyCars 220, 440
inflatables 110
insects 33, 59–63, 267, 314
International Criminal Court
    281
International Space Station 13
Internet 352–356, 489
  browsers 163;
  domain names 266;
  underwater broadcast 155
iPods 329
islands 28, 29, 49
  bottle 273;
  reed 32
Isle of Man TT races 442
Israel 222–224, 344
Italy 201–203

J

jackets 299, 358
jambalaya 257
Java, Indonesia 239
jaws 184
jazz 193
jeans 296, 299
jet fighters 201
jetskis *see* aquabikes
jet wings 321
jicama 132
jigsaw puzzles 268, 294
journeys 168–172, 293
  all seven continents 152;
  circumnavigations 164–168;
  cycling 189, 507;
  kite-surfing 419;
  motorcycle 132, 169;
  snowmobile 105;
  swimming 171, 313;

tractor 222;
train 168, 327
JPEGS 196
judo 460, 461
juggling 79
jumps
  BASE 129, 153;
  car 312;
  frog 64;
  horse 32;
  on ice skates 72;
  insect 314;
  minibike 506;
  Moto X step up 510;
  movie stunts 129, 130, 401;
  parachute 420;
  pogo sticks 423;
  quadbike 506;
  rabbit 238;
  skateboard 325, 512;
  track & field 526–529
Jupiter 14

K

K2 160, 163
karate 459, 460
kayaking 503
Kazakhstan 43, 236
kebabs 232
Keck Telescopes, Hawaii 5
keyboard, computer 270
Khardungla Pass, Kashmir 45
Khumbu Glacier, Himalayas 42
kick flips (skateboard) 504, 509
kidney stones 103, 104, 260
kidneys 105, 192, 245
Kilimanjaro, Mount 62, 356, 441
Kiribati 50
kissing xli, 200, 588
kite-sailing 159
kite-surfing 419
knee bends 140
knighthoods 471
knitting 216, 342
knives 128, 207
knots 206
korfball 442, 445, 546
Kosciuszko, Mount, Australia 47
Krakatoa, Indonesia xxv, 351
kung fu 391

L

lakebeds, dry 30, 31
lakes 32, 38, 54
Laki, Iceland 28
Lambert Glacier, Antarctica 53
lampreys 71
land speeds 4, 314, 424
languages 98
lanterns 344, 447

V

vacuum cleaners 267
vegetables 238, 360
vehicles 307–311
   human-powered 144;
   pulled 119, 120, 122, 128, 241
veils, bridal 408
Venezuela 271
Venus 12
Victoria, Lake 38
video gaming xxvi, 232, 412–415
violins 213, 243
vision 61
voice, human 431
volcanoes 27, 28, 32, 41, 43
volleyball 446, 546
vomit 42
voodoo 99
Vostok Lake, Antarctica 54
Voyager (aircraft) 164
Voyager (spacecraft) 14, 15, 31
vultures 80

W

waists 94, 95
wakeboarding 522, 546
Waldos (Wallys) 134
walking 209
   circumnavigation 165;
   Nordic 212;
   on all fours 99;
   over hot plates 373;
   race walking 428, 429, 524–525
wallpaper 199
walls 225, 227
waltzing 133, 167
war 283–287, 593
warships 315, 318
washing machines 123
Washington Monument, DC 332, 334
waste 274
watches 154, 208, 360
water 17, 18, 269, 272, 397
waterfalls xli, 24, 25, 28–29
watermelons 128
water parks 213
water polo 502
waterskiing 544–545
water slides 342
water sports 499–503
waterspouts 47
water striders 351
waxing 143
wealth 275, 276, 391
weapons 327–330;
   personal 176, 223
weather 8, 285
websites 147, 323
weddings xxxviii, 111, 253
weight-lifting 122, 140, 142, 143, 147

   by nipples 120;
   sports reference 540–543;
   by tongue 119;
   in teeth 121
weight loss 91
Wellington boots 514
welwitschia 38
wetlands 48
whale sharks 71
whales 60, 184
what's on TV? 372–376
wheel of death 145
wheel skills 503–507
wheelbarrow races 245, 246
wheelchairs, 106, 144, 168, 239
   backflips i, 421;
   basketball 544;
   tennis 499
wheelies 504, 505, 507
whistles 246
whoopee cushions 340
wicket-keeping 466, 468
wickets 464–467
wife-carrying 513
Wii Sports 414
Wimbledon 115, 263, 276, 499
wind farms 345, 348
windmills 217
windsurfing 503
wine 139, 228, 232, 268
wine bottles 260
wine flutes 343
wings, bird 77
Winnie Mae 167
witches 593
wonderful women 94–98
wood block game 135
wool 245
world championships *see specific sports*
World of Warcraft 412
World Wars 284, 286, 590
worm-charming 513
wrestling 460, 463
Wright Flyer viii
writing vi

X/Y/Z

X Games 508–512
yachts 157, 316
Yellowstone Park, USA 29
yoga 235
yo-yos 454
zombies 139

SUPERLATIVES

Bestselling
hybrid car 309
music xxvi, 404–406, 408, 410, 411
smartphone 358

ACKNOWLEDGMENTS/CREDITS

Guinness World Records would like to thank the following individuals, companies, groups, websites, societies, schools, colleges and universities for their help in the creation of the 2010 edition:

3run, Brenden Adams & family, Willie Adams, Bender Helper Impact (Susan Bender, Adam Fenton, Mark Karges, Chrissy Kelleher, Brian Reinert, Shannon Swaggerty and Sally Triebel), Oliver Blagden, Blue Peter Production, BBC1, Luke and Joseph Boatfield, Book Marketing Ltd. (Steve Bohme and Rachel Levin), Alfie Boulton-Fay, Ceri, Katie and Georgie Boulton, Olivia Boulton, Box Office Mojo, Brand Museum, Notting Hill, CCTV (Guo Tong), Chulalongkorn Hospital, Bangkok, Thailand, Clara and Camille Chambers, ChartTrack, Edd & Imogen China, Adam Cloke, Cobourg Fire Department, Ontario, Canada, Collaboration Inc. (Miho Goto, Suzuki-san), Mark Collins, Creo (Richard Saysell and Iain Johnstone), Kenneth & Tatiana Crutchlow (Ocean Rowing Society), Josh Cushins, Gordner Dan (X Games), Chi Danny (X Games), Davies Media (Ceri Davies and Charlotte O'Brien), Bryn Downing (INP Media), Malee Duangdee & family, Louis Epstein, Ermanno Pietrosemoli Escuela Latino-america de Redes, Europroducciones (Marco Fernandez de Araoz, Mar Izquierdo, Sheila Izquierdo, Maria Ligues, Stefano Torrisi, Gabriela Ventura), Amelia Ewen, Toby Ewen, explorersweb.com, Debbie Ezel, Rachel Falikoff, Imageworks, Molly and Isobel Fay, Flora London Marathon (Natasha Grainger and Nicola Okey), Kate Fisher (St. Pancras Press Officer), Rob Fraser, Ansley Fuks, Thomasina Gibson, Dorotka Girton, Gladstone Skate Park, Michigan, U.S.A., Ryan, Brandon and Jordan Greenwood, Victoria Grimsell, Greg Grusby (Industrial Light & Magic), Michael Hebranko, Stuart Hendry Hit Entertainment, Japan (Jun Otsuki and Frank Foley), Marsha Hoover, Anne-Mareike Homfeld (European Space Agency), Hotel Arts, Barcelona, Bill Hughes (unofficial engineering consultant), Simon Hughes (unofficial car consultant), Caroline Iggulden (*The Sun*), IMDb.com, Panoula Ioannidou (Manager, 40 Savile Row), ITV Productions (Laurence Blyth, Malcolm Donkin, Paul Ritz, Emma Wilkinson), Lodato Jason (NBA), Stokel John (Rob Dyrdek's Fantasy Factory), Richard Johnston, Simon Jones, Barberan Karen (NBA), Robshaw Kelly (X Games), Sultan Kosen & family, Lacey Leavitt, Don Levy (Sony Pictures), London Aquarium, All at Macmillan Distribution, Manda (Carey and Nick), Jim Manion (International Federation of Body Builders), Carla Maroussas (Ascent Media), metacritic.com, Morgan Middle School, Ellensburgh, WA, Motion Capture Society, Murphy Marc (X Games), Lori Mezhoff, Blackwell Michelle (NBA), Myrtle Beach Airport, South Carolina, U.S.A., Nationmaster.com, Nitro Circus (Smoler Barry and Zablow Shanna), Norddeich TV (York Altendorf, Thomas Goseberg, Rainer Noseck, Ollie Wieberg), Olga TV (Jude, Bert and Paul ady), Outline Productions (Rainer Chapman, Selina Ferguson, Ian ...ans, Diana Hunter, Steve Kidgell, Laura Mansfield, Jamie Starr, Janine ...ry, Helen Veale), Sullivan Patrick (NBA), Kate Perkins, Daniel Phillips, ...lia Pistor, POD Worldwide (Yip Cheong, Christy Chin, Alex Liew), Sean Porter, The Queens Head & Artichoke Public House, London, Buchholz Rachel (NGK), R&G Productions (Stéphane Gateau, Patrice Parmentier, Jean-Francois Peralta, Jerome Revon), Martyn Richards Research (Martyn Richards), Michael Rummery, Anna Rutherford, Sassy (Nikki Gillespie and Steve Kemsley), Robyn Scott, Austin Scott, Thomas Sergeant, Sky1 (Helen Devonald, Kirsty Howell, Emma Read, Louise Snell, Ben Tattersal-Smith, James Townley, Sophie Turner-Laing, Nicky White), Marcela Soukupova, Wacharasindhu Suttipong (Chulalongkorn Hospital, Thailand), Charlie Taylor, Holly Taylor, Television News Release (Amanda and Claire), Hand Theo (www.dannyway.com), Simon Thompson, TIHE (Peter Harper), Twin Galaxies, Jessica, Isabel and Samuel Way, Weezer, Kate White, Daniel Woods, Claire Woodward.

In memoria...
Amy, the **longest rabbit;** Sandy Allen, **tallest living woman;** Maria de Jesus, **oldest woman;** Edna Parker, **oldest woman.**

PICTURE CREDITS

vi–viii: Rex Features; Rex Features/Maurice McDonald/PA; **viii–ix**: Getty Images; NASA/AP/PA; **x**: Ranald Mackechnie/GWR; S. Blair Hedges; Richard Bradbury/GWR; Rick & Nora Bowers/Alamy

UK INTRO

xiv–xvi: Iain McLean; Andi Southam; **xvii–xviii**: Paul Michael Hughes/GWR; Richard Bradbury/GWR; Patrick Brown/GWR; **xix–xx**: Ken McKay/Rex Features; Jon Bond

USA INTRO

xiv–xvi: Nate Christenson; Rob Fraser/GWR; Paul Michael Hughes/GWR; **xvii–xviii**: Joe Murphy/Getty Images; Paul Michael Hughes/GWR; **xxi–xxiii**: Adam Bouska

CANADA INTRO

xiv–xvi: Ranald Mackechnie/GWR; **xxi–xxiii**: Ken Ardill; Richard Wahab

WORLD INTRO

xiv–xvi: Oleg Nikishin/Getty Images; Paul Michael Hughes/GWR; **xix–xx**: Richard Bradbury/GWR; Richard Bradbury/GWR; Rob Fraser/GWR; **xxiv–xxv**: Mary Evans Picture Library; Getty Images; Alamy; Charles Walker/Topfoto; J. Wood/showhistory.com; Getty Images; Patrice Fury/Rex Features; Getty Images; **xxv–xxvii**: Jeff Haynes/Getty Images; Getty Images; Getty Images; Getty Images; Getty Images; **xxviii–xxix**: Paul Michael Hughes/GWR; **xxix, xxxi–xxxii**: Paul Michael Hughes/GWR; **xxxiii–xxxv**: Griff Stefan Gregorowius/RTL; Stefan Gregorowius/RTL; Andi Southam/Sky1; Paul Michael Hughes/GWR; Paul Michael Hughes/GWR; **xxxvi–xxxvii**: Yolanda de Santos; John Wright/GWR; Paul Michael Hughes/GWR; **xxxviii–xl**: Paul Michael Hughes/GWR; Nick Hannes/Panos/GWR; **xl–xlii**: Dave Nelson; PA; **3**: NASA; **5**: Astrium (P. Dumas); NASA; Melinda Podor/Alamy; **6–7**: NASA; NASA; NASA; NASA; **8–9, 10**: NASA; **9, 11**: NASA; D. Ducros/CNES; NASA; **13–14**: NASA; NASA; Ralph Morse/Getty Images; **14, 15, 16**: NASA; NASA; NASA; **17–18**: NASA; NASA; NASA; Getty Images; **19–20**: Detlev Van Ravenswaay/Science Photo Library; NASA; NASA; NASA; **24**: David Welling/Nature PL; **23, 25**: Adam Woolfitt/Robert Harding; Science Photo Library; Alamy **26–27**: Stephen Alvarez/National Geographic; Fabrizio Villa/Getty Images; **29, 30**. Bill Dymire/Alamy; Paiwei Wei/Getty Images; W. Robert Moore/Getty Images; **30, 31**: Kevin Schafer/NHPA; Photolibrary; Dennis Flaherty/Getty Images; **33–34**: Galen Rowell/Alamy; Walter Bibikow/Reflex Stock;

Bosch/Getty Images; Guy Salter/Getty Images; Vivek Prakash/Reuters; **160, 161, 162**: Adrian Bitoiu; **162–163**: Michael Maloney/Corbis; Michael Maloney/Corbis; David Paterson/Alamy; **165, 166, 167**: Getty Images; AP/PA; Rex Features; **167, 168**: Thierry Martinez/Getty Images; Joe Raedle/Getty Images; **175**: Chuck Kennedy/Getty Images; Robert Nickelsberg/Getty Images; **176, 177, 178**: John Wright/GWR; Nate Christenson; Wally Pacholka; **179, 180**: Richard Bradbury/GWR; **181–182**: John Wright/GWR; Mireille Vautier/Alamy; Alamy; Holly Stein/Getty Images; Moviestore Collection; **183–184**: Roberto Schmidt/Getty Images; Corbis; Brad Mangin/Getty Images; Alamy; Yuri Cortez/Getty Images; **186–187**: Patrick Landmann/Science Photo Library; Eliseo Fernandez/Reuters; **188–189**: Mariana Bazo/Reuters; Pilar Olivares/Reuters; Paul Souders/ Getty Images; **190–191, 192**: Alamy; Mauro Azzura; **192, 193–194**: Bill Zygmant/Rex Features; Andre Jenny/Alamy; **195–196, 197**: WENN; Joe McGorty/GWR; **197, 198**: Rex Features; Darren Staples/Reuters; **199–201**: Franck Fife/Getty Images; Frank Micelotta/Getty Images; **202–203**: Clive Rose/Getty Images; **204–205**: PA Jasper Juinen/Getty Images; **209–210**: Peter Adams/Getty Images; **211, 212**: WENN; Nils-Johan Norenlind/Getty Images; **213–214**: John Wright/GWR; John Wright/GWR; **215–216**: Hoge Noorden/EPA; Alamy; **221–222**: Rex Features; Kazbek Basayev/Getty Images; Ziyah Gafic/Getty Images; **223, 224**: Eliana Aponte/Reuters; **225–226**: Khaled al-Harir/Reuters; **229–230**: Euan Denholm/Reuters; Dave M. Benett/Getty Images; Robert Hollingworth/Alamy; **231–232**: David Preston/Alamy; David Sacks/Getty Images; Schalk van Zuydam/AP/PA; **234–236**: Ray Tang/Rex Features; **237–238**: Chris Jackson/Getty Images; **239–240**: Roslan Rahman/Getty Images; David Longstreath/AP/PA; **241–242**: Rex Features; **243–244**: Menard Cosmetic Co. Ltd.; Yoshikazu Tsuno/Getty Images; **245, 246**: William West/Getty Images; **247–249**: Cameron Spencer/Getty Images; Adam Butler; Richard G. Robinson; **254**: Ranald Mackechnie/GWR; **255**: Ranald Mackechnie/GWR; Ranald Mackechnie/GWR; Ranald Mackechnie/GWR; **256**: John Wright/GWR; **258–259**: Guy Harrop/Barcroft Media; Warren Allott/MaxPPP; **257, 260–261**: Luis Acosta/Getty Images; Ranald Mackechnie/GWR; **263, 264**: Ray Tang/Rex Features; **266, 267, 268, 269**: WENN; **268, 269**: Paul Michael Hughes/GWR; Shaun Curry/Getty Images; **270–272**: Issouf Sanogo/Getty Images; Judith Erawati/Getty Images; James Balog/Getty Images; Mary Plage/Photolibrary; Eugenio Opitz/Alamy; **273–274**: Getty Images; **275, 276, 277**: Richard Drew/AP/PA; Craig Ruttle/AP/PA; Michael Buckner/ Getty Images; Mario Tama/Getty Images; **276, 277, 278**: Mike Clarke/Getty Images; Nigel R Barklie/Rex Features; Tsvangirayi Mukwazhi/AP/PA; **280, 282**: AP/PA; Timothy A. Clary/Getty Images; Corbis; **279, 281**: Michael

Kooren/Getty Images; John D. McHugh/Getty Images; **284, 285, 286**: Getty Images; South West News Service; Carlos Laprida/South West News Service; Alfred de Montesquiou/AP/PA; **285, 286, 287**: Susan Walsh/AP/PA; Qassim Abdul-Zahra/AP/PA; Getty Images; **288–289, 290**: Getty Images; Getty Images; WENN; Kin Cheung/AP/PA; **290–291**: Karim Sahib/Getty Images; Rex Features; **292, 294, 295**: Leonhard Foeger/Reuters; **297–298**: Paul Michael Hughes/GWR; Bart Joosen; John Wright/GWR; **296, 299, 300**: Mariana Bazo/Reuters; John Wright/GWR; **301, 302**: Ranald Mackechnie/GWR; **301, 303, 304**: Rex Features; **308**: Alexander Hassenstein/Getty Images; **310, 311**: Barcroft Media; **312–313**: Mykel Nicolaou; Shelley Mays/AP/PA; **316, 317**: Chris Ison/PA; **319, 320, 322**: Mark Wagner/aviation-images.com; IFAW; Getty Images; **319, 321**: Steven Day/AP/PA; David Paul Morris/Getty Images; Fabrice Coffrini/Getty Images; aviation-images.com; **323, 324–325, 326**: China Photos/Getty Images; Gareth Fuller/PA; **327, 329, 330**: Ho New/Reuters; QinetiQ; QinetiQ; **328, 330**: Linda Sikes/Alamy; **331, 332, 333**: Rex Features; Rex Features; Darkone; Lola Katania/Getty Images; Alamy; Mathias Beinling/Alamy; David Parker/Alamy; Paul Thompson/Photolibrary; **332, 334–335**: Rex Features; Roy Rainford/Getty Images; Alamy; David Shankbone; Nina Aldin Thune; Paul Springett/Alamy; Allan Baxter/Getty Images; Jonathan Martz; **336, 337, 338**: Martial Trezzini/AP/PA; Valentin Flauraud/Reuters; **337, 338, 339**: Science & Society; **340, 341, 342**: Ranald Mackechnie/GWR; Pat Wellenbach/AP/PA; Mykel Nicolaou/GWR; **341, 343**: Ranald Mackechnie/GWR; Ranald Mackechnie/GWR; Ranald Mackechnie/GWR; **344–346**: Dominion; Dr. I. J. Stevenson; Dr. I. J. Stevenson; **347–348**: Kevin Foy/Alamy; Susan Vogel/Getty Images; **350–351**: ESA—AOES Medialab; **353, 354, 356**: Reuters; Anwar Hussein/WENN; **354–355, 356**: Jae C. Hong/AP/PA; Andre Csillag/Rex Features; Chip Somodevilla/Getty Images; Ron Sachs/Getty Images; **357, 358, 359**: Paul Melcher/Rex Features; **358, 359, 360**: Ed Oudenaarden/Getty Images; Saeed Moghaddam; WENN; Denver Post; **364**: Edgar Mueller/Rex Features; **363, 365, 366**: Frederick Warne & Co./Sotheby's Francois Guillot/Getty Images; **365, 366**: Herbert Knosowski/AP/PA; Shaun Curry/Getty Images; Ragnar Th. Sigurdsson/Robert Harding; Ragnar Th. Sigurdsson/Robert Harding; Ragnar Th. Sigurdsson/Robert Harding; **369, 372**: J. Paul Getty Museum; North News; **370–371**: Kodak; Nicholas Kamm/Getty Images; **373, 374**: Lester Cohen/Getty Images; Frank Micelotta/Getty Images; Sci Fi Channel/Kobal; **374, 375–376**: BBC; Getty Images; Sergei Bachlakov/Getty Images; Rex Features; **377, 378**: NBC/Rex Features; 20th Century Fox/Rex Features; **378, 379–380**: ABC/Rex Features; Dave Hogan/Getty Images; John Wright/GWR; **381, 382, 383**: Rex Features; Ken McKay/Rex Features; Shirlaine Forrest/Getty Images; Getty Images; **382, 383, 384**: ITV/Rex Features; Rex Features; Rex Features; Ken McKay/Rex Features; **385–386**: United Artists; Rex Features; J. Vespa/Getty Images; Getty Images; **387–388**: Moviestore Collection; Moviestore Collection; Moviestore Collection; Ian West/PA; **389, 390**: Jason LaVeris/Getty Images; Jon Furniss/Getty Images; DreamWorks; 20th Century Fox; **390, 391–392**: Mike Marsland/Getty Images; John Wright/GWR; Jon Kopaloff/Getty Images; **393, 394**: Disney/

Moviestore Collection; AFP; Summit Entertainment; **394, 395**: Paramount
Pictures; Bridgit Folman Film Gang; Warner Bros/Kobal; **397, 398**: Rex
Features; Rex Features; Dreamworks/Ronald Grant; **398, 399–400**: Warner
Bros.; Clay Enos/Warner Brothers; Moviestore Collection; Moviestore Col-
lection; Columbia Pictures **401–402, 404**: Scott Myers/Rex Features;
United Artists; Eon Productions/Ronald Grant; United Artists/Kobal; Eon
Productions/Ronald Grant; Moviestore Collection; Rex Features; Rex Fea-
tures; Rex Features; **403**: Rex Features; Rex Features; Moviestore Collection; **404–406**: Gregg Delman/Rex Features; Joe Kohen/Getty Images; Rex
Features; Michael Caulfield/Getty Images; **407, 408**: WENN; Stefan Jere-
miah/Getty Images; Frank Micelotta/Getty Images; **408, 409**: Dave
Hogan/Getty Images; Walt Disney Pictures/Kobal; **410–411**: George Pi-
mentel/Getty Images; Patricio Garcia/Getty Images; John Wright/GWR;
414–415: Paul Michael Hughes/GWR; **419**: Adam Pretty/Getty Images;
420–421: Paul Michael Hughes/GWR; Stephen Sylvanie; **422–423**: Norman Kent/Barcroft Media; **425, 426**: Paul Spinelli/Getty Images; Jim
McIsaac/Getty Images; Mike Roemer/AP/PA; **426, 427–428**: Kevin Ter-
rell/Getty Images; Ben Liebenberg/Getty Images; Jamie Squire/Getty Images; **429–431**: Oleg Nikishin/Getty Images; Michael Steele/Getty Images;
Vladislav Galgonek/AP/PA; **432–433**: Nicolas Asfouri/Getty Images;
Michael Steele/Getty Images; Mark Dadswell/Getty Images; **434–435**:
Getty Images; Timothy A. Clary/Getty Images; Ranald Mackechnie/GWR;
439–440: Jonathan Ferrey/Getty Images; Chris Graythen/Getty Images;
Ross Land/Getty Images; **441**: Rusty Jarrett/Getty Images; Corbis; Clive
Mason/Getty Images; **442, 443**: Marco Spelten; Matt King/Getty Images;
443, 444–445: Reuters; Troy Fleece/AP/PA; Christian Petersen/Getty Im-
ages; International Handball Federation; **446–447, 448**: Jeff Gross/Getty
Images; Damian Strohmeyer/Getty Images; Al Bello/Getty Images; **448,
449–450**: Duane Burleson/AP/PA; John R. McCutchen/Getty Images; **451,
452, 453**: Fernando Medina/Getty Images; D. Clarke Evans/Getty Images;
Brian Babineau/Getty Images; **452, 453, 454**: Noah Graham/Getty Images;
David Liam Kyle/Getty Images; Garrett W. Ellwood/Getty Images; **456–457**:
Joe Murphy/Getty Images; **458, 459**: Christopher Ivey/Getty Images; Joe
Murphy/Getty Images; **460, 461**: Toshifumi Kitamura/Getty Images; John
Gichigi/Getty Images; **459, 461, 463**: Kazuhiro Nogi/Getty Images; Pekka
Sakki/Getty Images; George Pimentel/Getty Images; **464, 466, 468**:
Stephen Pond/PA; Marty Melville/Getty Images; Shakil Adil/AP/PA; **465,
467**: Duif du Toit/Getty Images; Simon Baker/Reuters; **469–470**: Steve
Buddendeck/ESPN; **471–472**: Stefan Rousseau/PA; Michael Kap-
peler/Getty Images; Phil Walter/Getty Images; Mike Hewitt/Getty Images;
474–475, 476: Doug Pensinger/Getty Images; Patrick Hertzog/Getty Im-
ages; Glyn Kirk/Getty Images; Patrick Hertzog/Getty Images; **476–477**:
Keith Turner/Turning Images; Ronald Martinez/Getty Images; Paul
Michael Hughes/GWR; **478, 479**: Getty Images; Itsuo Inouye/AP/PA;
Reuters; Darren Walsh/Action Images/Reuters; **479, 480–481**: PA; Matthew
Ashton/PA; Mirrorpix; Patrik Stollarz/Getty Images; **482–483**: Andy
Lyons/Getty Images; Andrew Redington/Getty Images; **484–485**: David
Cannon/Getty Images; Robert Laberge/Getty Images; Ross Kinnaird/Getty

Images; **486–487**: Jim McIsaac/Getty Images; Jeff Vinnick/Getty Images; **488–489**: Andre Ringuette/Getty Images; Jim McIsaac/Getty Images; Scott Audette/Getty Images; **490–491, 492**: Warren Little/Getty Images; Clive Rose/Getty Images; David Rogers/Getty Images; **492, 493, 494**: Warren Little/Getty Images; Toshifumi Kitamura/Getty Images; Lionel Bonaventure/Getty Images; **494, 496**: Laurent Fievet/Getty Images; Don Emmert/Getty Images; **497–498**: Pierre Verdy/Getty Images; **500, 501, 502**: Shaun Botterill/Getty Images; Mark Ralston/Getty Images; Speedo; **501, 503**: Getty Images; Manan Vatsyayana/Getty Images; Francois-Xavier Marit/Getty Images; **503, 504**: David Shepherd **505, 506–507**: Courtney Crow/Sport The Library; Jeff Crow/Sport The Library; **508–509, 510**: Jed Jacobsohn/Getty Images; Christian Pondella/ESPN; **510–511**: Tony Donaldson/Icon SMI/ESPN; Tony Donaldson/Icon SMI/ESPN; **512–513, 514**: Barry Batchelor/PA; Gaye Gerard/Getty Images; Maiju Saari; **514, 515, 516**: Paul Michael Hughes/GWR; Bradley Kanaris/Getty Images; Bradley Kanaris/Getty Images; **519, 521**: Michael Steele/Getty Images; Samuel Kuban/Getty Images; **525**: Mark Dadswell/Getty Images; **529**: Bob Thomas/Getty Images; **535**: Kiyoshi Ota/Getty Images; George Frey/Reuters; **537**: Gerard Julien/Getty Images; Clive Brunskill/Getty Images; **539, 541**: Olivier Morin/Getty Images; Andreas Rentz/Getty Images; **541, 543**: Shaun Botterill/Getty Images; Clive Brunskill/Getty Images; **545**: IWSF; **587–588**: Sang Tan/AP/PA; Ronaldo Schemidt/Getty Images; **589–590**: David Levenson/Getty Images; **591, 592**: Gerry Penny/Getty Images; Getty Images; The Art Archive; AKG Images; Adrian Dennis/Getty Images; **592, 593**: Corbis; Oxford University Museum of Natural History; NASA

STOP PRESS

★ **Largest shampoo bottle** A bottle of shampoo measuring 15 ft. 5 in. by 5 ft. 6 in. (4.70 m by 1.54 m) and weighing 2,303 lb. (1,045 kg) was produced by Ismail Abu Dawood Trading Co. at Al-Andalus Hyper store of Panda, in Jeddah, Saudi Arabia, on March 19, 2009.

☆ **Largest bowl of pasta** Wataniya restaurants-Sbarro (Qatar) made a bowl of pasta weighing 9,760 lb. (4,430 kg) at the Doha golf club in Doha, Qatar, on March 28, 2009.

☆ **Largest collection of nativity sets** The largest collection of nativity sets consisted of 1,802 different pieces, as of March 14, 2009. All are housed in the Museo dei Sogni e Della Memoria in Feltre, Italy.

★ **Longest stand-up comedy show by an individual** Funnyman Tommy Tiernan (Ireland) performed stand-up at Nuns Island Theatre, Galway, Ireland, for 36 hours 15 minutes. The event started at 3:00 p.m. on Friday, April 10, 2009, and finished at 3:15 a.m. on Sunday, April 12.

★ **Fastest 20 cone backward slalom on inline skates** Paul Randles (UK) completed a 20 cone backward slalom on inline skates in 5.62 sec. on the set of *Guinness World Records* in Madrid, Spain, on January 23, 2009.

☆ **Largest buffet** The Kuşadasi Professional Chefs Association displayed a buffet with 1,028 different dishes at the 5th Annual Kuşadasi Food Festival, held at the Pine Bay Holiday Resort, Kuşadasi, Turkey, on April 18, 2009.

☆ **LARGEST SOCCER SHIRT**
A Fenerbahçe soccer shirt measuring 234 ft. 1 in. by 259 ft. 8 in. (71.35 m by 79.15 m) was created by AVEA in an event organized by Efor Turizm Organizasyon VE TIC Ltd at the Sükrü Saracoglu Stadium, Istanbul, Turkey, on April 5, 2009.

FACT

Fenerbahçe Sports Club isn't just home to a soccer team. It also has teams for athletics, men's and women's basketball, boxing, swimming, and a variety of other sports, too.

☆**LONGEST TIME CONTROLLING A SOCCER BALL (MALE)** At an event organized by Sony PlayStation in Covent Garden, London, UK, on April 30–May 1 2009, Dan Magness (UK) controlled a soccer ball, keeping it up in the air and in constant motion, for 24 hours. He completed an estimated 250,000 touches in total during his feat.

☆**Driving to the highest altitude by motorcycle** The greatest altitude reached autonomously by a motorcycle is 6,245 m (20,488 ft. 9 in.), achieved by a team of six of the North Calcutta Disha Motorcycle Club (all India) with Hero Honda motorcycles on the Changchemno Range near Marsemikla, India, on August 29, 2008.

☆**Fastest time to put on a duvet cover** In just 42.97 seconds, Alan Hughes (Ireland) set a new record for the fastest time to put on a duvet cover on the set of *Ireland AM*, TV3 in Dublin, Ireland, on September 17, 2008.

★**Oldest boxing world champion (female)** Terri Moss (U.S.A., b. January 25, 1966) was 41 years 105 days when she defeated Stephanie Dobbs (U.S.A.) to win the Women's International Boxing Federation (WIBF) minimum weight title in Tulsa, Oklahoma, U.S.A., on May 10, 2007.

★ MOST EXPENSIVE MUSIC SINGLE SOLD AT AUCTION

A rare seven-inch copy of an unreleased 1965 single, "Do I Love You (Indeed I Do)" by Frank Wilson (U.S.A.), was sold at auction in April 2009 for $39,294 (£25,742) to a buyer who wished to remain anonymous.

☆**MOST PEOPLE KISSING SIMULTANEOUSLY** A total of 39,879 people kissed at the same time at an event organized by Gobierno del Distrito Federal in Mexico DF, Mexico, on February 14, 2009. The final figure is an odd number because kisses involving more than two people (such as two children kissing a parent) were allowed.

459 ft.² (42.69 M²): The size of the world's **largest postcard,** a record set in Krefeld, Germany, on May 10, 2009.

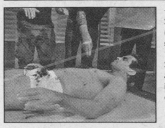

☆ **MOST SPIDERS ON A BODY FOR 30 SECONDS** Shane Crawford (Australia), an ex-professional sportsman and AFL champion, had 153 spiders placed on his body for 30 seconds on the set of *The Footy Show* in the Nine Network Studios in Melbourne, Victoria, Australia, on April 23, 2009.

☆ **Most step ups in one hour with a 40-lb. pack** One for fitness fanatics, the most step ups completed in one hour with an 18-kg (40-lb.) pack is 1,824 by Robin Simpson (UK) at the BT Heroes of Sport Exhibition at the GMEX Centre, Manchester, UK, on October 25, 2008.

This popular record has been broken three times this year alone. It was originally set by multiple record holder Paddy Doyle (UK) on November 9, 2006.

☆ **Largest silver-service dinner party** An epic silver-service dinner party took place on July 17, 2008, when 16,206 people were guests at the Alpha Kappa Alpha Sorority, Inc., Centennial Celebration Dinner hosted by the Walter E. Washington Convention Center (U.S.A.) in Washington D.C., U.S.A.

☆ **Longest concert by a solo artist** Canadian pianist Jason Beck, aka Gonzales, performed in a solo concert for 27 hr. 3 min. 44 sec. at the Cine 13 in Paris, France, on May 18, 2009. Jason was keen to avoid repeating songs during his attempt and promised his audience "I will break the record without sounding like a broken record."

☆ **LONGEST RABBIT** Alice, a Flemish giant rabbit owned by Annette Edwards (UK) and measuring 98 cm (3 ft. 3 in.), became the new longest rabbit after the sad news reached us of the death of Amy, the previous record holder, also owned by Annette. Alice was measured at Lowesmoor House Veterinary Centre, Worcester, UK, on April 29, 2009.

MOST POSITIONS HELD IN THE *NEW YORK TIMES* BESTSELLERS LIST Thriller writer James Patterson (U.S.A.) has had 43 of his books listed in the *New York Times* bestsellers chart, with 31 of them making it to the No.1 position. Pictured is Patterson receiving his certificate from GWR's Sam Fay.

☆**Largest choir** On May 12, 2009, a confirmed choir of 100,000 people (plus an unconfirmed 60,000 additional singers) gathered in Hyderabad, Andhra Pradesh, India. The mass sing-along in Telugu, the language of the Andhra Pradesh state, broke the previous 72-year-old record held by a choir of 60,000 at a contest held in what is now Wroclaw, Poland.

★**Largest physics lesson** A total of 5,401 students were taught by Steve Spangler Science (U.S.A.) during a presentation in Denver, Colorado, U.S.A., on May 7, 2009.

★**Fastest time to sort 500 g of Peanut M&Ms** The fastest time to sort 500 g (17.64 oz.) of Peanut M&Ms using one hand is 2 min. 37 sec. achieved by Debbie Nugent (UK) at Pinewood Studios, UK, on April 23, 2009.

☆**Most snails on the face** Mike Dilger (UK) managed to keep 37 snails on his face for the required 10 seconds while appearing on *The One Show* for BBC television in Covent Garden, London, UK, on May 13, 2009.

LAST...

★**World War II veteran to surrender** Private Teruo Nakamura (Taiwan), who served during World War II in the Imperial Japanese Army, did not surrender until 1974. He was stationed on Morotai Island in Indonesia, which was captured by the Allies in September 1944. Private Nakamura remained there, in hiding, long after the Allies departed.

★**Soldier to see action in both world wars** Francesco Domenico Chiarello (Italy, 1898–2008) was called up in 1918 during World War I and served as an infantryman, seeing action in Trentino, Italy. In 1940, he was

★ **TITANIC SURVIVOR** Elizabeth Gladys "Millvina" Dean (UK, February 2, 1912–May 31, 2009) was just 69 days old when she traveled third class on the cruise liner *Titanic* with her parents and 18-month-old brother, all hoping to start a new life in the U.S.A. She, along with her mother and brother, survived to return to the UK when the "unsinkable" ship sank on April 14, 1912, but her father, Bert, was among the 1,517 passengers who perished in the tragedy.

called up again at the age of 42 to fight in World War II at Reggio Calabria, Italy, but was discharged after a few months.

★ **Passenger pigeon** Martha, the last living passenger pigeon (*Ectopistes migratorius*), died in Cincinnati Zoo, U.S.A., on September 1, 1914. It was 29 years old and the very last of billions of these birds killed by mankind in less than a century.

The exact number of pink-breasted passenger pigeons that existed is impossible to determine, but an estimated 40% of the entire North American bird population was of this one species. The bird was largely shot for food, and a single shooter could easily kill 1,000 birds in one session. And incredible though it may seem today, dispatching pigeons was even a sport at one time. . . .

★ **ORIGINAL OLYMPICS** In A.D. 393, the original Olympic Games—first held c. 776 B.C.—were staged for the final time. Emperor Theodosius I disapproved of the Games' Ancient Greek pagan origins and had them banned in A.D. 394 for being anti-Christian. Olympia, the original site of the Games on the Greek Peloponnese peninsula, is where the modern Olympic flame is kindled to light the torch for today's Games.

★FLIGHT OF CONCORDE At 4:05 p.m. on October 24, 2003, Concorde made its last touchdown at the UK's Heathrow Airport. On its final transatlantic flight, it carried 100 celebrities from New York City, U.S.A., to mark the end of its 27 years of service. Before the flight, Captain Mike Bannister said, "What we have tried to do is to make the retirement of Concorde a celebration."

★**Olympic pigeon shoot** Live pigeon shooting was held for the first (and last) time in the extravagant 1900 Paris Olympics. Leon de Lunden (Belgium) snatched the gold, killing 21 birds in the process. France's Maurice Faure managed to down 20 birds, while Donald Mackintosh and Crittenden Robinson (both U.S.A.) tied for third place, with 18 pigeons each.

★**Death from smallpox** The last case of smallpox that resulted in death occurred in August 1978, when a medical photographer at Birmingham University, UK, was infected with a sample kept for research purposes. There have been no cases of the disease since then.

X-REF

You've read about some amazing lasts; don't forget to check out some incredible firsts on pp. vi–ix.

★LONDON PEA SOUPER When smoke from coal-burning fires mixes with fog, the result is a blinding, choking blanket of smog, known in London as a "pea souper." In December 1952, during the city's last pea souper, 3,500–4,000 people died from acute bronchitis. Visibility in the street was down to 12 in. (30 cm) and movie theaters closed because it was impossible to see the screens.

Last...

1890: the year of the Battle of Wounded Knee between the U.S. Cavalry and the tribal Sioux Indians, the **last battle on American soil.**

★ **DODO** The last known specimen of Mauritian dodo (*Raphus cucullatus,* formerly *Didus ineptus*) died in 1681. The single remaining closest relative—a *Rodrigues solitaire* from the nearby Rodrigues Island—died in 1790. The dodo's downfall was brought about by its fearlessness and flightlessness, as it would inquisitively approach strangers (and predators). Unfortunately for the dodo, it was also very tasty....

★ **Hieroglyph** The last known and datable hieroglyphs—the "sacred carved letters" engraved on monuments by Ancient Egyptians to communicate their religious beliefs—are those on Hadrian's Gate at the Temple of Philae, on Philae Island in the Nile, Egypt. They date back to August 24 in A.D. 394.

Use of the guillotine The last use of the guillotine in France, before its abolition on September 9, 1981, was for the execution of Hamida Djandoubi, a torturer and murderer aged 28, at Baumettes Prison, Marseille, on September 10, 1977.

Execution of a witch The last legal execution of a witch was that of Anna Göldi at Glarus, Switzerland, on June 18, 1782.

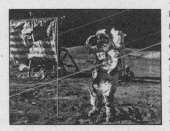

★ **MAN ON THE MOON** On December 14, 1972, the U.S.A.'s program of manned lunar exploration came to an end when Gene Cernan, commander of the *Apollo XVII* mission, stepped off the Moon's surface and boarded the lunar excursion vehicle, *Challenger.* This was the last of six successful manned lunar landings; the Moon has not experienced human footfall from that day to now.

British prime minister to be assassinated The last (and, to date, only) British prime minister to be assassinated was the Honorable Spencer Perceval (UK, 1762–1812), who was shot in the lobby of the House of Commons, London, UK, by John Bellingham (UK) on May 11, 1812.

Castrato The fashion for castrati—male opera singers whose testicles are removed before puberty, thus preserving their angelic boyhood voices—waned in the early 20th century. The last castrato was Alessandro Moreschi (Italy), who died in 1922. And on a similar note . . .

★**Eunuch** The last court eunuch—a male castrated in order to look after a harem of women without succumbing to sexual temptation—was Sun Yaoting (China), who died in 1996.